Advanced 1

Mikayla Wolford

Ms. Schroppe

4th period

ii

Currency and Coins Photos courtesy of Unit States Mint, Bureau of Engraving and Houghton Mifflin Harcourt.

Printed in the U.S.A.

ISBN 978-0-358-11582-3

4 5 6 7 8 9 10   0607   28 27 26 25 24 23 22 21

4500824323   C D E F G

Dear Students and Families,

Welcome to *Into Math*, Advanced 1! In this program, you will develop skills and make sense of mathematics by solving real-world problems, using hands-on tools and strategies, and collaborating with your classmates.

With the support of your teacher and by engaging with meaningful practice, you will learn to persevere when solving problems. *Into Math* will not only help you deepen your understanding of mathematics, but also build your confidence as a learner of mathematics.

Even more exciting, you will write all your ideas and solutions right in your book. In your *Into Math* book, writing and drawing on the pages will help you think deeply about what you are learning, help you truly understand math, and most important, you will become a confident user of mathematics!

Sincerely,
The Authors

Authors

Edward B. Burger, PhD
President, Southwestern University
Georgetown, Texas

Matthew R. Larson, PhD
Past-President, National Council
of Teachers of Mathematics
Lincoln Public Schools
Lincoln, Nebraska

Juli K. Dixon, PhD
Professor, Mathematics Education
University of Central Florida
Orlando, Florida

Steven J. Leinwand
Principal Research Analyst
American Institutes for Research
Washington, DC

Timothy D. Kanold, PhD
Mathematics Educator
Chicago, Illinois

Consultants

English Language Development Consultant

Harold Asturias
Director, Center for Mathematics
Excellence and Equity
Lawrence Hall of Science, University of California
Berkeley, California

Program Consultant

David Dockterman, EdD
Lecturer, Harvard Graduate School of Education
Cambridge, Massachusetts

Blended Learning Consultant

Weston Kiercshneck
Senior Fellow
International Center for Leadership in Education
Littleton, Colorado

STEM Consultants

Michael A. DiSpezio
Global Educator
North Falmouth, Massachusetts

Marjorie Frank
Science Writer and
Content-Area Reading Specialist
Brooklyn, New York

Bernadine Okoro
Access and Equity and
STEM Learning Advocate and Consultant
Washington, DC

Cary I. Sneider, PhD
Associate Research Professor
Portland State University
Portland, Oregon

Unit 1

Number Systems and Operations

Unit Opener 1

Build Conceptual Understanding Connect Concepts and Skills Apply and Practice

MODULE 4 Understand Addition and Subtraction of Rational Numbers

Build Conceptual Understanding   Connect Concepts and Skills   Apply and Practice

MODULE 5 Fluency with Rational Number Operations

© Houghton Mifflin Harcourt Publishing Company • Image Credits: ©studio023/iStock/Getty Images Plus/Getty Images

Sioux City, IOWA

−5 °F

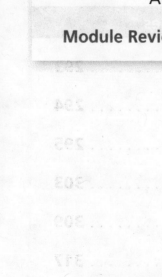

Unit 2

Expressions, Equations, and Inequalities

Build Conceptual Understanding   Connect Concepts and Skills   Apply and Practice

Ratios and Proportional Reasoning

MODULE 9 Ratios and Rates

Build Conceptual Understanding   Connect Concepts and Skills   Apply and Practice

MODULE 10 Apply Ratios and Rates to Measurement

© Houghton Mifflin Harcourt Publishing Company • Image Credit: ©Directphoto Collection/Alamy

© Houghton Mifflin Harcourt Publishing Company • Image Credit: ©Eric Isselee/Shutterstock

MODULE 13 Proportional Reasoning with Percents

Unit

4 Relationships in Geometry

Build Conceptual Understanding   Connect Concepts and Skills   Apply and Practice

© Houghton Mifflin Harcourt Publishing Company • Image Credit: Max Earey/Alamy

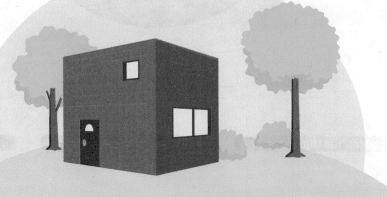

Unit 5

Data Collection and Analysis

Build Conceptual Understanding   Connect Concepts and Skills   Apply and Practice

Build Conceptual Understanding   Connect Concepts and Skills   Apply and Practice

My Progress on Mathematics Standards

The lessons in your *Into Math* book provide instruction for Mathematics Standards for Advanced 1. You can use the following pages to reflect on your learning and record your progress through the standards.

As you learn new concepts, reflect on this learning. Consider inserting a check mark or inserting a question mark if you have questions or need help.

Advanced 1	Student Edition Lessons	My Progress
Domain: RATIOS & PROPORTIONAL RELATIONSHIPS		
Cluster: Understand ratio concepts and use ratio reasoning to solve problems.		
Understand the concept of a ratio and use ratio language to describe a ratio relationship between two quantities.	9.1	
Understand the concept of a unit rate a/b associated with a ratio *a:b* with *b* ≠ 0, and use rate language in the context of a ratio relationship.	9.2, 9.4	
Use ratio and rate reasoning to solve real-world and mathematical problems, e.g., by reasoning about tables of equivalent ratios, tape diagrams, double number line diagrams, or equations.	9.5, 10.1 *See also below.*	
• Make tables of equivalent ratios relating quantities with whole-number measurements, find missing values in the tables, and plot the pairs of values on the coordinate plane. Use tables to compare ratios.	9.2, 9.3	
• Solve unit rate problems including those involving unit pricing and constant speed.	9.4, 9.5	
• Find a percent of a quantity as a rate per 100 (e.g., 30% of a quantity means 30/100 times the quantity); solve problems involving finding the whole, given a part and the percent.	12.1, 12.2, 12.3	
• Use ratio reasoning to convert measurement units; manipulate and transform units appropriately when multiplying or dividing quantities.	10.2, 10.3	

Interactive Standards

Cluster: Analyze proportional relationships and use them to solve real-world and mathematical problems.		
Compute unit rates associated with ratios of fractions, including ratios of lengths, areas and other quantities measured in like or different units.	9.4, 15.1	
Recognize and represent proportional relationships between quantities.	11.1 *See also below.*	
• Decide whether two quantities are in a proportional relationship, e.g., by testing for equivalent ratios in a table or graphing on a coordinate plane and observing whether the graph is a straight line through the origin.	11.2, 11.3	
• Identify the constant of proportionality (unit rate) in tables, graphs, equations, diagrams, and verbal descriptions of proportional relationships.	11.1, 11.2, 11.3, 11.4	
• Represent proportional relationships by equations.	11.2	
• Explain what a point (*x*, *y*) on the graph of a proportional relationship means in terms of the situation, with special attention to the points (0, 0) and (1, *r*) where *r* is the unit rate.	11.3	
Use proportional relationships to solve multistep ratio and percent problems.	11.4, 13.1, 13.2, 13.3, 13.4, 13.5	

Domain: THE NUMBER SYSTEM		
Cluster: Apply and extend previous understandings of multiplication and division to divide fractions by fractions.		
Interpret and compute quotients of fractions, and solve word problems involving division of fractions by fractions, e.g., by using visual fraction models and equations to represent the problem.	2.1, 2.2, 2.3, 2.4	
Cluster: Compute fluently with multi-digit numbers and find common factors and multiples.		
Fluently divide multi-digit numbers using the standard algorithm.	3.3	
Fluently add, subtract, multiply, and divide multi-digit decimals using the standard algorithm for each operation.	3.1, 3.2, 3.4, 3.5	
Find the greatest common factor of two whole numbers less than or equal to 100 and the least common multiple of two whole numbers less than or equal to 12. Use the distributive property to express a sum of two whole numbers 1–100 with a common factor as a multiple of a sum of two whole numbers with no common factor.	1.4, 1.5, 2.4	
Cluster: Apply and extend previous understandings of numbers to the system of rational numbers.		
Understand that positive and negative numbers are used together to describe quantities having opposite directions or values (e.g., temperature above/below zero, elevation above/below sea level, credits/debits, positive/negative electric charge); use positive and negative numbers to represent quantities in real-world contexts, explaining the meaning of 0 in each situation.	1.1	
Understand a rational number as a point on the number line. Extend number line diagrams and coordinate axes familiar from previous grades to represent points on the line and in the plane with negative number coordinates.	1.1, 14.1 *See also below.*	
• Recognize opposite signs of numbers as indicating locations on opposite sides of 0 on the number line; recognize that the opposite of the opposite of a number is the number itself, e.g., $-(-3) = 3$, and that 0 is its own opposite.	1.1	
• Understand signs of numbers in ordered pairs as indicating locations in quadrants of the coordinate plane; recognize that when two ordered pairs differ only by signs, the locations of the points are related by reflections across one or both axes.	14.1	

• Find and position integers and other rational numbers on a horizontal or vertical number line diagram; find and position pairs of integers and other rational numbers on a coordinate plane.	1.1, 1.2, 14.1, 14.2
Understand ordering and absolute value of rational numbers.	*See below.*
• Interpret statements of inequality as statements about the relative position of two numbers on a number line diagram.	1.2
• Write, interpret, and explain statements of order for rational numbers in real-world contexts.	1.2, 1.4, 1.5
• Understand the absolute value of a rational number as its distance from 0 on the number line; interpret absolute value as magnitude for a positive or negative quantity in a real-world situation.	1.1, 1.3
• Distinguish comparisons of absolute value from statements about order.	1.3
Solve real-world and mathematical problems by graphing points in all four quadrants of the coordinate plane. Include use of coordinates and absolute value to find distances between points with the same first coordinate or the same second coordinate.	14.1, 14.3

Cluster: Apply and extend previous understandings of operations with fractions to add, subtract, multiply, and divide rational numbers.		
Apply and extend previous understandings of addition and subtraction to add and subtract rational numbers; represent addition and subtraction on a horizontal or vertical number line diagram.	4.1, 4.2, 4.3, 5.1. 5.2, 5.6 *See also below.*	
• Describe situations in which opposite quantities combine to make 0.	4.3	
• Understand $p + q$ as the number located a distance $|q|$ from p, in the positive or negative direction depending on whether q is positive or negative. Show that a number and its opposite have a sum of 0 (are additive inverses). Interpret sums of rational numbers by describing real-world contexts.	4.1, 4.2, 4.3, 5.1	
• Understand subtraction of rational numbers as adding the additive inverse, $p - q = p + (-q)$. Show that the distance between two rational numbers on the number line is the absolute value of their difference, and apply this principle in real-world contexts.	5.1, 5.2	
• Apply properties of operations as strategies to add and subtract rational numbers.	5.6	
Apply and extend previous understandings of multiplication and division and of fractions to multiply and divide rational numbers.	*See below.*	
• Understand that multiplication is extended from fractions to rational numbers by requiring that operations continue to satisfy the properties of operations, particularly the distributive property, leading to products such as $(-1)(-1) = 1$ and the rules for multiplying signed numbers. Interpret products of rational numbers by describing real-world contexts.	5.3, 5.5	
• Understand that integers can be divided, provided that the divisor is not zero, and every quotient of integers (with non-zero divisor) is a rational number. If p and q are integers, then $-(p/q) = (-p)/q = p/(-q)$. Interpret quotients of rational numbers by describing real-world contexts.	5.3, 5.4	
• Apply properties of operations as strategies to multiply and divide rational numbers.	5.3, 5.6	

• Convert a rational number to a decimal using long division; know that the decimal form of a rational number terminates in 0s or eventually repeats.	5.4
Solve real-world and mathematical problems involving the four operations with rational numbers.	5.1, 5.2, 5.3, 5.5, 5.6, 5.7, 7.6

Domain: EXPRESSIONS & EQUATIONS

Cluster: Apply and extend previous understandings of arithmetic to algebraic expressions.

Write and evaluate numerical expressions involving whole-number exponents.	6.1, 6.2
Write, read, and evaluate expressions in which letters stand for numbers.	*See below.*
• Write expressions that record operations with numbers and with letters standing for numbers.	6.3
• Identify parts of an expression using mathematical terms (sum, term, product, factor, quotient, coefficient); view one or more parts of an expression as a single entity.	6.2, 6.3
• Evaluate expressions at specific values of their variables. Include expressions that arise from formulas used in real-world problems. Perform arithmetic operations, including those involving whole-number exponents, in the conventional order when there are no parentheses to specify a particular order (Order of Operations).	6.4, 15.1, 15.2, 16.2, 16.3
Apply the properties of operations to generate equivalent expressions.	6.5
Identify when two expressions are equivalent (i.e., when the two expressions name the same number regardless of which value is substituted into them).	6.5

Cluster: Reason about and solve one-variable equations and inequalities.

Understand solving an equation or inequality as a process of answering a question: which values from a specified set, if any, make the equation or inequality true? Use substitution to determine whether a given number in a specified set makes an equation or inequality true.	7.1, 7.5
Use variables to represent numbers and write expressions when solving a real-world or mathematical problem; understand that a variable can represent an unknown number, or, depending on the purpose at hand, any number in a specified set.	6.3

Solve real-world and mathematical problems by writing and solving equations of the form $x + p = q$ and $px = q$ for cases in which p, q and x are all non-negative rational numbers.	7.1, 7.2, 7.3, 7.4, 7.6
Write an inequality of the form $x > c$ or $x < c$ to represent a constraint or condition in a real-world or mathematical problem. Recognize that inequalities of the form $x > c$ or $x < c$ have infinitely many solutions; represent solutions of such inequalities on number line diagrams.	7.5

Cluster: Represent and analyze quantitative relationships between dependent and independent variables.

Use variables to represent two quantities in a real-world problem that change in relationship to one another; write an equation to express one quantity, thought of as the dependent variable, in terms of the other quantity, thought of as the independent variable. Analyze the relationship between the dependent and independent variables using graphs and tables, and relate these to the equation.	8.1, 8.2, 8.3

Cluster: Use properties of operations to generate equivalent expressions.

Apply properties of operations as strategies to add, subtract, factor, and expand linear expressions with rational coefficients.	6.6
Understand that rewriting an expression in different forms in a problem context can shed light on the problem and how the quantities in it are related.	6.6, 13.2

Domain: GEOMETRY

Cluster: Solve real-world and mathematical problems involving area, surface area, and volume.

Find the area of right triangles, other triangles, special quadrilaterals, and polygons by composing into rectangles or decomposing into triangles and other shapes; apply these techniques in the context of solving real-world and mathematical problems.	15.1, 15.2, 15.3
Find the volume of a right rectangular prism with fractional edge lengths by packing it with unit cubes of the appropriate unit fraction edge lengths, and show that the volume is the same as would be found by multiplying the edge lengths of the prism. Apply the formulas $V = lwh$ and $V = bh$ to find volumes of right rectangular prisms with fractional edge lengths in the context of solving real-world and mathematical problems.	16.2, 16.3

Draw polygons in the coordinate plane given coordinates for the vertices; use coordinates to find the length of a side joining points with the same first coordinate or the same second coordinate. Apply these techniques in the context of solving real-world and mathematical problems.	14.2, 14.3
Represent three-dimensional figures using nets made up of rectangles and triangles, and use the nets to find the surface area of these figures. Apply these techniques in the context of solving real-world and mathematical problems.	16.1

Domain: STATISTICS & PROBABILITY

Cluster: Develop understanding of statistical variability.

Recognize a statistical question as one that anticipates variability in the data related to the question and accounts for it in the answers.	17.1
Understand that a set of data collected to answer a statistical question has a distribution which can be described by its center, spread, and overall shape.	18.5
Recognize that a measure of center for a numerical data set summarizes all of its values with a single number, while a measure of variation describes how its values vary with a single number.	17.4, 18.4

Cluster: Summarize and describe distributions.

Display numerical data in plots on a number line, including dot plots, histograms, and box plots.	17.2, 17.3, 18.2
Summarize numerical data sets in relation to their context, such as by:	*See below.*
• Reporting the number of observations.	17.1, 17.4
• Describing the nature of the attribute under investigation, including how it was measured and its units of measurement.	17.1
• Giving quantitative measures of center (median and/or mean) and variability (interquartile range and/or mean absolute deviation), as well as describing any overall pattern and any striking deviations from the overall pattern with reference to the context in which the data were gathered.	18.1, 18.3, 18.4, 18.5
• Relating the choice of measures of center and variability to the shape of the data distribution and the context in which the data were gathered.	17.5, 18.4, 18.5

Unit 1

Number Systems and Operations

Event Organizer

Have you ever been to a wedding or other formal party? If so, there is a good chance that an event organizer helped make it happen. Event organizers plan all the details of big events like parties, banquets, concerts, conventions, and fundraisers. Event organizers face math problems every day, from calculating how to seat hundreds of guests to using geometry and measurement to plan decorations.

STEM Task:

Combinatorics is a branch of math focused on counting arrangements of objects. Jorge is an event organizer who must seat 102 guests. He has circular tables that seat 10 people each and square tables that seat 4 people each. He wants to use as many circular tables as possible but have no empty seats. Explain how he could arrange the tables he will need.

Learning Mindset

Perseverance Checks for Understanding

Learning is a process by which you constantly build new skills and knowledge through experience and study. Anything that you have already learned can help you learn new things now, and what you learn now will help you learn more in the future. When you first encounter a new topic, reflect upon past work and apply what you learned to new learning tasks.

- What knowledge do you already have that can help you understand the new topic?

- What strategies have you used to learn new topics in the past, and which ones might work now?

Reflect

Q What real-world knowledge did you use to understand the STEM Task?

Q What strategies or methods from your previous learning did you use to complete the STEM Task?

Rational Number Concepts

Which Fraction Does **Not Belong?**

Pizza slices are left over from a party. Each whole pizza was the same size, but was cut into a different number of equal slices.

For each pizza, write a fraction that represents the part of the pizza that is left over.

A. Cheese pizza _____

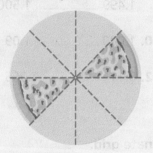

B. Olive pizza _____

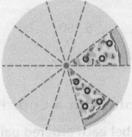

C. Mushroom pizza _____

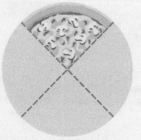

D. Spinach pizza _____

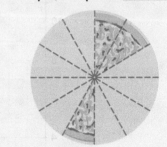

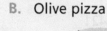 **Turn and Talk**

• Which fraction does not belong? Explain why.

• Which type of pizza has the least amount left over? Tell how you know.

• Can you make a whole pizza with the leftover pieces? Explain.

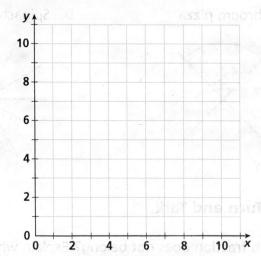

Are You Ready?

Complete these problems to review prior concepts and skills you will need for this module.

Compare and Order Whole Numbers

Use <, >, or = to compare the whole numbers.

1. 1,615 _____ 1,015

2. 549 _____ 2,986

3. 7,099 _____ 9,001

4. 14,999 _____ 15,000

5. 24,777 _____ 3,052

6. 98,455 _____ 98,450

Compare Decimals

Use <, >, or = to compare the decimals.

7. 0.993 _____ 0.421

8. 1.499 _____ 1.500

9. 5.16 _____ 5.160

10. 1.009 _____ 1.09

11. 4.087 _____ 3.987

12. 0.11 _____ 1.066

Identify Points on a Coordinate Grid

Graph and label each ordered pair on the coordinate grid.

13. (1, 4)

14. (2, 7)

15. (8, 1)

16. (5, 5)

17. (0, 3)

18. (6, 0)

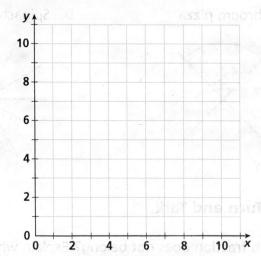

© Houghton Mifflin Harcourt Publishing Company

Name _____

Identify and Interpret Rational Numbers

(I Can) **graph rational numbers and find their opposites.**

Spark Your Learning

Fergal is recording the number of yards his school's football team gained or lost on successive plays. How can you model or represent the opposite of each loss or gain shown in the table?

Quantity	Opposite
gain of 2 yards	
loss of 13 yards	
loss of 8 yards	
gain of 4 yards	
loss of 2 yards	

© Houghton Mifflin Harcourt Publishing Company • Image Credit: ©Ilene MacConald/Alamy

Turn and Talk Write several pairs of your own opposite quantities. Explain how you know they are opposites.

Build Understanding

Positive numbers can be written with or without a positive sign (+), but they are usually written without it. Negative numbers are always written with a negative sign (−).

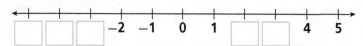

$$-5 \quad -4 \quad -3 \quad -2 \quad -1 \quad 0 \quad 1 \quad 2 \quad 3 \quad 4 \quad 5$$

Negative integers   Positive integers

Connect to Vocabulary

A **positive number** is a number greater than zero.
A **negative number** is a number less than zero.

1 The results of three football plays are shown in the table below.

Result	Net Yards
4 yard gain	4
1 yard loss	−1
4 yard loss	−4

A. What does 0 represent in this situation?

_____

B. What do negative numbers represent in this situation?

_____

C. What do positive numbers represent in this situation?

_____

D. Complete the number line. Then plot a point for each net yards value from the table.

$$\boxed{}\;\boxed{}\;\boxed{}\;-2 \quad -1 \quad 0 \quad 1 \quad \boxed{}\;\boxed{}\; 4 \quad 5$$

E. The integer 4 is 4 units from 0 on the number line. Which integer is also 4 units from 0 on the number line? How is this integer related to the integer 4?

_____

F. How many units from zero is 0 on the number line? What is the opposite of 0? Explain.

_____

_____

_____

Connect to Vocabulary

Two numbers are **opposites** if, on a number line, they are the same distance from 0 but on different sides of 0.

Integers are the set of all whole numbers and their opposites.

G. What is the opposite of the opposite of 5? This is written as −(−5). Explain.

_____

_____

2 In January, the average low temperature in Nome, Alaska, is the rational number −2.8 °F.

A. To graph integers, you can use marks on a number line that increase by ones. What marks would you need to graph −2.8 on a number line?

_____

_____

B. Between what two consecutive integers is −2.8 located on a number line?

−2.8 is between the integers ☐ and ☐ .

C. How would you graph −2.8 on a number line?

I would plot a point ☐ tenths to the _____ of −2.

D. Complete the statement to describe the position of −2.8 compared to 0.

−2.8 is ☐ units to the _____ of 0.

E. What is the opposite of −2.8?

The opposite of −2.8 will be ☐ units to the _____ of 0.

So, the opposite of −2.8 is ☐ .

F. Graph −2.8 and its opposite on the number line.

3 The legs of a swing set are buried as shown.

A. What marks on a number line would you need to graph $\frac{1}{2}$?

_____

B. Describe the position of $\frac{1}{2}$ on a number line.

$\frac{1}{2}$ is between the integers ☐ and ☐ .

$\frac{1}{2}$ is ☐ unit to the _____ of 0.

C. The opposite of $\frac{1}{2}$ will be ☐ unit to the _____ of 0.

So, the opposite of $\frac{1}{2}$ is ☐ .

D. Graph $\frac{1}{2}$ and its opposite on the number line.

Legs are buried $\frac{1}{2}$ foot in the ground.

Turn and Talk What marks on a number line would you need to graph −3.75? Explain.

4 The lowest elevation at Death Valley National Park is approximately −0.05 mile.

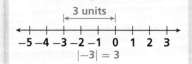
A. What distance is this from sea level?

_____

B. Between what two consecutive integers is −0.05 located on a number line?

_____

C. Graph −0.05 on the number line.

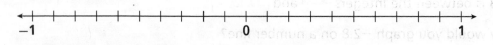

D. What is the distance from zero to −0.05?

_____

E. The absolute value of a number is written using the symbols | |. What is the absolute value of −0.05?

|−0.05| = ◻

 Turn and Talk How are the absolute value of a number and its opposite related?

Check Understanding

1. An investment gains $5 in value on one day. The next day, it loses $3 in value. Represent each of these changes using integers.

_____

2. Iman is playing a game. On one turn she earns 2 points and on the next turn she loses 5 points. Graph her points for each turn on the number line.

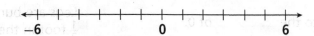

For Problems 3–6, find the opposite of the number.

3. 4.5 _____   4. −8 _____   5. −25 _____   6. $\frac{1}{4}$ _____

For Problems 7–9, find the absolute value of each number.

7. |−2.2| = _____   8. |−3| = _____   9. |7.29| = _____

On Your Own

For Problems 10–12, use the following information.

(MP) **Use Structure** Every week, Tiana runs 3 miles and records how long it takes her to complete the run. She also records the change in time from the previous week.

10. Last week, her time spent running decreased by 2 minutes.

What integer could represent this change? _____

11. This week, her time spent running increased by 1 minute.

What integer could represent this change? _____

12. In words, what is the opposite of "increased by 1 minute"?

What integer represents this opposite?

_____

13. STEM Atoms are made of tiny particles called protons, neutrons, and electrons. Protons and neutrons are in the center of the atom, making up the nucleus. The electrical charges on the protons and electrons are exactly the same size but opposite. If the protons in an atom have a total positive charge of 8, what is the total charge of the corresponding electrons?

_____

14. (MP) **Reason** Two integers are opposites of each other. One integer is 3 units to the right of 1 on a number line. What are the two integers?

_____

(MP) **Use Structure** For Problems 15–17, use the number line to graph the opposite of each number. Label each point.

15. −3.25 **16.** 0.25 **17.** −1.5

18. Rona starts at the base of a hill that has an elevation of 25 feet below sea level. Then Rona climbs to the top of the hill which has an elevation of 25 feet above sea level. Represent these elevations as integers. How are they related?

_____

19. (MP) **Use Structure** The low temperatures on three days are shown at the right. What are the opposites of the three temperatures? Graph the temperatures and their opposites on the number line.

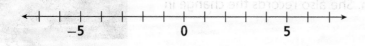

Monday: −2 °F

Tuesday: 4 °F

Wednesday: −7 °F

_____

_____

20. (MP) **Use Structure** Graph each number and its opposite on the number line.

$-1\frac{2}{10}, \ -\frac{5}{10}, \ \frac{3}{10}, \ \frac{9}{10}$

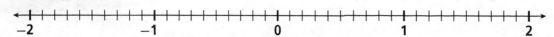

21. Graph the numbers on a number line: −2, 4.5, −5, 10.

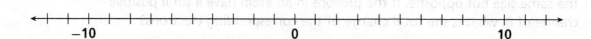

For Problems 22–25, find the absolute value of each number.

22. $\left|-5\right|$ _____

23. $\left|4.5\right|$ _____

24. $\left|-5.10\right|$ _____

25. $\left|-2\frac{3}{4}\right|$ _____

 I'm in a Learning Mindset!

What can I apply from previous work to better understand how to find opposites of negative numbers?

_____

_____

Name _____

Identify and Interpret Rational Numbers

1. Mila first stands on a diving board that is 3 feet above the surface of the water. She then dives to the bottom of the pool, to a depth of 10 feet.

   A. If the surface of the pool is 0, use integers to represent these two locations.

   _____

   B. Graph each of the integers on the number line. Then find the opposite of each integer and explain what it represents.

   _____
   _____
   _____
   _____

2. **(MP) Critique Reasoning** Hermes says that the opposite of 9 is 9 since each number is 9 units from zero on the number line. Is Hermes correct? Explain why or why not.

   _____
   _____

3. Graph 1.7, −0.3, and 0.5 and their opposites on the number line.

   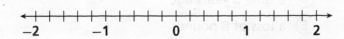

4. **(MP) Reason** On Friday, the value of one stock changed by −$2.75, and the value of a second stock changed by $2.75. How can you use a number line to show that these values are opposites?

   _____
   _____
   _____

For Problems 5–8, find the absolute value of each number.

5. $|2|$ 6. $|-3|$ 7. $\left|-\frac{1}{2}\right|$ 8. $|-0.5|$

_____

Test Prep

9. Jose collects baseball cards. Over the last year, the change in the value of his favorite card is −$7. Which best describes the meaning of this integer?

Ⓐ The card is now worth $7.

Ⓑ The value of the card has increased by $7.

Ⓒ The value of the card has decreased by $7.

Ⓓ The card is now worth −$7.

10. A stock market index drops by $1.38. What rational number represents the change in the index?

_____

11. Match each integer to its opposite.

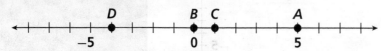

Integer A ●   ● −1
Integer B ●   ● −5
Integer C ●   ● 0
Integer D ●   ● 4

12. An ampere is a unit used to measure electrical current. The electrical current is −2.5 amperes in one part of a circuit and 0.6 ampere in another part. Graph the values and their opposites on the number line.

13. Which situation can be represented by −8? Choose all that apply.

Ⓐ a temperature drop of 8 °F   Ⓓ a time 8 years ago

Ⓑ a depth of 8 meters   Ⓔ a loss of 8 pounds

Ⓒ a growth of 8 centimeters   Ⓕ a gain of $8

Spiral Review

14. What is one tenth of 1,850?

_____

For Problems 15−17, use >, <, or = to compare the numbers.

15. 0.105 _____ 0.108   16. 0.002 _____ 0.040   17. 0.03 _____ 0.017

Lesson 2

Name _____

Compare Rational Numbers Using a Number Line

(I Can) compare positive and negative rational numbers with and without a number line.

Spark Your Learning

PAIRS

The thermometer shows a temperature that are above zero and temperatures that are below zero. Find a temperature to complete each statement. Then describe a thermometer to someone who may not have seen one.

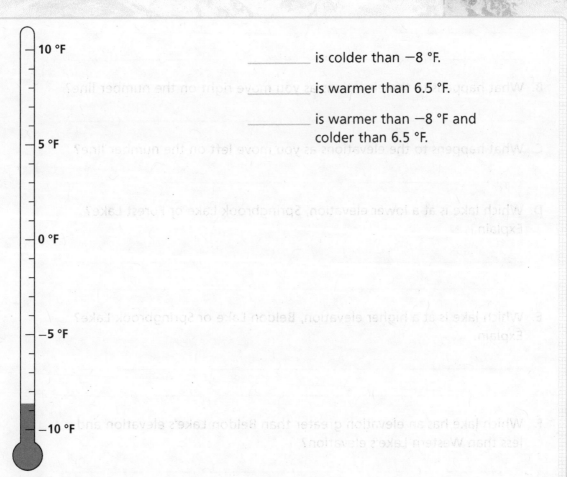

10 °F

5 °F

0 °F

−5 °F

−10 °F

_____ is colder than −8 °F.

_____ is warmer than 6.5 °F.

_____ is warmer than −8 °F and colder than 6.5 °F.

Turn and Talk Describe the location of a temperature warmer than 20.4 °F on a thermometer. Can you extend the drawing of the thermometer to show warmer and colder temperatures? Describe how.

Build Understanding

1 The table below shows the elevations above or below sea level of several lakes. Sea level is considered to be an elevation of zero feet.

Lakes	Elevation (feet)
Beldon Lake	−18.5
Forest Lake	90.7
Springbrook Lake	−75.2
Western Lake	44.5
Pleasant Lake	4.5

A. How could you use a horizontal number line to compare the elevations?

_____

_____

B. What happens to the elevations as you move right on the number line?

_____

C. What happens to the elevations as you move left on the number line?

_____

D. Which lake is at a lower elevation, Springbrook Lake or Forest Lake? Explain.

_____

_____

E. Which lake is at a higher elevation, Beldon Lake or Springbrook Lake? Explain.

_____

_____

F. Which lake has an elevation greater than Beldon Lake's elevation and less than Western Lake's elevation?

_____

 Turn and Talk Describe another situation that uses elevations to describe locations. Give an example.

Step It Out

The mathematical sentences $-3 < 5$ and $2 > -4$ are examples of *inequalities*.

The symbol "<" is read "is less than." So, $-3 < 5$ means "-3 is less than 5."

The symbol ">" is read "is greater than." So, $2 > -4$ means "2 is greater than -4."

You can compare fractions by graphing them on a number line.

> **Connect to Vocabulary**
>
> An **inequality** is a mathematical sentence that shows the relationship between quantities that are not equal.

2 ▶ Mrs. Smith and Mr. Jones each have 30 students in their class. If Mrs. Smith corrected $\frac{5}{8}$ of last week's math assignments and Mr. Jones corrected $\frac{3}{4}$ of last week's science assignments, which teacher corrected the greater portion of the assignments?

A. What marks on a number line would you need to graph $\frac{3}{4}$ and $\frac{5}{8}$?

_____

_____

B. Graph the fractions on the number line.

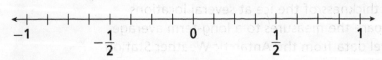

C. Note the locations of the numbers.

$\frac{3}{4}$ is to the _____ of $\frac{5}{8}$ on the number line,

so $\frac{3}{4}$ is _____ $\frac{5}{8}$.

D. Write an inequality statement.

$$\frac{3}{4} \ \boxed{} \ \frac{5}{8}$$

So, Mrs. Smith corrected | less than / more than | Mr. Jones.

E. Use the number line to help you write an inequality comparing $-\frac{5}{8}$ and $-\frac{3}{4}$.

_____

_____

Turn and Talk How do the numbers in Parts D and E compare? How can a number line help you to determine the relationship between the numbers in Parts D and E? Explain.

You can also compare decimals using a number line.

3 The record low temperatures for five cities are: Ashton −0.6 °F, Barres −2 °F, Carl 0.7 °F, Davison 0.4 °F, and Edgeville −1.5 °F. Graph the temperatures on the number line and label each with the first letter of the city's name.

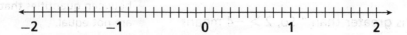

A. Note the locations of the numbers for Barres and Edgeville.

−2 is to the | left / right | of −1.5, so the low temperature for Barres is

| colder / warmer | than the low temperature for Edgeville.

B. Complete the inequality in two different ways.

−2 [ ] −1.5   −1.5 [ ] −2

Turn and Talk What do you notice about the rational numbers as you move from left to right on a number line? Use examples to support your answer.

Check Understanding

1. Researchers measure the thickness of the ice at several locations in the Antarctic and compare the measures to a long-term average thickness. A set of ice-level data from the Antarctic Weather Station is shown measured in meters.

−1.2, 2.6, −1.3, 1.8, 2.1, −0.9, 1.5

A. Graph the numbers on the number line to compare the data.

B. Use the number line to complete the inequalities.

2.6 [ ] −0.9   1.8 [ ] 2.1   −1.2 [ ] −1.3

C. Is 1.5 to the left or right of −0.9?

_____

D. Is −1.2 to the left or right of 2.1?

_____

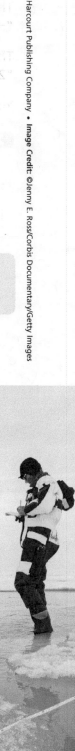

On Your Own

2. Diego is participating in a cooking competition in which the judges rate performance for various criteria using fractions between −1 and 2. The scores for four competitors are shown.

$\frac{1}{8}, -\frac{1}{4}, 1\frac{1}{2}, -\frac{3}{4}$

A. Complete the number line to compare the four scores.

B. How do the locations of $-\frac{3}{4}$ and $-\frac{1}{4}$ compare? Which number is less? Explain.

_____

3. **Health and Fitness** A sprint triathlon consists of a 750-meter swim, a 20-kilometer bicycle ride, and a 5-kilometer run. The race organizers recorded the difference between 5 athletes' times and the average time to complete the triathlon. Each value is the amount of time above or below the average in minutes.

2.5, −1.25, 0.8, 1.5, −1.2

A. Graph the athletes' differences from the average time on the number line.

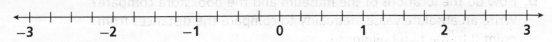

B. Complete the inequalities.

−1.2 ☐ −1.25   0.8 ☐ 1.5   2.5 ☐ −1.25

C. Which inequality in Part B is comparing the differences from the average time for the slowest and fastest athletes in the group? Explain.

_____

_____

4. **Open Ended** A cave system inside a mountain has caves at different elevations above and below sea level. One cave has an elevation of $-4\frac{1}{4}$ meters. How can you use a vertical number line to determine whether the elevation of a second cave is greater than or less than $-4\frac{1}{4}$ meters?

_____

_____

_____

_____

5. On this map of Main Street, distances are in miles. The plotted points indicate the locations of landmarks. The library is located at point 0.

A. Find the the locations of the other landmarks and record them in the table in decimal form.

Points of Interest	
Name	**Location**
city park	
courthouse	
bookstore	
museum	

courthouse   city park   library   museum   bookstore

-2   -1   0   1   2

B. How do the locations of the city park and the library compare? Write an absolute value inequality to compare the distances from point 0 to the two buildings.

_____

C. How do the locations of the bookstore and the courthouse compare? Write an absolute value inequality to compare the distances from point 0 to the two buildings.

_____

_____

D. How do the locations of the museum and the bookstore compare? Write an absolute value inequality to compare the distances from point 0 to the two buildings.

_____

Use the number line to compare the rational numbers.

-2   -1   0   1   2

6. $-1\frac{3}{4}$ ☐ $-\frac{1}{2}$ **7.** $-\frac{1}{10}$ ☐ $-\frac{4}{5}$

8. -1.5 ☐ -2 **9.** -1.25 ☐ -0.5

 I'm in a Learning Mindset!

What did I learn from Task 2 that I can use in my future learning?

_____

_____

Name _____

Compare Rational Numbers Using a Number Line

Name _____

LESSON 1.2
More Practice/ Homework

ONLINE
Video Tutorials and Interactive Examples

Compare Rational Numbers Using a Number Line

1. The high temperatures of four different towns in Norway were measured on the same day. The temperatures are 0.9 °C, −0.5 °C, −1.3 °C, and 1.2 °C.

   A. Graph the temperatures on the number line.

   B. Complete each statement.

   −0.5 °C is _____ than −1.3 °C, because −0.5 is to the _____ of −1.3.

   0.9 °C is _____ than 1.2 °C, because 0.9 is to the _____ of 1.2.

2. **STEM** A circuit board manufacturer rejects a 100-ohm resistor if its measured resistance is 0.15 ohm more than or less than 100 ohms. Resistors A and B are rejected. Resistor A's resistance differs from 100 ohms by 0.15 ohm. Resistor B's resistance differs from 100 ohms by −0.78 ohm. How do the resistances of these two resistors compare? Explain.

   _____

   _____

   _____

Resistors on a circuit board

3. Graph the numbers on the number line and complete the inequalities.
   $\frac{1}{20}$, $-\frac{1}{20}$, $\frac{6}{20}$, $-\frac{6}{20}$

   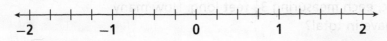

   $-\frac{6}{20}$ ▢ $-\frac{1}{20}$ $\frac{6}{20}$ ▢ $\frac{1}{20}$

For Problems 4–5, use the number line to write two different inequalities to compare the numbers.

4. −1.25 and −1$\frac{1}{8}$ 5. −$\frac{2}{5}$ and −0.5

   _____   _____

© Houghton Mifflin Harcourt Publishing Company • Image Credit: ©Artit Thongchuea/Shutterstock

Module 1 • Lesson 2

19

Test Prep

6. Use the number line to locate -0.4 and $-1\frac{1}{5}$. Then complete the inequality.

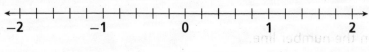

-0.4 [ ] $-1\frac{1}{5}$

7. Using the number line, select all the inequality statements that are true.

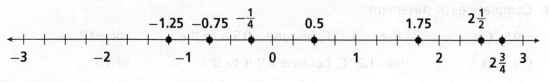

Ⓐ $2\frac{1}{2} < 2\frac{3}{4}$

Ⓑ $-1.25 < -0.75$

Ⓒ $1.75 < -\frac{1}{4}$

Ⓓ $1.75 > 0.5$

Ⓔ $2\frac{1}{2} > 2\frac{3}{4}$

Ⓕ $-1.25 > -\frac{1}{4}$

8. A water delivery service sells 5-gallon jugs of water to businesses. Each jug can differ in actual water volume by up to 1 cup. A set of jugs delivered to a business has the following differences: 0.6, -0.8, 0.5, 0.4, -0.3. Which inequality is correct?

Ⓐ $0.6 < -0.3$

Ⓑ $0.5 > 0.6$

Ⓒ $-0.8 > 0.4$

Ⓓ $-0.3 > -0.8$

Spiral Review

9. What number is 10 times as great as 450?

_____

10. Cynthia gave $\frac{1}{5}$ of her toys to her little sister. If she had 25 toys, how many did she give away?

_____

11. Laquan has 2 pieces of fabric, each measuring $3\frac{1}{4}$ feet long. How many feet of fabric does Laquan have in total?

_____

Name _____

Find and Apply Absolute Value

(I Can) find and use absolute value and magnitude to describe real-world situations.

Spark Your Learning

The table shows the low temperatures in Nome, Alaska, for five days in December. Find the distance from zero to each number.

Date	Dec. 18	Dec. 19	Dec. 20	Dec. 21	Dec. 22
Low temperature	−10 °F	−15 °F	−16 °F	8 °F	3 °F

Turn and Talk Name a real-world situation where finding the distance between two points can be useful.

© Houghton Mifflin Harcourt Publishing Company • Image Credit: ©Troutnut/Shutterstock

Build Understanding

1   The elevations of four fish in a lake are shown. The elevation of the top of a lifeguard stand is 6 feet. Graph the numbers on the number line.

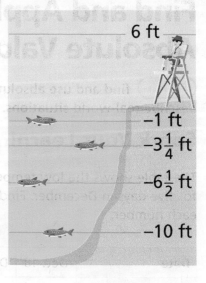

6 ft

−1 ft
−3$\frac{1}{4}$ ft
−6$\frac{1}{2}$ ft

−10 ft

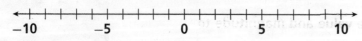

A. What is the distance from zero to each elevation on the number line?

_____

_____

_____

_____

B. Find the absolute value of each number.

The absolute value of −1 is _____.   The absolute value of 6 is _____.

The absolute value of −3$\frac{1}{4}$ is _____.   The absolute value of −10 is _____.

The absolute value of −6$\frac{1}{2}$ is _____.

2   Ms. Singh has a credit card balance of −$55. Mr. Singh has a credit card balance of −$70.

A. Write an inequality to show how the balances are related.

_____

B. Find the absolute value of each balance.

|−$55| = _____ |−$70| = _____

C. Write an inequality to show how the absolute values are related.

_____

D. Which person has the greater credit card balance? Which person has the greater debt? Explain why your answers are different.

_____

_____

_____

 Turn and Talk Can the absolute value of a number ever be negative? Explain.

Name _____

Step It Out

The **magnitude** of a number is its size or amount, without considering its sign. The magnitude of a number is the same as its absolute value.

3 ▸ Some insects produce a chemical that prevents the water in their bodies from freezing and helps them survive extreme cold. An insect's supercooling point is the lowest temperature at which it can survive. The table shows the supercooling points of several insects.

Insect	Supercooling Point (°C)
Pythid beetle	−54
Common banded hoverfly	−35
New Zealand alpine weta	−9
Pink rice borer moth	−6.8
Woolly bear caterpillar	−70

Woolly bear caterpillar

A. Graph the supercooling points on the number line.

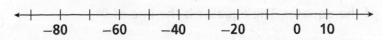

B. What are the magnitudes of −70, −54, and −35?

_____

_____

C. Complete these number sentences, which use absolute-value symbols to show the magnitude of each number from Part B.

$|-70| = \boxed{}$ $|-54| = \boxed{}$ $|-35| = \boxed{}$

D. Write an inequality to show the relationship between −70 and −35.

_____

E. Which supercooling point is closest to 0 on the number line? Explain.

_____

_____

F. Which insect has the lowest supercooling point?

_____

Check Understanding

1. A withdrawal, or money removed from a bank account, is listed on a bank statement as a negative number. Which represents a greater withdrawal, −$45.75 or −$50.25?

_____

2. What does the absolute value of −2.75 represent?

_____

On Your Own

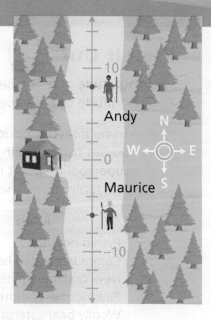

Andy

N
W ← → E
S

Maurice

3. (MP) **Reason** A model for the distance traveled from a cabin in a state park represents distances south of the cabin as negative numbers and distances north of the cabin as positive numbers. The number line shows the locations of two hikers. Distance is measured in miles.

A. Who walked farther from the cabin? Explain.

_____

B. How many miles is Maurice from the cabin?

_____

4. **Geography** The equator is an imaginary circle around Earth halfway between the North Pole and the South Pole. Lines of latitude are imaginary circles around Earth parallel to the equator, used to determine position north and south of the equator. The equator is the line of 0° latitude.

A. What latitude is opposite of 30° north latitude?

_____

B. How do these latitudes compare?

_____

5. The average low surface temperature for Mars is −80 °F. The average low surface temperature for Jupiter is −234 °F. Which temperature has the greater absolute value? Explain.

_____

For Problems 6–9, find the absolute value.

6. $|9.35|$ **7.** $|-1|$ **8.** $|-\frac{5}{6}|$ **9.** $|0|$

  I'm in a Learning Mindset!

What strategies do I use to stay on task when working on my own?

_____

_____

Name _____

LESSON 1.3
**More Practice/
Homework**

ONLINE

Video Tutorials and
Interactive Examples

Find and Apply Absolute Value

1. The change in the daily high temperature from Monday to Tuesday was −6.8 °F. The change in the daily high temperature from Thursday to Friday was −2.1 °F. Which represents a greater change in temperature?

_____

2. New memory is added to a computer so that it can run faster. The times it takes to open a graphics program and an e-mail program are recorded before and after the new memory is added. The change in the amount of time to open the graphics program is −8 seconds. The change in the amount of time to open the e-mail program is −5 seconds. Which shows more improvement? Explain.

_____

3. In baseball, the difference in the number of runs scored by a team and its opponent is studied by managers. In a Monday night game, the difference in the number of runs for a certain team is −3 runs. In a Wednesday night game, the difference in the number of runs for the same team is −9 runs. Which game shows the larger difference?

For Problems 4–7, determine which number has the lesser magnitude.

4. $\frac{1}{10}$ and $-\frac{6}{10}$

5. −2 and 10

6. −20 and −30

7. −4.05 and −5

For Problems 8 and 9, find each absolute value.

8. $\left|\frac{2}{9}\right|$ _____

9. $|-3.45|$ _____

For Problems 10–12, write a mathematical expression using absolute value symbols to match the verbal expression.

10. the opposite of the absolute value of negative one-eighth _____

11. the absolute value of negative one-eighth _____

12. the opposite of the absolute value of one-eighth _____

Test Prep

13. Each day, the total number of people who visit the library is recorded. The change from the same day last year is also recorded. The changes for four consecutive days are shown below.

Monday: +127, Tuesday: −18, Wednesday: +19, Thursday: −209

Which day had the largest change in the number of visitors compared to the same day last year?

(A) Monday

(B) Tuesday

(C) Wednesday

(D) Thursday

14. What is the absolute value of $-1\frac{1}{5}$?

_____

15. Which bank balance represents the greatest amount owed?

(A) a bank balance of −$20.50

(B) a bank balance of −$27.50

(C) a bank balance of −$50.75

(D) a bank balance of −$36.25

16. Which statement is correct?

(A) $|8| = -8$

(B) $|10.5| > |-9.75|$

(C) $|-2\frac{3}{5}| < |1\frac{7}{8}|$

(D) $|0| > 0$

Spiral Review

17. What is the product of 12 and 19?

_____

18. Write an inequality to compare the decimals 0.149 and 0.128.

_____

19. Find the sum: $1.23 + 4.99$.

_____

20. Find the quotient: $80 ÷ 8$.

_____

Name _____

Find and Apply LCM and GCF

(I Can) find and use the GCF or LCM to rewrite and compare fractions.

Step It Out

1 ▷ Three runners leave the starting line at the same time. Lena runs each lap in 3 minutes, Aria runs each lap in 5 minutes, and Tran runs each lap in 6 minutes. When is the first time, in minutes, that all three runners will cross the starting line together?

A. How many minutes does it take Lena to run 12 laps?

☐ laps × $\dfrac{\text{☐ minutes}}{\text{1 lap}}$ = ☐ minutes

B. Complete the table.

Lap	1	2	3	4	5	6	7	8	9	10	
Lena's time (min)	3	6			15			24			3-minute lap
Aria's time (min)	5	10		20					45		5-minute lap
Tran's time (min)	6	12				36		48		60	6-minute lap

C. Look at the results in the table. What do you notice about the times in each column? _____

D. Look at the rows for the three runners. Do they have any time in common? If so, what is it? _____

The first time in minutes that all three runners cross the starting line together is the least common multiple of their lap times.

_____ is the least common multiple of _____, _____, and _____.

Turn and Talk If you extended the table, what would the next common multiple be? What pattern do you notice in the common multiples?

Step It Out

2 ▷ Volunteers are making care packages for hurricane victims. Each volunteer has 24 granola bars and 16 bottles of water to put in the packages. Each package must contain the same number of granola bars and the same number of water bottles. What is the greatest number of care packages a volunteer can make?

A. Think about all the ways 24 granola bars and 16 water bottles can be divided equally among the packages. Complete the tables.

Care packages	Granola bars per package
1	24
2	
3	
	6
	4
8	
12	
	1

Care packages	Water bottles per package
1	16
2	
4	
	2
16	

24 granola bars

16 water bottles

B. In the first table, the numbers of packages and the numbers of granola bars per package are factors of _____.

In the second table, the numbers of packages and the numbers of water bottles per package are factors of _____.

Using the tables, list all the possible numbers of care packages for each item.

Granola bars: _____

Water bottles: _____

C. What numbers occur in both lists? _____

D. What is the greatest number of care packages a volunteer can make?

_____

E. The greatest common factor of 24 and 16 is _____.

F. You can use the greatest common factor to write the total number of bottles of water and granola bars, 24 + 16, as a sum of products.

24 + 16 = ☐(☐) + ☐(☐)

You can use the **Distributive Property** to write the total number of items as the product of the GCF and another sum.

☐(☐) + ☐(☐) = ☐(☐ + ☐) = ☐(☐)

3 Which is greater, $\frac{5}{6}$ or $\frac{7}{10}$?

A. Complete the lists of multiples of the denominators.

$\frac{5}{6}$: 6, ☐ , ☐ , ☐ ,

$\frac{7}{10}$: 10, ☐ , ☐ , ☐

B. The least common multiple (LCM) of the denominators is ____.

C. Rewrite the fractions using the LCM as the **common denominator**.

$\frac{5}{6} = \dfrac{\Box}{\Box}$ $\frac{7}{10} = \dfrac{\Box}{\Box}$

D. Use the new fractions to write an inequality to compare the original fractions.

$\dfrac{\Box}{\Box}$ ☐ $\dfrac{\Box}{\Box}$, so $\frac{5}{6}$ ☐ $\frac{7}{10}$.

4 Which is greater, $-\frac{13}{24}$ or $-\frac{7}{18}$?

A. Complete the lists of multiples for the denominators.

$-\frac{13}{24}$: 24, ☐ , ☐ , ☐

$-\frac{7}{18}$: 18, ☐ , ☐ , ☐

B. The least common multiple (LCM) of the denominators is ____.

C. Rewrite the fractions using the LCM of the denominators and complete the inequality to compare the original fractions.

$-\dfrac{\Box}{\Box}$ ☐ $-\dfrac{\Box}{\Box}$, so $-\frac{13}{24}$ ☐ $-\frac{7}{18}$

D. How would you compare the numbers using $-\frac{1}{2}$ as a benchmark?

_____

_____

Check Understanding

1. Paper cups are sold in packages of 6, and napkins are sold in packages of 8. Ted wants to buy the same number of each. What is the least number of cups and napkins he needs to buy?

_____

2. A florist has 60 tulips and 72 daffodils. She will make bouquets with the same number of tulips and the same number of daffodils in each, using all the flowers. What is the greatest number of bouquets the florist can make?

_____

On Your Own

3. Jamie makes plates and bowls. She needs to ship 48 plates and 54 bowls to a store. She wants to ship the same number of items in each box. Plates and bowls are shipped separately.

  A. What is the greatest number of items she can ship in each box?

  _____

  B. How many boxes of items will Jamie ship if she ships the greatest number possible in each box?

  Boxes of plates: ☐   Boxes of bowls: ☐

  C. (MP) **Use Structure** What is the greatest common factor of 48 and 54? Use the greatest common factor to write the total number of plates and bowls as a sum of products. Then use the distributive property to write the total number as a product.

  _____

4. Grant is making muffins for a reunion. The recipe for blueberry muffins makes 12 muffins. The recipe for bran muffins makes 18 muffins. He wants to make the same number of each kind of muffin using only full recipes of each.

  A. What is the least number of each type of muffin Grant can make?

  _____

  B. How many batches of each recipe will Grant make if he makes the least number of each type of muffin possible?

  Blueberry: _____ batches   Bran: _____ batches

5. A year is $\frac{1}{3}$ of the lifespan of a fire ant queen. A year is $\frac{1}{30}$ of a termite queen's lifespan. Write an inequality to compare the fractions of the insects' lifespans that a year represents.

Fire ant queen   Termite queen

6. (MP) **Reason** Cameron and Tatiana volunteer at the library. Cameron shelves one book every $\frac{1}{4}$ minute. Tatiana shelves one book every $\frac{3}{10}$ minute. Who is quicker at shelving books? Explain how you found your answer.

_____

7. Darnell helps to make lunches at a picnic. Each picnic basket will have the amounts of ham salad and potato salad shown in the illustration. Which is greater, the amount of ham salad or the amount of potato salad? Show your work.

8. (MP) **Critique Reasoning** Ryan is making biscuits. The recipe calls for 0.25 quart of milk and 2.5 cups of flour. He has $\frac{1}{5}$ quart of milk and $\frac{9}{4}$ cups of flour. Ryan makes the recipe with the milk and flour that he has. Explain his error.

9. Use the LCM to write the fractions $\frac{3}{8}$ and $\frac{1}{10}$ with a common denominator. Then write an inequality involving the rewritten fractions to show which is greater.

10. Groups of sixth graders and seventh graders compete in a race. The contestants include $\frac{3}{4}$ of the sixth graders and $\frac{4}{5}$ of the seventh graders. Which group has a greater fraction of their grade represented?

11. **Open Ended** How can you determine which of the fractions below is greatest?

$$\frac{13}{20}, \frac{5}{8}, \frac{3}{5}, \frac{3}{10}$$

12. The table shows the rainfall in four towns on the same day. Which town had more rain, Brighton or Springfield? Morristown or Pine Grove?

Town	Morristown	Brighton	Springfield	Pine Grove
Rainfall (inches)	$3\frac{9}{16}$	$3\frac{5}{16}$	$3\frac{8}{12}$	$3\frac{13}{24}$

13. (MP) **Use Structure** The table shows the distance below ground of items found at an archaeological site. Researchers also found a mouse fossil at the same site. Which, if any, of the items in the table were a greater distance below ground than the mouse fossil shown?

$5\frac{3}{4}$ feet deep

Item	Distance below ground (feet)
spoon	$5\frac{3}{8}$
key	$6\frac{3}{4}$
cup	$4\frac{3}{12}$
bowl	$5\frac{5}{6}$

For Problems 14–17, find the LCM of the number pair.

14. 8 and 4   **15.** 5 and 12   **16.** 6 and 21   **17.** 15 and 9

For Problems 18–21, find the GCF of the number pair.

18. 16 and 30   **19.** 24 and 32   **20.** 26 and 39   **21.** 54 and 36

For Problems 22–24, complete the inequality using the symbol $>$ or $<$.

22. $\frac{4}{10}$ ▢ $\frac{5}{6}$ **23.** $\frac{3}{33}$ ▢ $\frac{40}{100}$ **24.** $\frac{5}{12}$ ▢ $\frac{3}{20}$

For Problems 25–30, write an inequality to compare the fractions.

25. $\frac{24}{18}$ and $\frac{25}{15}$ **26.** $-\frac{3}{8}$ and $-\frac{5}{7}$

27. $-\frac{18}{42}$ and $-\frac{15}{21}$ **28.** $\frac{12}{16}$ and $\frac{16}{24}$

29. $\frac{5}{12}$ and $\frac{11}{28}$ **30.** $-\frac{7}{10}$ and $-\frac{5}{9}$

LESSON 1.4
**More Practice/
Homework**

ONLINE

Video Tutorials and
Interactive Examples

Find and Apply LCM and GCF

1. Martha ran $\frac{5}{8}$ of a mile and Terry ran $\frac{6}{15}$ of a mile. Who ran a larger portion of a mile? Write an inequality to compare the portions of a mile.

_____

2. (MP) **Reason** A radio station is giving away concert tickets to every 60th caller and a concert T-shirt to every 45th caller. What will be the number of the first caller to get both items? Explain.

_____

3. A cuckoo clock has birds that pop out of their nests every 6 minutes and dancers that pop out every 15 minutes. The birds and dancers have just popped out at the same time. When will this happen again in the next 60 minutes?

_____

4. String-cheese sticks are sold in packs of 10 and celery sticks in packs of 15. Mr. Deluca wants to give each of 30 students one string-cheese stick and one celery stick. How many packs of each food should he buy so there are no sticks left over?

_____

Math on the Spot Find the GCF of each set of numbers.

5. 8 and 12

6. 10, 15, and 30

7. 18, 36, and 60

_____

8. Use the GCF of 48 and 30 to write the sum of the two numbers as the product of their GCF and another sum.

$$\boxed{}\left(\boxed{}\right) + \boxed{}\left(\boxed{}\right) = \boxed{}\left(\boxed{} + \boxed{}\right) = \boxed{}\left(\boxed{}\right)$$

For Problems 9–11, compare the fractions using the LCM.

9. $\frac{1}{7}, \frac{2}{3}$

10. $\frac{3}{5}, \frac{1}{4}$

11. $\frac{4}{6}, \frac{4}{8}$

_____

For Problems 12–14, compare the fractions.

12. $\frac{10}{14}, \frac{3}{7}$

13. $-\frac{14}{21}, -\frac{3}{9}$

14. $\frac{30}{20}, \frac{8}{2}$

Test Prep

15. Which expression shows the sum of 72 and 96 as the product of the GCF and a sum of two numbers with no common factor?

- Ⓐ 12(6 + 8)
- Ⓑ 24(3 + 4)
- Ⓒ 24(6 + 8)
- Ⓓ 48(3 + 4)

16. Write an inequality to compare the numbers 12.7 and $12\frac{3}{4}$.

_____

17. Ambrose and Kaitlin are taking a pottery class. Kaitlin makes a bowl every 13 minutes. Ambrose makes a bowl every 7 minutes. If they start at the same time, after how many minutes will they finish bowls at the same time?

_____

18. Jewel has 20 apples and 16 bananas that she wants to arrange in baskets. There needs to be the same number of apples and the same number of bananas in each basket. What is the greatest number of baskets she can make? How many apples and bananas will be in each basket?

_____

Spiral Review

19. Which is greater, −13 or −10?

_____

20. Which is greater, 2.5 or $\frac{9}{4}$?

_____

21. What is the absolute value of −18?

_____

Name _____

Order Rational Numbers

(I Can) order positive and negative rational numbers of different forms.

Step It Out

1 ▷ The average weight of an adult African pygmy mouse is 0.27 ounce. Weights of the mice vary depending on age, diet, and whether the mouse is male or female. The differences from average weight in ounces for a set of African pygmy mice at a zoo are shown.

0.09, −0.14, 0.12, 0.06, −0.1

A. How can you use a number line to order the numbers?

_____

_____

B. Graph the numbers on the number line.

```
←++++++++++++++++++++++++++++++++++++++++→
 −0.2        −0.1         0         0.1        0.2
```

C. Complete the statements using the graph in Part B.

A number to the left of a second number on a number line is

| less / greater | than the second number.

D. Write an inequality to compare 0.09 and −0.1.

_____

E. Write the numbers in order from least to greatest.

_____

 Turn and Talk How are 0.5 and 0.29 related? Explain.

Step It Out

One way to compare rational numbers is to rewrite them in the same form.

2 ▷ Look at the list of numbers.

$-1\frac{2}{5}, -0.62, -1.18, -\frac{3}{5}$

A. Rewrite each decimal as a fraction.

$-0.62 = -\dfrac{\boxed{}}{100} = -\dfrac{\boxed{}}{50}$ $-1.18 = -1\dfrac{\boxed{}}{100} = -1\dfrac{\boxed{}}{50}$

B. What is the least common multiple, or LCM, of the denominators of all of the fractions?

_____

C. What are the numbers written with the LCM as the common denominator?

$-1\frac{2}{5} = -1\dfrac{\boxed{}}{50}$ $-0.62 = -\dfrac{\boxed{}}{50}$ $-1.18 = -1\dfrac{\boxed{}}{50}$ $-\frac{3}{5} = -\dfrac{\boxed{}}{50}$

D. Write the numbers in order in their new forms and then in their original forms from least to greatest.

_____

 Turn and Talk Is there another method you can use to order the numbers $2\frac{1}{2}$, -0.25, 1.5, and $-\frac{7}{8}$?

Check Understanding

1. Use the number line to graph the following numbers: 0.25, $-\frac{1}{2}$, -0.75, $\frac{3}{4}$. Then write the numbers in order from least to greatest.

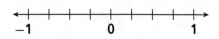

_____

2. Write the list of numbers in order from greatest to least:

$-\frac{5}{8}, 1.4, -0.6, \frac{1}{2}, 1\frac{3}{8}.$

_____

On Your Own

3. A musician uses water glasses to play music. The glasses contain 0.5 cup, $\frac{4}{6}$ cup, $\frac{1}{3}$ cup, and $\frac{4}{5}$ cup of water. To play the glasses, the musician lines them up from least amount of water to greatest amount of water. Write the amounts of water in order from least to greatest.

_____

4. Sakura is making a mobile for her room. She has a spool of twine that she cuts into lengths of $\frac{5}{6}$ foot, 0.75 foot, and $\frac{4}{5}$ foot. The mobile will have the pieces of twine with lengths in order from shortest to longest.

   A. What do you need to do before you can compare the lengths?

   _____

   _____

   B. In what order, from shortest to longest, will Sakura use the pieces of twine in the mobile?

   _____

5. The average human walking speed is 3.1 miles per hour. Shoe company employees measure people's walking speeds and record the difference from the average walking speed for each person. The results are shown.

Walker	Differences from average walking speed (mph)
A	−0.5
B	$\frac{3}{10}$
C	0.7
D	$-\frac{4}{5}$

Write the numbers in order from least to greatest.

_____

For Problems 6 and 7, order the rational numbers from least to greatest.

6. $\frac{7}{8}$, −0.25, $-\frac{1}{16}$, 0.75 _____

7. −2.1, $1\frac{2}{5}$, $-\frac{9}{10}$, 0.7 _____

8. The temperatures on four mornings are −8.5 °F, −2 °F, −11 °F, and 0.7 °F.

    A. Graph the temperatures on the number line.

    B. What was the temperature on the coldest morning?

    _____

    C. What was the temperature on the warmest morning?

    _____

    D. Use the number line to order the temperatures
       from least to greatest.

    _____

For Problems 9–11, graph the numbers. Then write the numbers in order from least to greatest.

9. $-1\frac{2}{5}$, 1.2, $-4\frac{4}{10}$, 0

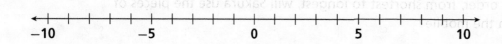

_____

10. −2, 1.1, −6.4, $-4\frac{1}{2}$

_____

11. $6\frac{1}{3}$, −4, 3.5, −6

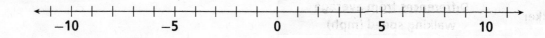

_____

Order Rational Numbers

1. A food company uses large coolers to store fresh food. The temperatures in the coolers are measured in degrees Celsius: −2.65°, −0.1°, −2.7°, 1.48°, 0.09°. Write the temperatures in order from coldest to warmest.

2. The daily changes in four stock prices are shown in the table. Write the changes from least to greatest in fraction form with a common denominator.

Stock	1	2	3	4
Change	$-2\frac{35}{100}$	−1.64	2.05	$1\frac{9}{50}$

3. **STEM** Air filters are rated based on the particle size that the filter will collect. Hospitals use air filters to remove dust and other particles from the air. The maximum particle sizes that a set of filters will collect (in units called microns) are $\frac{12}{10}$, 0.01, 0.38, $\frac{5}{10}$, and 0.07. Write the particle sizes in order from least to greatest.

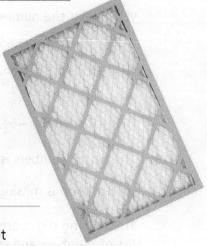

4. (MP) **Critique Reasoning** Margo lists the sizes, in inches, of a set of screws: $\frac{9}{64}$, $\frac{5}{32}$, $\frac{1}{16}$, $\frac{1}{8}$. She reasons that because the denominators are in order from greatest to least, the list is in order from least to greatest. Is Margo correct? Why or why not?

_____

_____

_____

For Problems 5–6, write the rational numbers in order from least to greatest.

5. −4.22, 0.8, $-4\frac{1}{2}$, 8.4, $\frac{4}{3}$

6. $\frac{1}{9}$, $-\frac{2}{3}$, $\frac{1}{18}$, $-\frac{3}{9}$

_____   _____

7. Write the numbers in order from least to greatest: 5.75, −3.25, 2.6.

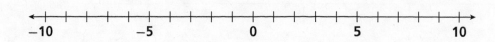

Test Prep

8. The average growth of a loblolly pine over its first ten years is 30 inches per year. The table shows the difference between the average yearly growth and the actual yearly growth for four trees.

Tree	Difference from average growth (in in.)
A	$-6\frac{3}{4}$
B	-6.6
C	$-6\frac{7}{8}$
D	-6.85

Which lists the numbers in order from least to greatest?

Ⓐ $-6\frac{3}{4}$, -6.6, -6.85, $-6\frac{7}{8}$

Ⓑ $-6\frac{7}{8}$, $-6\frac{3}{4}$, -6.85, -6.6

Ⓒ $-6\frac{3}{4}$, -6.6, $-6\frac{7}{8}$, -6.85

Ⓓ $-6\frac{7}{8}$, -6.85, $-6\frac{3}{4}$, -6.6

9. The list of numbers is in order from least to greatest, but some

information is missing: $-0.\blacksquare$, -0.41, $\frac{2}{\blacksquare}$, $\frac{3}{5}$, $1\frac{1}{\blacksquare}$.

The missing digits are 3, 4, and 5. Use each digit only once to complete the list of numbers and rewrite the list in order from least to greatest.

Spiral Review

10. Paige gave $\frac{1}{6}$ of her books to her friend. If she had 24 books, how many did she give away?

11. Complete the inequality with the correct comparison symbol.

-4 ☐ $|-4|$

12. What are the absolute values of -15, -7, and 3?

Vocabulary

Choose the correct term from the Vocabulary box.

Vocabulary

rational number
negative number
least common multiple
greatest common factor
positive number

1. The smallest number, other than zero, that is a multiple of two or more given numbers is the _____.

2. A _____ can be written in the form $\frac{a}{b}$, where a and b are integers and $b \neq 0$.

3. A number that is less than zero is a _____.

4. The _____ is the greatest number by which two or more given numbers can be evenly divided.

5. A number that is to the right of zero on a horizontal number line is a _____.

Concepts and Skills

6. What is the value of the integer A?

   _____

   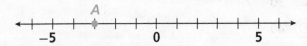

7. (MP) **Use Tools** At 3 a.m., the temperature is −6 °F. At 5 a.m., the temperature is −2 °F. Is the temperature at 3 a.m. warmer or colder than the temperature at 5 a.m.? State what strategy and tool you will use to answer the question, explain your choice, and then find the answer.

   _____

8. A thermometer in Grand Forks, North Dakota, reads −4.5 °F in January. The temperature on the same day in February is the opposite of the temperature in January. What is the temperature in February?

   _____ °F

9. Use the number line to match the statements to the point on the number line.

   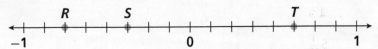

   Point R •   • The absolute value is $\frac{5}{8}$.

   Point S •   • The absolute value is $\frac{3}{8}$.

   Point T •   • The absolute value is $\frac{3}{4}$.

10. Positive and negative numbers are used to indicate elevations. Which statement is true about the elevations 30 feet and −30 feet?

Ⓐ They are both 30 feet above sea level.

Ⓑ The elevations are each the same distance from sea level.

Ⓒ They are both 30 feet below sea level.

Ⓓ The elevation of 30 feet is farther from sea level than the elevation of −30 feet.

For Problems 11–13, use the number line to complete each inequality.

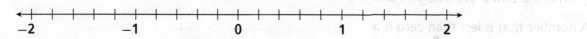

11. $-1\frac{8}{10}$ ☐ $|-1.8|$ **12.** $|0.4|$ ☐ $-\frac{4}{5}$ **13.** $-\frac{6}{5}$ ☐ -1.3

14. What is the least common denominator for the fractions $\frac{3}{4}$, $-\frac{2}{5}$, and $\frac{3}{2}$?

Ⓐ 10

Ⓑ 20

Ⓒ 30

Ⓓ 40

15. Which expression shows the sum of 54 and 36 as the product of their GCF and a sum of two numbers with no common factor?

Ⓐ 6(6 + 9)

Ⓑ 18(2 + 3)

Ⓒ 18(18 + 36)

Ⓓ 108(2 + 3)

16. Finches are small songbirds. The table lists the lengths of four finches, each of a different species. Order the finches from shortest to longest.

Finch species	Length (in.)
House finch	$5\frac{5}{8}$
Indigo bunting	4.9
Crimson finch	$5\frac{1}{10}$
Purple finch	5.9

2 Fraction Division

A Perplexing Pet Puzzle

30 pets

Ms. Tran wrote a set of clues about her pets.

Use the clues to complete the table with the number of each type of pet she owns.

I have 30 pets in all.

I have $\frac{1}{2}$ as many cats as mice.

I have $\frac{1}{3}$ as many dogs as cats.

Exactly $\frac{1}{5}$ of my pets are mice.

The rest of my pets are fish.

Type of Pet	Number
Cat	
Dog	
Mouse	
Fish	

Turn and Talk

- Which type of pet did you start with when completing the table? Why did you start with this pet?

- How could you tell that the number of dogs would be less than the number of mice without performing any calculations?

Are You Ready?

Complete these problems to review prior concepts and skills you will need for this module.

Factors

Find all factor pairs for each number.

1. 18

2. 21

3. 48

4. 65

Add Fractions and Decimals

Find each sum or difference.

5. $7.2 + 2.6$

6. $8.5 - 7$

7. $7.55 - 3.25$

8. $\frac{1}{3} + \frac{1}{5}$

9. $\frac{9}{10} - \frac{7}{8}$

10. $\frac{1}{6} + \frac{5}{12}$

Multiply Fractions

Find each product.

11. $\frac{3}{4} \times \frac{5}{8}$

12. $\frac{5}{6} \times \frac{9}{10}$

13. $\frac{1}{2} \times \frac{1}{4}$

Divide with Unit Fractions and Whole Numbers

Find each quotient.

14. $6 \div \frac{1}{3}$

15. $1 \div \frac{1}{10}$

16. $\frac{1}{4} \div 6$

Name _____

Explore Division of Fractions with Like and Unlike Denominators

(I Can) divide two fractions using at least two methods.

Spark Your Learning

PAIRS

Jayson is making sushi rolls. He has $\frac{5}{6}$ cup of rice and will use $\frac{2}{6}$ cup for each sushi roll. How many whole sushi rolls can he make?

Turn and Talk How many sushi rolls can Jayson make if he uses up all the rice? Explain.

Build Understanding

1   Malik is making egg rolls to share with Jayson. Malik has $\frac{4}{5}$ pound of chicken and will use the amount shown per batch. How many batches of egg rolls can Malik make?

$\frac{2}{5}$ pounds of chicken per batch

A. Previously, you divided a fraction by a whole number. Write an **expression** to show how you would divide a fraction by a fraction to solve this problem.

How many groups of _____ are in _____,

or _____ ÷ _____.

B. Show how you can use a model to represent $\frac{4}{5}$ pound of chicken. Use the model to show how to divide $\frac{4}{5}$ into groups of $\frac{2}{5}$.

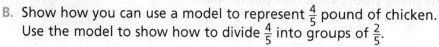

$\frac{1}{2}$	$\frac{1}{2}$

C. How many groups of $\frac{2}{5}$ are there in $\frac{4}{5}$? How do you know? How many batches of egg rolls can Malik make?

_____

_____

_____

    Turn and Talk How can you use the numerators to find the answer in Task 1? Explain.

2   Suppose Malik had $\frac{3}{4}$ pound of chicken and uses $\frac{3}{8}$ pound to make one batch of eggrolls. How many batches of egg rolls could he make?

A. What fraction strip could you use to represent both $\frac{3}{4}$ and $\frac{3}{8}$? Explain.

_____

B. Use your model to divide $\frac{3}{4}$ into groups of $\frac{3}{8}$. How many groups can you make? _____

C. How many batches of eggrolls can Malik make using this recipe?

_____

3 Roselyn needs to add $\frac{5}{8}$ cup of orange juice to make a sauce for her stir-fry. If she uses a $\frac{1}{4}$-cup measuring cup, how many measuring cups will she need to add?

A. How can you divide $\frac{5}{8}$ into groups of $\frac{1}{4}$? Complete the following statement.

Since $\frac{1}{4} = \frac{\boxed{}}{8}$, you can divide $\frac{5}{8}$ into groups of _____.

B. Use the number line to show the number of groups of $\frac{1}{4}$ in $\frac{5}{8}$.

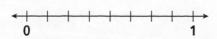

0   1

C. How many $\frac{1}{4}$-measuring cups of orange juice will Roselyn need to add?

$\frac{1}{4}$ cup

_____

D. How many measuring cups of juice will Roselyn need to add if she uses a $\frac{1}{8}$-cup measuring cup or a $\frac{3}{8}$-cup measuring cup? Use your results to complete the first column of the table.

E. *Reciprocals* can help you find quotients. You find the reciprocal of a fraction by switching the **numerator** and **denominator**. Complete the following equations with the correct reciprocals.

$\frac{1}{4} \times \dfrac{\boxed{}}{\boxed{}} = 1$ $\dfrac{\boxed{}}{\boxed{}} \times \frac{1}{8} = 1$ $\frac{3}{8} \times \dfrac{\boxed{}}{\boxed{}} = 1$

Quotient	Product
$\frac{5}{8} \div \frac{1}{4} = \frac{5}{2}$	$\frac{5}{8} \times \dfrac{\boxed{}}{1} = \frac{5}{2}$
$\frac{5}{8} \div \frac{1}{8} = \boxed{}$	$\frac{5}{8} \times \dfrac{\boxed{}}{1} = 5$
$\frac{5}{8} \div \frac{3}{8} = \dfrac{\boxed{}}{\boxed{}}$	$\frac{5}{8} \times \dfrac{\boxed{}}{3} = \frac{5}{3}$

F. Now complete the second column of the table. Look for a pattern in the table to complete the following statements.

In each row of the table, the **quotient** equals the

_____.

To find the quotient of two fractions, multiply the

_____ fraction by the reciprocal of the _____ fraction.

Connect to Vocabulary

Two numbers whose product is 1 are **reciprocals** or **multiplicative inverses**.

4 ▶ Tina feeds her dog $\frac{4}{7}$ pound of dog food per day. If she buys the bag of dog food shown, how many days will it last?

9 pounds

DOG FOOD

A. What expression could you use to solve the problem?

_____

B. What do you need to do first to find the quotient?

_____

C. What do you need to do next?

_____

_____

D. Show how to find a quotient to solve the problem.

_____

_____

The dog food will last _____ days.

 Turn and Talk About how many 9-pound bags of dog food will Tina need to feed her dog for an entire year? Explain.

Check Understanding

1. Marcus needs to measure out $\frac{2}{3}$ liter of a solution. He is using a container that holds $\frac{1}{6}$ liter.

   A. How many groups of $\frac{1}{6}$ are in $\frac{2}{3}$? _____

   B. How many times will Marcus need to fill the container?

   _____

2. Roberta bought $\frac{9}{10}$ pound of raisins. She is putting $\frac{2}{5}$ pound in bags for her lunch. How many $\frac{2}{5}$-pound bags can Roberta fill? Does she have any left over?

_____

For Problems 3–6, divide the fractions.

3. $\frac{6}{5} \div \frac{2}{5}$ _____

4. $\frac{3}{8} \div \frac{1}{3}$ _____

5. $\frac{5}{9} \div \frac{2}{3}$ _____

6. $10 \div \frac{2}{5}$ _____

On Your Own

7. Jasmine has $\frac{4}{5}$ pound of fertilizer. She wants to store the fertilizer in separate containers, each with $\frac{1}{5}$ pound of fertilizer. How many groups of $\frac{1}{5}$ are in $\frac{4}{5}$? How many containers will she need?

_____

8. (MP) **Reason** A city places street lights at equal intervals along a city street beginning $\frac{3}{8}$ mile from one end of the street. If the street is $\frac{7}{8}$ mile long, how many street lights will the city use? Explain.

_____

$\frac{3}{8}$ mile

9. Eric has $\frac{9}{16}$ pound of bird feed left. If he feeds his bird $\frac{1}{8}$ pound each day, how many days can he feed the bird before he needs to buy more food?

_____

(MP) **Model with Mathematics** For Problems 10–13, write an expression to model each situation. Then answer the question.

10. Mr. Duale would like to plant a vegetable garden. He has a part of an acre of land as shown, which he plans to divide into $\frac{2}{5}$-acre sections. How many sections will he have?

_____

$\frac{8}{10}$ acre of land

11. **STEM** The width of a single atom of aluminum is $\frac{7}{25}$ nanometer, which is more than 100,000 times smaller than a millimeter. Scientists sometimes use Ångströms to measure distances on an atomic scale. One Ångström is $\frac{1}{10}$ nanometer. How many Ångströms wide is a single atom of aluminum?

_____

12. At a school, each class period is $\frac{3}{4}$ hour long. If there are 6 hours of class time in a school day, how many class periods are there?

_____

13. A pitcher contains $\frac{8}{10}$ liter of juice and is used to fill cups that hold $\frac{1}{5}$ liter. How many cups can be filled?

_____

14. (MP) **Model with Mathematics** Diane had $\frac{15}{16}$ cup of butter. A recipe for a cake calls for $\frac{1}{4}$ cup of butter. Diane was able to make 3 whole cakes. How much butter did she use? How much butter does she have left over? Show how to model and solve this problem.

15. Sandy is a jeweler. She has 2 grams of gold. Each earring she makes contains $\frac{3}{16}$ gram of gold. How many earrings can she make? How many earrings could she make from a gold bar of 1,000 grams of gold? Show your work.

For Problems 16–19, find the reciprocal.

16. $\frac{5}{16}$ _____   17. $\frac{1}{5}$ _____   18. 4 _____   19. $\frac{4}{9}$ _____

For Problems 20–28, divide the fractions.

20. $\frac{5}{12} \div \frac{1}{3}$ _____   21. $\frac{2}{3} \div \frac{1}{6}$ _____   22. $\frac{1}{2} \div \frac{7}{8}$ _____

23. $\frac{11}{15} \div \frac{3}{5}$ _____   24. $\frac{1}{6} \div \frac{2}{3}$ _____   25. $\frac{5}{14} \div \frac{5}{7}$ _____

26. $\frac{4}{5} \div \frac{24}{25}$ _____   27. $\frac{5}{6} \div \frac{5}{9}$ _____   28. $\frac{7}{8} \div \frac{3}{16}$ _____

I'm in a Learning Mindset!

What strategies do I use to ensure I can complete my work on dividing fractions with different denominators?

LESSON 2.1
**More Practice/
Homework**

ONLINE
 **Video Tutorials and
Interactive Examples**

Explore Division of Fractions with Like and Unlike Denominators

1. A small bookshelf is $\frac{8}{12}$ yard long. How many books can fit on the shelf if the width of each book is $\frac{1}{24}$ yard? Explain.

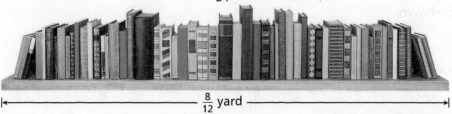

$\longleftarrow \frac{8}{12}$ yard $\longrightarrow$

_____

2. (MP) **Reason** Isabella owns a rectangular lot with an area of $\frac{9}{32}$ square mile. If the length of the western side of her lot is $\frac{3}{4}$ mile, what is the width of the northern side? How can you find the width?

_____

_____

3. **Math on the Spot** Show two methods for finding the quotient $\frac{3}{8} \div \frac{3}{4}$.

_____

_____

4. (MP) **Construct Arguments** When $\frac{9}{10}$ is divided by $\frac{2}{5}$, will the quotient be greater than 1 or less than 1? How do you know?

_____

_____

For Problems 5–8, find the reciprocal.

5. $\frac{7}{8}$ _____

6. $\frac{1}{10}$ _____

7. 12 _____

8. $\frac{14}{16}$ _____

For Problems 9–14, divide the fractions.

9. $\frac{3}{8} \div \frac{1}{8}$ _____

10. $\frac{9}{2} \div \frac{4}{10}$ _____

11. $\frac{5}{8} \div \frac{1}{24}$ _____

12. $\frac{5}{6} \div \frac{5}{24}$ _____

13. $12 \div \frac{18}{25}$ _____

14. $20 \div \frac{15}{16}$ _____

Test Prep

15. How many $\frac{1}{2}$ cups are in $\frac{7}{8}$ cup?

_____

16. An expression is shown.

$$\frac{2}{10} \div \frac{5}{4}$$

What is the value of the expression?

(A) $\frac{1}{50}$ (C) $\frac{8}{50}$

(B) $\frac{4}{10}$ (D) $\frac{1}{2}$

17. A large toy weighs $\frac{5}{8}$ pound. How many small toys that each weigh $\frac{5}{16}$ pound have a combined weight equal to the weight of the large toy?

_____

18. Select all the expressions that have the same value as $\frac{3}{5} \div \frac{6}{8}$.

(A) $\frac{3}{5} \div \frac{8}{6}$ (D) $\frac{24}{40} \div \frac{30}{40}$

(B) $\frac{3}{5} \times \frac{8}{6}$ (E) $\frac{24}{40} \times \frac{40}{30}$

(C) $\frac{5}{3} \times \frac{6}{8}$

Spiral Review

19. On Monday, the temperature was $-5\,°F$. On Tuesday, the temperature was $-8\,°F$. Which temperature has a greater absolute value? Which temperature is colder?

_____

20. What is the product of $2\frac{1}{2}$ and $1\frac{1}{4}$?

_____

21. Order the numbers from least to greatest.

$-\frac{9}{4}$, -2.5, $2\frac{1}{2}$, 0, $-2\frac{1}{3}$

_____

Name _____

Explore Division of Mixed Numbers

(I Can) divide a mixed number by a whole number, fraction, or mixed number.

Spark Your Learning

Four friends go hiking. They bring snacks, a compass, and $3\frac{1}{3}$ quarts of water. If they share the water equally, how many quarts will each person get?

 Turn and Talk How could you use a model to solve this problem? Explain.

Build Understanding

1 Three friends go on a hike that is $4\frac{1}{2}$ miles long. If they take breaks as shown, then how many breaks will they take?

taking a break every $\frac{3}{4}$ mile

A. Draw a bar model to represent the **mixed number** $4\frac{1}{2}$. How many equal-sized rectangles did you need? How many of them did you shade?

B. How can you find how many times the hikers must take a break?

C. Use your bar model to find how many breaks the three friends will take. How did you do it?

D. How many groups of $\frac{3}{4}$ are in $4\frac{1}{2}$? Use your model to count.

E. Write an expression to show what operation you would use to represent this situation.

 Turn and Talk How could you use another method to solve this problem?

Step It Out

2 Jamarion has $4\frac{2}{5}$ pounds of peanuts that he needs to divide evenly into 6 bins. How many pounds of peanuts will be in each bin?

A. What expression could you use to solve the problem?

$$\dfrac{\square}{\square} \div \square$$

B. Will the quotient be greater than or less than 1? How do you know?

_____

C. Write the mixed number as a fraction greater than 1.

$$4\frac{2}{5} = \frac{4 \cdot \square + 2}{5} = \frac{\square + 2}{5} = \frac{\square}{5}$$

D. Complete the steps to divide $4\frac{2}{5}$ by 6.

$$4\frac{2}{5} \div 6 = \frac{\square}{5} \div 6 = \frac{\square}{5} \times \frac{\square}{6}$$

$$= \frac{\square}{\square} = \frac{\square}{\square}$$

E. Complete the sentences to describe how to solve the division problem.

Write the _____ as a fraction greater than 1.

Change the operation to _____ and replace the

_____ with its reciprocal.

Multiply. There will be _____ pound of peanuts in each bin.

3 Consider the division problem $2\frac{1}{4} \div \frac{3}{8}$. Complete the steps to show how to divide the mixed number by the fraction.

$$2\frac{1}{4} \div \frac{3}{8} = \frac{\square}{4} \div \frac{3}{8}$$

$$= \frac{\square}{4} \times \frac{\square}{3}$$

$$= \frac{\square}{\square} = \square$$

 Turn and Talk When will the quotient be greater than the dividend in a division problem?

4 Phil works at a pet store where fish are sold. He has $5\frac{1}{4}$ liters of water to add to several aquariums. If each aquarium needs $\frac{7}{8}$ liter of water, how many aquariums can he fill?

A. What expression do you need to use to solve the problem?

_____

B. Will the quotient be greater than or less than 1? How do you know?

_____

C. Complete the steps to show how to divide the mixed number by the fraction. Then complete the solution.

$$5\frac{1}{4} \div \frac{7}{8} = \frac{\boxed{}}{\boxed{}} \div \frac{7}{8} = \frac{\boxed{}}{\boxed{}} \times \frac{\boxed{}}{\boxed{}} = \frac{\boxed{}}{\boxed{}} = \boxed{}$$

Phil can fill _____ aquariums with $5\frac{1}{4}$ liters of water.

D. In Part C, you multiplied the fractions and then divided to get the answer. However, you can **simplify** the solution before you multiply. Complete the steps to see how to do this.

$$5\frac{1}{4} \div \frac{7}{8} = \frac{21}{4} \times \frac{8}{7} = \frac{\overset{3}{\cancel{21}}}{\underset{1}{\cancel{4}}} \div \frac{\overset{\boxed{}}{\cancel{8}}}{\underset{1}{\cancel{7}}}$$

Divide numerator and denominator by common factor.

$$= \frac{\boxed{}}{\boxed{}} = 6$$

Check Understanding

1. Dion has a pitcher of lemonade holding $3\frac{1}{2}$ pints. He wants to make $\frac{1}{2}$-pint servings.

A. How many groups of $\frac{1}{2}$ are in $3\frac{1}{2}$?

_____

B. Write an expression to show what operation you would use to represent this situation.

_____

2. Jessica runs $2\frac{1}{2}$ miles in $16\frac{1}{4}$ minutes. What is Jessica's average time per mile in minutes?

_____

© Houghton Mifflin Harcourt Publishing Company • Image Credits: ©Glynsimages2013/Shutterstock

On Your Own

3. Javier exercises for $2\frac{1}{2}$ hours every Saturday. His exercise includes two parts. If he spends the same amount of time on each part how many hours does he spend weightlifting?

_____

_____

Javier's exercise: cardio and weightlifting

4. **(MP) Reason** A baker would like to store $12\frac{3}{4}$ pounds of flour in containers that each hold $3\frac{1}{2}$ pounds of flour. How many containers will the baker need? Explain.

5. A rectangular garden has an area of $46\frac{1}{2}$ square feet. If the garden is $7\frac{1}{2}$ feet long, how many feet wide is it?

_____

6. Kim is building a fence that is $32\frac{1}{2}$ feet long. She has already put the first post in place. There will be additional posts every $2\frac{1}{2}$ feet. How many additional posts will Kim need?

_____

7. Dana has a piece of lumber that is $22\frac{3}{4}$ feet long. She needs pieces that are $3\frac{1}{4}$ feet long. How many pieces can she cut from the $22\frac{3}{4}$-foot piece of lumber?

_____

For Problems 8–11, divide.

8. $2\frac{5}{6} \div \frac{1}{2}$ _____

9. $5\frac{1}{5} \div 3$ _____

10. $1\frac{1}{5} \div 2\frac{3}{10}$ _____

11. $\frac{3}{4} \div 2\frac{3}{8}$ _____

12. At a zoo, a tiger eats $8\frac{3}{4}$ pounds of a specially prepared ground beef every day. If the zookeeper buys $87\frac{1}{2}$ pounds of the ground beef, how many days will it last?

_____

13. At her bakery, Sherry has $6\frac{1}{2}$ pounds of cherries to make tarts. If she uses $\frac{1}{4}$ pound of cherries for each tart, how many tarts can she make?

_____

14. (MP) **Critique Reasoning** Dan says that $24\frac{1}{2} \div 12\frac{1}{2} = 2$, because $24 \div 12 = 2$. Sam disagrees and thinks there will be fewer than 2 groups of $12\frac{1}{2}$ in $24\frac{1}{2}$. Who is correct and why? What is $24\frac{1}{2} \div 12\frac{1}{2}$?

15. (MP) **Reason** Mason is laying tiles on an entryway. The tiles are each $\frac{2}{9}$ foot long, and the entryway is $7\frac{1}{2}$ feet long. How many tiles will Mason need to cover the length of the entryway? Explain.

_____

_____

For Problems 16–19, write the equivalent multiplication expression.

16. $2\frac{1}{6} \div \frac{3}{4}$ _____

17. $4\frac{5}{8} \div 2\frac{1}{2}$ _____

18. $3\frac{1}{3} \div \frac{9}{10}$ _____

19. $5\frac{2}{5} \div 1\frac{7}{8}$ _____

 I'm in a Learning Mindset!

What can I apply from my previous work with LCMs and GCFs to better understand division with mixed numbers?

_____

_____

Explore Division of Mixed Numbers

1. Darlene cuts a $9\frac{1}{2}$-foot-long pipe into pieces that are $2\frac{3}{8}$ feet long. How many pieces of pipe does she have? Explain.

_____

_____

$9\frac{1}{2}$ feet

2. (MP) **Attend to Precision** Jonathan will run a $6\frac{1}{4}$-mile relay with 4 other team members, where each team member runs an equal distance. How many miles will Jonathan run?

_____

_____

3. Every 14 days, Debbie's dog eats $4\frac{1}{5}$ pounds of dog food. If Debbie's dog eats the same amount of food each day, how many pounds does her dog eat per day?

_____

_____

4. **Math on the Spot** One serving of Roberto's favorite yogurt is $6\frac{1}{2}$ ounces. How many servings are in a $16\frac{1}{4}$-ounce container?

_____

_____

5. Jefferson reads his favorite book for $1\frac{1}{4}$ hours each day. If he has read the book for $22\frac{1}{2}$ hours so far, how many days has he read it? Show how you know.

For Problems 6–11, find the quotient.

6. $\frac{3}{4} \div 1\frac{1}{10}$ _____

7. $5\frac{1}{2} \div 6$ _____

8. $1\frac{2}{15} \div \frac{1}{5}$ _____

9. $2\frac{1}{2} \div 2\frac{5}{8}$ _____

10. $4\frac{2}{3} \div 2\frac{1}{3}$ _____

11. $2\frac{1}{5} \div 3\frac{1}{7}$ _____

Test Prep

12. Harley rides her bicycle the same distance every day for 4 days. The total distance she rides is $8\frac{1}{4}$ miles. How many miles does she ride each day?

_____

13. An equation is shown.

$1\frac{2}{3} \times \boxed{} = \frac{1}{4}$

What factor is missing from the equation?

- (A) $\frac{3}{20}$
- (B) $\frac{5}{12}$
- (C) $2\frac{2}{5}$
- (D) $6\frac{2}{3}$

14. An expression is shown.

$1\frac{3}{7} \div 1\frac{1}{3}$

What is the value of the expression as a mixed number? _____

15. What multiplication expression would you use to find the quotient of

$3\frac{1}{2} \div 2\frac{1}{5}$?

- (A) $\frac{2}{7} \times \frac{5}{11}$
- (B) $\frac{2}{7} \times \frac{11}{5}$
- (C) $\frac{7}{2} \times \frac{5}{11}$
- (D) $\frac{7}{2} \times \frac{11}{5}$

Spiral Review

16. Which number is greater, -18 or -16?

_____

17. An expression is shown.

$\frac{4}{3} \times \frac{4}{5}$

What is the value of the expression? _____

18. An expression is shown.

$\frac{4}{5} \div \frac{3}{5}$

What is the value of the expression? _____

© Houghton Mifflin Harcourt Publishing Company

Name _____

Practice and Apply Division of Fractions and Mixed Numbers

(**I Can**) solve real-world problems that require dividing with mixed numbers or fractions.

Step It Out

1 Kevin is making hamburgers for a cookout. He bought $10\frac{1}{4}$ pounds of ground meat. How many $\frac{1}{4}$-pound hamburger patties can he make?

A. Fill in the boxes to solve the division problem that answers this question.

$$10\frac{1}{4} \div \frac{1}{4} = \frac{\boxed{}}{4} \div \frac{1}{4}$$

$$= \frac{\boxed{}}{4} \times \frac{\overset{1}{\cancel{4}}}{1}$$

$$= \frac{\boxed{}}{1} = \boxed{}$$

B. Fill in the blank to answer the question: He can make

_____ $\frac{1}{4}$-pound patties.

2 Kevin's friend Justin is bringing juice to the cookout. If he brings $43\frac{3}{4}$ pints of juice, then how many $2\frac{1}{2}$-pint bottles can be filled?

A. Fill in the boxes to solve the division problem that answers this question.

$$43\frac{3}{4} \div 2\frac{1}{2} = \frac{\boxed{}}{4} \div \frac{\boxed{}}{2}$$

$$= \frac{\boxed{}}{4} \times \frac{\boxed{}}{\boxed{}} = \frac{\boxed{}}{\boxed{}}$$

$$= \boxed{}\frac{\boxed{}}{\boxed{}} = \boxed{}\frac{\boxed{}}{\boxed{}}$$

B. How many $2\frac{1}{2}$-pint bottles can be filled completely? Explain.

_____

Turn and Talk If Kevin made $\frac{1}{2}$-pound patties, how many could he make? How does this compare to the number of $\frac{1}{4}$-pound patties? Explain.

3 Cedric finished a 4-mile race as shown. If he ran each mile at the same pace, how many minutes did he average for each mile?

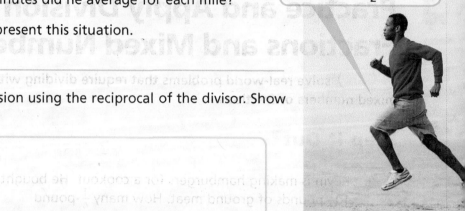

4 miles in $38\frac{1}{2}$ minutes

A. Write a expression to represent this situation.

_____

B. Solve the division expression using the reciprocal of the divisor. Show your work.

C. How many minutes did Cedric take to run each mile?

_____

Turn and Talk How could you use a model to find how many minutes it took Cedric to run each mile?

Check Understanding

1. Yousef is cutting pieces of construction paper so he can make cards for his friends. Each piece of paper is $11\frac{1}{2}$ inches wide. If he cuts that width so he would have two equal-sized smaller pieces, how wide will each smaller piece be?

_____

2. Marisol has $4\frac{1}{2}$ cups of flour. A biscuit recipe she wants to try requires $\frac{3}{4}$ cup of flour for a single batch of biscuits. How many batches of biscuits can Marisol make?

_____

For Problems 3–8, divide the mixed numbers or fractions.

3. $3\frac{1}{8} \div \frac{1}{8}$ _____

4. $6\frac{2}{5} \div 4\frac{1}{10}$ _____

5. $4\frac{1}{2} \div 3\frac{2}{3}$ _____

6. $2\frac{5}{8} \div 1\frac{3}{4}$ _____

7. $5\frac{3}{4} \div \frac{1}{2}$ _____

8. $7\frac{5}{6} \div 2\frac{1}{3}$ _____

Name _____

On Your Own

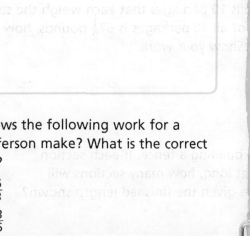

9. To paint a bedroom, Jade estimates she will need to buy $3\frac{1}{4}$ gallons of paint. How many $\frac{1}{2}$-gallon cans of paint should she buy? Explain.

10. **(MP) Critique Reasoning** Jefferson shows the following work for a division problem. What mistake did Jefferson make? What is the correct answer to his original division problem?

$$5\frac{2}{5} \div 2\frac{1}{3} = \frac{27}{5} \div \frac{6}{3}$$
$$= \frac{27}{5} \times \frac{3}{6}$$
$$= \frac{81}{30} = 2\frac{21}{30} = 2\frac{7}{10}$$

11. A cube has a surface area of $253\frac{1}{2}$ square inches. What is the area of one face of the cube in square inches? How do you know?

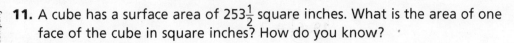

12. Darlene has $6\frac{3}{4}$ gallons of gasoline. Every time she mows a lawn, she uses $\frac{3}{8}$ gallon. How many times can she mow a lawn before she needs more gas?

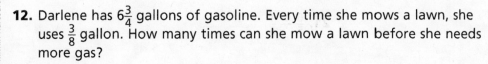

13. A rectangle has an area of $24\frac{1}{2}$ square feet. If the length of the rectangle is $4\frac{3}{8}$ feet, what is the width in feet?

© Houghton Mifflin Harcourt Publishing Company • Image Credit: ©goir/Shutterstock

Module 2 • Lesson 3

63

14. Open Ended Write a story problem that is modeled by the expression $10\frac{1}{2} \div 5\frac{1}{2}$. What is the answer to your problem?

_____

_____

_____

15. Jack mails 10 packages that each weigh the same amount. If the combined weight of all 10 packages is $67\frac{1}{2}$ pounds, how much does one package weigh? Show your work.

_____

_____

16. Peter is building a fence. If each section is $4\frac{1}{2}$ feet long, how many sections will there be given the finished length shown?

finished fence: $38\frac{1}{4}$ feet long

_____

_____

17. Jill has a pail of water that holds $6\frac{1}{2}$ quarts. She needs to give her plants $\frac{1}{8}$ quart each. How many of her plants can she water?

_____

_____

For Problems 18–23, divide.

18. $1\frac{1}{2} \div \frac{1}{2}$ _____

19. $6\frac{1}{5} \div 2$ _____

20. $3\frac{2}{5} \div \frac{1}{4}$ _____

21. $\frac{6}{5} \div \frac{1}{5}$ _____

22. $1\frac{4}{8} \div \frac{2}{3}$ _____

23. $10\frac{1}{5} \div 3\frac{3}{10}$ _____

Name _____

Practice and Apply Division of Fractions and Mixed Numbers

1. Andy works at a grocery store. The manager of the store would like Andy to set up a display of apples. Part of the display will include bags of apples as shown. If there are 39 pounds of apples in the back of the store, how many bags of apples can Andy make for the display?

APPLES
$1\frac{1}{2}$-pound bags

_____

_____

_____

2. (MP) **Attend to Precision** Gilbert needs to move $20\frac{3}{4}$ pounds of soil from a truck to a garden. His wheelbarrow can move 6 pounds at one time. How many loads of soil will he have to move? Explain.

_____

_____

_____

3. **Math on the Spot** The area of a rectangular garden is $53\frac{5}{6}$ square feet. The length of the garden is $9\frac{1}{2}$ feet. What is the width?

_____

4. Ramona is making book shelves. She bought a board that is $\frac{4}{5}$ meter long. She needs 5 shelves. If she cuts 5 equal-sized pieces from the board, how long is each piece?

_____

For Problems 5–10, divide.

5. $\frac{5}{4} \div \frac{1}{10}$ _____

6. $1\frac{1}{2} \div 8$ _____

7. $4\frac{1}{10} \div \frac{2}{5}$ _____

8. $5\frac{1}{2} \div 6\frac{1}{3}$ _____

9. $10 \div 3\frac{3}{4}$ _____

10. $9\frac{1}{5} \div \frac{1}{10}$ _____

11. Which expressions are equivalent to $4\frac{1}{2} \div 2\frac{1}{4}$?

(A) $4\frac{1}{2} \times 2\frac{4}{1}$

(B) $\frac{9}{2} \div \frac{9}{4}$

(C) $\frac{8}{2} \times \frac{8}{4}$

(D) $\frac{9}{2} \times \frac{4}{9}$

(E) $\frac{8}{2} \times \frac{4}{9}$

12. An expression is shown.

$$3\frac{1}{8} \div 2\frac{3}{4}$$

What is the value of the expression?

_____

13. Ms. Tsosie made $2\frac{3}{4}$ cups of white rice for a dinner party. She has 3 friends coming to the party and will give each person, including herself, the same amount of rice. How many cups of rice will she serve each friend and herself?

(A) $\frac{7}{20}$ cup

(B) $\frac{11}{16}$ cup

(C) $1\frac{7}{20}$ cups

(D) $1\frac{11}{16}$ cups

14. Foster needs to divide a plot of land covering $5\frac{3}{8}$ acres into plots covering $\frac{3}{4}$ acre each. How many whole plots can he make?

_____

15. An alligator is $11\frac{3}{4}$ feet long. Its tail is $5\frac{7}{8}$ feet long. What fraction of the alligator's total length is its tail?

_____

Spiral Review

16. Write the numbers in order from least to greatest: −5, 0, −10, 1, −18.

_____

17. Add the fractions: $\frac{1}{5} + \frac{1}{10}$.

_____

Name _____

Practice Fraction Operations

(**I Can**) use the LCM and GCF to solve fraction problems
with all four operations.

Step It Out

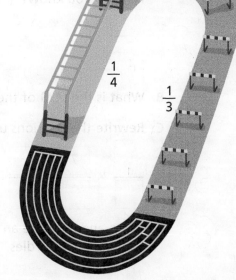

1▸ Tom is running an obstacle course. Monkey bars make up
$\frac{1}{4}$ of the course, and hurdles make up $\frac{1}{3}$ of the course. A
wall climb and sprint make up the rest. What fraction of
the course do the monkey bars and the hurdles make up?

  A. What operation do you need to use to solve this
  problem? How do you know?

  _____

  _____

  B. How is the least common multiple used when adding
  fractions with unlike denominators?

  _____

  _____

  C. What is the LCM of the two denominators? How do you know?

  _____

  D. Rewrite each fraction using the LCM of 3 and 4.

$$\frac{1}{4} = \frac{1}{4} \times \frac{3}{\boxed{}} = \frac{\boxed{}}{12} \qquad \frac{1}{3} = \frac{\boxed{}}{\boxed{}} \times \frac{\boxed{}}{\boxed{}} = \frac{\boxed{}}{\boxed{}}$$

  E. Write and evaluate an expression to find the fraction of the course the
  monkey bars and hurdles make up together.

$$\frac{\boxed{}}{\boxed{}} + \frac{\boxed{}}{\boxed{}} = \frac{\boxed{}}{\boxed{}}$$

 Turn and Talk Is there another way to solve this problem? Explain.

2 Tina takes $2\frac{1}{4}$ fewer seconds to finish the hurdles than to complete the monkey bars. How long does Tina take to finish the hurdles?

$7\frac{1}{2}$ seconds to complete monkey bars

A. What operation do you need to use to solve this problem? How do you know?

_____

_____

B. What is the LCM of the denominators in this problem? _____

C. Rewrite the fractions using the LCM.

$$\frac{1}{\square} \times \frac{\square}{\square} = \frac{\square}{\square} \qquad \frac{1}{4} \times \frac{\square}{\square} = \frac{1}{4}$$

D. Write and evaluate an expression to find how long it takes Tina to complete the hurdles.

$$\square\frac{\square}{\square} - \square\frac{\square}{\square} = \square\frac{\square}{\square} \text{ seconds}$$

3 Davon spent $\frac{2}{15}$ of his savings on a video game. He then spent $6\frac{1}{4}$ times as much on a new bike. What fraction of his original savings did he spend on the bike?

A. What operation do you need to use to solve this problem? Explain.

_____

_____

B. To multiply a fraction and a mixed number, convert _____ from a

_____ to a _____.

$$\square\frac{\square}{4} = \frac{\square}{4}$$

C. Write and evaluate an expression to find the fraction of his savings Davon spent on his bike. Use the GCF to write your answer in **simplest form**.

$$\frac{\square}{4} \times \frac{\square}{15} ; \qquad \frac{\square}{4} \times \frac{\square}{15} = \frac{\square}{\square} = \frac{\square}{6}$$

 Turn and Talk Explain how you used the GCF to write your answer in Part C of Task 3 in simplest form.

4 On Saturday, Pedro has $3\frac{1}{2}$ hours to practice on an obstacle course. If it takes him $\frac{1}{4}$ hour to complete the course, how many times can he go through the course in $3\frac{1}{2}$ hours?

A. What operation do you need to use to solve this problem? Explain your reasoning.

_____

_____

B. To divide $3\frac{1}{2}$ by $\frac{1}{4}$, first, convert _____ to a _____.

$$\dfrac{\boxed{}}{2} = \dfrac{\boxed{}}{2}$$

C. Write a division expression to represent this problem.

$$\dfrac{\boxed{}}{2} \div \dfrac{1}{\boxed{}}$$

D. Write an equivalent multiplication expression to represent this problem. You need to use the reciprocal of the divisor.

$$\dfrac{\boxed{}}{2} \div \dfrac{1}{\boxed{}} = \dfrac{\boxed{}}{2} \times \dfrac{4}{\boxed{}}$$

E. Evaluate the expression to find how many times Pedro can complete the obstacle course. Explain how you used the GCF to write the answer in simplest form.

$$\dfrac{\boxed{}}{2} \times \dfrac{4}{\boxed{}} = \dfrac{\boxed{}}{\boxed{}} = \boxed{}$$

_____

Check Understanding

1. At college, Tyrell has science for $5\frac{1}{2}$ hours per week. If his lab work takes up $\frac{2}{5}$ of his science class time, how many hours does Tyrell spend in the lab?

_____

For Problems 2–5, perform the operation shown.

2. $1\frac{5}{8} - \frac{3}{16}$ _____

3. $2\frac{2}{5} \div 3\frac{1}{5}$ _____

4. $3\frac{3}{5} \times 2\frac{1}{2}$ _____

5. $3\frac{1}{6} + 2\frac{5}{9}$ _____

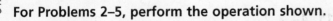

On Your Own

6. There are 12 miles of hiking trails in a county park. Each trail is rated for difficulty: $\frac{3}{8}$ of the trails are rated easy, $\frac{1}{6}$ are rated moderate, $\frac{1}{4}$ are rated hard, and $\frac{5}{24}$ are rated difficult. What fraction of the trails are rated easy or moderate?

_____

7. Terri peeled $2\frac{1}{6}$ pounds of potatoes for a stew. How many more pounds of potatoes does she need to peel so she peels $3\frac{3}{4}$ pounds of potatoes all together? What operation could you use to solve this problem?

_____

$3\frac{3}{4}$ pounds to peel

8. (MP) **Attend to Precision** Agatha drives $73\frac{1}{2}$ miles through two towns in $2\frac{1}{3}$ hours. What is her average speed in miles per hour? Show how you know.

9. Roy, Joseph, and Caitlyn have $3\frac{3}{4}$ pints of chicken soup.

   A. If they each eat the same amount of soup, how many pints will each person eat?

   _____

   B. If they decide to include one more of their friends, how many pints will each person eat?

   _____

For Problems 10–13, perform the given operation on $4\frac{4}{5}$ and $2\frac{1}{2}$.

10. $4\frac{4}{5} - 2\frac{1}{2}$ _____

11. $4\frac{4}{5} \times 2\frac{1}{2}$ _____

12. $4\frac{4}{5} \div 2\frac{1}{2}$ _____

13. $4\frac{4}{5} + 2\frac{1}{2}$ _____

14. A wall is $56\frac{1}{2}$ feet long. The art club will paint different murals that are each $14\frac{1}{8}$ feet long along the wall. How many murals will fit on the wall?

_____

15. (MP) **Attend to Precision** Patty rides her bike $2\frac{3}{4}$ miles to school. She rides $3\frac{5}{6}$ miles to get back home, because she needs to meet her brother at his school first. How many miles does Patty ride her bike? Explain how you know that your answer is reasonable.

16. William runs $6\frac{1}{5}$ miles daily. One day he ran $2\frac{1}{2}$ times as far. How many miles did he run that day?

_____

17. Music A note represents the pitch and duration of a musical sound. In a four/four measure, a whole note is equal to two half notes, four quarter notes, or eight eighth notes. In a given measure, a composer wants to divide a half note into sixteenth notes. How many sixteenth notes should be used? Write and evaluate an expression to represent this situation.

_____

18. (MP) **Reason** Alex is setting up an inline skating course 21 feet long to practice weaving around cones. He wants a cone every $3\frac{1}{2}$ feet, but not at the start or end of the course. How many cones will he need? Explain your reasoning.

_____
_____
_____

For Problems 19–22, perform the indicated operation.

19. $7\frac{1}{2} - \frac{3}{4}$ _____   **20.** $2\frac{2}{5} + 2\frac{1}{8}$ _____

21. $\frac{1}{4} \times 1\frac{3}{5}$ _____   **22.** $4\frac{1}{3} \div 1\frac{2}{3}$ _____

23. Beth participated in a triathlon that consisted of swimming, bicycling, and running. Her finishing time to complete the triathlon is shown. If she completed the swimming portion in $1\frac{1}{4}$ hours and the bicycling portion in $6\frac{1}{3}$ hours, how long did it take her to complete the running portion of the triathlon?

$12\frac{2}{3}$ hours to complete triathlon

24. (MP) **Construct Arguments** Raja claims that to add two fractions with unlike denominators, first you need to determine the smallest number that is a multiple of both denominators. Then change the denominators in both fractions and keep the numerators the same. What is incorrect about his claim?

25. A recipe for bread calls for $3\frac{1}{2}$ cups of flour, $\frac{1}{8}$ cup of salt, and $1\frac{1}{4}$ cups of milk. What is the total amount of the three ingredients? Explain the process you used to answer the question and how you used the LCM.

26. A gasoline tank holds $12\frac{1}{2}$ gallons of gasoline. If there are $5\frac{1}{5}$ gallons of gasoline in the tank, how many more gallons can it hold?

For Problems 27–29, perform the indicated operation.

27. $5\frac{1}{3} - \frac{2}{9}$ _____

28. $11\frac{2}{7} + 6\frac{1}{2}$ _____

29. $2\frac{1}{2} \div \frac{3}{4}$ _____

Practice Fraction Operations

1. Renee worked a total of $16\frac{1}{5}$ hours last week. She spent $\frac{1}{3}$ of that time reviewing reports. How many hours did she spend reviewing reports?

   $5 \quad \frac{2}{5}$

   $\frac{81}{5} \times \frac{1}{3} = \frac{81}{15}$

   $\frac{27}{5}$

2. Alisha added $5\frac{1}{4}$ quarts of water and $4\frac{2}{5}$ quarts of a cleaning solution to a large bucket. How much total liquid did she add to the bucket? Show your work.

   $\begin{array}{r} 1 \\ 26 \\ +26 \\ \hline 52 \end{array}$ $\begin{array}{r} 91 \\ \times \ 4 \\ \hline 4 \\ 360 \end{array}$

3. **Math on the Spot** Find the value of the expression. Write the answer in simplest form.

   $\frac{5}{12} - \frac{1}{10}$

4. Kyle runs $3\frac{1}{4}$ miles in $22\frac{3}{4}$ minutes. He runs each mile in the same number of minutes. How many minutes does it take Kyle to run a mile?

   7

   $\frac{91}{4} \times \frac{4}{13} = \frac{364}{52}$

5. Mary buys a bag of nuts that weighs $2\frac{1}{4}$ pounds. After a week, she has eaten $\frac{2}{3}$ of the nuts. How many pounds of nuts has she eaten?

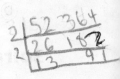

For Problems 6–11, perform the indicated operation.

6. $5\frac{3}{4} + \frac{1}{10}$ _____

7. $4\frac{3}{5} - 2\frac{1}{6}$ _____

8. $3\frac{1}{3} \times 2\frac{4}{5}$ _____

9. $4\frac{1}{2} \div 4\frac{5}{8}$ _____

10. $6\frac{1}{8} \div \frac{3}{16}$ _____

11. $3\frac{4}{5} \times 1\frac{2}{3}$ _____

Test Prep

12. Andrea finished her homework in $\frac{2}{3}$ the amount of time it took Dina to finish hers. Dina took $2\frac{4}{5}$ hours to finish her homework. Which expression shows how long Andrea took to finish her homework?

   Ⓐ $\frac{2}{3} + 2\frac{4}{5}$

   Ⓑ $2\frac{4}{5} - \frac{2}{3}$

   Ⓒ $2\frac{4}{5} \div \frac{2}{3}$

   Ⓓ $\frac{2}{3} \times 2\frac{4}{5}$

13. Which expression(s) have a value that is greater than 6? Select all that apply.

   Ⓐ $6 - \frac{1}{5}$

   Ⓑ $6 \times \frac{2}{3}$

   Ⓒ $6 \times 2\frac{1}{8}$

   Ⓓ $6 - \frac{1}{20}$

   Ⓔ $6 \div \frac{3}{4}$

14. Laurie is measuring crushed garlic for a recipe. Each serving requires $\frac{3}{4}$ teaspoon of garlic. If Laurie has $2\frac{5}{8}$ teaspoons of garlic, how many servings can she make?

_____

15. A hippo weighed $\frac{1}{20}$ ton when it was born. When the hippo turned 10 years old, it weighed $1\frac{1}{2}$ tons. Which expression shows the number of tons the hippo's weight increased between its birth and its tenth birthday?

   Ⓐ $1\frac{1}{2} - \frac{1}{20}$

   Ⓑ $\frac{1}{20} + 1\frac{1}{2}$

   Ⓒ $1\frac{1}{2} \times \frac{1}{20}$

   Ⓓ $\frac{1}{20} - 1\frac{1}{2}$

Spiral Review

16. What integer can be used to represent a diver's elevation if the diver is 40 feet below sea level?

_____

17. Add the decimals: $0.14 + 1.29$.

_____

18. What is the least common multiple of 18 and 27?

_____

Name _____

Vocabulary

Complete the following to review your vocabulary for this module.

Vocabulary
reciprocal
multiplicative inverse

1. Describe in your own words what it means for two numbers to be reciprocals, or multiplicative inverses.

   _____

   _____

2. Give an example of two numbers that are reciprocals, or multiplicative inverses.

   _____

Concepts and Skills

3. Which number sentences are true? Select **all** that apply.

   (A) $\frac{1}{2} \div 3 = 2 \times \frac{1}{3}$

   (B) $\frac{2}{3} \div \frac{4}{5} = \frac{3}{2} \times \frac{4}{5}$

   (C) $\frac{7}{10} \div \frac{1}{42} = \frac{7}{10} \times 42$

   (D) $\frac{5}{9} \div \frac{5}{6} = \frac{5}{9} \times \frac{6}{5}$

   (E) $\frac{5}{10} \div \frac{2}{10} = \frac{5}{10} \times \frac{2}{10}$

4. What is the value of the expression $1\frac{2}{3} \times 2\frac{1}{3}$?

   _____

5. (MP) **Use Tools** A piece of wood was 12 feet long. Kendra cut the wood into pieces $\frac{2}{3}$ foot long. How many pieces did Kendra make? State what strategy and tool you will use to answer the question, explain your choice, and then find the answer.

   _____

   _____

6. Which expression is equivalent to $\frac{2}{5} \div \frac{3}{5}$?

   (A) $\frac{2}{5} \times \frac{3}{5}$ (C) $\frac{5}{2} \times \frac{3}{5}$

   (B) $\frac{2}{5} \times \frac{5}{3}$ (D) $\frac{5}{2} \times \frac{5}{3}$

7. Mitchell spent $1\frac{3}{4}$ hours at the doctor's office and a total of $1\frac{1}{2}$ hours driving to and from the appointment. Which expression shows the total number of hours Mitchell spent away from home for his visit to the doctor?

(A) $1\frac{3}{4} - 1\frac{1}{2}$ (C) $1\frac{3}{4} \div 1\frac{1}{2}$

(B) $1\frac{3}{4} \times 1\frac{1}{2}$ (D) $1\frac{3}{4} + 1\frac{1}{2}$

8. On 5 days of every week, Jackie runs $2\frac{1}{2}$ miles in the morning. How many total miles does Jackie run every week?

_____

9. Andy rode his bicycle $2\frac{4}{5}$ miles on Monday and $1\frac{3}{10}$ miles on Tuesday.

A. Write each amount using the LCM.

_____

B. How many total miles did Andy ride on the two days?

_____

10. Find the quotient of $4\frac{4}{5} \div \frac{4}{5}$. Explain how you can use the GCF to write your answer in simplest form.

_____

_____

11. Lynda is making curtains. She has $2\frac{1}{3}$ yards of material. She wants to make 3 curtains. She needs $\frac{8}{9}$ yard for each curtain. Does she have enough material to make 3 curtains? Explain.

_____

12. Ken wants to install a row of ceramic tiles on a wall that is $21\frac{3}{8}$ inches wide. Each tile is $4\frac{1}{2}$ inches wide.

A. How many whole tiles does he need? _____

B. What fraction of a tile must he install at the end of the row to

totally fill the space? _____

13. How many times as long is a line measuring $9\frac{1}{3}$ yards as a line measuring $3\frac{1}{2}$ yards?

_____

14. A mural is $12\frac{5}{6}$ feet long and is divided into 7 equal-length panels. How many feet long is each panel?

_____

Fluency with Multi-Digit Decimal Operations

What's the Best Route?

A race will be held downtown. The diagram shows the lengths of the streets available for the race.

Plan a route that is approximately 10 kilometers long.

A. The race should begin and end at lettered points on the map. Trace your route on the map. Circle the starting and ending points.

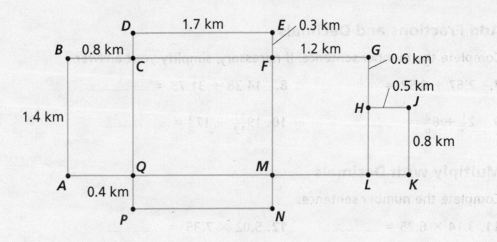

B. What is the total length of your race route? _____ kilometers

  Turn and Talk

- What strategies did you use to plan a route that is close to 10 kilometers in length?

- Compare your route with a partner's. How are they similar? How are they different?

Are You Ready?

Complete these problems to review prior concepts and skills you will need for this module.

Place Value of Decimals

Complete each statement.

1. The value of 3 in 10.31 is _____ times as much as the value of 3 in 10.13.

2. The value of 8 in 5.18 is _____ of the value of 8 in 5.81.

3. The value of 7 in 17.92 is _____ times as much as the value of 7 in 92.17.

Compare Decimals

Complete the inequality or equation using the symbols <, >, or =.

4. 0.54 _____ 0.6   5. 1.30 _____ 1.3   6. 0.22 _____ 0.18

Add Fractions and Decimals

Complete the number sentence. If necessary, simplify your answer.

7. $2.67 + 8.52 =$ _____   8. $14.38 + 31.73 =$ _____

9. $2\frac{1}{5} + 6\frac{2}{6} =$ _____   10. $19\frac{11}{12} + 17\frac{3}{8} =$ _____

Multiply with Decimals

Complete the number sentence.

11. $3.14 \times 6.25 =$ _____   12. $5.02 \times 7.35 =$ _____

13. $7.2 \times 8.09 =$ _____   14. $6.81 \times 5.64 =$ _____

Division

Find the quotient.

15. $7,296 \div 24 =$ _____   16. $9,216 \div 18 =$ _____

17. $9,765 \div 45 =$ _____   18. $8,064 \div 36 =$ _____

Name _____

Add and Subtract Multi-Digit Decimals

(I Can) **add and subtract decimals to thousandths.**

Step It Out

The 10 × 10 grid represents 1 whole. There are 100 squares, so each square represents 0.01 or $\frac{1}{100}$ of the whole.

1 ▶ Find the sum of 0.13 + 0.58 using a 10 × 10 grid.

   A. How can you represent 0.13 on the grid?

_____

   B. Shade the grid to represent 0.13.

   C. How can you represent 0.58 on the grid?

_____

   D. Shade the grid to represent 0.58.

   E. How many total squares are shaded?

_____

   So, 0.13 + 0.58 = _____.

Adding decimals is similar to adding whole numbers. You must first write the numbers so that like places are aligned. Then add from right to left and regroup when necessary.

2 ▶ While at a grocery store, Robert bought 0.26 pound of red grapes and 0.34 pound of green grapes. How many total pounds of grapes did Robert buy?

   A. You can use a table to align the places of decimals to make it easier to add. Write 0.34 in the table at the right. Add from right to left, regrouping when necessary.

   B. Did you need to regroup? Explain.

_____

_____

   C. Robert bought [   ] pounds of grapes.

0	.	2	6
+			

Turn and Talk How is adding decimals different from adding whole numbers?

3 Find the difference of 0.42 − 0.19 using a 10 × 10 grid.

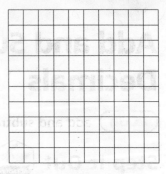

A. How can you represent 0.42 on the grid? How can you represent subtracting 0.19?

_____

_____

B. Perform the steps in your answer from Part A. How many shaded squares remain?

_____

C. So, 0.42 − 0.19 = _____.

4 A cardinal weighs 1.5 ounces. Find the difference between the weights of a cardinal and a bluebird. The weight of a bluebird is shown.

A. What subtraction problem can you write to represent this situation?

_____

B. Write 1.5 in the top row of the table. Write a zero in the hundredths place as a placeholder.

Bluebird
1.09 ounces

C. Write 1.09 in the table. Subtract from right to left, regrouping when necessary.

D. So, the weight of the cardinal is _____ ounce more than the weight of the bluebird.

 Turn and Talk How can you subtract a decimal from a whole number?

Check Understanding

1. Julia has $1 for a snack. She buys an apple for $0.49. How much does she have left after buying the apple?

_____

2. A group of friends spent $31.95 on movie tickets and $12.54 on refreshments. How much did they spend in all?

_____

Add and Subtract Multi-Digit Decimals

1. Deangelo babysits for his neighbor. Over a two-week period, he babysat 3.8 hours the first week and 5.25 hours the second week. How many total hours did Deangelo babysit over the two weeks?

_____

2. Babe Ruth, a professional baseball player known for hitting home runs, had a batting average of 0.342. Hank Aaron, another record home run hitter, had a batting average of 0.305. How much greater was Babe Ruth's batting average than Hank Aaron's?

_____

3. **STEM** The pH level of a substance is a measure of how acidic or alkaline it is. The pH of lemonade is 2.6, while orange juice has a pH of 4.09. What is the difference in the pH levels of orange juice and lemonade?

_____

4. A recipe for blintzes, a very thin type of pancake, calls for 0.06 liter of melted butter and 0.236 liter of milk. What is the total amount of butter and milk needed for the recipe?

_____

5. **Math on the Spot** Jared ran two sprints in track practice. His time for the first sprint was 4.64 seconds. His time for the second sprint was 4.3 seconds. What was Jared's total time for the two sprints?

_____

For Problems 6–11, find the sum or difference.

6.   4.105
     +3.685

7.   0.089
     −0.075

8.   12.15
     +6.832

9. 1.25 + 2.39

_____

10. 4.08 − 3.975

11. 0.91 − 0.487

_____

Test Prep

Use the following information for Problems 12 and 13.

Several teams, each consisting of 4 athletes, ran a relay race. The top two teams won ribbons. Team Rocket finished in 3.48 minutes and Team Jaguar finished in 3.471 minutes.

12. How much faster was Team Jaguar's finish than Team Rocket's finish?

13. Team Tortoise took twice as long to finish the race as Team Jaguar. How long did it take Team Tortoise to finish the race?

14. In 2018, the state sales tax in Maine was 5.5%, or 0.055. The state sales tax in Florida was 6%, or 0.06. How much greater was the sales tax in Florida than in Maine?

15. The Nürburgring in Germany is a racetrack that hosts racing events all year. Two of the fastest laps ever driven on the track were 6 minutes 47.30 seconds and 6 minutes 52.01 seconds. How much faster is the time of 6 minutes 47.30 seconds than the time of 6 minutes 52.01 seconds?

16. A hectare is a measure of area. There are 2.471 acres in 1 hectare. What is the area of 3 hectares?

    (A) 0.529 acre   (B) 4.942 acres   (C) 5.471 acres   (D) 7.413 acres

Spiral Review

17. What is the quotient of $\frac{1}{5} \div \frac{2}{3}$?

18. A garden bed has 4 sections of vegetables. The garden is $8\frac{1}{2}$ yards long. If each section is equal in length, what is the length of each section?

19. The elevation of a coral reef is 12 feet below sea level. The elevation of a snorkeler is 2 feet below sea level. Write an inequality to compare the elevations using integers.

Name _____

Multiply Multi-Digit Decimals

I Can multiply multi-digit decimals to thousandths.

Step It Out

One way to multiply decimals is by using a decimal grid. The grid represents 1 whole, where each square unit is 0.01.

1 ▸ Find the product of 0.5×0.4.

A. To represent 0.5, I can shade ☐ columns, which is ☐ squares.

B. To represent 0.4, I can shade ☐ rows, which is ☐ squares.

C. Shade the grid to represent 0.5 and 0.4. How many squares have been shaded twice?

_____

D. The double shaded squares represent the decimal ☐. So, $0.5 \times 0.4 = $ ☐.

Another way to multiply decimals is to use an area model.

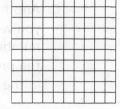
$3.50
PER POUND

2 ▸ Cara buys 11.2 pounds of pork chops for the price shown.

A. How can you find the total cost of the pork chops?

_____

B. An area model shows partial products using place values. Complete the area model by multiplying to find the partial products. List the partial products.

_____

C. What is the sum of the partial products?

_____

D. How much does Cara pay for the pork chops?

_____

	1	1	2
3	$3 \times 10 =$ 30	$3 \times 1 =$ 3	$3 \times 0.2 =$ ☐
5	$0.5 \times 10 =$ ☐	$0.5 \times 1 =$ 0.5	$0.5 \times 0.2 =$ ☐

 Turn and Talk What do the labels given on the area model represent?

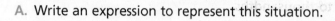

3 ▸ When Jared mows grass he uses the amount of gas per hour shown. How much gas does he use in 5.8 hours?

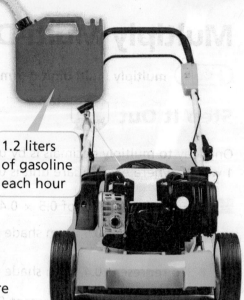

1.2 liters of gasoline each hour

A. Write an expression to represent this situation.

_____

B. Find an estimate of this product by rounding each factor to the nearest whole number and then multiplying.

_____

C. Another way to multiply decimals is to multiply as you would with whole numbers. Then count the number of decimal places in the factors. What is the product 58 × 12? How many decimal places are in the factors 5.8 and 1.2?

_____

_____

D. The product must have the same number of decimal places as the total number of decimal places in the factors. How many decimals places should there be in the product 5.8 × 1.2?

_____

E. What is the product of 5.8 × 1.2? Explain how you knew where to place the decimal point.

_____

_____

F. Check your answer for reasonableness.

My estimate of _____ is close to the product _____ so my answer is reasonable.

Check Understanding

1. Last summer Rachel worked 38.5 hours per week at a grocery store. She earned $9.70 per hour. How much did she earn in a week?

_____

2. Find the product of 2.3 × 0.6.

_____

	3	8	5
9	9 × 30 =	9 × 8 =	9 × 0.5 =
7	0.7 × 30 =	0.7 × 8 =	0.7 × 0.5 =
0	0 × 30 =	0 × 8 =	0 × 0.5 =

On Your Own

Denise runs
1 mile in
8.5 minutes.

3. Denise runs a 10-kilometer race (6.2 miles). Her time per mile is shown. What is her total time for the race? Explain.

_____

_____

4. **(MP) Critique Reasoning** Antwon says that he can multiply 14 and 12 to find the product of 0.14 × 0.12. Is Antwon correct? Explain your reasoning.

_____

_____

_____

5. **(MP) Attend to Precision** A city park is 0.85 mile long and 0.7 mile wide. The city wants to put in new plants and grass that need less watering.

A. Write an expression that can be used to find the area of the park. Then find the area of the park in square miles.

_____

B. The city calculates that only $\frac{6}{10}$ of the park will need plants and grass. What decimal can be used to calculate the area of the park that will have plants and grass?

_____

C. What is the total area of the park in square miles that will have plants and grass? Explain how you found your answer.

_____

For Problems 6–7, use the grid to find the product.

6. 0.2 × 0.7 = _____

7. 0.4 × 0.8 = _____

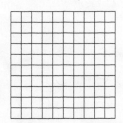

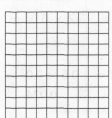

For Problems 8–9, find the product.

8. 10.05 × 5.6 = _____

9. 7.9 × 5.1 = _____

© Houghton Mifflin Harcourt Publishing Company • Image Credit: ©Michael Turner/Alamy

10. Nita will bake 3.2 batches of muffins for the school bake sale. Each batch uses 1.75 cups of flour. How much flour does Nita need to make the muffins?

1.75 c flour

A. Estimate the product by rounding each factor to the nearest whole number and multiplying.

_____

B. What is the actual product of 3.2 × 1.75? _____

C. Using your estimate, is your answer reasonable? Explain.

_____

_____

11. (MP) **Reason** How does estimating help you know whether you have placed the decimal point correctly in a product?

_____

_____

12. Colin needs 14.5 yards of fabric to cover a sofa. The fabric he likes costs $7.95 per yard. Write an expression that represents the cost of the fabric. Then simplify the expression to find the cost. Round to the nearest hundredth.

_____

13. **Open Ended** Describe a general method to multiply two decimals. Show an example.

_____

_____

_____

14. Use the area model to find the product 7.34 × 2.6.

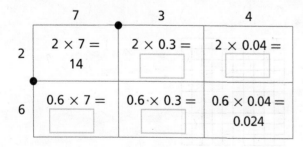

	7	3	4
2	2 × 7 = 14	2 × 0.3 =	2 × 0.04 =
6	0.6 × 7 =	0.6 × 0.3 =	0.6 × 0.04 = 0.024

The product is _____.

For problems 15–17, find the product.

15. 23.2 × 4.1 = _____   **16.** 0.05 × 0.07 = _____   **17.** 7.89 × 8.7 = _____

LESSON 3.2
**More Practice/
Homework**

ONLINE
 **Video Tutorials and
Interactive Examples**

Multiply Multi-Digit Decimals

1. At 3 years old, Javier was 36.5 inches tall. By age 13, he was 1.8 times as tall as he was at age 3. How tall was Javier at age 13?

_____

2. STEM The mass of an atom of helium is about 4.002 atomic units. The mass of an atom of beryllium is about 2.25 times the mass of an atom of helium. What is the approximate mass of a beryllium atom?

_____

3. (MP) **Reason** Shui's bedroom is 11.4 feet long and 12.5 feet wide. She wants to paint the floor. A gallon of paint will cover approximately 150 square feet. Will one gallon of paint be enough to paint Shui's bedroom floor with 2 coats of paint? Explain your reasoning.

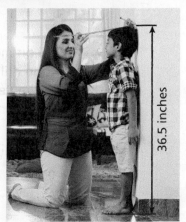

36.5 inches

_____

_____

4. The distance from Jupiter to the sun is 5.203 astronomical units. If the distance from Neptune to the sun is about 5.77 times Jupiter's distance from the sun, how far is Neptune from the sun in astronomical units? Round your answer to the nearest thousandth.

_____

5. Math on the Spot Reed bought 1.8 pounds of green beans. The green beans cost $1.27 per pound. What was the total cost of Reed's green beans? Round your answer to the nearest hundredth.

_____

For Problems 6–11, find the product.

6. 0.65×0.11

7. 0.281×0.6

8. 1.3×0.8

9. 2.54×3.7

10. 10.01×5.15

11. 13.49×0.806

Test Prep

12. A quart of water weighs about 2.09 pounds. What is the approximate weight of 15.5 quarts of water?

_____

13. A #15 drill bit measures 0.18 inch in diameter. The diameter of a large construction drill bit is about 2.3 times the diameter of a #15 bit. What is the approximate diameter of the large construction drill bit?

_____

14. Match the products to the expressions.

2.53×0.83 •   •   0.9282

0.70×0.02 •   •   2.0999

3.57×0.26 •   •   0.014

1.30×0.89 •   •   1.157

15. In 1930, the average movie was 1.5 hours long. In 1996, one of the longest movies made in America, _Hamlet_, was released. _Hamlet_ is about 2.69 times as long as the average 1930s movie. Approximately how long is _Hamlet_?

Ⓐ 1.19 hours

Ⓑ 1.793 hours

Ⓒ 4.035 hours

Ⓓ 4.19 hours

Spiral Review

16. A Dutch door is a door that is split in half to allow the top and bottom to open separately. The top section of a Dutch door is 3.25 feet tall and the bottom section is $3\frac{3}{4}$ feet tall. Write an inequality that compares the heights of the top and bottom sections of the door.

_____

17. Drew's gas tank is $\frac{3}{4}$-full. He uses $\frac{1}{6}$ of a full tank's gas per day driving to and from work. How many days can Drew drive to and from work with the gas he has in the tank? Explain.

_____

_____

18. Write the list of rational numbers in order from least to greatest.

$-2.15, \frac{3}{10}, -1.6, -1\frac{4}{5}, 0.8$

_____

Name _____

Divide Multi-Digit Whole Numbers

(I Can) divide multi-digit whole numbers and use a problem's context to interpret the remainder.

Step It Out

1 Mr. Soto buys a new phone for $432 on a payment plan. He pays $18 each month. How many months will it take him to pay for his phone?

A. Write an expression that could be used to find the number of months Mr. Soto will pay for the phone.

_____

B. Estimate the quotient. Explain how you found your estimate.

_____

C. Complete the division problem shown to find the number of months Mr. Soto will be paying for his new phone.

D. How many months will Mr. Soto be paying for his new phone?

_____

E. How can you use your estimate to check if your answer is reasonable?

```
         2 ☐
    18)432
      −36 ↓
          7
        − ☐
          ☐
```

2 An experimental airplane is flying at an altitude of 8,000 feet when it begins descending to land. If the plane descends at a constant rate of 125 feet per minute, how long will it take to land the plane?

A. Estimate the quotient. Explain how you found your estimate.

_____

B. How do you decide where to place the first number in the quotient?

_____
_____

C. How long will it take the plane to land? How can you use your estimate to check if your answer is reasonable?

_____
_____

```
        ☐
   125)8,000
    − ☐  ↓
        500
      − ☐
          0
```

Turn and Talk Why is it important to estimate before finding the exact answer?

3 ▶ An art class is making mosaics with glass squares. Each of the 121 students will get the same number of glass squares to use. There are a total of 1,240 glass squares for the students to use. How many glass squares will each student get?

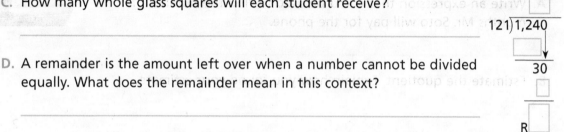

1,240 glass squares

A. Write an expression that can be used to find the number of glass squares each student will receive.

_____

B. Complete the given division problem to find the number of squares each student will receive.

C. How many whole glass squares will each student receive?

_____

D. A remainder is the amount left over when a number cannot be divided equally. What does the remainder mean in this context?

_____

_____

$$121\overline{)1{,}240}$$

```
         ___
121)1,240
    ___↓
      30
    ___
    ___
    R ___
```

 Turn and Talk What is another way you could find the total number of squares each student would get?

Check Understanding

1. It took the Pioneer 11 spacecraft 2,372 days to reach Saturn.

   A. How many whole years did it take Pioneer 11 to reach Saturn?
   Note: 1 year = 365 days.

   _____

   B. Is there a remainder? Explain what it means.

   _____

   _____

   _____

2. Ian has $4,032 he earned from working during the summer. If he earned $288 per week working on a construction project, how many weeks did he work? Complete the division problem to find the quotient.

   _____

```
        ___
288)4,032
   -___
    1,152
   -___
      ___
```

On Your Own

3. **(MP) Reason** A clothing company has 4,630 shirts to ship. It can fit 130 shirts in a shipping box.

   A. How many boxes are needed to ship all the shirts? _____

   B. What does the remainder mean in this context?

   _____

4. Trevor runs laps on the track. If he runs 9,200 meters total, and each lap is 400 meters, how many laps does he run?

   _____

5. A liter of water from the Dead Sea has 250 grams of salt. A tank of similarly salted water holds 5,750 grams of salt. How many liters of water are in the tank?

   _____

6. A gallon of water contains 128 fluid ounces. A rain barrel can hold 6,400 ounces of rain water. How many gallons of water can the barrel hold?

   _____

7. **(MP) Critique Reasoning** A high-speed train travels at a constant speed of 280 kilometers per hour. Keiko calculates the amount of time it would take to travel 3,360 kilometers. Her work is shown. Is Keiko's work correct? Explain your reasoning.

$$\begin{array}{r} 102 \\ 280\overline{)3{,}360} \\ \underline{280} \\ 56 \\ \underline{0} \\ 560 \\ \underline{560} \\ 0 \end{array}$$

For Problems 8–10, estimate. Then find the quotient.

8. $7{,}371 \div 189$

   Estimate _____

   Quotient _____

9. $5{,}104 \div 116$

   Estimate _____

   Quotient _____

10. $6{,}322 \div 109$

    Estimate _____

    Quotient _____

For Problems 11–13, estimate. Then find the whole-number quotient and remainder.

11. $640 \div 11$

    Estimate _____

    Quotient _____

    Remainder _____

12. $3{,}045 \div 850$

    Estimate _____

    Quotient _____

    Remainder _____

13. $101 \div 22$

    Estimate _____

    Quotient _____

    Remainder _____

14. **(MP) Reason** Simon buys a car for a total cost of $9,899. He can pay $206 a month but no more. He determines that he will make 49 payments. Is he correct? Explain your reasoning.

_____

_____

15. A blue whale can weigh up to 400,000 pounds. A standard school bus has a gross weight of 25,000 pounds. How many school buses are equivalent to the weight of a blue whale?

_____

16. **(MP) Attend to Precision** A jug contains 3,840 milliliters of water. How many cups of water does the jug contain? Show your work. Note: 1 cup is equivalent to 240 milliliters.

17. An office building is renting offices that each have an area of 500 square feet. The office building is renting a total of 7,000 square feet of offices. How many offices does the building have?

_____

For Problems 18–23, find the whole-number quotient and remainder, if there is one.

18. 7,874 ÷ 127

19. 4,995 ÷ 333

20. 945 ÷ 35

21. 8,588 ÷ 452

22. 880 ÷ 91

23. 6,800 ÷ 600

Name _____

Divide Multi-Digit Whole Numbers

1. At a paper mill, paper is placed into reams, or stacks of 500 sheets. A robot separates big stacks of sheets into reams. How many reams can the robot make with 9,500 sheets of paper?

_____

2. **STEM** Osmium is the densest chemical element. A cubic centimeter of osmium has a mass of about 23 grams. If a chemist has 2,530 grams of osmium, about how many cubic centimeters does the chemist have?

_____

3. The Burj Khalifa building in Dubai, United Arab Emirates, is one of the tallest buildings in the world at 2,722 feet tall. An American football field is 360 feet in length. Approximately how many football fields tall is the Burj Khalifa building? Round to the nearest tenth.

2,722 ft

_____

4. (MP) **Construct Arguments** The longest road in the United States is U.S. Route 20, measuring 3,365 miles long. A truck driver drives about 520 miles per day. How many days would it take her to drive from one end of U.S. Route 20 to the other end? Explain.

_____

_____

_____

5. **Math on the Spot** A total of 1,043 players signed up for a citywide soccer league. Each team in the league can have up to 18 members. How many teams will be needed?

_____

The Burj Khalifa is one of the tallest buildings in the world.

6. (MP) **Attend to Precision** There are 365 days in a year and 24 hours in a day. An airport video camera records for 18 hours and then automatically resets itself to start recording again.

A. How many times does the video camera reset itself in a year?

_____

B. If the camera is started at the beginning of a year, how many hours will it record in the following year before resetting again?

_____

For Problems 7–10, find the whole-number quotient and remainder, if there is one.

7. $3,760 \div 145$ 8. $500 \div 25$ 9. $646 \div 38$ 10. $9,311 \div 400$

_____

Test Prep

11. A cattle ranch has 1,400 acres of grazing land. The ranch has 140 cows, and no two cows graze on the same patch of land. How many acres of grazing land will each cow have on the ranch?

_____

12. A new amusement-park ride that lasts 1 minute can have up to 1,200 riders per hour of operation. How many riders can ride per minute?

_____

13. A small concert venue earned $6,804 in ticket sales. All tickets were the same price. If the venue sold 252 tickets, how much did each ticket cost?

_____

14. What is the whole-number quotient and remainder?

$7,810 \div 215$

Ⓐ 36 R 33   Ⓑ 36 R 70   Ⓒ 36 R 79   Ⓓ 36 R 170

15. Which is a reasonable estimate for $89,877 \div 31$?

Ⓐ 30   Ⓑ 300   Ⓒ 3,000   Ⓓ 30,000

Spiral Review

16. Bea withdraws $25 from her bank account. What integer represents the withdrawal?

_____

17. Which two points on the number line represent a number and its absolute value?

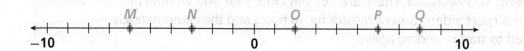

18. Naruto practices his harmonica $\frac{1}{4}$ hour, spends $\frac{2}{3}$ hour working on homework, and takes another $\frac{1}{2}$ hour to do chores every day. How much longer does Naruto spend practicing his harmonica and doing his chores than working on homework?

Name _____

Divide Multi-Digit Decimals

(I Can) find the quotient of multi-digit decimals.

Step It Out

1 ▶ Six toy blocks of the same length are lined up next to each other. What is the length of one toy block?

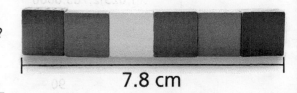

7.8 cm

A. What division problem models this situation?

_____

B. Divide to find the length of one toy block.

_____

2 ▶ Leo drives his car 443.75 miles and uses 12.5 gallons of gasoline. How many miles does Leo get per gallon?

A. Write a division problem to model this situation.

_____

B. In a previous lesson, you formed **equivalent fractions** by multiplying the numerator and denominator of a fraction by the same number. In a similar way, you can form an equivalent division problem by multiplying both parts of a given division problem by the same number. Write a division problem equivalent to the one you wrote in Part A, but with a whole number divisor.

_____

C. What power of 10 do you need to multiply by to make the divisor a whole number? Why is it helpful to make the divisor a whole number?

_____

_____

D. How do you show this change in long division?

443.75 × 10 = 4,437.5
12.5 × 10 = 125

12.5$\overline{)443.75}$ → 125$\overline{)4,437.5}$

E. Complete the given division problem to find the quotient.

F. How many miles does Leo get per gallon?

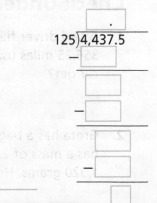

© Houghton Mifflin Harcourt Publishing Company • Image Credit: ©ozgurkeser/iStock/Getty Images Plus/Getty Images

3 A teacher drove a rental car 276.3 miles and used a total of 10.230 gallons of gas. Two students, Kierra and Shawna, both calculate how many miles the car got per gallon. Whose solution is correct? Explain the error(s) in the incorrect solution. How could you check the result?

Kierra's Solution	Shawna's Solution
2.7008 1,023)2,763.0000 −2,046 7170 −7161 90 − 0 9000 −8184 816	27.008 1,023)2,7630.000 −2,046 7170 −7161 90 − 0 900 − 0 9000 −8184 816
about 2.70 miles to the gallon	about 27.01 miles to the gallon

 Turn and Talk Why must you multiply the dividend and divisor by the same number? Explain.

Check Understanding

1. A taxi driver fills the gas tank and calculates that the car traveled 356.25 miles using 9.5 gallons of gas. How many miles per gallon did the car get?

2. Greta has a bag full of Lincoln pennies. She knows that a Lincoln penny has a mass of 2.5 grams. The total mass of the pennies in her bag is 1,320 grams. How many pennies does Greta have?

Divide Multi-Digit Decimals

1. Fiona can assemble a bookcase in 0.8 hour. She works for
   4 hours. How many bookcases can she assemble in this time?

   _____

2. **STEM** If 1 kg ≈ 2.2 lb, about how many kilograms are there in 34.76 pounds?

   _____

3. (MP) **Reason** Stanley can purchase a 15.4-ounce bottle of
   olive oil for $5.39 or a 23.6-ounce bottle of olive oil for
   $7.08. Which bottle is the better buy? Explain.

$7.08

$5.39

   _____

   _____

4. (MP) **Use Structure** Susan divided 38.08 by 23.80.

   A. Write an expression with a whole-number divisor to solve
      the problem. Will both the divisor and the dividend be
      whole numbers? Why or why not?

      _____

      _____

   B. Find the quotient. $38.08 \div 23.80 =$ _____

5. Donna is a pacer in a marathon. She finishes 26.2 miles in 3 hours 45
   minutes (3.75 hours) while running at a constant speed. What is Donna's
   speed in miles per hour to the nearest whole number?

   _____

6. **Math on the Spot** Sadie spent $12.46 to download songs that were on
   sale for $0.89 each. How many songs did she download?

   _____

For Problems 7–10, find the quotient.

7. $3.78 \div 12.6$ 8. $5.535 \div 1.23$

   _____   _____

9. $322.56 \div 25.6$ 10. $270.72 \div 6$

   _____   _____

Test Prep

11. Tabitha collects quarters from different states. The value of her collection is $17.75. How many quarters does she have in her collection?

_____

12. Roast beef at the neighborhood deli sells for $6.40 per pound. A package of the roast beef costs $16.64. How many pounds of roast beef are in the package?

_____

13. A grass fertilizer is sold in 5-pound bags. Stuart calculates that he needs enough fertilizer to cover 4,350 square feet. If each pound of fertilizer covers 362.5 square feet, how many 5-pound bags does Stuart need to buy?

_____

14. The perimeter of a square is 23.28 inches. What is the length of each side of the square?

(A) 5.28 inches   (C) 5.82 inches

(B) 5.43 inches   (D) 6.04 inches

15. Which expressions have a value of 21.06? Select all that apply.

(A) $63.18 \div 3$ (D) $6318 \div 0.3$

(B) $6.318 \div 3.0$ (E) $631.8 \div 0.03$

(C) $6.318 \div 0.3$ (F) $631.8 \div 30$

Spiral Review

16. Tom's rectangular driveway is 23.5 feet long and 9.25 feet wide. What is the area of the driveway in square feet?

_____

17. A stationery store ships 5,712 pounds of paper in boxes that each hold 24 pounds of paper. How many boxes are needed?

_____

18. Write the following numbers in order from least to greatest:

−5.6, 7.95, 2.06, 0, −6.89

_____

19. Shameka buys a blue garden hose that is 16.5 feet long and a green garden hose that is 14.75 feet long. How many feet of garden hose does she buy?

_____

© Houghton Mifflin Harcourt Publishing Company

Name _____

Apply Operations with Multi-Digit Decimals

(**I Can**) determine which operation is needed to solve a decimal word problem.

Step It Out

1 Harold bought 3.5 pounds of red apples that cost $1.79 per pound. How much did Harold spend on the red apples?

   A. Estimate the product by rounding each number to the nearest whole number and multiplying.

   _____ × _____ = _____

   pounds of red apples   cost per pound   total cost of apples

   (estimated)   (estimated)   (estimated)

   B. _____ to find out exactly how much Harold spent. Round your answer to the nearest cent.

   _____ × _____ = _____

   pounds of red apples   cost per pound   total cost of apples

   C. Since the estimate _____ is close to the exact product of _____, the answer is reasonable.

   D. So, Harold spent _____ on the red apples.

2 Tavon hikes 6.1 miles in 2.5 hours. Tavon says that he can find out how fast he hiked by subtracting 6.1 − 2.5.

   A. Explain Tavon's error.

   _____

   _____

   B. Write an expression Tavon could use to find out how fast he hiked.

   _____

   C. Tavon hiked _____ miles per hour.

 Turn and Talk How can you determine the correct operation to use when solving a word problem?

3 A "mole" is a standard unit used in chemistry for measuring large quantities of very small objects, such as atoms. One mole of hydrogen atoms has a mass of 1.0079 grams. One mole of oxygen atoms has a mass of 15.9994 grams. A mole of hydroxide is made up of 1 mole of hydrogen and 1 mole of oxygen. What is the mass of a mole of hydroxide?

A. Use _____ to find the mass of a mole of hydroxide atoms.

B. Add the mass of 1 mole of oxygen atoms and 1 mole of hydrogen atoms.

_____ + _____ = _____
mass of 1 mole of   mass of 1 mole of   mass of 1 mole of
hydrogen atoms   oxygen atoms   hydroxide

C. So, the mass of a mole of hydroxide is _____ grams.

 Turn and Talk Can you check your answer? Explain.

Check Understanding

1. The area of a rectangle is 69.75 square inches. Its length is 9.3 inches.

A. What operation should you use to find the width of the rectangle?

_____

B. What is the width of the rectangle?

_____

2. Three friends are going camping. They buy a pound of raisins costing $2.93 and a half of a pound of nuts costing $3.75.

A. What operation should you use to find the total cost of the raisins and nuts?

_____

B. What is the total cost of the nuts and raisins?

_____

3. The price of a gallon of gas is as shown. Write an equation that could be used to determine the cost of filling an empty 12.5-gallon gas tank and calculate the cost. Round your answer to the nearest cent.

$2.389
PER GALLON

_____

On Your Own

4. A sprinkler sprays 0.7 gallons of water per minute. If it takes 45 minutes to water a lawn, how many gallons of water does the sprinkler spray?

   _____

5. Petra buys a pair of jeans for $28.39 and a T-shirt that costs $6.40. How much does Petra spend?

   _____

6. A tailor spends $63.75 to buy 7.5 yards of satin. What is the cost of the satin fabric per yard?

   _____

7. (MP) **Critique Reasoning** Gael harvested 3 bags of potatoes that weigh 25.5 pounds, 32.25 pounds, and 27 pounds. He says that he harvested a total of 350.7 pounds. Explain and correct Gael's error.

Gael's work:
25.5
32.25
+ 27
350.7

   _____

8. Cassie volunteers at an animal shelter. She needs a total of 40 hours of volunteer time for a class. So far, she has volunteered for 18.5 hours. How many more hours does she need to volunteer?

9. An adult African elephant eats about 0.25 ton of food per day. If the zoo orders 2.3 tons of food for the elephant, how many full days will the food last?

   _____

African elephants

10. A collector purchased a rare book for $97.56, and then sold the book in an online auction for $141.82. The auction charged the collector $8.25 in fees for the use of its service. How much did the collector earn by selling the book?

    _____

11. A carpenter installing cabinets uses thin pieces of material called shims to fill gaps. The carpenter uses four shims to fill a gap that is 1.5 centimeters wide. The widths of three of the shims are 0.75 centimeter, 0.125 centimeter, and 0.1 centimeter. What is the width of the fourth shim?

    _____

12. How much fence is needed to surround a garden with side lengths of 2.1 meters, 3.5 meters, 1.9 meters, and 2.25 meters?

13. Simone Manuel, an American competitive swimmer, won a gold medal in the women's 100-meter freestyle event at the 2016 Rio Olympics. Her winning time was 52.70 seconds. Assuming she swam at a constant speed, how long did it take her to swim one meter?

14. When Renee first got her puppy, he weighed 4.5 pounds. Now he weighs 12.25 pounds. How much weight did the puppy gain?

15. A recipe for chicken soup calls for 3 boxes of chicken broth measuring 15.8 ounces each. How many ounces of broth are used in the recipe?

16. (MP) **Critique Reasoning** A box of cereal contains 98.7 grams of protein, and 1 serving contains 7.05 grams of protein. Kevin says there are about 1.4 servings in the box of cereal. Is he correct? Explain why or why not.

17. The speed at which the Hubble Telescope orbited Earth is given at the right. How far did the telescope travel in 3 seconds?

> 4.78 miles per second

18. Selma has to hike 11 miles to reach the top of Electric Peak in Yellowstone National Park. After hiking 2.4 miles, she takes a break. How much farther does she have to hike?

For Problems 19–24, add, subtract, multiply, or divide.

19. 10.26 + 7.55 = _____

20. 1.2 − 0.51 = _____

21. 5.5 × 1.3 = _____

22. 158.18 ÷ 5.5 = _____

23. 23.26 − 17.1 = _____

24. 231.65 + 0.45 = _____

Name _____

LESSON 3.5
**More Practice/
Homework**

ONLINE
Ed
Video Tutorials and
Interactive Examples

Apply Operations with Multi-Digit Decimals

1. The cost of a 12-ounce bag of cashews is $5.86. What is the cost per ounce of the cashews, to the nearest penny?

_____

2. (MP) **Reason** A table is 73.66 centimeters tall. An iguana tank on the table is 76.34 centimeters tall. Will the table and tank fit beneath a shelf that is 157.16 centimeters off the floor? Explain.

_____

_____

_____

_____

3. **STEM** A piece of brass contains 1.66 grams of copper and 0.34 gram of zinc. What is the mass of the piece of brass in grams?

_____

4. The temperature at 8:00 a.m. is 3.3 °C. At 4 p.m. the temperature is 7.22 °C. What is the change in temperature from 8:00 a.m. to 4:00 p.m.?

_____

5. Aniah printed 1-page fliers. She used a printer that can print 1 page every 4.25 seconds. How long did it take her to print 58 fliers?

_____

6. A track team has 4 runners on a relay team. If by coincidence each runner happens to take exactly 45.48 seconds to complete her leg of the relay, what is the total time to run the relay?

_____

7. **Math on the Spot** Darrell and Lyle are college basketball players. Darrell is 198.1 centimeters tall. Lyle is 190.5 centimeters tall. How much taller is Darrell than Lyle?

_____

8. The winner of a raffle will receive three-fourths, or 0.75, of the $530.40 raised from raffle ticket sales. How much money will the winner get?

Test Prep

9. A hectare is equal to 2.471 acres. A land developer buys a hectare of land to build homes. Each home will be built on 0.25 acre of land. How many homes can the land developer build on the hectare of space?

10. Glenn picked 3.45 pounds of Gala apples and 2.15 pounds of McIntosh apples at the orchard to make applesauce. How many pounds of apples did Glenn pick?

11. Ian rides bikes competitively. He practices his tricks 5.8 hours a week. How many hours does he spend practicing his tricks in a 4.5-week period?

12. Find the difference.

    $16.58 - 8.793$

    Ⓐ 7.787

    Ⓑ 8.213

    Ⓒ 8.865

    Ⓓ 25.373

Spiral Review

13. What is the quotient of $\frac{4}{5} \div \frac{1}{2}$?

14. A state fair uses $3\frac{5}{6}$ pallets of lemons for lemonade and $3\frac{7}{12}$ pallets for lemon ice. Which uses a greater amount of lemons?

15. The lowest point of Death Valley in California is 86 meters below sea level. What is the elevation written as an integer?

16. What is the quotient of $1\frac{2}{3} \div 2\frac{1}{2}$?

Vocabulary

Choose the correct term from the Vocabulary box.

Vocabulary

difference
dividend
divisor
equivalent
product
remainder
sum

1. In the problem $3.8 \div 0.7$, the number 3.8 is the
   _____ and the number 0.7 is the

   _____ .

2. In the problem $1.34 + 8.2 = 9.54$, 9.54 is the

   _____ .

3. The solution to a subtraction problem is called the

   _____ .

4. Which word correctly describes the value 15 in
   $2.5 \times 6 = 15$?

   (A) remainder

   (B) sum

   (C) product

   (D) difference

Concepts and Skills

5. The distance from Jose's home to school is 1.85 miles. The school is
   2.34 miles from the local library, which is 1.9 miles from Jose's home. If
   Jose goes from his home to school, from school to the library, and then
   home, how far does he travel?

   _____ miles

6. (MP) **Use Tools** An airplane flew a total of 6,240 miles. Its speed was
   520 miles per hour. How many hours did the plane fly? State what strategy
   and tool you will use to answer the question, explain your choice, and
   then find the answer.

   _____

   _____

7. Telegraphs were used to send messages before the telephone was
   invented. A telegraph operator could interpret about 40 words sent in
   Morse Code per minute. Approximately how many words sent in Morse
   Code could the operator interpret in 12.5 seconds?

   (A) 8 words

   (B) 10 words

   (C) 12 words

   (D) 16 words

8. Which has a quotient of 0.6?

(A) $0.204 \div 0.034$ (C) $2.04 \div 0.034$

(B) $0.204 \div 0.34$ (D) $2.04 \div 0.34$

9. The ocean rises and falls each day due to tides. The Bay of Fundy in Canada has some of the highest tides in the world. Its tidewater rises about 53.478 feet and falls the same amount afterwards, twice a day.

    A. Write an expression that can be used to find the total feet the tide rises and falls each day.

    B. Write an expression that can be used to find the total feet the tide rises and falls over a one-week period.

    C. How many total feet does the tide rise and fall over a one-week period?

10. A 0.5-pound bunch of bananas costs $0.22 and 1 pound of oranges cost $2.39. If a person has $20, which expression could be used to determine how much change the person would get after purchasing the 0.5-pound bunch of bananas and 3.25 pounds of oranges?

(A) $20 - 0.22 + (2.39 \times 3.25)$ (C) $20 - [0.22 + (3.25 \times 2.39)]$

(B) $0.22 + (2.39 \times 3.25) - 20$ (D) $0.22 + (0.5 \times 3.25) - 20$

11. A bag of equally-sized rhinestones weighs 16 ounces. Each rhinestone weighs 0.016 ounce. If you have 2 bags of rhinestones, how many rhinestones do you have?

12. What is the value of the expression?

$7.09 - (1.36 \times 4.125) + (3.28 \div 0.04)$

(A) 8.85   (B) 9.68   (C) 83.39   (D) 83.48

13. Remy is saving money to buy a new video game console. The console costs $199.95. Remy makes $40.50 each week babysitting. How many total weeks will he need to babysit to save up enough money for the video game console? Explain your reasoning.

© Houghton Mifflin Harcourt Publishing Company

Understand Addition and Subtraction of Rational Numbers

What's the Pattern?

Five explorers are each at different elevations in a cave. The rational numbers given show their elevations in kilometers. The signs of the numbers indicate the elevation above (+) or below (−) ground level.

Plot each rational number on the number line given.

A. $-1\frac{3}{5}$

B. $-\frac{9}{10}$

C. $-\frac{1}{5}$

D. $\frac{1}{2}$

E. $1\frac{1}{5}$

 Turn and Talk

What pattern is formed by the five elevations? Explain your reasoning.

Are You Ready?

Complete these problems to review prior concepts and skills you will need for this module.

Add and Subtract Fractions

Find the sum or difference.

1. $\frac{2}{5} + \frac{1}{2}$ _____   **2.** $\frac{5}{6} + \frac{1}{3}$ _____   **3.** $2\frac{3}{4} - 1\frac{5}{6}$ _____

Opposites and Absolute Value

Complete the table by describing the opposite of the given situation and representing it with a positive or negative number.

	Quantity	Opposite Quantity
4.	A football team gains 6 yards on a play. Number: +6	
5.	A penguin is $2\frac{1}{2}$ feet below sea level. Number: $-2\frac{1}{2}$	
6.	Marci deposits $38 into her bank account. Number: +38	

Rational Numbers on a Number Line

For Problems 7–14, use the given number line.

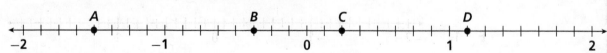

Write the rational number in fraction form for each point on the number line.

7. A _____   **8.** B _____   **9.** C _____   **10.** D _____

Plot and label each number on the number line.

11. $\frac{7}{8}$ **12.** $-1\frac{5}{8}$ **13.** $-\frac{3}{4}$ **14.** $1\frac{3}{4}$

Name _____

Add or Subtract a Positive Integer on a Number Line

(I Can) use a number line to add and subtract positive integers.

Spark Your Learning

John has an account balance of $20. He receives his weekly paycheck for work at his part-time job in the amount of $110. He can't find a bike he wants, so he buys some comic books for $40. Then John finds his dream bike with a price tag of $80. If he buys the bike now, what will his account balance be?

 Turn and Talk What happens when you subtract a greater positive number from a lesser positive number?

Build Understanding

1 Use the thermometer as a number line to answer the following questions.

A. On Monday morning, it was 35 °F outside. Plot this on the thermometer.

B. By afternoon, the temperature rose 20 **degrees**.

What distance will you move on the thermometer? _____

In which direction will you move? _____

C. What was the temperature Monday afternoon? _____

Show the change in temperature on the thermometer.

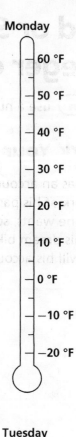

D. Tuesday's high temperature was 25 °F. The temperature dropped by 30 °F overnight. What direction on the number line is this?

_____

Show this on the number line. What is the resulting temperature?

_____

E. Explain why Tuesday's temperature drop resulted in a negative temperature.

_____

_____

_____

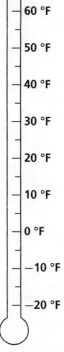

Turn and Talk Is it possible to start with a positive temperature and then have a rise in temperature which leads to a negative temperature? Explain.

2 Use a number line to answer the following questions.

A. Thursday's low temperature was −5 °F. The temperature rose 20 degrees by mid-afternoon. At what point do you start on the number line? _____

What distance do you move? _____

In which direction do you move? _____

Show this on the number line. What is the temperature Thursday afternoon?

_____

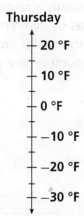

Thursday

20 °F
10 °F
0 °F
−10 °F
−20 °F
−30 °F

B. Friday's low temperature is −10 °F. During the day, the temperature rises by 5 degrees. Show the movement on the number line for Friday and give the result.

_____

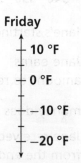

Friday

10 °F
0 °F
−10 °F
−20 °F

C. Sunday's high temperature is −10 °F. During the day, the temperature drops 2 degrees. What is the temperature Sunday afternoon?

_____

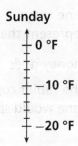

Sunday

0 °F
−10 °F
−20 °F

D. Explain why the temperatures on Friday and Sunday afternoons are both negative, even though one is the result of an increase in temperature and one is the result of a decrease in temperature.

_____

_____

_____

_____

Turn and Talk How can you predict whether the sum of a positive and a negative number will be positive or negative by comparing the two numbers?

3 ▸ Jane wants to buy a new tablet that costs $100. She keeps a record of the money she earns and spends as shown. Will Jane have enough money to buy the tablet on Sunday? Follow the steps using the number line given.

Earning / Spending
Monday:
  Starting balance $60
Tuesday:
  Earned babysitting + $25
Friday:
  Weekly allowance   + $20
Saturday:
  Food at football game – $10

```
←──┼───┼───┼───┼───┼───┼───┼───┼───┼───┼───┼───┼───┼───┼───┼──→
  –$40 –$30 –$20 –$10  $0  $10  $20  $30  $40  $50  $60  $70  $80  $90 $100 $110
```

A. Jane's starting balance is _____. Plot the amount on the number line.

B. Jane earns _____ babysitting. Draw an arrow from the starting amount to represent the amount Jane earns by babysitting. How much money does Jane have now? _____

C. Jane received _____ for a weekly allowance. Draw another arrow from the end of the arrow from Step B to represent Jane's allowance.

How much money does Jane have now? _____

D. Jane spent _____ at the football game. Draw another arrow to represent the amount Jane spent at the football game. How much money does Jane have now? _____

E. The tablet costs _____. Draw an arrow to represent the amount Jane would spend on the tablet. Does she have enough money? Explain.

_____

_____

Check Understanding

1. A business has $10,000 in its bank account. In order to build an addition onto their office, they take out a loan for $30,000.

A. What is their new account balance? Use the number line.

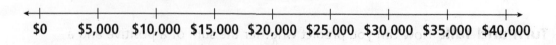

```
←─┼─────┼─────┼─────┼─────┼─────┼─────┼─────┼─────┼──→
 $0   $5,000 $10,000 $15,000 $20,000 $25,000 $30,000 $35,000 $40,000
```

B. If the amount required to build the addition is actually $45,000, will the business have enough to do it? Explain.

_____

On Your Own

2. **MP Use Tools** Use the number line for Parts A and B.

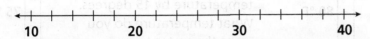

A. It is first down in the football game, your team has the ball at your 25-yard marker, and the play is a successful run for 6 yards. Where does the ball end up? Where is the ball relative to where it started?

_____

B. On second down, your quarterback drops back to pass but is sacked for a 10-yard loss. Where does the ball end up?

_____

C. **MP Reason** Review the actions covered in Parts A and B. Over these two plays, has your team gained or lost total ground? How much? Explain using an addition statement.

_____

In Problems 3–5, use the given number line to answer the question.

3. What is the sum of 18 and 20?

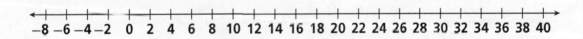

4. What is the result of subtracting 35 from 25?

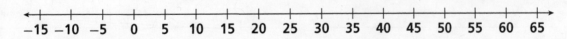

5. What is the result of subtracting 35 from 40?

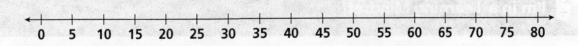

(MP) Use Tools Use the thermometers provided for Problems 6–7.

6. Your home feels cold to you at 60 °F. You turn up the heat in order to raise the temperature by 15 degrees. What will the resulting temperature be?

_____

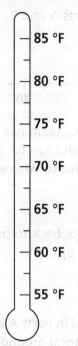

7. You have a beaker of water that is currently at 70 °F. You add some ice to lower the temperature by 15 degrees. What temperature do you want the water to go down to?

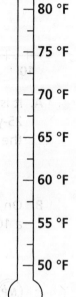

8. **(MP) Use Tools** John has $50 in his bank account. He gets his usual allowance of $20 and mows two lawns, earning $10 each. He puts that money in the bank. Then John spends $45 on a video game. How much money does he have after that purchase? Use the number line to help you find the answer.

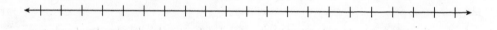

Use the number line for Problems 9–12.

$$-30 \quad -20 \quad -10 \quad 0 \quad 10 \quad 20 \quad 30 \quad 40 \quad 50 \quad 60 \quad 70$$

9. What is the result of 20 plus 30 minus 60?

_____

10. What is the result of −10 plus 30?

_____

11. What is the result of 70 minus 50 plus 20?

_____

12. What is the result of 20 minus 50?

_____

 I'm in a Learning Mindset!

How did I apply prior knowledge to subtracting positive integers?

_____

_____

LESSON 4.1
**More Practice/
Homework**

ONLINE

Video Tutorials and
Interactive Examples

Add or Subtract a Positive Integer on a Number Line

1. Ms. Howard buys a car for $500 and adds a music system that costs $200. Then she adds the seat covers shown. How much has Ms. Howard spent on the car so far?

_____

2. At the beginning of the week, Tideland Manufacturing had an inventory of 60,000 rivets. This week they received a shipment of 30,000 more rivets. Then they used 50,000 rivets to make their Tideland mowers. How many rivets do they have left in inventory?

_____

3. **STEM** A chemical reaction is *endothermic* if it absorbs heat from its surroundings and thereby lowers the temperature. It is *exothermic* if it gives off heat to its surroundings. In her chemistry class, Lily is given a salt (ammonium nitrate) and a beaker of water at 60 °F. She dissolves the salt in the water and sees that the temperature of the solution is now 50 °F. Did the temperature of the solution increase or decrease? By how many degrees? What kind of reaction has occurred? Use the thermometer provided.

_____

_____

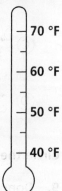

4. (MP) **Use Tools** At the beginning of the month, Joe has $180 in his bank account. He wants to buy a new gaming system for $250 in two weeks. His parents have offered to loan him money if he needs it. He gets $20 a week for an allowance. Will he have enough money at the end of two weeks to make the purchase on his own? If not, how much will he have to borrow from his parents? Use the number line and explain.

5. (MP) **Reason** Can you ever add two positive integers and get a negative integer? Explain.

_____

_____

6. (MP) **Reason** Can you subtract a positive integer from a positive integer and get a negative result? Explain your answer.

_____

_____

_____

Test Prep

7. Marcus owes his mother $10. He babysits his little sister and earns $25. Then he cleans the garage and earns $32. After he pays his mother, how much money does Marcus have?

_____

8. The water in a lake is 4 feet above its usual level. Then the level of the lake drops 7 feet. If 0 represents its usual level, which number line shows the final level in feet of the water in the lake?

Ⓐ
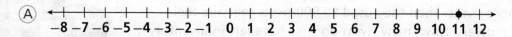

Ⓑ
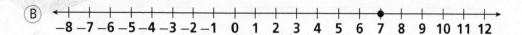

Ⓒ
$$-8\ -7\ -6\ -5\ -4\ -3\ -2\ -1\ \ 0\ \ 1\ \ 2\ \ 3\ \ 4\ \ 5\ \ 6\ \ 7\ \ 8\ \ 9\ \ 10\ 11\ 12$$

Ⓓ
$$-8\ -7\ -6\ -5\ -4\ -3\ -2\ -1\ \ 0\ \ 1\ \ 2\ \ 3\ \ 4\ \ 5\ \ 6\ \ 7\ \ 8\ \ 9\ \ 10\ 11\ 12$$

Circle the word that best completes the sentence.

9. Donna subtracts a positive number from a greater positive number. The resulting difference will be positive / negative .

10. Devon subtracts a positive number from a lesser positive number. The resulting difference will be positive / negative .

Spiral Review

11. Find the sum.

$1.208 + 6.45 = $ _____

12. Raoul makes shell necklaces to sell at a craft fair. The supplies for each necklace cost $3.75. Raoul sells the necklaces for $11.25. How much does Raoul earn from each necklace he sells?

_____

13. Neveah goes out to dinner at a restaurant with 4 friends. The bill for dinner is $57.25, including the tip. If they split the bill evenly, how much does each person owe?

_____

Name _____

Add or Subtract a Negative Integer on a Number Line

(I Can) use a number line to add and subtract negative integers.

Spark Your Learning

The scores of three contestants on a game show are shown. The final question is worth 50 points. A correct answer adds 50 points to a contestant's score. An incorrect answer deducts 50 points.

Show the possible final scores for each contestant. What circumstances are necessary for each contestant to win?

| 30 | 50 | -20 |
| MORGAN | CARLOS | KAYLEE |

Turn and Talk How can you add a number to each score to show a loss?

Build Understanding

1 The table shows the scores of three contestants on a game show.

Game Show Scores		
Latrell	**Mayumi**	**Scott**
8	6	3

A. Latrell spins a wheel to find out how many points he adds to his score. The wheel stops on "−5 points." Use the number line to add −5 points to Latrell's score. Then complete the equation.

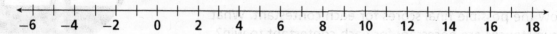

$8 + (-5) =$ _____

B. Mayumi spins the wheel next. The wheel stops on "−11 points." Use the number line to add −11 points to her score. Complete the equation.

```
←+--+--+--+--+--+--+--+--+--+--+--+--+--+--+--+--+--+--+--+→
  -10   -8    -6    -4    -2    0     2     4     6     8     10
```

$6 + (-11) =$ _____

C. How do Latrell's and Mayumi's final scores compare to their starting scores? Explain why this is reasonable.

_____

_____

_____

D. Because Scott started with the lowest score, he plays a penalty round. In the penalty round, the wheel determines the number of points that are *subtracted* from a player's score. The result of Scott's spin is shown. Use the number line to subtract −7 points from Scott's score. (Hint: To subtract a negative integer you move to the right.) Then complete the equation.

Penalty Round

Subtract:

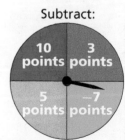

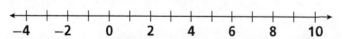

$3 - (-7) =$ _____

 Turn and Talk Is it possible to subtract a loss from a positive number and result in a negative number? Why or why not?

2 ▶ The table shows the scores of three contestants on a game show.

Game Show Scores		
Natalie	Gina	Tyler
−2	−6	−6

A. Natalie spins a wheel to find out how many points she adds to her score. The wheel stops on "−6 points." Use the number line to add −6 points to Natalie's score. Then complete the equation.

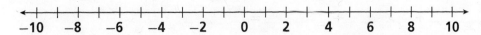

$$-2 + (-6) = \underline{\hspace{1cm}}$$

B. Gina and Tyler both started with the lowest score, so they each play a penalty round. In the penalty round, the wheel determines the number of points that are *subtracted* from a player's score. The result of Gina's spin is shown. Use the number line to find Gina's score. Then complete the equation.

Penalty Round

Subtract:

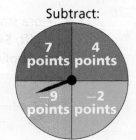

$$-6 - (-9) = \underline{\hspace{1cm}}$$

C. Explain which direction to move on the number line when you subtract a negative integer.

_____

_____

_____

D. The result of Tyler's spin is shown. Use the number line to find Tyler's score. Then complete the equation.

Penalty Round

Subtract:

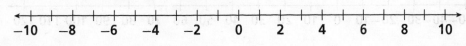

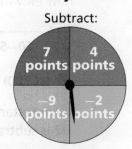

$$-6 - (-2) = \underline{\hspace{1cm}}$$

 Turn and Talk Is it possible to add a loss to a negative number and result in a positive number? Why or why not?

3 ▶ Jackson and Flora both have bank accounts, and they use credit cards. Use the number line to determine if they can pay off their credit card bills.

A. Jackson has $20 in his account. He uses a credit card to spend $30 on a coat and $10 on a movie. Jackson then deposits $50 into his account. How much will Jackson have left after he pays the credit card bill? Use the number line.

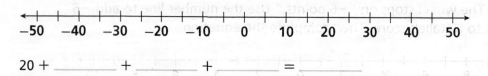

20 + _____ + _____ + _____ = _____

Can Jackson pay his credit card bill? Explain.

_____

_____

B. Flora starts with $10 in her account. She uses a credit card to spend $20 on a gift, $40 on some shoes, and then returns a $30 appliance for a refund to be applied to her card. Use the number line to show these transactions.

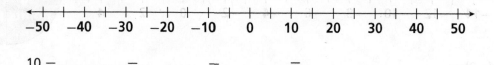

10 − _____ − _____ − _____ = _____

Can Flora pay her credit card bill? Explain.

_____

_____

Check Understanding

Use the number lines to find the answers. Then complete the equations.

1. Jessica starts at an elevation of 40 feet. She descends 60 feet. What is her new elevation in feet?

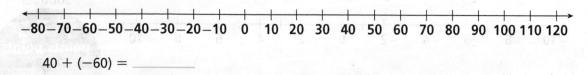

40 + (−60) = _____

2. A contestant on a game show has a score of −4. After spinning the wheel, −2 is subtracted from her score. What is her new score?

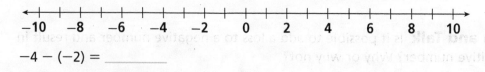

−4 − (−2) = _____

124

On Your Own

3. (MP) **Use Tools** Denny has a balance of $7 on his transit card. Each train ride debits $3, which is the same as adding −$3 to the card. Use the number line to add −$3 to Denny's balance. Then complete the equation.

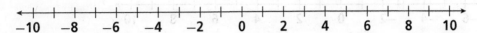

$7 + (−$3) = _____

(MP) **Use Tools** Three friends are playing a board game. The table shows their current scores. Each player draws two cards. The first card says "add" or "subtract." The second card says a number of points. Use a number line and complete the equation to find each player's final score.

Player	Score
Andrew	−4
Saleema	−3
Cassie	−9

4. Andrew's cards say "add" and "−4 points."

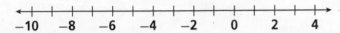

$-4 + (-4) =$ _____

5. Saleema's cards say "subtract" and "−7 points."

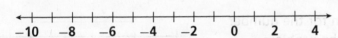

$-3 - (-7) =$ _____

6. Cassie's cards say "subtract" and "−8 points."

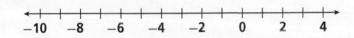

$-9 - (-8) =$ _____

7. (MP) **Use Tools** Tomas and a friend are hiking in Death Valley National Park in California. They start at an elevation of −10 meters. During the hike they ascend 30 meters, then descend 40 meters, and then descend another 20 meters. Use the number line and complete the equation to find their final elevation.

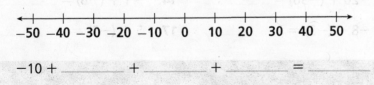

$-10 +$ _____ $+$ _____ $+$ _____ $=$ _____

Final elevation: _____

In the United States, the lowest point of elevation is found in Death Valley in California.

8. **(MP) Use Tools** The temperature at midnight is −7 °F. Before noon, the temperature decreases by 2 °F, then increases by 5 °F, and then increases by 4 °F. Use the number line and complete the equation to find the temperature at noon.

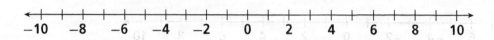

−7 °F − _____ + _____ + _____ = _____   Temperature at noon: _____

9. **(MP) Critique Reasoning** Leah said that when you add two negative integers the result must be negative. Do you agree or disagree? Use a number line to help explain your answer.

10. **Open Ended** Write a story problem for the number line shown. Provide the answer to the problem.

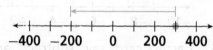

_____

_____

_____

11. **STEM** The freezing point of seawater is −2 °C. The freezing point of nitric acid is −42 °C. How much greater is the freezing point of seawater than the freezing point of nitric acid?

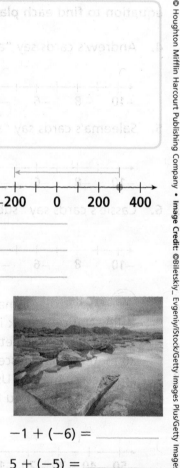

For Problems 12–17, use a number line to add or subtract.

12. 7 − (−3) = _____   13. −20 + (−30) = _____   14. −1 + (−6) = _____

15. 5 − (−4) = _____   16. −8 − (−5) = _____   17. 5 + (−5) = _____

 I'm in a Learning Mindset!

What strategies do I have for subtracting negative integers?

_____

_____

Name _____

Add or Subtract a Negative Integer on a Number Line

1. **(MP) Use Tools** Brad has 8 points during a trivia game. He answers a question incorrectly and −12 points are added to his score. Use the number line to add −12 points to Brad's score. Then complete the equation to show his final score.

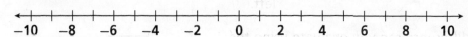

$8 + (-12) =$ _____

2. **Math on the Spot** A dolphin is swimming 3 feet below sea level. It dives down 9 feet to catch some fish. Then it swims 4 feet up toward the surface with its catch. What is the dolphin's final elevation relative to sea level?

_____

3. **(MP) Use Tools** Dario is scuba diving. He is currently at an elevation of −20 feet. He descends 20 feet. What is his elevation in relation to the other diver shown? Use the number line and complete the equation to find his relative elevation.

−30 ft

Dario

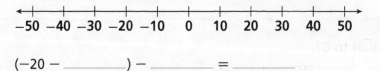

$(-20 -$ _____ $) -$ _____ $=$ _____

Relative elevation: _____

4. **(MP) Use Tools** Latisha has $40 in her checking account. She makes a withdrawal of $20 and then writes a check for $40. Then she deposits $30. Use the number line and complete the equation to find her final balance.

$$\text{(number line: } -30, -20, -10, 0, 10, 20, 30, 40, 50, 60, 70, 80, 90, 100 \text{)}$$

$40 +$ _____ $+$ _____ $+$ _____ $=$ _____

Final balance: _____

For Problems 5–10, use a number line to add or subtract.

5. $2 - (-4) =$ _____   6. $-2 + (-7) =$ _____

7. $-10 + (-60) =$ _____   8. $3 - (-1) =$ _____

9. $-7 - (-7) =$ _____   10. $2 + (-9) =$ _____

© Houghton Mifflin Harcourt Publishing Company • Image Credit: ©JonMilnes/Shutterstock

Test Prep

11. Elena wants to use a number line to find the difference 5 − (−7). Which is the best description of how she should do this?

Ⓐ Start at −7 and move 5 units right.

Ⓑ Start at −7 and move 5 units left.

Ⓒ Start at 5 and move 7 units right.

Ⓓ Start at 5 and move 7 units left.

12. Which sum or difference can you evaluate using the number line model shown?

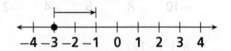

Ⓐ −3 − (−2)

Ⓑ −3 − 2

Ⓒ −1 + 3

Ⓓ −1 − (−3)

13. Aaron is playing a board game and has a score of 20 points. He spins a spinner to see how many points will be added to his score. The spinner lands on "−50 points." Find Aaron's final score. Show your work.

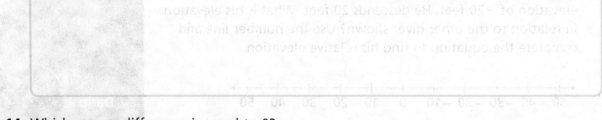

14. Which sum or difference is equal to 0?

Ⓐ −7 − 7

Ⓑ 4 − (−4)

Ⓒ −1 + (−1)

Ⓓ 6 + (−6)

Spiral Review

15. At a restaurant, Brianna and Naomi each order an appetizer for $6.50 and an entree for $9.75. The sales tax is $0.98 and they leave a tip of $5.85. How much did Brianna and Naomi spend in all?

16. Colton has a balance of $6 on his transit card. He takes several bus rides over the weekend for a total cost of $9. Use the number line to subtract $9 from Colton's balance. Then complete the equation.

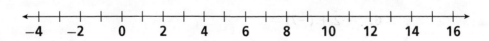

$6 − $9 = _____

Name _____

Use a Number Line to Add and Subtract Rational Numbers

(**I Can**) use a number line to add and subtract rational numbers.

Spark Your Learning

When a person owes money on a credit card, the credit card holder can think of it as a negative balance.

Devin has a balance of −$9.50 on a credit card. Which two items can he purchase without his balance going below −$15.00? Find all the pairs of items Devin can purchase.

Dinner rolls
$0.50

Pizza dough
$3.00

Cinnamon bread
$4.50

Turn and Talk If the cinnamon bread was on sale for $2.00, could he purchase all three items? Explain.

© Houghton Mifflin Harcourt Publishing Company

Build Understanding

1 An underwater camera is dropped from a helicopter flying $4\frac{1}{2}$ feet over the water. The camera has an elevation change of −8 feet. Where is the camera now in relation to the surface of the water?

4½ feet

A. The number line represents distance from sea level.

What do positive numbers represent?

_____

What do negative numbers represent?

_____

_____

What does 0 represent?

_____

_____

B. On the number line, draw an arrow representing the camera's change in elevation. Where is the camera after the change in elevation of −8 feet from the helicopter?

$4\frac{1}{2} + (-8) =$ _____

C. Later, the camera is at $-5\frac{1}{2}$ feet and has an elevation change of +3 feet. What is the camera's final elevation in relation to the surface?

On the number line a line would start at _____ and go _____ 3 units. Draw an arrow representing the camera's change in elevation.

$-5\frac{1}{2} + 3 =$ _____

D. Now the camera is at $-5\frac{1}{2}$ feet again, and it sinks $2\frac{1}{2}$ feet. What is the camera's final elevation in relation to the surface? Use the number line to show your work.

$-5\frac{1}{2} + \left(-2\frac{1}{2}\right) =$ _____

Elevation (ft)

13
12
11
10
9
8
7
6
5
4
3
2
1
0
−1
−2
−3
−4
−5
−6
−7
−8
−9
−10

Turn and Talk If the camera is at −2.5 feet and undergoes a change of elevation of 0 feet, where will the camera be then? Will it be at the surface?

Name _____

Step It Out

2 Carmela is playing with a ball.

A. The ball is on a platform 2.3 meters above the ground, then the ball falls to the ground. Use the number line to represent the change in height of the ball.

Begin at _____ to represent the height of the ball on the platform, then show the decrease in height.

B. Complete the equation to represent the situation in Part A.

$2.3 -$ _____ $=$ _____

C. The ball fell into a pit 1.5 feet below ground level. Carmela grabs the ball and puts it back on ground level.

Begin at _____ to represent the height of the ball in the pit, then show the increase in height on the number line.

D. Complete the equation to represent the situation in Part C.

$-1.5 +$ _____ $=$ _____

E. Carmela stands on the ground and kicks the ball 4.5 meters up into the air. It falls down and goes in another pit that is 3.5 meters deep.

Use the number line to show the changes in the height of the ball.

Begin at _____ to represent the height of the ball on the ground, and show the increase followed by the decrease.

F. Complete the equation to represent the situation in Part E.

_____ $+ 4.5 -$ _____ $= -3.5$

G. Using the number line model in Parts C and D as an example, explain the **Addition Property of Opposites** which states that the sum of a number and its **opposite** equals zero. Another name for opposite is **additive inverse**.

_____

_____

_____

 Turn and Talk How can you interpret the model in Parts A and B as a sum to show that the sum of a number and its opposite is 0?

© Houghton Mifflin Harcourt Publishing Company

3 ▶ Describe each situation in words.

A. Margarita has $50 in her bank account. What transaction would result in an account balance of $0?

_____

B. The temperature is 15 °F. What change in temperature would result in the temperature being 0 °F?

_____

C. A kite is 25 feet in the air. What needs to happen to the kite in order for it to be at ground level?

_____

D. Describe a situation in which opposite quantities combine to make 0.

_____

Check Understanding

1. From an elevation of 2.5 feet above a lake's surface a bird dives 4 feet to catch a fish. How far below the surface is the fish?

A. Represent this situation on the number line shown.

B. Complete the equation to represent the situation.

2.5 − 4 = _____

2. Pietro used a number line to subtract $-\frac{1}{8} - \left(-\frac{1}{4}\right)$. The figure shows the arrow he drew to represent the subtraction. Is he getting the right result? Explain.

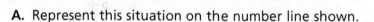

_____

_____

3. The overnight low temperature is −3 °F. By morning, the temperature increases by 13 degrees. Draw an arrow on the thermometer to represent this situation, and find the morning temperature.

_____

4. Mr. Anderson has a credit card balance of −$80.23 at the end of the month. Use Mr. Anderson's credit card balance to describe a situation in which opposite quantities combine to make 0.

_____

_____

_____

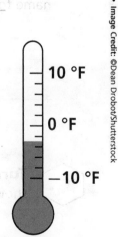

On Your Own

MP **Use Tools** The temperature in Mittenville is changing. Use the thermometer to help solve each problem.

5. In the morning, the temperature is −5 °F. The temperature increases by 13 °F, then decreases by 5 °F. Write an equation to represent the situation.

_____

6. The high temperature for the day is 28 °F. The record high for the day was 54 °F. What is the difference in temperatures?

_____

7. The high temperature for the day is 28 °F. The record low for the day was −12 °F. What is the difference in temperatures?

_____

8. This morning the temperature was −5 °F. How much must the temperature change to reach 0 °F?

_____

9. **MP** **Reason** Evan added $\left(-2\frac{1}{2}\right) + 4$ and got $6\frac{1}{2}$. Draw arrows on the number line to represent the problem. Then explain Evan's error.

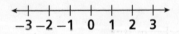

_____

_____

10. The number line shows the elevation of the bottom of a harbor and the elevation of a fish swimming close to the surface.

    A. What change in elevation is necessary for the fish to reach bottom?

    _____

    B. Once the fish reaches the bottom, what change in elevation will bring it back up to the surface?

    _____

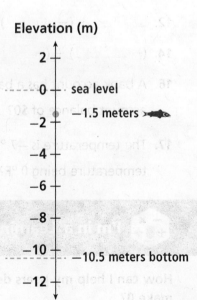

Elevation (m)

© Houghton Mifflin Harcourt Publishing Company

11. Financial Literacy Stock in Boomer Branding, Inc. started the week at $26.50 per share. During the week the following changes in the share price were registered:

(+$2.75), (+$3.00), (−$9.25), (+$1.50), (−$5.25)

A. Show the changes on the number line.

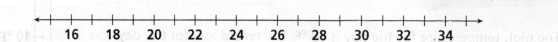

16   18   20   22   24   26   28   30   32   34

B. What was the price per share at the end of the week? _____

C. Open Ended Describe a situation using stocks in which opposite quantities combine to make 0.

_____

_____

For Problems 12–15, find rational numbers to complete each equation. Use the number line to help.

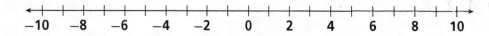

−10   −8   −6   −4   −2   0   2   4   6   8   10

12. _____ + (−_____) = −8.75   **13.** _____ − _____ = $-1\frac{3}{4}$

14. (−_____) + (−_____) = −19.25   **15.** _____ + _____ = 0

16. A bank account has a balance of $135. What transaction would result in an account balance of $0? _____

17. The temperature is −7 °F. What change in temperature would result in the temperature being 0 °F? _____

 I'm in a Learning Mindset!

How can I help my peers describe situations in which opposites combine to make 0?

_____

© Houghton Mifflin Harcourt Publishing Company • Image Credit: ©mdfiles/Fotolia

Use a Number Line to Add and Subtract Rational Numbers

1. **(MP) Use Tools** Caleb rode his bike $3\frac{1}{2}$ miles in the morning. Then he rode his bike another $2\frac{1}{2}$ miles in the afternoon. How many miles did Caleb ride altogether? Draw an arrow on the number line to show how to find the answer, then write the answer.

_____

```
←——|——|——|——|——|——|——|——|——|——|——|——→
   −2     0     2     4     6     8
```

2. **(MP) Critique Reasoning** Jasmine evaluated the expression $10 - (-3)$ and says it is equal to 7. Is she right? If not, what was her mistake?

_____

3. On a number line, what other number is the same distance from -2.8 as -7.2?

_____

4. A number line is drawn left to right with integers spaced 1 centimeter apart. An ant crawls onto the number line at $+2$. It then crawls 3.5 centimeters left, 4.8 centimeters right, and 7.9 centimeters left.

   A. Where is the ant on the number line now? _____

   B. How far is it from its original position? _____

   C. What is the total distance the ant crawled along the number line? _____

   D. **Open Ended** Describe a situation in which the ant crawls in a way that results in opposite quantities combining to make 0.

   _____

   _____

   _____

For Problems 5–6, draw arrows on the number line to show the operations indicated and fill in the answer.

5. $0.5 + (-1.5) - (-5.5) =$ _____

6. $-1\frac{1}{2} - \left(+3\frac{1}{2}\right) - \left(-\frac{5}{8}\right) =$ _____

```
←——|——|——|——|——|——|——|——|——|——|——|——→
  −5 −4 −3 −2 −1  0  1  2  3  4  5
```
```
←——|——|——|——|——|——|——|——|——|——|——|——→
  −5 −4 −3 −2 −1  0  1  2  3  4  5
```

Test Prep

7. If the temperature was 0 °C and then there was a temperature change of +5 °C, what temperature change would return the temperature to 0 °C?

(A) −10 °C

(B) −5 °C

(C) 0 °C

(D) 5 °C

8. Find the sum.
$$-\frac{1}{8} + \frac{1}{8} + \frac{5}{8}$$

(A) $\frac{1}{8}$

(B) $\frac{3}{8}$

(C) $\frac{5}{8}$

(D) $\frac{7}{8}$

9. Which set of operations corresponds to the arrows shown on the number line?

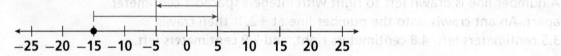

(A) $-15 - (+20) + (-10)$

(B) $-15 + (+20) - (-10)$

(C) $-15 - (+20) - (+10)$

(D) $-15 - (-20) + (-10)$

Spiral Review

10. A box of cereal contains 14.25 ounces. One serving is equal to 1.5 ounces. How many servings are in the box?

11. In an inspection, a bag of rice that was supposed to contain 5 kilograms was found to contain 4.8 kilograms. How many kilograms need to be added to the bag?

12. Mrs. Hernandez deposits $45.50 from every paycheck into a savings account. If she receives 26 paychecks in one year, how much will she deposit in one year?

136

© Houghton Mifflin Harcourt Publishing Company

Review

Vocabulary

For each number, select the terms that apply to it.

		Positive integer	Negative integer	Rational number
1.	23	☐	☐	☐
2.	$-\frac{3}{10}$	☐	☐	☐
3.	1.4	☐	☐	☐
4.	−7	☐	☐	☐

Concepts and Skills

5. **(MP) Use Tools** Name two numbers that are 7 units from 3. State what strategy and tool you will use to answer the question, explain your choice, and then find the answer.

_____

_____

6. A school, a bookstore, and a park are on the same straight street. The bookstore (*B*) is 2.25 miles from the school (*S*). The park (*P*) is 1.75 miles from the school.

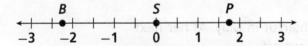

What is the distance from the park to the bookstore? _____ miles

7. Paolo is using number lines to find the value of $\frac{1}{6} + \frac{2}{3} + \left(-1\frac{1}{3}\right)$.

A. Paolo's first two steps are shown. Draw an arrow on the number line provided to show the last step.

Step 1: Start at $\frac{1}{6}$.	
Step 2: Add $\frac{2}{3}$.	
Last step: Add $\left(-1\frac{1}{3}\right)$.	

B. What is the value of the expression $\frac{1}{6} + \frac{2}{3} + \left(-1\frac{1}{3}\right)$? _____

8. A number line is shown. Eric knows that *n* is the opposite of *m*. Which statement about *m* and *n* is true?

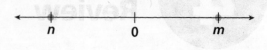

Ⓐ $m = n$ Ⓑ $m = -(-n)$ Ⓒ $m + n = 0$ Ⓓ $m - n = 0$

9. The difference $a - b$ is equal to *c*. The number line shows *a* and *b*. Select all statements about *c* that are true.

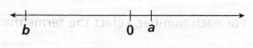

Ⓐ $c < 0$

Ⓑ $c = 0$

Ⓒ $c > 0$

Ⓓ *c* is closer to 0 than *a*.

Ⓔ *c* is the same distance from 0 as *a*.

Ⓕ *c* is farther from 0 than *a*.

10. On a quiz show, Anabel started with 0 points. She gained 10 points on her first turn and lost 10 points on her second turn. What is her combined score after her first two turns? Use addition of integers to explain your reasoning.

_____

_____

_____

11. An equation is shown, where $s > 0$ and $t < 0$.

$$r - s = t$$

Plot and label two points on the number line to show possible locations of *s* and *t*.

12. Ivy's hair has grown $\frac{5}{8}$ inch since her last haircut in May. At her next haircut in June, she has $1\frac{1}{2}$ inches of hair cut off.

A. Which expressions represent the total change, in inches, in the length of Ivy's hair since her haircut in May? Select all that apply.

Ⓐ $\frac{5}{8} - 1\frac{1}{2}$ Ⓓ $-1\frac{1}{2} - \frac{5}{8}$

Ⓑ $\frac{5}{8} + \left(-1\frac{1}{2}\right)$ Ⓔ $1\frac{1}{2} - \frac{5}{8}$

Ⓒ $\frac{5}{8} + 1\frac{1}{2}$

B. Plot a point on the number line to represent the total change, in inches, in the length of Ivy's hair since her haircut in May.

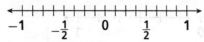

Fluency with Rational Number Operations

Can YOU Find the Mystery Number?

Missing a Number?

Can't find x?

Call the Math Detective Agency!

You are the new investigator for the Math Detective Agency. Your first case depends on finding a mystery number. Follow these steps.

A. Find each sum or difference.

$-7 + 9 =$ _____

$-5 - (-4) =$ _____

$-\frac{4}{5} - \frac{4}{5} =$ _____

$-\frac{1}{10} + \frac{3}{5} =$ _____

$-1 + 1\frac{1}{10} =$ _____

$-\frac{1}{5} - \frac{1}{2} =$ _____

B. Plot and label each sum or difference from Part A on the number line.

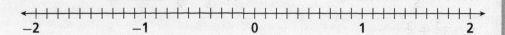

-2   -1   0   1   2

 Turn and Talk

The mystery number is the distance between the two closest points that you plotted. What is the mystery number? Explain how you found it.

Are You Ready?

Complete these problems to review prior concepts and skills you will need for this module.

Write and Interpret Numerical Expressions

Write a numerical expression to express the calculation. Do not simplify the expression.

1. The comic books in Cora's favorite series regularly cost $2.99. Today, they are on sale for $0.50 off the regular price. Cora subtracts $0.50 from $2.99 and multiplies the result by 4 to find the cost of 4 comic books at the sale price.

_____

Add Fractions and Decimals

Find each sum.

2. $8.04 + 4.15$ _____

3. $\frac{5}{6} + \frac{2}{3}$ _____

Multiply with Decimals

Find each product.

4. 1.68×2.5 _____

5. 0.45×0.08 _____

Divide Fractions and Mixed Numbers

Find each quotient.

6. $3 \div \frac{1}{5}$ _____

7. $\frac{7}{8} \div \frac{1}{2}$ _____

8. $3\frac{2}{3} \div \frac{3}{5}$ _____

9. One serving of rice is equal to $\frac{3}{4}$ cup. Gerardo makes 4 cups of rice. How many servings of rice did Gerardo make?

_____

Name _____

Compute Sums of Rational Numbers

(I Can) compute sums of rational numbers with the same or different signs, and for real-world problems, I can interpret the results.

Spark Your Learning

A research submarine was stationed 700 feet below sea level. It ascends 250 feet every hour. If the submarine continues to ascend at the same rate, when will the submarine be at the surface?

Turn and Talk How can you express the position of the submarine as an integer to show that the submarine is below sea level? Explain.

© Houghton Mifflin Harcourt Publishing Company • Image Credit: ©Photomarine/Shutterstock

Build Understanding

1 ► A submarine descends to 800 feet below sea level. Then it descends another 200 feet. What is the submarine's final elevation? First use a number line to find out. Then use **absolute value** to solve the same problem without a number line.

A. Write an addition expression, and use the number line to determine the final elevation of the submarine.

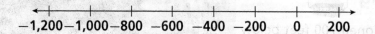

−1,200 −1,000 −800 −600 −400 −200 0 200

B. Recall that the absolute value of a number is the number's distance from 0 on the number line. For example, the absolute value of −4 is 4 because −4 is 4 units from 0.

Because the arrows you drew for −800 and −200 in Part A both point in the same direction, you can find the submarine's final distance from 0 by adding the absolute values of these numbers.

$|-800| + |-200| = \boxed{} + \boxed{} = \boxed{}$

C. How does the sum of the absolute values compare to the sum of −800 and −200?

D. How can you use the sum of absolute values in Part B to find the final elevation—that is, to find the sum of −800 and −200?

E. Find −100 + (−300) by first adding the absolute values. Use the number line in Part A to check your answer.

$|-100| + |-300| = \boxed{} + \boxed{} = \boxed{}$, so −100 + (−300) = $\boxed{}$.

F. Complete the rule for adding rational numbers with the same signs:

_____ the absolute values of the numbers and use the _____ of the addends.

 Turn and Talk Use a number line to explain why adding two rational numbers with the same sign will always result in a sum that has the same sign as the addends.

2 ▸ The temperature in the morning in Sioux City, Iowa, is shown. By the afternoon, the temperature had risen 25 °F. What was the temperature in the afternoon? First use a number line to find out. Then use absolute value to solve the same problem without a number line.

Sioux City,
IOWA

−5 °F

A. Write an addition expression and use the number line to determine the temperature in the afternoon.

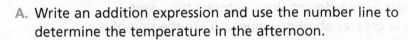

The temperature in the afternoon is _____ °F.

B. Use absolute value to find the distance of the final temperature from 0. Because the first number moves you left on the number line and the second number moves you right, subtract the lesser absolute value from the greater absolute value. How does the result compare to the sum in Part A?

_____

_____

C. On another day, the temperature was 30 °F but a severe ice storm caused a temperature drop of 35 °F. Write an addition expression and use the number line to determine the temperature after the ice storm.

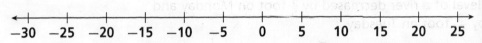

The temperature after the ice storm was _____ °F.

D. Use absolute value to find the distance of the final temperature from 0. Because the first number moves you right on the number line and the second number moves you left, subtract the lesser absolute value from the greater absolute value. How does the result compare to the sum in Part C?

_____

_____

E. Complete the rule for adding rational numbers with different signs:

_____ the lesser absolute value from the greater absolute value

and use the sign of the addend with the _____ absolute value.

Step It Out

Here are the rules for adding rational numbers:

- To add rational numbers with the same sign, add their absolute values and use the sign of the addends.
- To add rational numbers with different signs, subtract the lesser absolute value from the greater absolute value and use the sign of the addend with the greater absolute value.

3 The water level of a river decreased by $\frac{1}{5}$ foot on Monday and increased by $\frac{3}{10}$ foot on Tuesday.

A. Write an addition expression for the number of feet gained or lost.

B. Use the rules above to find and interpret the sum of your expression in Part A.

C. Explain why your answer is reasonable.

D. Use the Commutative Property of Addition to show that the result is the same if the two changes happened in reverse order.

E. The water level of a canal decreased by 4.8 meters and then decreased by another 3.5 meters. Write an addition expression for the number of meters gained or lost.

F. Use the rules above to find and interpret the sum of your expression in Part E.

Check Understanding

1. A football player averages 16.4 yards in his first game. During his second game, his average changes by −2.3 yards. Write and evaluate an addition expression to find the player's new average.

2. Evaluate $-7\frac{1}{3} + \left(-\frac{2}{5}\right)$.

© Houghton Mifflin Harcourt Publishing Company

144

On Your Own

3. Belle's dad lends her $10. Then Belle borrows another $15 from him. Write and evaluate an expression that shows the change in the amount of money Belle's dad has.

_____

4. The changes in the elevation of a plane while it was flying are shown. Write and evaluate an expression that shows the plane's change in elevation compared to its altitude before the first descent.

_____

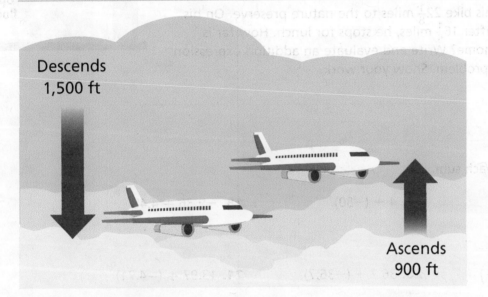

Descends 1,500 ft

Ascends 900 ft

5. In the stock market, changes in value used to be indicated by fractions, which represented portions of $1. If a stock had a value of $11.50, write and evaluate an addition expression to find how much the stock is worth after an increase of $\frac{1}{4}$.

_____

6. Jayvon has 33.6 points in a competition. He loses 5.5 points. Write and evaluate an addition expression to determine Jayvon's current score.

_____

For 7–12, find each sum.

7. $-7 + 10$

8. $-42 + (-6)$

9. $-\frac{5}{7} + \left(-\frac{3}{14}\right)$

10. $-21.6 + (-5.6)$

11. $12\frac{2}{3} + \left(-9\frac{1}{6}\right)$

12. $-15.23 + 6.23$

13. (MP) **Reason** Blake's journey on the elevators of his building is shown. Write and evaluate an addition expression that shows Blake's location compared to his starting point.

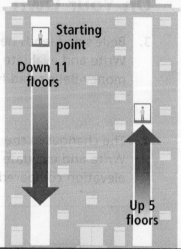

Starting point

Down 11 floors

Up 5 floors

_____

14. Seth earned $76.50 and spent $42.95. Write and evaluate an addition expression that shows how much money Seth has left.

_____

15. Brock rides his bike $22\frac{1}{8}$ miles to the nature preserve. On his way home, after $16\frac{1}{5}$ miles, he stops for lunch. How far is Brock from home? Write and evaluate an addition expression to solve the problem. Show your work.

_____

_____

For 16–21, find each sum.

16. $\frac{3}{8} + \left(-\frac{1}{2}\right)$

17. $4 + (-50)$

18. $-9.36 + 4.48$

19. $-6\frac{3}{8} + \left(-5\frac{3}{4}\right)$

20. $36.7 + (-36.7)$

21. $13.97 + (-4.71)$

22. **Financial Literacy** A bank account had a balance of $1,184.57. Then the customer withdrew $455.75. Write and evaluate an addition expression showing the new account balance.

_____

 I'm in a Learning Mindset!

What can I do to check my understanding when I solve problems in which I add rational numbers?

_____

_____

Compute Sums of Rational Numbers

ONLINE

Video Tutorials and Interactive Examples

1. (MP) **Use Structure** Joni climbed $75\frac{1}{2}$ feet up a hill and then rappelled down $92\frac{1}{4}$ feet into a valley.

   A. Write an addition expression to represent the situation.

   _____

   B. Evaluate the expression to determine how far Joni was from where she started.

   _____

   _____

2. (MP) **Model with Mathematics** The temperature at 8:00 a.m. on a winter day was −2 °F. By noon, the temperature had increased by 28 °F. Write and evaluate an expression to find the temperature at noon.

   _____

   _____

3. **Math on the Spot** Andrea's income from a lemonade stand was $28. Supply expenses were $9. Write and evaluate an expression to find Andrea's profit or loss.

   _____

   _____

For Problems 4–12, find each sum.

4. $14 + 8$

5. $20 + (-5)$

6. $-19 + 2$

7. $27.81 + (-13.97)$

8. $-3\frac{2}{3} + 14\frac{2}{3}$

9. $-5\frac{2}{7} + (-2\frac{1}{5})$

10. $100 + (-26)$

11. $-22.8 + 22.8$

12. $15 + (-3\frac{7}{9})$

13. Leandra bought two shirts for a total of $46.72. She returned one of the shirts for a refund of $24.61. Write and evaluate an addition expression to show what Leandra paid for the shirt she kept.

   _____

Test Prep

14. Melissa has $37.25 and spends $15.65. Which expression represents this situation?

Ⓐ 37.25 + 15.65

Ⓑ −37.25 + (−15.65)

Ⓒ −37.25 + 15.65

Ⓓ 37.25 + (−15.65)

15. A rock climber descends $22\frac{1}{2}$ feet into a small canyon. The climber then climbs up $7\frac{1}{2}$ feet. What is his final position relative to where he started?

Ⓐ 30 ft

Ⓑ 15 ft

Ⓒ −15 ft

Ⓓ −30 ft

16. Write and evaluate an expression for the following number line.

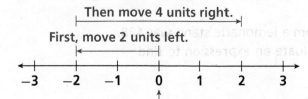

Spiral Review

17. Lauren plots the rational numbers shown below on a number line. Which of the numbers is farthest left on the number line?

-1.4 $2\frac{2}{3}$ -0.99 $-2\frac{1}{3}$ $\frac{99}{100}$

18. Pablo has a piece of ribbon that is $41\frac{1}{4}$ feet long. As part of an art project, he wants to cut the ribbon into smaller pieces that are each $3\frac{3}{4}$ feet long. How many smaller pieces of ribbon can he make?

19. Jamal buys 3.45 kilograms of tomatoes to make sauce. The tomatoes cost $2.75 per kilogram. What is the cost of the tomatoes? Round your answer to the nearest cent.

Name

3 A scuba diver jumps in the water and continues to descend until reaching −10.75 feet. How far did the diver descend?

The diver is 4.5 ft above the water's surface.

A. Use the number line to find the distance the diver descended. Explain how you got your answer.

<---|---|---|---|---|---|---|---|---|---|---|---|---|---|---|---|---|---|---|---|---|---|---|---|---|---|---|---|---|---|---|---|---|---|---|---|---|---|---|---|---|---|---|---|---|---|---|---|---|---|---|---|---|---|---|---|---|---|---|--->
      −13−12−11−10 −9 −8 −7 −6 −5 −4 −3 −2 −1 0 1 2 3 4 5 6 7

_____

_____

_____

_____

B. Write and evaluate a subtraction expression to find the distance the diver traveled, starting from the diver's elevation of 4.5 feet above sea level.

_____

C. Now write and evaluate an expression to find the difference between the diver's ending point and starting point.

_____

D. How are your answers to Parts B and C alike, and how are they different? Are they equal or opposites?

_____

_____

E. Distance is always expressed as a positive number because it does not indicate direction. When you subtract to find the distance between two locations, how can you make sure that your result is always positive?

_____

_____

Turn and Talk How can you use subtraction and absolute value to find the distance between any two numbers on a number line?

Step It Out

To subtract a positive or negative rational number, add its opposite.

4 ▸ Complete the equivalent addition expression for each subtraction expression. Then evaluate.

A. $3.2 - 6.8 = 3.2 +$ ☐ ; ☐

B. $5\frac{1}{3} - \left(-4\frac{1}{2}\right) = 5\frac{1}{3} +$ ☐ ; ☐

C. $-8.42 - 7.3 = -8.42 +$ ☐ ; ☐

D. $-6\frac{2}{5} - \left(-6\frac{2}{5}\right) = -6\frac{2}{5} +$ ☐ ; ☐

E. Complete each statement.

After rewriting subtraction as addition, a statement that adds two negative numbers results in a _____ number.

After rewriting subtraction as addition, a statement that adds two positive numbers results in a _____ number.

After rewriting subtraction as addition, a statement that adds opposites results in _____ .

Check Understanding

1. Elise had a credit card balance of −$120. She made a payment of $70. Write and evaluate a subtraction expression to find her new balance.

_____

2. Use subtraction and absolute value to find the distance between the numbers −7.3 and 2.1 on a number line.

_____

3. Complete the equivalent addition expression for each subtraction expression. Then evaluate.

A. $7\frac{2}{7} - \left(-15\frac{2}{7}\right) = 7\frac{2}{7} +$ ☐ ; ☐

B. $-14\frac{1}{6} - 4 = -14\frac{1}{6} +$ ☐ ; ☐

4. How do you subtract a rational number from another rational number without using a number line? Give an example.

_____

_____

On Your Own

5. The temperature is 2 °F and drops to −15 °F overnight. Write and evaluate a subtraction expression to determine the change in temperature.

_____

_____

6. A submarine descended 500 feet below sea level. It then descended another 275 feet. Write and evaluate a subtraction expression to determine the new position of the submarine relative to sea level.

_____

7. (MP) **Reason** Ingvar is playing a video game that takes away points for losing treasures. His current score is shown. Then he loses treasure worth 27.7 points.

    A. Write and evaluate a subtraction expression to find Ingvar's new score.

_____

_____

    B. Is your answer reasonable? Why?

_____

_____

_____

Ingvar's current score is −56.2.

8. Malik earns an average of $4\frac{1}{2}$ points on his daily homework quizzes. Near the end of the quarter, his average decreases by $\frac{3}{4}$ point. Write and evaluate a subtraction expression to find his current quiz grade average.

_____

_____

9. **Financial Literacy** Miss Aliyah's checking account balance is $15.50. She withdraws $5.37. Write and evaluate a subtraction expression to find the new balance.

_____

_____

For Problems 10–13, find the distance in units between the numbers on a number line.

10. $\frac{5}{8}$ and $\frac{1}{4}$

11. −12 and 14

_____

12. $1\frac{1}{2}$ and $-2\frac{5}{6}$

13. −5.75 and −6.42

_____

14. The West High football team gained 7 yards but then lost 15 yards. Write and evaluate a subtraction expression to determine the overall change in yardage.

_____

15. Financial Literacy Amy had a $9.78 monthly fee for music streaming due when she received her paycheck. After paying for the music streaming service, she had $65.02 remaining from her paycheck. Write and evaluate a subtraction expression to determine the original value of Amy's paycheck.

_____

16. At the beginning of a game, April had a score of −150 points. April played for another 20 minutes, and her final score was −355 points. Write and evaluate a subtraction expression to determine the change of her score from the beginning of the game to the end of the game.

_____

_____

For Problems 17–24, write each subtraction expression as an equivalent addition expression and evaluate it.

17. $41.7 - 41.7$

_____

18. $36 - 48$

19. $-13\frac{1}{4} - \left(-10\frac{3}{4}\right)$

_____

20. $-33\frac{5}{8} - 7\frac{1}{2}$

21. $21.85 - 6.03$

_____

22. $-9 - (-13.11)$

23. $0 - (-5)$

_____

24. $1.9 - 1.9$

 I'm in a Learning Mindset!

What did I learn by discussing strategies for subtracting rational numbers with my peers?

_____

Compute Differences of Rational Numbers

1. Wednesday morning, the temperature was −12 °F. By the afternoon, the temperature was 23 °F. Write and evaluate a subtraction expression to determine the number of degrees of change in temperature between the morning and the afternoon.

_____

2. **STEM** Scientists are studying the effects of increased temperature, which causes bleaching on coral reefs. A scientist dives at two different reefs, one located 34.5 feet below sea level and one at 26.25 feet below sea level. Represent the position of each reef as a rational number. Then use subtraction and absolute value to find the vertical distance between the reefs.

_____

Coral reef that has been affected by bleaching

Coral reef that has not been affected by bleaching

3. Savana walks $3\frac{1}{3}$ miles to a park. On her way home, she stops at Ray's house after $1\frac{2}{3}$ miles to pick up a book. Write and evaluate a subtraction expression to find how much farther Savana must walk to get home.

_____

4. Joseph removes $\frac{5}{8}$ gallon of white paint from a can. Then he adds $\frac{5}{8}$ gallon of blue paint to the can. Write and evaluate an addition expression to find the overall increase or decrease in the amount of paint in the can.

_____

For Problems 5–8, evaluate the expression.

5. $\frac{1}{4} - \left(-\frac{1}{6}\right)$

6. $-4\frac{1}{2} - 2\frac{3}{4}$

7. $-233.2 - 25.8$

8. $27.81 - (-13.97)$

© Houghton Mifflin Harcourt Publishing Company • Image Credits: [(t)] ©Ethan Daniels/Shutterstock; [(b)] ©Ethan Daniels/Alamy

Test Prep

9. Maya's bank account had $55.29. She wrote a check for $42. Which expression represents the situation?

    (A) $55.29 + 42$

    (B) $-42 - 55.29$

    (C) $55.29 - 42$

    (D) $42 - 55.29$

10. George had a score of 25 points in a game. During the rest of the game, he lost 59 points. What score did George have at the end?

    (A) 34 points

    (B) −34 points

    (C) 84 points

    (D) −84 points

11. The highest elevation in California is 14,505 feet, and the lowest elevation is −282 feet. Write and evaluate an expression to determine the distance between the lowest and highest elevations.

_____

12. Evaluate $-13\frac{1}{2} - \left(-17\frac{1}{2}\right)$.

    (A) −31

    (B) −4

    (C) 4

    (D) 31

13. Evaluate $23 - (-9)$.

_____

Spiral Review

14. What is the value of $|-6.8|$?

_____

15. On Friday, Lakesha jogs 3.21 miles. On Saturday, she jogs 3.75 miles. On Sunday, she jogs 1.94 miles. What is the total distance she jogs over the three days?

_____

16. Alex wants to model $-4 + (-3)$ on a number line. He starts at −4. What should he do next to find the sum?

© Houghton Mifflin Harcourt Publishing Company

Name _____

Understand and Compute Products and Quotients of Rational Numbers

(**I Can**) apply the rules for multiplying and dividing rational numbers.

Spark Your Learning

Arnot wins a $50 gift card for a virtual reality arcade. If he does not use the card for a whole year, the balance on the card will be reduced by $5 each month that it continues to go unused. What will be the change in the value of the card if Arnot doesn't use it for 18 months?

Turn and Talk Did you use the same method as your partner? If not, explain your reasoning to make sure both methods are correct.

Build Understanding

1 Jordan is scuba diving and stops each time she descends 15 feet to take a photo. Starting at the surface, she does this 4 times. What is her overall change in elevation?

A. Write an addition equation to represent the overall change in elevation.

_____

B. Adding [ ] units [ ] times can be written as

the multiplication expression [ ]([ ]).

C. How should your answer in Part A compare to the value of the multiplication expression? Explain your reasoning.

_____

D. We want the Commutative Property of Multiplication to hold for all rational numbers. So if $(4)(-15) = -60$, then $(-15)(4) = $ [ ].

E. Complete the last column in the table indicating the sign of the product pq.

F. Write a rule for multiplication of rational numbers with different signs.

The product of two rational numbers with different signs is a | positive / negative | number.

Products of Rational Numbers

Sign of factor p	Sign of factor q	Sign of product pq
+	−	
−	+	

G. We want the Distributive Property to hold for all rational numbers. Use your rule from Part F to show that the Distributive Property holds for $3(6 + (-4))$. Then determine what the value of $(-3)(-4)$ must be for the Distributive Property to hold for $-3(6 + (-4))$.

$$3(6 + (-4)) \stackrel{?}{=} 3(6) + 3\left(\boxed{}\right)$$

$$3(2) \stackrel{?}{=} 18 + \left(\boxed{}\right)$$

$$6 = \boxed{}$$

$$-3(6 + (-4)) = (-3)(6) + (-3)(-4)$$

$$-3(2) = -18 + \boxed{}$$

$$-6 = -6$$

This means that $(-3)(-4) = $ [ ].

H. Complete the table.

I. Write a rule for multiplication of rational numbers with the same sign.

The product of two rational numbers with the same sign is a | positive / negative | number.

Products of Rational Numbers

Sign of factor p	Sign of factor q	Sign of product pq
+	+	
−	−	

2 You can use what you know about multiplying signed numbers to figure out the rules for dividing signed numbers.

A. Use the fact that division and multiplication are **inverse operations** to complete the number statements in the table.

Multiplication	Related division
$2 \times 4 = 8$	$8 \div \boxed{} = 4$ and $8 \div 4 = \boxed{}$
$-2 \times 4 = -8$	$-8 \div \boxed{} = 4$ and $-8 \div 4 = \boxed{}$
$2 \times (-4) = -8$	$-8 \div \boxed{} = -4$ and $-8 \div (-4) = \boxed{}$
$-2 \times (-4) = 8$	$8 \div \boxed{} = -4$ and $8 \div \boxed{} = -2$

B. Use your results from Part A to complete the table.

C. Complete the rules for division of rational numbers.

- The quotient of two rational numbers with different signs is a _____ number.
- The quotient of two rational numbers with the same sign is a _____ number.

Quotients of Rational Numbers		
Sign of dividend p	Sign of divisor q	Sign of quotient $\frac{p}{q}$
$+$	$-$	
$-$	$+$	
$+$	$+$	
$-$	$-$	

3 You can multiply pairs of factors to find the product of three or more rational numbers.

A. Complete the table.

Product	Number of negative factors	Sign of product
$(-3)(4)(7)$		
$(-5)(-5)(2)(6)$		
$(-1)(-3)(-10)$		
$(3)(-2)(-1)(-2)(-3)$		

B. What relationship do you see between the number of negative factors and the sign of the corresponding product?

_____

_____

Turn and Talk How do the rules you learned previously for multiplying two numbers with the same sign and two numbers with different signs support your answer to Part B?

Step It Out

4 ▷ Find each product or quotient.

A. $\left(-\frac{1}{3}\right)(-7)(-9) = \left(\boxed{}\right)\left(-\frac{1}{3}\right)(-9)$

$= \left(\boxed{}\right)\left[\left(-\frac{1}{3}\right)(-9)\right]$

$= \left(\boxed{}\right)(3)$

$= -21$

B. $-135 \div 15$

This is a quotient of two rational numbers with different signs, so the quotient is a $\boxed{\text{positive / negative}}$ number.

$-135 \div 15 = \boxed{}$

C. $-\frac{3}{4} \div \left(-\frac{5}{4}\right)$

This is a quotient of two rational numbers with the same sign, so the quotient is a $\boxed{\text{positive / negative}}$ number.

$-\frac{3}{4} \div \left(-\frac{5}{4}\right) = -\frac{3}{4} \times \left(\boxed{}\right) = \boxed{}$

Check Understanding

1. Jared writes a multiplication expression with eight rational factors. Half of the factors are positive and half are negative. Is the product positive or negative? Why?

2. The expression $(8)(-1.5)$ represents the change in a scuba diver's elevation in meters after 8 minutes. Find the change in elevation.

Find each product or quotient.

3. $-1 \div (-0.25)$ _____

4. $(10)(-3)\left(-\frac{4}{5}\right)\left(-\frac{5}{6}\right)$ _____

5. Compare the rules for finding the signs of products and quotients.

On Your Own

(MP) **Model with Mathematics** In Problems 6–7, model the situation with a multiplication expression and an addition expression involving negative numbers. Then evaluate.

All-Day Parking $5

6. Every day that Annabelle takes the train to work, she uses an app to charge the parking fee shown to her credit card. What will be her card balance for commuter parking if she parks and takes the train to work 10 times?

_____

_____

7. Alejandro makes $100 donations to five of his favorite charities every December. He pays for the donations by check. What is the change in his checking account balance after making these donations?

_____

_____

For Problems 8–13, identify the sign of the product or quotient. Do not evaluate.

8. $253 \times (-185)$

9. -59×819

10. $-1{,}200 \times (-490)$

_____

_____

_____

11. $1{,}242 \div (-18)$

12. $-1{,}890 \div (-15)$

13. $-18{,}175 \div 125$

_____

_____

_____

14. DeMarcus multiplies all of the integers from -10 to -1, including -10 and -1. Should his answer be positive or negative? Explain your thinking.

_____

_____

_____

For Problems 15–23, find each product or quotient.

15. $(-4)(-8)(-5)$

16. $(-4)(-2)(5)(3)$

17. $-270 \div (-3)$

_____

_____

_____

18. $(0.2)(50)(-0.9)$

19. $(0.1)(-0.2)(10)(-10)$

20. $14.7 \div (-3.5)$

_____

_____

_____

21. $\left(-\frac{1}{3}\right)\left(\frac{3}{5}\right)\left(-\frac{5}{7}\right)$

22. $\left(\frac{2}{7}\right)\left(\frac{14}{15}\right)\left(-\frac{1}{2}\right)$

23. $-\frac{3}{2} \div \frac{1}{4}$

Module 5 • Lesson 3

161

24. (MP) **Construct Arguments** Complete each step to show that $(-1)(-1) = 1$.

$(-1)(0) = \boxed{}$ Multiplication Property of Zero

$(-1)(-1 + 1) = 0$ Addition Property of Opposites

$(-1)(-1) + (-1)(1) = 0$ _____

$(-1)(-1) + \boxed{} = 0$ Identity Property of Multiplication

$(-1)(-1) + (-1) + \boxed{} = 0 + \boxed{}$ Addition Property of Equality

$(-1)(-1) + (-1 + 1) = 0 + 1$ _____

$(-1)(-1) + \boxed{} = 0 + 1$ Addition Property of Opposites

$(-1)(-1) = \boxed{}$ Identity Property of Addition

25. The value of a collectible baseball card decreased as shown.

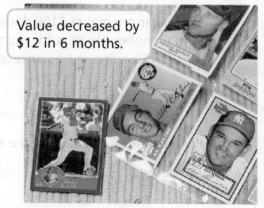

Value decreased by $12 in 6 months.

A. (MP) **Use Tools** To find the average monthly change in the value of the card, use the number line to find $-12 \div 6$.

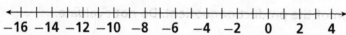

$-12 \div 6 =$ _____

B. (MP) **Construct Arguments** What is the sign (positive or negative) of the quotient? Explain why this makes sense in the context of the problem.

_____

_____

26. **Open Ended** Write a different division problem involving negative numbers that can be solved using the number line given in Problem 25.

_____

 I'm in a Learning Mindset!

How can I use my understanding of rational number multiplication to help support my understanding of rational number division?

_____

_____

Name _____

Understand and Compute Products and Quotients of Rational Numbers

(MP) Model with Mathematics For Problems 1 and 2, model the situation with a multiplication expression and an addition expression involving negative numbers. Then evaluate.

1. After a gymnastics competition, the coaches reviewed all the gymnasts' scores to identify areas for improvement. A missed landing on an aerial cartwheel deducts 2 points from the score. The coaches found that aerial cartwheels were missed 5 times across the competition. How did these missed landings affect the scores overall?

_____

_____

2. The temperature fell by 3°F every hour during a 6-hour period. What was the overall change in temperature during the 6-hour period?

_____

_____

For Problems 3–5, identify the sign of the product. Do not evaluate.

3. $-819 \times (-324)$ 4. $-1,201 \times 54$ 5. $10,005 \times (-84)$

6. **(MP) Critique Reasoning** Dario said that if the dividend and divisor have the same sign, then the quotient also has that same sign. Do you agree or disagree? Explain.

_____

_____

7. **(MP) Use Structure** Explain how you can use the fact that multiplication and division are inverse operations to help you determine whether the quotient $-10 \div (-5)$ is positive or negative.

_____

_____

For Problems 8–11, find each product or quotient.

8. $(3)(5)(-3)(-2)(10)(-1)$ 9. $-4300 \div (-100)$

_____   _____

10. $\left(\frac{2}{3}\right)\left(-\frac{9}{8}\right)\left(-\frac{4}{5}\right)(-1)$ 11. $-3\frac{1}{2} \div \frac{3}{4}$

_____   _____

Test Prep

12. Which quotients are negative? Select all that apply.

   Ⓐ $\dfrac{-52}{13}$ Ⓓ $\dfrac{-20}{-5}$

   Ⓑ $14 \div (-2)$ Ⓔ $-27 \div 3$

   Ⓒ $-36 \div (-9)$ Ⓕ $\dfrac{7}{-1}$

13. Marley's bank charges a $3 service fee each time money is withdrawn from another bank's ATM. Marley is traveling and must withdraw money from another bank's ATM 4 times. Which expressions model the change in the balance of her account due to the service fees? Select all that apply.

   Ⓐ $-3 + (-3) + (-3) + (-3)$ Ⓓ $-4 \times (-3)$

   Ⓑ $-4 + (-4) + (-4)$ Ⓔ 3×4

   Ⓒ $4 \times (-3)$

14. An equation is shown.

$$a \times b = c$$

Which statement is true?

   Ⓐ If $a > 0$ and $b > 0$, then $c < 0$.   Ⓒ If $a < 0$ and $b > 0$, then $c > 0$.

   Ⓑ If $a > 0$ and $b < 0$, then $c < 0$.   Ⓓ If $a < 0$ and $b < 0$, then $c < 0$.

Spiral Review

15. Miguel takes $50 to the mall. He buys a flannel shirt for $18.99 and a hat for $12.49. On his way home, he stops at the bank and withdraws $25. How much money does Miguel have now?

_____

16. Callie bought 4 pies from a bakery for a holiday dinner. The total cost was $75.80. If each pie cost the same, how much did one pie cost?

_____

17. The temperature at 6:00 a.m. on a winter day is $-6\ °F$. The temperature rises by $7\ °F$ by noon. Use the number line to represent the situation. Then complete the equation.

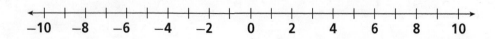

$-6\ °F + 7\ °F = $ _____ $°F$

Write Rational Numbers as Decimals

(I Can) show that a number is rational by writing it as a ratio of integers, and I can convert a rational number to a decimal. I can show that $-\left(\frac{p}{q}\right) = \frac{(-p)}{q} = \frac{p}{(-q)}$ for specific values of p and q.

Spark Your Learning

Hayley is buying herbs. She wants to buy $\frac{5}{6}$ ounce of basil. The scale she is using to weigh the basil displays the weight as a decimal. How will she know when the display on the scale is correct to the tenths place? Explain your reasoning.

Turn and Talk What do you think the digit in the hundredths place of the display will be? Explain your reasoning.

Build Understanding

1 ▶ Hayley wants to buy the amounts of herbs shown. How can you convert these fractions to decimals?

$\frac{3}{4}$ oz oregano, $\frac{2}{3}$ oz thyme

A. You can use **equivalent fractions** to convert a fraction to a decimal. Does that method work well for these fractions? Why or why not?

_____

_____

_____

_____

B. You can also use long division to convert a fraction to a decimal, because $\frac{a}{b} = a \div b$ for all fractions $\frac{a}{b}$.

Think about dividing 3 ounces into 4 equal parts as shown. How many tenths and hundredths will there be in each part?

```
    0.7 5
4)3.0 0
 -2 8
    2 0
  -2 0
      0
```

_____

_____

C. How can you use the decimal form of $\frac{3}{4}$ ounce to find what Hayley will pay for basil that costs $5.80 per ounce?

_____

_____

D. Use long division to find the decimal equivalent of $\frac{2}{3}$ ounce to the thousandths place. Do not round.

_____

E. Describe the pattern in the quotient. Will the pattern continue if you write a zero in the ten-thousandths place of the dividend and continue dividing? Why or why not?

_____

_____

_____

_____

 Turn and Talk Can the number 20 be divided evenly by 3? What does your answer imply about the quotient in Part E? Explain.

Step It Out

2 Every quotient of integers is a **rational number**, provided that the divisor is not zero. A rational number can be written as a fraction in which the numerator and the denominator are integers. The decimal form of a rational number either *terminates* (ends) or *repeats*.

Examples: terminating decimal: $\frac{3}{4} = 0.75$

repeating decimal: $\frac{2}{3} = 0.666...$, or $0.\overline{6}$

The bar over the 6 means that it repeats forever.

$$
\begin{array}{r}
2.\boxed{}\boxed{}\boxed{} \\
6\overline{)1\ 7.\ 0\ \boxed{}\ \boxed{}} \\
-1\ 2 \\
\hline
5\ 0 \\
-\boxed{} \\
\hline
2\ 0 \\
-\boxed{} \\
\hline
2\ 0 \\
-\boxed{} \\
\hline
2
\end{array}
$$

A. Suppose Hayley wants to buy $2\frac{5}{6}$ ounces of basil. Complete the statement to show that $2\frac{5}{6}$ is a rational number.

$2\frac{5}{6} = \dfrac{\boxed{}}{6}$, and _____ and _____ are integers.

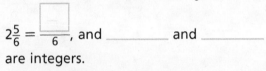

B. Complete the long division shown to write $2\frac{5}{6}$ as a decimal. Then complete the statement.

$2\frac{5}{6} =$ _____, which is a

terminating / repeating decimal.

3 Use the rules you've learned for dividing negative numbers.

A. Find each quotient. Then complete the statement.

$\dfrac{15}{-3} =$ _____ ÷ _____ = _____

$\dfrac{-15}{3} =$ _____ ÷ _____ = _____

$-\left(\dfrac{15}{3}\right) =$ _____

The rational numbers $\dfrac{15}{-3}$, $\dfrac{-15}{3}$, and $-\left(\dfrac{15}{3}\right)$ are / are not equivalent.

B. If p and q are integers and q is not zero, what is true about $\dfrac{-p}{q}$, $\dfrac{p}{-q}$, and $-\left(\dfrac{p}{q}\right)$? _____

C. The value of a share of stock decreased by $15 in 3 days. If it decreased the same amount each day, which expression in Part A best represents the daily change in the stock's value? Explain.

_____

 Turn and Talk Is the number $-2\frac{5}{6}$ a rational number? Why or why not?

4 What are some different ways you can express the rational number $\frac{100}{-11}$?

A. Express the rational number as a fraction in different ways.

$$\frac{100}{-11} = \frac{\boxed{}}{\boxed{}} = -\frac{\boxed{}}{\boxed{}}$$

B. Express the rational number as a mixed number.

$$\frac{100}{-11} = -9\,\frac{\boxed{}}{\boxed{}}$$

C. Complete the division to express the rational number as a decimal.

$$\frac{100}{-11} = \underline{\hspace{4cm}}$$

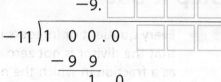

$$-11\,\overline{)1\ \ 0\ \ 0\ .\ 0}$$
$$\underline{-\ 9\ 9}$$
$$\ \ \ \ \ 1\ \ 0$$
$$\ \ \ \ \ \ \underline{0}$$

 Turn and Talk Predict the decimal value of the rational number $\frac{-200}{11}$. Explain your reasoning.

Check Understanding

1. Eloise needs $3\frac{5}{8}$ yards of fabric to make a costume.

   A. Show that the amount of fabric is a rational number.

   _____

   B. Write the amount of fabric as a decimal.

   _____

2. **A.** Write the mixed number $-5\frac{4}{9}$ as a fraction in three different ways. Then write it as a decimal.

   _____

   B. Explain why $-5\frac{4}{9}$ is a rational number.

   _____

3. The temperature outside dropped 27 degrees over a period of 3 hours. Find the quotient $-27 \div 3$, and explain what it means in this context.

   _____

On Your Own

4. Rafael is buying $1\frac{3}{8}$ pounds of salad at a salad bar that charges the amount shown.

Salad bar:
**$6.80
per lb**

A. Show that the amount of salad is a rational number.

_____

B. Write the amount of salad as a decimal.

_____

C. What will Rafael pay for the salad?

_____

5. Mariana drives for $\frac{9}{20}$ hour at a constant speed of 52 miles per hour.

A. Write the amount of time Mariana drives as a decimal.

_____

B. What is the total distance Mariana drives?

_____

6. Write the rational number $\frac{-55}{99}$ in at least four different ways.

_____

7. (MP) **Use Repeated Reasoning** Use the table shown.

A. Convert each fraction in the table to a decimal. Describe a pattern in the results.

Fraction	Decimal
$\frac{1}{8}$	
$\frac{2}{8}$	
$\frac{3}{8}$	

_____

_____

B. Does this pattern continue? Why or why not?

_____

_____

_____

8. (MP) **Use Structure** Michelle has to find the decimal equivalent of $15\frac{1}{8}$. How can she do this without first writing the mixed number as a fraction?

_____

_____

9. The value of a gift card to a rock climbing gym decreased by $34 after 4 equal charges to the card. Jamar represented this as $\frac{-34}{4}$. Write the rational number as a decimal and explain what it means in this context.

_____

_____

10. (MP) **Reason** Are all integers rational numbers? Explain.

_____

_____

_____

For Problems 11–16, convert each number to a decimal.

11. $\frac{5}{8}$ _____

12. $\frac{5}{16}$ _____

13. $\frac{7}{9}$ _____

14. $1\frac{1}{6}$ _____

15. $10\frac{4}{11}$ _____

16. $7\frac{3}{11}$ _____

For Problems 17–18, write two fractions equivalent to the given fraction.

17. $\frac{-3}{5}$ _____

18. $-\left(\frac{7}{10}\right)$ _____

19. Explain why $-7\frac{3}{5}$ is a rational number.

_____

_____

Write each rational number as a decimal.

20. $\frac{-69}{-11}$ _____

21. $\frac{60}{-8}$ _____

22. **Open Ended** Write two rational numbers that can be converted to terminating decimals and two that can be converted to repeating decimals.

_____

 I'm in a Learning Mindset!

How effective was using long division to write a rational number as a decimal? What questions do I still have?

_____

_____

Write Rational Numbers as Decimals

1. Sean is buying $\frac{9}{16}$ pound of tea at a teashop. The cost of the tea is shown.

A. Write the amount of tea as a decimal.

_____

B. What will Sean pay for the tea?

_____

$24 per lb

For Problems 2–3, convert each number to a decimal.

2. $\frac{1}{3}$

3. $4\frac{7}{8}$

_____

_____

4. Write two fractions that are equivalent to $\frac{50}{-17}$. Then explain why it is a rational number.

_____

_____

For Problems 5–8, write each rational number as a decimal.

5. $\frac{42}{-70}$

6. $\frac{-56}{800}$

_____

_____

7. $\frac{-27}{5}$

8. $\frac{35}{-3}$

_____

_____

9. (MP) **Use Repeated Reasoning** Use the table shown.

A. Convert each fraction in the table to a decimal. Describe a pattern in the results.

_____

_____

B. Does this pattern continue? Why or why not?

_____

_____

_____

Fraction	Decimal
$\frac{1}{9}$	
$\frac{2}{9}$	
$\frac{3}{9}$	

Test Prep

10. Which of the following are equivalent to $-\left(\frac{a}{b}\right)$? Select all that apply.

(A) $\frac{a}{b}$

(B) $\frac{-a}{-b}$

(C) $\frac{-a}{b}$

(D) $\frac{a}{-b}$

(E) $-\left(\frac{a}{-b}\right)$

11. Match each fraction to its integer value.

$\frac{-64}{8}$ •   • -8

$\frac{-48}{-6}$ •   • -6

$\frac{-36}{-6}$ •   • 6

$\frac{24}{-4}$ •   • 8

Spiral Review

12. Use the number line to show how to find the given difference. Then write an equivalent addition expression.

$1 - 6 =$ _____

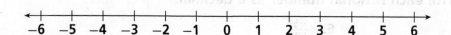

13. In 2016, the price of a stock decreased by $11. In 2017, the price decreased by $13. Write a sum of two integers that represents the overall change in the price of the stock for the two years. Then find the sum and explain what it tells you about the price of the stock.

14. Audra has a subscription to a news site. To pay for the subscription, $8 is automatically deducted from her checking account once per month.

A. Write a product of three or more integers that represents the change in Audra's account after three years.

B. What integer represents the change in Audra's account after three years?

Multiply and Divide Rational Numbers in Context

(I Can) solve word problems that require multiplying and dividing rational numbers.

Step It Out

1 Dashon is flying a hot air balloon at an altitude of 570 meters. He releases air from the balloon in order to change the altitude by −2.5 meters every second for 4 seconds. What is the new altitude of the balloon?

A. Write and use a model to find the change in altitude.

Change in altitude	=	Number of seconds	×	Change per second
	=	☐	×	☐
	=	☐		

The altitude changes by _____ meters.

B. Write and use a model to find the new altitude.

New altitude	=	Original altitude	+	Change in altitude
	=	☐	+	☐
	=	☐		

The new altitude is _____ meters.

C. Use a number line to show that your answer is reasonable.

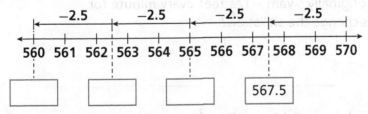

Turn and Talk Write and solve your own multiplication problem based on this situation.

© Houghton Mifflin Harcourt Publishing Company • Image Credit: ©Ocean/Corbis

2 In $4\frac{1}{2}$ minutes, a scuba diver swims from the surface to an elevation of −85 feet, swimming at a constant speed. Later, she swims upward 5 feet following a fish. Finally, she takes $10\frac{2}{3}$ minutes to ascend to the surface, swimming at a constant speed.

A. Write and use a model to find how many feet her elevation changes every minute during her descent.

$$\frac{\boxed{\text{Change in elevation}}}{\boxed{\text{Number of minutes}}} = \frac{\boxed{} \text{ feet}}{4\frac{1}{2} \text{ minutes}} = \boxed{} \div \frac{9}{2}$$

$$= \boxed{} \times \frac{\boxed{}}{\boxed{}}$$

$$= \boxed{}$$

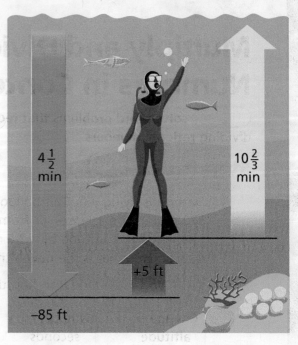

$4\frac{1}{2}$ min

$10\frac{2}{3}$ min

+5 ft

−85 ft

Her elevation changes by about _____ feet every minute.

B. How do you know that your answer is reasonable?

_____

_____

 Turn and Talk What is the scuba diver's change in elevation in feet per minute during her final ascent? Explain.

Check Understanding

1. If the scuba diver in Task 2 originally swam $-12\frac{1}{2}$ feet every minute for $4\frac{1}{2}$ minutes, how would this change the situation?

_____

_____

2. Susan has $\frac{3}{4}$ cup of raisins and she is dividing it into $\frac{3}{8}$ cup servings. Complete the following. What does the answer represent?

$$\frac{\frac{3}{4}}{\frac{3}{8}} = \boxed{} \div \frac{3}{8} = \boxed{} \times \boxed{} = \boxed{}$$ _____

Name _____

On Your Own

3. **STEM** Air temperature changes as you move away from Earth's surface. Under certain conditions in Earth's lower atmosphere, the temperature changes with increase in elevation as shown. Use this relationship to solve each problem.

Temperature change: about −18.8 °F for each mile increase in elevation

   A. Find and interpret the change in temperature for an increase in elevation of 0.2 mile.

   _____

   _____

   B. Find and interpret the change in temperature for a decrease in elevation of 0.2 mile.

   _____

   _____

   C. How are your answers to Parts A and B related?

   _____

4. A butterfly is flying $8\frac{3}{4}$ feet above the ground. It descends at a steady speed to a spot $6\frac{1}{4}$ feet above the ground in $1\frac{2}{3}$ minutes. What is the butterfly's change in elevation each minute?

   _____

5. One scuba diver's elevation changed by $-15\frac{5}{8}$ feet every minute. This was $1\frac{1}{4}$ times as fast as the elevation of a second diver changed. How much did the second diver's elevation change every minute? Show your work.

   _____

   _____

6. **Open Ended** Write a real-world problem based on one of the contexts in the lesson that can be solved using multiplication or division of negative fractions or decimals.

   _____

   _____

7. Carl has $3\frac{1}{2}$ cups of blueberries. He is storing them in containers that each hold $\frac{2}{3}$ cup. How many containers can he fill? Find the answer and interpret the result.

_____

_____

8. Mrs. Anderson writes a check for $10.50 to each of her four nieces. What will be the total change in Mrs. Anderson's checking account balance after all four checks are cashed?

_____

_____

9. The denominator of a fraction is $\frac{-3}{4}$. The numerator is $\frac{1}{4}$ more than the denominator. Identify the fraction. Then show that it is a rational number.

For Problems 10–15, find each quotient.

10. $\dfrac{\frac{7}{10}}{\frac{-1}{5}}$ _____

11. $\dfrac{\frac{-5}{6}}{\frac{-6}{7}}$ _____

12. $\dfrac{\frac{252}{4}}{\frac{3}{-8}}$ _____

13. $\dfrac{2.8}{-4}$ _____

14. $-\dfrac{5.5}{0.5}$ _____

15. $\dfrac{0.72}{-0.9}$ _____

I'm in a Learning Mindset!

What questions can I ask my teacher to help me understand how to set up a problem that involves division?

_____

_____

LESSON 5.5
**More Practice/
Homework**

ONLINE
Ed
Video Tutorials and
Interactive Examples

Multiply and Divide Rational Numbers in Context

1. **Math on the Spot** Sarah drove her police car at a constant speed down a mountain. Her elevation decreased by 200 feet over a 10-minute period. What was the change in elevation during the first minute?

_____

2. A submarine descends $\frac{1}{120}$ mile every minute. Write a product of three or more rational numbers to represent the change in the submarine's elevation after 3 hours. Then find the value of the product, and explain what it represents.

_____

_____

3. **Financial Literacy** Tanisha takes a dance class that is priced as shown. The charge appears as negative on her account balance until she makes her monthly payment.

   A. Show how to find the balance of Tanisha's account for dance classes during a 4-week period in which she attends 3 classes per week.

   _____

   B. (MP) **Reason** Suppose the balance on Tanisha's account for a 2-week period is –$100. If Tanisha attended at least 1 dance class per week, how many classes could she have attended each week? Explain your reasoning.

   _____

   _____

   _____

$12.50 per class

   C. Evaluate the expression $-112.50 \div (-12.50)$ and interpret what it could mean in this context.

   _____

   _____

For Problems 4–6, find each quotient.

4. $\dfrac{\frac{-5}{8}}{\frac{15}{16}}$ _____

5. $\dfrac{-\frac{2}{3}}{\frac{4}{-9}}$ _____

6. $\dfrac{\frac{24}{7}}{\frac{-6}{35}}$ _____

Test Prep

7. Salton Sea Beach in California has an elevation of about −230 feet. This is about 11.5 times the elevation of Indio, California. What is the elevation of Indio, California?

about _____ feet

8. During a winter cold spell, the temperature change was −1.2 °F per hour for a period of 4.5 hours. Which expressions can be used to find the overall change in temperature during that time period?

Ⓐ 4.5 ÷ (−1.2) degrees Fahrenheit

Ⓑ 4.5 × (−1.2) degrees Fahrenheit

Ⓒ 4.5 − (−1.2) degrees Fahrenheit

Ⓓ (−1.2) + (−1.2) + (−1.2) + (−1.2) degrees Fahrenheit

Ⓔ 4(−1.2) + (0.5)(−1.2) degrees Fahrenheit

9. Which expression is equivalent to $\dfrac{-\frac{5}{6}}{\frac{10}{3}}$?

Ⓐ $-\dfrac{5}{6} \div \dfrac{3}{10}$ Ⓒ $-\dfrac{5}{6} \times \dfrac{10}{3}$

Ⓑ $-\dfrac{5}{6} \div \dfrac{10}{3}$ Ⓓ $-\dfrac{6}{5} \times \dfrac{3}{10}$

Spiral Review

10. What is the difference when −2 is subtracted from 2?

_____

11. Complete the number line diagram. What addition problem does the diagram represent?

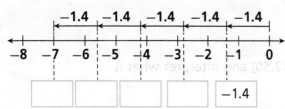

_____

_____

Name _____

Apply Properties to Multi-Step Problems with Rational Numbers

(**I Can**) apply properties of operations to evaluate multi-step expressions with positive and negative rational numbers.

Step It Out

1 ▶ Andy usually skates for about 6 hours per week. On Monday, he spent $1\frac{1}{5}$ hours skating; on Wednesday, he spent $2\frac{3}{5}$ hours skating; and on Thursday, he spent $1\frac{5}{6}$ hours skating. Andy wrote the following expression to find the number of hours he spent skating. He grouped Wednesday and Thursday together because those were his best days, without thinking too much about what would be easiest to add.

$$1\frac{1}{5} + \left(2\frac{3}{5} + 1\frac{5}{6}\right)$$

A. Rewrite the expression to make it simpler to add.

$$\left(\boxed{} + 2\frac{3}{5}\right) + \boxed{}$$

B. What property is demonstrated by rewriting the expression?

_____

C. Regrouping makes the problem simpler because it associates

two mixed numbers with _____.

D. To add the numbers in parentheses,

Add the whole numbers: $1 + \boxed{} = \boxed{}$

Add the like fractions: $\frac{1}{5} + \boxed{} = \boxed{}$

Combine the results: _____

E. Use your result from Part D to finish evaluating the expression.

$$3\frac{4}{5} + \boxed{} = \frac{\boxed{}}{5} + \frac{11}{6} = \frac{114}{\boxed{}} + \frac{55}{\boxed{}} = \frac{\boxed{}}{30} = \boxed{}$$

Turn and Talk Is there another way to solve this problem? Explain.

2 ▶ Rae goes scuba diving in the lake, starting at the water's surface. Her change in elevation in the lake is described. She:

- descends 15.5 feet and takes some pictures of fish;
- ascends $8\frac{1}{5}$ feet to explore another area;
- descends 1.6 feet to capture video while following a fish;
- descends 20.4 feet to find some feeding bass; and finally,
- ascends 15.5 feet to take more pictures.

How far does Rae have left to ascend before reaching the surface?

A. Write an expression involving addition and subtraction to represent Rae's change in elevation from the water's surface.

_____

B. Write your expression from Part A as an addition expression.

_____

C. Rewrite the expression to make it simpler to find the sum by first adding opposites.

_____

D. What properties of operations did you use to rewrite your expression in Part C?

_____

_____

E. Add the opposites in your expression in Part C, and write the resulting expression.

_____

F. Evaluate your expression in Part E to find Rae's elevation relative to the water's surface. Identify the property used in the second line.

$8\frac{1}{5} +$ ⬜ $+$ ⬜

$= 8\frac{1}{5} +$ ⬜   _____ Property

$= 8.2 +$ ⬜

$=$ ⬜

Rae needs to ascend ⬜ feet to reach the water's surface.

Turn and Talk How are the properties of addition used to evaluate the expression in Task 2?

3 ▶ A dot symbol in an expression indicates multiplication. Use properties to evaluate $\frac{4}{7}\left(-\frac{3}{5}\right) \cdot \frac{5}{3}\left(-\frac{9}{10} - \frac{3}{10}\right)$.

$\frac{4}{7}\left[\left(-\dfrac{\boxed{}}{\boxed{}}\right) \cdot \dfrac{\boxed{}}{\boxed{}}\right]\left(-\frac{9}{10} - \frac{3}{10}\right)$ _____ Property of Multiplication

$= \frac{4}{7} \cdot \left(\boxed{}\right)\left(-\frac{9}{10} - \frac{3}{10}\right)$ Inverse Property of Multiplication

$= \boxed{}\left(-\frac{9}{10} - \frac{3}{10}\right)$ Identity Property of Multiplication

$= \boxed{}\left(\boxed{}\right)$ Subtraction

$= \boxed{}$ Multiplication

4 ▶ Max has 6 ounces of white paint. He gives $\frac{1}{3}$ of the paint to a friend. He uses the rest to paint model cars. The amount he uses is shown. Write and evaluate an expression to find the number of cars Max can paint.

Paint Required: 0.02 oz for each car

$\left[6 - \left(\boxed{}\right) \cdot 6\right] \div \boxed{}$

$= \dfrac{6 - \boxed{}}{\boxed{}} = \dfrac{\boxed{}}{\boxed{}} = \boxed{}$ cars

Check Understanding

1. Soojin is flying his drone. First the drone ascends to an altitude of $20\frac{2}{3}$ feet. Then it descends $7\frac{3}{4}$ feet. Finally, it ascends $5\frac{3}{4}$ feet. Write and evaluate an addition expression to determine the drone's current altitude.

_____

2. Suresh has 4 coupon books, each with 6 coupons. He keeps $\frac{1}{3}$ of the coupons and gives the rest away. Fifty percent of those he keeps are for the movie theater. Write and evaluate an expression to show how many movie theater coupons he has.

_____

3. Explain how to use properties to evaluate the expression mentally.
$-\frac{3}{21} \cdot \frac{3}{5} \cdot 7 \cdot 15$

_____

On Your Own

4. **(MP)** **Use Structure** Dena cuts wood for a treehouse. She has five pieces of wood left over with the following lengths in centimeters: 12.7, $26\frac{3}{10}$, $15\frac{4}{5}$, $21\frac{1}{4}$, and 19.2.

   A. Write and evaluate an expression to find the total length of wood left over.

   _____

   B. Dena wants to make a birdhouse with the leftover wood. She needs $105\frac{3}{5}$ centimeters of wood for the birdhouse. Write and evaluate an expression to determine how much more wood she will need.

   _____

5. **(MP)** **Use Repeated Reasoning** The table shows the highest and lowest elevations in four states.

   A. Write and evaluate an expression to find the difference in elevation in each state.

   _____

   _____

State	Highest elevation (ft)	Lowest elevation (ft)
Louisiana (LA)	535	−8
California (CA)	14,505	−282
Indiana (IN)	1,257	320
Florida (FL)	345	0

   B. Roger says the difference between the lowest elevation in California and the lowest elevation in Louisiana is 290 feet. Determine if his answer is reasonable.

   _____

6. The high temperatures for a 4-day holiday weekend were: −2.6 °F, 16.7 °F, −3.4 °F, 6.1 °F Use properties of addition to help you find the sum.

   _____

   _____

For Problems 7–12, evaluate each expression.

7. $2.6 + (-3.7 - (-1.5))$

8. $-15 - 2\frac{3}{4} - 1.7 - \left(-2\frac{2}{5}\right)$

9. $-1\frac{1}{5} + 2.9 - \left(-3\frac{3}{8}\right)$

10. $2\frac{3}{4} + (-8.34) + \left(-7\frac{3}{10}\right)$

11. $-11.5 + 15\frac{2}{5} - 10.1$

12. $5\frac{1}{4} - (-3.55) + \left(-3\frac{2}{5}\right)$

13. (MP) **Model with Mathematics** Liu Tse is 6 years older than four times the age of her daughter, Lan. Lan will be 9 years old in 3 years.

A. Write and evaluate an expression that shows Lan's age.

_____

B. Use Lan's age to write and evaluate the expression for Liu Tse's age.

_____

14. (MP) **Reason** Ella has $\frac{1}{3}$ as many trading cards as Kip. Adira has 3 more than half of the number of cards that Kip has. Kip has 18 cards.

A. Write an expression for the total number of cards the group has.

_____

B. Evaluate the expression.

_____

15. Tamir bought $2\frac{1}{2}$ pounds of fish at $5.50 per pound, and two bananas at the price shown.

A. Write an expression to show how much change he received from a $20 bill.

Bananas: $0.45 each

_____

B. Evaluate the expression to show his change.

_____

16. Tre earns $16 per hour. An expression for the amount of money she earned in one week is $16\left(3\frac{1}{2}\right) + 16\left(2\frac{1}{4}\right) + 16\left(5\frac{3}{4}\right) + 16\left(4\frac{1}{2}\right)$. Rewrite the expression so that it only has one multiplication operation, and then evaluate the expression.

Earns $16 per hour

17. (MP) **Attend to Precision** Erin has 10 bags of cherries. These are the weights of the bags in pounds: $2\frac{1}{2}$, $2\frac{3}{4}$, $2\frac{1}{2}$, $2\frac{1}{4}$, $1\frac{1}{4}$, $2\frac{1}{2}$, $2\frac{1}{2}$, $1\frac{1}{4}$, $2\frac{1}{4}$, $2\frac{1}{4}$. She wants to redistribute the cherries so that each bag weighs the same. Write an expression to find the weight of each bag after she does this. Evaluate the expression.

18. Rewrite the expression $6 \cdot \left(-\frac{1}{3}\right) + 2\left(\frac{1}{2}\right) - 2\left(\frac{3}{4}\right)$ using the Distributive Property. Then evaluate the expression.

$$6 \cdot \left(-\frac{1}{3}\right) + 2\left(\frac{\boxed{}}{\boxed{}} - \frac{\boxed{}}{\boxed{}}\right) = \boxed{}$$

19. Evaluate the expression $[0.75 \cdot (-12)] - \left(-6 \div \frac{2}{3}\right)$. _____

20. Rewrite the expression $-\frac{1}{4} \cdot 3\frac{1}{3} \cdot 8 \cdot \left(-1\frac{1}{5}\right)$ using the Commutative Property of Multiplication. Then evaluate the expression.

21. Rewrite the expression $\frac{1}{2} \cdot 33 \cdot \frac{1}{11}$ using the Associative Property of Multiplication. Evaluate the expression.

22. What property was used to rewrite the expression below? What is the sum?

$$-5.5 + 10.63 + (-3.7) = -5.5 + (-3.7) + 10.63$$

Name _____

Apply Properties to Multi-Step Problems with Rational Numbers

1. Brian is adding the lengths of wood posts that he has left from building a pen for his chickens. The lengths are $3\frac{2}{3}$, $2\frac{1}{4}$, and $2\frac{1}{3}$ feet. Brian began with 20 feet of wood. Write and evaluate an expression to determine how much wood he used for the pen.

_____

_____

2. At dinner time, the temperature outside was −13.9 °F. The temperature decreased by 12.8 °F overnight. Write and evaluate an expression to determine the temperature in the morning.

_____

_____

3. Evaluate the expression. Identify the property used in each step.

$$\frac{3}{4} + \left(-\frac{3}{8}\right) + \left(-\frac{1}{4}\right) = \left(-\frac{3}{8}\right) + \frac{3}{4} + \left(-\frac{1}{4}\right)$$ _____ Property of Addition

$$= -\frac{3}{8} + \left[\frac{3}{4} + \left(-\frac{1}{4}\right)\right]$$ _____ Property of Addition

$$= \boxed{}$$

4. (MP) **Model with Mathematics** Mr. Chung's math class is 1 hour long. Today, he spent 6 minutes taking attendance and collecting homework. Then he spent 18 minutes teaching. After that, the class worked on 4 problems. For each problem, the class spent 3 minutes working and 6 minutes discussing the answer. Write and evaluate an expression to find how much class time was left after this.

_____

5. **Math on the Spot** Sophia uses $3\frac{3}{4}$ cups of flour for each loaf of bread she makes. She has a 10-pound bag of flour that cost $8.79 and contains 152 quarter-cup servings. How many loaves can Sophia make if she uses all the flour? How much does the flour for one loaf cost?

_____

_____

6. Evaluate $5 - 44 \cdot (-0.75) - 18 \div \frac{2}{3} \cdot 0.8 + \left(-\frac{4}{5}\right)$.

_____

7. The sum of 7 and 2.6 is multiplied by 9. Then this product is divided by the result of 4 − 2.8. Add parentheses to the expression, $9 \cdot 7 + 2.6 \div 4 - 2.8$, to show the correct order for the calculations described.

_____

Test Prep

8. While Jackie was in Hawaii, she dove for shells. One afternoon she dove 7.8 feet. Her next two dives were each $2\frac{1}{8}$ feet deeper than the dive before it. What were the elevations relative to sea level of her second and third dives?

9. Which expression has a value of 7?

Ⓐ $4 + 0.5 \times 8 - 2$

Ⓑ $(4 + 0.5) \times 8 - 2$

Ⓒ $4 + 0.5 \times (8 - 2)$

Ⓓ $(4 + 0.5) \times (8 - 2)$

10. Chandra bought twice as many plants as Marvin. Kira bought $\frac{1}{3}$ as many plants as Chandra. Marvin bought 6 plants. Write an expression that shows the total number of plants purchased. Who bought the most plants?

11. This morning, the temperature was $13\frac{1}{2}$ °F. During the day, the temperature increased by 5.6 °F. At night, the temperature decreased by 23.8 °F. What was the temperature after it decreased?

Ⓐ 18.2 °F

Ⓑ 4.7 °F

Ⓒ −4.7 °F

Ⓓ −18.2 °F

12. Evaluate the expression: $-7\frac{7}{8} + 3.7 - (-15.9)$.

Spiral Review

13. Overnight, the temperature decreased by $17\frac{1}{2}$ °F. If the temperature began at −3.6 °F, what is the current temperature?

14. Pauline plots the numbers $4\frac{1}{3}$ and $-5\frac{1}{8}$ on a number line. Explain how she can use the number line to determine which number is greater. Then write an inequality to compare the numbers.

© Houghton Mifflin Harcourt Publishing Company

Name _____

Solve Multi-Step Problems with Rational Numbers in Context

(I Can) solve multi-step problems that involve rational numbers in different forms and multiple operations.

Step It Out

1 Sandi is one of 4 friends who will go to the park together 3 times this year. She says they will save about $200 if they buy the season pass. Use estimation to determine whether her statement is reasonable.

A. Estimate the cost of 4 season passes.

$ [   ] · 4 = $ [   ]

Season pass:	$249.99
Day pass:	$82.99

B. Overestimate the cost of 4 day passes for 3 days. Use the Distributive Property to make calculations easier.

4 day passes:

$ [   ] · 4 = ([   ] + [   ])4 = [   ] + [   ] = $ [   ]

4 day passes for 3 days:

$ [   ] · 3 = ([   ] + [   ])3 = [   ] + [   ] = $ [   ]

C. Sandi's estimation of saving about $200 [is / is not] reasonable. Explain.

_____

_____

_____

 Turn and Talk If the 4 friends visited the park 4 times, would season passes save them money? Explain.

2 Estimate $-3.8 \cdot \frac{14}{5} - \frac{117}{20}$ using integers. Tell whether your estimate is an underestimate or an overestimate. Explain.

$-3.8 \cdot \frac{14}{5} - \frac{117}{20} \approx$ [   ] · [   ] − [   ] ≈ [   ]

_____

_____

Charise collects antique salt and pepper shakers. She bought 3 sets of cactus salt and pepper shakers. The value of each set at the time of purchase is shown.

During the next 5 years, Charise tracked the value of the salt and pepper shakers on an auction website. The annual changes in the value of each set are shown in the table. What is the total value of the 3 sets of salt and pepper shakers at the end of the 5-year period?

$56.28

A. What was the total value of the 3 sets of salt and pepper shakers at the beginning of the 5-year period?

3 × $ ☐ = $ ☐

B. What is the total change in the value of one set of salt and pepper shakers over the 5-year period? How did you find your answer?

_____

_____

Year	Change in value ($)
1	2.52
2	−1.40
3	−5.65
4	0.80
5	1.75

C. Did the value of a set of salt and pepper shakers increase or decrease during the 5-year period? Explain how you know.

_____

D. In Part B you found the total change in the value of one set of salt and pepper shakers. What is the total change, in dollars, in the value of all 3 sets of shakers?

3 × ☐ = ☐

E. What is the total value of the 3 sets of salt and pepper shakers at the end of the 5-year period? Explain how you found your answer.

_____

_____

_____

Turn and Talk A student said you can solve this problem by finding the total change in the value of one set of shakers, adding the total change to $56.28, and then multiplying the result by 3. Does this method work? Explain.

4 ▷ Suppose the aquarium shown developed a leak at the bottom corner and lost water at an average rate of $6\frac{3}{4}$ fluid ounces per minute. How many hours, to the nearest tenth, would it take for the aquarium to be empty?

20-gallon tank

A. There are 128 fluid ounces in 1 gallon. How many fluid ounces of water are in the tank?

_____ · _____ = _____

There are _____ fluid ounces in the tank.

B. Find the number of minutes, to the nearest tenth, that it takes for the aquarium to empty.

_____ ÷ $6\frac{3}{4}$ = 2,560 ÷ _____ ≈ _____ minutes

C. What remaining work do you need to do to solve the problem? Solve the problem and show your work.

_____

_____

D. Explain how you can check your answer for reasonableness.

_____

_____

_____

_____

Check Understanding

1. A block of clay contains twenty 4-ounce portions of clay. A ceramics teacher wants to use the block to make as many spheres of clay as possible, each weighing $\frac{2}{5}$ pound. How many spheres can she make?

_____

2. A laptop computer costs $356.75 when it is new. The value of the computer is expected to change by −$35.50 per year during the first 3 years. What is the expected value of the computer after 3 years? Is your answer reasonable? Use estimation to show why.

_____

_____

On Your Own

3. Luis is hiking at a park. He sees the sign shown and decides to hike to Wandering Twin Lake. Luis knows that he can hike at an average rate of $\frac{1}{3}$ mile in 6 minutes.

Wandering Twin Lake
4.9 mi

   A. How many hours will it take Luis to reach Wandering Twin Lake?

   _____

   B. Explain how you know your answer is reasonable.

   _____

   _____

   _____

4. **Financial Literacy** Mr. Liling bought 10 shares of stock in QJZ Software at the beginning of 2016 for $198.58 per share. The table shows how the value of the stock changed during 2016 and during 2017.

   A. What was the total value of Mr. Liling's shares at the end of 2016?

   _____

QJZ Software	
Year	Change in stock price
2016	−$9.73
2017	+$19.36

   B. What was the total value of Mr. Liling's shares at the end of 2017?

   _____

   C. Explain how you know your answers are reasonable.

   _____

   _____

   _____

5. According to Denise's recipe, each batch of granola requires 1.75 cups of shelled sunflower seeds. She has 3 bags of shelled sunflower seeds that each contain eleven $\frac{1}{4}$-cup servings. What is the maximum number of batches of granola that Denise can make with the sunflower seeds?

   _____

6. A desert tour includes 305 people traveling by van. Each van can transport 18 people.

   A. Estimate the number of vans needed.

   _____

   B. (MP) **Construct Arguments** Is your answer an overestimate or an underestimate? In this situation, would it be better to overestimate or underestimate? Explain your choice.

   _____

   _____

7. (MP) **Critique Reasoning** A bag of dry pet food costs the pet store $18.66. A case of canned food costs $11.43. The owner puts in an order for 27 bags of dry food and 34 cases of canned food. The owner thinks he owes $1,835.49.

   A. Estimate the total amount of the order.

   _____

   B. Is the owner's total reasonable? Explain your answer.

   _____

8. **STEM** Sound travels about 1,125.33 feet in a second. An engineer detects the sound of an explosion from a test site 8 seconds after the blast.

   A. To find the distance the engineer was from the blast, you can multiply the speed of sound, 1,125.33 feet per second, by 8 seconds. Estimate this distance in feet and then in miles.

   _____

   _____

You can use the speed of sound to calculate the distance away from a visible loud object.

   B. If the engineer wants to find the exact spot of the blast, should she use an estimate or an exact answer? Explain your choice.

   _____

   _____

9. Gianna is taking a walking tour in her city. The entire tour is $10\frac{1}{10}$ kilometers long. According to an app on her phone, Gianna's average walking rate is 1.6 meters per second.

A. How many meters does Gianna walk each hour?

_____

B. How many kilometers does Gianna walk each hour?

_____

C. About how long will it take Gianna to complete the walking tour? Express your answer in hours and minutes.

_____

D. (MP) **Construct Arguments** Explain how you know your answer is reasonable.

_____

_____

10. **Open Ended** A container of oatmeal costs $3.79 and contains about 17 servings of the size shown. Write a word problem involving the serving size, the number of servings per container, and the price of the oatmeal.

Serving size: $\frac{1}{4}$ cup uncooked

_____

_____

_____

_____

11. (MP) **Attend to Precision** A snail is moving along a path that is 4 meters long. The snail moves $3\frac{3}{10}$ inches each minute.

A. Find the length of the path to the nearest inch. (*Hint:* 1 in. = 2.54 cm)

_____

B. To the nearest minute, how long does it take the snail to reach the end of the path?

_____

Vocabulary

Choose the correct term from the Vocabulary box.

Vocabulary

absolute value

opposite

1. The number −4 is the _____ of 4.

2. The _____ of a number always represents the distance of that number from zero on a number line.

3. Complete the Venn diagram by writing at least three numbers in each oval as examples of the types of numbers described.

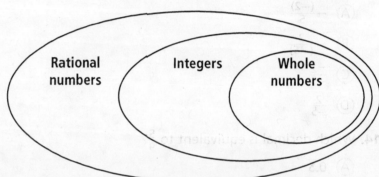

Rational numbers

Integers

Whole numbers

Concepts and Skills

4. When subtracting two numbers, you add the _____ of the number being subtracted.

(MP) Use Tools Find the value of each expression. State what strategy and tool you will use to answer the questions, explain your choice, and then find the answers.

5. $10 + (-6)$

6. $-1 + (-7)$

7. $3 - 8\frac{2}{3}$

_____

_____

8. $-2.7 - 1.8$

9. $5\frac{1}{5} \div \left(-2\frac{4}{15}\right)$

10. $(-0.4)(-3.8)$

_____

_____

_____

11. In the equation $p \cdot q = r$, $p < 0$.

   A. Assume $r > 0$. Plot a point on the number line to identify a possible location for q.

   B. Assume $r < 0$. Plot a point on the number line to identify a possible location for q.

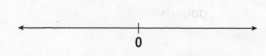

0

0

12. The depth of water in a swimming pool decreases by $\frac{1}{8}$ inch per day due to evaporation. No water is added to the pool for a 2-week period. What is the total change in the depth of the water during this time period?

Ⓐ $-1\frac{3}{4}$ inches

Ⓑ $-\frac{1}{4}$ inch

Ⓒ $\frac{1}{16}$ inch

Ⓓ $1\frac{1}{2}$ inches

13. Which expression is equivalent to $-\left(\frac{2}{5}\right)$?

Ⓐ $-\frac{(-2)}{5}$

Ⓑ $-\frac{2}{(-5)}$

Ⓒ $\frac{-2}{-5}$

Ⓓ $\frac{2}{-5}$

14. Which decimal is equivalent to $\frac{5}{9}$?

Ⓐ $0.\overline{5}$

Ⓑ 0.6

Ⓒ 1.8

Ⓓ 5.9

15. Kyle plans to make 15 turkey burger patties, each weighing $\frac{1}{4}$ pound, for a cookout. At the store, ground turkey meat is priced at $3.66 per pound. If Kyle orders the exact amount of meat he needs, how much will it cost, rounded to the nearest cent?

$ _____

16. An aquarium can hold 3,744 cubic inches of water. Ben fills the aquarium $\frac{9}{10}$ full of water. Water weighs about 0.036 pound per cubic inch. Which estimate of the weight of the water in the aquarium is closest to the exact value?

Ⓐ 2 pounds

Ⓑ 120 pounds

Ⓒ 165 pounds

Ⓓ 3,370 pounds

17. A rectangular backyard has a length of 68 feet and a width of $40\frac{1}{2}$ feet. The owner wants to plant $\frac{3}{4}$ of the yard with grass seed. The directions say to plant 1.5 pounds of seed for every 1,000 square feet of area. To the nearest tenth of a pound, how much grass seed will the owner need to plant?

_____ pounds

Expressions, Equations, and Inequalities

Visual Artist

Edna Andrade was an American artist and educator. She began her teaching career as an elementary school art teacher in Virginia. She later taught at the University of the Arts in Philadelphia and Tulane University in New Orleans. As an artist, Andrade was an early pioneer in the op art movement. Op art features geometric patterns that create optical illusions such as a sense of motion, flashing, or vibration.

STEM Task:

Visual artists may mix paints to match a color they used before or to create new colors. Matthew is an artist. He mixes 4 pints of blue paint with 2 pints of yellow paint to make 6 pints of green paint. After he uses all of the green paint, he wants to make 3 more pints of the same shade. How much blue and yellow paint should he mix? Explain.

HRW/Houghton Mifflin Harcourt, (b) ©Africa Studio/Shutterstock

© Houghton Mifflin Harcourt Publishing Company • Image Credits:

Learning Mindset

Resilience Monitors Emotions

Artists may be frustrated as they strive to achieve a particular result, or sad when their work receives negative criticism. What emotions do you experience when you are learning something new? Do you feel excited, or do you feel discouraged and want to give up? It's normal to experience negative emotions at times, but learning to recognize and address these feelings will help prevent them from being obstacles to learning. As you work, monitor your thoughts and feelings by asking yourself these questions.

- How am I feeling about this task? Am I frustrated, bored, or tired? Am I worried or embarrassed about how others perceive my work?

- Is there a fixed-mindset voice in my head that is contributing to my negative feelings? If so, what is that voice telling me? What is triggering that voice?

- How can I activate my growth-mindset voice to counter messages from the fixed-mindset voice?

Remember, feelings often shift and change. If you find yourself struggling with negative emotions, take a few deep breaths. You may also want to take a short break or talk to someone about your feelings.

Reflect

Q As you worked on the STEM Task, how did you feel about your learning?

Q Did any part of the STEM Task trigger a fixed-mindset voice in your head? If so, what part(s)? How did you use self-talk to activate a growth-mindset voice?

6

Numerical and Algebraic Expressions

Guess the Number

Ethan discovered a number game. Follow the directions to see if it works for any number.

A. Try Ethan's number game.

I predict that your final answer is **3!**

Think of a number. _____

Add 5. _____

Double the result. _____

Subtract 4. _____

Divide by 2. _____

Subtract the original number.

_____

B. How does your final number compare with Ethan's prediction?

_____

C. Use your original number to write a single numerical expression that represents the steps of the game.

_____

 Turn and Talk

- How does your expression show the order in which the operations should be performed?

- How could you change your expression so that it would model the game no matter which number you start with?

Are You Ready?

Complete these problems to review prior concepts and skills you will need for this module.

Write and Interpret Numerical Expressions

Write the expression.

1. 3 times the sum of 4 and 9: _____

2. Divide 12 by 4 and add 5: _____

3. Subtract 6 from 13, then multiply by 2: _____

4. The quantity 12 times 5 divided by 7: _____

5. The quantity 32 minus 16 multiplied by 9: _____

Write a statement to represent each expression.

6. $3 \times 2 + 5$: _____

7. $6(5 + 7)$: _____

8. $24 - 8 \div 4$: _____

9. $(9 + 5) \div 7$: _____

Evaluate Simple Numerical Expressions

Find the value of each expression.

10. $4 \times (3 + 5) =$ _____

11. $7 + (3 \times 2) =$ _____

12. $(45 \div 9) \times 2 =$ _____

13. $(3 + 9) \div 3 =$ _____

14. $(12 + 6) \div 2 + 4 =$ _____

15. $(20 - 11) \times 5 + 1 =$ _____

Name _____

Understand and Apply Exponents

(I Can) **write exponential expressions to represent repeated-multiplication situations, and I can find the value of an exponential expression.**

Spark Your Learning

Brianna needs to contact members of the softball league. She calls 4 members in the morning. Those 4 people each call 4 more people in the afternoon. That evening, those additional people each call 4 others. How many people are called that evening?

Turn and Talk Is there another way to solve this problem? Explain.

Build Understanding

1. A small company uses a phone tree to notify employees of cancellation due to bad weather. The manager calls 2 people. Then each of those people calls 2 more people, and so on.

A. Complete the table. What pattern(s) do you see?

_____

_____

Round	Number of Calls
1	2
2	2 × 2
3	2 × 2 × ☐
4	2 × 2 × ☐ × ☐
5	2 × 2 × ☐ × ☐ × ☐

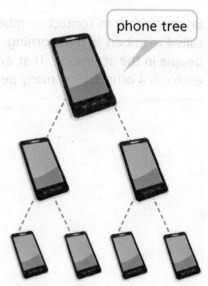

phone tree

B. Complete each statement to describe the pattern.

In the second round of calling, the total number of calls in that round is equal to the product of two 2s.

In the third round of calling, the total number of calls in that round is equal to the product of _____ 2s.

In the fourth round of calling, the total number of calls in that round is equal to the product of _____ 2s.

In the fifth round of calling, the total number of calls in that round is equal to the product of _____ 2s.

C. How is the number of the round of calling related to the number of times 2 is used as a factor?

_____

_____

 Turn and Talk Look at how the number of calls changes from round to round. Do you see a pattern? If so, describe it.

Step It Out

You can use an exponent and a base to show repeated multiplication of a factor.

$$\underbrace{7 \times 7 \times 7 \times 7 \times 7}_{\text{5 repeated factors}} = 7^5 \xleftarrow{\quad} \text{exponent}$$

base

Connect to Vocabulary

When a number is raised to a power, the number that is used as a factor is the **base**.
An **exponent** is the number that indicates how many times the base is used as a factor.

The expression 7^5 is read as "7 to the 5th power."

There are two specially named powers:

8^2 can be read as "8 to the 2nd power" or as "8 squared."

9^3 can be read as "9 to the 3rd power" or as "9 cubed."

2 Look at the expression $5 \times 5 \times 5 \times 5$.

A. How many times is the factor 5 used? _____

B. Complete each statement by writing an exponent.

$5 \times 5 \times 5 \times 5 = 5^{\boxed{}}$ $8 \times 8 \times 8 \times 8 \times 8 = 8^{\boxed{}}$

C. Write an equivalent repeated multiplication expression.

$2^3 = \boxed{} \times \boxed{} \times \boxed{}$ $\left(\dfrac{1}{3}\right)^5 = \boxed{} \times \boxed{} \times \boxed{} \times \boxed{} \times \boxed{}$

3 Recall that a dot symbol can be used to show multiplication. Find the value of each expression.

A. $5^3 = \boxed{} \cdot \boxed{} \cdot \boxed{} = \boxed{}$

B. $4^5 = \boxed{} \cdot \boxed{} \cdot \boxed{} \cdot \boxed{} \cdot \boxed{} = \boxed{}$

Check Understanding

1. A community begins with one resident. Then every year, the number of residents multiplies by 10. Write an expression with an exponent for the number of residents after 5 years.

_____

2. On a tree, the trunk splits into 5 branches. Then each branch splits into 5 smaller branches, and each of those branches splits into 5 very thin branches. How many very thin branches are on the tree?

_____

3. Explain the expression 2^{10}. Complete the sentences.

A. The number $\boxed{}$ is used as a repeated factor $\boxed{}$ times.

B. The base of the expression is $\boxed{}$, and the exponent is $\boxed{}$.

C. The value of 2^{10} is $\boxed{}$.

On Your Own

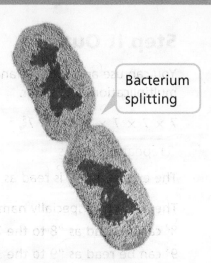

Bacterium splitting

4. **STEM** A certain bacterium splits itself into 2 identical cells in 1 day. Each of those new cells is capable of splitting itself into 2 identical cells in 1 day. So the first day there are 2 cells, the second day there are 2 × 2 cells, and so on. Write and evaluate an expression using a base and an exponent to represent the number of cells present at the end of the seventh day.

_____

5. Write each expression in exponential form.

A. $9 \times 9 \times 9 \times 9 \times 9 =$ _____

B. $\frac{1}{8} \times \frac{1}{8} \times \frac{1}{8} =$ _____

For Problems 6–7, write the exponential expression as an equivalent repeated multiplication expression.

6. $\left(\frac{5}{6}\right)^5 =$ _____

7. $\left(\frac{1}{3}\right)^4 \times \left(\frac{1}{3}\right)^3 =$ _____

8. Explain the expression 10^5. Complete the sentences.

The number ⬜ is used as a repeated factor.

⬜ is used as a factor ⬜ times.

9. (MP) **Use Repeated Reasoning** Carrie recruits 3 of her friends to sell candles to raise money for new playground equipment. The next day each of her 3 friends recruits 3 more friends. This pattern continues for 5 days. How could you write an exponential expression to represent the number of new recruits on the fifth day?

A. The number ⬜ would be used as a factor ⬜ times.

B. Express the number of recruits on the 7th day as repeated multiplication and with an exponent.

⬜ × ⬜ × ⬜ × ⬜ × ⬜ = ⬜

🔷 I'm in a Learning Mindset!

What facts about exponents can I talk about?

_____

_____

Name _____

Understand and Apply Exponents

1. Explain the expression 12^8. Complete the sentences.

   The number ☐ is used as a repeated factor.

   ☐ is used as a factor ☐ times.

2. (MP) **Use Repeated Reasoning** At 4 o'clock, Devon contacted 6 friends to let them know that the weather forecast called for snow. At 6 o'clock, each of his friends contacted 6 other friends. At 8 o'clock, each of those friends contacted 6 of their other friends.

   A. Write an expression to represent the number of people contacted at 6 o'clock using a base and an exponent. _____

   B. Write an expression to represent the number of people contacted at 8 o'clock using a base and an exponent. _____

   C. How many people were contacted in all? Explain.

   _____

3. (MP) **Reason** Use the properties of multiplication to compare the expressions 3^8 and $3^5 \times 3^3$. What do you notice?

4. **Math on the Spot** Write the expression in exponential form.

   A. $7 \cdot 7 \cdot 7 \cdot 7 =$ _____   B. $3 \cdot 3 \cdot 3 \cdot 3 \cdot 3 \cdot 3 =$ _____

For Problems 5–6, write the exponential expression as an equivalent repeated multiplication expression, and then evaluate the expression.

5. $2^8 =$ _____

6. $15^3 \times 15^2 =$ _____

For Problems 7 and 8, write each repeated multiplication expression using a single exponent.

7. $8 \cdot 8 \cdot 8 \cdot 8 \cdot 8 =$ _____

8. $4 \cdot 4 \cdot 4 \cdot 4 \cdot 4 \cdot 4 \cdot 4 =$ _____

Test Prep

9. Select all expressions equivalent to $3 \cdot 3 \cdot 3 \cdot 3 \cdot 3 \cdot 3 \cdot 3 \cdot 3$.

Ⓐ 8^3

Ⓑ 3^8

Ⓒ $3^5 \cdot 3^3$

Ⓓ $3^4 \cdot 3^4$

Ⓔ $3^7 \cdot 3^2$

10. Select all expressions equivalent to $11 \cdot 11 \cdot 11$.

Ⓐ 11^3

Ⓑ 3^{11}

Ⓒ $11^1 \cdot 11^3$

Ⓓ $3^5 \cdot 3^6$

Ⓔ $11^1 \cdot 11^2$

11. Write two equivalent expressions, one exponential and one a product of factors, for "4 to the 5th power." Evaluate the expressions.

12. Select the expression that is equivalent to 7^5.

Ⓐ $7 \times 7 \times 7 \times 7 \times 7 \times 7 \times 7$

Ⓑ $7 \times 7 \times 7 \times 7 \times 7$

Ⓒ $5 \times 5 \times 5 \times 5 \times 5 \times 5 \times 5$

Ⓓ $5 \times 5 \times 5 \times 5 \times 5$

Spiral Review

13. Gustus bought three pairs of shoes that each cost $19.98. What is the total amount he spent on shoes, before tax?

14. A bucket can hold a total of 5 gallons of water. If the bucket is $\frac{9}{20}$ full, how much water is in the bucket?

15. A cube is 6 centimeters on each side. What is its volume in cubic units?

Name _____

Write and Evaluate Numerical Expressions for Situations

(**I Can**) write numerical expressions to represent situations, identify terms in expressions, and use the order of operations to evaluate expressions.

Spark Your Learning

Two tour groups are visiting an aquarium. There are 20 children in one group and 22 children in the other. Along with the 2 group leaders, there are 5 additional adults. If the cost per child is $9.00 among the two groups and the total for both groups is $490, what is the cost per adult? Explain your reasoning.

Turn and Talk If the aquarium discounted the price for both groups by one-tenth, what would the total cost be? Explain.

© Houghton Mifflin Harcourt Publishing Company • Image Credit: ©Vlad61/Shutterstock

Build Understanding

The parts of an expression that are added or subtracted are called **terms**.

1 ▶ Consider the expressions in Parts A–D.

A. How many terms does the expression $14 + 9$ have? What are they? Explain how you know.

_____

B. How many terms does the expression $6 + 20 - 9$ have? What are they? Explain how you know.

_____

_____

C. The expression $25 + (4 \times 5)$ has _____ terms, namely _____ , because it is a _____ of those expressions.

The expression 4×5 has two _____ , namely _____ , because it is a _____ of those expressions.

D. The expression $\frac{7}{10} - \frac{11}{20}$ has _____ terms, namely, _____ and _____ , because it is a _____ of those expressions.

The fraction expression $\frac{7}{10}$ is also a _____ because it represents 7 _____ by 10.

2 ▶ How can you write a numerical expression to represent a phrase?

A. Consider the phrase, "the product of 7 and the sum of 5 and 4."

The sum of 5 and 4 is written as _____ .

The product of 7 and the sum of 5 and 4 is written as _____ .

B. Consider the phrase, "the square of the difference of 9 and 3."

The difference of 9 and 3 is written as _____ .

The square of the difference of 9 and 3 is written as _____ .

 Turn and Talk Compare and explain the meanings of 2^3 and $2(3)$.

Name _____

Step It Out

You learned about the **order of operations** in a previous grade. Now we need to add exponents into our order of operations. Exponents are calculated after performing operations in parentheses or brackets.

Connect to Vocabulary

Evaluate means to find the value of a numerical or algebraic expression.

3 ▶ The correct order of operations has been used to evaluate the given expressions. Identify the operation used in each step.

A. $3^3 + 12 \times 2$

$27 + 12 \times 2$ Evaluate exponents.

$27 + 24$ _____

51 _____

B. $72 \div (15 - 6) + 3 \times 2^2$

$72 \div 9 + 3 \times 2^2$ _____

_____

$72 \div 9 + 3 \times 4$ _____

$8 + 3 \times 4$ _____

$8 + 12$ _____

20 _____

C. $15 + 32 - 6 + (5 + 2)^2$

$15 + 32 - 6 + 7^2$ _____

$15 + 32 - 6 + 49$ _____

$47 - 6 + 49$ _____

$41 + 49$ _____

90 _____

Order of Operations

Perform operations in parentheses.
( )

Find the value of numbers with exponents.
exponents

Multiply and divide from left to right.
× ÷

Add and subtract from left to right.
+ −

Turn and Talk Why is it important to follow the order of operations?

4 A staff member is buying beds for all the dogs in a shelter. There are 10 dogs in one building and 14 dogs in another building. The price of a bed is shown.

DOG BED
$12

A. Complete the numerical expression to find the total cost.

☐ (☐ + ☐)

B. What is the first step for evaluating this expression? Complete the step.

_____

( )

C. What is the next step for evaluating the expression using the order of operations? Complete the step.

_____

D. Use the **Distributive Property** to evaluate your expression from Part A and show it is equal to your result from Part C.

☐ + ☐

E. What is the total cost of the beds?

_____

Check Understanding

1. The softball coach is buying new jerseys for the varsity and junior varsity teams. Each jersey costs $18. There are 12 students on the varsity team and 14 students on the junior varsity team. Write and evaluate a numerical expression to find the total cost.

_____

2. Write a numerical expression to represent the phrase "the quotient of 12 and the product of 4 and 5." How many terms does it have?

_____

3. Use the order of operations to evaluate the expression.

$4(7 + 9) + 8^2 - 7$ _____

On Your Own

4. Lamar drinks 8 ounces of water with breakfast, 6 ounces of water with his vitamins, 16 ounces of water with his lunch, 16 ounces of water with his dinner, and 32 ounces of water from a bottle he carries throughout the day. Write and evaluate a numerical expression for the amount of water in ounces that he drinks in a week.

_____

5. (MP) **Use Structure** Kyle rides his bicycle to school 5 days a week. He also rides from school to the soccer field twice a week. Every day, he rides his bicycle home on the same paths. Write and evaluate a numerical expression for the total number of miles Kyle bikes during the week.

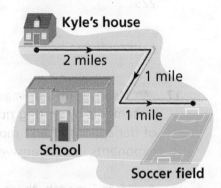

Kyle's house

2 miles

1 mile

1 mile

School

Soccer field

   A. Write an expression for the number of miles Kyle bikes on a day when he does not go to the soccer field.

   _____

   B. Write an expression for the number of miles Kyle bikes on a day when he does go to the soccer field.

   _____

   C. Write and evaluate an expression for the total number of miles Kyle bikes during the week.

   _____

For Problems 6–9, evaluate each expression.

6. $25 - 21 \div 3 =$ _____

7. $8 + 8 \div 8 =$ _____

8. $10 - 4 \times 1 + 7 =$ _____

9. $18 \div 3 - 1 \times 4 =$ _____

For Problems 10–11, complete the sentence using *sum*, *difference*, *product*, *quotient*, or *factors*.

10. The expression $20 + (8 \div 2)$ is the _____ of 20 and $(8 \div 2)$. The expression $8 \div 2$ is the _____ of 8 and 2.

11. The expression 11×6 has two _____, namely 11 and 6, because it is the _____ of those expressions.

For Problems 12–15, write a numerical expression to represent the phrase.

12. the sum of 6 and the square of 12 _____

13. the quotient of 30 and the sum of 5 and 7 _____

14. the difference of 4 cubed and 25 _____

15. 5 more than the product of 12 and 8 _____

16. (MP) **Critique Reasoning** Aman and Jennifer both evaluated the same numerical expression. They got different answers. Who simplified the expression correctly? Explain.

Aman	Jennifer
$1 + 4 \cdot 3^2$	$1 + 4 \cdot 3^2$
$5 \cdot 3^2$	$1 + 4 \cdot 9$
15^2	$1 + 36$
225	37

_____

_____

17. (MP) **Use Repeated Reasoning** A field has 11 dandelions. Complete the statements by writing numerical expressions to show the total number of dandelions after 1 month, 2 months, 3 months, and 4 months. Use exponents in your answers for Part A.

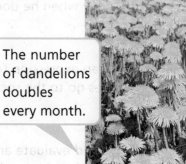

The number of dandelions doubles every month.

A. After 1 month, there are $11 \times \boxed{}$ dandelions.

After 2 months, there are $11 \times \boxed{}^{\boxed{}}$ dandelions.

After 3 months, there are _____ dandelions.

After 4 months, there are _____ dandelions.

B. Evaluate the last expression in Part A. Show your work.

For Problems 18–21, evaluate the expression.

18. $7 + 15 \div 3 \cdot 2 - 12$ _____   **19.** $6(9 - 6) - 2^3 + 4$ _____

20. $(7 - 6) + 9 - 2 \cdot 5$ _____   **21.** $7 + (2 - 1)^5 \cdot 8$ _____

© Houghton Mifflin Harcourt Publishing Company • Image Credit: ©Vaclav Volrab/Shutterstock

 I'm in a Learning Mindset!

How did I apply prior knowledge to evaluate numerical expressions using order of operations?

_____

LESSON 6.2
**More Practice/
Homework**

ONLINE
Ed Video Tutorials and
Interactive Examples

Write and Evaluate Numerical Expressions for Situations

1. **STEM** Margarite is building 3 prototypes of a robot she designed. Each robot includes a body and a remote control. She needs 450 inches of wire for each body and 120 inches for each remote control. In addition, she is going to build one master remote to run all three robots at once. The master remote will require 380 inches of wire. Write and evaluate a numerical expression to find the total length of wire she will need.

    A. Write an expression for the amount of wire needed for a robot.

    _____

    B. Write an expression for the total amount of wire needed for all 3 robots.

    _____

    C. Write an expression for the amount of wire needed for all 3 robots and the master remote.

    _____

    D. How much wire will Margarite need to complete her project?

    _____

2. For a school picnic, Todd fills 30 paper cups with ketchup and Yuki fills 27 paper cups with ketchup. Each paper cup holds 1 ounce. Later, Todd and Yuki learn that two other students completed exactly the same task. How many ounces of ketchup did the four students prepare?

    _____

3. (MP) **Reason** At football practice on Monday, Brandon threw a football into the target 5 times. The next Monday, he tripled the number of times he hit the target. On the following Monday, his hits doubled that of the week before. Write and evaluate a numerical expression to find how many times he hit the target during those three weeks.

    _____

    _____

4. **Math on the Spot** For Problems 4–7, evaluate the expression.

    A. $25 - 21 \div 3$

    B. $50 + 12 \div 3 \times 5 - 2$

    C. $7 + 3^3 \times 10$

    D. $40 - 4^2 \times 2 + 1$

Test Prep

5. Evaluate the expression.

$13 - 2 \times 5 + 7^2$

(A) 104

(B) 594

(C) 100

(D) 52

6. Mrs. Kershner is a school nurse. She uses, on average, 24 self-adhesive bandages during each spring month: March, April, and May. She also knows that in June there are several field days, and she will need 4 times the number of bandages for that month. How many bandages should she order for March through June? If the bandages cost 3 cents each, what is her total cost for March through June?

7. To evaluate the expression, what is the first step to follow?

$2(7 + 3 \div 3 \times 7)^2 - 100$

(A) Divide $3 \div 3$.

(B) Multiply 3×7.

(C) Multiply by 2.

(D) Add $7 + 3$.

8. Evaluate $15 \times 3 + 7(4 + 1) - 5^2$. What is the second step according to order of operations?

Spiral Review

9. Which expressions are equal to 4? Select all that apply.

(A) $9 + (-5)$

(B) $6 - 10$

(C) $(-12) \div (-8)$

(D) $8 + (-4) + 1$

(E) $(-2)(-2)$

10. Alex paid $3.59 for 1.35 pounds of chicken. To the nearest cent, how much did Alex pay per pound?

11. Which correctly orders the numbers from least to greatest?

(A) $-5, -1, -3, 0$

(B) $-3, 0, -1, 5$

(C) $-12, -1, 0, 3$

(D) $5, -2, 1, 7$

Name _____

Write Algebraic Expressions to Model Situations

(I Can) write algebraic expressions to represent situations, and I can identify variables, coefficients, and constants.

Spark Your Learning

Viola is helping to plant a rectangular community garden. A plant handbook states that 1 plant requires 8 square inches of soil. Given the dimensions of the rectangular garden below, how many plants can Viola plant in the garden? Explain.

24 in.

84 in.

$\frac{1}{2}$ $\frac{1}{2}$

 Turn and Talk If Viola increased the width of her garden to 36 inches, how many more plants could she put in her garden? Explain.

Build Understanding

An **algebraic expression** is an expression that contains one or more variables.

A **variable** is a letter or symbol used to represent one or more unknown quantities.

A **constant** is a specific number whose value does not change.

$2x + 75$ is an example of an algebraic expression.

2 is a coefficient. x is a variable.   75 is a constant.

Connect to Vocabulary

A **coefficient** is a number that is multiplied by a variable in an algebraic expression.

1 ▷ Trista has 2 baskets of dolls. One basket has 8 dolls, and the other basket has an unknown number of dolls in it. What expression can you use to represent the total number of dolls?

A. Can you write a numerical expression to represent the total number of dolls? Explain.

_____

B. What do you know about this situation?

There are ☐ baskets. One has ☐ dolls in it.

Do you know the number of dolls in the other basket? _____

C. If you do not have all the information you need, can you still write an expression to represent the total number of dolls? Explain.

_____

_____

D. Complete the bar model to represent this situation. Then write an expression to represent the bar model.

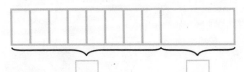

The expression is ☐ + ☐ .

E. Explain why the expression in Part D is an algebraic expression. Identify the coefficient.

_____

_____

Turn and Talk Does it matter which letter you choose for the variable when you write an algebraic expression? Explain.

© Houghton Mifflin Harcourt Publishing Company

Step It Out

2 Kristen works at a supermarket. She wants to divide a box of apples equally among 3 displays.

A. Let f represent the total number of apples. Complete the bar model to express the number of apples each display will have.

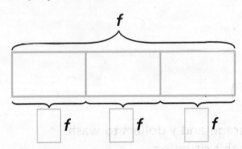

B. Write an algebraic expression that represents the number of apples each display will have. Write your answer as a product and a quotient.

_____

C. Kristen decides to use an additional 12 apples for each display. What is the new algebraic expression that represents the number of apples each display will have?

_____

 Turn and Talk How would the algebraic expression change if instead of putting an additional 12 apples in each display, Kristen decided to keep 6 apples from the total number before she divided them among the 3 displays? Explain.

Check Understanding

1. Raj is 3 inches taller than Howard. Let h represent Howard's height. Write an algebraic expression to represent Raj's height.

_____

2. Marcus has 4 times the sum of 6 and the number of marbles David has. Let d represent the number of marbles David has. Write an algebraic expression to represent how many marbles Marcus has.

_____

Write an algebraic expression for the words. Identify the coefficient(s).

3. the quotient of t and 13

4. the product of g and 2, plus m

On Your Own

5. (MP) **Use Tools** Larry and Zach both want to buy the latest video game. Let x represent the price of the video game.

   A. Larry's mom pays him $7 for each of the 3 flower beds he weeds and y dollars to edge the yard. Complete the model to show this situation.

   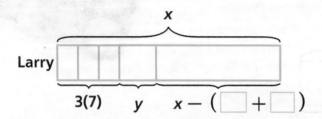

   Larry

   $3(7)$ y $x - (\boxed{} + \boxed{})$

   B. Zach's dad pays him $25 to clean out the garage and y dollars to wash his mom's car. Complete the model to show this situation.

   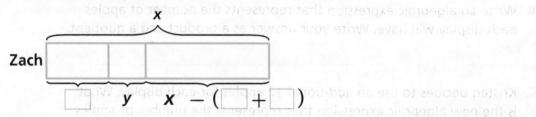

   Zach

   $\boxed{}$ y $x - (\boxed{} + \boxed{})$

   C. (MP) **Reason** Who has more money left to earn before he can buy the video game? Explain.

6. Jayden begins with 25 cups of soil at the greenhouse. Each day his goal is to fill 5 cups more. Write an algebraic expression to represent the number of cups he will have after n days. Identify the coefficient.

For Problems 7–9, write an algebraic expression for the word expression.

7. 32 divided by b

8. the sum of 112 and m

9. the product of $\frac{1}{2}$ and x

I'm in a Learning Mindset!

What about writing algebraic expressions triggers a fixed-mindset voice in my head?

Write Algebraic Expressions to Model Situations

1. **Financial Literacy** Clyde rents a tuxedo for several days. Let *d* represent the number of additional days Clyde uses the tuxedo. Write an algebraic expression to represent the total cost of the rental after *d* additional days.

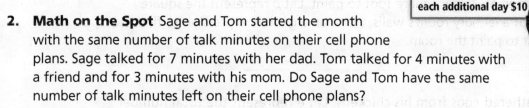

TUXEDO RENTAL
First day $75
each additional day $10

_____

2. **Math on the Spot** Sage and Tom started the month with the same number of talk minutes on their cell phone plans. Sage talked for 7 minutes with her dad. Tom talked for 4 minutes with a friend and for 3 minutes with his mom. Do Sage and Tom have the same number of talk minutes left on their cell phone plans?

   A. Complete the models to represent Sage's and Tom's minutes. Then write an algebraic expression to represent the number of minutes each has left.

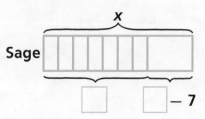

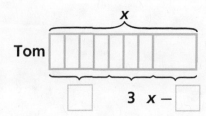

   _____

   B. Do Sage and Tom have the same number of talk minutes left on their cell phone plans? Explain your reasoning.

   _____

   _____

3. **Open Ended** Nola fits together *p* pieces a day of a 5,000-piece puzzle. Write an algebraic expression for this situation and explain what it represents.

   _____

   _____

Write an algebraic expression for the word expression.

4. the product of *c* minus 13 and 7

5. the quotient of 10 times *m* and 7

_____

Identify the variable, coefficient, and constant term of the expression.

6. $4b + 24$
   variable: _____
   coefficient: _____
   constant: _____

7. $11y + 4.5$
   variable: _____
   coefficient: _____
   constant: _____

Test Prep

8. Alix's mom gives her x dollars per week for lunch. Alix spends $3 on lunch at school every weekday. Write an algebraic expression to represent how much money she has left over at the end of the school week.

_____

9. The Color My Room painting company charges a fixed set-up fee of $20 per job and then $0.25 per square foot to paint. Let p represent the square footage of a laundry room's walls. Write an algebraic expression to find the total cost to paint the room.

_____

10. Gabe gathered eggs from his chickens. Let e represent the total number of eggs he collected. He gives a third of the eggs to a friend, 7 of the eggs to another friend, and the rest to his cousin. Which algebraic expression represents the number of eggs he gives to his cousin?

Ⓐ $\frac{1}{3}e + 7$

Ⓑ $e - \frac{1}{3}e - 7$

Ⓒ $7 - \frac{e}{3}$

Ⓓ $\frac{e}{3} - 7$

11. Let g represent the total number of hours Greg will travel on his trip across the country to attend his cousin's wedding. The first day he travels 8 hours. The second day he travels 9 hours. The third day he had mechanical problems and drove for only 4 hours. Write an algebraic expression to represent how much time he has left to drive.

_____

Spiral Review

12. An expression is shown. 5[8(7 − 4) ÷ 6]

    What is the value of the expression? _____

13. An expression is shown: 2.54 × 5.5

    What is the value of the expression? _____

14. Haru is putting lace around the edge of a rectangular pillow case that has a length of 12.75 inches and a width of 15.5 inches. How much lace does he need?

_____

© Houghton Mifflin Harcourt Publishing Company

Name

Interpret and Evaluate Algebraic Expressions

(I Can) evaluate an algebraic expression for given values of the variables.

Step It Out

You can **evaluate** an expression with a variable by substituting a known value for the variable.

1 Evaluate each expression for the given value of the variable.

A. The area of the rug in square feet can be represented by the expression $6w$.

Find the area when $w = 4$.

Substitute 4 for w.

$6\left(\boxed{}\right)$

Multiply.

$\boxed{}$

When $w = 4$, $6w = \boxed{}$. The area is 24 ft².

B. Evaluate $18y$ when $y = \frac{2}{3}$.

Substitute $\frac{2}{3}$ for y.

$18\left(\dfrac{\boxed{}}{\boxed{}}\right)$

Multiply.

$\boxed{}$

When $y = \frac{2}{3}$, $18y = \boxed{}$.

C. Evaluate $x - 12$ when $x = 18.6$.

Substitute 18.6 for x.

$\boxed{} - 12$

Subtract.

$\boxed{}$

When $x = 18.6$, $x - 12 = \boxed{}$.

 Turn and Talk For the expression in Part A, how is the value of the expression related to the value of the variable? Explain.

6 ft

w ft

Sometimes expressions have more than one variable.

2 The **perimeter** of a rectangular swimming pool can be written as $2\ell + 2w$, where ℓ is the length and w is the width. Find the perimeter when $\ell = 7.5$ meters and $w = 4.5$ meters.

Substitute 7.5 for ℓ and 4.5 for w. $2\left(\boxed{}\right) + 2\left(\boxed{}\right)$

Multiply. $\boxed{} + \boxed{}$

Add.

When $\ell = \boxed{}$ and $w = \boxed{}$, $2\ell + 2w = \boxed{}$ meters.

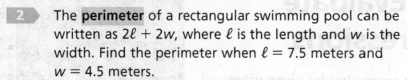

3 Evaluate each expression for the given values of the variables.

A. Evaluate $4x^3 - 3y$ when $x = 2$ and $y = 10$.

Substitute 2 for x and 10 for y. $4\left(\boxed{}\right)^3 - 3\left(\boxed{}\right)$

Evaluate the exponent. $4\left(\boxed{}\right) - 3\left(\boxed{}\right)$

Multiply. $\boxed{} - \boxed{}$

Subtract.

When $x = \boxed{}$ and $y = \boxed{}$, $4x^3 - 3y = \boxed{}$.

B. Evaluate $6s + \dfrac{d}{2}$ when $s = \dfrac{5}{12}$ and $d = 15$.

Substitute $\dfrac{5}{12}$ for s and 15 for d. $6\left(\dfrac{\boxed{}}{\boxed{}}\right) + \dfrac{\boxed{}}{2}$

Multiply. $\dfrac{\boxed{}}{\boxed{}} + \dfrac{\boxed{}}{\boxed{}}$

Add. $\dfrac{\boxed{}}{\boxed{}}$

Divide. $\boxed{}$

When $s = \underline{}$ and $d = 15$, $6s + \dfrac{d}{2} = \boxed{}$.

 Turn and Talk How is evaluating algebraic expressions similar to evaluating numerical expressions? How is it different? Explain.

C. Evaluate $4x^2y$ when $x = 3$ and $y = 0.5$.

Substitute 3 for x and 0.5 for y. $4\left(\Box\right)^2\left(\Box\right)$

Evaluate the exponent. $4\left(\Box\right)\left(\Box\right)$

Multiply. $\Box$

When $x = \Box$ and $y = 0.5$, $4x^2y = \Box$.

4 ▶ The expression $1.8C + 32$ gives the temperature in degrees **Fahrenheit** (°F) for a given temperature C in degrees **Celsius** (°C). Find the temperature in degrees Fahrenheit that is equivalent to 30 °C.

Substitute 30 for C. $1.8\left(\Box\right) + 32$

Multiply. $\Box + 32$

Add. $\Box$

$30\ °C = \Box\ °F$

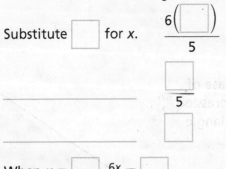

Thermometer scale: 50 °C, 40 °C, 30 °C, 20 °C, 10 °C, 0 °C, −10 °C, −20 °C, −30 °C, −40 °C

Check Understanding

1. Evaluate the expression $\frac{6x}{5}$ when $x = 20$.

   Substitute $\Box$ for x. $\dfrac{6\left(\Box\right)}{5}$

   $\dfrac{\Box}{5}$

   $\Box$

   When $x = \Box$, $\frac{6x}{5} = \Box$.

2. The expression $\frac{k}{8}$ shows the cost per person of splitting a restaurant bill k among 8 people. Evaluate the expression when $k = 72$ dollars.

   Substitute 72 for k. $\dfrac{\Box}{8}$

   Divide. $\Box$

   When $k = \Box$ dollars, $\frac{k}{8} = \Box$ dollars.

For Problems 3–6, evaluate the expression when $x = 4$ and $y = 3$.

3. $3x - 4y$ 4. $2x^2$ 5. $\dfrac{30}{y}$ 6. $\dfrac{3x}{4y}$

On Your Own

7. The volume of a right rectangular prism is ℓwh, where ℓ is the length, w is the width, and h is the height. What is the volume of a right rectangular prism with length 6 inches, width 4 inches, and height $\frac{3}{4}$ inch?

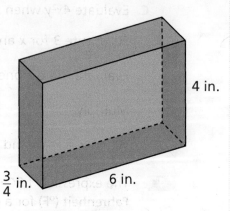

4 in.

Substitute 6 for ℓ, 4 for w, and $\frac{3}{4}$ for h.

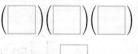

Multiply. ☐

The volume is _____.

$\frac{3}{4}$ in.   6 in.

8. Jasper needs fencing for a rectangular vegetable garden. The garden will be 8 feet by 4.5 feet. He knows the perimeter is found using the expression $2\ell + 2w$, or $2(\ell + w)$, where ℓ and w are the length and width of the garden. How many feet of fencing should Jasper buy?

_____

9. The expression $6s^2$ gives the surface area of a cube with edge length s, and the expression s^3 gives the volume. What are the volume and surface area of the cube with edge length 5 cm?

surface area = ☐ cm²

volume = ☐ cm³

10. (MP) **Use Structure** The area of a triangle with a base of 6 inches and a height of h inches, is given by the expression $\frac{6h}{2}$. Complete the table to show how the area of the triangle changes with height:

Height (in.)	4	5	6	7	8
Area (in²)	12				

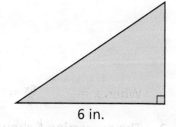

6 in.

How does the area change as the height increases? Why do you think this happens?

_____

_____

In Problems 11–14, evaluate the expression for $n = 0.75$.

11. $4n$ _____

12. $6 - n$ _____

13. $n + 12.5$ _____

14. $0.5n$ _____

15. (MP) **Critique Reasoning** Bill and Tia are trying to evaluate the expression $5x^2$ when $x = 3$. They both agree that 3 should be substituted for x. Tia says they should multiply 3 by 5, and then square the result. Bill says they should square 3, and then multiply by 5. Who is correct and why? What is the value of the expression?

_____

_____

16. STEM The expression $(F - 32)\frac{5}{9}$ gives the temperature in degrees Celsius (°C) for a given temperature F in degrees Fahrenheit (°F).

A. Find the temperature in degrees Celsius that is equivalent to 77 °F.

_____

B. Water freezes at 32 °F. At what temperature does water freeze in degrees Celsius?

_____

17. To find approximately how many pounds are equivalent to a given number of kilograms, use the expression $2.2n$, where n represents the number of kilograms. How many pounds are equivalent to 6.5 kilograms?

_____

18. To find the perimeter of a regular octagon, use the expression $8s$, where s represents side length. If the side length of a regular octagon is 1.5 feet, what is its perimeter in feet?

_____

1.5 ft

19. A rectangle is twice as long as it is wide. If the width is w, the length is $2w$. The area of the rectangle can be found using the expression $2w^2$. If the rectangle is 10 centimeters wide, what is its area in square centimeters?

_____

For Problems 20–25, evaluate the expression for the given value.

20. $6w$; $w = 0.1$

21. $x + 5\frac{1}{4}$; $x = 3\frac{1}{2}$

22. $1.4y$; $y = 5$

23. $\frac{48}{k}$; $k = 3$

24. z^5; $z = 2$

25. $2.5g^2$; $g = 4$

26. 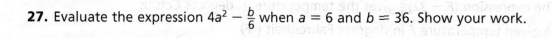 **(MP) Critique Reasoning** To evaluate the expression $(r + 6)^2$ for $r = 7$, Sayid says that r should be squared and 6 should be squared, and then the results should be added. Explain why Sayid is incorrect. Then find the value of the expression when $r = 7$.

_____

_____

_____

27. Evaluate the expression $4a^2 - \dfrac{b}{6}$ when $a = 6$ and $b = 36$. Show your work.

28. Rosa sells pens. She pays $0.75 for each pen and sells them for $1.25 each. She uses the expression $1.25p - 0.75p$, where p is the number of pens she sells, to calculate her profit. If Rosa sells 48 pens, what is her profit?

_____

29. Steve is playing a carnival game. He wants to win a prize, but he thinks he has about a 20% chance of winning. He uses the expression $0.2t$ to calculate the number of games he can expect to win if he plays t times. If he plays the game 12 times, about how many times can he expect to win?

For Problems 30–35, evaluate the expression s^3 for the given value.

30. $s = 4$ **31.** $s = \dfrac{1}{2}$

_____   _____

32. $s = 0.3$ **33.** $s = 10$

_____   _____

34. $s = 1.2$ **35.** $s = \dfrac{1}{6}$

_____   _____

LESSON 6.4
**More Practice/
Homework**

ONLINE
Video Tutorials and
Interactive Examples

Interpret and Evaluate Algebraic Expressions

1. Every day Jin reads for 0.75 hour in the morning and 1.25 hours
   in the evening. He uses the expression $0.75d + 1.25d$ to keep track
   of the number of hours he has read for any number of days, d. If
   Jin reads for 20 days, how many hours has he read? Show your work.

2. There are 16 ounces in 1 pound, so the expression $\frac{z}{16}$, where z
   represents the number of ounces, can be used to find the number
   of pounds for any given number of ounces. How many pounds
   are in 40 ounces?

1 lb

1 pound = 16 ounces

3. Jeffrey is 5 years older than his brother. If j represents Jeffrey's
   age, the expression $j - 5$ can be used to find his brother's age.
   If Jeffrey is 23, how old is his brother?

4. **Math on the Spot** For Problems 4–6, evaluate each expression.

   A. $4x - 5$ for $x = 10$

   B. $w \div 5 + w$ for $w = 20$

   C. $3z^2 - 6z$ for $z = 5$

For Problems 5–8, evaluate each expression for $b = 5$.

5. $2.1b$ 6. $5b - 12.4$ 7. $7.4b$ 8. $4b^2$

_____   _____   _____   _____

Test Prep

9. What is the value of the expression $8w - 4j^2$ when $w = 0.25$ and $j = 0.5$?

_____

10. What is the first step in evaluating an expression for given variable values?

_____

_____

11. Shade the correct box to identify the value of x that gives the expression the given value.

	$x = 2$	$x = 3$	$x = 4$	$x = 5$
$4x^2 - 2x, 30$	☐	☐	☐	☐
$5x + 20, 45$	☐	☐	☐	☐
$\frac{8x}{2} - 3x, 4$	☐	☐	☐	☐

12. Evaluate the expression $4(n + 3) - 5r$ for $n = \frac{1}{4}$ and $r = \frac{1}{5}$.

- (A) 3
- (B) 5
- (C) 8
- (D) 12

13. The surface area for a square prism is given by the expression $2s^2 + 4sh$, where s is the side length of the square base and h is the height of the prism. What is the surface area in square feet of a square prism when $s = 4$ feet and $h = 6$ feet?

_____

Spiral Review

14. One-third of 250 is what number?

_____

15. Rob has $45.75. How many neckties can he buy if each tie costs $15.25?

_____

16. A kilogram is equal to approximately 2.2 pounds. A cinder block weighs x kilograms. Write an expression for the approximate weight in pounds of the cinder block.

_____

Name

Identify and Generate Equivalent Algebraic Expressions

(I Can) use properties of operations to generate and identify equivalent algebraic expressions.

Step It Out

1 Substitute the given value into both expressions, and determine if the expressions have the same value.

A. Evaluate when $x = 6$.

$x^2 - 5x$

Substitute. $\left(\boxed{}\right)^2 - 5\left(\boxed{}\right)$

Evaluate exponent. $\boxed{} - 5\left(\boxed{}\right)$

Multiply. $\boxed{} - \boxed{}$

Subtract. $\boxed{}$

$x(x - 5)$

Substitute. $\boxed{}\left(\boxed{} - 5\right)$

Subtract. $\left(\boxed{}\right)$

Multiply. $\boxed{}$

The expressions | do / do not | have the same value when $x = 6$.

B. For the hexagon shown, Linda says the perimeter can be found using the expression $4\left(\frac{s}{2}\right) + 2s$. David says that he can use the expression $4s$ to find the perimeter. Do the expressions have the same value when $s = 8$?

$4\left(\frac{s}{2}\right) + 2s$

Substitute. $4\left(\dfrac{\boxed{}}{2}\right) + 2\left(\boxed{}\right)$

Divide. $4\left(\boxed{}\right) + 2\left(\boxed{}\right)$

Multiply. $\boxed{} + \boxed{}$

Add. $\boxed{}$

$4s$

Substitute. $4\left(\boxed{}\right)$

Multiply. $\boxed{}$

The expressions | do / do not | have the same value when $s = 8$.

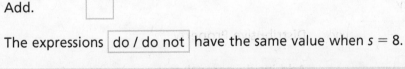

Turn and Talk Do the expressions $4s$ and $5s$ have the same value when $s = 0$? Do they have the same value for all values of the variable? Explain.

© Houghton Mifflin Harcourt Publishing Company

Equivalent expressions are expressions that have the same value for all possible values of the variable. Of course, you can't check every possible value! Fortunately, there is an easier way to show that expressions are equivalent. You can use the properties of operations. If you can apply the properties to one expression to get the other, then the two expressions are equivalent.

Properties of Operations	Examples
Commutative Property of Addition: When adding, changing the order of the numbers does not change the sum.	$a + b = b + a$
Commutative Property of Multiplication: When multiplying, changing the order of the numbers does not change the product.	$ab = ba$
Associative Property of Addition: When adding more than two numbers, the grouping of the numbers does not change the sum.	$(a + b) + c = a + (b + c)$
Associative Property of Multiplication: When multiplying more than two numbers, the grouping of the numbers does not change the product.	$(ab)c = a(bc)$
Distributive Property: Multiplying a number by a sum or difference is the same as multiplying by each number in the sum or difference and then adding or subtracting.	$a(b + c) = ab + ac$ $a(b - c) = ab - ac$

2 ▶ Identify the properties used to determine if the expressions are equivalent.

A. $4(a + 2b) + 4a$ and $8(a + b)$

$4(a + 2b) + 4a = 4a + 8b + 4a$ _____ Property

$= 4a + 4a + 8b$ _____ Property of Addition

$= (4 + 4)a + 8b$ _____ Property

$= \boxed{}\,a + 8b$ Add inside parentheses.

$= 8(a + b)$ _____ Property

$4(a + 2b) + 4a$ ┌ is / is not ┐ equivalent to $8(a + b)$.

B. $8xy + 5xy$ and $3xy$

$8xy + 5xy = \left(\boxed{} + \boxed{}\right)xy$ Distributive Property

$= \left(\boxed{}\right)xy$ Add inside parentheses.

$8xy + 5xy$ ┌ is / is not ┐ equivalent to $3xy$.

Like terms have the same variables raised to the same exponents. For example, $2p$ and $3p$ are like terms, as are $7x^2y$ and $5x^2y$. Constant terms such as 4 and 6 are also like terms. You can combine like terms using properties of operations.

3 ▶ The expression $s + (s + 1) + (s + 2)$ gives the perimeter of the triangle shown. The s terms are like terms and can be combined.

$s + (s + 1) + (s + 2)$

$= (s + s) + 1 + (s + 2)$ _____ Property of Addition

$= (s + s) + (s + 2) + 1$ _____ Property of Addition

$= (s + s + s) + 2 + 1$ _____ Property of Addition

$= (1 + 1 + 1)\ \boxed{} + 2 + 1$ _____ Property

$= \left(\boxed{}\right)s + \boxed{}$ Add.

$s + (s + 1) + (s + 2) = \boxed{}\,s + \boxed{}$.

4 ▶ Are the expressions $6w + 3z + 4w + 7z$ and $8(w + z)$ equivalent?

In the expression $6w + 3z + 4w + 7z$, the terms $6w$ and $4w$ are _____,

and the terms ____ and ____ are like terms.

$6w + 3z + 4w + 7z$

$= 6w + 4w + 3z + 7z$ _____ Property of Addition

$= (6 + 4)\boxed{} + \left(\boxed{} + \boxed{}\right)z$ _____ Property

$= \boxed{}\,w + \boxed{}\,z$ Add inside parentheses.

$= 10\left(\boxed{} + \boxed{}\right)$ _____ Property

$6w + 3z + 4w + 7z$ | is / is not | equivalent to $8(w + z)$.

 Turn and Talk How can you show that $8(xy + xy)$ is equivalent to $16xy$?

Check Understanding

Rewrite the first expression to determine whether the expressions are equivalent.

1. $8x + 4y = $ _____

$8x + 4y$ is _____ to $4(2x + 1)$.

2. $3(k + 3) = $ _____

$3(k + 3)$ is _____ to $3k + 9$.

On Your Own

3. (MP) **Use Structure** To find the perimeter of a rectangle, you can use different expressions: $\ell + w + \ell + w$, $2\ell + 2w$, or $2(\ell + w)$. Show that the expressions are equivalent.

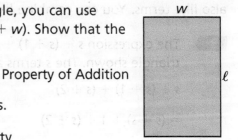

$\ell + w + \ell + w = \ell + \ell + w + w$ _____ Property of Addition

$\ell + \ell + w + w = \boxed{} + \boxed{}$ Combine like terms.

$2\ell + 2w = \boxed{}$ Distributive Property

4. (MP) **Reason** Marcus wrote an expression equivalent to $7(x + 8)$. Liz wrote a different expression that has the same value as Marcus's expression when $x = 2$. What could Liz's expression be?

_____

5. (MP) **Critique Reasoning** On a math test, students earn 4 points for each correct answer and lose 1 point for each incorrect answer. If there are 50 questions on the test, a student's score is shown by the expression $4(50 - w) - w$, where w is the number of wrong answers. Chris says that the expression $5(40 - w)$ could also be used. Is he correct? Why or why not? Show your work.

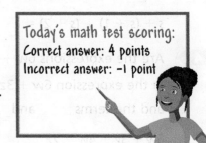

Today's math test scoring:
Correct answer: 4 points
Incorrect answer: –1 point

6. What property of operations is used to show that $12x + 6y$ is equivalent to $6(2x + y)$?

_____

7. **Open Ended** Write an expression that is equivalent to $5(d + 2f) + 5d$.

_____

For Problems 8–13, combine like terms.

8. $8w^2 - 3w^2 =$ _____

9. $x + 5 + 7x =$ _____

10. $6p^3 + 2p^2 + p^3 =$ _____

11. $2(x + 4) - 5 =$ _____

12. $g + 3 + 4(g + 2) =$ _____

13. $3(x^2 + 2) + 8 =$ _____

14. (MP) **Construct Arguments** Determine whether $6y + 18 + 3y$ is equivalent to $9(y + 2)$. Use properties of operations to justify your answer.

15. $6(4x + 3y)$ and $3(8x + 6y)$ are equivalent expressions. Explain why this is true.

_____

_____

$7.50/ hour babysitting

16. Sarah earns $7.50 per hour babysitting and $5.00 per hour walking dogs. Last week she worked h hours babysitting and twice as many hours walking dogs. Write an expression to show the amount of money Sarah earned last week. Then multiply and combine like terms to write the expression as one term.

_____

17. (MP) **Reason** If $2n$ is added to an expression, it will be equivalent to $6(2n + 3)$. For which expression is this true: $12n + 21$, $10 + 9$, $2(5n + 9)$, or $12n + 1$? Show how you know.

_____

_____

18. Determine whether the expressions $6x + 2 + 4x$ and $8x + 4$ have the same value when $x = 2$.

$6x + 2 + 4x$ is equal to ☐ when $x = 2$.

$8x + 4$ is equal to ☐ when $x = 2$.

Do the expressions have the same value when $x = 2$? _____

19. Identify the property used in each step.

$6x + (19 + 5x) = 6x + (5x + 19)$ _____ Property of Addition

$= (6x + 5x) + 19$ _____ Property of Addition

$= 11x + 19$

For Problems 20–21, determine if the expressions are equivalent.

20. $4m + 3m$ is _____ to $7m$.

21. $3j + 3k$ is _____ to $\frac{1}{4}(8j + 12k)$.

22. Which expression is NOT equivalent to the others? Explain.

$12p + 8$ $6p + 8 + 6p$ $4(p + 2) + 3p$ $4(3p + 2)$

23. A rectangle is 4 units wide and $6 + x$ units long. Write two expressions to represent the area of the rectangle.

_____

$\frac{3}{4}$ hour
morning run

24. Open Ended Each weekday, Ana runs in the morning and the afternoon. Write an expression to show how long Ana runs for any number of days d. Then multiply and combine like terms to write the expression as one term.

$\frac{1}{2}$ hour
afternoon run

_____

25. (MP) **Use Structure** Determine if $4x$ and $3x + 3$ have the same value when $x = 3$ and when $x = 0$.

$4x = \boxed{}$ when $x = 3$. $3x + 3 = \boxed{}$ when $x = 3$.

$4x = \boxed{}$ when $x = 0$. $3x + 3 = \boxed{}$ when $x = 0$.

The expressions have the same value when $x = \boxed{}$,

but not when $x = \boxed{}$. This means that $4x$ and $3x + 3$

_____ equivalent expressions.

For Problems 26–31, find an equivalent expression using the Distributive Property.

26. $25w + 30x$ **27.** $x(4 + y)$ **28.** $0.25(8r - 4m)$

_____   _____   _____

29. $24 + 8k$ **30.** $4xy - 16x$ **31.** $g^3(7 + h)$

_____   _____   _____

For Problems 32–33, determine if the expressions are equivalent.

32. $7(x + 4)$ is _____ to $7x + 4$.

33. $3r + 11 + 5r$ is _____ to $2(4r + 3) + 5$.

Name _____

LESSON 6.5
More Practice/ Homework

Identify and Generate Equivalent Algebraic Expressions

ONLINE

Video Tutorials and Interactive Examples

1. **(MP) Use Tools** A pattern of squares is shown. It changes by the same amount in each step. Kwan has determined that he can use the expression $2(n + 1) - 3$ to find the number of squares for any step number n. Find an equivalent expression that Kwan can also use.

   _____

2. Determine if the expressions have the same value when $x = 5$.

   $6x + 9$ and $3(2x + 3)$

   The value of $6x + 9$ when $x = 5$ is ☐ .

   The value of $3(2x + 3)$ when $x = 5$ is ☐ .

   Do the expressions have the same value when $x = 5$? _____

3. **(MP) Critique Reasoning** Trisha says that since $4(3s + 2)$ and $5(7s - 3)$ both equal 20 when $s = 1$, the expressions are equivalent. Is she correct? Explain.

   _____

   _____

   _____

4. A stained glass sun catcher in the shape of a pentagon is shown. Write and simplify an expression to find the perimeter of the pentagon.

   _____

   _____

   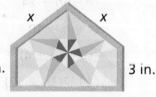

   3 in.   3 in.

   $x + 3$

5. The surface area of a rectangular prism with length ℓ, width w, and height h is given by the expression $2\ell w + 2\ell h + 2wh$. Write an equivalent expression using the Distributive Property.

   _____

6. **Math on the Spot** Identify the property.

   A. $3(6 \cdot 5) = (3 \cdot 6)5$ _____ Property of Multiplication

   B. $w + z = z + w$ _____ Property of Addition

For Problems 7–8, determine whether the expressions are equivalent.

7. $6r + 3w - 2r + 5w$ is _____ to $4(r + 2w)$.

8. $12d + 8r$ is _____ to $2(5d + 4r) + 4d$.

© Houghton Mifflin Harcourt Publishing Company

Module 6 • Lesson 5

235

Test Prep

9. What property of operations can be used to justify that the two expressions in this equation are equivalent? $6x^2 + 4x = 4x + 6x^2$

_____

10. Do the expressions $6x - 4x$ and $12x \div 6$ have the same value when $x = 6$?

$6x - 4x = \boxed{}$ when $x = 6$. $12x \div 6 = \boxed{}$ when $x = 6$.

$6x - 4x$ and $12x \div 6$ $\boxed{\text{do / do not}}$ have the same value when $x = 6$.

11. For the expression in each row, select the equivalent expression.

	$2(3x + 2y)$	$2(5x + 4y)$	$3(2x + 3y)$
$2(4x + 3y) - 2x - 2y$	☐	☐	☐
$2(4x + 3y) + 2(x + y)$	☐	☐	☐
$2(4x + 4y) - 2x + y$	☐	☐	☐

12. Which expressions are equivalent to $6(h + 4)$? Select all that apply.

Ⓐ $6h + 4$

Ⓑ $6h + 24$

Ⓒ $h + 10$

Ⓓ $4(h + 4) + 2(h + 4)$

Ⓔ $2(3h + 12)$

13. Write an expression that is equivalent to $24x + 36y$.

_____

Spiral Review

14. Amanda earns \$12 an hour babysitting. She spends \$8 of her earnings on dinner while babysitting. Write an expression to represent her total earnings after x hours of babysitting.

_____

15. What integer is the opposite of 12?

_____

16. Write $5 \times 5 \times 5 \times 5 \times 5 \times 5 \times 5$ as an expression with an exponent.

_____

236

Name _____

Add, Subtract, Factor, and Expand Algebraic Expressions

(**I Can**) add, subtract, factor, and expand algebraic expressions with
rational coefficients, and apply these skills to real-world problems.

Step It Out

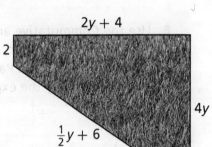

2y + 4

3y − 2

4y + 1

$\frac{1}{2}y + 6$

1 ▶ A yard is shaped like a **quadrilateral**.

A. Write an expression that shows the perimeter
of the yard as the sum of its side lengths.

$(2y + 4) + \boxed{} + \left(\frac{1}{2}y + 6\right) + \boxed{}$

B. How can you identify like terms in an expression?

_____

C. Remove the parentheses and rewrite the expression as a sum of
eight terms.

$2y + 4 + \boxed{} + \boxed{} + \frac{1}{2}y + 6 + \boxed{} + \boxed{}$

D. Use the Commutative Property to rearrange the addends so that all the
y-terms are together and all the integer terms are together.

$2y + \boxed{} + \frac{1}{2}y + \boxed{} + \boxed{} + \boxed{} + \boxed{} + (-2)$

E. How can the Associative Property of Addition be applied to simplify this
expression? Explain.

_____

_____

F. Simplify the expression by combining like terms.

$\boxed{} + \boxed{}$

Turn and Talk What is the advantage of the expression in Part A? What is
the advantage of the expression in Part F?

2 A path in a park forms the shape of an **equilateral triangle** with the side length shown.

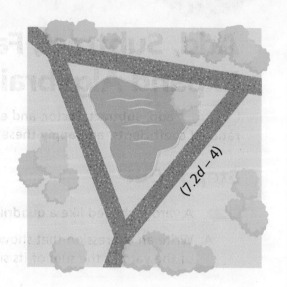

(7.2d − 4)

A. Write an expression that represents the length of the triangular path as a sum of the lengths of the three sides.

[ ] + [ ] + [ ]

B. Use the Commutative and Associative Properties of Addition to reorder and group like terms in your expression from Part A. Then combine like terms to simplify the expression.

$$\left(7.2d + \boxed{} + \boxed{}\right) +$$

$$\left(\left(-4\right) + \boxed{} + \boxed{}\right) = \boxed{}$$

C. Write an expression for the length of the path using the factor 3 and the length of one side.

$$3\left(\boxed{}\right)$$

D. Use the Distributive Property to *expand* the expression from Part C, and then simplify it.

$$3\left(\boxed{}\right) = 3\left(\boxed{}\right) - 3\left(\boxed{}\right) = \boxed{}$$

 Turn and Talk How do your results from Parts B and C show that the two expressions you wrote for the path's length are equivalent?

3 Another path in the park goes around a square playground. The length of the entire path can be represented by the expression $20x + 8$.

A. Divide by 4 to find an expression that represents the length of each side of the square.

$$\frac{20x + 8}{4} = \frac{\boxed{}}{4} + \frac{8}{4}$$

$$= \boxed{} + \boxed{}$$

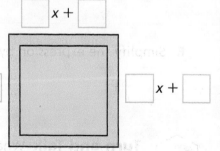

B. Complete the expressions for the side lengths the diagram.

C. Complete the equivalent expression for the length of the path, $20x + 8$.

$$20x + 8 = 4\left(\boxed{}\right)$$

4 Apply what you have learned about adding, subtracting, factoring, and expanding algebraic expressions to rewrite the following expressions.

A. Simplify $(-t - 5) + (-2t + 3)$.

$(-t - 5) + (-2t + 3)$

$= -t + \boxed{} + \boxed{} + 3$ Rewrite as the sum of terms.

$= \boxed{}\, t + \boxed{}$ Combine like terms.

$= \boxed{} - \boxed{}$ Combine like terms.

B. Simplify $(7 + 3d) - (5d - 5)$.

$(7 + 3d) - (5d - 5)$

$= 7 + \boxed{} + \boxed{} + \boxed{}$ Rewrite as the sum of terms.

$= \boxed{}\, d + \boxed{}$ Combine like terms.

C. Factor $30x - 5$ using the greatest common factor (GCF).

$30x - 5$

$= \boxed{} \left(6x - \boxed{} \right)$ The GCF is 5.

D. Expand $-7(3x + 1)$.

$-7(3x + 1)$

$= -7\left(\boxed{} \right) + (-7)\left(\boxed{} \right)$ Use the Distributive Property.

$= \boxed{} - \boxed{}$ Simplify.

Check Understanding

1. A playground is shaped like a pentagon with side lengths of x, $(2x + 3)$, $4x$, $(3x - 2)$, and $(2x + 4)$. Write an expression to represent the perimeter of the playground. Then, use the Commutative and Associative Properties to simplify the expression by combining like terms.

_____

_____

2. Use the Distributive Property to expand the expression $3(3x + 6)$. Then simplify the expression.

_____

3. Factor $24x - 20$ using the GCF.

_____

On Your Own

4. Recall that a regular polygon has sides that are all equal in length and angles that all have the same measure. A regular decagon has side lengths as shown.

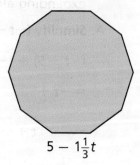

$5 - 1\frac{1}{3}t$

A. (MP) **Model with Mathematics** Write an expression for the perimeter of the regular decagon as a product of the number of sides and one side length. Explain.

_____

_____

_____

B. Use the Distributive Property to expand the expression from Part A. Then simplify.

_____

5. Factor $14f + 21$ using the GCF.

_____

6. (MP) **Model with Mathematics** A pentagon has these side lengths: $(12 + 4x)$, $(10 + 8x)$, $(15 + 3x)$, $(9 + 2x)$, and $(14 + 3x)$.

Write a simplified expression that represents the perimeter of the pentagon. Use the Distributive Property to factor the expression.

For Problems 7–8, factor the expressions using 3 as one factor.

7. $3x - 30$ 8. $3x + 15$

_____   _____

For Problems 9–10, simplify the expressions using properties of operations.

9. $(4x - 7.2) + (-5.3x - 8)$ 10. $(t - 1) - (-7t + 2)$

_____   _____

For Problems 11–12, expand the expressions using the Distributive Property. Then simplify the expressions.

11. $4(7x + 3)$ 12. $9(3y - 5)$

_____   _____

240

13. Emilio buys liter bottles of shampoo when the store has the promotion shown. Write an expression in two different ways to represent the total cost of 3 liters of shampoo.

Buy 2 liters, **get $1 off** 3rd liter.

_____

14. A plumber charges a customer a one-time service fee of $79, $62 per hour for labor, and a surcharge of $15 per hour due to the call being an emergency. Write an expression in two different ways that represents the total charges for the plumber.

_____

15. ⓂⓅ **Reason** Gavin uses x yards of material to make quilts. A customer requests 3 such quilts plus 5 additional quilts that are twice as large as his normal pattern.

A. Write an expression in two different ways that represents the total yards of material needed for the customer's quilts.

_____

B. What information does each expression from Part A give you?

_____

_____

_____

16. Maribelle works two part-time jobs to pay for college. She works 8 hours each week tutoring and 10 hours each week in the dining hall. She gets paid the same wage at each job. She is also provided $50 per week for expenses. Maribelle writes this expression, $18w + 50$, where w represents her hourly wage, to represent her total weekly income. Write another expression equivalent to Maribelle's.

_____

For Problems 17–20, decide whether the expressions are equivalent. Circle Yes or No.

17. $3n + 4n + 1 + 2n - 3$ and $9n - 2$

Yes   No

18. $0.85b - 0.2b$ and $0.65b$

Yes   No

19. $13x - 7x + 4$ and $20x + 4$

Yes   No

20. $26 - 0.9y + 0.32y - 4$ and $22 - 0.58y$

Yes   No

21. (MP) **Model with Mathematics** The width of a rectangle is shown. The length is twice the width. Write an expression for the perimeter that shows each side length. Simplify the expression.

$5 - \frac{1}{4}x$

22. (MP) **Model with Mathematics** Katelyn drew a pentagon. The side lengths are $(6.7t + 4.3)$, $(-t + 11)$, $(4.8t + 3)$, $(9.7t - 0.4)$, and $(8.6t - 0.2)$.

    A. Write an expression for the perimeter. Group the like terms. Then combine like terms to simplify.

    B. What two properties allowed you to reorder and regroup the terms?

For Problems 23–24, simplify the expressions using properties of operations.

23. $\left(-6s - 7\frac{2}{5}\right) + (-6s + 6)$

24. $5(y - 7) - (2y + 9)$

For Problems 25–26, expand and simplify the expressions using properties of operations.

25. $8(3x - 7)$

26. $14(3b + 2)$

For Problems 27–28, simplify using properties of operations and then factor the expressions using the GCF.

27. $(10p + 10) + (8p - 1)$

28. $(2g + 2) - (-4g - 7)$

29. Wesley wrote the following equivalent expressions for the perimeter of a rectangular garden plot.

    $2(7x) + 2(3x)$ $14x + 6x$ $20x$

    Which expression gives the most information about the dimensions of the rectangle? Explain.

Name _____

Add, Subtract, Factor, and Expand Algebraic Expressions

ONLINE
Video Tutorials and Interactive Examples

1. **(MP) Model with Mathematics** Write a simplified expression that represents the perimeter of a quadrilateral with side lengths $\left(2\frac{1}{4}t - 5\right)$, $(4t + 3)$, $\left(\frac{1}{2}t - 1\right)$, and $(3t + 2)$.

_____

2. **(MP) Reason** The length of a rectangle is represented by $4 + 6x$. The width is half the length. What expression represents the perimeter of the rectangle? Explain your reasoning.

_____

_____

3. **(MP) Model with Mathematics** A regular octagon has a perimeter represented by the expression shown. Write an expression to represent the length of one side of the octagon.

_____

Perimeter $= 48y - 40$

4. **Math on the Spot** Simplify the expressions using properties of operations.

   A. $5(x - 4) + 2x$

   _____

   B. $18t - 3 - 5t + 8$

   C. $7.5 + 5f + 16.2 + 2t$

   D. $-8(1 + x) + 7x$

   _____

   E. $7\frac{1}{3}t - \left(10\frac{2}{3}t - 6\right)$

   F. $(-r - 5) - (-2r - 4)$

   _____

For problems 5–6, expand and simplify the expressions using properties of operations.

5. $7(11c + 3)$

6. $6(7y - 8)$

_____

Test Prep

7. A square has a perimeter represented by the expression $8.8s - 20$. Write an expression to represent the length of one side of the square.

_____

8. Simplify $-5(7 + x) + 2\frac{5}{6}x$.

_____

9. Which expression is equivalent to $9y + 2(1 - 5y)$?

Ⓐ $4y + 2$

Ⓑ $19y + 2$

Ⓒ $y + 2$

Ⓓ $-y + 2$

10. A pentagon has side lengths of $(x + 3)$, $(2x - 4)$, $(4x + 5)$, $(3x - 1)$, and x. Which simplified expression represents the pentagon's perimeter?

Ⓐ $11x - 3$

Ⓑ $24x + 60$

Ⓒ $11x + 3$

Ⓓ $-9x + 3$

11. Leon orders sheets of metal for an art class he teaches. He needs 12 sheets for his Tuesday night class and 8 sheets for his Thursday night class. There is also a $7.95 delivery fee. Select all the expressions that represent the total cost of Leon's order, if x is the cost of one sheet.

Ⓐ $12x + 8x$

Ⓑ $12x + 8x + 7.95$

Ⓒ $20x + 7.95$

Ⓓ $12x + 8x - 7.95$

Ⓔ $12x + 8x + 7.95x$

Spiral Review

12. Jovan is 15 years old. His sister is 6 years older than $\frac{1}{3}$ his age. How old is Jovan's sister?

_____

13. Steven finds the product of all the integers from -99 to -90, including -99 and -90. Should his answer be positive or negative? Explain.

_____

_____

_____

Review

Vocabulary

Complete the following to review your vocabulary for this module.

Vocabulary
algebraic expression
base
coefficient
constant
equivalent expression
evaluate
exponent
numerical expression
term
variable

1. For the expression 6^4:

   A. The _____ is 6 and the _____ is 4.

   B. A(n) _____ using repeated

   multiplication is $6 \times 6 \times 6 \times 6$.

2. A(n) _____ expression contains at least one variable,

   while a(n) _____ expression contains only numbers

   and operations.

3. For the expression $4x + 7$, the _____ is 4, the

   _____ is x, and the _____ is 7.

4. To _____ an algebraic or numerical expression, find its value.

Concepts and Skills

For Problems 5–6, write an equivalent expression and evaluate.

5. $5 \times 5 \times 5 \times 5 =$ _____ = _____

6. _____ $= 4^3 =$ _____

7. (MP) **Use Tools** Howard buys 5 pounds of apples at $2.50 per pound and
   3 pounds of grapes at $1.50 per pound. Find the total cost of the fruit.
   State what strategy and tool you will use to answer the question, explain
   your choice, and then find the answer.

   _____

For Problems 8–9, identify the variable, coefficient, and constant term of the expression.

8. $12p + 47$

   variable: _____

   coefficient: _____

   constant: _____

9. $m + 7.5$

   variable: _____

   coefficient: _____

   constant: _____

10. Write an equivalent expression using the Distributive Property.

$35 + 21 = 7\left(\boxed{} + \boxed{}\right)$

11. Write an algebraic expression to represent 24 more than the product of 2 and a number.

_____

12. Evaluate the expression $5(m - 2) + 10w$ when $m = 8.4$ and $w = 1.25$.

- (A) 8.75
- (B) 44.5
- (C) 52.5
- (D) 80.25

13. Simplify $(y - 2) - (-6y + 1)$.

- (A) $7y - 1$
- (B) $7y - 3$
- (C) $-5y - 1$
- (D) $-5y - 3$

14. Which expressions are equivalent to $8(2s + 6)$? Select all that apply.

- (A) $16s + 6$
- (B) $16s + 48$
- (C) $10s + 48$
- (D) $4(4s + 12)$
- (E) $2(4s + 1) + 4(2s + 1)$

15. Write three expressions that are equivalent to $24k + 12k$.

_____

_____

16. A triangle has these side lengths:

$(7 + x)$, $(6 + x)$, and $(5 + 4x)$.

Write a simplified expression that represents the perimeter of the triangle.

_____

17. A bag of plums costs $3 per pound, and a bag of oranges costs $2 per pound. If Cammie buys x pounds of plums and y pounds of oranges, what expression could she write to find the total amount she will spend?

_____

© Houghton Mifflin Harcourt Publishing Company

Solve Problems Using Equations and Inequalities

EXPRESSION DARTS

Write expressions to match the scenario given.

The dartboard has sections numbered 1 to 20. You can "hit" a number on the dartboard by writing an expression equal to the number. Each expression must include each of the numbers 1, 2, 3, and 4 exactly once, but no other numbers. Try to get as many hits as you can. An example is shown.

1. $(4 + 2) \div 3 - 1 = 1$ 2. _____

3. _____   4. _____

5. _____   6. _____

7. _____   8. _____

9. _____   10. _____

11. _____   12. _____

13. _____   14. _____

15. _____   16. _____

17. _____   18. _____

19. _____   20. _____

 Turn and Talk

- Describe a strategy you used to hit different numbers.

- How did grouping symbols help you hit different numbers?

Are You Ready?

Complete these problems to review prior concepts and skills you will need for this module.

Expressions with Variables

For Problems 1–10, find the value of the expression. Show your work.

1. $25 - m$ if $m = 9$

2. $50 + t$ if $t = 18$

3. $105 - a$ if $a = 75$

4. $112 + c$ if $c = 35$

5. $15 \times r$ if $r = 5$

6. $36 \div y$ if $y = 3$

7. $64 \div d$ if $d = 4$

8. $24 \times n$ if $n = 8$

9. $125 \div k$ if $k = 25$

10. $120 \times b$ if $b = 10$

Plot Points on a Number Line

For Problems 11–16, plot and label each integer on the number line.

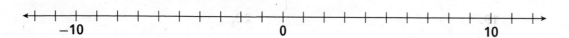

11. -2

12. 1

13. 4

14. -9

15. 10

16. -5

Name _____

Write Equations to Represent Situations

(I Can) write an equation to model a situation and determine
whether a given value is a solution of an equation.

Spark Your Learning

Bella and Tia began the week with the same amount of
money. Bella paid $9 to go to the movies. Tia spent $2 on
snacks and $7 on a new T-shirt. Do Bella and Tia have the
same amount of money left? Explain how you know.

Turn and Talk How would your representation of the problem change if
both people earned money instead of spending money?

Build Understanding

1 You can think of an equation as a balance scale that is level with equal weight on both sides. The scale shows two quantities that have equal weight.

Connect to Vocabulary

An **equation** is a mathematical sentence that shows that two expressions are equivalent.

A. What does the left side of the scale show? Write your answer in words. Then write a mathematical expression using addition that represents the weight on the left side.

_____

_____

B. What does the right side of the scale show? Write your answer in words. Then write an integer that represents the weight on the right side.

_____

_____

C. What equation does the scale represent? _____

D. If the 2-unit weight is removed, will the scale remain balanced? What would the scale show if the 2-unit weight were removed?

_____

_____

2 If a scale is balanced but a value is unknown, you can solve for the unknown value.

A. What equation does the scale represent?

_____

B. How can you find the value of x? That is, how can you find the solution of the equation.

_____

_____

_____

Connect to Vocabulary

A **solution of an equation** is a value of the variable that makes the equation true.

C. Would other values of x keep the scale balanced? Explain.

_____

_____

_____

Turn and Talk Do you think an equation with one variable can have more than one solution? Explain.

Step It Out

4 tickets to skate = $72

3 ▶ Ben buys tickets for the outdoor skating rink as shown. Each ticket costs the same amount. How much does one ticket cost?

A. What information do you know?

Ben bought ☐ tickets. Ben spent $ ☐ .

B. What do you need to find out?

_____

C. You can represent the cost of a ticket with the variable *c*. How are the unknown amount *c* and the amount Ben spent related?

_____

D. Model the situation using an equation, thinking about the different parts. Write the value or variable for each part of the model.

Number of tickets bought	×	Cost per ticket	=	Total amount spent

☐ × ☐ = 72

E. Substitute values for *c* to find the solution. Try $c = 20$.

When $c = 20$, the left side of the equation is _____ 72, so $c = 20$ | is / is not | a solution of the equation.

F. Try other values for *c*, thinking about how close your result is to 72. What is the solution for the equation? How much does a ticket cost?

When $c =$ ☐ , $4 × c = 72$. Each ticket costs ☐ .

Check Understanding

1. There are 30 students in a class. Today, 26 students are present. Write and solve an equation to show how many students are absent.

_____

For Problems 2–4, determine whether the given value is a solution for the equation. Answer *yes* or *no*.

2. $x - 8 = 12$, $x = 4$ **3.** $12w = 36$, $w = 3$ **4.** $\frac{y}{8} = 40$, $y = 5$

_____   _____   _____

On Your Own

5. **MP** **Model with Mathematics** The number of red marbles in a jar is 3 times the number of blue marbles. There are 27 red marbles and b blue marbles. Write an equation to represent this situation. How many blue marbles are there?

_____

6. **MP** **Model with Mathematics** Martha's daughter is $\frac{1}{4}$ Martha's age. If Martha's daughter is 12 years old, how old is Martha? Write an equation to represent this problem and explain your reasoning. Then find Martha's age.

_____

_____

7. Shan exercises daily. Today he did 85 pushups, which is 20 more than he usually does. How many pushups p does Shan usually do? Write an equation to represent this situation, and then solve the problem.

_____

8. **MP** **Critique Reasoning** Phillip writes the following equation to show how many hours h he needs to work to earn $108 at $12 per hour: $\frac{h}{12} = 108$. Is his equation correct? Explain.

_____

_____

9. **MP** **Attend to Precision** How are expressions different from equations?

_____

_____

For Problems 10–15, determine whether $x = 3$, $x = 4$, or $x = 5$ is the solution.

10. $8x = 32$, $x = \boxed{}$ 11. $42 - x = 37$, $x = \boxed{}$ 12. $\frac{20}{x} = 4$, $x = \boxed{}$

13. $0.5x = 2$, $x = \boxed{}$ 14. $\frac{x}{3} = 1$, $x = \boxed{}$ 15. $x + 13 = 16$, $x = \boxed{}$

I'm in a Learning Mindset!

How do I keep myself motivated to write equations for real-world situations?

_____

_____

© Houghton Mifflin Harcourt Publishing Company

Write Equations to Represent Situations

1. **Math on the Spot** At Glencliff High School, the photography club has 23 members, which is 12 fewer than the hacky sack club. Does the hacky sack club have 35 members or 11 members? Write an equation to model the problem.

   _____

2. (MP) **Model with Mathematics** Tilda buys a shirt for d dollars. She uses a $50 gift card and receives the change shown. Write an equation for this situation.

   _____

3. **Open Ended** Write an equation that has a solution of 4. Use the variable n and multiplication.

   _____

4. (MP) **Model with Mathematics** One pound is equal to 0.454 kilogram. If Jim has a mass of 100 kilograms, write an equation to represent how many pounds p he weighs.

   _____

$22.50 in change

5. **Open Ended** Write a word problem that could be modeled by the equation $x + 5 = 12$.

   _____

   _____

   _____

6. (MP) **Model with Mathematics** Jon bought a pizza as shown. Write an equation involving the cost per slice c.

BIG DEAL! Large pizza $20

For Problems 7–12, write whether the given value _is_ or _is not_ a solution for the equation.

7. $9x = 45$, $x = 5$

   5 _____ a solution.

8. $k - 6 = 8$, $k = 2$

   2 _____ a solution.

9. $n + 12 = 20$, $n = 32$

   32 _____ a solution.

10. $\frac{r}{5} = 25$, $r = 125$

    125 _____ a solution.

11. $\frac{16}{a} = \frac{1}{2}$, $a = 8$

    8 _____ a solution.

12. $24x = 6$, $x = \frac{1}{4}$

    $\frac{1}{4}$ _____ a solution.

Test Prep

13. Jennifer reads p pages every day. After 15 days, she has read 300 pages. Write an equation for this situation.

_____

14. Jermaine has t trading cards. Jasmine has 7 trading cards. Together, Jermaine and Jasmine have 13 trading cards. Which equation could represent the problem? Select all that apply.

(A) $t + 7 = 13$ (D) $7 + t = 13$

(B) $7 + t = 7$ (E) $13 \div t = 7$

(C) $7t = 13$ (F) $13 - 7 = t$

15. Lily is 5 inches shorter than Dan. If Dan is 67 inches tall, how tall is Lily? Write an equation to model the problem using h for Lily's height.

_____

16. Which value is a solution for the equation $\frac{m}{4} = 16$?

(A) $m = 4$ (C) $m = 20$

(B) $m = 12$ (D) $m = 64$

17. Derrick has 72 inches of ribbon to make bows. He uses all of his ribbon to make 9 bows of equal length L. How many inches of ribbon does each bow use? Write an equation to model the situation. Then solve the problem.

_____

Spiral Review

18. A batting average in baseball equals a player's number of hits divided by the number of times at bat, rounded to the nearest thousandth. What is Amaya's batting average if she gets 3 hits in 7 times at bat?

_____

19. What is the cost of 2.3 pounds of salmon at $9.70 a pound?

_____

20. Turkey hot dogs come in packages of 6 and buns come in packages of 8. What is the least number of packages that can be bought of each so that there are the same number of hot dogs and buns?

_____

For Problems 21–23, find the quotient.

21. $5\frac{1}{4} \div \frac{1}{4}$ **22.** $1\frac{1}{3} \div \frac{2}{3}$ **23.** $9\frac{3}{4} \div 3\frac{1}{4}$

Use Addition and Subtraction Equations to Solve Problems

(I Can) solve one-step addition and subtraction equations by applying the same operation to both sides.

Spark Your Learning

Thomas has four jugs of different sizes. One holds 1.2 liters, one holds 1.3 liters, one holds 2.3 liters, and one holds 2.6 liters. He has to fill a large barrel with exactly 5 liters of water. How can he use the jugs to pour this amount into the barrel? Find as many ways as possible.

 Turn and Talk Explain how you could measure exactly 0.1 liter, exactly 1 liter, and exactly 1.4 liters by pouring water from one jug to another.

Build Understanding

When solving an addition equation, you can model the equation on a balance scale. For the equation to remain true, both sides must remain equal or, in the case of a balance scale, be the same weight. If you remove something from one side, you must remove the same amount from the other side.

1 Weights are shown on the scale. Each square is 1 unit, but the value of the triangle x is unknown. The sides of the scale are balanced.

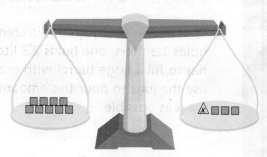

A. Describe the weights on the left side of the scale and on the right side of the scale using both words and mathematical expressions.

_____

_____

_____

B. What equation represents what is shown on the scale?

_____

C. How could you remove weights, making sure that the scale is still balanced, and use that to find the value of x?

D. How much must the weight labeled x weigh? Explain how you know.

_____

_____

E. Check your answer by substituting the value of x into the equation from Part B. Explain your work.

_____

_____

_____

 Turn and Talk If one side of a balance is lower than the other side, what mathematical symbol could you use to describe what the balance shows?

Step It Out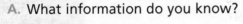

2 ▶ A plant is 6 inches tall. After 2 weeks, the plant is
14 inches tall. How many inches did the plant grow?

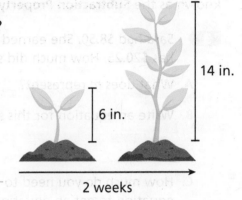

14 in.

6 in.

2 weeks

A. What information do you know?

The plant starts at ☐ inches.

The plant grows to ☐ inches.

B. What do you need to find out?

_____

_____

C. You can represent how many inches the plant grew in two weeks
with a variable x. How can you describe the relationship between the
unknown amount x and the height of the plant at the start?

_____

_____

D. Write an equation you can solve in order to answer the problem.

☐ + ☐ = ☐

E. You can also model the problem using algebra
tiles. The sets of tiles on both sides of the gray
rule are equal. Just like with a scale, if you
remove one tile from one side, you must also
remove one tile from the other side. Cross out
tiles until x is by itself. How many tiles did you
cross out on each side? How many tiles remain
on the right side of the model?

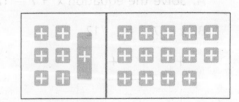

☐ 1-tiles were crossed out on each side.

☐ 1-tiles remain on the right side.

F. What is the solution to the equation? _____

G. Check your answer by substituting the value for x into the equation
from Part D and simplifying. Is your answer correct?

_____

 Turn and Talk Which model do you prefer, the scale or algebra tiles? Explain.

Instead of using a scale or algebra tiles, you can subtract the same amount from both sides of an equation and the two sides will remain equal. This is known as the **Subtraction Property of Equality**.

3 Sara had $8.50. She earned *m* dollars babysitting and now she has $20.25. How much did she earn babysitting?

A. What does *m* represent? _____

B. Write an equation for this situation.

$ [___] + [___] = $ [___]

C. How much do you need to subtract from both sides of the equation to get an equation with only *m* on the left side?

_____

D. Subtract [___] from both sides to isolate *m*.

$$8.50 + m = 20.25$$
$$\underline{- [\ \ ] \qquad\quad - [\ \ ]}$$
$$[\ \ ] = [\ \ ]$$

E. Sara earned $ [___] babysitting.

4 You can also add the same amount to both sides of an equation and the two sides will remain equal. This is the **Addition Property of Equality**.

A. Solve the equation $x - 7 = 12$ by adding [___] to each side.

B.
$$x - 7 = 12$$
$$\underline{+ [\ \ ] \qquad + [\ \ ]}$$
$$[\ \ ] = [\ \ ]$$

Check Understanding

1. Jerry has two dogs. The older one weighs 95 pounds. Their combined weight is 120 pounds. Write and solve an equation to find the younger dog's weight *d*. What number did you subtract from both sides?

_____

_____

For Problems 2–4, add or subtract to solve the equation, circle the correct word, and state the number that you added or subtracted.

2. $x - 15 = 29$, $x =$ [___]   I added / subtracted [___] .

3. $12.26 + w = 39$, $w =$ [___]   I added / subtracted [___] .

4. $y - \frac{3}{4} = 4\frac{1}{4}$, $y =$ [___]   I added / subtracted [___] .

258

On Your Own

5.

   (MP) Model with Mathematics Annie is the height shown. She is 49 centimeters taller than her brother. Write and solve an equation to find her brother's height b in centimeters.

   > Annie is 152.5 cm tall.

   _____

6. **(MP) Critique Reasoning** For the equation $z - 14 = 29$, Juan says that the solution is 33. Check Juan's solution by substituting it into the equation and simplifying. Is his solution correct?

   _____

7. William buys a book for $14.85. If he pays with a $20 bill, what will be his change c? Write and solve an equation to find out.

   _____

8. Yan had 5 trading cards, and then his friend gave him more cards. Now he has 16 trading cards. Let t represent the number of cards his friend gave him. Complete both an addition equation and a subtraction equation to model the problem.

   $\boxed{} + t = \boxed{}$ $\boxed{} - \boxed{} = t$

9. The scale shows the equation $7 = r + 5$. Cross out the same number of tiles on each side to get r by itself. What is the value of r?

   $r =$ _____

For Problems 10–15, circle whether you add or subtract to solve the equation. Then find the value.

10. $8 + x = 42$, | add / subtract |, $x = \boxed{}$ 11. $w - 61 = 14$, | add / subtract |, $w = \boxed{}$

12. $n - 81 = 67$, | add / subtract |, $n = \boxed{}$ 13. $m + 3.89 = 9.02$, | add / subtract |, $m = \boxed{}$

14. $y + 2.4 = 6.7$, | add / subtract |, $y = \boxed{}$ 15. $c + \frac{5}{9} = \frac{8}{9}$, | add / subtract |, $c = \boxed{}$

16. **(MP) Model with Mathematics** Jasmine is training for a race. Her goal is to cover 28 miles this week. So far this week, she has gone the distances shown. Write and solve an equation to find the number of miles m Jasmine has left to meet her goal.

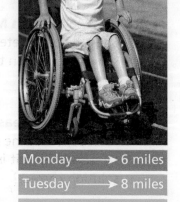

Monday ⟶ 6 miles
Tuesday ⟶ 8 miles
Wednesday ⟶ 6 miles

_____

_____

17. Aviva has collected 56 cans of food for disaster relief. Her goal is to collect 200 cans. Write and solve an equation to show how many more cans c she needs to reach her goal.

_____

_____

18. The Gateway Arch in St. Louis, Missouri, is 630 feet tall. It is 75 feet taller than the Washington Monument in Washington, D.C. Write and solve an equation to find the height h of the Washington Monument.

_____

19. Show that 1.27 is not a solution for the equation $g + 3.74 = 5.1$. Then find the correct solution and show why it is correct.

_____

_____

20. The scale shows the equation $b + 6 = 10$. What is the value of b?

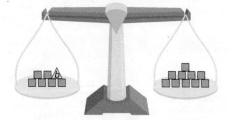

$b =$ _____

For Problems 21–22, add or subtract to solve the equation.

21. $8.7 + x = 12.05$, $x =$ _____   22. $a - 34 = 60$, $a =$ _____

🔢 I'm in a Learning Mindset!

How do I know when solving addition and subtraction equations triggered a fixed-mindset response in a classmate?

_____

_____

LESSON 7.2
**More Practice/
Homework**

ONLINE

Video Tutorials and
Interactive Examples

Use Addition and Subtraction Equations to Solve Problems

1. **Math on the Spot** Solve each equation.

   A. $s - 5 = 12$ _____

   B. $35 = y - 6$ _____

   C. $x - 22 = 44$ _____

2. (MP) **Model with Mathematics** Mary compares the heights of two trees. Their heights are shown. Write and solve an equation to find the height h of the taller tree.

   _____

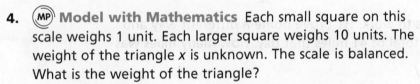

12 feet

45 feet

3. **Open Ended** Write an equation with a solution of 25. Use the variable x and addition.

   _____

4. (MP) **Model with Mathematics** Each small square on this scale weighs 1 unit. Each larger square weighs 10 units. The weight of the triangle x is unknown. The scale is balanced. What is the weight of the triangle?

   A. Write an equation to represent the weights shown on the scale.

   _____

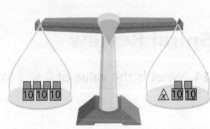

10 10 10   10 10

   B. Cross out the same weights on each side until x is alone. What is the total weight that you crossed out on each side?

   _____

   C. Write the simplified equation represented by the scale now. What is the weight of the triangle?

   _____

For Problems 5–6, determine whether the given value is a solution. Write *is* or *is not* on the line.

5. $x - 14 = 42$, $x = 56$

   56 _____ a solution.

6. $k + 66 = 98$, $k = 28$

   28 _____ a solution.

For Problems 7–8, solve the equation.

7. $55 + s = 110$, $s =$ _____

8. $n - 52 = 12$, $n =$ _____

Module 7 • Lesson 2

Test Prep

9. What value for w makes the equation $76 + w = 100$ true?

_____

10. Which equations have $x = 15$ as a solution? Select all that apply.

   Ⓐ $x + 14 = 29$ Ⓓ $x + 17 = 32$

   Ⓑ $25 + x = 10$ Ⓔ $x - 8 = 7$

   Ⓒ $x - 38 = 23$ Ⓕ $35 - x = 25$

11. How can you solve the equation $g - 24 = 36$? Circle the correct responses and fill in the blank.

   | Add / Subtract | ☐ | to / from | both sides.

12. Which value is a solution for the equation $\frac{7}{12} + n = \frac{5}{6}$?

   Ⓐ $n = \frac{10}{7}$ Ⓒ $n = \frac{1}{3}$

   Ⓑ $n = \frac{1}{4}$ Ⓓ $n = \frac{17}{12}$

13. Mr. Renner drove 18 miles to work. He drove home a different way and saw that he had driven a total of 41 miles that day. How many miles was the drive home?

_____

Spiral Review

14. What is the value of $\frac{4}{5} \times \frac{3}{4}$ in simplest form?

_____

15. A carpenter charges $50 an hour plus $75 for materials. Write an expression for his total charge if the job takes t hours.

_____

For Problems 16–19, evaluate the exponential expression.

16. 2^3 _____

17. 3^4 _____

18. 1^{10} _____

19. 10^3 _____

© Houghton Mifflin Harcourt Publishing Company

Name _____

Use Multiplication and Division Equations to Solve Problems

(I Can) solve one-step multiplication and division equations by applying the same operation to both sides.

Spark Your Learning   PAIRS

Diana is preparing lunch for her friends. She has 0.75 pound of ham and 0.5 pound of cheese. She uses 0.15 pound of ham and 0.08 pound of cheese to make a ham and cheese sandwich. Is there enough ham and cheese to make 5 sandwiches if she uses the same amount of ham and cheese for each sandwich? Explain.

Turn and Talk If ham costs $5.79 per pound and cheese costs $4.29 per pound, how can you find the total amount you pay for the ham and cheese in each sandwich? Can you stay within a budget of $1.50 per sandwich? Explain.

Build Understanding

In the previous lesson, you learned to solve addition equations with a variable by subtracting. How can you solve a multiplication equation?

1 A group of 4 people goes apple picking. They pick the amount shown. If they share the apples equally, how many pounds of apples does each person get? Let x represent the weight in pounds of apples per person.

20 lb of apples

A. Complete the diagram.

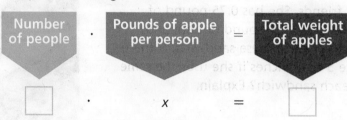

| Number of people | · | Pounds of apple per person | = | Total weight of apples |

☐ · x = ☐

B. Write an equation to represent this problem.

_____

C. Model the equation using algebra tiles. How many x-tiles are in your model? How many 1-tiles?

D. How many equal groups do you need to divide your model into? Explain.

_____

E. Draw circles around the tiles you drew for Part C to separate the tiles into equal groups.

F. How many 1-tiles are in each group? How many pounds of apples does each person get?

_____

 Turn and Talk What other method can you use to find how many pounds of apples each person gets? Explain.

Name _____

Step It Out

The **Division Property of Equality** states that you can divide both sides of an equation by the same nonzero number and the two sides will remain equal.

2 ▷ What is the value of x in the equation $7x = 119$?

A. Divide both sides of the equation by the same nonzero number to get x alone on one side.

$$\frac{7x}{\boxed{}} = \frac{119}{\boxed{}}$$

$$x = \boxed{}$$

B. To check the solution, substitute your answer in the original equation.

$$7\left(\boxed{}\right) \overset{?}{=} 119$$

$$\boxed{} = \boxed{}$$

Does your solution check? _____

The **Multiplication Property of Equality** states that you can multiply both sides of an equation by the same number and the two sides will remain equal.

3 ▷ What is the value of x in the equation $\frac{x}{6} = 9$?

A. Multiply both sides of the equation by the same number to get x alone on one side.

$$\frac{x}{6} = 9$$

$$\boxed{} \times \frac{x}{6} = \boxed{} \times 9$$

$$x = \boxed{}$$

B. To check the solution, substitute your answer in the original equation.

$$\frac{\boxed{}}{6} \overset{?}{=} 9$$

$$\boxed{} = \boxed{}$$

Does your solution check? _____

C. Find the value of x if you know that $\frac{x}{10} = 9$. Describe how you found the solution.

_____

Turn and Talk Why can't you divide both sides of an equation by zero? Explain.

$1.85 per pound

4 ▶ A bag of 5 plum tomatoes weighs 1 pound and costs $1.85. If each tomato weighs the same amount, what is the cost of one tomato? Use the equation $5x = 1.85$.

A. To solve the equation $5x = 1.85$, _____ both sides of the equation by the number ☐.

B. The result of performing the same operation to both sides of the equation leads to the solution $x =$ ☐.

C. Graph your solution on the number line.

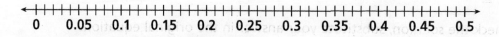

```
←++++++++++++++++++++++++++++++++++++++++++++++++++++++→
   0    0.05  0.1  0.15  0.2  0.25  0.3  0.35  0.4  0.45  0.5
```

D. To check the solution, put your answer into the original equation.

$5\left(\boxed{}\right) \overset{?}{=} 1.85$

$\boxed{} = \boxed{}$ Does your solution check? _____

E. Interpret your answer. _____

_____

🐃 **Turn and Talk** How is solving a multiplication equation with rational numbers like solving a multiplication equation with whole numbers?

Check Understanding

1. Mr. Poyser uses $4\frac{2}{3}$ cups of flour to make 7 dozen oatmeal-raisin cookies. How many cups of flour does he need to make a dozen cookies? Use the equation $7c = 4\frac{2}{3}$. Graph the solution on a number line.

_____

```
←+++++++++++++++++++++++++++++++++++++++→
  0     1     2     3     4     5
```

2. Four friends equally share the cost of lunch. Each person pays $14.00. How much is the total bill? Use the equation $\frac{b}{4} = 14$.

A. To find the total bill, I _____ each side by ☐.

B. $b =$ ☐

C. Graph the solution on a number line.

```
←++++++++++++++++++++++++++++++++++++++++++++++++++++++→
  0   5   10  15  20  25  30  35  40  45  50  55  60
```

© Houghton Mifflin Harcourt Publishing Company • **Image Credit:** ©Oleksandr Perepelytsia/Alamy

On Your Own

3. (MP) **Model with Mathematics** Preston earns $33.00 for babysitting his neighbor's children for 2.4 hours.

   A. Write an equation you can use to find out how much Preston earns per hour.

   _____

   B. How much does Preston earn in one hour? _____

4. Henri has exactly enough quarters to wash 3 loads of laundry. It takes 8 quarters to wash one load of laundry. How many quarters does Henri have? Use the equation $\frac{x}{8} = 3$.

5. (MP) **Use Tools** Carlos has 6 mugs on a shelf as shown. The mugs all have the same weight. The equation $6x = 84$ represents this situation.

   Total weight = 84 ounces

   A. What visual model could you use to solve the equation $6x = 84$? Explain.

   _____

   _____

   B. How much does each mug weigh? _____

For Problems 6–9, find each solution and graph it on the number line.

6. $\frac{x}{3} = 4$

   $x = \boxed{}$

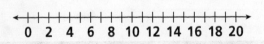

7. $1.9x = 4.75$

   $x = \boxed{}$

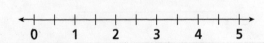

8. $12x = 60$

   $x = \boxed{}$

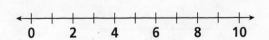

9. $\frac{x}{5} = 3$

   $x = \boxed{}$

10. (MP) **Model with Mathematics** Glenn is 5 feet tall. He is $\frac{4}{5}$ as tall as his brother. How tall is Glenn's brother?

A. Write an equation to find Glenn's brother's height, using x to represent the height.

B. How can you solve this equation for x?

C. How tall is Glenn's brother in feet?

11. Iris made bracelets with string and beads. She used x centimeters of string and made 7 bracelets. She used 17.8 centimeters of string for each bracelet. How much string did she use in all? Write an equation and use it to solve this problem.

12. (MP) **Model with Mathematics** The price of a can of beans is shown. Jason has $8.69 to spend on beans. Write an equation to represent the situation, and solve the equation to find number of cans Jason can buy.

COST $0.79

For Problems 13–16, find each solution.

13. $9x = 171$

14. $\frac{x}{6} = 15$

15. $\frac{9}{5}x = 2\frac{7}{10}$

16. $\frac{x}{4} = 28.80$

I'm in a Learning Mindset!

How can I help a classmate develop a growth-mindset response?

Use Multiplication and Division Equations to Solve Problems

1. (MP) **Model with Mathematics** Selena buys 4 peaches that weigh 1 pound in all. Each peach weighs the same amount. Peaches are on sale for $2.24 per pound. Write and solve an equation to find the cost p of one peach. Graph the solution on a number line.

   _____

2. **STEM** A 120-volt battery is connected to a circuit with 30 ohms of resistance. The current in amperes c flowing through the circuit can be found using the equation $30c = 120$. How many amperes of current are in the wire?

   _____

3. **Math on the Spot** Solve each equation. Check your answer.

   A. $\frac{x}{7} = 2$ _____

   B. $36 = \frac{w}{4}$ _____

4. Mr. Falco baked several batches of blueberry muffins using the recipe shown. He used $3\frac{3}{4}$ cups of milk in all. How many batches of muffins did he bake? Use the equation $\frac{1}{4}x = 3\frac{3}{4}$.

   _____

Blueberry Muffin Recipe

$1\frac{1}{2}$ cups flour $\frac{3}{4}$ cup sugar
$\frac{1}{4}$ cup milk   1 egg
1 cup blueberries $\frac{1}{3}$ cup corn oil
$\frac{1}{2}$ teaspoon salt   2 teaspoons baking powder

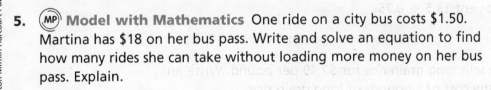

5. (MP) **Model with Mathematics** One ride on a city bus costs $1.50. Martina has $18 on her bus pass. Write and solve an equation to find how many rides she can take without loading more money on her bus pass. Explain.

   _____

For Problems 6–9, find each solution.

6. $\frac{x}{3} = 16$

   $x =$ ☐

7. $4x = 76$

   $x =$ ☐

8. $15x = 105$

   $x =$ ☐

9. $\frac{x}{8} = 10$

   $x =$ ☐

Test Prep

10. Bonnie buys 4 ounces of loose-leaf tea as a gift. The total cost of the tea is $25.00. Use the equation $4t = 25$. How much does each ounce of tea cost?

_____

11. Santos cuts a length of ribbon into 2-inch-long pieces. He has enough ribbon to make 10 pieces. What is the total length of the ribbon that Santos has? Use the equation $\frac{x}{2} = 10$.

_____

12. What is the solution to the equation $5x = 6$?

Ⓐ 1.2   Ⓒ 1

Ⓑ 0.83   Ⓓ 30

13. Mr. Nakamoto's gas tank is empty. He refills the 11.6-gallon tank in his car with gasoline that costs $2.58 per gallon. Which point on the number line shows how much Mr. Nakamoto pays for the gasoline? Use the equation $\frac{x}{11.6} = 2.58$.

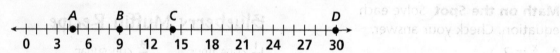

Ⓐ Point *A*

Ⓑ Point *B*

Ⓒ Point *C*

Ⓓ Point *D*

Spiral Review

14. What is the quotient $13.5 \div 0.75$?

_____

15. A grocery store sells long grain rice for $2.49 per pound. Write an expression for the cost of *y* pounds of long grain rice.

_____

16. Order the fractions from least to greatest.

$\frac{3}{8}, \frac{4}{12}, \frac{4}{9}, \frac{3}{6}, \frac{1}{4}$

_____

Name

Use One-Step Equations to Solve a Variety of Problems

(I Can) solve problems by writing and solving one-step equations.

Step it Out

1 The sum of the measures of the two **angles** shown is 180°. What is the unknown angle measure?

A. In the diagram, the unknown angle measure is labeled $x°$. What is the given angle measure?

_____

$x°$ $67°$

B. Write an equation to represent the relationship in the diagram.

□ + □ = 180

C. Solve the equation using the Subtraction Property of Equality.

□ + □ = 180

− □ − □

x = □

D. The unknown angle measure is □.

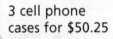
3 cell phone cases for $50.25

2 A store sells 3 cell phone cases for the price shown. Write and solve an equation to find how much money the store charges for each case.

A. Write an equation to represent this situation.

□ x = $ □

B. Solve the equation using the Division Property of Equality. What does x represent?

_____

Turn and Talk The sum of the measures of two angles is 90°. If the angles have the same measure, what is the measure of each angle? Explain.

3 ▶ Paul has his laptop open at a 105° angle. If he closes his laptop to a 19° angle or less, the laptop will go into sleep mode. How many **degrees** x does Paul need to close his laptop before it will go into sleep mode?

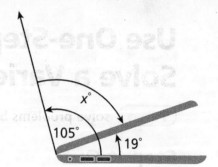

A. Write an equation you can use to solve for the unknown angle measure.

$x + \boxed{} = \boxed{}$

B. Solve the equation using the Subtraction Property of Equality.

$x + \boxed{} = \boxed{}$

$\quad - \boxed{} \quad - \boxed{}$

$\rule{3cm}{0.4pt}$

$\quad\quad x = \boxed{}$

C. The measure of the unknown angle is $\boxed{}$.

4 ▶ The picture shows the flat and angled positions that Kat likes her tablet in when drawing. The first viewing angle measures 180°. What is the measure of the unknown angle?

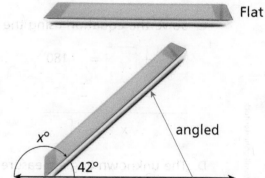

A. Write an equation you can use to find the second viewing angle.

$\boxed{} + x = \boxed{}$

B. Solve the equation.

$\boxed{} + x = \boxed{}$

$- \boxed{} \quad - \boxed{}$

$\rule{3cm}{0.4pt}$

$\boxed{} = \boxed{}$

C. The measure of the unknown angle is $\boxed{}$.

Check Understanding

1. The perimeter of a square is 68 inches. Write and solve an equation to find the length of each side.

2. Kamal makes $18.00 an hour at his job. Last week he earned $585. Write and solve an equation to determine how many hours Kamal worked last week.

© Houghton Mifflin Harcourt Publishing Company • Image Credit: ©Pakhnyushchyy/Shutterstock

On Your Own

3. **(MP) Model with Mathematics** In a pack of pretzel sticks, $\frac{1}{4}$ of the total number of pretzel sticks is 14. Write and solve an equation to find the total number of pretzel sticks in the pack x.

_____

_____

_____

4. The sum of Ryan's and Rene's ages is 35. If Ryan is 16 years old, how old is Rene?

   A. Let x represent Rene's age. Write and solve an equation for x.

   _____

   B. How old is Rene? _____

5. The triangular-shaped walking path in the park shown has a perimeter of 990 feet.

   A. Write an equation to find the length x of the third side of the path.

   _____

   B. Solve the equation. How long is the third side of the path? Show your work.

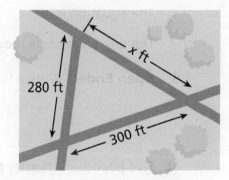

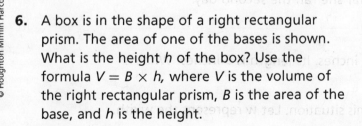

6. A box is in the shape of a right rectangular prism. The area of one of the bases is shown. What is the height h of the box? Use the formula $V = B \times h$, where V is the volume of the right rectangular prism, B is the area of the base, and h is the height.

$V = 121$ cubic inches

_____

7. The formula for the area A of a rectangle is $A = \ell \times w$. The formula for the perimeter P of a rectangle is $P = 2\ell + 2w$. The area of the front of a rectangular window flower box is shown.

$A = 10\frac{1}{2}$ square inches $w = 2\frac{1}{4}$ inches

ℓ

A. What is the length of the flower box? _____

B. What is the perimeter of the front of the flower box? _____

8. The sum of the measures of the two angles shown is 180°. Write and solve an equation to find the unknown angle measure.

43° $x°$

The equation is _____

The unknown angle measure is _____.

9. Open Ended Write a word problem for the equation $x - 6 = 20$.

_____

_____

10. Five pounds of cherries cost $14.95. Write and solve an equation to determine how much each pound of cherries costs.

_____

11. Sophie buys milk and vegetables at the grocery store. She spends $3.29 on milk and has a total bill of $15.56. Write and solve an equation to determine how much Sophie spends on the vegetables.

_____

12. Crystal ran 21.7 miles over two days. She ran 13.2 miles the first day. Write and solve an equation to find how far she ran the second day.

_____

13. The area of a rectangle is 36 square inches. Its length is 9 inches. What is its width?

A. Write an equation to represent this situation. Let w represent the width.

_____

B. What is its width? _____

LESSON 7.4
**More Practice/
Homework**

ONLINE
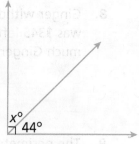
Video Tutorials and
Interactive Examples

Use One-Step Equations to Solve a Variety of Problems

1. The two angles shown have a combined measure of 90°. Write and solve an equation to find x. Show your work.

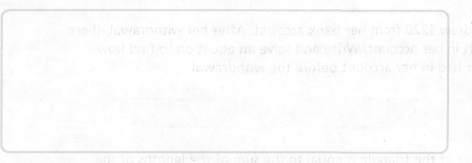

2. Janelle weighed an unknown substance. It had a mass of 20.609 grams. She exposed the substance to a flame and carefully weighed the substance again. The substance then had a mass of 17.39 grams. Write and solve an equation to determine the amount of mass x the substance lost.

_____

_____

3. (MP) **Model with Mathematics** Rosario is working on an 8 foot by 8 foot floor covered with 64 white tiles. She replaces x white tiles with blue tiles. After she's finished, there are 40 white tiles left. Write and solve an equation to find the number of blue floor tiles Rosario used.

4. **Math on the Spot** The distance between Professor Burger's house and Chris's house is 12 miles. Lila's house is on the way from Professor Burger's house to Chris's house. The distance between Lila's house and Chris's house is 5 miles. Write and solve an equation to find the distance x between Professor Burger's house and Lila's house.

_____

_____

5. (MP) **Model with Mathematics** A store had a sale on baseball cards, so Percy bought several baseball cards to give away as gifts. He gave a total of x baseball cards away to 5 friends. Each friend got 4 baseball cards. Write and solve an equation to figure out how many baseball cards Percy gave away.

_____

6. A swinging door opens to form a 90° angle. If the door is swung 36° closed, how many more degrees can the door close?

_____

Test Prep

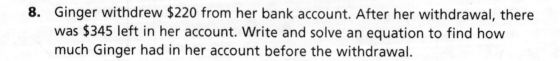

7. The area of a rectangle is 120 square inches. Its length is 15 inches. Write an equation to find its width. What is its width?

_____

8. Ginger withdrew $220 from her bank account. After her withdrawal, there was $345 left in her account. Write and solve an equation to find how much Ginger had in her account before the withdrawal.

_____

_____

9. The perimeter of the triangle is equal to the sum of the lengths of the three sides. The perimeter is 194.2 centimeters. Find the value of b.

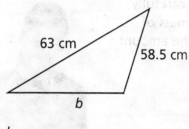

63 cm

58.5 cm

b

$b = $ _____

10. The sum of the measures of two angles is 90°. One angle has a measure of 32.8°. The measure of the other angle is represented by x. What is the value of x?

$x = $ _____

Spiral Review

11. Plot the following integers on the number line: −4, 6, −2, 5, −8.

$$\xleftarrow{\qquad}\overset{\displaystyle-10\ -8\ -6\ -4\ -2\quad 0\quad 2\quad 4\quad 6\quad 8\quad 10}{|\ \ |\ \ |\ \ |\ \ |\ \ |\ \ |\ \ |\ \ |\ \ |\ \ |\ \ |}\xrightarrow{\qquad}$$

12. A relay race covers a distance of $2\frac{1}{2}$ miles. Each runner on the team will run $\frac{1}{4}$ mile. How many runners are needed for the team to cover the total distance of the race?

_____

Name

Write and Graph Inequalities

(I Can) solve a one-step equation with negative integers, fractions, and decimals.

Step it Out

You can write inequalities using inequality symbols and variables to describe quantities that have many values.

Symbol	Meaning	Word phrases
<	Is less than	Fewer than, below
>	Is greater than	More than, above
≤	Is less than or equal to	At most, no more than
≥	Is greater than or equal to	At least, no less than

> **Connect to Vocabulary**
>
> An **inequality** is a mathematical sentence that shows the relationship between quantities that are not equal.

1 ▶ The temperature in Seminole, Texas, reached a record-setting low of −23 °F on February 8, 1933.

A. Find −23 and graph it on the number line.

$$-24\ -22\ -20\ -18\ -16\ -14\ -12\ -10\ -8\ -6\ -4\ -2\quad 0\quad 2\quad 4$$

B. The temperatures 4 °F, −3 °F, −14 °F, 1 °F, and −19 °F have also been recorded in Texas. How do these temperatures compare to −23 °F?

_____

C. Give examples of other numbers that are greater than −23. How many such numbers exist?

_____

D. Let x represent the temperatures greater than −23 °F. Complete the inequality to describe these temperatures.

x ☐ −23

 Turn and Talk How is a number line not like a thermometer? Explain.

The solutions of the inequality $x > 2$ are all numbers greater than 2, but not including 2.

An inequality such as $x > 2$ represents a **constraint**. A constraint is a condition that restricts the values of a quantity to a given value or range of values. For the inequality $x > 2$, the values of x must be greater than 2. So, 2 and numbers less than 2 are not solutions of $x > 2$.

For the inequality $x \leq 4$, the values of x must be less than or equal to 4. So, 4 is a solution of $x \leq 4$, but numbers greater than 4 are not solutions.

You must be 54 inches or taller.
$h \geq 54$

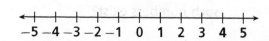
CAN YOU RIDE THIS RIDE?
YES
54"

2 ▷ Graph the inequalities.

A. $y \leq -3$

Step 1 Draw a solid circle at -3 to show that -3 is a solution.

$$-5\ -4\ -3\ -2\ -1\ \ 0\ \ 1\ \ 2\ \ 3\ \ 4\ \ 5$$

Step 2 Shade the number line to the left of -3 to show that numbers less than -3 are also solutions.

Step 3 Check your answer. Choose a number that is on the shaded section of the number line, such as -4. Substitute -4 for y. Since the inequality $-4 \leq -3$ is true, the graph on the number line appears to be correct. You can never check all the possible values for the variable, but checking one or two values helps assure that you have shaded the correct side of the number line.

B. $1 < m$

Step 1 Draw an empty circle at 1 to show that 1 is *not* a solution.

$$-5\ -4\ -3\ -2\ -1\ \ 0\ \ 1\ \ 2\ \ 3\ \ 4\ \ 5$$

Step 2 Shade the number line to the right of 1 to show that numbers greater than 1 are solutions.

Step 3 Check your answer. Pick a number for m that falls on the shaded section of the number line. $1 < \boxed{}$. Is the inequality you have written true? _____

Turn and Talk Think of a situation you have faced where something must be greater than a certain amount. Think of a second situation where something must be greater than or equal to a certain amount. Explain each scenario and then write inequalities to represent each situation.

You can write inequalities to represent certain real-world situations.

3 ▶ Use inequalities to solve these problems.

A. The temperature is at most −2 °F. What could be the temperature *t*?

Are numbers less than −2 part of the solution? _____

Are numbers greater than −2 part of the solution? _____

Is −2 part of the solution? _____

Write the inequality. *t* [ ] −2

B. Raphael needs to buy more than 4 concert tickets. How many tickets *t* could he buy?

Are numbers less than 4 part of the solution? _____

Are numbers greater than 4 part of the solution? _____

Is 4 part of the solution? _____

Write the inequality. *t* [ ] 4

How many tickets can Raphael buy?

Graph the inequality. Use an open circle at 4 because the value 4 is not a solution.

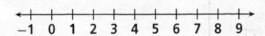

Check Understanding

1. A pilot needs to log at least 500 flying hours before earning a pilot's license. Write and graph an inequality to show the number of flying hours *h* a pilot needs to get a license.

_____

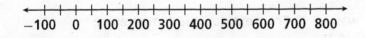

For Problems 2–3, graph each inequality.

2. $r \leq 8$

‹—+—+—+—+—+—+—+—+—+—+—›
−1 0 1 2 3 4 5 6 7 8 9

3. $z < -3$

‹—+—+—+—+—+—+—+—+—+—›
−7 −6 −5 −4 −3 −2 −1 0 1

On Your Own

4. When cooking chicken, the recommended internal temperature of the chicken is the temperature shown. A lower internal temperature will undercook the chicken. Write an inequality that is true only for temperatures *t* at which the chicken will be undercooked. _____

   internal temp. 165 °F

   Graph the inequality.

   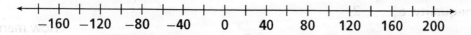
   ```
   ←――+――+――+――+――+――+――+――+――+――+――→
     −160 −120  −80  −40   0   40   80  120  160  200
   ```

5. **STEM** The speed of sound is approximately 761 miles per hour. For an object to produce a sonic boom, it must travel faster than the speed of sound. Write an inequality that is true only for speeds *s* at which a moving object will produce a sonic boom. _____

6. To find the area *A* of a rectangle, the length ℓ must be multiplied by the width *w*. A farmer needs to build a fence to enclose a chicken pen with an area greater than or equal to 50 square feet. The length of the fence must be 10 feet.

   ℓ = 10 feet

   | A ≥ 50 square feet |

   w

   A. Write an inequality that is true only for the widths *w* that will yield a fenced-in area of at least 50 square feet. _____

   B. Graph the inequality.

   ```
   ←+――+――+――+――+――+――+――+――+――+――+――→
    −1  0   1   2   3   4   5   6   7   8   9
   ```

7. The temperature in Minneapolis was −9 °F. The next day, the temperature in Minneapolis was warmer than −9 °F.

   A. Write an inequality which is true only for temperatures *t* that were warmer than −9 °F.

   _____

   B. Could the temperature have been −12 °F in Minneapolis on the next day? Why or why not?

   _____

   _____

8. A. Graph the inequality $d \leq -2$.

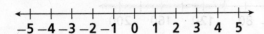

-5 -4 -3 -2 -1 0 1 2 3 4 5

B. **Reason** Name three solutions for d. How many possible solutions does this inequality have?

_____

9. Write an inequality that describes the graph. Use y for the variable.

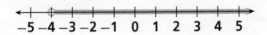

-5 -4 -3 -2 -1 0 1 2 3 4 5

_____

10. To have enough orange juice for all the campers, the camp cook will need at least 9 gallons.

A. Write an inequality that is true only for the number of gallons g the cook needs.

_____

B. Graph the inequality.

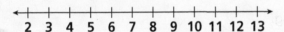

2 3 4 5 6 7 8 9 10 11 12 13

C. If the cook buys 4 gallons, will he have enough? _____

11. According to government guidelines, drones are limited to how high they can legally fly above the ground as shown. See the image for the maximum height.

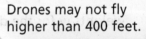

Drones may not fly higher than 400 feet.

A. Write an inequality that is true only for the height h a drone can fly above the ground.

_____

B. If a drone flies 430 feet above the ground, will it violate government guidelines? Explain.

_____

_____

12. Write an inequality that represents the graph. Use x for the variable.

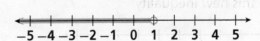

-5 -4 -3 -2 -1 0 1 2 3 4 5

_____

13. A. Write an inequality that represents the graph. Use x for the variable.

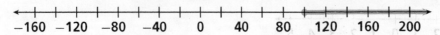

B. Choose a number from the shaded part of the number line to check your inequality. State the number you picked and explain why it is a possible solution.

_____

_____

14. Graph the inequality on the number line: $b \geq -14$.

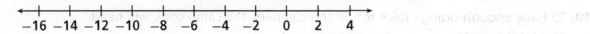

15. Graph the inequality on the number line: $d < 25$.

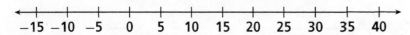

16. A dog weighs less than 15 pounds.

A. List three possible weights for the dog.

_____

B. Write an inequality that is true only for the possible weights w for the dog. _____

C. Some puppies can be born with a weight of $\frac{1}{5}$ of a pound. Can any dog ever weigh 0 pounds or

less? _____

D. An inequality can be written with a variable between two numbers if that variable must be greater than one number and less than another number. Write a new, more accurate inequality to describe the dog's possible weight by writing an inequality symbol in each blank.

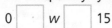

E. Graph this new inequality.

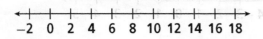

less than
15 pounds

17. Open Ended Describe a situation that can be modeled by the inequality $x < 7$.

_____

Solve One-St..p Equations Involving Negative N..mbers

(I Can) solve a one-s..p equation with negative integers, fra..ons, and decimals.

Step It Out

To keep a balan.. ..evel, you must add or subtract the sa.. amount of weight to or from each side. Sim..rly, when solving an equation, you isolate ..e variable by applying the same operation.. each side of the equation.

1 W..te operation symbols and numbers to solve each equation.

A. $x + 11 = -5$

$x + 11 - \boxed{} = -5 \bigcirc \boxed{}$

$x + 0 = \boxed{}$

$x = \boxed{}$

B. $x - 10 = -3$

$x - 10 + \boxed{} = -3 \bigcirc \boxed{}$

$x = \boxed{}$

C. $x + \frac{7}{10} = \frac{3}{5}$

$x + \frac{7}{10} - \boxed{} = \frac{6}{10} \bigcirc \boxed{}$

$x = -\dfrac{1}{\boxed{}}$

D. $x - 4.2 = -9.6$

$x - 4.2 + \boxed{} = -9.6 \bigcirc \boxed{}$

$x = \boxed{}$

 Turn and Talk How is solving a one-step equation involving negative numbers like solving a one-step equation with positive numbers?

© Houghton Mifflin Harcourt Publishing Company • Image Credit: ©Vaniato/Shutterst..

2 Select the words that complete the statements. Then solve the equation.

A. $-4x = -20$

In this equation, x is [multiplied / divided] by -4.

To solve the equation, [multiply / divide] each side of the equation by -4.

$x = \boxed{}$

B. $\frac{x}{-2.1} = 3$

In this equation, x is [multiplied / divided] by $\boxed{}$.

To solve the equation, [multiply / divide] each side of the equation

by $\boxed{}$.

$x = \boxed{}$

C. $-\frac{3}{4}x = 15$

In this equation, x is [multiplied / divided] by $\boxed{}$.

To solve the equation, multiply each side of the equation by $\boxed{}$.

$x = \boxed{}$

Turn and Talk To solve the equation in Part C of Task 2, why do you think both sides were multiplied by $-\frac{4}{3}$, instead of being divided by $-\frac{3}{4}$?

Check Understanding

Solve each equation. Simplify your answer.

1. $x + \frac{7}{18} = \frac{2}{9}$

2. $k + (-1.7) = -1.9$

3. $y - 5 = -12$

4. $7t = -21$

5. $-\frac{4}{13}z = -\frac{1}{3}$

6. $\frac{a}{-5.4} = 30$

On Your Own

For Problems 7–10, identify operations that will solve the equation in one step when performed on each side. Select all that apply.

7. $x + 23 = 17$

Ⓐ Add 23.

Ⓑ Add −23.

Ⓒ Subtract 23.

Ⓓ Subtract −23.

Ⓔ Add 17.

Ⓕ Subtract 17.

8. $x - 8.5 = 12.7$

Ⓐ Add 8.5.

Ⓑ Subtract 8.5.

Ⓒ Add −8.5.

Ⓓ Subtract −8.5.

Ⓔ Add 12.7.

Ⓕ Subtract 12.7.

9. $6x = -42$

Ⓐ Multiply by 6.

Ⓑ Multiply by $\frac{1}{6}$.

Ⓒ Multiply by $-\frac{1}{42}$.

Ⓓ Divide by 6.

Ⓔ Divide by $\frac{1}{6}$.

Ⓕ Divide by −42.

10. $-\frac{5}{7}x = \frac{25}{14}$

Ⓐ Multiply by $-\frac{5}{7}$.

Ⓑ Divide by $-\frac{5}{7}$.

Ⓒ Multiply by $-\frac{7}{5}$.

Ⓓ Divide by $-\frac{7}{5}$.

Ⓔ Multiply by $\frac{25}{14}$.

Ⓕ Divide by $\frac{25}{14}$.

11. Ⓜⓟ **Model with Mathematics** Katie lives in the Florida Keys. She loves to dive and take pictures of marine life. During her last dive, she used her depth gauge to change her position relative to sea level by −4.5 feet to reach her goal, −12 feet. Let x represent her initial position. Write and solve an equation to find x.

© Houghton Mifflin Harcourt Publishing Company • Image Credit: ©sirtravelalot/Shutterstock.com

For Problems 12–27, solve the equation. Simplify your answer.

12. $y + 8 = -25$

_____

13. $-17 + b = 68$

_____

14. $d + 4.4 = -11.7$

_____

15. $7m = -4$

_____

16. $-24p = 60$

_____

17. $-1.8b = -12.6$

_____

18. $\frac{x}{18} = -5$

_____

19. $\frac{h}{-3} = -14$

_____

20. $\frac{n}{-4} = 10.4$

_____

21. $-21 + j = -50$

_____

22. $s - \frac{21}{25} = \frac{3}{5}$

_____

23. $z + 62 = 54.8$

_____

24. $-\frac{11}{3}r = -44$

_____

25. $\frac{5}{12} + k = -\frac{1}{3}$

_____

26. $\frac{x}{1.5} = -14$

_____

27. $m - 3.52 = -1.47$

_____

28. A. Open Ended Write a word problem that can be represented by the equation $\frac{3}{4}p = -60$.

_____

_____

_____

_____

B. Solve the equation, and give the solution to your problem.

_____

_____

Solve One-Step Equations Involving Negative Numbers

1. **(MP) Critique Reasoning** Scott solves the equation $y - (-9.7) = -2.8$. When he checks his work, he realizes that he made a mistake. Identify Scott's error and find the correct solution.

$$y - (-9.7) = -2.8$$
$$y - (-9.7) + 9.7 = -2.8 + 9.7$$
$$y = 6.9$$

Check:
$$6.9 - (-9.7) \stackrel{?}{=} -2.8$$
$$16.6 \neq -2.8$$

_____

_____

_____

2. Tolu, Abram, and Nevis are partners in a new business. The bank account for the business currently shows a balance of −$123.45, so the partners agree to pay equal amounts to bring the balance to $0. Write and solve an equation using negative numbers to find each partner's share of the balance.

Our balance is −$123.45.

Let's bring it up to 0.

_____

_____

For Problems 3–11, solve the equation. Simplify your answer.

3. $x - 4 = -25$

4. $-8y = -70$

5. $z + 18 = -43$

_____

6. $\frac{a}{2.5} = -30$

7. $-1.15 + b = 2.37$

8. $0.6b = -19.2$

_____

9. $p + \frac{1}{4} = -\frac{1}{7}$

10. $-\frac{4}{3}q = \frac{8}{9}$

11. $-\frac{15}{16} + r = \frac{3}{8}$

Test Prep

12. What is the solution of $-\frac{7}{12} + k = -\frac{2}{3}$?

(A) $-\frac{5}{4}$

(B) $-\frac{3}{5}$

(C) $-\frac{5}{9}$

(D) $-\frac{1}{12}$

13. What is the solution of $\frac{x}{8} = -6.4$?

(A) -51.2

(B) -0.8

(C) 0.8

(D) 51.2

14. What is the solution of $s + 5.3 = -9.1$?

(A) 14.4

(B) 3.8

(C) -3.8

(D) -14.4

15. What is the solution of $-\frac{10}{21}d = \frac{12}{35}$?

(A) $-\frac{18}{25}$

(B) $-\frac{8}{49}$

(C) $\frac{8}{49}$

(D) $\frac{18}{25}$

Spiral Review

16. The temperature at 7:00 p.m. decreases by 20 °F to −12 °F at 3:00 a.m. Which equation can be used to find the temperature T at 7:00 p.m.?

(A) $T - 12 = -20$

(B) $T - 20 = -12$

(C) $T - 12 = 20$

(D) $20 - T = -12$

17. Find the quotient.

$253.26 \div 20.1$

_____

18. Simplify the expression.

$(4x - 9) - (-3x + 17)$

_____

19. Andrea is enjoying the novel she is reading. She had read 431 pages when she checked yesterday. She read more this afternoon and has now read a total of 487 pages. Write and solve an equation to find how many pages Andrea read today.

_____

Module 7 Review

Vocabulary

Choose the correct term from the Vocabulary box.

Vocabulary
equation
inequality
solution
solution of the inequality

1. a mathematical sentence that shows the relationship between quantities that are not equal _____

2. a mathematical sentence that shows that two expressions are equivalent _____

3. 3 is the _____ of the equation $b + 2 = 5$.

4. 8 is a _____ $x < 10$.

Concepts and Skills

5. A Komodo dragon can grow to be 120 inches long. One Komodo dragon is 92 inches long.

   A. Write an equation you can use to find the number of inches x it still needs to grow to be 120 inches long.

   _____

   B. Solve the equation. How many inches does the Komodo dragon still need to grow to be 120 inches long?

   _____

6. (MP) **Use Tools** Dakota has been assigned 80 math problems that are due in 5 days.

   A. Write an equation you can use to find how many problems she should do each day if she wants to do the same number each day. Choose any letter for the variable and explain what it represents.

   _____

   _____

   _____

   B. How many problems should Dakota do each day? State what strategy and tool you will use to answer the question, explain your choice, and then find the answer.

   _____

   _____

7. Karen used one-third of her total stamps on a campaign for charity. Karen used 60 stamps on the charity campaign.

    A. Write an equation you could use to find how many stamps she had at the start. Choose any letter for the variable and explain what it represents.

    _____

    _____

    B. Solve the equation. How many stamps did Karen start with?

    _____

8. Denise used 22.5 gallons of water in the shower. This amount is 7.5 gallons less than the amount she used for washing clothes. Write and solve an equation to find the amount of water x Denise used to wash clothes.

    _____

    _____

9. In a visit to Glacier National Park in Montana, Vera hiked a total of 138 miles in 12 days. She hiked the same distance each day. Write and solve an equation to find the number of miles m she hiked each day.

    _____

10. The temperature underwent a change of -18 degrees Fahrenheit between noon and midnight. It changed by the same amount each hour. Write and solve an equation to find h, the hourly change in temperature.

    _____

For Problems 11–13, write and graph an inequality for each situation.

11. The width w is at least 10 inches.

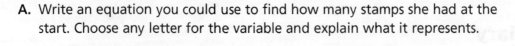

12. The truck has a weight t of more than 2 tons.

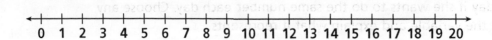

13. The temperature t was below 12 °C.

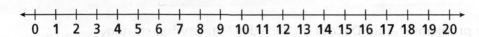

Real-World Relationships Between Variables

Which Relationship Does NOT Belong?

Describe the pattern shown by each relationship.

A.

Number of markers	Cost ($)
5	3
10	6
15	9

C.

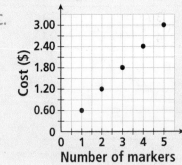

_____

_____

_____

_____

B.

> **Package of 8 markers: $4**
> **Package of 16 markers: $8**

D.

_____

_____

_____

 Turn and Talk

- Which relationship does not belong? Explain why.

- Which relationship represents the best deal? Explain your reasoning.

Are You Ready?

Complete these problems to review prior concepts and skills you will need for this module.

Generate Patterns and Relationships

Describe a pattern you see in each table. Use the pattern to complete each table.

1.

x	y
0	0
1	6
2	12
3	
4	

2.

x	y
0	8
1	13
2	18
3	
4	

_____

_____

_____

Identify Points on a Coordinate Grid

Write the ordered pair for each point.

3. A _____

4. B _____

5. C _____

6. D _____

7. E _____

8. F _____

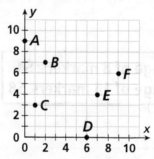

Graph and label each ordered pair on the coordinate grid.

9. G(0, 7)

10. H(3, 8)

11. I(5, 5)

12. J(1, 0)

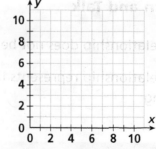

Name _____

Represent Equations in Tables and Graphs

(I Can) make a table to represent the equation for a real-world relationship, and I can graph the ordered pairs from the table.

Spark Your Learning

PAIRS

A baby gorilla had a mass of 2,620 grams at birth, 2,960 grams after 10 days, and 3,300 grams after 20 days. What is the average number of grams that the baby gorilla grew each day during the first 10 days and during the next 10 days? Show your work.

x	y

Turn and Talk If the baby gorilla continued to grow the same average number of grams each day for the first month after birth, what would be the baby gorilla's mass 30 days after birth? Explain how you found your answer.

Build Understanding

Many real-world situations involve two variable quantities in which one quantity depends on the other. The quantity that depends on the other quantity is the **dependent variable**, and the quantity that it depends on is the **independent variable**. The dependent variable is typically recorded on the y-axis.

1 ▷ The Jackson family is driving to visit family members who live out of state. They record the following information about their trip.

Hours	Miles
2	130
3	195
4	260
5	325

A. Which of the two quantities is the independent quantity, and which is the dependent quantity? Explain.

_____

_____

_____

B. How far does the car travel each hour? How do you know?

_____

_____

_____

C. Suppose that *d* represents the distance traveled by the car in miles and that *t* represents the time in hours the car has been traveling. How can you model the relationship between the distance traveled, in miles, by the car and the time, in hours, using an equation? Use *d* for distance and *t* for time in hours.

Distance traveled (miles)	=	Distance traveled each hour	·	Time (hours)
⬇	⬇	⬇	⬇	⬇
☐	=	☐	·	☐

D. A student represented this relationship as $65t = d$. Is this student correct? Why or why not?

_____

_____

_____

Name _____

Step It Out

When one variable depends on a second variable, the relationship between the variables can be represented in a table or by an equation. An equation can be used to express the dependent variable in terms of the independent variable.

Pablo walks dogs to earn money.

2 Pablo walks dogs after school. His earnings e, in dollars, are represented by the equation $e = 24h$, where h is the number of hours he works.

A. Complete the table.

Hours worked, h	1	2	3	4
Earnings, e			$72	

B. To determine values in the table, multiply each value of the independent

variable, ☐, by ☐ to find the corresponding value of the

dependent variable, ☐.

3 Each egg carton holds one dozen eggs. The equation $n = 12c$ shows the number of eggs n in c cartons.

A. Use the equation to complete the table.

Number of cartons, c	1		5	
Number of eggs, n	12	24		96

B. To find the missing values in the table, sometimes I multiplied a value

of the independent variable, ☐, by ☐ to get each corresponding

value of the dependent variable, ☐. Other times I divided a value of

the dependent variable by ☐ to get the value of the independent
variable, c.

Turn and Talk In Tasks 2 and 3, do the equations and the tables describe the same relationships? Explain how you know.

© Houghton Mifflin Harcourt Publishing Company

Module 8 • Lesson 1

297

4 The distance in meters that Kaycia hikes in *x* minutes is represented by the equation $y = 75x$.

A. Complete the table.

Minutes, *x*	Meters, *y*
5	
15	
	1,500
	2,250

75 meters per minute

B. How did you find the value of *y* when *x* = 5?

_____

_____

C. How did you find the value of *x* when *y* = 1,500?

_____

_____

_____

D. Write the ordered pairs from the table.

(☐ , ☐), (☐ , ☐), (☐ , ☐)

(☐ , ☐)

E. Graph the ordered pairs on the **coordinate grid**.

F. Your points should follow a straight line pattern. Because Kaycia is hiking between the times represented by the points, you can draw a line through points. Draw this line on the graph.

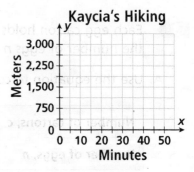

Kaycia's Hiking

y-axis: Meters — 0, 750, 1,500, 2,250, 3,000
x-axis: Minutes — 0, 10, 20, 30, 40, 50

 Turn and Talk Why might graphing a set of paired values be better than displaying them in a table?

Check Understanding

1. The equation $p = \frac{2}{5}m$ shows the number of book pages *p* Ellen reads in *m* minutes. What is the dependent variable? What is the independent variable?

   Complete the table. _____

2. A box of cereal costs $3. Write an equation to relate the number of boxes *b* to total cost *T*. _____

m	*p*
10	
	8
	12
60	

On Your Own

3. The total cost C, in dollars, to dry clean a certain number of shirts s is given by the equation $C = 3.25s$.

   A. What is the dependent variable? _____

   What is the independent variable? _____

   B. Complete the table to relate the total cost to the number of shirts dry cleaned.

Shirts, s	3			10
Cost, C		$16.25	$26.00	

   C. Plot the points on a graph.

   D. (MP) **Reason** Should you draw a straight line through the points on the graph, or should you leave them as separate points? Explain.

Dry Cleaning

_____

_____

4. (MP) **Model with Mathematics** Dennis is floating down the river on a raft. The table shows the distance he travels over time. Write an equation that represents the number of kilometers k he travels in h hours.

Hours, h	0.5	2	3	5
Kilometers, k	0.75	3	4.5	7.5

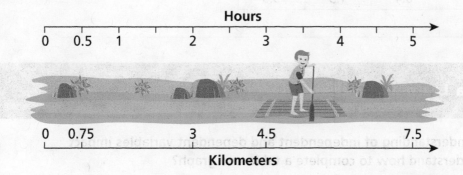

5. Gary has a sister named Tina. Their ages are related by the equation $G = T + 4.5$ where G stands for Gary's age and T stands for Tina's age.

   A. Complete the table to show Gary's and Tina's ages over time.

Tina			7	10
Gary	7	10		

   B. Write the ordered pairs from the table.

   (☐ , ☐), (☐ , ☐), (☐ , ☐), (☐ , ☐),

   C. Graph the ordered pairs on the coordinate grid.

   D. (MP) **Reason** Should you draw a straight line through the points on the graph, or should you leave them as separate points? Explain.

   _____

   _____

Sibling Ages

(Graph with x-axis "Tina's age" 0 to 20 and y-axis "Gary's age" 0 to 20.)

6. The equation $y = 1.19x$, gives the cost y, in dollars, of x pounds of pasta. Complete the table to represent the relationship.

x	2	3	5	8
y				

PASTA $1.19 PER POUND

For Problems 7–8, write an equation to represent each table of values.

7.

t	4	6	9	15
d	228	342	513	855

_____

8.

x	3.8	4.2	5.1	7.3
y	0	0.4	1.3	3.5

_____

 I'm in a Learning Mindset!

How does my understanding of independent and dependent variables impact my ability to understand how to complete a table and graph?

_____

_____

Represent Equations in Tables and Graphs

1. The price of green beans at a supermarket is shown in the table. Write an equation for the total cost *C*, in dollars, of *p* pounds of green beans.

Pounds of green beans, *p*	0.8	1.2	1.5	0.6
Total cost, *C*	$2.40	$3.60	$4.50	$1.80

_____

2. **STEM** Joules and calories are two different units of energy. The equation $j = 0.239c$ relates the measures, where *c* stands for calories and *j* stands for joules. Complete the table.

c	3	7	10	50
j				

3. **Math on the Spot** A car wash attendant counted the number of cars washed and the total amount of money earned. The company charged the same price for each car washed and earned $165 for 15 cars, $231 for 21 cars, and $275 for 25 cars. Write an equation for the relationship between the number of cars washed *n* and the number of dollars earned *m*.

n	15	21	25
m	165	231	275

4. Data for the fastest long-distance train in the United States as of 2018 are shown, where *t* is the time in minutes, and *d* is the distance in miles.

$d = 2.5t$

A. What is the dependent variable? What is the independent variable? _____

B. Complete the table.

t	3		10	
d		15		28

For Problems 5–6, write an equation representing each table of values.

5.
x	17	14	29
y	25	22	37

6.
d	9	12	16
g	135	180	240

_____

7. The perimeter p of a regular hexagon is found using the equation $p = 6s$. The length of each side is s. Complete the table to represent the relationship.

s	5	12		
p		72	21	54

8. Does the graph match the values in the table?

x	4	8	12	16
y	12	24	36	48

The graph ⎣ does / does not ⎦ match the values in the table.

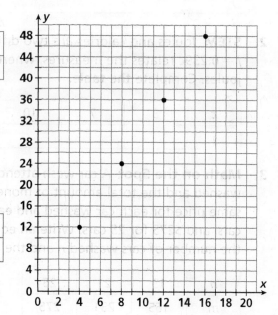

9. The distance m in miles, traveled by an airplane in h hours of flying is shown in the table. What equation represents the situation?

h	1.5	2.5	4	7
m	810	1,350	2,160	3,780

10. Write an equation to represent each table of values.

n	2.5	3.2	4.5	5.4
p	3.0	3.7	5.0	5.9

Spiral Review

11. Write an inequality that represents the sentence, "y is less than 3." Then graph the inequality.

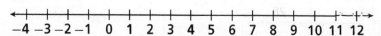

12. Sally pays $50.00 for a meal that costs $38.13. She tells the server to keep the difference as a tip. How much is the tip?

Name _____

Write Equations from Verbal Descriptions

(I Can) write linear equations from verbal descriptions and use them to solve problems.

Step It Out

1 ▷ Ms. Tran tutors students in mathematics. Her rate is shown. How much does Ms. Tran earn tutoring for any number of hours?

Tutoring rate: $25.50 per hour

A. Identify the independent and dependent variables.

Let x represent the number of hours Ms. Tran tutors.

Let y represent the number of dollars per hour Ms. Tran earns for tutoring.

☐ is the independent variable.

☐ is the dependent variable.

B. Write an equation to represent the situation.

Ms. Tran's total earnings in dollars	=	Number of dollars earned per hour	·	Number of hours spent tutoring
☐	=	25.5	·	☐

The equation that represents the situation is _____.

 Turn and Talk How did you determine which variable is the independent variable?

2 An orchestra will give a concert. There are 1,500 seats in the concert hall. Some tickets have been sold. How many tickets remain?

A. Identify the independent and dependent variables.

Let x represent the number of tickets sold.

Let y represent the number of tickets that remain.

[ ] is the independent variable.

[ ] is the dependent variable.

Conductor and Orchestra

B. Write and solve an equation representing the situation.

Number of tickets that remain	$=$	Number of seats in the concert hall	$-$	Number of tickets sold

[ ] $=$ 1,500 $-$ [ ]

The equation that represents the situation is _____.

C. So far, 847 tickets have been sold. How many tickets remain?

Substitute 847 for x in the equation. $y = 1{,}500 - $ [ ]

Subtract to solve for y. $y = $ [ ]

Given that 847 tickets to the concert have been sold, [ ] tickets remain.

 Turn and Talk Are there other equations that you can write to represent this situation? Explain.

Check Understanding

1. Jim gives the cashier at the pharmacy a $20 bill. Let b be the cost of his purchases in dollars, and let c be the change he gets back in dollars. Which variable is the independent variable? Write an equation for this situation. How much change does he get back if his purchases total $12.83?

_____

2. A hot-air balloon is 45 meters above the top of the tallest building in a city. Write an equation to show the height b of the balloon in meters if the tallest building is t meters tall.

_____

On Your Own

3. Rosa earns $12.25 per hour working at an ice-cream shop.

   A. Write an equation that shows Rosa's earnings e, in dollars, for h hours of working at the ice-cream shop.

   _____

   B. How much does Rosa earn for working $19\frac{1}{2}$ hours? Round your answer to the nearest cent.

   _____

4. Lin is running a marathon.

   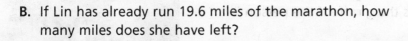

   A marathon is 26.2 miles long.

   A. Write an equation that shows the number of miles y she has left to run after running x miles.

   _____

   B. If Lin has already run 19.6 miles of the marathon, how many miles does she have left?

   _____

5. (MP) **Use Structure** You want to make $2\frac{1}{2}$ times as many muffins as your friend's recipe makes. Write an equation that shows how to find the amount of each ingredient you will need for the adjusted recipe. Let x represent the amount of each ingredient in the original recipe and y represent the amount of each ingredient in the adjusted recipe.

   _____

(MP) **Model with Mathematics** For Problems 6–9, write an equation to represent each situation.

6. Neil pays $19.99 for each shirt he buys. How many total dollars p does he pay for s shirts?

   _____

7. Omar has been practicing violin for $4\frac{1}{2}$ years longer than his sister. If his sister has been practicing for x years, how many years y has Omar been practicing violin?

   _____

8. A coupon discounts the total grocery bill by $3.50. How many dollars g is the bill after the discount if the bill before the discount is b dollars?

   _____

9. Tickets for a local dog show cost $9.75 each. What is the total cost c, in dollars, for t tickets?

   _____

10. **STEM** Scientists measure temperature in degrees Celsius and in kelvin. The temperature in kelvin is 273.15 greater than the temperature in degrees Celsius.

    A. What is an equation that relates the temperature K, in kelvins, to the temperature C, in degrees Celsius?

    _____

    B. What is the temperature in kelvins of a gas that has a temperature of 5 °C? _____

11. **Open Ended** Describe a scenario that matches the equation $y = \frac{3}{2}x$.

    _____

    _____

12. A giraffe is 3 times as tall as a person. Write an equation for the height g, in meters, of a giraffe if the person is t meters tall. How tall is the giraffe if the person is 1.85 meters tall?

    _____

13. Kayla walked 1,392 fewer steps than her mother walked. Write an equation for the number of steps w Kayla walked if her mother walked s steps. If her mother walked 11,258 steps, how many steps did Kayla walk?

    _____

14. The diameter of a tree increases by about $\frac{1}{8}$ inch each year. Write an equation that represents x, the increase in the diameter of the tree, in the last y years. How much has the diameter increased in the last 15 years?

    _____

15. (MP) **Model with Mathematics** Ramon wants to collect $250 in donations to support his favorite charity. He has collected f dollars from his friends and family but has not reached his goal. Write an equation that describes the number of dollars d Ramon still needs to collect to meet his goal.

    _____

16. Ms. Quinn pays $16.99 per person to take several friends to lunch. Write an equation that represents the cost C, in dollars, that Ms. Quinn pays for f friends. How much does she pay for 7 friends?

    _____

Write Equations from Verbal Descriptions

1. (MP) **Model with Mathematics** The area of a floor in square yards is one-ninth the area of the floor in square feet. Write an equation relating y, the area in square yards, to f, the area in square feet.

_____

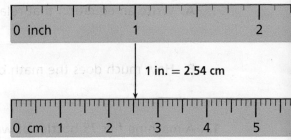

1 in. = 2.54 cm

2. Write an equation that relates the number of centimeters c to the number of inches i. Determine the height in centimeters of a chair that is 32 inches tall.

_____

3. (MP) **Model with Mathematics** Michael practiced his harmonica 3 times as long as Timothy did. Write an equation that represents the relationship between the amount of time Timothy practiced x and the amount of time Michael practiced y.

_____

4. Caleb has read 17 more books than his friend Liana. Write an equation that represents the relationship between n, the number of books Caleb has read, and p, the number of books Liana has read.

_____

(MP) **Model with Mathematics** For Problems 5–10, write an equation for each description.

5. Felix sold 35 fewer raffle tickets than Helene. How many tickets F did Felix sell if Helene sold H tickets?

_____

6. Sloane works $7\frac{1}{2}$ hours each day. How many hours h does Sloane work in d days?

_____

7. A grocery store charges $2.49 per pound for organic apples. What is the cost c, in dollars, of p pounds of organic apples?

_____

8. Paula used $1\frac{3}{4}$ cups of flour for a recipe. How many cups y of flour does Paula have if she had x cups before making the recipe?

_____

9. Each crate holds 135 avocados. How many avocados a are in c crates?

_____

10. Every delivery order from a pizzeria has a delivery charge of $1.50. How many dollars b is the total bill for a delivery of one pizza if the pizza costs p dollars?

_____

Test Prep

11. Edith bought a science book and a math book for her college classes. The cost *s*, in dollars, of the science book is $28.75 more than the cost *m*, in dollars, of the math book.

    A. Write an equation that relates the prices of the two books.

    B. How much does the math book cost if the science book cost $78.50?

12. A machine fills 75 bottles of water each minute. Write an equation to represent the number of bottles *b* of water the machine can fill in *m* minutes.

13. Ken said he would sell 30 tickets to the school play. Write an equation to relate the number of tickets *t* he has left to sell to the number of tickets *s* he has already sold. Which variable is the dependent variable?

14. Viola is making bracelets to sell at a craft fair. Each bracelet will have 20 beads. Write an equation to relate the number of beads *b* she has to the number of bracelets *x* she can make.

Spiral Review

15. Roberto paid $35.75 for dinner at a restaurant, plus an additional $7.15 tip. Idil paid a total of $41.13 for dinner, including the tip. Who paid more? How much more?

16. Write an equation to represent the values in the table.

x	3	8	13	18
y	0	5	10	15

17. A 5-pound bag of organic brown rice costs $12.99. A 12-pound bag of the same type of rice costs $31.99. How much does each cost per pound?

Write Equations from Tables and Graphs

(I Can) use a table or graph to write an equation for a linear relationships.

Step It Out

1 Use the table to complete each statement.

x	y
2	10
3.25	11.25
4.5	12.5
5.75	13.75
7	15

A. Look at the table for patterns. Describe the patterns found in the table.

As x increases by ☐ , y increases by ☐ .

Each value of y is _____ units _____ than the corresponding value of x.

B. Write a verbal model describing an equation in the form $y = x + p$ to represent the relationship between the values in the table.

_____

_____

C. Write an equation using the verbal model.

_____

> **Turn and Talk** What would be the value of x in the table if the corresponding value of y were 25.2? Explain.

2 Mara is making bracelets. For every red bead, she uses 4 green beads. The graph represents this situation. Use the graph to complete each part.

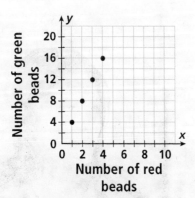

A. Read the ordered pairs from the graph. Use them to complete the table.

Red beads, x	Green beads, y

B. Look at the table for patterns. Describe the patterns found in the table.

As x increases by _____, y increases by _____.

Each value of y is _____ the corresponding value of x.

C. Write a verbal model of the form y = px to represent the relationship between the values in the table

_____

_____

D. Write an equation using the verbal model.

_____

 Turn and Talk In Task 2, would it make sense to draw a line through the points on the graph? Explain why or why not.

You can model real-world situations using an equation.

3 The graph shows the distance d, in miles, a car traveled over time t, in hours.

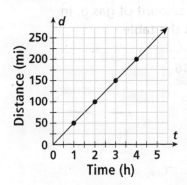

A. Write the coordinates of the points on the graph as ordered pairs.

(☐ , ☐), (☐ , ☐), (☐ , ☐), and (☐ , ☐)

B. Complete the sentence to describe the pattern shown in the graph.

As the first coordinate of a point increases by _____, the second coordinate of the point increases by _____.

C. The value of the distance d, in miles, is always _____ times the value of the time t, in hours. So the equation that models the relationship is

_____

 Turn and Talk In Task 3, explain why it makes sense to draw a line through the points.

Check Understanding

Write an equation representing each table or graph.

1.

x	y
0	12
1	13
2	14
3	15
4	16

2.

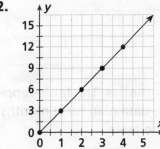

On Your Own

3. (MP) **Construct Arguments** The table below represents the distance driven on different amounts of gas. Write an equation that models the relationship between the distance d, in miles, and the amount of gas g, in gallons. Explain your answer by describing a pattern in the table.

Distance (d) in miles	120	144	168	192	216
Gas (g) in gallons	5	6	7	8	9

4. The graph represents the relationship between the total cost, in dollars, of a city taxi and the number of miles driven.

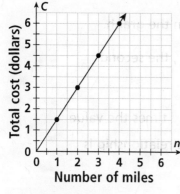

CITY CAB
Miles 0002.0
Fare 0003.00

A. Write an equation that relates C, the cost in dollars, to n, the number of miles driven.

B. (MP) **Reason** Suppose the second coordinate of each point in the graph is increased by 3 dollars. Write an equation that relates C, the new cost in dollars, to n, the number of miles driven. Explain how you found the new equation. If the number of miles driven is 6, what would the cost be?

5. (MP) **Model with Mathematics** The table represents the cost C, in dollars, of a smartphone data plan for n months. Write an equation that represents the data in the table.

n	1	2	3	4
C	45.25	90.50	135.75	181.00

312

6. Write an equation representing each table or graph.

A.

x	y
0	14
1	15
2	16
3	17
4	18

_____

B.

x	y
0	0
1	13
2	26
3	39
4	52

_____

C.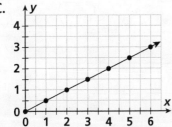

_____

D.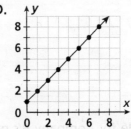

_____

E.

x	y
0	16
1	17
2	18
3	19
4	20

_____

F.

x	y
0	0
1	14
2	28
3	42
4	56

_____

G. (MP) **Use Repeated Reasoning** Examine the tables and graphs in Parts A–F. What do you notice about the equations for the tables and graphs that include the point (0, 0)? What do you notice about the equations for the tables and graphs that do not include the point (0, 0)?

_____

_____

_____

_____

_____

7. The table shows the monthly costs for a smartphone plan with Company A. The advertisement shows the cost of Company B's plan.

NEW CELL PHONE PLAN

$7.50 lower per month than our competition!

START-UP FEE: $35.00

months, n	1	2	3	4
cost, C	32.50	65.00	97.50	130.00

A. (MP) **Use Structure** Write an equation that models the total cost C, in dollars, for n months of Company B's plan. Explain.

_____

_____

_____

_____

B. Complete the table for Company B's plan.

months, n	1	2	3	4
cost, C				

C. After how many months will Company B's plan cost less than Company A's plan? Explain how you arrived at your answer.

_____

_____

_____

For Problems 8–9, write an equation representing each table or graph.

8.
x	y
0	0
2	12
5	30
8	48
12	72

9.
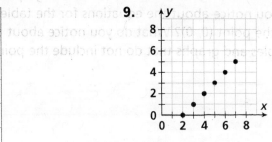

_____   _____

Write Equations from Tables and Graphs

1. (MP) **Model with Mathematics** The graph at the right shows the total sales of tickets to a school performance.

   A. Write an equation that relates the total sales to the number of tickets sold? Use T for the total sales and n for the number of tickets.

   _____

   B. If the number of tickets sold is 125, what will be the total sales? _____

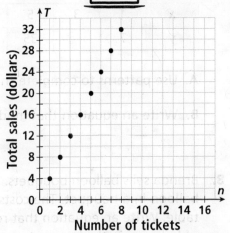

2. **STEM** The table shows the relationship between the mass m and the force w of weights on the ground. Write an equation representing this relationship.

Force (newtons)	9.8	19.6	29.4	39.2
Mass (kilograms)	1	2	3	4

For Problems 3–6, write an equation representing each graph or table.

3.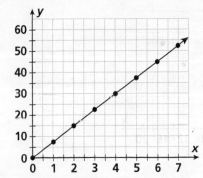

4.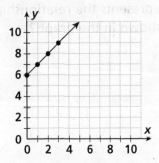

5.

x	y
0	11.2
3	14.2
6	17.2
9	20.2
12	23.2
15	26.2

6.

x	y
0	0
2	17
4	34
6	51
8	68
10	85

7. The partially completed table contains some values for x and y.

x	1	3	5		9
y	7		35		

   A. Use patterns to complete the table.

   B. Write an equation that models the relationship between x and y.

   _____

8. Brenda sells balloon bouquets. She charges the same price for each balloon in a bouquet. The costs for several bouquets are shown in the table. Write an equation that relates the cost of a bouquet to the number of balloons in the bouquet.

Number of balloons, x	6	9	12
Cost ($), y	3	4.50	6

   _____

9. Which equation represents the relationship between x and y shown in the graph?

   Ⓐ $y = 0.25x$

   Ⓑ $y = 0.5x$

   Ⓒ $y = 2x$

   Ⓓ $y = 4x$

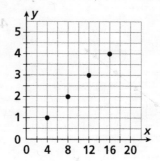

Spiral Review

10. Evaluate the expression for $a = 3$ and $b = \frac{1}{4}$.

    $5a - 16b + 7$

    _____

11. What is the opposite of -3.5?

    _____

12. Combine like terms: $4(x^2 - 3) + 2x^2 + 8$

    _____

Review

Vocabulary

Identify the dependent and independent variables.

1. For every hour of reading, Cameron earns 10 minutes on the computer.

	Dependent	Independent
Hours of reading	☐	☐
Minutes of computer time	☐	☐

2. A city charges an 8% sales tax.

	Dependent	Independent
Amount spent on purchases	☐	☐
Amount paid in sales tax	☐	☐

Concepts and Skills

3. **(MP) Use Tools** Willow works at a grocery store. She earns $10.50 per hour. Write an equation to represent Willow's total earnings t if she works h hours. How much will she earn if she works 12 hours? State what strategy and tool you will use to answer the question, explain your choice, and then find the answer.

_____

_____

4. Becka can make a bracelet in 2 minutes. Write an equation that relates the number of bracelets she makes x to the number of minutes it takes her to make them y. Complete the table and graph.

x	y
1	
2	
3	
4	

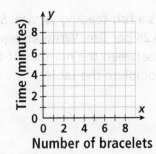

5. Tag's uncle gave him 25 baseball cards to start his collection. Every week, Tag buys 5 more cards. Write an equation that represents the total number of baseball cards Tag has in his collection *y* after he has bought cards for *x* weeks. Complete the table and the graph.

x	y
1	
2	
3	
4	
5	

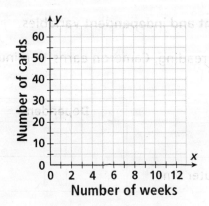

For Problems 6–8, write an equation representing the given graph.

6.
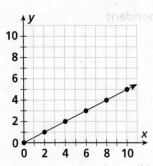

7.
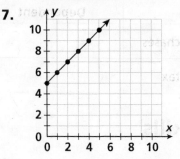

8.
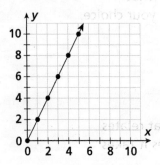

9. A pet sitter offers a fish-feeding service. She charges $8 for each visit plus $0.25 per fish. Write an equation to express the relationship between the number of fish *f* and the total charge *C*. Then complete the table.

f	C
1	
2	
3	
4	

© Houghton Mifflin Harcourt Publishing Company

Ratios and Proportional Reasoning

Astronomer

STEM
POWERING INGENUITY

Michael E. Brown is a professor of planetary astronomy at the California Institute of Technology and the author of the book *How I Killed Pluto and Why It Had It Coming*. Brown and his team discovered a number of objects in our solar system farther away than Neptune. One of these objects, the dwarf planet Eris, is more massive than Pluto (shown above). This discovery resulted in the International Astronomical Union demoting Pluto to a dwarf planet.

STEM Task:

We often use ratios to describe scale models. If a model rocket has a scale 1 inch = 12 feet, that means for every part of the model that measures 1 inch the corresponding part of the rocket measures 12 feet. Use this scale to calculate the height of a rocket if the model is 26 inches tall. Explain your reasoning.

Learning Mindset

Perseverance Applies Learning Strategies

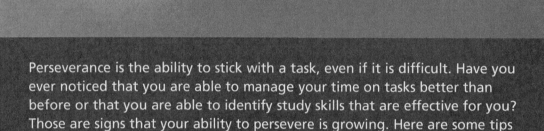

Perseverance is the ability to stick with a task, even if it is difficult. Have you ever noticed that you are able to manage your time on tasks better than before or that you are able to identify study skills that are effective for you? Those are signs that your ability to persevere is growing. Here are some tips for helping you persevere through difficult tasks.

- Get rid of distractions, such as your cell phone, while you are working. Your brain is less effective when you try to multitask. All human brains are! That's because multitasking doesn't really let you do two things at once. Your brain is actually shifting attention between the activities, and that slows you down. It can also decrease the quality of your work.

- Divide complex tasks into smaller steps. This helps you focus your efforts. It also makes it easier to spot mistakes.

- Even if your effort is unsuccessful, look at what you can learn from each attempt and adjust your strategy.

- Check for a fixed-mindset voice in your head telling you that you're not good with certain content or with certain tasks. Activate your growth-mindset voice telling you that you can learn more about the content and get better at the tasks.

Reflect

Q What are some strategies you used to manage your time while working on the STEM Task?

Q How have you kept yourself on task in the past? What is your plan for improving your ability to stay focused as you face math challenges?

Ratios and Rates

USE *PAINT* PATTERNS

The cafeteria is being painted sky blue. The table shows the amounts of bright blue paint that must be mixed with different amounts of white paint to make sky-blue paint.

Use number patterns to complete the table and answer the questions.

Mixing Sky-Blue Paint					
Bright blue paint (gallons)	2	4		8	10
White paint (gallons)	3		9	12	

The painting crew needs 40 gallons of sky-blue paint for the cafeteria. What amounts of bright blue paint and white paint should they mix?

_____ gallons of bright blue paint and _____ gallons of white paint

 Turn and Talk

• Describe the patterns you used to complete the table.

• How did you use patterns in the table to find the amounts of bright blue paint and white paint needed for the cafeteria?

Are You Ready?

Complete these problems to review prior concepts and skills you will need for this module.

Multiply or Divide to Find Equivalent Fractions

Multiply or divide to find the equivalent fraction.

1. $\frac{5}{8} = \frac{\boxed{}}{32}$

2. $\frac{45}{55} = \frac{9}{\boxed{}}$

3. $\frac{\boxed{}}{7} = \frac{16}{28}$

Find two equivalent fractions, one by multiplying and one by dividing.

4. $\frac{12}{16}$

5. $\frac{8}{10}$

6. $\frac{9}{15}$

_____

_____

Analyze Patterns and Relationships

Complete each pattern.

7. 10, 15, 20, _____, _____, _____, _____, _____

8. 17, 22, 27, _____, _____, _____, _____, _____

9. How are the patterns related?

_____

_____

_____

_____

Division Involving Decimals

Find the quotient.

10. $11.6 \div 4$ _____

11. $48 \div 0.6$ _____

12. $1.18 \div 0.2$ _____

13. $4.96 \div 1.6$ _____

14. $5.4 \div 3.6$ _____

15. $7.67 \div 1.3$ _____

Name _____

Understand the Concept and Language of Ratios

(I Can) find and express ratios.

Spark Your Learning

Jace and Keiko each have several birdhouses. Jace thinks his birdhouses are more popular, but Keiko disagrees. They decide to test their conjectures. They both count the number of birds that visit their birdhouses in one afternoon. They find that 12 birds visit Jace's 5 birdhouses, while 15 birds visit Keiko's 6 birdhouses. Whose birdhouses are more popular?

Turn and Talk Share your solutions. Did you all use the same method? If not, explain your reasoning to make sure all methods are correct.

Build Understanding

1 ▸ Tyree's cat has a litter of black and orange kittens. The tape diagram shows the number of each color kitten in the litter, with each section representing 1 kitten. What are different ways that Tyree can compare the numbers of kittens?

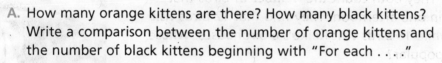

Black kittens

Orange kittens

A. How many orange kittens are there? How many black kittens? Write a comparison between the number of orange kittens and the number of black kittens beginning with "For each . . . ."

_____

_____

B. How does the number of orange kittens compare to the total number of kittens in the litter? Write the comparison beginning with "For every . . . ."

_____

_____

C. How does the number of black kittens compare to the total number of kittens in the litter? Write the comparison beginning with "For every . . . ."

_____

_____

D. Suppose each section of the tape diagram represents 2 kittens rather than 1 kitten. Will that change the comparisons in Parts A and B? Why or why not?

Part A: _____

_____

_____

Part B: _____

_____

_____

 Turn and Talk Suppose the model represents a group of orange and black kittens with 16 orange kittens. How many kittens are there in all? Explain.

A ratio can be written in several different ways.

5 to 4   5:4 $\frac{5}{4}$

A ratio can compare a part to a part, a part to the whole, or the whole to a part. The quantities in a ratio are sometimes called *terms*.

> **Connect to Vocabulary**
>
> A **ratio** is a comparison of two quantities by division, $a : b$; $\frac{a}{b}$; or a to b, where b is not equal to 0 ($b \neq 0$).

2 ▶ Aaron is making a quilt for a craft fair. The quilt is made with four different fabric colors as shown in the picture.

A. Complete the tape diagram to model the ratio of the number of blue squares to the number of white squares in the quilt.

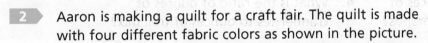

B. Complete the statements below to describe the ratio of blue squares to white squares in Part A.

☐ to ☐   ☐ : ☐ $\frac{\square}{\square}$

For every _____ there are _____ .

C. Write a part-to-whole or whole-to-part comparison about the quilt using symbols and using ratio language, such as "for each," "for every," or "per."

_____

_____

D. For every small green square, there are 2 large green squares. Does this mean that 1 out of every 2 green squares is small? Why or why not?

_____

_____

Check Understanding

1. At a summer camp, there are 8 campers and 2 counselors in each cabin. How does the number of campers compare to the number of counselors? Write the comparison beginning with "For every . . . ."

_____

2. A recipe that makes 8 cups of limeade uses 2 cups of lime juice. Describe the related ratio 2:8 using ratio language. Does the ratio involve only parts, or does it involve a part and the whole?

_____

_____

On Your Own

In Problems 3 and 4, a bag of trail mix contains 3 ounces of peanuts, 6 ounces of cranberries, 2 ounces of almonds, and 2 ounces of raisins. Write each ratio three different ways.

3. What is the ratio of ounces of peanuts to ounces of almonds?

4. What is the ratio of ounces of cranberries to ounces of trail mix?

In Problems 5 and 6, a carpenter is buying materials. The carpenter needs 36 screws that are 1.5 inches long, 24 screws that are 2 inches long, and 12 screws that are 2.5 inches long. Write each ratio in three different ways.

5. What is the ratio of 1.5-inch screws to 2.5-inch screws?

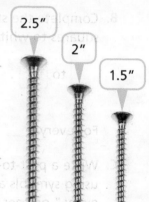

6. What is the ratio of the total length of the 2-inch screws to the total length of all the screws?

7. (MP) **Critique Reasoning** Alfred mixes 1 part cleanser with 3 parts water to make a cleaning solution. Alfred says that the ratio of cleaning solution to cleanser is 3:1. Is he correct? Why or why not.

8. **Open Ended** Use ratio language to describe a real-world situation that can be represented by the part-to-whole ratio 7:10.

© Houghton Mifflin Harcourt Publishing Company • Image Credits: ©Rudmer Zwerver/Shutterstock

![I'm in a] **I'm in a Learning Mindset!**

What can I apply from previous work to better understand ratios?

Name _____

Understand the Concept and Language of Ratios

1. An aquarium contains 20 African cichlids and 7 botia loaches. Compare the number of botia loaches to African cichlids beginning with the words "For every . . . ."

_____

2. **Math on the Spot** Carrie collects antique chess pieces. The table gives the number of each type of piece she has in her collection. Use the data to write each ratio in three different ways.

Queen	19
King	33
Knight	10
Rook	7
Bishop	23
Pawn	57

   A. Pawn to queens: _____

   B. Rooks to total pieces: _____

3. The ratio of tires to cars is 4 to 1. Use the words *for every*, *for each*, and *per* to complete the statements.

There are [ ] tires _____ car.

There are [ ] tires _____ car.

There are [ ] tires _____ car.

4. A survey asks 25 people if they prefer Brand A or Brand B laundry detergent. The data show that 12 people prefer Brand A. Write a ratio, in three ways, to describe the relationship between the people who prefer Brand B and all the people surveyed.

_____

5. (MP) **Attend to Precision** The amount of food a dog should eat daily is based on its weight. The picture shows the correct amount of food for the dog. What is the ratio of cups of dog food to the dog's weight in pounds? If a 100-pound dog is fed 4 cups of food a day, is this the correct ratio? Why or why not?

50 pounds

_____

_____

6. **Open Ended** Use ratio language to describe a real-world situation that can be represented by the part-to-part ratio 4:7.

2 cups

_____

_____

Test Prep

7. Marta has a bracelet made up of 3 red, 5 yellow, and 24 green beads. What is the ratio of yellow beads to beads that are not yellow?

Ⓐ 5:3

Ⓑ 5:24

Ⓒ 5:27

Ⓓ 5:32

8. A furniture builder pays $100 for the materials necessary to build one porch swing. A store sells the swing for $250. What is the ratio of the cost in dollars of the materials to the sale price in dollars?

_____

9. Andre is writing a paper for science class. He can type 30 words per minute. What is the ratio of words to minutes?

_____

10. A bread recipe uses 2 cups of white flour and 5 cups of whole wheat flour. Which statements are true? Select all that apply.

Ⓐ The ratio of white flour to whole wheat flour is 2 to 5.

Ⓑ The ratio of whole wheat flour to total flour is 5:7.

Ⓒ For every 2 cups of white flour, there are 3 cups of whole wheat flour.

Ⓓ For every 7 cups of flour, there are 2 cups of white flour.

Ⓔ For each cup of white flour, there are 4 cups of whole wheat flour.

Spiral Review

11. Viktor purchases a car for $10,608. He makes monthly payments for 48 months in order to pay off the car. He does not pay interest. What is his payment each month?

_____

12. A professional running track has two straight sections that are each 328.084 feet long. The total distance around the track is 1,312.34 feet. What is the length of the part of the track that is not straight?

_____

13. What is the greatest common factor of 72 and 34?

_____

Name _____

Represent Ratios and Rates with Tables and Graphs

(I Can) use tables and graphs to represent ratios and rates, and I can find equivalent ratios and unit rates.

Spark Your Learning

Cameron cleans her kitchen with an eco-friendly cleaning solution. She uses 4 tablespoons of baking soda for every 1 quart of warm water. She made a table to help her mix different amounts of the cleaning solution, but the table has faded over time and some of the values are illegible. A copy of the table is shown. Complete the table and describe the strategies you used to fill in the missing quantities.

Water (qt)	Baking soda (Tbsp)
1	4
	8
4	

Turn and Talk What is another method you could use to complete the table?

© Houghton Mifflin Harcourt Publishing Companyy • Image Credit: ©zeljkosantrac/E+/Getty Images

Build Understanding

1 ▶ Hank has a recipe that calls for the ingredients shown per batch. The table shows the amount of sour cream and milk he will need if he doubles the recipe.

1 cup sour cream and 4 cups milk per recipe

A. Describe a pattern you see in the amount of sour cream and the amount of milk when the recipe is doubled.

_____

_____

Sour cream (cups)	Milk (cups)
1	4
2	8

B. Complete the table for 3 and 4 times the original recipe. What did you do to find the answer?

_____

_____

C. Write the ratio of cups of sour cream to cups of milk for the given number of batches of the recipe.

1 Batch   **2 Batches**   **3 Batches**   **4 Batches**

   □/□

D. Are the ratios you wrote in Part C equivalent ratios? How do you know?

_____

_____

_____

> **Connect to Vocabulary**
>
> **Equivalent ratios** are ratios that name the same comparison.

E. Complete the statements.

You can _____ both terms of a ratio by the same _____ to find an equivalent ratio. So, equivalent ratios have a

multiplicative / additive relationship.

F. Describe a consistent pattern relating the number of cups of sour cream to the number of cups of milk. How can you use this pattern to help you find the amount of milk needed for 8 batches?

_____

_____

_____

2 ▶ Ken teaches ballet classes. The dance
studio offers classes in blocks.

Connect to Vocabulary

A **rate** is a ratio that
compares two quantities
that have different units.

A **unit rate** is a rate
in which the second
quantity in the
comparison is one unit.

Number of classes in a block	5	8	10
Cost ($)	90	120	140

A. Ken's students pay $90 for every block of 5 ballet classes.
Express this as a rate.

_____

B. Complete the diagram to find the unit rate for classes in
the 5-class block. What is the cost per class?

_____

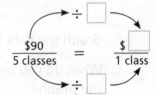

C. Explain in words what you did to find the cost per class
in Part B.

_____

D. Complete the diagram to find the unit rate
for classes in the 8-class block. What is the cost
per class?

_____

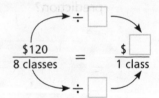

E. Draw your own diagram to find the cost per class in
the 10-class block. What is the cost per class?

F. Compare the unit rates you found for the blocks of
classes.

_____

_____

_____

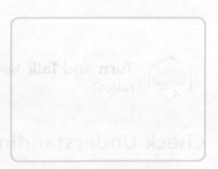

Turn and Talk Describe the difference between a ratio and a rate. Is a ratio
always a rate? Is a rate always a ratio? Explain.

Step It Out

 3 Tovah earns money pet sitting for friends and neighbors. She earns the same amount per hour.

A. Complete the table to show how much Tovah earns for different numbers of hours.

Time pet sitting (h)	Money earned ($)
2	40
4	
	120

B. Graph the data from the table.

C. What do you notice about the points on the graph?

_____

D. Use the graph to predict the unit rate, or amount that Tovah earns per hour. How can you use the table to check your prediction?

_____

_____

_____

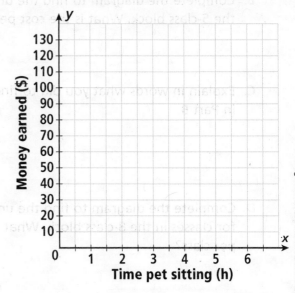

Turn and Talk How can you find unknown values in a table of equivalent ratios?

Check Understanding

1. A troop leader will give 2 packs of trail mix and 3 bottles of water to each scout. Complete the table of equivalent ratios.

Trail mix packs	2	4		20
Bottles of water	3		18	

2. A train travels at a constant speed for 420 miles. If it takes the train 7 hours to travel that distance, what is the unit rate at which the train travels?

_____

© Houghton Mifflin Harcourt Publishing Company • Image Credit: ©kikovic/iStock/Getty Images Plus/Getty Images

On Your Own

3. **Open Ended** A grocery store charges $6 for every 2 boxes of a certain cereal. Complete the table of equivalent ratios.

Boxes	2			
Cost ($)				

4. A hotel advertises vacation packages on its website. Each package costs the same amount per night. The table shows the total costs of stays for different numbers of nights.

Length of stay (nights)	Total cost ($)
2	210
3	315
4	420

A. What is the unit rate per night? _____

B. What is the total cost for 5 nights? _____

5. The table shows the number of beads a jeweler used to make bracelets. Each bracelet used the same number of beads.

A. Complete the table. Then graph the data.

Bracelets	2		4
Beads	32	48	

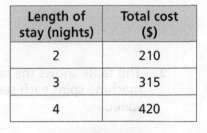

Beads Used for Bracelets

B. Write a ratio to show the number of beads necessary to make one bracelet.

_____

C. How many beads would the jeweler need to make 10 bracelets?

_____

6. **STEM** Calcium chloride is a salt used in the production of cheese. It consists of calcium (Ca) and chlorine (Cl) atoms. A single calcium chloride molecule is shown in the illustration. Complete the table of equivalent ratios relating the number of calcium atoms to the number of chlorine atoms in 1, 2, 3, 4, and 5 molecules of calcium chloride.

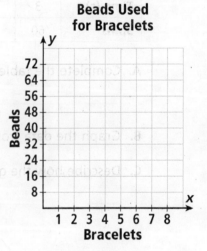

Calcium atoms	1	2	3	4	5
Chlorine atoms					

7. Each week, Sachi has 3 soccer practices that each last 45 minutes. Write the unit rate in minutes per practice. Then find the total time she practices soccer each week.

_____

8. **(MP)** **Critique Reasoning** Mark bought 2 pounds of apples as shown in the figure. He says that the unit cost is $\frac{2}{3.50} \approx \$0.57$ per pound. Find and correct his error.

2 pounds for $3.50

_____

_____

_____

9. The table shows the number of times a washing machine spins each second when operating at its top speed.

Time (s)	3	6	
Spins	60	180	

A. Complete the table. Then find the unit rate.

_____

B. Graph the data from the table.

C. Describe how the graph shows patterns in the table.

_____

_____

_____

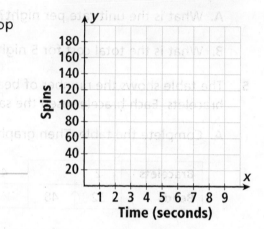

For Problems 10–13, find the unit rate.

10. 16 steps for every 2 floors

11. 36 grams for every 4 servings

12. $12 for every 4 containers

13. $960 for 12 months

 I'm in a Learning Mindset!

Did my strategy for representing ratios work? How did I adjust my strategy when I got stuck?

_____

Name _____

Represent Ratios and Rates with Tables and Graphs

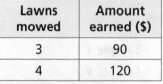
1. The table shows the amount of money that Roberto earns mowing lawns.

   A. How much does Roberto earn per lawn mowed? Show your reasoning using ratios.

   _____

Lawns mowed	Amount earned ($)
3	90
4	120

   B. (MP) **Reason** When finding the unit rate, does it matter whether you use the values for 3 lawns mowed or the values for 4 lawns mowed? Explain.

   _____

   _____

   _____

For Problems 2–3, complete the table using equivalent ratios.

2. 8 pairs of black shoes for every 3 pairs of red shoes

Red shoes	Black shoes
3	8
6	16
9	
	32

3. $50 for every 2-hour art class

Time (h)	Cost ($)
2	50
4	
6	
	200

4. **Math on the Spot** Eric lays tile on a floor at a constant rate. He covers a 150-square-foot floor in 3 hours.

   A. Complete the table to show the area Eric can cover in various amounts of time.

Time (h)	3	4	4.5	5	6.5
Area covered (sq ft)					

   B. Graph the information from the table.

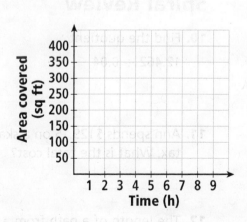

For Problems 5–6, find the unit rate.

5. 56 ounces for every 2 cans
   _____

6. $5.15 per 5-pound bag
   _____

Test Prep

In Problems 7–8, use this information. Steel is a mixture of iron, carbon, and other elements. The table shows the number of parts of each element in two different-sized samples of steel.

	Iron	Carbon	Other elements
Sample # 1	90	3	7
Sample # 2	45	1.5	3.5

7. What is the unit rate of parts iron to parts carbon?

_____

8. What is the unit rate of parts iron to parts all other elements, including carbon?

_____

9. The graph shows the cost of pairs of headphones. Which ratios are represented by a point on the graph? Select all that apply.

Ⓐ $2 for every 24 pairs of headphones

Ⓑ $5 for every 60 pairs of headphones

Ⓒ $6 per pair of headphones

Ⓓ $12 per pair of headphones

Ⓔ 2 pairs of headphones for $24

Ⓕ 5 pairs of headphones for $54

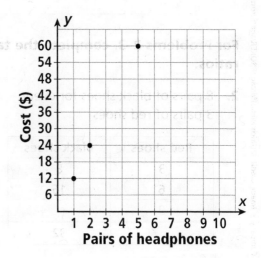

Spiral Review

10. Find the quotient.

    12.462 ÷ 0.04

_____

11. Ann spends $129.15 on a skateboard and $38.95 on a helmet, including tax. What is the total cost?

_____

12. The length of a path from a picnic area to a playground is $\frac{3}{4}$ mile. The path has signs with arrows pointing to the playground every $\frac{1}{8}$ mile. How many signs are placed along the path, assuming that there is a sign at the beginning of the path but not at the end?

_____

Name

Compare Ratios and Rates

(I Can) analyze tables to compare ratios and rates.

Step It Out

1 ▸ Amari makes orange juice from frozen concentrate and water. The amounts needed for one pitcher are shown in the picture.

A. Amari wants to make 4 pitchers of orange juice. Complete the table to find how many cups of water and cups of frozen concentrate she will need.

Pitchers	Frozen concentrate (cups)	Water (cups)
1		
2	4	
		9
4		
		15

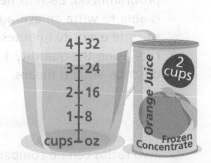

B. Amari's friend Gabriela also makes orange juice from frozen concentrate. Using the table at the right, write a rate to represent Gabriela's recipe.

[ ] cups of concentrate

[ ] cups of water

Pitchers	Frozen concentrate (cups)	Water (cups)
1	3	4
2	6	8
3	9	12
4	12	16
5	15	20

C. Whose orange juice has a weaker flavor, Amari's or Gabriela's?

Step 1 Find ratios in the two tables that have the same amount of frozen concentrate.

Row _____ of Amari's table has _____ cups of concentrate.

Row _____ of Gabriela's table also has _____ cups of concentrate.

Step 2 Compare the amount of water used for this amount of concentrate.

Amari uses _____ cups of water, while Gabriela uses _____ cups of water. _____ uses more water for the same amount of concentrate.

So, _____ orange juice will have a weaker flavor.

 Turn and Talk Is there another way you could have compared the recipes for orange juice? Explain.

© Houghton Mifflin Harcourt Publishing Company

2 Mrs. Morales teaches computer programming. Each student writes an average of 9 lines of code per hour.

A. Complete the double number line to find how many lines of code a student could write in a given number of hours.

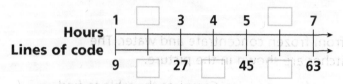

| Hours | 1 | ☐ | 3 | 4 | 5 | ☐ | 7 |

Lines of code: 9, ☐, 27, 45, ☐, 63

9 lines of code per hour.

B. Ms. Sanchez also teaches computer programming. Each of her students is able to write an average of 4 lines of code every 20 minutes. Write a rate using the quantity 1 hour. Then describe what it means.

Hours: $\frac{1}{3}$, $\frac{2}{3}$, $\frac{3}{3}$, $\frac{4}{3}$, $\frac{5}{3}$, $\frac{6}{3}$

Lines of code: 4, 8, 12, 16, 20, 24

C. Two ratios can be compared if both ratios have the same amount of one of the two quantities being compared. Which class writes code faster? Explain.

Check Understanding

1. Compare the ratios in the tables. Which trail mix is more "peanuty"? Explain.

Sam's Trail Mix		Liam's Trail Mix	
Cups of peanuts	Cups of raisins	Cups of peanuts	Cups of raisins
5	3	3	2
10	6	6	4
15	9	9	6
20	12	12	8

2. Kanesha saves $6 for every $50 that she earns. Liana saves $3 for every $20 that she earns. Who saves more of the money she earns? Explain.

Name _____

On Your Own

3. A track coach has runners perform drills to practice for a track meet. Each runner is supposed to run 5 sprints for every 4 full laps. Megan runs 11 sprints for every 8 full laps. Did Megan use the correct ratio for her running drills?

A. Complete each table.

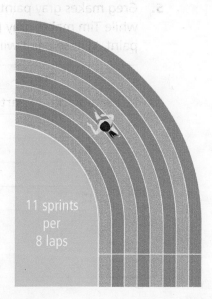

11 sprints per 8 laps

Ratio for Each Runner	
Sprints	Laps
5	4
10	
	12
	16

Ratio for Megan	
Sprints	Laps
11	8
	16
33	
44	

B. Compare the ratio of sprints to laps that each runner is supposed to run to the ratio of sprints to laps that Megan ran during practice. What row in each table has the same first or second quantity? How can you use that quantity to compare the ratios?

_____

_____

C. Did Megan use the same ratio of sprints to laps that her coach asked her to run?

_____

_____

D. (MP) **Reason** Suppose that Megan wants to run more sprints and laps. How many of each could she run so that her total sprints and total laps are in the ratio that the coach wanted? Explain.

_____

_____

_____

_____

4. Vivian scored 8 out of 10 on a quiz. Ramona scored 3 out of 4. Did Vivian and Ramona get equivalent scores? Explain.

_____

_____

© Houghton Mifflin Harcourt Publishing Company

5. Greg makes gray paint by mixing 3 parts black paint to 8 parts white paint, while Tim makes gray paint by mixing 4 parts black paint to 9 parts white paint. Whose paint will be darker? Explain.

Greg's	
Parts black	Parts white
3	8
6	16
9	24
12	32

Tim's	
Parts black	Parts white
4	9
8	18
12	27
16	36

_____

_____

_____

6. Two pet stores both sell canaries and parrots. The ratio of canaries to parrots for each store is shown in the double number lines. Are the ratios equivalent? Explain how you know.

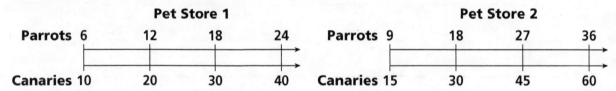

Pet Store 1

Parrots 6   12   18   24

Canaries 10   20   30   40

Pet Store 2

Parrots 9   18   27   36

Canaries 15   30   45   60

_____

_____

7. A wildlife manager is stocking fish in several ponds. She wants to put 6 yellow perch for each pair of largemouth bass in each pond. Her assistant put 54 yellow perch and 16 largemouth bass in one of the ponds. Did the assistant use the correct ratio of perch to bass? Explain your reasoning.

_____

_____

_____

Name _____

LESSON 9.3
More Practice/ Homework

ONLINE
Video Tutorials and Interactive Examples

Compare Ratios and Rates

1. Two farms grow lettuce and tomatoes as shown on the labels.

A. Complete the double number line to find ratios equivalent to 3 acres of lettuce to 7 acres of tomatoes.

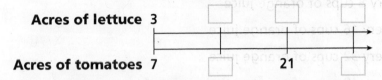

Brookberry Farms

Acres of lettuce 3 □ □ □

Acres of tomatoes 7 □ **21** □

B. Complete the double number line to find ratios equivalent to 2 acres of lettuce to 5 acres of tomatoes.

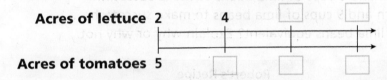

Madsen Farms

Acres of lettuce 2 **4** □

Acres of tomatoes 5 □ □ □

C. Which farm has a greater ratio of acres of lettuce to acres of tomatoes? How do you know?

_____

Brookberry
—Farms—
3 acres lettuce
7 acres tomatoes

MADSEN
FARMS
2 acres lettuce
5 acres tomatoes

For Problems 2–3, use the following information.

Four students in Mr. Morales's math classes are conducting surveys in their school. They each handed out 100 surveys. The table shows the response rates of each student's survey.

Response Rates	
Min-seo	4 out of 5 students responded.
Orlando	8 out of 10 students responded.
Jian	3 out of 4 students responded.
Leona	10 out of 12 students responded.

2. Did Min-seo and Orlando get the same ratio of responses? Explain.

_____

3. Did Jian and Leona get the same ratio of responses? Explain.

_____

_____

4. At Wild Bill's Wildlife Sanctuary, there are 3 elephants for every 2 rhinos. At Westside Wildlife Sanctuary, there are 15 elephants for every 8 rhinos. Do the two wildlife sanctuaries have the same ratio of elephants to rhinos? Explain.

_____

_____

© Houghton Mifflin Harcourt Publishing Company

Module 9 • Lesson 3

341

Test Prep

5. Mark uses 10 cups of apple juice and 16 cups of orange juice to make fruit punch. Deon uses an equivalent ratio of apple juice to orange juice when he makes fruit punch. Which ratio of apple juice to orange juice could Deon use? Choose all that apply.

   (A) 5 cups of apple juice for every 8 cups of orange juice

   (B) 15 cups of apple juice for every 16 cups of orange juice

   (C) 20 cups of apple juice for every 32 cups of orange juice

   (D) 30 cups of apple juice for every 48 cups of orange juice

   (E) 40 cups of apple juice for every 56 cups of orange juice

6. Gabby uses 5 cups of corn and 6 cups of lima beans to make succotash. Robert uses 7 cups of corn and 9 cups of lima beans to make succotash. Are the ratios of corn to lima beans equivalent? Explain why or why not.

Gabby's Recipe	
Corn	Lima beans
5	6
10	12
15	18
20	24

Robert's Recipe	
Corn	Lima beans
7	9
14	18
21	27
28	36

7. Milla ran 3 miles in 21 minutes. Fatima ran 5 miles in 35 minutes. Are the ratios of miles to minutes equivalent? Explain why or why not.

Spiral Review

8. What is the magnitude of −9? _____

9. Write an inequality to compare −10 and |−10|.

10. Find the quotient of $\frac{3}{7} \div \frac{1}{3}$. _____

Name _____

Find and Apply Unit Rates

 find and use unit rates.

Step It Out

1 Jack is at the supermarket. He finds a
5-pound bag of flour that costs $2.69 and
a 2-pound bag of flour that costs $1.89.
Which of the two bags of flour is the
better buy?

COST
$2.69

COST
$1.89

A. Write a rate that compares the cost to
the weight for the 5-pound bag of flour.

$\dfrac{\$\;\boxed{}}{\boxed{}\;\text{pounds}}$

B. Find the unit cost of the 5-pound bag of flour in dollars per pound.
Round your answer to the nearest cent.

$\dfrac{\$\;\boxed{}\;\div\;\boxed{}}{\boxed{}\;\text{pounds}\;\div\;\boxed{}}\;=\;\dfrac{\$\;\boxed{}}{1\;\text{pound}}\;=\;\$\;\boxed{}\;\text{per pound}$

C. Find the unit cost of the 2-pound bag of flour in dollars per pound.
Round your answer to the nearest cent.

$\dfrac{\$\;\boxed{}\;\div\;\boxed{}}{\boxed{}\;\text{pounds}\;\div\;\boxed{}}\;=\;\dfrac{\$\;\boxed{}}{1\;\text{pound}}\;=\;\$\;\boxed{}\;\text{per pound}$

D. Which of the two bags of flour offers the better value? Explain.

_____

_____

_____

 Turn and Talk Why is it helpful to use unit rates to compare prices? Explain.

2 It takes Kendra 27 minutes to run 3 miles.

A. Write a unit rate to represent Kendra's running rate in minutes per mile.

$$\frac{27 \text{ minutes}}{3 \text{ miles}} = \frac{27 \text{ minutes} \div \boxed{}}{3 \text{ miles} \div \boxed{}} = \frac{\boxed{} \text{ minutes}}{1 \text{ mile}}$$

B. Write Kendra's rate as a unit rate in miles per minute.

If Kendra runs at a rate of $\dfrac{\boxed{} \text{ minutes}}{1 \text{ mile}}$, she runs 1 mile every $\boxed{}$ minutes.

$$\frac{1 \text{ mile}}{\boxed{} \text{ minutes}} = \frac{\boxed{} \text{ mile} \div \boxed{}}{\boxed{} \text{ minutes} \div \boxed{}} = \frac{\dfrac{\boxed{}}{\boxed{}} \text{ mile}}{1 \text{ minute}}, \text{ or } \frac{\boxed{}}{\boxed{}} \text{ mile per minute}$$

C. Kendra can run at this rate for 45 minutes. How many miles can she run in 45 minutes?

$$\frac{1 \text{ mile}}{\boxed{} \text{ minutes}} \cdot 45 \text{ minutes} = \frac{1 \text{ mile}}{\boxed{} \text{ minutes}} \cdot \frac{45 \text{ minutes}}{\boxed{}} = \boxed{} \text{ miles}$$

3 A recipe says to use $\frac{2}{3}$ cup of milk to make $\frac{4}{5}$ serving of pudding. How many cups of milk are in 1 serving?

A. Recall that *reciprocals* are two numbers whose product is 1. Read the example below. Explain how reciprocals are used to find the unit rate.

$$\frac{\frac{2}{3} \text{ cup of milk}}{\frac{4}{5} \text{ serving of pudding}} = \frac{\frac{2}{3} \times \frac{5}{4}}{\frac{4}{5} \times \frac{5}{4}} = \frac{\frac{5}{6}}{1}, \text{ or } \frac{5}{6} \text{ cup of milk per serving}$$

_____

_____

B. How can you use division to find this unit rate?

_____

_____

 Turn and Talk How can you find the number of servings of pudding for every cup of milk?

4 ▶ Jaylan makes limeade using $\frac{3}{4}$ cup of water for every $\frac{1}{5}$ cup of lime juice. Rene's limeade recipe is different. He uses $\frac{2}{3}$ cup of water for every $\frac{1}{6}$ cup of lime juice. Whose limeade has a weaker flavor?

A. Compute the unit rate of water to lime juice in each limeade.

Jaylan: $\dfrac{\frac{3}{4}\text{ cup water}}{\frac{1}{5}\text{ cup lime juice}}$

Rene: $\dfrac{\frac{2}{3}\text{ cup water}}{\frac{1}{6}\text{ cup lime juice}}$

$\dfrac{3}{4} \div \dfrac{1}{5} = \dfrac{\boxed{}}{4} \times \dfrac{\boxed{}}{1}$

$\dfrac{2}{3} \div \dfrac{1}{6} = \dfrac{2}{\boxed{}} \times \dfrac{6}{\boxed{}}$

$= \dfrac{\boxed{}}{\boxed{}}$, or $\boxed{}$

$= \dfrac{\boxed{}}{\boxed{}}$, or $\boxed{}$

$\boxed{}$ c water per c lime juice

$\boxed{}$ c water per c lime juice

B. Whose limeade has a weaker lime flavor? Explain.

_____

_____

Check Understanding

1. A recipe for 12 servings of soup calls for 8 cups of chicken broth. How many cups of broth are needed to make 30 servings of the soup?

_____

2. A store sells two different-sized packages of AA batteries. Which package is the better buy? Explain.

Number in package	36	24
Cost in dollars	$19.19	$16.98

_____

_____

3. Write $2\frac{1}{4}$ miles in $\frac{3}{4}$ hour as a unit rate.

_____

On Your Own

4. **STEM** A Rube Goldberg machine consists of a series of needlessly complex devices that perform a simple task. Kate is drawing a scale model of her Rube Goldberg machine, which she plans to build and enter into a contest. A bicycle wheel on the scale model is $\frac{3}{4}$ inch in diameter, while in the actual machine, it will be $28\frac{1}{2}$ inches in diameter.

    A. Based on the measures of the wheel diameter, what is the unit rate of inches of machine per inch of the model?

    B. What would be the actual length of a rope that is 4 inches long in the model?

5. Chen bought a 20-foot chain for $36.50.

    A. What is the price per foot? Round the unit rate to the nearest cent.

    B. At this rate, what would be the price of a 30-foot chain?

6. **(MP) Reason** A pool is being drained by a pump at a rate of 4 gallons per minute. A second, identical pump is added to help drain the pool. How does the second pump affect the rate of drainage? Explain.

7. Melanie and her cousin Grace are arguing about who is the faster swimmer. The distance each can swim in a certain number of minutes is shown in the photo.

    A. How fast does Melanie swim in meters per minute?

    B. How fast does Grace swim?

    C. Who is the faster swimmer?

Melanie: 300 m in 5 minutes

Grace: 325 m in 5.5 minutes

© Houghton Mifflin Harcourt Publishing Company • **Image Credit:** ©Purdue9394/iStock/Getty Images Plus/Getty Images

8. Jorge measured his heart rate after jogging. He counted 11 beats during a 6-second interval. What was Jorge's heart rate in beats per minute?

_____

9. Ava bikes $2\frac{1}{2}$ miles in $\frac{5}{12}$ hour. What is Ava's unit rate in miles per hour?

_____

10. Amal can run $\frac{1}{8}$ mile in $1\frac{1}{2}$ minutes.

   A. If he can maintain that pace, how long will it take him to run 1 mile?

   _____

   B. How long would it take Amal to run 3 miles at that pace?

   _____

   C. Naomi can run $\frac{1}{4}$ mile in 2 minutes. Does Amal or Naomi run faster? How do you know?

   _____

   _____

11. **Open Ended** When both quantities in a rate are fractions, what strategy do you use to write the rate as a unit rate?

   _____

   _____

12. (MP) **Reason** What is the ratio of dried fruit to sunflower seeds in the granola recipe? If you need to triple the recipe, will the ratio change? Explain.

   _____

   _____

Granola

2 cups old fashioned oats   3 tablespoons honey
2/3 cup raw nuts   2 tablespoons sunflower oil
1/8 cup sunflower seeds   1/2 teaspoon vanilla
1/2 cup dried fruit, chopped   1/8 teaspoon salt

Preheat oven to 300 °F. Combine and mix ingredients in a bowl.
Spread on baking sheet. Bake for 10 minutes. Cool.
Store in closed container in the refrigerator.

13. Jordan is a tailor. He found cloth for $7.50 per yard. How much would his total cost be if he needed 12 yards of cloth?

_____

14. Out of every 8 loaves of bread that Markelle bakes, 5 of them are pumpkin bread. At this rate, how many loaves of pumpkin bread would he have if he baked a total of 40 loaves of bread?

_____

15. Open Ended The table gives the costs of two different-sized cartons of eggs, one of which is pictured. Suppose a supermarket wants to sell eggs individually. Is there a price the supermarket can charge per egg that is between the prices per egg for the two different-sized cartons? Explain.

18 EGGS
$4.32

Number of eggs in carton	12	18
Cost in dollars	$3.00	$4.32

_____

_____

_____

_____

For Problems 16–18, A) find each unit rate and B) use it to fill in the blank.

16. 1 yard in 6 minutes

A. _____ **B.** _____ per 18 minutes

17. $72 for $7\frac{1}{2}$ hours

A. _____ **B.** _____ per 40 hours

18. $130.50 for 18 hours

A. _____ **B.** _____ per 40 hours

For Problems 19–22, find each unit rate.

19. $\frac{5}{8}$ mile in $\frac{1}{4}$ hour

20. $68 for $8\frac{1}{2}$ hours

21. $1\frac{1}{4}$ cups of flour per $\frac{1}{8}$ cup of butter

22. $2\frac{1}{2}$ miles in $\frac{3}{4}$ hour

Name _____

Find and Apply Unit Rates

1. Dandelion's Lawn Service can mow 8 lawns in 5 hours. At this rate, how long does it take for the service to mow 12 lawns?

_____

2. **STEM** Density is measured in units of mass per unit of volume. It can be thought of as a unit rate. The mass of a block of aluminum is 9.45 grams. The volume is 3.5 cubic centimeters (cm³). What is the density of the aluminum?

_____

3. **Math on the Spot** Jen and Kamlee are walking to school. After 20 minutes, Jen has walked $\frac{4}{5}$ mile. After 25 minutes, Kamlee has walked $\frac{5}{6}$ mile. Find their speeds in miles per hour. Who is walking faster?

_____

4. It takes Tyreke 28 minutes to bike to his school, which is 7 miles away. If Tyreke is able to pedal at this pace, how long would it take for him to get from the school to the soccer field, which is 8.8 miles away from the school?

28 minutes to bike 7 miles

_____

5. (MP) **Attend to Precision** Maria and Franco are draining water troughs on their farms. Maria's trough drained 60 gallons of water in 75 minutes. Franco's trough drained 75 gallons of water in an hour and a half. Explain whose trough drained faster.

_____

_____

For Problems 6–7, A) find each unit rate and B) use it to find an equivalent rate.

6. 3 feet in 4 minutes

   A. _____ B. _____ per 16 minutes

7. 473 heartbeats in $5\frac{1}{2}$ minutes

   A. _____ B. _____ per 3 minutes

For Problems 8–9, find the unit rate.

8. $\frac{1}{4}$ kilometer in $\frac{1}{3}$ hour

9. $\frac{7}{8}$ square foot in $\frac{1}{4}$ hour

Test Prep

For Problems 10–11, use the following information. A store sells two packages of the same brand of biodegradable water bottles.

Package	48-pack of 8-ounce bottles	28-pack of 10-ounce bottles
Cost ($)	5.88	5.98

10. Which package has the better unit price per bottle?

_____

11. Which package has the better unit price per ounce?

12. Jordan cooked a $16\frac{1}{5}$-pound turkey in $5\frac{2}{5}$ hours. How many minutes per pound did it take to cook the turkey? Express your answer as a unit rate.

13. Orlo uses a spool of wire to make 15 necklaces. At this rate, how many spools of the same size would he need to make 50 necklaces?

14. Preston is buying 1-gallon cans of paint to paint a room. The information on the paint can says that a gallon of paint can cover 400 square feet. The room's walls are 688 square feet combined. How many 1-gallon cans of paint does he need to buy to put 2 coats of paint on the walls?

(A) 4 cans

(B) 3 cans

(C) 2 cans

(D) 1 can

Spiral Review

15. Juan is a chef who bought 7.8 pounds of seedless red grapes for $2.85 per pound. How much did Juan spend on seedless red grapes?

_____

16. Mrs. Kelly bought a bag of flour that holds $16\frac{2}{3}$ cups of flour. Each loaf of banana bread uses $\frac{2}{3}$ cup of flour. How many loaves of banana bread can she make?

_____

17. The elevation at the top of a mountain is +150 feet. A reef's elevation is −75 feet. Is the top of the mountain or the reef closer to sea level?

_____

Solve Ratio and Rate Problems Using Proportional Reasoning

(I Can) use ratio reasoning to solve problems.

Step It Out

1 Lemons are sold in bags of 6 lemons for $4. If you bought 24 lemons, how much would you spend?

LEMONS
6 for $4

A. Write a ratio of 6 lemons to the cost of 6 lemons in dollars.

_____

B. What is the unknown value you are looking for?

_____

C. One way to find the unknown number is to use a table. Complete the table using equivalent ratios.

D. Look at the results in the table. What do you notice about the number of bags of lemons, the number of lemons, and the cost?

Bags of lemons	Number of lemons	Cost ($)
1	6	4
2	12	
		12
	24	

_____

_____

E. Another way to find the unknown number is to find a factor that generates the equivalent ratio. When both quantities are multiplied by the same number, the result is an equivalent ratio. Find the unknown number using this method.

$$\frac{6 \text{ lemons}}{\$4} = \frac{24 \text{ lemons}}{\$\boxed{}}$$
× 4, × 4

F. What is the cost of 24 lemons?

_____

Turn and Talk How could you use the relationship between 6 lemons and $4 to find the relationship between 24 lemons and the cost for 24 lemons?

2 ▶ Jarrah wants to make a batch of slime. The diagram shows the ratio of hot water to cold water needed to make the slime. He wants to use 18 parts of water in total. How many parts of cold water does he need to make the slime?

Hot water | | | | | | |

Cold water | | | |

A. Look at the tape diagram. What are the total parts of water shown?

_____

B. Write the ratio of total parts of water to parts of cold water.

☐ total parts of water
☐ parts of cold water

C. What is the relationship between the quantities in the ratio in Part B?

D. How can you use the relationship between the quantities in Part B to find the parts of cold water needed for a total of 18 parts of water?

_____

E. How many parts of cold water will Jarrah need if he wants to use a total of 18 parts of water?

_____

F. If Jarrah wanted to make a larger batch of slime using 36 total parts of water, how many parts of cold water would he need?

_____

G. How many parts of hot water will Jarrah need if he uses a total of 18 parts of water?

_____

H. How many parts of hot water will Jarrah need if he uses 36 total parts of water?

_____

 Turn and Talk How can you use the tape diagram to check your answers? Explain.

© Houghton Mifflin Harcourt Publishing Company • **Image Credit:** ©Jarabee123/Shutterstock

3 A race car driver completes 5 laps of a race in 3 minutes and 30 seconds and then continues driving at this rate. How many laps will the driver complete in 17.5 minutes?

A. What is the ratio of laps to minutes? Explain.

_____

_____

B. You can use a double number line to find the unknown quantity. Complete the double number line diagram. Explain how you found the missing numbers of laps and minutes.

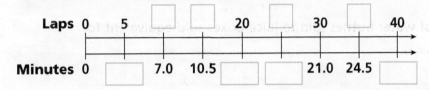

Laps 0   5   ☐   ☐   20   ☐   30   ☐   40

Minutes 0   ☐   7.0   10.5   ☐   ☐   21.0   24.5   ☐

_____

_____

C. Another way to find the unknown quantity is to find a factor that generates the equivalent ratio. What number multiplied by 3.5 minutes will result in 17.5 minutes? _____

Multiply both quantities of the first ratio by this factor to find the quantities of the second, equivalent ratio.

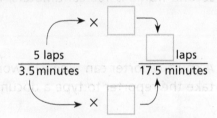

$\dfrac{5 \text{ laps}}{3.5 \text{ minutes}}$ $\dfrac{\text{laps}}{17.5 \text{ minutes}}$

D. How many laps will the race car driver complete in 17.5 minutes? _____

Check Understanding

1. A garden center is running a special on houseplants. A selection of any 2 plants costs $7. If a designer buys 22 plants for new homes, how much does the designer spend on plants?

_____

2. A scale model of the Eiffel Tower uses the scale shown. The Eiffel Tower is 324 meters tall to the tip. What is the height of the model?

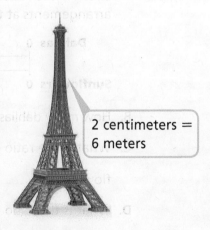

2 centimeters = 6 meters

_____

3. A hybrid car can drive 53 miles in the city on 1 gallon of gas. How many gallons of gas will it use to drive a total of 371 city miles?

_____

On Your Own

4. The table shows the numbers of biodegradable water bottles and juice boxes sold at two events.

Item sold	Event 1	Event 2
Water bottles	24	36
Juice boxes	54	108

   A. What is the ratio of water bottles sold to juice boxes sold at Event 1?

   _____

   B. What is the ratio of water bottles sold to juice boxes sold at Event 2?

   _____

   C. Are the ratios of water bottles sold to juice boxes sold equivalent for each event?

   _____

   _____

5. Elsa builds her own frames for paintings. She has one frame with a length of 60 centimeters and a width of 45 centimeters. She builds a second frame with an equivalent ratio of length to width. If the length of her second frame is 100 centimeters, what is its width?

   _____

6. A court reporter can type 215 words per minute. How many minutes will it take the reporter to type a document that is 1,505 words long?

   _____

7. The ratio of dahlias to sunflowers is the same in all of the flower arrangements at a banquet.

   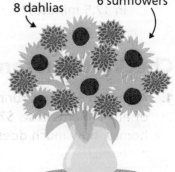
   8 dahlias   6 sunflowers

   A. (MP) **Use Structure** Complete the double number line to show the ratios of dahlias to sunflowers in flower arrangements at the banquet.

   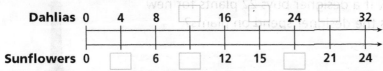

   Dahlias 0   4   8   ☐   16   ☐   24   ☐   32

   Sunflowers 0   ☐   6   ☐   12   15   ☐   21   24

   B. How many dahlias will there be when there are 33 sunflowers? _____

   C. What is the ratio of dahlias to all flowers when there are 21 total

   flowers? _____

   D. What is the ratio of sunflowers to all flowers in a bouquet with

   70 total flowers? _____

8. Nadine shops at three different grocery stores. She uses the ads to determine where to buy certain items. The table shows the cost of a brand of laundry detergent at each store.

Store	Detergent size	Cost
Fresh Grocers	48 ounces	$5.76
Jim's Corner Store	26 ounces	$3.38
City Market	54 ounces	$5.94

A. What is the cost per ounce of detergent at each grocery store?

Fresh Grocers: _____ Jim's Corner Store: _____ City Market: _____

B. Where should Nadine shop to get the lowest price per ounce?

_____

9. The tape diagram shows the ratio of turkey burgers to veggie burgers served at a family reunion.

Turkey burgers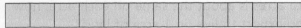

Veggie burgers

A. What is the ratio of veggie burgers served to turkey burgers served?

_____

B. If 30 veggie burgers were served, how many turkey burgers were served?

_____

10. (MP) **Reason** A pack of 140 stickers contains sheets of 28 stickers. Each sheet has star and heart stickers. There are 16 heart stickers.

A. How many heart stickers does a pack of 140 stickers have? Write equivalent ratios to show your reasoning.

_____

B. How many star stickers does a pack of 140 stickers have? Write equivalent ratios to show your reasoning.

_____

C. What is another way you could have found the number of star stickers in a pack of 140 stickers?

_____

11. Kyle recorded the results of his basketball free-throw practice for three different sessions in the table shown. Any attempt not missed is a free throw he made.

Misses	3	6	9
Attempts	10	20	30

A. Are the ratios of misses to attempts in the table equivalent ratios? Explain how you know.

_____

_____

_____

B. If the ratio remains the same, how many free throws would Kyle make if he misses 15 free throws in his next practice session?

_____

_____

12. Geography On a small island, 63 people live on 21 acres of land.

A. If the ratio of people to acres is about the same on each acre, how many people would you expect to live on 1 acre of land?

_____

_____

B. If another 42 people move to the island and the ratio of people to acres is equivalent to the original ratio, how many acres will the 105 people live on?

_____

_____

_____

13. The length-to-width ratios of three rectangles are equivalent. One of the rectangles has a width of 2.5 centimeters and a length of 15 centimeters.

A. The second rectangle has a length of 9 centimeters. What is its width?

_____

_____

B. The third rectangle has a width of 6 centimeters. What is its length?

_____

_____

C. Open Ended Write the length and width of two more rectangles whose length-to-width ratios are equivalent to that of the three rectangles. Explain how you found the length and width of each of your rectangles.

_____

_____

_____

_____

356

LESSON 9.5
**More Practice/
Homework**

ONLINE
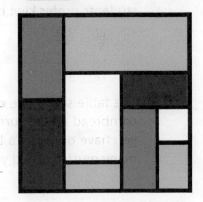
Video Tutorials and
Interactive Examples

Solve Ratio and Rate Problems
Using Proportional Reasoning

For Problems 1–4, use the following information. Piet Mondrian, a Dutch artist, painted images of rectangles and squares. The image shown is an example of art similar to Mondrian's art.

1. What is the ratio of orange rectangles to green rectangles?

   _____

2. What is the ratio of green rectangles to white rectangles?

   _____

3. What is the ratio of orange rectangles to white rectangles?

   _____

4. Describe in words two ratios from the image that are equivalent.

   _____

   _____

5. (MP) **Reason** Carmen can make 9 bracelets a day. She needs to make at least 120 bracelets to sell at a craft fair. She estimates she will need more than 13 days to make enough bracelets. Is she correct? Explain.

   _____

   _____

6. A catering company mixes taco seasoning and sour cream to make a vegetable dip. The table shows the amounts of taco seasoning for various amounts of sour cream.

   A. Complete the table.

Taco seasoning (tsp)	3	9	
Sour cream (c)	2		9

   B. How much taco seasoning will the catering company use if it makes a dip with 15 cups of sour cream? _____

7. **Math on the Spot** On the map, the distance between the trailhead and the campground is 4 inches. What is the actual distance? _____

8. The speed of an object is the ratio of its distance traveled to time. If the speed of a bicycle is 4.5 meters per second, what is the distance traveled in 9 seconds? _____

River

Campground

Trailhead

Ranger
station

1 in. : 3 mi

Test Prep

9. The ratio of students who prefer pineapple to students who prefer kiwi is 12 to 5. Which pair of equivalent ratios could be used to find how many students prefer kiwi if there are 357 total students?

Ⓐ $\frac{12}{5} = \frac{357}{?}$ Ⓒ $\frac{5}{12} = \frac{?}{357}$

Ⓑ $\frac{12}{17} = \frac{?}{357}$ Ⓓ $\frac{5}{17} = \frac{?}{357}$

10. The table shows the ratio of boxes of cornbread mix to cornbread muffins. If you have only half a box of mix, how many muffins could you make?

Cornbread mix (boxes)	1	2	4	5
Cornbread muffins	10	20	40	50

11. Jackson answered every 7 out of 9 questions correctly on a Spanish quiz. If the quiz had 63 questions, how many questions did Jackson answer correctly?

12. The double number line shows the cost of different quantities of cheddar cheese at a grocery store. One large wheel of cheddar cheese weighs a total of 15 pounds. How much would it cost to buy one large wheel?

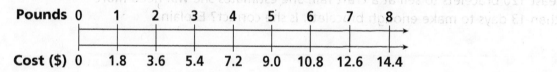

Pounds	0	1	2	3	4	5	6	7	8
Cost ($)	0	1.8	3.6	5.4	7.2	9.0	10.8	12.6	14.4

Spiral Review

13. A blue ribbon has a length of 1.694 yards. A red ribbon is 1.228 yards long. How much longer is the blue ribbon than the red ribbon?

14. What is the greatest common factor of 54 and 72? _____

15. What integers are represented by the points on the number line?

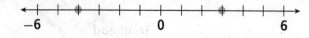

Review

Vocabulary

Complete the following to review your vocabulary for this module.

Vocabulary
ratio
equivalent ratios
rate
unit rate

1. $\frac{12}{20}$ is an example of a _____.

2. _____ are ratios that name the same comparison.

3. How can a ratio be like a fraction? How can it be different from a fraction?

_____

_____

_____

4. A ratio that compares two quantities with different units is called a _____. If the second quantity in the comparison is one unit, the comparison is a _____.

Concepts and Skills

5. Write the ratio three different ways: 1 table for every 4 students.

_____

6. A florist makes a bouquet with 7 roses, 12 carnations, and 5 lilies. What is the ratio of roses to flowers that are not roses?

Ⓐ $\frac{7}{24}$

Ⓑ $\frac{7}{17}$

Ⓒ $\frac{7}{12}$

Ⓓ $\frac{7}{5}$

7. (MP) **Use Tools** Sixteen watermelons cost $48. The ratio of the number of watermelons to the cost in dollars is 16:48. Name another ratio that is equivalent to this ratio. State what strategy and tool you will use to answer the question, explain your choice, and then find the answer.

_____

_____

8. In a smoothie, the ratio of ounces of blueberries to ounces of yogurt is 2 to 5. How many ounces of yogurt would be needed for a smoothie with 10 ounces of blueberries?

(A) 4

(B) 25

(C) 13

(D) 70

9. At the produce store, Wendy sees that grapes cost $13.50 for 3 pounds. What is the unit rate?

10. The double number line shows the number of minutes it takes Stan to run different numbers of miles. At the given unit rate, how many minutes would it take him to run 3 miles?

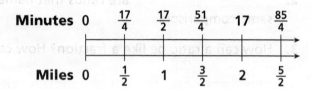

(A) 25

(B) $\frac{25}{2}$

(C) 51

(D) $\frac{51}{2}$

11. A plant grows at a constant rate. The table shows the height of the plant for different numbers of days of growth.

Which of the following pairs of days and heights could also be included in the table? Choose all that apply.

(A) Day 4: 8 in.

(B) Day 9: 16 in.

(C) Day 11: 22 in.

(D) Day 15: 30 in.

(E) Day 21: 44 in.

Day number	Height (in.)
3	6
7	14
8	16
10	20

12. A paint store makes lime-green paint by mixing 3 parts yellow paint to 1 part blue paint. A clerk mixes 4 parts yellow paint to 3 parts blue paint. Did the clerk use the correct ratio of yellow paint to blue paint? Explain your answer.

Lime-Green Paint	
Yellow paint	Blue paint
3	1
6	2
9	3
12	4

Clerk's Paint Mixture	
Yellow paint	Blue paint
4	3
8	6
12	9
16	12

10 Apply Ratios and Rates to Measurement

How **Many** Ways Can You **Write** Equivalent Ratios?

The cost per hour of renting a photo booth for a party is the same no matter how many hours the booth is rented.

Write four pairs of equivalent ratios based on the information presented on the flyers.

Party Package
• Booth rental for 2 hours
• Unlimited prints
Only **$110**

Party **Plus** Package
• Booth rental for 3 hours
• Unlimited prints
Only $165

_____   _____

_____   _____

 Turn and Talk

• Choose one of the answers you wrote and explain how the two ratios make similar comparisons.

• Choose one of the answers you wrote, and use mathematics to explain how you know that the two ratios are equivalent.

Are You Ready?

Complete these problems to review prior concepts and skills you will need for this module.

Multiply or Divide to Find Equivalent Fractions

Multiply or divide to find the equivalent fraction.

1. $\frac{21}{60} = \frac{\blacksquare}{360}$ ________

2. $\frac{51}{120} = \frac{\blacksquare}{360}$ ________

3. $\frac{143}{180} = \frac{\blacksquare}{360}$ ________

Ratio Language

There are 8 sixth-graders and 16 seventh-graders in a class. Complete each ratio for this class.

4. The ratio of sixth-graders to seventh-graders is 8 to ________.

5. There is 1 sixth-grader for every ________ seventh-graders.

6. The ratio of seventh-graders to students is ________ :3.

7. 1 out of every ________ students is a sixth-grader.

Representing Equivalent Ratios

Complete the table of equivalent ratios.

8. Maris is making a necklace. She uses 4 silver beads for each gold bead.

Silver	4	8		
Gold	1		3	

9. Kendra is making trail mix. She uses 3 cups of peanuts for each cup of raisins.

Raisins (cups)	1	2		4	
Peanuts (cups)	3		9		

Name _____

Use Ratio Reasoning with Circle Graphs

(I Can) use reasoning about equivalent ratios
to make and interpret a circle graph.

Spark Your Learning

In a music competition, the ratio of guitarists to all
musicians is 5:8. There are 64 musicians in the competition.
Of the guitarists, 32 play jazz solos and the rest play
classical solos. How could you represent the portion of all
musicians who play jazz guitar solos and the portion who
play classical guitar solos both visually and numerically?

Turn and Talk Is there another visual representation that could be used to
display this situation? Explain.

Build Understanding

A **circle graph** shows how a whole set of data is divided into parts or categories. The size of the angle for a section indicates the portion of the whole that category makes up. The sum of the angle measures of all the sections is 360°, the measure of one full rotation around a circle.

1 ▶ Kara conducted a survey of 120 students. She asked how they get to school. The results are shown in the circle graph.

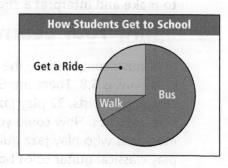

How Students Get to School

A. What do the sizes of the sections tell you about how the number of students who walk to school compares to the number who take the bus?

_____

_____

B. How can you find the angle measure of each section? What are the angle measures?

_____

_____

C. Write part-to-whole ratios comparing the angle measure for each section to the angle measure for the whole circle, 360°.

_____

D. Use your part-to-whole ratios from Part C to find the number of students represented by each section.

Bus

$$\frac{\boxed{}}{360} = \frac{\boxed{}}{120}$$

_____ students

Walk

$$\frac{\boxed{}}{\boxed{}} = \frac{\boxed{}}{\boxed{}}$$

_____ students

Get a Ride

$$\frac{\boxed{}}{\boxed{}} = \frac{\boxed{}}{\boxed{}}$$

_____ students

Step It Out

2 ▶ There are 45 vehicles in a parking lot. There are 25 cars, 5 trucks, and 15 SUVs. How can you make a circle graph to represent these data?

A. For each type of vehicle, write the ratio of the number of vehicles of that type to the total number of vehicles.

Cars   **Trucks**   **SUVs**

_____   _____   _____

Name _____

B. Use your part-to-whole ratios from Part A to find the angle measure for each section in the graph.

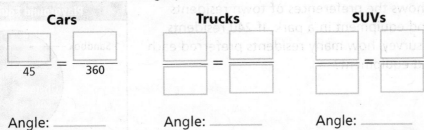

Cars

$$\frac{}{45} = \frac{}{360}$$

Angle: _____

Trucks

$$\frac{}{} = \frac{}{}$$

Angle: _____

SUVs

$$\frac{}{} = \frac{}{}$$

Angle: _____

C. What is the sum of the angle measures you found in Part B? What does this tell you?

_____

_____

D. Make a circle graph of the parking lot data. Use a protractor to draw each angle using the angle measures from Part B. Label each section with the type of vehicle it represents.

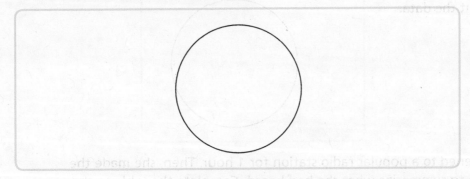

 Turn and Talk How does changing the order in which you graph each category affect the circle graph? Explain.

Check Understanding

1. Sara collected information from 60 students in the sixth grade about their pets. She represented the results in the circle graph shown. How many students own a dog?

2. Max asked students at his school what their favorite subject is. Of the 60 students he surveyed, 24 students said math, 12 said science, 18 said English, and 6 said social studies. Max wants to make a circle graph of these data. What angle measure should he use for the math section?

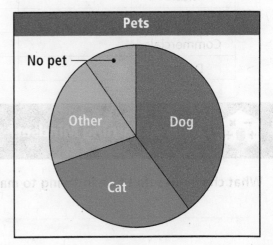

Pets

No pet

Other

Dog

Cat

Module 10 • Lesson 1

365

© Houghton Mifflin Harcourt Publishing Company

On Your Own

3. The circle graph shows the preferences of town residents for new playground equipment in a park. If 240 residents responded to the survey, how many residents preferred each type of playground equipment?

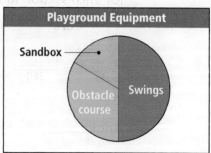

Playground Equipment

Swings: _____

Sandbox: _____

Obstacle Course: _____

4. Mr. Perez's science students conducted a wildlife count in the local forest. The results of their work are shown in the table.

   A. Find the angle measure for each section.

   _____

   B. Make a circle graph to represent the data.

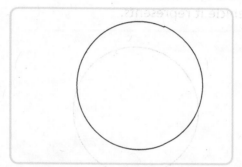

Animal	Count
Squirrel	25
Rabbit	10
Deer	10
Raccoon	5

5. Daniela listened to a popular radio station for 1 hour. Then, she made the circle graph to summarize what she had heard. Complete the table to show the angle measure for each section and the number of minutes that section represents.

Category	Angle measure (degrees)	Time (minutes)
Music		
News		
Commercials		
DJ talk		

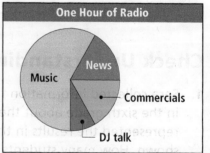

One Hour of Radio

I'm in a Learning Mindset!

What challenges do I face in trying to master making a circle graph?

_____

_____

LESSON 10.1
**More Practice/
Homework**

ONLINE
⊙ Ed   Video Tutorials and
Interactive Examples

Use Ratio Reasoning with Circle Graphs

1. **Health and Fitness** Kahlil asks his doctor how much of his daily diet should come from carbohydrates, protein, and fat. His doctor recommended 900 calories from carbohydrates, 360 calories from protein, and 540 calories from fat. Kahlil wants to make a circle graph of this information.

A. What is the total number of calories Kahlil should have each day?

   _____

B. What is the angle measure for each section?

   _____

C. Use your answers from Part B to make a circle graph.

2. (MP) **Attend to Precision** Sara collected information from students in her school about their favorite type of movie. She represented the results in a circle graph. If 200 students expressed their preference, complete the table below to show how many students picked each type of movie. Use a protractor to find the angle measure of each section.

Movie Type	Number of People
Comedy	
Action	
Horror	
Romance	
Drama	

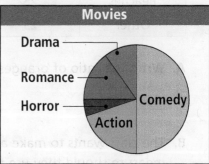

Movies

Drama
Romance
Horror
Action
Comedy

3. **Open Ended** Make up your own trail mix recipe.

Ingredient	Weight (ounces)
Nuts	
Yogurt raisins	

My Trail Mix

A. The trail mix will include nuts, yogurt-covered raisins, and two ingredients of your choice. Write the ingredients you will use in the first column of the table.

B. Your recipe should make a total of 24 ounces of trail mix. In the second column, record the weight, in ounces, of each ingredient in your recipe.

C. Make a circle graph to show the portion of the whole recipe each ingredient makes up.

Test Prep

4. Jon asked people what their favorite type of exercise is. Of the 180 people he surveyed, 60 said jogging, 40 said cycling, and 80 said aerobics. Jon wants to make a circle graph of these data. What angle measure should he use for the aerobics section?

Ⓐ 80°

Ⓑ 120°

Ⓒ 160°

Ⓓ 240°

5. Ms. Hager's math class kept a record of the fruit sold in the school cafeteria over the course of a week. The results are shown in the table.

Fruit	Number sold
Apples	150
Bananas	100
Oranges	200
Peaches	25
Other	25

A. Write the ratio of oranges sold to total pieces of fruit sold.

B. The class wants to make a circle graph of the data. What angle measure should they use to represent the oranges section?

Spiral Review

6. Bob buys some apples for $16.50. If Bob buys 4.4 pounds of apples, what is the price per pound?

7. Sara wants to make dinner for herself. The recipe she will use calls for $13\frac{1}{2}$ ounces of chopped nuts. However, the recipe feeds 6 people. How many ounces of chopped nuts does Sara need for one serving?

8. How many inches are in 8 feet?

Name _____

Use Rate Reasoning to Convert Within Measurement Systems

(I Can) convert measurements within a measurement system by using equivalent ratios or conversion factors.

Spark Your Learning

Milo is making $1\frac{1}{2}$ batches of muffins for a bake sale. If each batch of muffins calls for $1\frac{3}{4}$ cups of flour, how much flour will he need?

 Turn and Talk How is multiplying fractions similar to multiplying whole numbers or decimals? How is it different? Explain.

© Houghton Mifflin Harcourt Publishing Company • Image Credit: ©Rawpixel.com/Shutterstock

Build Understanding

You can use equivalent rates to convert units of measurement in the **customary system** and the **metric system**. Use the table to convert one unit to another unit within the same measurement system.

Customary Measurements		
Length	**Weight**	**Capacity**
1 ft = 12 in. 1 yd = 36 in. 1 yd = 3 ft 1 mi = 5,280 ft 1 mi = 1,760 yd	1 lb = 16 oz 1 T = 2,000 lb	1 c = 8 fl oz 1 pt = 2 c 1 qt = 2 pt 1 qt = 4 c 1 gal = 4 qt

Metric Measurements		
Length	**Mass**	**Capacity**
1 km = 1,000 m 1 m = 100 cm 1 cm = 10 mm	1 kg = 1,000 g 1 g = 1,000 mg	1 L = 1,000 mL

1 ▶ Heather needs to mail the package shown. The weight on the display is in pounds. The shipping company charges by the ounce. How many ounces does the package weigh?

A. How many ounces are in one pound?

_____

B. What rate could you use to convert 4 pounds into ounces?

_____

C. Use equivalent rates to convert 4 pounds into ounces.

$$\frac{\boxed{} \text{ ounces} \times \boxed{}}{1 \text{ pound} \times \boxed{}} = \frac{\boxed{} \text{ ounces}}{4 \text{ pounds}}$$

D. How many ounces are in 4 pounds?

$\boxed{}$ pounds is equal to $\boxed{}$ ounces.

 Turn and Talk How can you convert units within a measurement system? Explain.

Step It Out

Another way to convert measurements is by using a *conversion factor*.

2 In Paris, the sculpture Long-Term Parking, made by Armand Fernandez, contains 60 cars embedded in 40,000 pounds of concrete. How many tons of concrete are in 40,000 pounds?

A. Find the conversion factor comparing tons to pounds.

$$\frac{\boxed{}\text{ ton}}{\boxed{}\text{ pounds}}$$

B. Multiply 40,000 pounds by the conversion factor.

$$\frac{\boxed{}\text{ ton}}{\boxed{}\text{ pounds}} \times 40{,}000 \text{ pounds}$$

C. Simplify the expression.

$$\frac{\boxed{}\text{ ton}}{\boxed{}\text{ pounds}} \times \frac{40{,}000 \text{ pounds}}{1} = \frac{\boxed{}\text{ tons}}{\boxed{}} = \boxed{}\text{ tons}$$

Long-Term Parking
Sculpture by
Armand Fernandez

D. How many tons of concrete are in 40,000 pounds?

_____

Turn and Talk Explain how you know how to set up the conversion factor.

3 A bag of flour has a mass of 4.5 kilograms. How many grams are in 4.5 kilograms?

A. Write a conversion factor comparing kilograms to grams.

$$\frac{\boxed{}\text{ g}}{\boxed{}\text{ kg}}$$

B. Multiply 4.5 kilograms by the conversion factor.

$$\frac{\boxed{}\text{ g}}{\boxed{}\text{ kg}} \cdot 4.5 \text{ kg}$$

C. Simplify the expression.

$$\frac{\boxed{}\text{ g}}{\boxed{}\text{ kg}} \cdot \frac{\boxed{}\text{ kg}}{1} = \boxed{}\text{ g}$$

D. How many grams are in 4.5 kilograms? _____

4 ▸ A camel can drink 25 gallons of water in 10 minutes. How many cups of water can the camel drink in 10 minutes?

A. You need to find the conversion factor for gallons to cups, but the conversion table does not show this conversion. The table does show that

☐ cups = 1 quart, and that ☐ quarts = 1 gallon.

Complete the table of equivalent ratios to compare cups to quarts.

cups	2	4	8	16
quarts		1		

B. How many cups are in 1 gallon?

☐ quarts = 1 gallon, so 1 gallon = ☐ cups

C. Multiply 25 gallons by the conversion factor.

$$\frac{\boxed{} \text{ cups}}{\boxed{} \text{ gallon}} \times 25 \text{ gallons}$$

D. How many cups are in 25 gallons?

Check Understanding

1. The 1,600-meter race in the Olympics is very close to 1 mile long. How many kilometers is 1,600 meters? Show your work using equivalent ratios.

1,600-meter race

2. Scott is 72 inches tall. How many feet tall is Scott? Use a conversion factor. Show your work.

3. Jill has 15 feet of ribbon. How many yards of ribbon does she have? Use a conversion factor. Show your work.

© Houghton Mifflin Harcourt Publishing Company • Image Credit: ©petesaloutos/iStock / Getty Images Plus/Getty Images

On Your Own

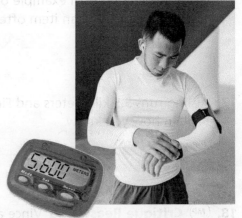

4. Karen is preparing 4.5 liters of punch. How many milliliters are in 4.5 liters?

_____

5. Chen's pedometer says he has walked 5,600 meters today. How many kilometers has Chen walked today?

_____

6. (MP) **Critique Reasoning** Doug says that 3,000 kilometers is the same distance as 3 meters. What mistake did he make converting 3 meters to kilometers?

_____

_____

_____

7. (MP) **Reason** A truck weighs 9,000 pounds. A repair shop sends a tow truck that can pull up to 5 tons. Can the tow truck tow the truck? Explain.

_____

_____

8. Morgan has 42 inches of rope, Malcolm has 4 feet of rope, and Roberto has 2 yards of rope. Express the total length of rope the three friends have in inches, feet, and yards.

[ ] inches = [ ] feet = [ ] yards

9. What conversion factor can you use to convert miles to inches? Explain how you found it.

_____

_____

For Problems 10–15, convert the units.

10. 8 ft = [ ] in.

11. 12 yd = [ ] ft

12. [ ] km = 11,250 m

13. [ ] mg = 3.5 g

14. 150 mL = [ ] L

15. [ ] in. = 0.5 ft

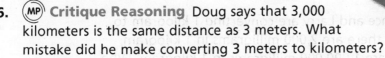

16. **Open Ended** Give an example of an item often measured with customary units and an item often measured with metric units.

_____

_____

17. Aisling runs 5.5 kilometers and Fiona runs 6,250 meters. Who runs farther? Explain how you know.

_____

_____

18. 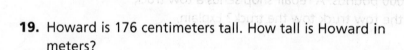 **Critique Reasoning** Vince and Larry are converting 1 kilogram to milligrams. Larry reports that there are 2,000 milligrams in 1 kilogram, and Vince reports that there are 1,000,000 milligrams in 1 kilogram. Who is correct and why? Explain.

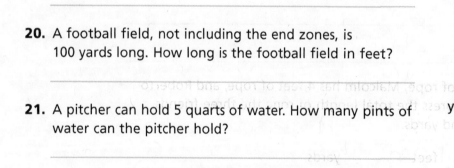

19. Howard is 176 centimeters tall. How tall is Howard in meters?

_____

20. A football field, not including the end zones, is 100 yards long. How long is the football field in feet?

_____

21. A pitcher can hold 5 quarts of water. How many pints of water can the pitcher hold?

_____

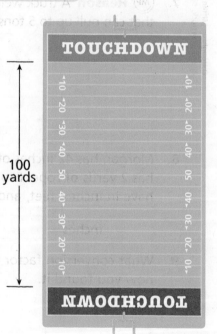

For Problems 22–25, compare the measurements using <, =, or >.

22. 75 in. ☐ 7 ft

23. 8,465 lb ☐ 4 T

24. 2.7 m ☐ 270 cm

25. 10 mi ☐ 10,000 ft

 I'm in a Learning Mindset!

What specific evidence do I have that I solved Task 1 correctly?

_____

_____

Use Rate Reasoning to Convert Within Measurement Systems

1. Angela has 3 gallons of milk. How many quarts of milk does she have?

_____

2. **Math on the Spot** Use conversion factors.

   A. Convert 40 yards to feet. B. Convert 20 quarts to gallons.

   _____ _____

3. A sink can hold 10 gallons of water. How many quarts of water can the sink hold?

   _____

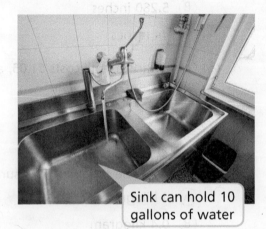

Sink can hold 10 gallons of water

4. A box weighs 64 ounces. What is the weight of the box in pounds?

   _____

5. **(MP) Reason** Greg already has 2 gallons of paint to paint a living room. He estimates that he will need 10 quarts of paint. Does he have enough paint? Show your work.

   _____

   _____

6. Two bottles of water have a total mass of 4 kilograms. How many grams is 4 kilograms?

   _____

Convert to the unit indicated in parentheses. Then compare the measurements using <, =, or >.

7. 5,000 m ☐ 4.9 km (meters)   8. 4 lb ☐ 60 oz (ounces)

   _____

9. 3 mi ☐ 15,840 ft (feet)   10. 72 in. ☐ 2 yd (feet)

   _____

11. 0.45 L ☐ 4,200 mL (milliliters)   12. 1.2 g ☐ 950 mg (milligrams)

Test Prep

13. Write the following measurements in order from least to greatest:
0.04 kilometer, 420 centimeters, 4,600 millimeters, 4.3 meters

14. Which of the following measurements is equivalent to 528 feet? Select all that apply.

   (A) 176 yards

   (B) 5,280 inches

   (C) 44 inches

   (D) 0.1 mile

   (E) 10 miles

15. One quart of milk costs $1.05, and 1 gallon of milk costs $3.89. Which is a better buy? Explain.

16. Which of the following measurements is equivalent to 400 grams?

   (A) 4 kilograms

   (B) 0.4 kilogram

   (C) 0.04 kilogram

   (D) 0.004 kilogram

17. Mairead jogs 2,700 feet, while Paula jogs 0.5 mile. Who jogs farther, and by how many feet?

Spiral Review

18. Kelly is trying to decide which plan to use to download songs. Rates for two plans are shown. Which plan offers the lowest cost per song? Explain.

   Plan A: 8 songs for $9.60   Plan B: 10 songs for $12.50

19. There are 10 children and 15 adults on the bus. What is the ratio of children to people on the bus?

20. Polly buys 6.8 yards of fabric for $28.90. What is the cost per yard?

21. What is the distance between −7 and its opposite on a number line?

© Houghton Mifflin Harcourt Publishing Company

Name _____

Use Rate Reasoning to Convert Between Measurement Systems

(I Can) convert measurements between measurement systems by using equivalent rates or conversion factors.

Spark Your Learning

At Winnie's restaurant, one serving of chicken soup is $1\frac{1}{2}$ cups. The chef makes 48 cups of soup each night. How many servings of chicken soup are in 48 cups? Explain how you know.

Turn and Talk How is dividing fractions related to multiplying fractions?

Build Understanding

Many countries use only the metric system of measurement. In the United States, however, we use measurements in both metric units and customary units. Sometimes we need to convert between the two systems.

The table below shows equivalences between customary and metric systems. You can use these equivalences to convert a measurement in one system to a measurement in the other system.

Length	Weight/Mass	Capacity
1 inch = 2.54 centimeters 1 foot ≈ 0.305 meter 1 yard ≈ 0.914 meter 1 mile ≈ 1.61 kilometers	1 ounce ≈ 28.4 grams 1 pound ≈ 0.454 kilogram	1 fluid ounce ≈ 29.6 milliliters 1 quart ≈ 0.946 liter 1 gallon ≈ 3.79 liters

The systems are not related so the conversions are approximate, as indicated by the symbol ≈.

1 ▸ Daniel is 6 feet tall. He wants to know how tall he is in meters.

6 feet

A. One way to solve this problem is to use a bar diagram. Each part represents 1 foot.

6 feet

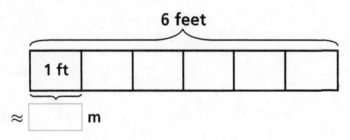

| 1 ft | | | | | |

≈ [ ] m

B. How does the diagram help you solve the problem?

_____

_____

C. You could also use a unit rate as a conversion factor.

$$\frac{\boxed{}\,m}{1\ ft} \times 6\ ft \approx \boxed{}\ m$$

D. There are about [ ] meters in 6 feet.

 Turn and Talk How would the steps to solve the problem be different if you converted a metric height to feet? Explain.

Step It Out

2 In the metric system, the mass of 1 milliliter of water is 1 gram. A gallon of water weighs about 8 pounds. What is the mass of a gallon of water to the nearest tenth of a kilogram?

1 gallon

Method 1: Solve using equivalent ratios.

A. The first ratio is the conversion factor, which is found in the table.

$$\frac{1\,\text{lb}}{\boxed{}\,\text{kg}}$$

B. The second ratio relates the known amount to the unknown converted amount.

$$\frac{\boxed{}\,\text{lb}}{x\,\text{kg}}$$

C. Set the ratios equal to one another.

$$\frac{1\,\text{lb}}{\boxed{}\,\text{kg}} = \frac{\boxed{}\,\text{lb}}{x\,\text{kg}}$$

D. Multiply both parts of the left ratio by a factor that will make the number of pounds in the two ratios the same.

$$\frac{1\,\text{lb} \times \boxed{}}{\boxed{}\,\text{kg} \times \boxed{}} = \frac{\boxed{}\,\text{lb}}{\boxed{}\,\text{kg}}$$

E. A gallon of water has a mass of about $\boxed{}$ kilograms.

Method 2: Solve using the conversion factor.

F. Write the conversion factor as a ratio.

$$\frac{\boxed{}\,\text{kg}}{\boxed{}\,\text{lb}}$$

G. Multiply 8 pounds by the conversion factor. Round the result to the nearest tenth of a kilogram.

$$\frac{\boxed{}\,\text{kg}}{\boxed{}\,\text{lb}} \times 8\,\text{lb} \approx \boxed{}\,\text{kg}$$

H. Notice the _____ units cancel, resulting in an answer given

in _____ .

I. When you choose a conversion factor, the unit you are converting to should

be in the | first / second | quantity, and the unit to cancel out should be in

the | first / second | quantity.

Turn and Talk Which method is easier to use, the equivalent ratios method or the conversion factor method? Explain.

Many water bottles contain 16 fluid ounces, or 1 pint, of water. Drink labels often show the number of fluid ounces and the number of milliliters in a container. How many milliliters are in a 16-fluid-ounce drink?

Solve using equivalent ratios.

A. One ratio is the conversion factor.

$$\frac{\boxed{}\text{ mL}}{1\text{ fl oz}}$$

B. The other ratio relates the known amount to the unknown converted amount.

$$\frac{x\text{ mL}}{\boxed{}\text{ fl oz}}$$

16 fluid ounces

C. Set the ratios equal to one another.

$$\frac{\boxed{}\text{ mL}}{1\text{ fl oz}} = \frac{x\text{ mL}}{\boxed{}\text{ fl oz}}$$

D. Multiply both parts of the left ratio by a factor that will make the number of fluid ounces in the two ratios the same.

$$\frac{\boxed{}\text{ mL} \times \boxed{}}{1\text{ fl oz} \times \boxed{}} = \frac{\boxed{}\text{ mL}}{\boxed{}\text{ fl oz}}$$

There are about $\boxed{}$ milliliters in 16 fluid ounces.

 Turn and Talk When converting units using equivalent ratios, does it matter which unit is in the first part of the ratio? Explain.

Check Understanding

1. Robert enters a race. The race is 10 kilometers long, but he is more familiar with miles than kilometers. How many miles are in 10 kilometers to the nearest tenth of a mile?

_____

2. Scott is 72 inches tall, and Chris is 185 centimeters tall. Who is taller? Show your work.

_____

_____

_____

On Your Own

3. (MP) **Reason** Kathy is following a recipe for punch that calls for 3 liters of juice. She has 3 quarts of juice. Without using an equation, does Kathy have enough juice for the punch? Explain.

_____

_____

4. Simon measures the length of an insect that is 2.5 inches long for a science project. He needs to record his data in centimeters. How long is the insect in centimeters?

_____

5. An Olympic-size swimming pool is 50 meters long. How many yards long is the pool, to the nearest tenth of a yard?

_____

6. How many kilograms are in 1 ton, or 2,000 pounds?

_____

7. (MP) **Attend to Precision** Many newborn babies have a mass between 2,500 grams and 4,000 grams. How many pounds does a 2,500-gram baby weigh, to the nearest tenth of a pound? [16 ounces = 1 pound] Show your work.

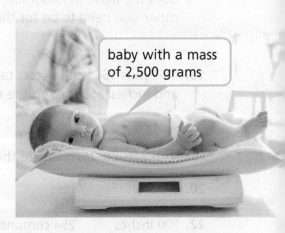

baby with a mass of 2,500 grams

8. Shane is following an English recipe for scones. The recipe calls for 1.2 kilograms of flour. How many pounds of flour, to the nearest tenth of a pound, does he need?

_____

For Problems 9–14, convert the units to the nearest tenth.

9. 10 feet ≈ _____ meters

10. _____ yards ≈ 25 meters

11. _____ kilometers ≈ 50 miles

12. _____ grams ≈ 10 ounces

13. 8 fluid ounces ≈ _____ milliliters

14. 6 inches = _____ centimeters

15. 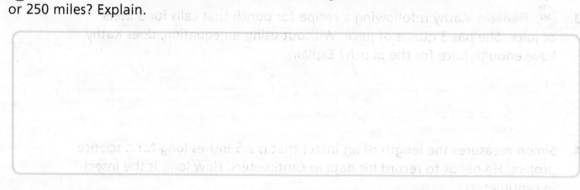 **Construct Arguments** Which distance is longer, 500 kilometers or 250 miles? Explain.

16. The tank in Mary's car holds 10 gallons of gas. How many liters does the tank hold?

_____

17. Wendy drives her car 110 kilometers per hour. What is this rate, in miles per hour, to the nearest tenth?

_____

18. Jim sits on a seesaw. If Jim weighs 100 pounds, what does the mass, in kilograms, of the person on the other side need to be for the seesaw to balance?

100 pounds

_____

19. Caitlyn is 160 centimeters tall. How tall is she in feet and inches, rounded to the nearest inch?

_____

For Problems 20–25, compare the measurements using <, =, or >.

20. 2 meters [ ] 7 feet

21. 50 pounds [ ] 25 kilograms

22. 100 inches [ ] 254 centimeters

23. 10 miles [ ] 6.2 kilometers

24. 6 liters [ ] 2 gallons

25. 24 ounces [ ] 600 grams

© Houghton Mifflin Harcourt Publishing Company

 I'm in a Learning Mindset!

What prior knowledge of measurement can I use to solve Problem 8?

_____

_____

Use Rate Reasoning to Convert Between Measurement Systems

1.  **(MP) Reason** An elevator can hold at most 2,500 pounds. If 10 adults with an average mass of 80 kilograms each get on the elevator, can the elevator carry them? Show your work.

_____

2. **Math on the Spot** Find the weight, to the nearest tenth of a pound, of a dog that has a mass of 5,400 grams.

_____

3. **(MP) Critique Reasoning** Dwayne estimated his mass as 6 kilograms. Is his estimate reasonable? Explain your answer.

_____

4. A long-distance runner ran 5,000 meters (5 kilometers) in 12 minutes, 37.5 seconds. What is this distance to the nearest tenth of a mile?

_____

5. How many meters longer to the nearest tenth is 100 meters than 100 yards?

_____

6. **(MP) Health and Fitness** The average adult has 1.2 to 1.5 gallons of blood in their body. How much blood does the average adult have in liters? Round your answer to the nearest tenth liter.

_____

For Problems 7–12, convert to the unit indicated in parentheses. Then compare the measurements using <, =, or >. (Round to nearest tenth if necessary.)

7. 100 inches ☐ 250 centimeters (centimeters) **8.** 4 pounds ☐ 2 kilograms (pounds)

_____

9. 3 miles ☐ 5 kilometers (miles) **10.** 5 feet ☐ 2 meters (meters)

_____

11. 5 liters ☐ 5 quart (liters) **12.** 6 inches ☐ 15.24 centimeters (centimeters)

_____

13. Write the following measurements in order from least to greatest: 600 centimeters, 200 inches, 4 meters, 10 feet.

_____

14. About how many kilograms are in 2,000 pounds (1 ton)?

Ⓐ 90.8 kilograms   Ⓒ 908 kilograms

Ⓑ 440.5 kilograms   Ⓓ 4,405 kilograms

15. Which rate gives the lower price, $4.89 per kilogram or $4.89 per pound? Justify your answer.

_____

_____

16. Match each measurement on the left with the measurement that is closest to it on the right.

6 in. ●   ● 3.94 in.

10 cm ●   ● 5.08 cm

8 cm ●   ● 3.15 in.

2 in. ●   ● 15.24 cm

Spiral Review

17. A jar contains 3 red marbles for every 1 blue marble.

A. If there are 12 blue marbles, how many red marbles are there?

_____

B. If there are 12 red marbles how many blue marbles are there?

_____

C. If there are 12 marbles in all, how many red marbles and how many blue marbles are there?

_____

18. A wall is $4\frac{1}{2}$ feet long and has an area of $15\frac{3}{4}$ square feet. What is its height in feet?

_____

19. Adam runs 6.75 kilometers each day for 4 days. On the fifth day, he runs 9.5 kilometers. How many kilometers has he run altogether?

_____

Vocabulary

Complete the following to review your vocabulary for this module.

1. A rate in which two quantities are equal, but use different units, is called a(n) _____.

2. A graph that uses sections of a circle to compare parts to the whole and parts to other parts is called a(n) _____.

3. A comparison of two quantities by division is a(n) _____.

4. How is a conversion factor like a unit rate? How are they different?

_____

_____

_____

_____

Concepts and Skills

5. (MP) **Use Tools** Sanjib collected information from students in the sixth grade about their favorite sport. He represented the results in a circle graph. If there are 240 students in the sixth grade, how many students preferred soccer? State what strategy and tool you will use to answer the question, explain your choice, and then find the answer.

_____

_____

_____

_____

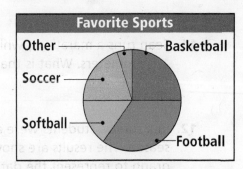

Favorite Sports

6. Frieda makes a batch of punch using the recipe shown. She wants to compare the ingredients using a circle graph. Find the angle measure for each section of the circle graph.

Cranberry juice: _____

Pineapple juice: _____

Orange juice: _____

Ginger ale: _____

Fruit Punch

64 ounces of cranberry juice

24 ounces pineapple juice

24 ounces orange juice

32 ounces ginger ale

7. Match each measurement with its equivalent measurement.

360 in. •   • 36 ft

12 yd •   • 288 in.

24 ft •   • 440 yd

0.25 mi •   • 10 yd

8. To convert a quantity from kilograms to pounds using a conversion factor, pounds should be in the ☐ first / second ☐ quantity of the conversion factor and kilograms should be in the ☐ first / second ☐ quantity of the conversion factor.

9. 3,500 milligrams is equivalent to which of the following measurements? Select all that apply.

Ⓐ 0.0035 kg   Ⓓ 35 kg

Ⓑ 0.35 g   Ⓔ 3,500,000 g

Ⓒ 3.5 g

10. Fu Haifeng of China set a badminton world record with a smash of 332 kilometers per hour. A kilometer is about $\frac{5}{8}$ mile. What is the speed in miles per hour, to the closest whole number?

11. Sean runs a marathon, which is 26.2 miles long. A mile is about 1.6 kilometers. What is that distance to the nearest kilometer?

12. In a survey, students were asked about their favorite season. The results are shown in the table. Make a circle graph to represent the data.

Favorite Season	
Season	# of Students
Spring	30
Summer	54
Fall	24
Winter	12

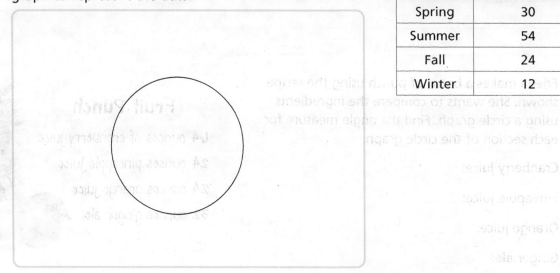

Identify and Represent Proportional Relationships

WHICH RATIO DOES NOT BELONG?

Express each ratio of apples to oranges shown below in words and as a fraction. Share with a partner or a small group.

A.

_____

B.

_____

C.

Apples	Oranges
8	18
32	72
56	126

_____

_____

D.

A grocer displays
4 dozen apples
9 dozen oranges

_____

_____

 Turn and Talk

- Explain how the ratios are related and how they are different.

- Which ratio does not belong? Explain why.

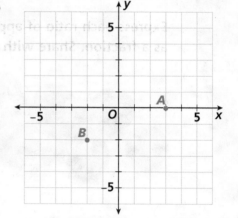

Are You Ready?

Complete these problems to review prior concepts and skills you will need for this module.

Solve One-Step Equations

Solve the equation.

1. $8x = 56$ _____

2. $4a = 23$ _____

Ordered Pairs on the Coordinate Plane

Write the ordered pair for each point.

3. A _____

4. B _____

Plot and label the ordered pairs on the graph.

	Point	(x, y)
5.	C	(−3, 2)
6.	D	(1, −2)

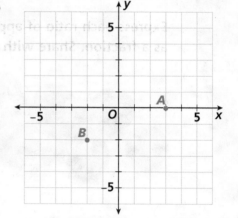

Divide Fractions and Mixed Numbers

Divide.

7. $\frac{3}{4} \div \frac{3}{5}$ _____

8. $7\frac{1}{2} \div \frac{5}{8}$ _____

9. $\frac{3}{8} \div \frac{1}{2}$ _____

Ratio Language

10. Jasper has a jar of marbles. Complete the table to show the ratios of marbles.

blue:red	
blue:yellow	
red:blue	
yellow:red	

Name _____

Explore Relationships

(I Can) recognize when a relationship presented in a table, diagram, or
verbal description can be represented by a constant unit rate.

Spark Your Learning

These salsas are made for a competition.

On Fire!

2 tablespoons peppers; 5 tablespoons tomatoes

Blazin'

4 tablespoons peppers; 12 tablespoons tomatoes

Kickin'

6 tablespoons peppers; 15 tablespoons tomatoes

Feel the Burn

3 tablespoons peppers; 6 tablespoons tomatoes

If peppers and tomatoes are the only ingredients in the salsas
and the names are based on taste, which two salsas should have
the same name? Show your work and explain.

 Turn and Talk Using the ratios described in the salsa recipes, identify which
salsa is the hottest and which is the mildest. Explain your reasoning.

© Houghton Mifflin Harcourt Publishing Company • **Image Credit:** (t) ©lizakorobkova/iStock/Getty Images Plus/Getty Images; (b) ©Torresigner/iStock/Getty Images Plus/Getty Images

Build Understanding

1 The table shows how many ounces of salsa you get when buying small jars of salsa.

Small jars of salsa	4	8	12	16	
Ounces of salsa	32	64	96		

A. Describe patterns you see in the rows of the table.

_____

_____

B. Describe a pattern you see in the columns of the table.

_____

_____

C. Use the patterns described in Parts A and B to fill in the blank cells in the table.

D. You previously learned that a unit rate is a rate in which the second quantity in the comparison is one unit, such as 4 ounces per 1 serving. Describe the relationship between ounces of salsa and small jars of salsa using a unit rate.

_____

_____

E. The diagram shows how many ounces of salsa you get when buying medium jars of salsa. Describe the relationship using a unit rate.

48 ounces

_____

_____

 Turn and Talk Is the relationship represented in the table the same as the relationship represented in the diagram in Part E? Why or why not?

2 ▶ The tables show the price and weight of avocados.

Avocados	Price
1	$1.25
2	$2.50
3	$3.75
4	$5.00
5	$6.25

Avocados	Weight
1	7 oz
2	13 oz
3	20 oz
4	26 oz
5	34 oz

An avocado is classified as a fruit, and in particular, as a one-seeded berry.

A. Can the relationship between the price and the number of avocados be described with a constant rate? Explain.

_____

_____

B. Can the relationship between the weight and the number of avocados be described with a constant rate? Explain.

_____

_____

Check Understanding

1. A 2-pound package of hamburger costs $7.00, and you pay $10.50 for a 3-pound package of hamburger. Complete the table. Then decide whether it makes sense to use a unit rate to describe the relationship. Explain.

Weight (lb)	2	3	4	5
Cost ($)	7.00		14.00	17.50

_____

_____

2. The table shows the total cost of different numbers of tickets. Decide whether it makes sense to use a constant rate to describe the relationship. Explain.

Number of Tickets	6	8	10	14	25
Total Cost ($)	34.50	44.00	52.50	73.50	131.25

_____

_____

On Your Own

3. **(MP) Reason** Flo measures the amount of water her high pressure sprayer uses and finds that it uses 20 gallons of water in 4 minutes and 30 gallons in 6 minutes. Complete the table. Then decide whether it makes sense to use a constant rate to describe the relationship. Explain.

Time (min)	2	4		10	18
Water (gal)	10		30	50	90

_____

_____

For Problems 4–5, use the information and the data in the tables.

Ken rode his bike on Monday and Tuesday. Each table shows the distance that he was from home at various times.

Monday	
Time (min)	Distance (km)
20	5
40	10
60	12
80	14
100	16

Tuesday	
Time (min)	Distance (km)
20	4
40	8
60	12
80	16
100	20

4. Can the relationship in Monday's table be described by a constant unit rate? Explain.

_____

5. Can the relationship in Tuesday's table be described by a constant unit rate? Explain.

_____

_____

I'm in a Learning Mindset!

What can I apply from previous work with ratios and rates to recognize when a relationship between two quantities can be described by a constant unit rate?

_____

_____

LESSON 11.1
**More Practice/
Homework**

ONLINE
Video Tutorials and
Interactive Examples

Explore Relationships

1. The amount of money Chaz earned for walking dogs is given in the table. Can the relationship be described by a constant rate? Explain.

Dogs walked	6	8	11
Money earned ($)	112.50	150.00	206.25

_____

_____

2. **STEM** The diagram shows the structure of a molecule of sulfur dioxide. The ratio of oxygen atoms to sulfur atoms in sulfur dioxide is always the same. How many oxygen atoms (O) are there when there are 6 sulfur atoms (S)? Explain how you got your answer.

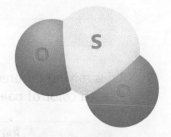

_____

_____

_____

3. (MP) **Reason** Three different sizes of sports-drink mix are shown with their prices. Can the relationship between price and volume (in grams) be described by a constant rate? Explain.

_____

_____

For Problems 4–5, use the values in the table.

Servings of cereal	Cups of cereal	Cups of milk
16	12	4
24	18	6

4. Can the relationship between cups of milk and cups of cereal be described by a constant ratio? Why or why not?

_____

_____

5. Can the relationship between cups of cereal and servings of cereal be described by a constant rate? Why or why not?

_____

_____

Test Prep

6. Jane is saving to buy a cell phone. She is given a $100 gift to start and saves $35 a month from her allowance. So after 1 month, Jane has saved $135. Does it make sense to represent the relationship between the amount saved and the number of months with one constant rate? Why or why not? Explain your answer.

_____

_____

_____

7. Raj is mixing different colors of paint. The table shows the amount of each color of paint Raj uses for each mixture.

Raj's Paint Mixtures		
Mixture	**Red (ounces)**	**Blue (ounces)**
1	2	1
2	7	3.5
3	4.5	2
4	5.5	2.5

Select the two mixtures that will produce the same color.

(A) mixtures 1 and 2

(B) mixtures 3 and 4

(C) mixtures 1 and 3

(D) mixtures 2 and 4

Spiral Review

8. At 1:00 p.m., a diver's elevation is −30 feet relative to sea level. At 2:00 p.m., the diver's elevation is −45 feet. At which time is the diver farther from sea level?

_____

9. A share of stock costs $83.60. The next day, the price increases by $15.35. The following day, the price decreases by $4.75. What is the final price?

_____

© Houghton Mifflin Harcourt Publishing Company

Name

Recognize Proportional
Relationships in Tables

(I Can) identify a proportional relationship, find its constant of proportionality,
and write an equation to represent it.

Spark Your Learning

For which tables can you predict the cost of 100 units of the item? Explain why
you can make that prediction for some of the tables and not for others. For
the tables that let you predict the cost of 100 units, find the cost.

Peanut butter (oz)	Total cost ($)
8	3
16	4
40	6

Binder clips	Total cost ($)
12	2
36	5
50	6

Trail mix (lb)	Total cost ($)
2	6
8	24
12	36

Shower sponges	Total cost ($)
4	8
8	16
10	20

Turn and Talk What characteristic of the table allows you to predict the cost
of any number of items?

Build Understanding

© Houghton Mifflin Harcourt Publishing Company • **Image Credit:** ©Nadezhda V Kulagina/Shutterstock

> **Connect to Vocabulary**
>
> Two quantities have a **proportional relationship** if the ratio of one quantity to the other is a constant. In a proportional relationship, the constant unit rate is called the **constant of proportionality** and is usually represented by the letter k.

1 Maxine walks dogs to earn extra money. The table of values shows the proportional relationship between the number of dogs Maxine walks and the amount of money she earns.

Dogs walked	2	4	6
Amount ($)	7	14	21

A. Show that the ratio of dogs walked to amount earned is a constant ratio.

_____

B. Show that the ratio of amount earned to dogs walked is a constant ratio.

_____

_____

C. What is the unit rate of dogs walked per dollar earned? Does it make sense? Explain.

_____

_____

D. What is the unit rate of dollars earned per dog walked? Does it make sense? Explain.

_____

_____

_____

E. What is the constant of proportionality k in this situation?

_____

_____

F. Describe what the constant of proportionality k represents in this situation.

_____

_____

_____

 Turn and Talk In a table of values that represents a proportional relationship, how can you find the constant of proportionality?

396

Name

Step It Out

2 Two relationships are represented in the tables. Which table shows a proportional relationship, and which does not? Explain.

Table 1

Windows washed, x	3	6	7
Amount earned ($), y	36	72	84

Table 2

Windows washed, x	4	5	8
Amount earned ($), y	48	55	64

Table 1

The ratios $\frac{\text{amount earned (\$), } y}{\text{windows, } x}$ are

$$\frac{36}{\Box} = \Box \quad \frac{\Box}{6} = \Box \quad \frac{\Box}{7} = \Box$$

The ratios $\frac{y}{x}$ are / are not equivalent. Therefore, the relationship shown in this table is / is not proportional.

Table 2

The ratios $\frac{\text{amount earned (\$), } y}{\text{windows, } x}$ are

$$\frac{48}{\Box} = \Box \quad \frac{\Box}{5} = \Box \quad \frac{\Box}{8} = \Box$$

The ratios $\frac{y}{x}$ are / are not equivalent. Therefore, the relationship shown in this table is / is not proportional.

3 The number of students whom Malcolm tutors is proportional to the amount he earns. The calendar shows Malcolm's earnings from tutoring in one week.

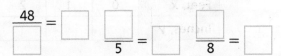

Tutoring Schedule

Mon	Tue	Wed	Thu	Fri
Clive	Justice	Rance	Molly	Janis
Bray	Krissy	Kimee	Rick	$30
Jen	Eve	Yuri	Sharona	
Haley	Nolan	$90	Mikay	
$120	Armond		Paco	
	Landree		$150	
	$180			

A. Complete the table.

Number of students, x		3		5	
Amount earned ($), y	30		120		180

B. Find the constant of proportionality k.

$$k = \frac{y}{x} = \frac{\Box}{\Box} = \Box$$

C. The equation for a proportional relationship is $y = kx$, where k is the constant of proportionality. Use the value of k you found in Part B to write an equation for this proportional relationship.

$$y = \Box x$$

© Houghton Mifflin Harcourt Publishing Company

Module 11 • Lesson 2

397

4 ▸ The equation $y = 12x$ represents the number of inches y in x feet.

A. The equation $y = 12x$ [does / does not] represent a proportional relationship. If the equation represents a proportional relationship, what is the constant of proportionality? How do you know?

_____

_____

B. Use the equation to complete the table of values for the relationship between inches and feet.

Feet, x	0	1	2			5
Inches, y				36	48	

 Turn and Talk When would it be better to use an equation to represent a proportional relationship? When would it be better to use a table?

Check Understanding

1. There are 4 quarters in $1.00.

   A. Make a table of values to represent this relationship.

Dollars, x					
Quarters, y					

   B. Is this a proportional relationship? If so, identify k and explain what it represents. If not, explain why not.

   _____

   C. Write an equation for the situation. _____

2. The equation $y = 7x$ gives the cost y of x pounds of chicken at the grocery store. Complete the table for the given weights of chicken.

Weight (lb), x	1	2	5	8
Cost ($), y				

3. Is the relationship in the table proportional? If it is, write its equation.

x	1	2	3	4
y	5	10	15	20

On Your Own

4. (MP) **Model with Mathematics** Reanna is making a scrapbook which holds 14 photos on each 2-page spread. Complete the table of values to represent this relationship. Write an equation for the situation.

2-page spreads, x				
Photos, y				

For Problems 5–6, tell whether each table represents a proportional relationship. If it does, identify the constant of proportionality.

5.

x	3	7	9
y	63	147	189

6.

x	14	15	16
y	21	22.5	15

7. Determine whether the table represents a proportional relationship. If it does, find the constant of proportionality and use it to write an equation to represent the table of values.

x	1	2	3	4	5
y	7	14	21	28	35

8. The equation $y = 8x$ gives the number of slices y in x pizzas. Complete the table of values using the equation. Identify the constant of proportionality. Then complete each sentence.

Pizzas, x				
Slices, y				

There are _____ slices in 3 pizzas. There are 16 slices in _____ pizzas.

9. (MP) **Reason** The table shows the relationship between the number of workers painting apartments in an apartment building and the number of days it takes to paint the apartments. Determine whether the relationship is proportional. Explain your reasoning.

Workers, x	5	10	15	20	25
Duration of job (days), y	60	30	20	15	12

For Problems 10–12, use the description of a proportional relationship to complete the table. Then identify the constant of proportionality, and write an equation for the situation.

10. A 2-cup serving of chicken noodle soup has 1.5 ounces of noodles.

Cups of soup, x	Ounces of noodles, y

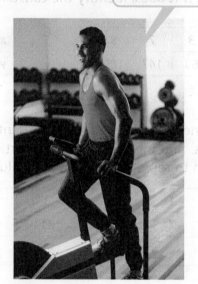

126 steps every 3 minutes

11. Rick is exercising at a constant pace.

Time (min), x	Steps, y

12. Colin is preparing equal-sized care packages. He placed 34 items in 2 care packages he made.

Packages, x				
Items, y				

13. The equation $y = 100x$ gives the number of centimeters y in x meters. Complete the table of values using the equation. Identify the constant of proportionality. Then complete each sentence.

Meters, x				
Centimeters, y				

$k =$ _____; There are _____ centimeters in 3 meters. There are 200 centimeters in _____ meters.

I'm in a Learning Mindset!

What strategies do I use to decide if a relationship displayed in a table is proportional? How do I know when I am finished?

_____

_____

© Houghton Mifflin Harcourt Publishing Company • Image Credit: ©Realstock/Shutterstock

Recognize Proportional Relationships in Tables

For Problems 1–2, tell whether each table represents a proportional relationship. If it does, identify the constant of proportionality.

1.

x	2	5	7
y	18	45	63

2.

x	3	4	5
y	42	60	80

3. **Math on the Spot** Determine whether the table of values represents a proportional relationship. If it does, find the constant of proportionality and use it to write an equation to represent the table.

Number of lawns, x	1	2	3	4
Amount earned ($), y	24	48	72	96

4. The equation $y = 6x$ gives the cost y of x of the tickets shown. Complete the table of values. Identify the constant of proportionality. Then complete each sentence.

Tickets, x				
Cost ($), y				

ADMIT ONE $6

It costs _____ for 5 movie tickets.

It costs $24 for _____ movie tickets.

(MP) **Model with Mathematics** For Problems 5–6, use the description of a proportional relationship and the table. Identify the constant of proportionality, and then write an equation to represent the situation in the table.

5. Alison earned $24 by stocking shelves at the grocery store for 3 hours.

Time (h), x	1	2	3	6
Total pay ($), y	8	16	24	48

6. Each cooler holds 18 water bottles.

Coolers, x	1	2	4	7
Water bottles, y	18	36	72	126

Test Prep

7. Which table represents a proportional relationship?

Table 1			
Carrots (lb)	2	3	4
Number of carrots	23	33	43

Table 2			
Deli meat (lb)	2	3	4
Total cost ($)	23	34.50	46

8. Use the proportional relationship in the table.

Milk (gal), x	2	4	8
Servings, y	32	64	128

 A. Write an equation for the relationship.

 _____

 B. There are 4 quarts in a gallon and 4 cups in a quart. How many cups are in one serving?

 _____

 C. There are 8 fluid ounces in a cup. How many fluid ounces are in one serving?

 _____

9. What is the meaning of the constant of proportionality in the situation represented by the table?

Rocking chairs, x	2	3	5
Time to build (h), y	48	72	120

_____

10. Describe a method for determining whether a table represents a proportional relationship.

_____

_____

_____

11. Kevin uses $\frac{2}{3}$ cup of flour to make 2 servings of biscuits. How many cups of flour are there per serving? How many cups of flour should Kevin use to make 7 servings?

 Ⓐ $\frac{1}{3}$ cup; $2\frac{1}{3}$ cups Ⓒ $\frac{2}{3}$ cup; $4\frac{2}{3}$ cups

 Ⓑ $\frac{2}{3}$ cup; $2\frac{1}{3}$ cups Ⓓ $1\frac{1}{3}$ cups; $4\frac{2}{3}$ cups

Spiral Review

12. Donya ran a 3-kilometer race at a constant speed in 21 minutes 30 seconds. At this speed, how long does it take her to run 1 kilometer?

_____

13. It costs $20 for 4 play tickets and $35 for 7 play tickets. Is the cost per ticket constant? Why or why not?

_____

© Houghton Mifflin Harcourt Publishing Company

Name _____

Recognize Proportional Relationships in Graphs

(I Can) identify a proportional relationship from a graph and use the graph to find the constant of proportionality and equation.

Spark Your Learning

Jake makes custom-painted sneakers. He makes 6 pairs in 4 hours. On a graph of this proportional relationship, what point would represent 6 pairs in 4 hours? Justify your answer with a description or a model.

x	y

Turn and Talk How did you decide which axis represents which variable? Explain.

Build Understanding

1 ▶ The table shows the proportional relationship between pairs of sneakers Jake makes to sell at a craft fair and the revenue from selling them.

Pairs of sneakers, x	0	1	2	3	4	5
Revenue ($), y	0	40	80	120	160	200

A. How do you know the data in the table show a proportional relationship? What is the constant of proportionality?

_____

B. Write the data in the table as ordered pairs and graph them.

_____

C. Do the points all lie along a straight line? _____

D. Does the graph pass through the origin? _____

Sneakers

Revenue ($) vs *Pairs of sneakers*

> **Turn and Talk** Describe the characteristics of the graph of a proportional relationship.

2 ▶ Maya sells homemade spice mixes in different sizes at the craft fair. The graph shows the proportional relationship between teaspoons of cumin and teaspoons of chili powder in one recipe.

A. What does the origin represent?

_____

_____

B. What are the coordinates of the point at x = 1, and what do they represent?

_____

_____

C. Explain why the graph shows a proportional relationship.

_____

_____

D. Why is the graph a solid line?

_____

_____

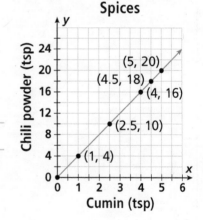

Spices

Chili powder (tsp) vs *Cumin (tsp)*

(5, 20)
(4.5, 18)
(4, 16)
(2.5, 10)
(1, 4)

Step It Out

3 Parker sells lemonade at the craft fair. The relationship between the number of servings and cups of water used is shown.

Servings, x	2	3	6	8
Water (c), y	1	$1\frac{1}{2}$	3	4

A. Graph the relationship, and tell whether it is a proportional relationship. Explain how you know.

_____

_____

_____

Lemonade

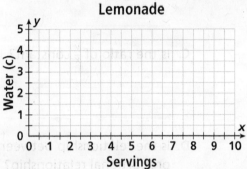

B. The graph of the line should be [solid / dashed] because x and y can be any nonnegative numbers.

C. What is the constant of proportionality? Write an equation for the relationship.

_____

4 Angel was in charge of ordering graphic T-shirts for the craft fair. The graph shows the relationship between the number of boxes of T-shirts Angel ordered x and the total number of T-shirts y.

A. Is the relationship in the graph a proportional relationship? Explain how you know.

_____

_____

Graphic T-Shirts

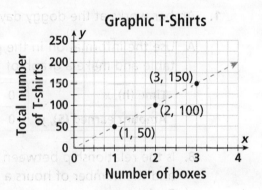

(3, 150)
(2, 100)
(1, 50)

B. What is the constant of proportionality? How do you know based on the graph?

_____

_____

C. Write an equation to represent the relationship.

_____

_____

D. Why is the graph dashed rather than solid?

_____

5 Alonso pays a fee of $4 plus a percent of his sales to participate in the crafts fair. The table shows the amount Alonso pays in relationship to his sales.

Sales ($), x	10.00	20.00	35.00	45.00	50.00
Fee ($), y	4.50	5.00	5.75	6.25	6.50

A. Graph the relationship.

B. What does the point (0, 4.00) represent?

_____

_____

C. Is the ratio of $\frac{y}{x}$ constant? Justify your answer.

_____

_____

D. Is the relationship between the total fees and the amount of sales a proportional relationship? Explain.

_____

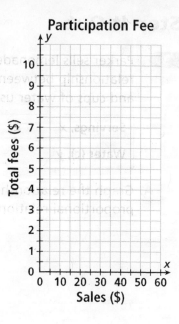

Participation Fee

Check Understanding

1. Amber works at the doggy daycare after school.

A. Use the information in the photograph to complete the table and make a graph of the data.

Time (h), x	0	1	2	3		5
Amount earned ($), y	0			32		

B. Is the relationship between the amount Amber earns and the number of hours a proportional relationship? Explain.

_____

_____

C. The y-coordinate of which point represents the constant of proportionality?

_____

D. What is the ratio $\frac{y}{x}$ for each point on the graph?

_____

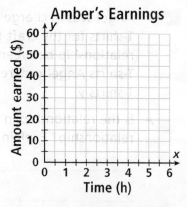

Amber's Earnings

$8 PER HOUR

On Your Own

2. **(MP)** **Model with Mathematics** The table
shows the number of cups of cherries used to
bake pies.

   Make a graph of the data. Tell whether the
relationship between the amount of cherries
and the number of pies is a proportional
relationship. Explain.

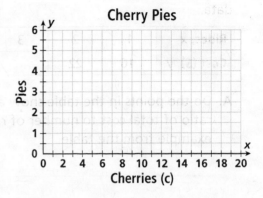

Cherry Pies

Cherries (c), x	4	8	12	16
Pies, y	1	2	3	4

_____

_____

_____

3. The graph shows the distance x Yazmin jogs and the
amount of time y that it takes her.

   A. What is the meaning of the point (1, 16) on the graph?

   _____

   _____

   _____

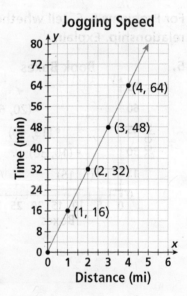

Jogging Speed

   B. Does the graph show a proportional relationship? If so,
what is the constant of proportionality k? What is the
equation of the graph? Explain your reasoning.

   _____

   _____

   _____

   _____

   C. **Open Ended** Describe how the graph would be different if Yazmin's
jogging rate were a different constant.

   _____

   _____

   _____

4. Henry goes to the town fair. Use the prices on the photograph to complete the table and graph the data.

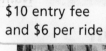
$10 entry fee and $6 per ride

Rides, x	1	2	3	4
Cost ($), y	16	22		34

A. Do the points in the table show a constant ratio of total cost to number of rides? Give an example from the table.

_____

_____

B. Does the graph show a proportional relationship? Why or why not?

_____

_____

Town Fair

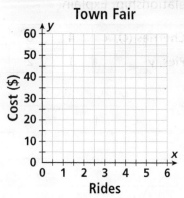

For Problems 5–6, tell whether the graph shows a proportional relationship. Explain.

5.

Book Boxes

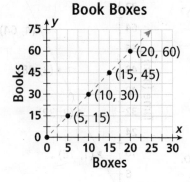

6.

Rental Costs

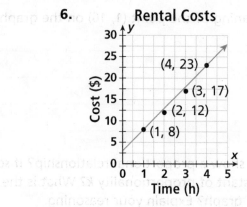

_____   _____

_____   _____

_____   _____

I'm in a Learning Mindset!

How can I make the process of writing a proportional relationship for a graph more efficient?

_____

_____

Recognize Proportional Relationships in Graphs

1. The graph shows the area y that can be covered by a given amount of paint x when using a paint sprayer.

  A. Does the graph show a proportional relationship? Explain.

  _____

  _____

  _____

  B. Using the point (3, 45), find the constant of proportionality k and write an equation that describes the proportional relationship.

  _____

2. (MP) **Construct Arguments** Graph the data from the table.

x	2	4	6	8	10
y	4	6	8	10	12

Does the graph show the relationship is a proportional relationship? Does the relationship have a constant of proportionality? Justify your answer using any two points from the table.

_____

_____

_____

Paint Usage

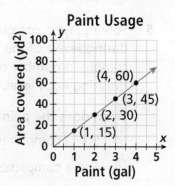

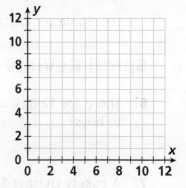

3. **Open Ended** Think of a proportional relationship you may see in your daily life. Make a table of data and graph the data. Explain how you know that the data show a proportional relationship.

Test Prep

4. The table and graph show the costs of books at the library book sale. Select all the ordered pairs that lie on the line in the graph.

Books, x	2	4	6	8	10
Cost ($), y	5	10	15	20	25

Ⓐ (3, 7.5)

Ⓑ (12, 33)

Ⓒ (9, 22.5)

Ⓓ (11, 27)

Ⓔ (5, 12.5)

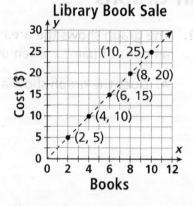

Library Book Sale

5. Sonia plays a computer game and completes puzzles during levels of the game. The graph shows the combined number of puzzles she completed after finishing each level.

What does the point (1, 3) on the graph represent?

Ⓐ Sonia completes 1 puzzle every 3 levels.

Ⓑ Sonia completes 3 puzzles on each level.

Ⓒ Sonia completes 1 puzzle on level 3.

Ⓓ Sonia completes puzzles 1 to 3.

Computer Game Puzzles

Spiral Review

6. There are 12 girls and 14 boys in class today. What is the ratio of girls to boys?

7. A bakery charges $14.00 for 4 croissant sandwiches. What is the unit rate?

8. The table shows how many pages Andy reads over time. Does Andy read at a constant rate? Explain.

Time (min), x	10	20	30	40	50
Pages, y	4	9	10	15	20

Name

Use Proportional Relationships to Solve Rate Problems

(**I Can**) identify the constant of proportionality and write an equation for a proportional relationship presented in various forms and use them to solve multi-step ratio problems.

Step It Out

1 ▷ The bar diagram shows how many inches a garden snail travels over time. At this rate, how many feet would the snail travel in 0.75 hour?

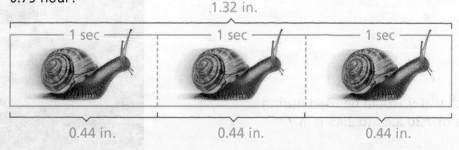

1.32 in.

1 sec   1 sec   1 sec

0.44 in.   0.44 in.   0.44 in.

A. What is the unit rate in inches per second? Use conversion factors to convert the unit rate to feet per hour.

$$\frac{\boxed{}\ \text{in.}}{1\ \text{s}} \times \frac{\boxed{}\ \text{s}}{1\ \text{min}} \times \frac{\boxed{}\ \text{min}}{1\ \text{h}} = \frac{\boxed{}\ \text{in.}}{1\ \text{h}} \times \frac{1\ \text{ft}}{\boxed{}\ \text{in.}} = \frac{\boxed{}\ \text{ft}}{1\ \text{h}}$$

B. Write an equation for the number of feet y the snail travels in x hours, and use it to solve the problem.

$y = kx$

$y = \underline{\hspace{2cm}}\ x$

$y = \underline{\hspace{2cm}}\ (\underline{\hspace{1cm}}) = 99$ feet in 0.75 hour

C. What is the unit rate in miles per hour? Write an equation for the number of miles y the garden snail travels in x hours. (5,280 ft = 1 mi)

$$\frac{\boxed{}\ \text{ft}}{1\ \text{h}} \times \frac{1\ \text{mi}}{5,280\ \text{ft}} = \frac{\boxed{}\ \text{mi}}{1\ \text{h}} \qquad y = \underline{\hspace{1.5cm}}\ x$$

 Turn and Talk Explain how you converted the unit rate to miles per hour.

2 The graph shows the number of gallons of water used over time in one lane of a car wash. At this rate, how much water would be used if the lane were used continuously from 8:00 a.m. to noon?

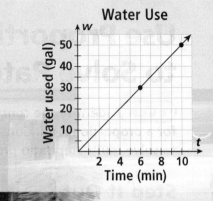

Water Use

A. What is the unit rate in gallons per minute? Use conversion factors to convert the unit rate to gallons per hour.

$$\frac{\boxed{}\ \text{gal}}{1\ \text{min}} \times \frac{\boxed{}\ \text{min}}{1\ \text{h}} = \frac{\boxed{}\ \text{gal}}{1\ \text{h}}$$

B. Write an equation for the number of gallons of water y used in x hours, and use it to solve the problem.

$y = kx$

$y = \underline{\hspace{2cm}} x$

$y = \underline{\hspace{1.5cm}} (\underline{\hspace{1.5cm}}) = \underline{\hspace{1.5cm}}$ gallons

C. How much water would be used during the hours of 7:30 a.m. to 3:45 p.m.?

$y = \underline{\hspace{1.5cm}} x$

$y = \underline{\hspace{1.5cm}} (\underline{\hspace{1.5cm}}) = \underline{\hspace{1.5cm}}$ gallons

Turn and Talk In Parts B and C, how did you find the number to put in the parentheses?

3 The graph shows Michaela's earnings over time. Marcus's hourly rate is represented in the table. Who has a greater rate of pay, and how much more than the other will that person earn in 40 hours of work?

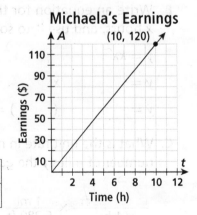

Michaela's Earnings

A. Complete the table, write an equation, and graph Marcus's earnings A over time t.

Marcus's Earnings

Time (h)	2	4	5		
Earnings ($)	19.00			57.00	76.00

$k = \frac{19}{2} = \underline{\hspace{2cm}}$

$A = \underline{\hspace{2cm}}$

Name _____

B. Use the graph to determine who is earning a greater rate of pay. Explain how you know.

_____
_____

C. What information do you still need in order to solve the problem? Solve the problem and show your work.

I still need: _____

Michaela

$$\frac{\boxed{}}{10} = k, \text{ or } k = \underline{}$$

$A = kt$

$A = \underline{} t$

$A = \underline{} (\underline{}) = \underline{}$

Marcus

$A = kt$

$A = \underline{} t$

$A = \underline{} (\underline{}) = \underline{}$

_____
_____

 Turn and Talk What happens to the difference in their earnings over time?

Check Understanding

1. Solve the problems using the diagrams.

Rate A

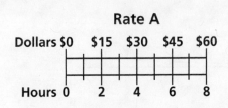

Dollars $0 $15 $30 $45 $60

Hours   0   2   4   6   8

Rate B

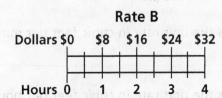

Dollars $0 $8 $16 $24 $32

Hours   0   1   2   3   4

A. Write an equation for the number of dollars *y* earned from working *x* hours for each rate.

_____

B. What is the difference between the total dollars earned from 40 hours of work at these rates? Show your work.

_____

On Your Own

2. Use the diagram of distance traveled at a constant rate.

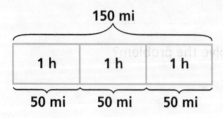

   A. What is the unit rate?

   _____

   B. Convert the rate to feet per minute.

   _____

   C. Convert the rate to inches per second.

   _____

3. The graph shows the number of cubic feet of water used over time at a water park that is open during the hours in the table. At this rate, how many cubic feet of water would be used at the water park on a Sunday?

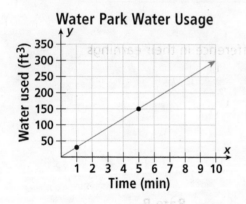

Water Park Hours of Operation	
Days	**Hours**
Monday to Thursday	11:00 a.m. to 7:30 p.m.
Friday and Saturday	11:00 a.m. to 9:00 p.m.
Sunday	12:00 p.m. to 6:00 p.m.

   A. What is the unit rate in cubic feet per minute?

   _____

   B. What is the unit rate in cubic feet per hour?

   _____

   C. Write an equation for the number of cubic feet of water y used in x hours, and use it to solve the problem.

   _____

   D. How many cubic feet of water would be used at the water park on a Tuesday?

   _____

4. **(MP) Model with Mathematics** The distance Dan jogs over time is shown in the graph. Pattie's constant jogging speed is represented in the table. Who has a faster jogging speed? How much more distance will that jogger have traveled in a total of 22 hours jogging?

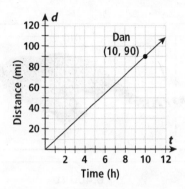

Dan

Time (h)	Distance (mi)
2	12
3	
5	
	42
	60

Pattie

A. Use the table to find Pattie's jogging speed k. Complete the table.

_____

B. Write an equation for the distance in miles d that Pattie jogs in t hours. Graph the equation on the grid with Dan's graph.

_____

C. Solve the problem and show your work.

5. A cheetah, the world's fastest land animal, cannot maintain its top speed for very long. This bar diagram shows a cheetah's top speed, in feet per minute. Suppose a racecar is driven at the cheetah's top speed. How many miles would the racecar travel in 3 hours?

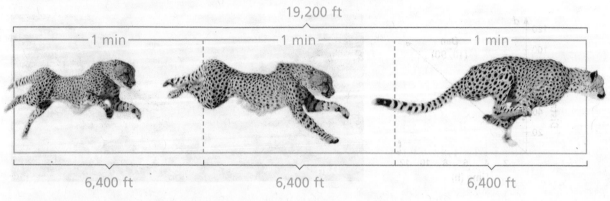

19,200 ft

1 min   1 min   1 min

6,400 ft   6,400 ft   6,400 ft

A. What is the unit rate in feet per hour?

B. What is the unit rate in miles per hour, to the nearest tenth?

C. Write an equation for the number of miles *y* that the racecar travels in *x* hours, and use it to solve the problem.

6. Rhoni reads at a rate of 75 pages per hour. The number of pages Rie reads over time is shown in the table.

Time (h)	3	5	9	10
Pages	195	325	585	650

A. What is Rie's rate of reading? Whose rate is greater?

B. At these rates, what is the difference in the number of pages they will read in 4 hours?

C. How long will it take each student to read a book with 780 pages? Show your work.

LESSON 11.4
**More Practice/
Homework**

ONLINE

Video Tutorials and
Interactive Examples

Use Proportional Relationships
to Solve Rate Problems

For Problems 1–4, give each rate in miles per hour. Round to the nearest tenth.

1. Dev jogs $8\frac{1}{2}$ miles in $1\frac{1}{2}$ hours.

_____

2. Caroline walks $9\frac{1}{2}$ inches per second.

_____

3. Dhruv jogs 8 feet per second.

_____

4. Rachel jogs 20 feet in 3 seconds.

_____

5. A bald eagle flies 43.2 meters in 3 seconds. The graph shows the distance a typical peregrine falcon flies over time. At these rates, what is the difference in the distances flown by these two birds after 3 hours of flight? Show your work.

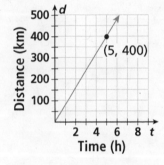

(5, 400)

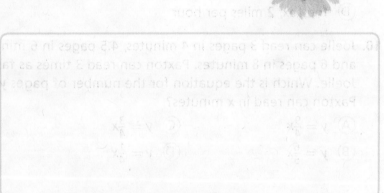

6. Two water tanks are leaking. Tank A has leaked $\frac{1}{16}$ of a gallon in $\frac{1}{12}$ minute, and Tank B has leaked $\frac{3}{80}$ of a gallon in $\frac{1}{30}$ minute. Which tank is leaking faster?

_____

7. Write an equation for each boat-rental company that gives the cost in dollars y of renting a kayak for x hours. What is the difference in cost between the company that charges the most and the one that charges the least for 4 hours? Show your work.

Company B The cost y of renting a kayak for x hours is $9.00 for each half hour.

Company C The cost y of renting a kayak is $14.25 per hour.

_____

_____

Company A	
Hours	Total cost ($)
2	$33.00
3	$49.50
4	$66.00
5	$82.50

Test Prep

8. James walked at a constant rate for 3 hours as shown in the graph. Jaycee walked 14.5 miles in 3 hours at a constant rate. Who walked farther, and how much farther? Explain.

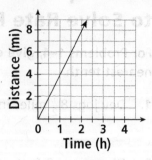

_____

_____

_____

9. A squirrel can run a short distance at a rate of $4\frac{3}{4}$ miles in 15 minutes. A fox can run a short distance at a rate of 21 miles in half an hour. Which is faster, and how much faster in miles per hour?

Ⓐ the squirrel; 23 miles per hour

Ⓑ the fox; 23 miles per hour

Ⓒ the squirrel; 2 miles per hour

Ⓓ the fox; 2 miles per hour

10. Joelle can read 3 pages in 4 minutes, 4.5 pages in 6 minutes, and 6 pages in 8 minutes. Paxton can read 3 times as fast as Joelle. Which is the equation for the number of pages y that Paxton can read in x minutes?

Ⓐ $y = \frac{9}{4}x$ Ⓒ $y = \frac{3}{4}x$

Ⓑ $y = \frac{6}{5}x$ Ⓓ $y = \frac{1}{4}x$

Spiral Review

For Problems 11–12, compare. Write < or >.

11. −3 _____ −15

12. $-\frac{5}{8}$ _____ $-\frac{1}{4}$

13. List the numbers in order from least to greatest.

−2, 8, −15, −5, 3, 1

_____

For Problems 14–16, graph each number on the number line. Then use your number line to find the absolute value of each number.

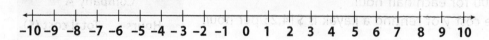

14. 2 _____   15. −8 _____   16. −5 _____

Vocabulary

For Problems 1–3, choose the correct term from the Vocabulary box.

1. the quantity k in a relationship described by an equation of the form $y = kx$

   _____

2. a rate in which the second quantity is one unit

   _____

3. a relationship between two quantities in which the rate of change or the ratio of one quantity to the other is constant

   _____

Concepts and Skills

4. Which ratio is equivalent to $\frac{3}{1}$?

   Ⓐ $\frac{\frac{1}{4}}{\frac{2}{3}}$ Ⓑ $\frac{2}{\frac{2}{3}}$ Ⓒ $\frac{4}{\frac{5}{6}}$ Ⓓ $\frac{5}{6}$

5. A news radio program has 3 commercial breaks per half-hour of programming. What is the unit rate of commercials to hours of programming?

   _____

6. (MP) **Use Tools** A recipe calls for 2 cups of sugar for $\frac{1}{4}$ cup of butter. What is the unit rate for sugar to butter? State what strategy and tool you will use to answer the question, explain your choice, and then find the answer.

   _____

   _____

7. Jana and Jenn are training to run a race. Jana runs 3 miles in $\frac{1}{3}$ hour. Jenn runs 5 miles in $\frac{3}{4}$ hour. Who runs faster, and what is the unit rate of her speed in minutes per mile?

   _____

8. Which of the following tables represents data that have a proportional relationship?

Ⓐ
x	y
0	0
1	1.5
3	3.5
6	6.5
8	8.5

Ⓑ
x	y
0	0
1	1.5
3	4.5
6	9.0
8	12.0

Ⓒ
x	y
0	0.5
1	1
3	3
6	6
8	8

Ⓓ
x	y
0	0
1	0.5
3	1.5
6	3
8	5

For Problems 9–10, write an equation of the form $y = kx$ for the relationship shown in the graph or table.

9.

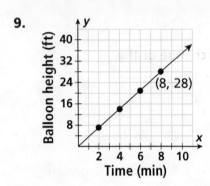

_____

10.

x	6	10	12
y	45	75	90

11. A store sells beans for 80¢ per pound.

A. Graph the proportional relationship that gives the cost y in dollars of buying x pounds of beans.

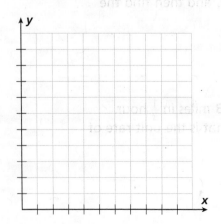

B. Write an equation of the form $y = kx$ to represent this relationship.

_____

_____

C. A farmers' market sells organic locally-grown beans for $1.25 per pound. How much more would it cost to buy 3 pounds of beans at the farmers' market than at the store?

_____

_____

12 Understand and Apply Percent

TIME TO CLEAN UP

A nature club held a beach cleanup. Four club members described the length of the beach that they each cleaned.

I cleaned 0.16 mile.

I cleaned 0.3 mile.

I cleaned 0.28 mile.

I cleaned 0.2 mile.

Kurt   Maria   Eddie   Celia

Find the total amount of beach the club cleaned.

A. Write a fraction with a denominator of 10 or 100 that is equal to each decimal.

$0.16 =$ _____ $0.28 =$ _____

$0.3 =$ _____ $0.2 =$ _____

B. What length of the beach did the club clean? _____

 Turn and Talk

• How does the length of beach cleaned compare with 1 mile? How do you know?

• How would the length of beach cleaned change if Kurt cleaned $\frac{6}{100}$ mile more? Justify your response.

Are You Ready?

Complete these problems to review prior concepts and skills you will need for this module.

Relate Fractions and Decimals

Write each fraction as a decimal.

1. $\frac{7}{10}$ = _____   **2.** $\frac{3}{10}$ = _____

3. $\frac{9}{10}$ = _____   **4.** $\frac{5}{10}$ = _____

5. $\frac{12}{100}$ = _____   **6.** $\frac{73}{100}$ = _____

7. $\frac{45}{100}$ = _____   **8.** $\frac{90}{100}$ = _____

Write Decimals as Fractions

Write each decimal as a fraction with a denominator of 10 or 100.

9. 0.6 = _____   **10.** 0.8 = _____

11. 0.16 = _____   **12.** 0.25 = _____

13. 0.3 = _____   **14.** 0.24 = _____

15. 0.52 = _____   **16.** 0.44 = _____

Name _____

Understand, Express, and Compare Percent Ratios

(**I Can**) use three different methods to write a ratio as a percent.

Spark Your Learning

A race car uses 2 gallons of gas to travel 25 miles. How many miles can the race car travel on 8 gallons of gas?

> **Turn and Talk** How can you use the ratio of 2 gallons of gas to 25 miles to write a ratio for the number of miles the race car travels on 1 gallon of gas? How could this be useful?

Build Understanding

1 Eleanor, Tillie, and Caleb earn money training dogs to surf. For every dollar they earn, Caleb gets 20 cents, Tillie gets 30 cents, and Eleanor gets 50 cents.

A. Write a ratio that shows how much each trainer earns from a dollar.

Caleb: ☐ : 100

Tillie: ☐ : 100

Eleanor: ☐ : 100

B. Caleb's portion of each dollar earned is shaded on the 10 × 10 grid. How many boxes do you need to shade to represent Tillie's portion? Shade in Tillie's portion of each dollar on the grid.

_____

C. A percent is a part-to-whole ratio with a whole of 100. You can write 25% as 25 : 100 or $\frac{25}{100}$. Write percents to represent the amounts Caleb and Tillie earn from each dollar. Explain how you found them.

_____

_____

_____

_____

D. What does the part of the grid that isn't shaded represent? Write a percent to represent this portion of the grid.

_____

_____

_____

 Turn and Talk Devon says that the ratios 2:10, 3:10, and 5:10 represent Caleb's, Tillie's, and Eleanor's portions. Is Devon right? If so, explain how he found these ratios. If not, explain Devon's error.

2 A survey says that 13 out of 20 people have pets. Write this ratio as a percent.

A. One way to write a ratio as a percent is to use a table. Complete the table to write equivalent ratios for the ratio 13:20.

People who have pets	13				
Total number of people	20	40		80	

B. Use the table to write the percent of people who own pets. What is $\frac{13}{20}$ as a percent? Explain.

_____

_____

_____

C. You also can use equivalent ratios to find the percent. What is $\frac{13}{20}$ as a percent?

$$\frac{13}{20} = \frac{\boxed{}}{100}$$

$$\frac{13}{20} = \underline{} \%$$

Turn and Talk Could you use any of the ratios in the table to find the percent?

3 A recipe for pie crusts includes 1 cup of sugar for every 4 cups of flour. Find the ratio of sugar to flour as a percent.

> pie crust: 1 cup of sugar per 4 cups of flour

A. What fraction can represent the ratio of sugar to flour? Convert this fraction to a decimal. Explain how you did the conversion.

_____

_____

B. Write the decimal as a percent. Explain how you found the percent.

_____

Step It Out

4 The diagram shows quiz results in red for John and Vince. Who received the higher score, John or Vince?

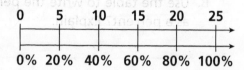

John (20/25)
1.
2.
3.
4.
5.
6.
7.

Vince (82.5%)
1.
2.
3.
4.
5.
6.
7.

A. What can you do to solve this problem?

_____

_____

B. Many test scores are written as percents. Use the double number line to convert John's score to a percent. John's score is a part-to-whole ratio with a whole of 25. So 25 is aligned with 100% on the double number line.

```
0     5    10    15    20    25
|-----|-----|-----|-----|-----|---->
0%  20%  40%  60%  80%  100%
```

Mark John's score on the top number line.

On the bottom number line, mark the percent that aligns with John's score.

C. Use the numbers you marked in Part B to write $\frac{20}{25}$ as a percent.

$$\frac{20}{25} = \boxed{}\,\%$$

D. Who received the higher score?

_____

 Turn and Talk How else could you find out who had the higher score?

Check Understanding

1. A basketball player made 12 out of the 30 shots she attempted. What percent of shots did the basketball player make? Explain.

_____

_____

For Problems 2–7, write each ratio as a percent.

2. 1 to 20 _____

3. $\frac{45}{75}$ _____

4. 160 : 400 _____

5. $\frac{12}{60}$ _____

6. 5 to 250 _____

7. $\frac{1}{8}$ _____

Name _____

On Your Own

8. Rachel hits one home run every 40 times she bats.

 A. About how many times at bat should it take Rachel to hit 5 home runs?

 _____

 B. Write a ratio showing her home runs for every 40 times she's at bat.

 _____

 C. What percent of the time does Rachel hit a home run?

 _____

9. **Financial Literacy** Compared to the money he made last year, Zach made 115% as much this year. Use the 10-by-10 grids to show 115%.

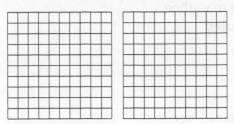

 Did he make more or less money than last year?

 _____

10. (MP) **Construct Arguments** Ryan got 36 out of 40 questions right on a test. Tessa got 92% on the same test. Who got a better score? Explain.

 _____

 _____

11. **Open Ended** Write three ratios that are equivalent to 75% and three ratios that are equivalent to 100%.

 _____

For Problems 12–17, write each number as a percent.

12. $\frac{3}{24}$ _____

13. 0.95 _____

14. 8.37 _____

15. $6\frac{1}{5}$ _____

16. $\frac{70}{50}$ _____

17. 0.340 _____

18. Ricardo threw rings over bottles in a ring-toss competition. The diagram shows the number of bottles Ricardo got rings around.

A. Write a ratio of the number of bottles with rings to the total number of bottles.

_____

B. Complete the double number line to show the percentage of rings that successfully landed around a bottle.

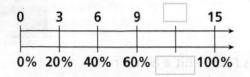

C. What percent of the bottles have rings on them?

_____

19. Two marathon runners run the full distance of the marathon, approximately 26 miles, in 4 hours at a constant speed.

A. About how many miles did they run in 1 hour?

_____

B. What percent of the full distance have they run in 1 hour?

_____

20. The ratio of sixth-graders to seventh-graders on a chess team is 5 to 3.

A. The ratio of sixth-graders to total chess players is $\dfrac{5}{\boxed{}}$.

B. What percent of the players on the chess team are sixth-graders?

21. Kari has one day each week (7-day week) to research the decline in bee populations. Approximately what percent of each week does she have to research this topic? Round your answer to the nearest hundredth of a percent.

Bee populations are in decline.

I'm in a Learning Mindset!

How did I adjust my strategy for converting ratios?

_____

LESSON 12.1
**More Practice/
Homework**

ONLINE

Video Tutorials and
Interactive Examples

Understand, Express, and Compare
Percent Ratios

1. In a chili cook-off, 18 of the 40 chilis included two types of
    beans. What percentage the chilis did *not* include two types
    of beans?

    _____

chili cook-off

2. (MP) **Attend to Precision** The ratio of roses to lilies in a
    garden is 3 to 2. If lilies and roses are the only flowers in the
    garden, what percentage of the garden's flowers are roses?

    _____

3. The picture shows the blue and white tiles of an outdoor
    patio. What percent of the tiles are blue? Explain.

    _____

    _____

4. A movie studio keeps 240 dresses in its wardrobe for historical films.
    Three-fifths of them can be used for movies that take place in the 1700s and
    15% of them can be used for movies in the Civil War era.

    A. What percent of the dresses are for films set in the 1700s?

        _____

    B. What percent of the dresses are for films *not* set in the 1700s? Explain
        how you found your answer.

        _____

        _____

        _____

    C. What percent of the dresses are for films set in the 1700s *or* during the
        Civil War era? Explain how you found your answer.

        _____

        _____

For Problems 5–8, write each number as a percent.

5. $\frac{1}{5}$ _____

6. $\frac{9}{10}$ _____

7. 0.33 _____

8. $\frac{11}{2}$ _____

Test Prep

9. A hotel puts out 3 apples for every 1 orange as the fruit for their breakfast buffet. Assume that apples and oranges are the only fruit served.

   A. Write a ratio of apples compared to all the fruit.

   _____

   B. What percent of the fruit in the breakfast buffet are apples?

10. On a necklace of 100 beads, 45 of the beads are round. The rest of the beads are rectangular. What percent of the beads are round? What percent are rectangular?

   _____

11.

R	S	T	A	E

V	O	A	G	S

   What percent of the tiles are vowels?

   (A) 25%   (B) 40%   (C) 60%   (D) 400%

12. A chorus has 50 singers. There are 16 altos and 10 tenors. What percent of the singers are altos? What percent of the singers are tenors?

   (A) 8%; 5%   (B) 16%; 10%   (C) 32%; 20%   (D) 68%; 80%

Spiral Review

13. On the first move, a game piece is moved ahead 2 spaces. On the next move, the game piece is moved back 5 spaces. What integer represents the overall result of the two moves?

   _____

14. Alex paid $3.59 for 1.35 pounds of chicken. To the nearest cent, how much did Alex pay per pound?

   _____

15. One-third of an orchestra's musicians play violin or viola and another one-quarter play cello or contrabass. What fraction of the orchestra's musicians play either violin, viola, cello, or contrabass?

   _____

© Houghton Mifflin Harcourt Publishing Company

Name

Use Strategies to Find a Percent of a Quantity

I Can find the percent of a quantity by using equivalent ratios, models, or multiplication.

Spark Your Learning

In a school football game, Marcus completes 3 out of 4 pass attempts. Terry completes 7 out of 10 pass attempts. Who has the better record of successful pass attempts? Explain.

 Turn and Talk Is there another way you could have solved this problem?

© Houghton Mifflin Harcourt Publishing Company • Image Credit: ©Matthew J. Lee/The Boston Globe via Getty Images

Build Understanding

1 What is 32% of 25?

A. You can use equivalent ratios to find 32% of 25. One ratio is the percent. How can you express 32% as a ratio?

_____

B. The other ratio is a part-to-whole ratio. The whole is 25, and the part is unknown. Complete the equation to show the equivalent ratios. The gray box represents the unknown.

C. What multiplication fact will help you to find the unknown number? Explain how.

_____

_____

D. Use the multiplication fact you wrote in Part C to find equivalent ratios.

32% of 25 is _____.

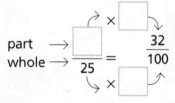

2 Bree wants to save 40% of her weekly pay as a lifeguard. How much does she plan to save each week?

You can use a bar model to solve this problem.

A. What number should you enter into the top bar of the model? What number should you enter into each section on the bottom bar? Explain.

_____

_____

B. How much money does Bree plan to save each week? Explain.

_____

_____

_____

Bree earns $250 per week.

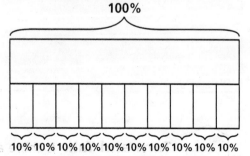

100%

10% 10% 10% 10% 10% 10% 10% 10% 10% 10%

© Houghton Mifflin Harcourt Publishing Company • **Image Credit:** ©Daniel Dempster Photography/Alamy

Step It Out

3 ▶ Use multiplication to find 45% of 80.

A. Write 45% as a fraction. ⬚/⬚

B. I can _____ 80 by the fraction in Part A to find 45% percent of 80.

C. Complete the multiplication to show how you can use the fraction from Part A to find 45% of 80.

$$\frac{\boxed{}}{100} \text{ of } 80 = \frac{\boxed{}}{100} \times 80$$

$$= \frac{\boxed{}}{100}$$

$$= \boxed{}$$

 Turn and Talk Is there another way to find 45% of 80? Explain.

4 ▶ Alyssa has to make 250 invitations for a party. She has completed 72% of them. How many invitations has she completed?

> 250 invitations to make

A. Write a ratio to represent the percent. ⬚/⬚

B. What operation does the word "of" indicate?

_____

C. Write a multiplication problem to find the number of completed invitations.

$$\frac{\boxed{}}{\boxed{}} \times \boxed{} = \boxed{}$$

You're Invited

D. How many invitations has Alyssa completed? _____

E. Check your answer using decimal multiplication. Write a decimal to represent 72%. _____

F. Write a decimal multiplication problem to find the number of completed invitations.

$$\boxed{} \times \boxed{} = \boxed{}$$

 Turn and Talk What is 100% of any amount? What is 50% of any amount?

5 Scott planted 20% of a garden with roses. What is the area of the part of the garden planted with roses?

10 ft

5 ft

A. How can you find the total area of the garden? What is the total area?

_____

_____

B. You know that the rose garden is 20% of the total garden.

Write 20% as a ratio. $\dfrac{\square}{100}$

C. Complete this ratio to represent the unknown area of the garden planted with roses compared to the total area of the garden. The gray

box represents the unknown area.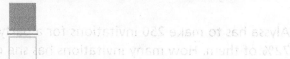

D. Use equivalent ratios to find 20% of the rose garden's area.

E. What is the area of the rose garden? _____

> **Turn and Talk** What percent of the garden is not planted with roses? Explain how you know.

Check Understanding

1. Shonda has $125. She spends 35% of the money she has on a concert ticket. How much does Shonda pay for the concert ticket?

_____

For Problems 2–5, find the percent of each number.

2. 10% of 70 _____

3. 75% of 8 _____

4. 55% of 55 _____

5. 90% of 20 _____

On Your Own

6. A football team scored 70% of a total of 400 points in the first 11 games of the season.

A. Fill in the model to show 70% of 400.

100%

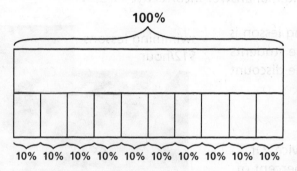

10% 10% 10% 10% 10% 10% 10% 10% 10% 10%

B. How many points did the football team score in the first 11 games of the season? Explain how you found your answer.

_____

7. Cassie is painting a rectangular wall in her bedroom. The wall is 12 feet by 15 feet. She plans on painting the top 20% of the wall green and the rest of the wall tan. What is the area of the part of the wall that she plans to paint green?

_____

8. (MP) **Reason** Stephon and Marcy are saving money to buy new bikes. If Stephon suddenly has to spend 12% of his savings and Marcy has to spend 8% of her savings, who spent more money? Explain how you found your answer.

Stephon has saved $200.

Marcy has saved $350.

_____
_____
_____

9. The regular price of a pair of sneakers is $40. The sale price is 25% off the regular price. What is the sale price? Explain.

_____

For Problems 10–15, find the percent of each number.

10. 13% of 400 _____

11. 80% of 14,236 _____

12. 60% of 50 _____

13. 30% of 70 _____

14. 45% of 20 _____

15. 75% of 804 _____

16. A quiz has 30 problems. Kamal answered 80% of the problems correctly.

   A. How many problems did Kamal answer correctly? _____

   B. How many problems did Kamal answer incorrectly? _____

   C. What percent of the problems did Kamal answer incorrectly? _____

17. The regular price of a 1-hour swimming lesson is shown. The discount price for first-time students is 75% of the regular price. What is the discount price?

swimming lessons $12/hour

_____

18. Maya has 200 songs on her mobile device. Of these songs, 48 are jazz songs. What percent of Maya's songs are jazz songs?

_____

19. Financial Literacy The sales tax in the town where Georgia lives is 8%. Georgia wants to buy a table saw that costs $300. How much sales tax will she pay?

_____

20. Parson City Middle School has 1,340 students. About 38% of the students are in the seventh grade. About how many seventh-graders attend Parson City Middle School?

_____

For Problems 21–26, find the percent of each number.

21. 25% of 500 _____   **22.** 80% of 10 _____

23. 10% of 100 _____   **24.** 100% of 60 _____

25. 105% of 220 _____   **26.** 120% of 40 _____

 I'm in a Learning Mindset!

How effective were my strategies for solving percent problems?

_____

_____

436

Name _____

Use Strategies to Find a Percent of a Quantity

ONLINE
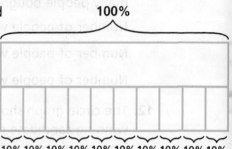
Video Tutorials and
Interactive Examples

1. A football team scored 80% of a total of 500 points in the first 11 games of the season. Fill in the model to show 80% of 500 and then write the number.

100%

10% 10% 10% 10% 10% 10% 10% 10% 10% 10%

2. **STEM** About 71% of Earth's surface is covered in water.

   A. If the surface area of Earth is about 196,900,000 square miles, about how many square miles are covered in water?

   _____

   B. About what percent of Earth's surface is not covered in water? How many square miles is this?

   _____

For Problems 3–4, use the following information. The metal bar shown is an alloy of silver and other metals.

7.5 ounces

3. If the silver accounts for 84% of the bar's weight, what is the weight of the silver? _____

4. (MP) **Attend to Precision** If 9% of the bar's weight is iron, how much does the iron weigh?

   _____

5. **Math on the Spot** Find 30% of 180. _____

6. (MP) **Use Repeated Reasoning** Find 10% of each number. What pattern do you notice?

   A. 10% of 30 is _____.   B. 10% of 47 is _____.

   C. 10% of 240 is _____.   D. 10% of 10.8 is _____.

   E. Describe the pattern that you notice.

   _____

   _____

For Problems 7–10, find the percent of each number.

7. 10% of 90 _____   8. 50% of 14 _____   9. 30% of 90 _____   10. 80% of 40 _____

© Houghton Mifflin Harcourt Publishing Company • Image Credit: ©Rashevskyi Viacheslav/Shutterstock

11. Of 140 people at a movie, 40% of the people bought popcorn, 30% of the people bought pretzels, and 10% of the people bought milkshakes. How many people bought each item?

Number of people who bought popcorn: _____

Number of people who bought pretzels: _____

Number of people who bought milkshakes: _____

12. The circle graph shows the percent of votes the winning candidate received in a local election. About how many votes did the winning candidate receive?

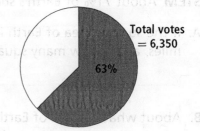

Total votes = 6,350

63%

    Ⓐ 630 votes

    Ⓑ 2,350 votes

    Ⓒ 4,000 votes

    Ⓓ 6,350 votes

13. There are 80 marbles in a bag. If 30% of the marbles are green, how many marbles are *not* green?

_____

14. Lamar earns 40% of his money moving furniture. If he earns $150 in total, how much money did he earn moving furniture?

    Ⓐ $110   Ⓑ $60   Ⓒ $40   Ⓓ $90

15. Barry entered a singing competition. Three of 15 judges voted for him to go on to the semifinals. What percent of the judges voted for him?

_____

Spiral Review

16. A bakery packages 868 muffins into 31 boxes. The same number of muffins are put into each box. How many muffins are in each box?

_____

17. Order the numbers 0, 3, −12, and −1 from least to greatest.

_____

Find the quotient. Round to the nearest thousandth, if necessary.

18. 560 ÷ 1.4 _____   **19.** 9.5 ÷ 500 _____   **20.** 0.80 ÷ 46 _____

© Houghton Mifflin Harcourt Publishing Company

Name _____

Solve a Variety of Percent Problems

(I Can) solve real-world percent problems that require me to find the part, the percent, or the whole.

Step It Out

1 ▶ Liz is collecting aluminum cans for a school fundraiser. So far, she has collected 16 cans, which is 20% of her goal. How many cans must she collect to reach her goal?

A. Use a double number line to solve the problem. When Liz reaches 100%, she has reached her goal. Complete the double number line until you reach 100%.

Cans 0   16   ☐   ☐   ☐   ☐

Percent 0% 20% ☐ ☐ ☐ ☐

B. For every 16 cans Liz collects, she adds ☐ % toward her goal.

If she reaches 40% of her goal she will have ☐ cans. Liz must

collect ☐ cans to reach her goal.

2 ▶ Jose is in the same class as Liz, and he is also collecting aluminum cans. He has collected 36 cans, which is 18% of his goal. How many cans must Jose collect to reach his goal?

A. Use equivalent ratios to solve the problem. One ratio is the percent: $\frac{☐}{100}$. The second ratio is the number of cans already collected compared to the total number of cans that must be collected. You know the first number, the *part* of the ratio. You must find the second number, the *whole* of the ratio. Complete the ratio. The gray box represents

the unknown number.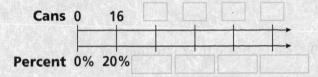

B. Find equivalent ratios: $\frac{☐}{100} = \frac{☐}{☐}$. Eighteen is multiplied by ☐ to

get ☐ . Multiply 100 by the same number to find the answer.

$100 \times ☐ = ☐$. Jose must collect ☐ cans to reach his goal.

Turn and Talk Which method do you think is easier to use: a double number line or finding equivalent ratios? Explain.

© Houghton Mifflin Harcourt Publishing Company • Image Credit: (t) ©tobkatrina/YAY Media AS/Alamy

3   In Big Bog in Maui, Hawaii, about 400 inches of rain falls during a normal year. It is the seventh wettest place in the world, judging by annual rainfall. If 364 inches of rain have fallen so far and you expect the rainfall to reach the usual yearly amount, what percent of the year's rain has already fallen? Use equivalent ratios to find the solution.

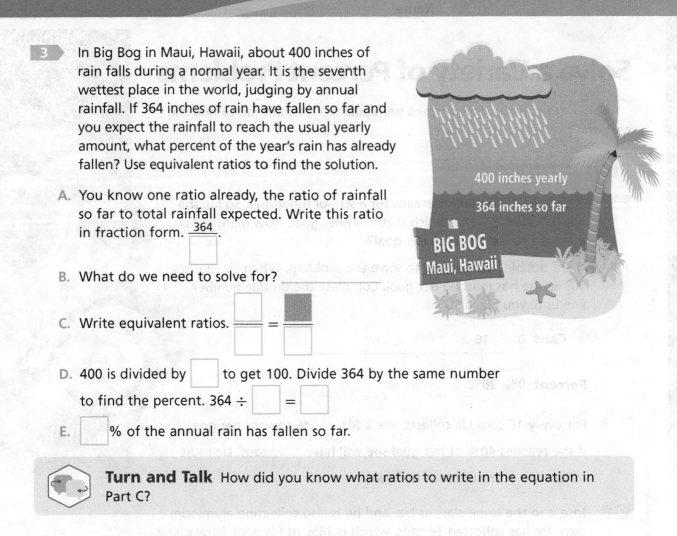

400 inches yearly

364 inches so far

BIG BOG
Maui, Hawaii

A. You know one ratio already, the ratio of rainfall so far to total rainfall expected. Write this ratio in fraction form. $\dfrac{364}{\boxed{}}$.

B. What do we need to solve for? _____

C. Write equivalent ratios. $\dfrac{\boxed{}}{\boxed{}} = \dfrac{\boxed{}}{\boxed{}}$

D. 400 is divided by $\boxed{}$ to get 100. Divide 364 by the same number to find the percent. $364 \div \boxed{} = \boxed{}$

E. $\boxed{}$ % of the annual rain has fallen so far.

> **Turn and Talk** How did you know what ratios to write in the equation in Part C?

Check Understanding

1. In a city election, 5,000 people voted for mayor. If the winning candidate received 60% of the votes, how many people voted for her? Show how you know.

_____

_____

2. At King School, 55% of the students are girls. If there are 220 girls at the school, how many students are there in total? _____

3. Randy is 3 years old and is 90 centimeters tall. His father is 180 centimeters tall. What percent of his father's height is Randy's height?

_____

4. On a math test, Janice answers 85% of the questions correctly. If she answered 17 questions correctly, how many questions are on the test?

_____

On Your Own

5. There are 8 equally sized slices in a pizza. If Ken eats 5 of the slices, what percent of the pizza has he eaten? Show your work.

_____

6. 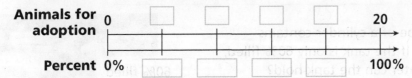 **Use Structure** An animal shelter offers kittens and puppies each day for adoption. The shelter director wants 40% of the animals offered to be kittens. Fill in the double number line to find out how many kittens should be included if the shelter offers 20 animals for adoption.

Animals for adoption   0 ☐ ☐ ☐ ☐ 20

Percent   0% ☐ ☐ ☐ ☐ 100%

7. A zoo has a ratio of 1 giraffe for every 4 zebras. What percent of this grouping of animals are giraffes? What percent of this grouping are zebras?

1 giraffe for every 4 zebras

8. **STEM** About $\frac{39}{50}$ of Earth's atmosphere is made up of nitrogen. Use equivalent ratios to find about what percent of the atmosphere is nitrogen.

_____

9. **Critique Reasoning** Andy has read 126 pages of a biography that has 300 pages. He says that he has read 60% of the book. Is this percent reasonable? Why or why not?

_____

10. **STEM** The average adult is about 60% water. One liter of water has a mass of 1 kilogram. If a person's body contains 45 liters of water, what is the person's mass in kilograms? _____

For Problems 11–16, find the unknown value.

11. 25% of 48 = ☐

12. 75% of 60 = ☐

13. 40% of 72 = ☐

14. 100% of ☐ = 30

15. 30% of ☐ = 30

16. 120% of ☐ = 18

17. (MP) **Reason** Lily is using equivalent ratios to find the unknown whole value. What factor should she multiply 100 by? Explain how you found the factor.
$\dfrac{7}{100} = \dfrac{77}{\blacksquare}$

_____

_____

18. If the gas tank in Glen's car can hold 12 gallons and it is 80% full, how many gallons of gas are in the gas tank?

_____

19. A water tank in the shape of a cylinder contains 54,000 gallons of water. If the tank is only 60% filled, how many gallons of water can the tank hold?

60% filled

_____

20. Financial Literacy Melinda earned $550 in one month and saved 30% of her earnings. She is saving for a new bicycle that costs $825. How much has Melinda saved so far? At this rate, how long will it take her to save enough money to buy the bicycle?

_____

21. In a survey of 560 students, 35% chose math as their favorite subject. Use multiplication to find the number of students who chose math.

A. Write the percent in fraction form. $35\% = \dfrac{\square}{100}$

B. How many students chose math? Show your work.

_____

C. Double-check your answer by converting the percent to a decimal and using decimal multiplication. Write the percent in decimal form.
$35\% = $ _____

D. Multiply the decimal by the total number of students surveyed.

_____

E. Open Ended Which method do you prefer, converting the percent to a fraction and multiplying or converting the percent to a decimal and multiplying? Why?

_____

_____

Name _____

Solve a Variety of Percent Problems

ONLINE

Video Tutorials and Interactive Examples

1. Nancy hopes to collect 100 oysters from the ocean. She has collected 15% of her goal. How many does she have?

_____

2. **Math on the Spot** Hal is downloading a file from the internet. So far, he has downloaded 25% of the file. If 10 minutes have passed since he started, how long will it take to download the rest of the file?

_____

3. Sally eats lunch at a restaurant and her bill is $24. She would like to leave a 15% tip for the waiter. How much money should she leave?

_____

4. A town spends 43% of its annual budget on education. If the town's budget is one million dollars, how much will be spent on education?

_____

5. Matt hopes to score 120 points this season. He has scored 80% of his goal so far. Fill in the double number line diagram to find out how many points he has scored so far and write the answer.

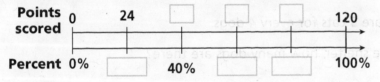

6. (MP) **Attend to Precision** On a test, Jenna gets 85% of the questions correct, Linda gets 32 out of 40 questions correct, Karl gets $\frac{7}{8}$ of the questions correct, and Julie gets 0.83 of the questions correct. List the students in order from lowest to highest score.

_____

7. Students are auditioning for a school play. Only 18 of the 45 students auditioning will get a part in the play. What percent of the students who audition will be in the play? _____

8. The first lap of an auto race is 2,500 meters. This is 10% of the total race distance. What is the total race distance? _____

For Problems 9–12, find the unknown value.

9. 200% of 500 is [ ] .

10. 35% of 500 is [ ] .

11. [ ] % of 500 is 100.

12. 5% of [ ] is 25.

© Houghton Mifflin Harcourt Publishing Company • Image Credit: ©Muellek Josef/Shutterstock

Test Prep

13. In a jar, 25% of the marbles are red. If there are 45 red marbles in the jar, how many marbles are in the jar altogether?

Ⓐ 70
Ⓒ 60
Ⓑ 180
Ⓓ 1,125

14. On a 747 airplane, 20% of the seats are business class. If 80 passengers can ride in business class, how many passengers can the plane carry?

Ⓐ 160
Ⓒ 320
Ⓑ 100
Ⓓ 400

15. About 10% of people are left-handed. If there are 480 people in a movie theater, about how many of them are likely to be left-handed?

_____

16. Mr. Ramos pays 22% of his income for housing. If Mr. Ramos pays $8,800 for housing, how much money did he earn during the year?

_____

Spiral Review

17. At an animal shelter, there are 3 cats for every 4 dogs.

A. If there are 15 cats at the shelter, how many dogs are there?

_____

B. If there are 32 dogs at the shelter, how many cats are there?

_____

C. If there are 21 animals at the shelter, how many cats are there?

_____

18. A rectangular mural on the side of a building is 25 meters long and 12.8 meters high. What is the area of the mural in square meters?

_____

19. A cube is 6 centimeters on each edge. What is its volume in cubic units?

_____

20. Find the values and complete the statement.

A. $|-18| =$ ☐ $|4| =$ ☐ $|97| =$ ☐

B. In Part A, I found the _____ of each integer.

Review

Vocabulary

Complete the statements to review your vocabulary for this module.

Vocabulary

equivalent ratios
percent

1. _____ is a ratio that compares a part to a whole of 100.

2. Six out of 20 is 30% because $\frac{6}{20}$ and $\frac{30}{100}$ are _____.

Concepts and Skills

3. What percent of the 10-by-10 grid is shaded? _____

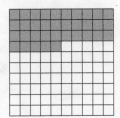

4. Shade 80% of the grid.

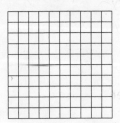

5. Complete the percents in the double number line. Shade $\frac{3}{8}$ of the double number line. What percent is equivalent to $\frac{3}{8}$?

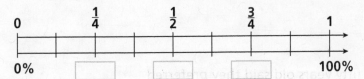

$\frac{3}{8}$ = _____ %

6. (MP) **Use Tools** Write the ratio 7 to 8 as a fraction, decimal, and percent. State what strategy and tool you will use to answer the question, explain your choice, and then find the answer.

_____

_____

7. On a history test, Robert gets 23 questions correct out of 25. What is Robert's percent score for the test? Show how you know.

_____

8. Write the following ratios in order from least to greatest: 82%, $\frac{16}{20}$, 35 out of 40.

_____

9. A group of film students in college shot 420 short videos and 40% of the videos included background music. How many included background music?

_____ videos included background music.

10. At a birthday party, 20% of the guests wear glasses. If there are 30 guests, how many wear glasses?

Ⓐ 10 guests

Ⓑ 24 guests

Ⓒ 6 guests

Ⓓ 20 guests

11. In a school, 135 students out of 900 are in the 6th grade. Out of every 100 students, how many students are 6th grade students?

_____

12. In a vaulting contest during gymnastics camp, Kylie made 75% of her 12 attempts. How many successful vaults did she make?

Ⓐ 3 vaults

Ⓑ 6 vaults

Ⓒ 9 vaults

Ⓓ 12 vaults

13. In a survey, 36% of people over fifty years old said they preferred chocolate ice cream to other flavors. If 63 people over fifty preferred chocolate ice cream, how many people over fifty were surveyed?

_____

Proportional Reasoning with Percents

THE CASE OF THE MISSING DIAGRAM

The Bounceville Table Tennis Club holds a 50-game tournament each year.

The shaded portion of each diagram represents the games won by a table tennis team during the tournament.

Write a sentence for each diagram that describes the percent of the whole that is shown. The first one is done for you.

A. Team Dachshunds: 10% of 50 is 5.

B. Team Ferrets _____

C. Team Tigers _____

D. Team Honey Badgers _____

 Turn and Talk

What diagram do you think is missing from the sequence of figures above? Explain your reasoning using a diagram.

Are You Ready?

Complete these problems to review prior concepts and skills you will need for this module.

Multiply Decimals by Whole Numbers

Find each product.

1. 0.3(12) _____   **2.** 0.75(68) _____   **3.** 1.25(40) _____

Find a Percent or a Whole

Solve each problem.

4. What is 60% of 120? _____   **5.** Find 8% of 65. _____

6. 50% of what number is 27? _____   **7.** 63% of what number is 252? _____

8. Carl scored 35% of his basketball team's 40 points during a game. How many points did Carl score?

_____

Use Ratio and Rate Reasoning

Solve each problem.

9. The ratio of fish to snails in an aquarium is 3 to 2. There are 18 fish in the aquarium. How many snails are in the aquarium?

_____

10. Irina ran 0.25 mile in 2 minutes. At this rate, how many minutes will it take her to run 2 miles?

_____

11. A painter mixes gray paint by using 1 gallon of black paint for every 7 gallons of white paint. How much black paint and how much white paint will the painter need to mix 20 gallons of gray paint?

_____

Name _____

Percent Change

(I Can) solve multi-step problems involving percent change.

Step It Out

1 When a quantity increases or decreases, you can use number sense and proportional reasoning to compare the amount of change to the original amount.

A. Janis earns $7.00 per hour at Pizza King. After 6 months, her salary increases to $7.70 per hour. What is the percent increase in her hourly rate of pay?

The original amount is $_____. The new amount is

$_____. The amount of change is $_____.

Write the ratio of the amount of change to the original amount as a percent. This is the **percent change**. Note that the original amount is 10 times the amount of change.

$$\frac{\text{amount of change}}{\text{original amount}} = \frac{0.7}{7} = \frac{1}{\boxed{}} = \underline{\qquad} = \underline{\qquad}\%$$

B. Pizza King decides to decrease the price of a large pizza as shown on their sign. What is the percent decrease in the cost of a large pizza?

The original amount is $_____. The new amount is $_____. The amount of change is $_____.

$$\frac{\text{amount of change}}{\text{original amount}} = \frac{4}{16}$$

$$= \frac{1}{\boxed{}}$$

$$= \underline{\qquad}$$

$$= \underline{\qquad}\%$$

 Turn and Talk How can you use number sense to write $\frac{1}{8}$ as a percent?

2 A population of cheetahs has decreased 30% over the last 18 years. If there were originally about 12,000 cheetahs, how many cheetahs are there now?

A. Find the change in the number of cheetahs. Write the percent as a decimal.

Percent of decrease × Original amount = Decrease

_____ × _____ = _____

B. How many cheetahs are there now?

_____ − _____ = _____, so there are about _____ cheetahs now.

 Turn and Talk What is another way to determine how many cheetahs there are now?

3 A machine cuts lumber into 8-foot planks. Company regulations allow the lengths to vary by $\frac{1}{2}$%, which can be either an increase or decrease of $\frac{1}{2}$%. Find the range of values allowed by the company's regulations.

A. How do you express $\frac{1}{2}$% as a decimal?

☐ ÷ 100 = ☐

B. What are the lengths of the shortest and the longest allowable planks?

Shortest: ☐ − (☐ × 8) = ☐ feet

Longest: ☐ + (☐ × 8) = ☐ feet

The range of allowable lengths is ☐ feet to ☐ feet.

Check Understanding

1. Peggy earned $20 for each lawn she mowed last summer. This summer, she raised her price to $23 per lawn. What is the percent increase?

_____

2. Robert is inspecting a shipment of 22-inch pipes. The lengths of the pipes may vary by 1%. What is the range of allowable lengths of the pipes?

_____

3. When Bart bought his car, it averaged 28 miles per gallon of gas. Now, the car's average miles per gallon has decreased by 14%. What is the car's average miles per gallon now? Round your answer to the nearest mile per gallon.

_____

On Your Own

4. The population of deer in a protected area is 225. If the population increases at a rate of 24% per year, how many deer will be in the area next year?

5. There are 75 students enrolled in a camp. The day before the camp begins 8% of the students cancel. How many students actually attend the camp?

6. Two years ago, a car was valued at $24,000. This year, the value of the car is $23,160. What was the percent decrease in the value of the car?

7. (MP) **Use Structure** Mr. Milton had $1,200 in his savings account at the beginning of the year. If his account has a balance of $1,230 at the end of the year, what is the percent increase of his balance?

8. Last year, 140 people in a community had cell phones. This year the number of people in the community with cell phones has increased by 65%.

A. What is the change in the number of people who have cell phones?

B. How many people in the community have cell phones this year?

9. A library has 300 feet of shelves for books. The library will increase the number of feet of shelves by 18%.

A. How many feet of shelves are being added?

B. (MP) **Reason** The library plans to add 1,000 books to its collection. If the library can fit 15 books on each foot of shelving, will the library have enough room on the new shelves for all the new books? Explain.

10. Last year, 360 students walked to school each day. This year the number of students who walk to school decreased by 25%. What is the change in the number of students who walk to school each day? How many students walk to school each day this year?

_____

Find each percent change. State whether it is an increase or decrease.

11. From 50 to 22

12. From 50 to 43

_____

13. From 20 to 35

14. From 112 to 140

_____

15. (MP) **Attend to Precision** A display for rolls of tape indicates that each roll contains 150 yards of tape. If the actual length of tape can vary by 2.5% of that amount, what is the range for the length of tape on a roll?

_____

16. (MP) **Attend to Precision** An airline states that a flight between two cities takes 2.5 hours. The airline also says that the actual flying time can change by up to 15% of that amount. What are the shortest and longest times for the airplane flight? Round your answers to the nearest tenth of an hour.

_____

Find the range of allowable values based on the given information. Round to the nearest tenth.

17. 15; can vary by 2%

18. 24; can vary by 3.5%

_____

19. The _percent error_ of a measurement tells how close the measurement is to the actual value. Dani ran four times around the track, which is 1,600 meters. Her GPS watch recorded the distance as 1,592 meters.

A. To find the percent error, first find the absolute value of the difference between the distance recorded on Dani's watch and the actual distance.

_____

B. Now express the difference from Part A as a percent of the actual value. This is the percent error.

_____

C. When Cam ran 800 meters, his watch recorded the distance as 810 meters. What is the percent error?

_____

Percent Change

1. Five years ago, a typical 70″ TV cost about $2,400. Now a similar TV costs approximately $1,680. What is the percent decrease in TV price?

   _____

2. **Financial Literacy** Antoine made $33,284 last year. He received a 4.5% annual raise. What will his new salary be for the coming year?

   _____

3. **STEM** A scientist observes and counts the bacteria in a culture as 155. Later the scientist counts again and finds that the number has increased by 40%. How many bacteria are there now?

   _____

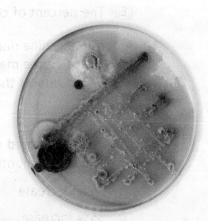

4. The number of veggie burgers sold at a restaurant in Houston, Texas, went from 425 in April to 357 in May. What was the percent decrease of the number of veggie burgers sold from April to May?

   _____

5. **(MP)** **Attend to Precision** A warehouse worker fills 150 orders per day on average. From day to day, the number of orders varies by 2%. What is the range of the number of orders the worker fills each day?

   _____

6. Find the percent change from 96 to 93. State whether it Is an increase or decrease.

   _____

7. Find the percent change from 32 to 60. State whether it is an increase or decrease.

   _____

8. **(MP)** **Attend to Precision** Find the range of allowable values based on a measure of 130 inches if the values can vary by 1.4%.

   _____

Test Prep

9. A collector bought a rare coin for $30. The coin is now valued at $37.50.
   Select all the true statements.

   (A) The scenario represents a percent increase.

   (B) The scenario represents a percent decrease.

   (C) The percent of change was 20%.

   (D) The percent of change was 25%.

   (E) The percent of change was 75%.

10. A coffee machine dispenses 8-ounce cups of coffee automatically. The
    amount of coffee may vary by 3%. What are the least and greatest
    number of ounces the coffee machine will dispense?

    Least number: _____ ounces   Greatest number: _____ ounces

11. A German shepherd puppy weighed 25 pounds at 4 months old and
    31 pounds at 5 months old. What is the percent increase or decrease?

    (A) 35% decrease   (C) 24% decrease

    (B) 35% increase   (D) 24% increase

12. The butterfly population at Glen Arbor Farms was 250 last year. This year
    there are 100 butterflies. What is the percent increase or decrease?

    (A) 50% decrease   (C) 60% decrease

    (B) 50% increase   (D) 60% increase

Spiral Review

13. There is a proportional relationship between time in hours and time in days.

    A. What is the constant of proportionality?

    _____

    B. What equation describes this relationship?

    _____

14. Kate walks 3.5 kilometers along a hiking trail. How far does Kate walk
    in meters?

    _____

Markups and Discounts

(I Can) calculate markups, markdowns, and retail prices and write
equations for markup and markdown situations.

Step It Out

1 ▶ Music Enterprise buys digital downloads of music albums
for $5.00. The markup rate is 30%. How much will you pay
if you want to buy the latest album of your favorite artist,
not including tax?

Connect to Vocabulary

Markup is the amount of
increase in a price. The
markup rate is similar to
percent increase but more
specific to selling items.
Retail price is the amount
an item is sold for after
a company adds the
markup.
Markdown is the amount
of decrease in a price.

A. Calculate the amount of the markup. Show your work.

[   ] × 5 = [   ]   The markup amount is $ _____ .

B. Calculate the retail price, which is the price you will pay.

$5.00 + $[   ] = $[   ]

C. Express the ratio of the retail price to the cost of the download as a
percent. How does this percent relate to the markup rate?

$\dfrac{[\quad]}{[\quad]}$ = [   ]   or   [   ] %   _____

D. What is another way you could find the percent of the original amount
that the retail price represents?

original amount + markup = retail

100% + [   ] % = [   ] %

After New Year's Day, Music Enterprise marks down their
albums as shown in their ad. How much will the album cost
after this markdown?

E. The retail price is $[   ] . The markdown percent is [   ] %.

F. Find the amount of the markdown.

[   ] × $6.50 = $[   ]

G. Calculate the album price after the markdown.
Is this cost reasonable? Explain.

_____

_____

Turn and Talk Would the final price be $5 if there were a markdown of 30%
and then a markup of 30%? Explain.

© Houghton Mifflin Harcourt Publishing Company

2 You can also use equations to solve problems involving markups, markdowns, and discounts.

Penelope buys bracelets in bulk to sell at her store. She uses a markup rate of 125% which is added to the bracelet cost. What is the retail price of a bracelet with an original cost of $8?

A. The markup rate is _____. The equation $m =$ _____ x gives the markup amount y in dollars for the bracelets in terms of the original amount x in dollars.

B. Use the equation to find the markup amount for a bracelet with an original cost of $8.

$$m = \boxed{} \times \$ \boxed{} = \$ \boxed{}$$

C. Calculate the retail price of the bracelet.

$$\$8 + \$ \boxed{} = \$ \boxed{}$$

D. The markup amount is _____ x. An equation for the retail price r in dollars in terms of the original amount x in dollars is

$$r = \text{\_\_\_\_} x + \text{\_\_\_\_} x = \text{\_\_\_\_} x.$$

3 Penelope marked down the price of necklaces in her store as shown.

A. Calculate what percent the sale price is of the retail price.

$$\frac{\text{sale price}}{\text{retail price}} = \frac{\$\boxed{}}{\$\boxed{}} = \boxed{} = \boxed{} \%$$

$25
$22

B. What is an equation in the form $y = kx$ that relates the sale price to the retail price x?

_____

 Turn and Talk Discuss how you find the markup and markdown amounts. Which concept did you find more challenging to understand, and why?

Check Understanding

1. A grocery store buys organic apples for $0.75 per apple. The grocery store marks up the cost of each apple by 18%. To the nearest cent, how much will one organic apple cost at the grocery store?

_____

2. A store is selling all toaster ovens at 15% off. Write an equation in the form of $y = kx$ to represent the sale price y in dollars of a toaster with a retail price of x dollars. Then find the amount Jill paid for a toaster with a retail price of $40.

_____

On Your Own

3. A hobby store marks up remote-controlled cars 20%. The original cost was $35. What is the retail price to purchase a remote-controlled car at the hobby store?

_____

4. Organic hot dogs at the grocery store cost $2.00 each. At a major league baseball game, an organic hot dog costs $6.50. By what percent are the organic hot dogs marked up?

_____

5. **Financial Literacy** The Bakers want to sell their house for $145,500. After 2 months, the Bakers decided to mark down the price of their house 8% to sell more quickly. How much are the Bakers selling their house for now?

_____

6. (MP) **Reason** What is the retail price of a pair of shoes if there is a 10% discount and the sale price is $76.50?

_____

7. A convenience store sells prepaid mobile phones. It purchases them for $12 each and uses a markup rate of 250%.

   A. (MP) **Model with Mathematics** The markup rate is the constant of proportionality in the equation $y = kx$. Write an equation that can be used to find the amount of markup on the cost x of a phone.

   _____

   B. Use the equation to calculate the markup amount. What is the retail price of a phone?

   _____

   C. Next week the store is going to reduce the price to $31.50. Calculate what percent the sale price is of the retail price. Show your work.

   _____

   D. (MP) **Model with Mathematics** Based on your answer to Part C, what is an equation in the form $y = kx$ that relates the sale price to the retail price x?

   _____

For Problems 8–9, find the new price for the markup or discount given. Round to the nearest cent if necessary.

8. $3.00 marked up 72%

_____

9. $125.49 discounted 30%

_____

10. The thrift store is selling their old DVDs. When the DVDs first came out, they sold for $19. They have now been marked down as shown. What is the sale price of a DVD?

_____

11. (MP) **Attend to Precision** A manufacturer makes hand-woven scarves for $10 and then ships them to retail boutiques around the country. The boutiques sell the scarves for $25. What percent markup do the boutiques charge their customers?

_____

12. (MP) **Model with Mathematics** Melissa makes apple pies and sells them with a markup of 78%. Write an equation representing the retail price y of Melissa's apple pies in terms of the original cost x.

_____

13. All of last year's car models were marked down 40%. Tracy wants to buy a car that now costs $18,000. What was the retail price of the car?

_____

14. A video game store buys used games and marks them up 25% for resale.

A. (MP) **Model with Mathematics** If the store pays x dollars for a used game, the expression $x + 0.25x$ gives the price the store charges for the game. Simplify this expression.

_____

B. Complete this statement: Increasing a quantity by 25% is the same as multiplying the quantity by _____ .

15. For a sale, a video game store discounts the prices of all games by 8%.

A. (MP) **Model with Mathematics** If p is the retail price of a game, write two expressions that each represent the sale price.

_____

B. Complete this sentence: Decreasing a quantity by 8% is the same as multiplying the quantity by _____ .

Name _____

Markups and Discounts

1. (MP) **Attend to Precision** A local nonprofit organization is selling popcorn to raise money for hurricane relief. The organization paid $4 per bag for the popcorn and sold it for $5 per bag. What was the percent markup on each bag of popcorn?

_____

2. A high school decided to buy new uniforms for the girls and boys basketball teams. They plan to buy 35 uniforms with a total retail cost of $1,235. The store offers discounts based on the number of items the school buys, as shown. What will the discounted price be for the high school?

_____

3. Professor Burger bought a DVD player with an original price of $150 that was reduced by 20%. What was the reduced price?

_____

**BASKETBALL UNIFORM
GROUP DISCOUNTS**

10% off	Buy 10–24 items **Get 10% off** Use code: 10
15% off	Buy 25–49 items **Get 15% off** Use code: 15
20% off	Buy 50+ items **Get 20% off** Use code: 20

For Problems 4–7, find the new price for the markup, markdown, or discount given. Round to the nearest cent if necessary.

4. $6.25 marked up 25%

_____

5. $13.50 discounted 75%

_____

6. $112 marked down 40%

_____

7. $220 marked up 60%

_____

8. **Open Ended** Describe a real-life situation involving markup, markdown, or discount that the equation $y = x + 0.4x$ could represent.

_____

_____

9. A local jewelry store sells class rings. The store engraves a name and date on the ring and sells it using a markup rate of 340%. Write an equation that can be used to find the amount of markup on the cost of a ring.

_____

10. Nate just started working at a clothing store. He receives a 40% discount on any item, once a month. This month Nate decided to buy a jacket with a retail price of $74.99. How much did Nate pay for his jacket?

- (A) $29.99
- (B) $34.99
- (C) $44.99
- (D) $104.99

11. Cup o' Coffee buys its coffee for $1.25 a cup. The coffee shop then sells each cup for $3.75. What is the percent markup for a cup of coffee?

- (A) 300%
- (B) 200%
- (C) 66.6%
- (D) 33.3%

12. Write an equation that represents a discount of 18% on a retail price of $55. Let p represent the new price.

_____

_____

13. Brooke needs a new computer. On Friday, the computer was $200. On Saturday, the price of the computer was $149. Determine if there was a markup or markdown and by what percent.

- (A) markup; 25.5%
- (B) markup; 34.5%
- (C) markdown; 25.5%
- (D) markdown; 34.5%

Spiral Review

14. Determine whether the cost of grapes is proportional to the number of pounds.

Grapes (lb)	1	2	3	4
Cost ($)	3	6	9	12

15. Find the range of allowable masses for a ball bearing with an expected mass of 250 grams for which values are allowed to vary by 5%.

_____

© Houghton Mifflin Harcourt Publishing Company

Name _____

Taxes and Gratuities

(I Can) find taxes, gratuities, and total costs by writing and using equations of the form $y = kx$, and assess the reasonableness of results.

Step It Out

1 ▶ Jeremy paid a barber $15 for a haircut. He also paid 15% as a tip. What is the total amount that Jeremy paid?

A. What percent of the cost did Jeremy pay the barber, including the tip? _____

B. Calculate the total cost of the haircut, including the tip. Show your work. _____

2 ▶ Kelsey and Jamal went to lunch on Saturday. Their lunch cost $17.60, they gave the waiter a 15% gratuity, and they were charged a 5% sales tax rate. No tax is charged on the gratuity. What was the total cost of the lunch?

A. Write an equation in the form $y = kx$ to find the amount of the gratuity y in dollars on an amount of x dollars.

$y =$ _____ x

Use the equation to find the gratuity.

$y =$ _____ $\times 17.60 =$ _____

The gratuity was $_____.

B. Write an equation in the form $y = kx$ to find the tax y in dollars on an amount of x dollars.

$y =$ _____ x

Use the equation to find the tax on Kelsey and Jamal's bill.

$y =$ _____ $\times 17.60 =$ _____

The tax was $_____.

C. Find the total cost of the lunch.

$17.60 + $_____ + $_____ = $_____.

> **Connect to Vocabulary**
>
> A **gratuity** is a percent that is given or paid in addition to the price of a service. It is also referred to as a **tip**.

Haircuts $15

> **Connect to Vocabulary**
>
> **Sales tax** is a percent that is added to the price of goods or services.

Turn and Talk Round up the cost of the meal before tax and tip. Explain how to use mental math to estimate a tip of at least 15% rounded to the nearest dollar.

3 Nolan buys office supplies for his home business. Nolan paid a total of $210, which included a sales tax rate of 5%. What was the cost of the supplies before tax was added?

A. What was the total cost of the office supplies including sales tax in terms of the original cost *x*? Express the answer using a percent and using a decimal.

_____

B. Write an equation in the form $y = kx$ to find the cost *y* in dollars including sales tax for items with a cost of *x* dollars without the sales tax.

$y =$ _____ x

C. Use the equation to find the cost of Nolan's office supplies without the tax.

$210 =$ _____ x

_____ $= x$

The cost of the office supplies without the sales tax was $ _____ .

D. Does your answer seem reasonable? Explain.

_____

_____

 Turn and Talk Explain another way you could have justified in Part D the reasonableness of your answer to Part C.

Check Understanding

1. Ella buys a computer for $785. Her local tax rate is 7%. How much does Ella pay for the computer, including tax?

_____

2. Kim works as a DJ and earns $1,250 to play music for 6 hours at a wedding reception. At the end of the night, she gets an 18% tip. How much in total did she earn?

_____

3. Adrian shops for school clothes and spends a total of $93.42. If the local tax rate is 8%, how much was the cost without tax?

_____

Name _____

On Your Own

DEEP-SEA FISHING

Full-Day Trips **$850**

4. The amount that a charter boat captain charges a group to go deep-sea fishing is shown. If the group tips the captain 17%, what is the total amount that the captain receives for the fishing trip?

_____

5. (MP) **Reason** The school secretary orders a new printer and pays $310.30 after tax. The tax rate is 7%. What was the original price of the printer?

_____

For Problems 6–7, find the total amount given the original price and tax rate. Round to the nearest cent if necessary.

6. $15.25, 7%

7. $31.69, 6%

_____

8. Miguel buys a car for $14,999. The tax rate is 6%. What is the total purchase price of the car?

_____

9. The music boosters have their year-end banquet at a hotel that charges $750. The president of the boosters tips the banquet team 20%. What is the total amount spent?

_____

10. (MP) **Model with Mathematics** A family used a professional decorator to help furnish their new home. The decorator selected $1,580 worth of furnishings. In addition to paying for the purchases, the family paid 4.5% tax on the purchases. The decorator's fee was 12% of the purchases, not including the tax.

A. Write an equation in the form of $y = kx$ to represent the decorator's fee. Then use the equation to calculate the amount of that fee. Round to the hundredths place if necessary.

_____

B. Write an equation in the form of $y = kx$ to represent the tax. Then use the equation to calculate the amount of tax. Round to the hundredths place if necessary.

_____

C. What is the total cost that the family paid? Show your work.

_____

For Problems 11–12, find the total amount given the original price and tip rate. Round to the nearest cent if necessary.

11. $22.22, 10%

12. $41.32, 15%

13. (MP) **Use Structure** A group of friends receives a dinner bill of $287.50 at a restaurant. The bill includes a 15% tip for the server. How much was the bill before the tip was added? Explain how you found your answer.

For Problems 14–15, find the original price given the total amount and tip rate.

14. $51.84, 20%

15. $38.35, 18%

16. Jayme buys the painting shown for his apartment. The tax rate is 6.5%. How much did Jayme spend? Round to the nearest cent if necessary.

$179.99

17. A business traveler buys a round-trip plane ticket for $629. The tax rate is 7.5%. How much was the cost after tax? Round to the nearest cent if necessary.

For Problems 18–19, find the tax amount given the original price and tax rate. Round to the nearest cent if necessary.

18. $58.73, 6.5%

19. $73.81, 7.5%

20. Three coworkers buy a baby shower gift for $60. The local tax rate is 6%. How much was the tax?

For Problems 21–22, find an equation for the total amount y after the given rate of increase is added to the original amount x.

21. 20%

22. 8.5%

23. (MP) **Model with Mathematics** The cost x of the Sennet family's meal at a restaurant is $172.65, and they tip 20%. Write and use an equation to find the total cost y of the dinner.

Name _____

LESSON 13.3
**More Practice/
Homework**

ONLINE

Video Tutorials and
Interactive Examples

Taxes and Gratuities

1. Beau buys a skateboard with a price tag of $82.50 not including tax. The tax rate is 8%. How much does he pay, including tax?

   _____

2. Professor Burger orders flowers to be delivered to his mother. The flowers cost $59.95, not including tax. If there is a 6% sales tax, what is the total cost of the flowers to the nearest cent?

   _____

3. Monty takes a cab to work and pays a fare of $12.75. He tips the driver 20% and the tax rate is 8%. How much does he spend on the trip?

   _____

4. (MP) **Reason** Mary Jo takes her son to get a haircut at the barbershop. The total cost of the haircut is $12.60, including a 20% tip. How much was the haircut before the tip?

   _____

5. Derek and Jeannine buy a car for a total price, including tax, of $19,795. The price of the car without tax was $18,500. What is the tax rate?

   _____

For Problems 6–7, find the total amount given the original price and tax or tip rate. Round to the nearest cent if necessary.

6. $123.28, 7.5%

7. $156.67, 6%

   _____   _____

For Problems 8–9, find the total amount given the original price, tax rate, and tip rate. Round to the nearest cent if necessary.

8. $90.34, 3.5%, 20%

9. $101.33, 6.7%, 18%

   _____   _____

For Problems 10–11, find the original price given the total amount and tax or tip rate.

10. $128,500, 5.5%

11. $307.32, 20%

   _____   _____

Test Prep

12. Match the amounts and tip or tax rates in the first column to the total cost with the tip or tax included in the second column.

$123.01, 7.5% •   • $1,336.66

$52.48, 6.5% •   • $57.86

$1,261, 6% •   • $258.19

$224.51, 15% •   • $132.24

$48.22, 20% •   • $55.89

13. Brett plays an acoustic guitar at an event for $500. At the end of the event, the sponsor tips him 20%. How much does Brett make at this event?

_____

14. Carmine buys a canoe priced at $478. He pays a total, including tax, of $509.07. What was the tax rate?

Ⓐ 6%

Ⓑ 6.5%

Ⓒ 7%

Ⓓ 7.5%

15. Kenton buys a tool box, drill set, and socket set. He spends a total of $564.45 after tax, and the tax rate is 6%. What was the total cost before tax?

Ⓐ $540.04

Ⓑ $537.50

Ⓒ $534.99

Ⓓ $532.50

Spiral Review

16. An 8-ounce cup of juice costs $1.20. A 12-ounce cup of the same juice costs $1.44. Can the relationship between cost and ounces of juice be described by a constant rate? Explain.

_____

_____

17. Last year, 320 students were members of Pine Hill Middle School clubs. This year, there was a 20% increase in members. How many students are members this year?

_____

Commissions and Fees

(**I Can**) calculate commissions, fees, and total earnings and assess the reasonableness of my results.

Step It Out

1.75% commission

1 ▷ Harlan is a real estate agent whose total annual earnings are the sum of his annual salary and the commission shown. Last year, Harlan sold 10 homes that totaled $2,500,000 in sales. How much commission did Harlan earn?

A. The amount of Harlan's sales for the year is $_____ .

Harlan will receive _____ % of his sales as his commission amount.

B. Calculate Harlan's commission.

$_____ × _____ = $_____

C. How do you know your answer is reasonable?

_____

_____

> **Connect to Vocabulary**
>
> A **commission** is a fee a person earns for sales or services. It is often a percent of an amount of sales. The person may or may not also earn a salary.

2 ▷ A **fee** is a payment to someone for a service. Fees can be paid as a fixed amount or as a percent of an amount.

Yuan is an insurance salesman who makes a base monthly salary of $1,500 with a commission of 1% of the value of each policy he sells. In addition, each time his client makes an investment transaction, Yuan receives a $5.00 service fee.

This month, Yuan sells one policy valued at $50,000 and his client makes 4 investment transactions. How much does Yuan earn this month?

Base Salary + Commission Amount + Earnings from Fees = Total Earnings

$$1,500 + 50,000\left(\underline{\quad}\right) + 5\left(\underline{\quad}\right) = \text{total earnings}$$

$$1,500 + \underline{\quad} + \underline{\quad} = \underline{\quad}$$

Yuan's total earnings this month are $_____ .

 Turn and Talk How do the payments vary for the people described in this lesson so far?

© Houghton Mifflin Harcourt Publishing Company • Image Credit: ©PhotosIndia.com LLC/Getty Images

3 A loan officer makes a base salary of $22,500 per year, with a commission of 0.4% of the amount of the loans he processes. He also gets a service fee of $1.75 on every loan preapproval application he processes. Assume the loan officer processes an average of $100,000 in loans and completes 8 preapproval applications each week. How much will he earn this year?

✓ $22,500 base salary
✓ 0.4% commission
✓ $1.75 service fee

LOAN APPROVED

A. The total amount of the loans he processes this year is 52 × $_____ = $_____.

B. The total commission the loan officer earns is

0.004 × $_____ = $_____.

C. The total number of preapproval applications he processes this year is

8 × _____ = _____.

D. The total of the fees he earns for preapproval applications this year is

$1.75 × _____ = $_____.

E. Find the loan officer's total earnings this year.

_____

 Turn and Talk How are the amounts earned in Tasks 1, 2, and 3 different, and how are they the same?

Check Understanding

1. Anna sells computer software and makes a salary of $50,000 annually and 6.5% commission on total sales. If Anna sells $3 million in computer software this year, how much does she make?

_____

2. Dirk is a broker who earns a salary of $41,000 annually, 3.5% commission on his clients' investments of $2.4 million, and a fee of $5.25 on each online transaction. If Dirk processes 1,250 online transactions this year, what are his annual earnings?

_____

3. Brenton is a phone sales specialist who makes $33,000 per year plus an $8 fee for each sale he makes. If Brenton makes 15 sales per week, what are his annual earnings?

_____

On Your Own

4. A literary agent makes $30,000 a year plus 13% commission on the sales of her clients' books to publishers. The agent sold 4 books for $175,000 each for her clients this year. Find her total earnings.

_____

5. An insurance agent earns a base salary of $28,000, a commission of 2% of sales, and receives an additional fee of $9.00 for each sale of an investment policy. The agent had total sales of $75,000 and 6 investment policies this month. Find the commission and fees earned.

_____

6. Find the commission based on total sales of $98,000 and a commission of 1.5%.

_____

7. Find the total fees: Applications: 48, Fee: $2.95 per application.

_____

8. Find the total earnings based on the given information.
Base Salary: $42,000; Total Sales: $175,000; Commission: 4%

_____

9. **Financial Literacy** A stockbroker earns $53,000 annually plus 0.8% of his clients' total investment portfolios. If his clients' investments total $1.2 million, what is his commission this year?

_____

10. (MP) **Reason** A home sold for $286,000. The amount the homeowner received, before taxes and closing costs, was the selling price minus the commission to the real estate agent, which was 6%. How much commission did the real estate agent earn on the sale? How do you know your answer is reasonable?

_____

_____

_____

_____

_____

11. (MP) **Construct Arguments** An oil painting was sold at an auction house for $6,550. The buyer agrees to pay that price plus a commission called the buyer's premium. For the painting, the rate for the buyer's premium was 25%. Calculate the amount of the commission. How do you know your answer is reasonable?

_____

_____

_____

12. A golf equipment salesperson earns a base salary plus commission on golf equipment sold as shown. If the salesperson sells $78,000 worth of equipment in a year, what is the total annual salary earned?

$47,000 base salary

4% commission

_____

13. Irma works for a service that delivers groceries and pet supplies. She earns a base monthly salary of $1,900. In addition, she gets a commission of 1.8% of the cost of each grocery order, and she also gets a delivery fee of $11 for each delivery of pet supplies.

A. How is calculating Irma's total monthly earnings different from calculating earnings based on salary and commission?

_____

B. (MP) **Attend to Precision** Last month Irma's deliveries consisted of $33,600 in groceries, and she made 140 deliveries of pet supplies. What are Irma's total earnings for the month?

_____

Next year the delivery service is going to change the way it pays its delivery drivers. Irma will make a base monthly salary of $2,750. She will also earn a commission of 2.1% of the cost of groceries and a commission of 10.2% of the cost of pet supplies.

C. How will next year's pay structure differ from this year's pay structure?

_____

_____

_____

_____

D. Suppose Irma's deliveries during a month next year consist of $35,100 in groceries and $1,080 in pet supplies. How much will her earnings be that month?

_____

Name _____

Commissions and Fees

1. Maryanne sells cruise vacations. She makes a base salary of $2,500 per month plus 5% of the cost of each vacation. This month she sold $80,000 in cruises. What are her total monthly wages?

_____

2. (MP) **Use Structure** A realtor sells 3 houses this month for a total of $825,000, and each buyer uses her company to process their loan. She earns a base pay of $2,600 each month plus 1.5% of her total house sales. She also gets a fee of $12 for each loan she gets serviced through her company. What are her total earnings for the month?

_____

3. A pharmaceutical sales representative gets paid $50,000 annually plus 3.5% commission on total sales. This year he sold $420,000 in pharmaceuticals. What are his annual total earnings?

_____

4. **Open Ended** Write and solve a problem about base pay and commission. Show your work.

_____

_____

_____

For Problems 5–8, find the requested information based on the given facts.

5. The commission is 3.5% of the total sales of $55,000. Find the commission.

_____

6. The fee is $2.75 per transaction for 175 transactions. Find the total fees.

_____

7. The base salary is $54,300. The commission is 2.75% of the total sales of $950,000. Find the total earnings.

_____

8. The base salary is $48,000. The commission is 9% of the total sales of $256,000. The fee is $7.25 per transaction for 325 transactions. Find the total earnings.

_____

Test Prep

For Problems 9 and 10, mark all the statements that are true.

9. Marcus works for base pay: $25,000, commission: 2%, and fees: $3.75 per transaction.

   Ⓐ Commission on $50,000 is $1,000.

   Ⓑ Commission on $35,000 is $800.

   Ⓒ Fees for 25 transactions are $93.75.

   Ⓓ Total earnings for $75,000 in sales and 10 transactions are $1,537.50.

   Ⓔ Total earnings for $75,000 in sales and 10 transactions are $26,537.50.

10. Maddy works for base pay: $37,555 and commission: 5.5%.

    Ⓐ Commission on $155,000 is $852.50.

    Ⓑ Commission on $155,000 is $8,525.

    Ⓒ Total earnings for $85,000 in sales are $42,230.

    Ⓓ Total earnings for $45,000 in sales are $40,300.

    Ⓔ Total earnings for $115,000 in sales are $43,880.

11. Veronica sells Internet ads over the phone. She is paid $12 per hour plus $15 for every ad she sells. She works 4 hours a day 5 days a week and sells on average 13 ads per day. What are her average weekly earnings?

_____

12. A trampoline salesman makes $25,000 annually plus 6% commission on his total sales. If he sold $40,000 worth of trampolines this year, what are his total earnings?

_____

Spiral Review

13. Haley scored 93% on her first math test and 86% on her second test. What is her percent decrease from Test 1 to Test 2 to the nearest tenth?

_____

14. It takes Camden 45 minutes to complete $\frac{1}{5}$ of his art project. How many hours will it take him to complete the whole project if he works at the same rate?

_____

15. Maggie eats at a restaurant and gets a bill for $23.50. She wants to leave a 20% gratuity. What is Maggie's total cost?

_____

Name _____

Simple Interest

(**I Can**) calculate simple interest and the total value of an account after any period of time. I understand and can apply the equation $I = Prt$.

Step It Out

1 ▷ Big Money Bank loans $12,000 to Carlotta. This initial amount borrowed is called the **principal**.

At the end of 8 years, Carlotta has to repay the loan to the bank at a rate of 5.5% simple interest per year. What is the total amount of interest she will have to pay on her loan?

A. Find the amount of simple interest *I* that Carlotta owes after one year by finding 5.5% of $12,000.

$I =$ ☐ $\times\ 12,000 =$ ☐

Carlotta owes $ _____ in interest after one year.

B. Calculate the total interest Carlotta owes for the 8 years of the loan.

Interest for one year   ×   8 years = Interest for 8 years

_____   ×   8   = _____

Over 8 years Carlotta will pay _____ in simple interest on her loan.

> **Connect to Vocabulary**
>
> **Simple interest** is a fixed percent of the principal. It is calculated using the formula $I = Prt$, where *P* represents the principal, *r* the rate of interest, and *t* the time.

2 ▷ Melanie deposits $8,200 in a bank account paying 4.4% simple interest. How much is in her account after 5 years and 6 months?

A. Use the equation $I = Prt$ to find the amount of interest Melanie earns after 5.5 years.

$I = \left(8{,}200\right)\left(\text{——}\right)\left(\text{——}\right) = \$ \text{———}$

B. The total amount of money in Melanie's account after 5 years and 6 months will be $P + I$: her original principal *P* plus the interest earned *I*.

P   +   *I*   =   account total

8,200   + _____ = _____

Melanie's account will contain $ _____ after 5 years and 6 months.

 Turn and Talk Which of the following changes would increase Melanie's balance the most: increasing the time to 10 years, increasing the interest rate to 6.5%, or increasing the principal to $9,000.00? Explain.

3 Gregory borrowed money to buy a used car, which he paid back at the end of the loan period. It cost him $10,650 to repay the loan. How many years was the loan period?

- $7,500 loan
- annual simple interest rate of 6%

A.

P	+	I	=	Total repayment
7,500	+	_____	=	_____

Gregory paid a total of _____ in interest.

B. To find the loan period t, solve $I = Prt$ for t.

$$I = P \times r \times t$$

$$\underline{\hspace{1cm}} = 7{,}500 \times \underline{\hspace{1cm}} \times t$$

$$\underline{\hspace{1cm}} = 450 \times t$$

$$\boxed{} = t$$

$$\boxed{} = t$$

The loan period was _____ years.

 Turn and Talk Suppose you know the amount of a loan, the amount repaid, and the number of years of the loan period. How could you find the interest rate?

Check Understanding

1. Arisia puts $500 into a savings account with an annual simple interest rate of 4.5%.

A. How much interest does she earn per year?

_____

B. If the interest rate stays the same, how much interest will Arisia's account earn after 15 years?

_____

C. If the interest rate stays the same, how much money will be in Arisia's account after 20 years?

_____

D. If the savings account pays 5% simple interest, how much interest will Arisia earn on her $500 principal over 20 years?

_____

474

On Your Own

2. **Financial Literacy** Marcus borrows $3,000 from his local credit union, to be repaid with 3.5% annual simple interest at the end of 4 years. What are the principal, interest rate, and time in this situation?

Principal	
Interest rate	$\dfrac{\Box}{100} = \Box$
Time	$\Box$ years

3. Inez opens a savings account with $2,400. The account pays her 2.4% annual simple interest.

   A. Find the amount of interest that the account will earn per year.

   _____

   B. Calculate the total interest Inez would earn in 10 years.

   _____

4. Barry opens a savings account after seeing the ad shown. He deposits $1,300.

   A. (MP) **Model with Mathematics** Write an equation that relates the amount of time t in years that Barry holds his account to the amount of simple interest I that Barry earns.

   _____

   B. How much interest does Barry earn in 7 years?

   _____

Savings accounts over $1,000 earn 2.2% annual interest.

5. Avram borrows $14,500 at 5.4% annual simple interest to open up a small business. He must pay back the borrowed money and interest at the end of 9 years.

   A. How much interest will Avram have to pay on the loan?

   _____

   B. How much money will Avram have to repay in all?

   _____

Use the information for Problems 6 and 7.

Financial Literacy Regina is buying a new car. She sees two advertisements for the same car at different prices from different dealerships. Both dealers are offering a simple-interest loan for the price of the car.

Ad A

$24,200
6.5% interest
XX years

Ad B

$XXXX
5.3% interest
9 years

6. Regina calculates that to buy the car in Ad A, the loan would ultimately cost her $41,503. After how many years is the loan in Ad A to be paid back?

_____

7. Regina calculates that to buy the car in Ad B, the loan would ultimately cost her $38,402. What is the price of the car offered in Ad B?

_____

8. (MP) **Model with Mathematics** Write an equation to find the simple interest rate when $450,000 earns $31,500 interest in 2 years.

_____

9. (MP) **Use Structure** A savings account pays an annual simple interest rate of 1.5%.

   A. How much interest would you earn in 1 year on $2,000?

_____

   B. What would be the balance in your account after 5 years?

_____

   C. How long would it take to earn $500 or more in interest?

_____

10. (MP) **Use Structure** It costs $36,736 to repay a loan of $20,500 at 6.6% annual simple interest.

   A. How much interest would you pay each year?

_____

   B. After how many years must you repay the loan?

_____

Simple Interest

1. **Financial Literacy** Rena's grandfather opened a savings account as a college fund for her. His initial deposit and the yearly simple interest rate are shown. How much will Rena have in the account after 2 years and 6 months?

4 years

$?

3.25%
simple
interest

$3,500

2. (MP) **Use Structure** If you deposit $5,000 in a savings account, you will earn 6.5% simple interest over the first 10 years.

   A. How much interest will the account earn over this period?

   _____

   B. How much will be in the account after the 10-year period?

   _____

   C. At the Town Savings Bank, you will earn $2,950 in simple interest on a $5,000 deposit over the first 10 years. What rate of interest does that bank pay?

   _____

3. (MP) **Use Structure** Dream Loan Bank offers loans. Carrie borrows $10,500 to help start a business. The loan must be repaid at 4.5% annual simple interest after 10 years. How much money will Carrie have to pay back?

   _____

4. **Financial Literacy** Kevin is going to open a savings account with $4,000.

   Bank A offers an account that will pay 6% annual simple interest for 6 years.

   Bank B offers an account that will pay 7% annual simple interest for 3 years. After the 3 years, Kevin would have to transfer all his money to a regular account that will pay 5% annual simple interest on the *new* transferred principal. Which offer will leave Kevin with more money after 6 years? Explain.

   _____

5. Delilah deposits $8,255 in an account that pays 4.2% simple interest. How much money will be in her account after 8 years?

Ⓐ $2,773.69

Ⓑ $11,028.68

Ⓒ $12,254.66

Ⓓ $27,736.80

6. Edgar takes out a loan of $5,540, to be repaid after 7 years at 8.5% simple interest. How much interest will Edgar have to pay on the loan?

Ⓐ $470.90

Ⓑ $3,296.30

Ⓒ $3,775.60

Ⓓ $8,836.30

7. Gregoria borrowed $2,450, to be paid back at 3.5% annual simple interest. She repays $3,221.75. How many years was the loan period?

Spiral Review

For Problems 8 and 9, use the number line.

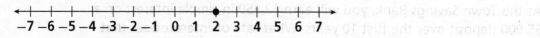

8. What number is 3 units to the right of 2 on the number line?

9. What number is 3 units to the left of 2?

10. Bianca had a weekly allowance of $8.50 two years ago. Last year, her weekly allowance was $9.75. This year, Bianca's weekly allowance is $12.00. Does it make sense to represent the relationship between the amount of her allowance and the year with a constant rate? Why or why not? Explain your answer.

Vocabulary

Choose the correct term from the Vocabulary box.

Vocabulary
commission
gratuity
markdown
principal
sales tax

1. The amount by which a price is reduced so that an item will sell:

   _____

2. An amount of money that is deposited or borrowed and that earns or is charged interest:

   _____

3. An amount of money given as a tip to someone who has performed a service:

   _____

4. An amount paid to an employee that represents a percent of the employee's sales:

   _____

Concepts and Skills

5. (MP) **Use Tools** All sweaters at a store are on sale at a 20% discount. What would be the sale price of a sweater regularly priced $40? State what strategy and tool you will use to answer the question, explain your choice, and then find the answer.

   _____

   _____

6. Match each verbal description with all equivalent expressions.

	$0.97d$	$1.03d$	$d - 0.03$	$d + 0.03d$	$(1 - 0.03)d$
d increased by 3%	☐	☐	☐	☐	☐
d decreased by 3%	☐	☐	☐	☐	☐

7. Phillip wants to buy a baseball cap. Sales tax is 8%. Select the prices of all caps Phillip could buy for less than or equal to $20 once sales tax is added.

   (A) $18.18   (B) $18.50   (C) $18.68   (D) $19.00   (E) $19.90

8. Amy and two of her friends eat lunch at a restaurant. Their bill comes to $27.63. They decide to split the bill equally. Amy wants to leave a 20% tip for her portion. What is the total amount Amy should pay, including tip? Round to the nearest cent.

$ _____

9. Mr. Bauer deposits $600 in an account that earns simple interest at an annual rate of 2%. Use three of the numbers from the box at right to complete an expression that represents the amount, in dollars, that will be in Mr. Bauer's account after 3 years.

0.02
0.2
2
3
100
600

_____ (1 + _____ · _____)

10. A salesperson earns $8 per hour plus 6% commission on her sales. In a week when she worked 40 hours, her total earnings were $692. What was the amount of her sales for the week?

$ _____

11. The owner of an art supply store buys tubes of magenta oil paint for $10.80 and marks up the cost by 110% to determine the retail price. The tubes of paint do not sell well, so the owner marks down the retail price by 20%. To the nearest cent, what is the marked-down price of a tube of magenta oil paint?

(A) $9.50   (B) $11.88   (C) $18.14   (D) $22.68

12. A ticket company charges a service fee of 5% of the ticket price for each ticket to a concert. Use this information to complete the table.

Ticket Price ($)	Service Fee ($)	Total Cost with Service Fee ($)
19.00		
	1.40	
		47.25

13. For a scale to pass inspection, the scale's reading can vary by at most 0.1% from the actual mass of an object on the scale. A test mass has an exact mass of 250.00 grams. In what range must the scale's reading be for the scale to pass inspection?

_____

14. This year, 17,884 people attended a basketball team's first game, and 17,150 people attended their second game. What is the percent decrease from the first game to the second game in the number of people who attended? Round to the nearest tenth of a percent.

_____%

© Houghton Mifflin Harcourt Publishing Company • Image Credits: (t) ©Sitthiphong/Essentials Collection/iStock/Getty Images; (b) ©vik1003mike/Shutterstock

Unit 4 Relationships in Geometry

Marketing Manager

Marketing managers are responsible for making a company's products appeal to customers. They often do this using information gathered from focus groups and surveys. To do their job effectively, marketing managers must analyze not only *how* people react to products and advertising, but also *why* they react the way they do. The managers then use their analyses to develop and implement marketing strategies.

STEM Task:

Market researchers study people's reactions to product logos. One study found that circular logos suggest softness and comfort, while angular logos convey strength and durability. RunWalk, an athletic shoe company, found that consumers think their shoes do not last very long. Design a logo for RunWalk to address this issue. Explain your thinking.

Learning Mindset

Strategic Help-Seeking Identifies Need for Help

Do you ask for help when you need it? Sometimes, struggling with a concept or task is the best way to learn. But other times, you may find that you are unable to make progress despite your efforts. When this happens, you may need to seek help from other people or resources. No one knows better than you do when your effort is unproductive, so it is important to recognize when to ask for help. Here are some questions to consider when you are struggling with a new concept.

- Do you understand enough of the concept to keep moving forward on your own? How do you know?

- What parts of the concept are you struggling with? What resources can you use to increase your understanding?

- Who might be able to help you? Who can you go to with questions?

Reflect

Q Were there any parts of the STEM Task that you did not understand? If so, how did you get the help you needed to complete the task?

Q Think about times you have asked for and received help in the past. What kinds of help best support your learning? How do you communicate the kind of help you need?

Polygons on the Coordinate Plane

Polygon **Seek** and **Find**

Find an example of each polygon in the design and label it with its letter.

In this figure, assume that what appear to be right angles, parallel lines, or segments with equal lengths are actually so.

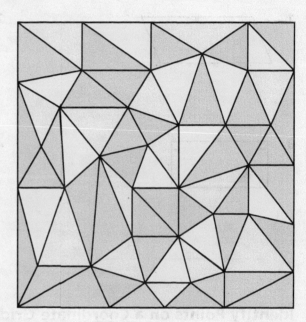

A. square

B. rectangle
(that is not a square)

C. rhombus
(that is not a square)

D. parallelogram
(that is not a rectangle or a rhombus)

E. quadrilateral
(that is not a parallelogram)

F. isosceles triangle
(that is not equilateral)

G. right triangle

H. acute triangle

I. obtuse triangle

 Turn and Talk

- Explain the characteristics you used to identify a rhombus that is not a square.

- Explain the characteristics you used to identify a quadrilateral that is not a parallelogram.

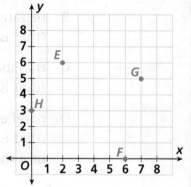

Are You Ready?

Complete these problems to review prior concepts and skills you will need for this module.

Quadrilaterals

Classify each figure using the most specific term from the list.

quadrilateral, parallelogram, rectangle, square

1.

_____

2.

_____

3.

_____

4.

_____

Identify Points on a Coordinate Grid

Graph and label each ordered pair on the coordinate grid.

5. $A(3, 4)$

6. $B(1, 1)$

7. $C(5, 2)$

8. $D(6, 7)$

Write the ordered pair for each point shown on the coordinate grid.

9. E _____

10. F _____

11. G _____

12. H _____

Name _____

Graph and Find Distances Between Points on the Coordinate Plane

I Can plot a point with rational number coordinates and locate its reflection over the *x*- or *y*-axis, and I can use absolute value to find the distance between points with the same *x*- or *y*-coordinate.

Spark Your Learning PAIRS

The Robinsons' family home is located at (3, 7) on the coordinate plane, where the units are miles. They begin their vacation by driving to a restaurant located at (3, 1). From the restaurant, the family drives to a campground located 5 miles due west of the restaurant to spend the night. Then the family drives 6 miles due south to visit their grandparents. What are the coordinates of the campground and their grandparents' home? Explain how you found the coordinates of each location.

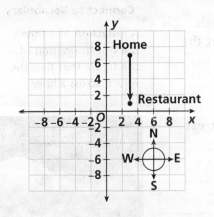

Turn and Talk A number line displays ordered numbers along a straight line. Explain how the coordinate grid above relates to number lines.

Build Understanding

A **coordinate plane** is formed by the intersection of a horizontal number line, called the **x-axis**, and a vertical number line, called the **y-axis**. The **origin** is the point where the x-axis and y-axis intersect. Notice that the coordinate plane is divided into four regions called **quadrants**. An **ordered pair** is a set of two numbers in the form (x, y) used to locate a point on a coordinate plane.

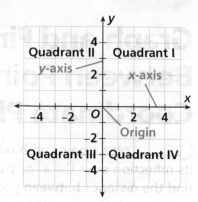

1 How do you identify the **coordinates** of a point?

A. The **x-coordinate** and **y-coordinate** of an ordered pair in Quadrant I are both positive numbers. Write + or − to show the sign of each coordinate in the other quadrants.

Quadrant I: (+, +)   Quadrant III: (⬚ , ⬚)

Quadrant II: (⬚ , ⬚)   Quadrant IV: (⬚ , ⬚)

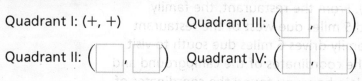

B. What are the coordinates of Points A, B, C, and D, shown?

A point on a coordinate plane can be reflected across an axis. The reflection is located on the opposite side of the axis, at the same distance from the axis.

2 Use the table to record your work.

Point	Reflection across y-axis	Reflection across x-axis
(3, −2)		
(−5, 1.5)		
$\left(2\frac{1}{3}, 4\right)$		
(−1, −3)		

reflection of a mountain in a lake

A. Draw a coordinate plane on graph paper. Graph the points listed in the table. Then find the reflections by folding the paper first along the y-axis, and then along the x-axis. Record the coordinates of each reflection.

B. What is the relationship between the coordinates of a point and the coordinates of its reflection across each axis?

Step It Out

3 What is the distance between Points *F* and *G* on the coordinate plane, measured by units of the coordinate plane?

A. Plot and label Points *F*(3, 6) and *G*(3, −2) on the coordinate plane.

B. The *x*-coordinate of Point *F* is
   the same as / different from the
   x-coordinate of Point *G*.

C. Draw a line segment that connects the two points. What is the distance between Point *F* and the point where the line segment intersects the *x*-axis?

_____

D. What is the absolute value of the *y*-coordinate of Point *F*?

_____

E. What is the distance between Point *G* and the *x*-axis? What is the absolute value of the *y*-coordinate of Point *G*?

_____

F. What do you notice about the absolute value of each point's *y*-coordinate and the distance of the point to the *x*-axis?

_____

G. The points are / are not in the same quadrant.

H. Because the points are in different quadrants, add the absolute values of the points' *y*-coordinates to find the distance between Points *F* and *G*.

   $\boxed{} + \boxed{} = \boxed{}$

I. Plot and label Point *H*(3, −6) on the coordinate plane. Complete the statement below to calculate the distance between Points *G* and *H*.

   $\left|\boxed{}\right| - \left|-2\right| = \boxed{} - 2 = \boxed{}$

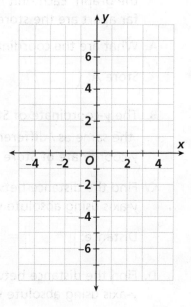

 Turn and Talk Explain how you might find the distance between two points with the same *x*-coordinate that are both in Quadrant III.

4 A wholesale chain has two stores as shown on the graph. Each unit represents 10 miles. How far apart are the stores?

A. What are the coordinates of each store?

Store A: (☐ , ☐); Store B: (☐ , ☐)

B. The y-coordinate of Store A is ____ .
   [the same as / different from] the y-coordinate of Store B.

C. Find the distance between Store A and the y-axis using absolute value.

Distance: | ☐ | = ☐ units

D. Find the distance between Store B and the y-axis using absolute value.

Distance: | ☐ | = ☐ units

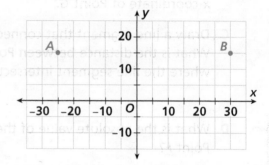

E. Find the distance, in miles, between the two stores.

Distance (units): ☐ + ☐ = ☐ units

Distance (in miles): ☐ × ☐ = ☐ miles

 Turn and Talk How could you use absolute value to find the distance between two points that have the same y-coordinate and lie in the same quadrant?

Check Understanding

1. Point (−6.2, 5) is reflected across the y-axis. What are the coordinates of its reflection? _____

2. Are the points P(80, −75) and Q(−35, −75) in the same quadrant or different quadrants? What is the distance between the points? Explain how you found the distance.

_____

_____

3. Are the points A(−4, −10) and B(−4, −2) in the same quadrant or different quadrants? What is the distance between the points? Explain how you found the distance.

_____

On Your Own

4. The locations of two neighboring train stations are shown. Each unit on the coordinate plane is equal to 1 mile. How far apart are the two stations?

A. What are the coordinates of each station?

Station *M*: ([   ] , [   ]); Station *N*: ([   ] , [   ])

B. What is the distance in miles between Station *M* and the *x*-axis?

_____

C. What is the distance in miles between Station *N* and the *x*-axis?

_____

D. What is the distance in miles between the two stations?

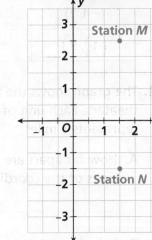

For Problems 5–8, use the coordinate plane.

5. What are the coordinates for the six points shown?

_____

_____

6. What is the distance between Points *S* and *T*? Are they in the same quadrant?

_____

7. What is the distance between Points *R* and *T*? Are they in the same quadrant?

_____

8. What is the distance between Points *Q* and *U*? Are they in the same quadrant?

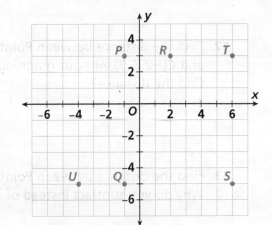

_____

9. (MP) **Critique Reasoning** Theo says that the point (−5, 7) and its reflection across the axis are always 10 units apart. Is he correct? Explain.

_____

_____

_____

_____

10. (MP) **Use Repeated Reasoning** Write the coordinates of each point after each reflection.

Point	Reflection across *x*-axis	Reflection across *y*-axis
(2, −5)		
(−6, −3.2)		
(−4, 1)		
$\left(1\frac{3}{4}, 9\right)$		

11. The graph shows the locations of two movie theaters. Each unit of the coordinate plane represents 8 miles.

    A. How far apart are the movie theaters in units of the coordinate plane?

    _____

    B. How far apart are the movie theaters in miles?

    _____

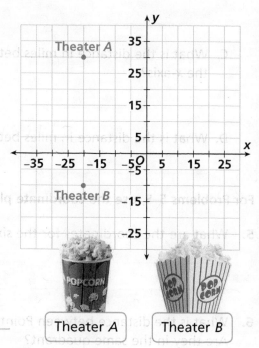

12. Find the distance between Points $B(−2.7, −8)$ and $C(−2.7, 3)$ without graphing. How did you find the distance?

    _____

    _____

13. Find the distance between Points $P\left(3\frac{1}{5}, 9\right)$ and $R\left(7\frac{4}{5}, 9\right)$ without graphing. Why do you subtract instead of adding to find the distance?

    _____

    _____

    _____

I'm in a Learning Mindset!

What is challenging about finding distance in a coordinate plane? Can I work through it on my own or do I need help?

_____

_____

© Houghton Mifflin Harcourt Publishing Company • Image Credits: (l) ©Fotofermer/Shutterstock; (r) ©Stephen Mcsweeny/Shutterstock

Graph and Find Distances Between Points on the Coordinate Plane

1. Each unit on the grid shown represents 20 miles.

   A. Airport *A* is located at (125, −325) and Airport *B* is located at (125, 125). Plot and label points to represent the locations of the two airports.

   B. What is the distance between the two airports in miles?

   _____

   C. Plot and label the point for Airport *C*: (−250, 350).

   D. Which quadrant of the coordinate plane does not have an airport?

   _____

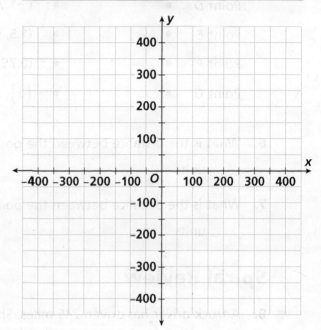

2. What are the coordinates of Point *Z*(−3.9, −9.3) after a reflection across the *y*-axis?

   _____

3. **Math on the Spot** Find the distance between the points.

   A.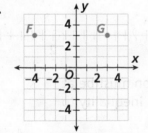

   B.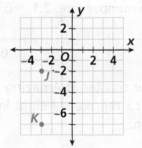

   _____   _____

4. (MP) **Use Structure** Find the distance between Points *D*(−5, −3) and *E*(9, −3) without graphing. How did you find the distance?

   _____

   _____

Test Prep

5. Draw a line to match each label to the correct ordered pair.

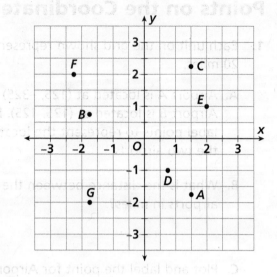

Point A   ●   ●   (−2.25, 2)

Point B   ●   ●   (2, 1)

Point C   ●   ● $\left(-1\frac{3}{4}, -2\right)$

Point D   ●   ●   (−1.75, 0.75)

Point E   ●   ●   (1.5, −1.75)

Point F   ●   ●   (0.75, −1)

Point G   ●   ● $\left(1\frac{1}{2}, 2\frac{1}{4}\right)$

6. What is the distance between the points (−2.5, 6.5) and (2.5, 6.5)?

_____ units

7. What is the distance between the points (3, 4.1) and (3, 1.2)?

_____ units

Spiral Review

8. A truck driver has driven 245 miles. She needs to drive *m* miles in all. Write an equation for the number of miles *d* that the driver has left to drive.

_____

9. Plot the points on the number line. 2.1, −0.4, 1.3, −1.8

10. In order to ride a roller coaster at Amazing Rides Fair, a person must be at least 42 inches tall. Let *x* represent height in inches. Write an inequality to represent this situation.

_____

Name _____

Graph Polygons on the Coordinate Plane

(I Can) graph polygons on a coordinate plane, classify them, and identify a vertex that completes a specified polygon.

Spark Your Learning

Marisol is designing a vegetable garden. The coordinate plane shows the area where the garden will be planted where 1 grid square equals 1 square meter. She has 24 meters of fencing to put around her garden. The garden can be any shape as long as she uses all of the fencing to make a border around the garden. Use the coordinate plane to show a possible design for her vegetable garden. Name the coordinates of the corners of the garden. Explain your reasoning.

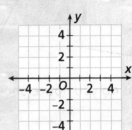

Turn and Talk What do you notice about the coordinates of the corners of rectangles? Explain.

Build Understanding

A **vertex** is the point where two sides of a polygon intersect.
The plural of *vertex* is vertices.

Connect to Vocabulary

A **polygon** is a closed plane figure formed by three or more line segments that intersect only at their endpoints.

1 ▷ Look at the figures shown.

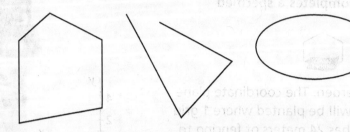

A. What do you notice about the first figure? Is it a polygon?

_____

B. What do you notice about the second figure? Is it a polygon?

_____

_____

C. What do you notice about the third figure? Is it a polygon?

_____

_____

You can classify polygons by the number of sides they have. Triangles, quadrilaterals, **pentagons**, and **hexagons** are all examples of polygons.

2 ▷ Describe the polygon with vertices *F*(2, 5), *G*(7, 1), *H*(2, −6), and *J*(−3, 1).

A. Plot the points on the coordinate plane.

B. Draw segments connecting *F* to *G*, *G* to *H*, *H* to *J*, and *J* to *F*. Classify the polygon you drew by the number of sides.

C. How many vertices does it have?

_____

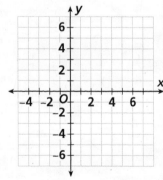

Turn and Talk Is there another way to classify the figure you drew in Part B? Explain.

Name _____

Step It Out

3 An architect is drawing a plan for part of a bridge that makes a **right triangle**. The coordinates of two vertices of the right triangle are $A(-3, 5)$ and $B(2, 4)$. Sides AC and BC will form the **right angle** of the triangle. What are the coordinates of Vertex C?

right triangle

A. Plot Points A and B on the coordinate plane.

B. What must be true about a right triangle?

_____

C. Is there more than one possible location for Vertex C? What are the possible coordinates of C?

_____

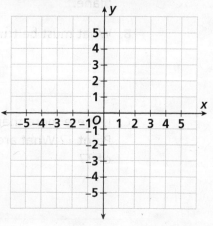

D. Plot Point C and draw Triangle ABC.

E. At which vertex is the right angle? _____

F. Draw a second right triangle in the fourth quadrant of the coordinate plane. What are the coordinates of each vertex of the triangle?

_____

_____

G. Label the vertices of your triangle with letters. What is the vertex of the right angle in your triangle?

_____

H. Are the right triangles you drew polygons? Explain.

_____

_____

I. Can you plot three points on a coordinate plane that cannot be the vertices of a triangle? If so, how?

_____

_____

 Turn and Talk Can you make a right triangle ABC with a right angle at Vertex B instead of at Vertex C? How could you find where to place Point C?

4 An architect is designing a plan for a new building inspired by the Nykredit Krystallen building in Copenhagen, Denmark. The building will have faces that are parallelograms without right angles. The architect plots three of the four corners of one face at $Q(-5, -2)$, $R(1, -2)$, and $S(-2, 3)$. What are the coordinates of Point T if T is the fourth corner of that face of the building?

Nykredit Krystallen building, Copenhagen, Denmark

A. Plot Points Q, R, and S on the coordinate plane.

B. What must be true about a parallelogram?

_____

_____

C. Is there more than one possible location for Point T? What are the possible coordinates of T?

_____

_____

D. Plot Point T and draw the parallelogram.

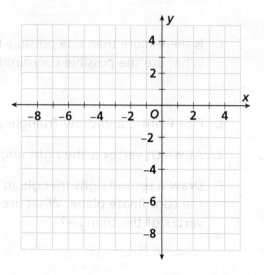

Check Understanding

1. You can classify polygons by the number of sides they have.

A. Graph Points $A(-3, 4)$, $B(-4, -2)$, $C(1, -2)$, and $D(0, 4)$. Connect A to B to C to D to A. What names can you use to describe this polygon? Explain.

_____

_____

_____

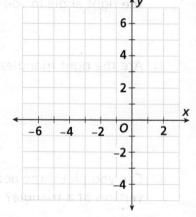

B. Use the points you graphed in Part A. What are the possible coordinates of a Point E if ADE is a right triangle where Angle D is the right angle? Explain.

_____

_____

_____

On Your Own

2. Art Wesley designs a shark fin for a costume. He chooses the points $K(1, 7)$, $L(3, 5)$, $M(6, -3)$, $N(-5, -2)$, and $P(-1, 1)$ to model the fin.

A. Graph the points on the coordinate plane.

B. Connect the points in order from K to L to M to N to P, and back to K.

C. How many sides does the polygon that you drew have? Classify the polygon by the number of sides.

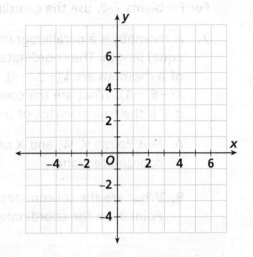

(MP) Construct Arguments For Problems 3–4, tell whether the figure is a polygon. If it is a polygon, give the number of sides and classify it. If it is not, explain why not.

3.

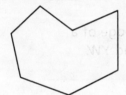

_____

_____

_____

4.

_____

_____

_____

For Problems 5–6, use the coordinate plane.

5. Consider Points $K(1, 2)$ and $L(3, 5)$. What possible coordinates for Point J will make Figure JKL a right triangle with the right angle at Point J? Graph Triangle JKL on the coordinate plane.

_____

6. (MP) Use Tools An isosceles triangle has two sides of the same length. Isosceles triangle DEF has Vertices $D(4, -5)$ and $E(-2, -5)$. What are possible coordinates for Point F in the section of Quadrant IV shown in the coordinate plane? Explain how you could check your answer.

_____

_____

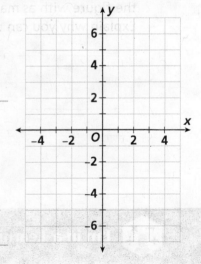

For Problems 7–8, use the coordinate grid.

7. A rhombus is a parallelogram with sides of equal length. The coordinates of three vertices of a rhombus are V(−2, −4), W(3, −4), and X(−6, −1). What are the coordinates of Point Y if Y is the fourth vertex of the rhombus?

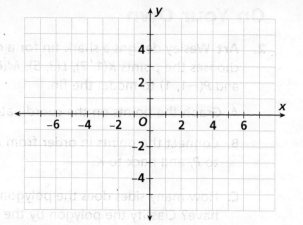

   A. Plot Points V, W, and X on the coordinate plane.

   B. What are the coordinates of Point Y? Plot Point Y on the coordinate plane.

   _____

   C. To check that all four sides are the same length, first use the coordinate plane to find the lengths of Sides VW and XY.

   _____

   D. (MP) **Use Tools** Next, mark off a scale of grid units on the edge of a sheet of paper and use it to find the lengths of Sides XV and YW.

   _____

8. **Open Ended** Graph a square on the coordinate plane with sides of length 3 units.

   _____

   _____

9. (MP) **Construct Arguments** Carla drew the figure shown on the coordinate plane. Classify the figure with as many terms as possible. Explain why you can use each term.

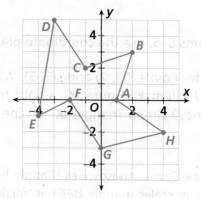

   _____

   _____

   _____

© Houghton Mifflin Harcourt Publishing Company

 I'm in a Learning Mindset!

What tools can I use to solve Problem 6?

_____

_____

Graph Polygons on the
Coordinate Plane

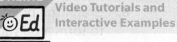
(MP) Construct Arguments For Problems 1–2, tell whether the figure
is a polygon. If it is a polygon, classify it. If it is not, explain why not.

1.

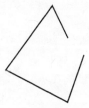

_____

2.

_____

3. Points A(3, 3), B(−6, 1), and C(−3, 1) are
three vertices of a parallelogram.

A. Plot the points on the coordinate plane.

B. Find one possible point in the part of the
coordinate plane shown that could be the
fourth vertex, D, of the parallelogram.
Give its coordinates

_____

C. Plot Point D and draw the parallelogram on the coordinate plane.

_____

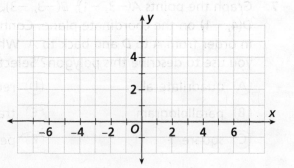

4. (MP) Reason Suppose you want to give the coordinates of three points that
are vertices of a right triangle. How can you do this without looking at a
coordinate plane?

_____

_____

_____

5. A right triangle XYZ has Vertices X(−2, −1) and Y(1, 1)
and a right angle at Vertex Z. What could the coordinates
of Vertex Z be? Use the coordinate plane to decide.

_____

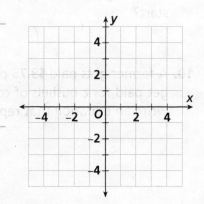

Test Prep

6. Graph the points (1, 3), (5, −4), and (−4, 2) and connect them to form a polygon.

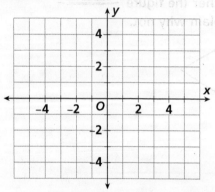

7. Graph the points $A(−3, −1)$, $B(−3, −3)$, $C(4, −3)$, and $D(4, −1)$ on the coordinate plane. Connect the points in order from A to D and back to A. What names can you use to describe this polygon? Select all that apply.

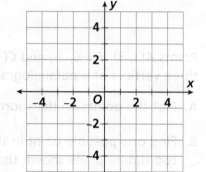

- (A) quadrilateral
- (B) parallelogram
- (C) square
- (D) rectangle
- (E) trapezoid
- (F) pentagon

8. Diana is drawing a parallelogram on a coordinate plane. She plots vertices at (−2, −2), (2, −2), and (0, 1). Select all the possible coordinates for the fourth vertex.

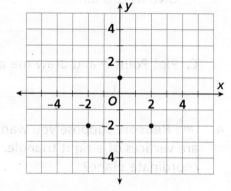

- (A) (4, 1)
- (B) (1, 0)
- (C) (−3, 1)
- (D) (−4, 1)
- (E) (0, −5)
- (F) (2, −5)

Spiral Review

9. The population of a certain bacteria doubles every 24 hours. How many times as great is the population after 5 days as the population was at the start?

_____

10. A farmer gets paid $3.75 per bushel of corn. How much does the farmer get paid for c bushels of corn? Use p to represent the farmer's pay and write an equation that represents this situation.

_____

Name _____

Find Perimeter and Area on the Coordinate Plane

(**I Can**) find the perimeter and area of polygons in the coordinate plane.

Step It Out

You can use what you learned about finding the distance between points to find areas and perimeters of figures on the coordinate plane.

1 Recall that the **formula** for the **area** of a rectangle is $A = b \times h$, where b is the length of the **base** and h is the **height**.

A. If we consider Side *EF* to be the base of the rectangle, which side's length is the height?

_____

B. To find the length of the rectangle's base, add the absolute values of the _____-coordinates of Point *E* and Point *F*.

$$\left|\ \boxed{}\ \right| + \left|\ \boxed{}\ \right|$$

The length of the rectangle's base is $\boxed{} + \boxed{} = \boxed{}$ units.

C. To find the rectangle's height, add the absolute values of the _____-coordinates of Point *E* and Point *D*.

$$\left|\ \boxed{}\ \right| + \left|\ \boxed{}\ \right|$$

The rectangle's height is $\boxed{} + \boxed{} = \boxed{}$ units.

D. Find the area of the rectangle.

$A = b \times h = \boxed{} \times \boxed{}$

$\qquad = \boxed{}$ square units

Turn and Talk What are two ways to find the area of a rectangle on a coordinate plane?

2 Alex is designing a rectangular piece of art. He draws a rectangle on a coordinate plane to begin the piece.

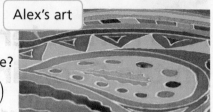
Alex's art

A. What are the coordinates of the vertices of the rectangle?

(☐ , ☐), (☐ , ☐), (☐ , ☐), (☐ , ☐)

B. What are the length and width of the rectangle?

_____

C. Find the perimeter of the rectangle.

$P =$ ☐ $+$ ☐ $+$ ☐ $+$ ☐ $=$ ☐ units

D. Find the area of the rectangle.

$A =$ ☐ $\times$ ☐ $=$ ☐ square units

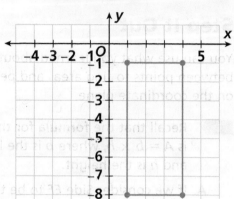

3 Figures *PQRS* and *TUVW* are squares. Find the shaded area.

A. Find the length of Side *PS*.

☐ $+$ ☐ $=$ ☐ units

B. Find the length of Side *TW*.

☐ $+$ ☐ $=$ ☐ units

C. Find the shaded area.

Shaded area = Area of *PQRS* − Area of *TUVW*

$=$ ☐ $-$ ☐ $=$ ☐ square units

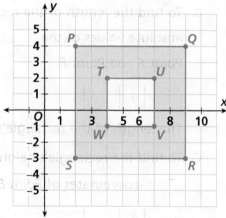

Check Understanding

1. A blueprint of a rectangular pool is shown. What are the area and perimeter of the pool?

_____

_____

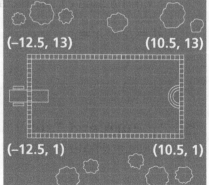

(−12.5, 13)   (10.5, 13)

(−12.5, 1)   (10.5, 1)

2. What is the area of a rectangle *ABCD* with vertices at *A*(−8, 5), *B*(−8, −4), *C*(3, −4), and *D*(3, 5)?

_____

On Your Own

3. Gina is growing lettuce in a section of her garden. She represents this section with Rectangle *JKLM*. Each unit in the coordinate grid represents 1 foot.

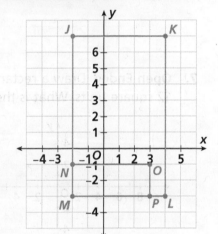

lettuce plants

A. What is the area of the section where lettuce grows?

$A =$ ☐ $\times$ ☐ $=$ ☐ square feet

B. Gina plants each head of lettuce with 2 square feet around it. How many heads of lettuce can Gina plant?

C. Next year Gina plans to plant carrots in the section of her garden represented by rectangle *MNOP*. Find the area of this section of her garden.

$A =$ ☐ $\times$ ☐ $=$ ☐ square feet

D. Gina can plant 8 carrots per square foot. How many carrots can Gina plant?

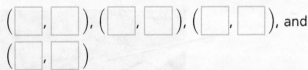

4. What are the area and perimeter of the quadrilateral?

A. What are the coordinates of the quadrilateral's vertices?

(☐ , ☐), (☐ , ☐), (☐ , ☐), and
(☐ , ☐)

B. Find the perimeter of the quadrilateral.

$P =$ ☐ $+$ ☐ $+$ ☐ $+$ ☐ $=$ ☐ units

C. Find the area of the quadrilateral.

$A =$ ☐ $\times$ ☐ $=$ ☐ square units

5. The length of one rectangle in a quilt is 6 inches. Its width is 3 inches. About how many of these rectangles do you need to cover an area of 7,500 square inches? Explain.

6. Use the figure on the coordinate plane.

  A. What is the area of Rectangle *FGHK*?

  _____

  B. What is the area of Rectangle *PQRS*?

  _____

  C. What is the area of the shaded region? Explain how you found your answer.

  _____

  _____

  _____

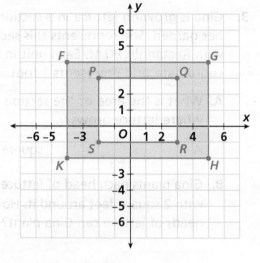

7. **Open Ended** Draw a rectangle on the coordinate plane with an area of 12 square units. What is the rectangle's perimeter?

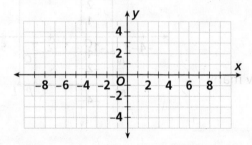

_____

_____

8. The pattern for the two wings of a hang glider is shown on the grid. The unit is inches. What is the total area of the wings? What is the area of each wing?

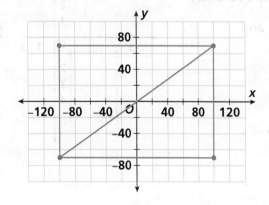

_____

9. What is the area of the rectangle shown on the coordinate plane?

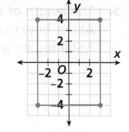

_____

Find Perimeter and Area on the Coordinate Plane

For Problems 1–2, use the following information.

An engineer is tasked with doubling the length and width of a city park. The engineer draws the park on a coordinate plane and labels it *ABCD*.

1. Find the area of the park before and after the expansion.

    A. What is the area of the park before the expansion? _____

    B. What is the area of the park after the length and width are doubled? _____

    C. By what factor did the area change? _____

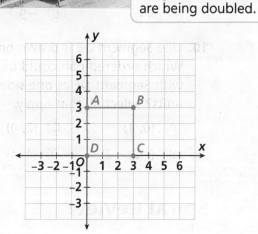

Length and width are being doubled.

2. Find the perimeter of the park before and after the expansion.

    A. What is the perimeter of the park before the length and width are doubled? _____

    B. What is the perimeter of the park after the length and width are doubled? _____

    C. By what factor did the perimeter change? _____

3. **Math on the Spot** What is the perimeter of the rectangle shown?

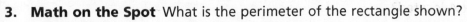
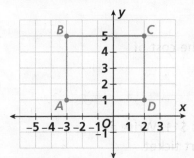

For Problems 4–7, find the length of the segment with the given endpoints.

4. (−12, 4), (21, 4)

5. (−6, 9), (−6, 13)

6. (17.1, 3), (21.4, 3)

7. (−3, −12.5), (−3, 16.5)

© Houghton Mifflin Harcourt Publishing Company • Image Credit: ©Shutterstock

Test Prep

8. Find the area of the shaded region in square units.

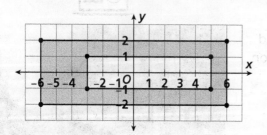

9. Rectangle *ABCD* has perimeter of 22 units. The coordinates of the rectangle's vertices are *A*(−4, 5), *B*(3, 5), *C*(3, *x*), and *D*(−4, *x*). Which could be the value of *x*?

   (A) 4   (B) −9   (C) 1   (D) 7

10. Line Segment *DE* is drawn on the coordinate plane. Which ordered pair could be the vertex of a rectangle with Segment *DE* as one side and an area of 28 square units? Select all that apply.

   (A) (0, 1)   (C) (2, 0)   (E) (−3, 1)

   (B) (−2, −2)   (D) (4, 4)   (F) (4, 1)

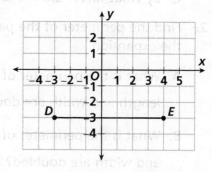

Spiral Review

11. A triangle has vertices at *A*(−2, −1), *B*(−2, 4), and *C*(7, −1). In what quadrant is Vertex *A* located?

12. A dozen donuts cost $2.99. To the nearest cent, what is the cost of 1 donut?

13. Mr. Lee had $67. He bought a concert ticket and now has $11. Write an equation that can be used to find the cost *c* of the concert ticket.

14. List three solutions of the inequality $h < -34$.

Review

Vocabulary

Choose the correct term from the Vocabulary box to complete each statement.

Vocabulary

coordinate plane
axes
x-axis
y-axis
origin
quadrant
coordinates
polygon
vertex
reflection

1. A(n) _____ is a closed plane figure formed by three or more line segments that intersect only at their endpoints.

2. An ordered pair describes a point on a(n) _____.
The first number in an ordered pair describes the distance from the origin along the _____. The second number in an ordered pair describes the distance from the origin along the _____.

3. The numbers in an ordered pair are called _____

4. The point (0, 0) on the coordinate plane is called the _____.

5. A(n) _____ of a figure is a transformation that flips the figure across a line.

6. The point on a polygon where two sides intersect is a(n) _____.

7. The point (1, 1) is located in _____ I of the coordinate plane.

Concepts and Skills

Use the coordinate plane to answer Problems 8–11.

8. What type of figure has vertices at *R*, *S*, *T*, and *U*?

_____

9. What is the area of Figure *RSTU*?

_____

10. What is the perimeter of Figure *RSTU*?

11. (MP) **Use Tools** Name the point that is the reflection of the point $\left(1\frac{1}{4}, -2\frac{1}{2}\right)$ across the *x*-axis. State what strategy and tool you will use to answer the question, explain your choice, and then find the answer.

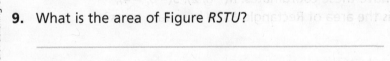

_____

Use the coordinate plane to answer Problems 12–16.

12. Write the ordered pair for each of the points on the graph.

Point *G* _____

Point *H* _____

Point *L* _____

Point *J* _____

13. What figure is formed by Points *G, H,*

L, and *J*? _____

14. Point *K* is reflected across the *x*-axis. What are the coordinates of the reflection?

_____

15. What is the distance from *J* to *G*?

[ ] grid units, which equals [ ]

16. What is the distance from *L* to *H*? [ ] grid units, which equals [ ]

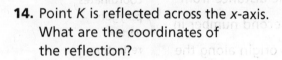
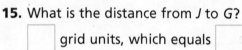
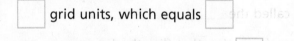
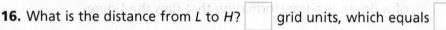
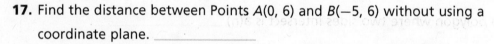
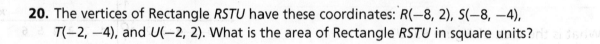

17. Find the distance between Points *A*(0, 6) and *B*(−5, 6) without using a coordinate plane. _____

18. Find the distance between Points *V*(12, 14.5) and *W*(12, −15.5) without using a coordinate plane. _____

19. The vertices of Rectangle *DEFG* have these coordinates: *D*(4, 6), *E*(4, 1), *F*(0, 1), and *G*(0, 6). What is the area of Rectangle *DEFG* in square units?

_____

20. The vertices of Rectangle *RSTU* have these coordinates: *R*(−8, 2), *S*(−8, −4), *T*(−2, −4), and *U*(−2, 2). What is the area of Rectangle *RSTU* in square units?

_____

21. The points *M*(−3, 2), *N*(−3, −4), *P*(2, −4), and *Q*(2, 2) form a rectangle.

A. What is the rectangle's perimeter? _____

B. What is the rectangle's area in square units? _____

22. Which point is a reflection of (−5, 1.8) across the *y*-axis on a coordinate plane?

(A) (5, 1.8) (C) (−5, 1.8)

(B) (−5, −1.8) (D) (5, −1.8)

Area of Triangles and Special Quadrilaterals

NEW AT THE ZOO

A zoo is adding three new cages to its bird exhibit. The floors of the cages will be rectangles with the same perimeters but different areas. The floor plan for one of the cages is shown on the grid.

Draw possible floor plans for the other two cages with the same perimeter.

A. Each unit on the grid represents 5 feet.
What is the perimeter of the floor of each cage?

_____

B. Label the floor plan for each cage with its area.

Cage 1

 Turn and Talk

- What happens to the floor area of a cage as the difference between the length and width decreases?

- What is the largest possible floor area for one of the new cages?

Are You Ready?

Complete these problems to review prior concepts and skills you will need for this module.

Estimate and Find Area

For Problems 1–2, find the area of each rectangle.

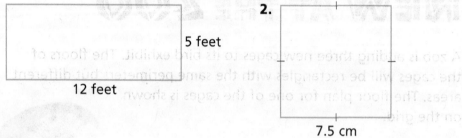

1.

5 feet

12 feet

2.

7.5 cm

_____   _____

3. A rectangular swimming pool has a length of 25 meters and a width of 12 meters. Find the area of the pool.

_____

4. A high school basketball court is a rectangle with a length of 84 feet and a width of 50 feet. Find the area of the basketball court.

_____

5. Find the area of a rectangular painting that has a length of 7.2 feet and a width of 4.5 feet.

_____

Triangles

Complete each statement.

6. A triangle that has three acute angles is called a(n) _____ triangle.

7. A triangle that has one obtuse angle is called a(n) _____ triangle.

8. A triangle with a 90° angle is called a(n) _____ triangle.

Name _____

Develop and Use Formulas for Areas of Quadrilaterals

(I Can) use formulas to find areas of parallelograms and trapezoids.

Spark Your Learning

The tabletops in a restaurant are parallelograms and rectangles with the same distance between parallel sides. The approximate side lengths are shown. Is the area of a parallelogram-shaped tabletop the same as the area of a rectangular one? Explain.

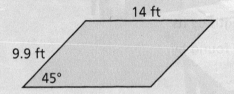

14 ft

9.9 ft

45°

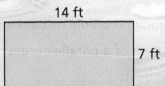

14 ft

7 ft

 Turn and Talk Suppose the restaurant also has square tabletops. What are the approximate side lengths of one of the square tabletops if it has the same area as the rectangular tabletop? Explain.

Build Understanding

A quadrilateral is a polygon with four sides and four angles. Examples of quadrilaterals include **parallelograms** and trapezoids.

1 ▷ How can you find the area of a parallelogram?

A. Look at the parallelogram shown. The **base** and **height** are labeled. The dashed segment forms a right triangle. If you move the right triangle as shown, you get a new figure. What is the new figure?

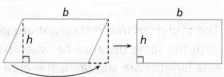

_____

B. Complete the statements.

To find the area of a rectangle, multiply its base length by its

_____. So, the area of a parallelogram is found by

multiplying its base length by its _____.

C. Fill in the boxes to find the area of the parallelogram shown.

$A = b \times h$

$A = \boxed{}$ cm $\times \boxed{}$ cm

$A = \boxed{}$ cm^2

$b = 6$ cm

$h = 3$ cm

2 ▷ The **bases of a trapezoid** are a pair of parallel sides. The **height of a trapezoid** is the perpendicular distance from one base to the other. How can you find the area of a trapezoid?

base 2

height

base 1

A. Notice that two copies of the same trapezoid fit together to form a parallelogram. How does the area of one of the trapezoids compare to the area of the parallelogram?

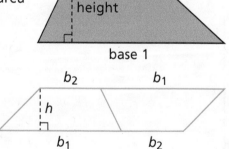

_____

_____

B. Fill in the blanks to find a formula for the area A of a trapezoid.

$A = \frac{1}{2}$ (area of parallelogram)

$= \frac{1}{2}$ (_____ of parallelogram)(height of parallelogram)

$= \frac{1}{2} \left(\boxed{} + \boxed{} \right) \cdot h$

So, the area formula for a trapezoid can be written as

$A = \dfrac{\boxed{}}{\boxed{}} h \left(\boxed{} + \boxed{} \right)$.

Step It Out

3 An interior designer sketched a floor made up of parallelogram-shaped tiles. Each tile has an actual base length of $8\frac{1}{2}$ inches and an actual height of $3\frac{1}{2}$ inches. In the sketch, each tile has an area of 1.75 square centimeters. What is the unit rate of actual area to area in the sketch?

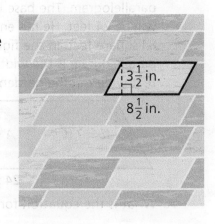

$3\frac{1}{2}$ in.

$8\frac{1}{2}$ in.

A. What is the formula for the area of a parallelogram?

_____

B. Substitute the actual dimensions of each tile for b and h in the formula:

$$A = \boxed{\frac{\boxed{}}{\boxed{}}} \text{ in.} \times \boxed{\frac{\boxed{}}{\boxed{}}} \text{ in.}$$

C. Find the area:

$$A = \boxed{\frac{\boxed{}}{\boxed{}}} \text{ in}^2$$

D. Each tile has an actual area of _____ square inches.

E. The unit rate of actual area to area in the sketch is _____ in^2 per cm^2.

4 What is the area of the trapezoid shown? Remember, the bases are the two parallel sides.

A. What is the formula for the area of a trapezoid?

_____

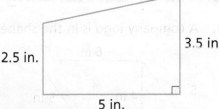

3.5 in.

2.5 in.

5 in.

B. What are the dimensions of the trapezoid? Assume b_1 is the shorter base.

$b_1 = \boxed{}$ in. $b_2 = \boxed{}$ in. $h = \boxed{}$ in.

C. Substitute the values for b_1, b_2, and h into the formula:

$$A = \frac{1}{2}\left(\boxed{}\right)\left(\boxed{} + \boxed{}\right)$$

D. Simplify.

$$A = \boxed{} \text{ square inches}$$

E. The trapezoid has an area of _____ square inches.

 Turn and Talk Without calculating, how do you know that the area of the trapezoid in Task 4 is less than 3.5 × 5 square inches?

5 Harry wants to build a garden in the shape of a parallelogram. The base length of the parallelogram will be 24 feet. He has enough materials to cover 84 square feet. In the figure shown, the height of the parallelogram is the width of the garden. How many feet wide can the garden be?

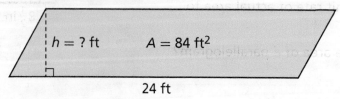

$h = ?$ ft $A = 84$ ft^2

24 ft

A. What is the equation for the area of a parallelogram?

$A = $ ☐ $\times$ ☐

B. Substitute the known values.

☐ $=$ ☐ $\times h$

C. To solve for h, _____ each side of the equation by ☐.

D. $\dfrac{☐}{☐} = h$, so $h = $ ☐

E. The garden can be _____ feet wide.

Check Understanding

1. A company logo is in the shape of the parallelogram shown. Find its area.

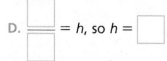

6 in.

5 in.   4 in.   5 in.

6 in.

_____

2. In a trapezoid, the length of one base is equal to the height and the length of the other base is twice the height. If the height is 10 centimeters, what is the area of the trapezoid? Explain how you found your answer.

_____

_____

_____

3. A trapezoid has an area of 24 square feet. If the height is 6 feet, what is the sum of the lengths of the bases in feet?

_____

Name _____

On Your Own

4. On a baseball field, the area inside the base path is the infield. For a major league field, the infield must be a square that is 90 feet on each side. Each base is a corner of the square. Note that a square, like a rectangle, is a special type of parallelogram. What is the area of the infield in square feet?

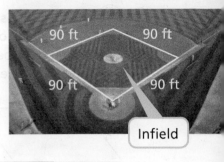

Infield

5. A parallelogram has an area of 125 square inches. If its base is 25 inches long, what is its height in inches?

6. A trapezoid has a base that is 10.2 centimeters long and another base that is 9.8 centimeters long. Its height measures 5 centimeters. What is the area of the trapezoid?

7. A window frame in the shape of a trapezoid has bases 4 feet and 3 feet long. Its height is 3 feet. What is the area of the glass needed for the window?

For Problems 8–9, find the area of a parallelogram with the given base and height.

8. $b = 10$ m $h = 4.5$ m

9. $b = 3\frac{1}{4}$ in. $h = 2\frac{1}{2}$ in.

For Problems 10–11, find the area of a trapezoid with the given measures.

10. $b_1 = 16$ m, $b_2 = 8$ m, $h = 4.5$ m

11. $b_1 = 3.5$ cm, $b_2 = 6.5$ cm, $h = 8.4$ cm

12. (MP) **Use Structure** In an aerial photo, a parallelogram-shaped cornfield has a base length of 1 inch and a height of $\frac{1}{2}$ inch. The actual field has a base length of $\frac{1}{2}$ mile and a height of $\frac{1}{4}$ mile.

A. Find the area of the field in the photo in square inches. Then find the area of the actual field in square miles.

B. Find the unit rate of actual area per square inch of photo area.

C. A second field in the aerial photo has an area of 2 square inches. What is its actual area in square miles?

13. (MP) **Critique Reasoning** For the two quadrilaterals shown, Dan says that the one on the left has a larger area than the one on the right because it is longer. Bob says that both quadrilaterals have the same area. Who is correct? Why?

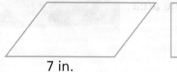
7 in.

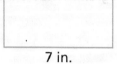
7 in.

Who is correct?

_____

_____

_____

14. A scientist is studying a photo of a trapezoid-shaped feature on the surface of another planet. The actual area of the feature is $\frac{1}{4}$ square mile, and its area in the photograph is $\frac{5}{2}$ square inches. What is the unit rate of actual area per square inch of photo area?

_____

15. A square has an area of 144 in². How long is each side of the square?

_____

For Problems 16–17, find the unknown height for each parallelogram.

16. $b = 9$ cm $A = 108$ cm²

   $h =$ _____

17. $b = 8.5$ ft $A = 68$ ft²

   $h =$ _____

For Problems 18–19, find the unknown height for each trapezoid.

18. $b_1 = 5$ m, $b_2 = 3$ m, $A = 30$ m²

   $h =$ _____

19. $b_1 = 5$ in., $b_2 = 4$ in., $A = 20.25$ in²

   $h =$ _____

 I'm in a Learning Mindset!

How did I apply what I know about parallelograms to write an area formula for a trapezoid?

_____

_____

Develop and Use Formulas
for Areas of Quadrilaterals

1. The Shanghai World Financial Center is one of the tallest
buildings in the world. It features a large trapezoidal opening to
allow wind to pass through. The opening is about 35 meters tall.
It is about 40 meters along the bottom and 50 meters along
the top. What is the approximate area of the opening?

Opening is
35 m tall

_____

2. (MP) **Reason** A trapezoid's longer base is three times the length of
its shorter base. If the trapezoid has an area of 32 square feet and a
height of 4 feet, what is the length of each base?

_____

3. A panel in a stained-glass window in the shape of
a parallelogram has the actual dimensions shown.
In a blueprint, the area of the panel is 2.75 square
centimeters. What is the unit rate of actual area to
the area in the blueprint?

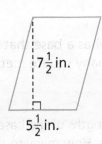

$7\frac{1}{2}$ in.

$5\frac{1}{2}$ in.

_____

For Problems 4–7, find the area of the figure.

4.

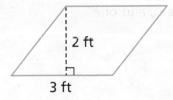

2 ft

3 ft

5.

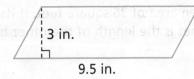

3 in.

9.5 in.

6.

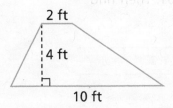

2 ft

4 ft

10 ft

7.

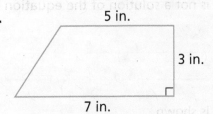

5 in.

3 in.

7 in.

_____

Test Prep

8. Which quadrilateral has the largest area?

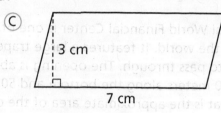

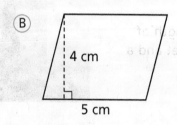

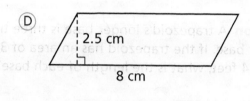

9. A parallelogram has a base that measures 4.8 meters. Its height measures 5 meters. How many square meters is the area of the parallelogram?

_____

10. The sum of the lengths of the bases of a trapezoid is 6.4 meters. The trapezoid's height is 4 meters. How many square meters is the area of the trapezoid?

_____

11. A trapezoid has an area of 36 square feet. If its height is 8 feet, and one base is 4 feet, what is the length of the other base?

_____

Spiral Review

12. Write two expressions that are equivalent to $4(6x + 8y)$.

_____

13. Show that 9.1 is not a solution of the equation $n - 6.4 = 2.61$. Then find the solution.

_____

_____

14. An expression is shown.

3.4×6.25

What is the value of the expression?

_____

Name _____

Develop and Use the Formula for Area of Triangles

(I Can) use a formula to find the area of a triangle.

Spark Your Learning

A farmer has a rectangular paddock for his horses, as shown. He wants to reconfigure his fields and change the paddock so that it is square. However, he wants it to have the same area as the rectangular paddock. What should the side length of the square paddock be? Justify your answer.

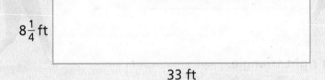

$8\frac{1}{4}$ ft

33 ft

Turn and Talk Will the rectangular paddock and the square paddock use the same amount of fencing? Explain.

© Houghton Mifflin Harcourt Publishing Company • Image Credit: ©klagyivik/iStock / Getty Images Plus/Getty Images

Build Understanding

1 How can you find the area of a right triangle?

A. The **base of a triangle** can be any side. The **height of a triangle** is the perpendicular distance from the base to the opposite vertex.

You can put together two copies of a right triangle to form a rectangle as shown. How does the area of each right triangle compare to the area of the rectangle?

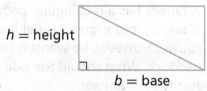

h = height

b = base

_____

_____

B. How can you use the area formula for a rectangle, $A = b \times h$, to write an area formula for a right triangle?

_____

_____

C. Write the area formula for a right triangle.

$$A = \frac{b \times h}{\square} = \frac{\square}{\square} bh$$

2 How can you find the area of a non-right triangle?

A. You can put together two copies of a non-right triangle to form a parallelogram as shown. How can you use the area formula for a parallelogram, $A = b \times h$, to write an area formula for a triangle?

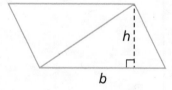

h

b

_____

_____

_____

B. Write the area formula for a non-right triangle.

$$A = \frac{\square \times \square}{\square} = \frac{\square}{\square} \times \square \times \square$$

 Turn and Talk Do you need to know the angle measures of a triangle to find its area? Explain.

Name _____

Step It Out

3 The segment that represents the height of a triangle is perpendicular to the base. Sometimes it is shown outside of the triangle. Find the length of the base of the triangle shown in meters.

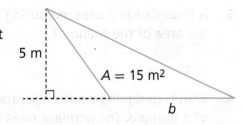

5 m

$A = 15 \text{ m}^2$

b

A. Substitute the known values into the formula for the area of a triangle.

$$\boxed{} = \frac{1}{2} \times b \times \boxed{}$$

B. To solve for b, _____ each side of the equation by $\frac{2}{5}$.

$$\frac{2}{5} \times \frac{\boxed{}}{1} = \frac{2}{5} \times \frac{1}{2} \times b \times \boxed{}$$

$$\boxed{} = b$$

The base is _____ meters long.

4 Many cities are planned with a grid pattern for the streets. Often there are one or more diagonal streets that cut across the grid, forming right triangles. What is the area of the triangle shown, in square feet?

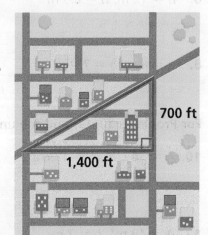

700 ft

1,400 ft

A. What are the dimensions of the triangle?

$b =$ ⬚ ft, $h =$ ⬚ ft

B. Substitute the values for b and h into the formula for the area of a triangle. Then find the area.

$$A = \frac{1}{2} \times \boxed{} \times \boxed{} = \boxed{} \text{ ft}^2$$

C. The area of the triangle is _____ square feet.

Check Understanding

1. An isosceles right triangle has a base and height of 5 inches. Find its area.

_____

2. Find the height of a triangle with an area of 12 square centimeters and a base of 8 centimeters.

_____

© Houghton Mifflin Harcourt Publishing Company

Module 15 • Lesson 2

521

On Your Own

3. A triangle has a base measuring $8\frac{1}{2}$ inches. If its height is $4\frac{1}{2}$ inches, what is the area of the triangle?

_____

4. Walt is designing a school pennant in the shape of a triangle. The pennant must have a height of 11 inches and an area of 66 square inches. What is the length of the base?

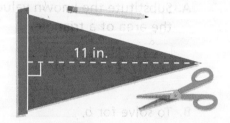

11 in.

_____

5. (MP) **Reason** A rectangle has a perimeter of 22 feet and a length 5 feet greater than its width. If a right triangle has a height of 3 feet, what length would its base be if it has the same area as the rectangle?

_____

For Problems 6–9, find the area of a triangle with the given base and height.

6. $b = 12$ m, $h = 6.5$ m

7. $b = 4\frac{1}{4}$ in., $h = 8$ in.

_____

8. $b = 8$ ft, $h = 7$ ft

9. $b = 4.4$ cm, $h = 6.5$ cm

_____

For Problems 10–13, find the unknown base length for each triangle.

10. $A = 44$ cm^2, $h = 11$ cm

11. $A = 34$ ft^2, $h = 8.5$ ft

_____

12. $A = 49$ m^2, $h = 7$ m

13. $A = 31.5$ in^2, $h = 7$ in.

_____

I'm in a Learning Mindset!

I want to increase my understanding of using formulas to find the area of a right triangle. What clarifying questions can I ask?

_____

_____

Name _____

Develop and Use the Formula for Area of Triangles

1. **STEM** A geodesic dome is made up of triangles, most of which are equilateral. The surface uses less material and allows for more open space than traditional buildings. An equilateral panel of a geodesic dome has a base of 6 feet and a height of about 5.2 feet. What is its area in square feet?

_____

A geodesic dome is made up of mostly equilateral triangles.

2. **(MP) Reason** A triangle has a height of 3 meters and an area of 9 square meters. Is there a unique triangle represented by these measurements? Explain.

_____

_____

_____

3. An isosceles right triangle has a base and height with the same length. If the area of an isosceles right triangle is 32 square centimeters, how long are the base and height?

_____

4. **Math on the Spot** The diagram shows the outline of the triangular foundation of a front porch. What is the area of the foundation?

_____

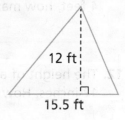

12 ft
15.5 ft

For problems 5–8, find the area.

5.

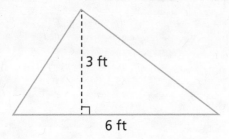

3 ft
6 ft

6.

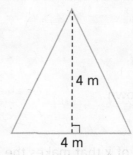

4 m
4 m

7.

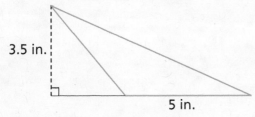

3.5 in.
5 in.

8.

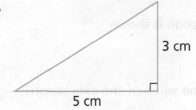

3 cm
5 cm

© Houghton Mifflin Harcourt Publishing Company • Image Credit: Ted Foxx/Alamy

Test Prep

9. Which triangle has the largest area?

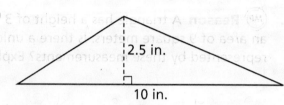

(A) 3 in. 7 in.

(C) 4 in. 6 in.

(B) 3 in. 8 in.

(D) 2.5 in. 10 in.

10. A triangle has a base that measures 6.4 feet. Its height measures 5 feet. How many square feet is the area of the triangle?

11. A triangle has an area of 42 square feet. If the height of the triangle is 4 feet, how many feet is the length of the base?

12. The height of a triangle is one-tenth of its base. The base measures 12 inches. How many square inches is the area of the triangle?

Spiral Review

13. An equation is shown.

$$64x = 8$$

What is the value of x that makes the equation true?

14. An expression is shown.

$$2\frac{3}{4} \div 4\frac{1}{2}$$

What is the value of the expression?

Name _____

Find Area of Composite Figures

(**I Can**) find the area of a composite figure by breaking it into familiar figures.

Step It Out

You can find the area of composite figures by breaking them into familiar figures such as triangles or quadrilaterals.

1 ▸ The figure shown gives the dimensions of a city park. What is the area of the city park?

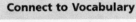

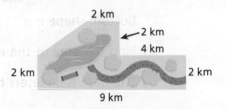

A. What different shapes could the figure be divided into?

_____

_____

B. There are several ways to divide the figure. The figure is divided into two quadrilaterals with a horizontal segment. What are the two quadrilaterals?

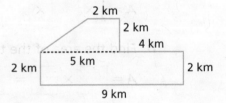

_____

_____

C. Find the area of the top shape.

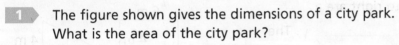

$A = \frac{1}{2} \times \boxed{} \left(\boxed{} + \boxed{} \right) = \boxed{}$ km²

D. Find the area of the bottom shape.

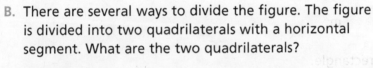

$A = \boxed{} \times \boxed{} = \boxed{}$ km²

E. Total area = Area of top shape + Area of bottom shape

$= \boxed{}$ km² $+ \boxed{}$ km²

$= \boxed{}$ km²

The area of the park is _____ square kilometers.

 Turn and Talk In what other ways could you divide the figure? Explain.

2   The roof of a building is shown. What is its area?

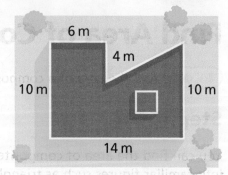

A. What different shapes could the roof be divided into?

_____

_____

B. The figure represents the roof. The figure is divided with a horizontal segment.

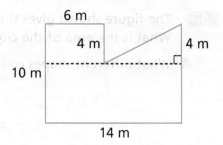

The top shapes from left to right are a

_____ and a _____. The

bottom shape is a _____.

C. Find the area of the right triangle.

The base is 8 meters because ⬜ − ⬜ = 8.

$A = \frac{1}{2} \times$ ⬜ $\times$ ⬜ $=$ ⬜ m²

D. Find the area of the top rectangle.

$A =$ ⬜ $\times$ ⬜ $=$ ⬜ m²

E. Find the area of the bottom rectangle.

The width is 6 meters because ⬜ − ⬜ = 6.

$A =$ ⬜ $\times$ ⬜ $=$ ⬜ m²

F. Total area = Area of triangle + Area of top rectangle + Area of bottom rectangle

= ⬜ m² + ⬜ m² + ⬜ m² = ⬜ m²

G. The area of the roof is _____ square meters.

H. How else could you divide the figure to find the area?

_____

_____

_____

Turn and Talk How could you find the area of the figure using subtraction? What figures would you use? Explain.

3 Paula is painting the side of a house and needs to know how much paint to buy. Each gallon of paint will cover a certain number of square feet. How many square feet need to be painted?

A. The side of the house is divided into two shapes. The top shape is

a _____, and the bottom shape is a _____.

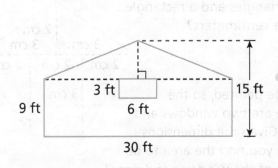

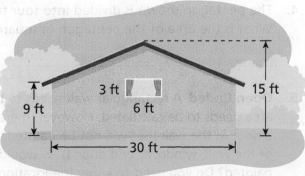

B. Find the area of the rectangle.

$A = \boxed{} \times \boxed{} = \boxed{}$ ft²

C. Find the area of the triangle.

The triangle has a height of 6 feet because $15 - \boxed{} = 6$.

$A = \frac{1}{2} \times \boxed{} \times \boxed{} = \boxed{}$ ft²

D. Find the area of the rectangular window.

$A = \boxed{} \times \boxed{} = \boxed{}$ ft²

E. Total area = Area of rectangle + Area of triangle − Area of window

$= \boxed{}$ ft² $+ \boxed{}$ ft² $- \boxed{}$ ft² $= \boxed{}$ ft²

Check Understanding

1. Find the area of the figure shown.

_____

_____

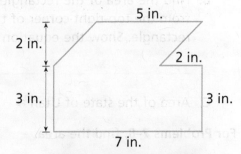

2. What is the area of the picture frame in square inches? Show how you solved the problem.

_____

_____

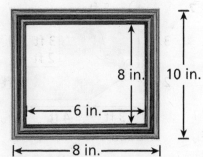

On Your Own

3. The outline of Sara's family room, including the entry, is shown. Sara wants to carpet the family room. How many square feet of carpet does she need? _____

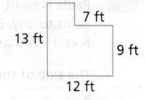

4. The pentagon shown is divided into four triangles and a rectangle. What is the area of the pentagon in square centimeters?

_____

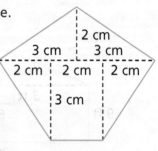

5. Open Ended A rectangular wall needs to be painted, so the area needs to be calculated. However, there are two windows and a door in the wall that will not be painted. Given the dimensions of the wall, windows, and door, how would you find the area to be painted? Do you need to know the location of the windows and door?

_____

_____

_____

6. Geography The state of Utah is shown. All the angles measure 90°. What is the area, in square miles, of the state?

A. Find the area of the dashed rectangle that contains the state. Show the equation you used.

_____ square miles

B. Find the area of the rectangle that is missing from the top-right corner of the dashed rectangle. Show the equation you used.

_____ square miles

C. Area of the state of Utah ≈ _____ square miles

For Problems 7–8, find the area.

7.

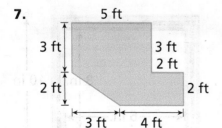

8.

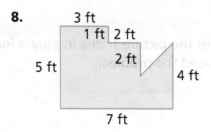

9. (MP) **Construct Arguments** The two figures shown have the same area. Without calculating the area, explain why this is so.

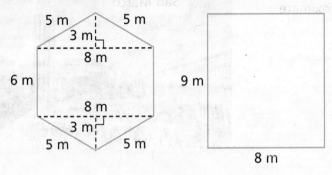

_____
_____
_____

10. In the compass rose shown, each triangle has the same area, and the center is a square. What is the area of the figure in square inches?

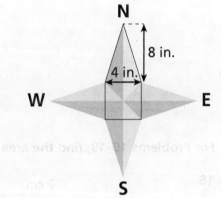

_____

11. Sandy has built a triangular pool and wants to add a rectangular deck around it as shown in the figure.

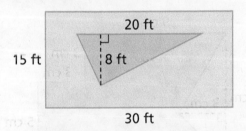

How many square feet of wood does Sandy need for the deck?

_____

For Problems 12–13, find the area of the figure.

12.

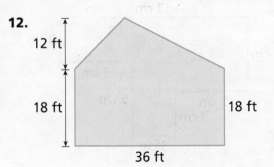

13.

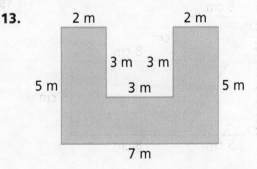

14. (MP) **Reason** Piazza San Marco is a famous open plaza in Venice, Italy. It is about 574 feet long. How would you find the approximate area of the plaza?

Piazza San Marco

_____

_____

_____

_____

15. Open Ended Draw a composite figure with at least one slanted side and an area of 24 square units.

For Problems 16–19, find the area of the figure.

16.

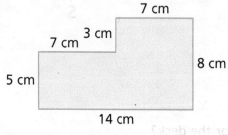

7 cm
3 cm
7 cm
8 cm
5 cm
14 cm

17.

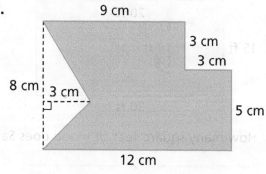

9 cm
3 cm
3 cm
8 cm
3 cm
5 cm
12 cm

18.

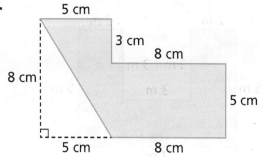

5 cm
3 cm
8 cm
8 cm
5 cm
5 cm
8 cm

19.

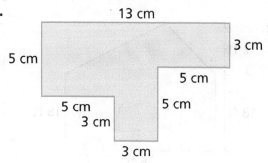

13 cm
3 cm
5 cm
5 cm
5 cm
5 cm
3 cm
3 cm

Find Area of Composite Figures

1. The floor plan for a house is shown. Vertical lengths and horizontal lengths are given.

What is the floor area in square feet?

_____

2. On a baseball field, home plate is where the batter stands to hit and where a runner scores a run. What is the area of the home plate diagram shown in square inches?

_____

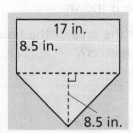

3. **Math on the Spot** Kirsten wants to buy wooden flooring for her bedroom. The diagram shows the bedroom's shape and dimensions. One case of flooring will cover 25 square feet. How many cases of flooring will Kirsten need to buy? Explain.

_____

_____

_____

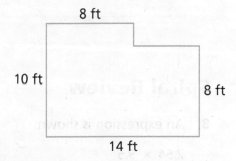

4. (MP) **Attend to Precision** Robert is designing hexagonal tiles that are made up of 12 identical right triangles, as shown. Write three equations Robert can use to find the area A of the hexagonal tile in square centimeters.

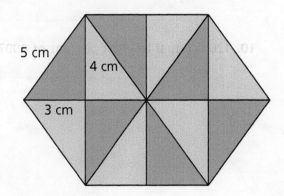

Test Prep

5. A figure is shown.

Which equations could be used to find the area *A* of the figure in square centimeters? Select all that apply.

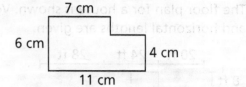

7 cm

6 cm

4 cm

11 cm

Ⓐ $A = 6 \times 11$

Ⓑ $A = 7 \times 6 + 4 \times 4$

Ⓒ $A = 4 \times 11 + 2 \times 7$

Ⓓ $A = 7 \times 6 + 4 \times 11$

Ⓔ $A = 6 \times 11 - 4 \times 2$

6. A figure is shown.

What is the area of the figure in square meters?

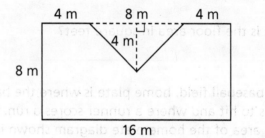

4 m   8 m   4 m

4 m

8 m

16 m

_____

7. A figure is shown.

Write an equation to find the area *A* of the figure in square feet.

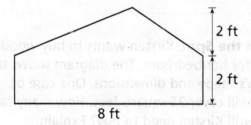

2 ft

2 ft

8 ft

_____

Spiral Review

8. An expression is shown.

2.54 × 5.5

What is the value of the expression?

_____

9. Write $\frac{12}{15}$ as a decimal.

_____

10. 120 is equal to what percent of 400?

_____

Review

Vocabulary

Choose the correct term from the Vocabulary box.

1. A _____ is a shape that can be divided into more than one of the basic shapes.

2. A _____ is a four-sided figure with opposite sides that are parallel.

3. A _____ is a four-sided figure with at least one pair of parallel sides.

Concepts and Skills

4. **(MP) Use Tools** On a park map, a parallelogram-shaped campsite has an area of $4\frac{1}{10}$ square inches. The actual dimensions of the campsite are shown. What is the unit rate of actual area per square inch of map area? State what strategy and tool you will use to answer the question, explain your choice, and then find the answer.

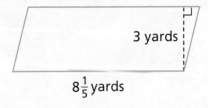

3 yards

$8\frac{1}{5}$ yards

_____

_____

5. A square has a side length of $10\frac{1}{4}$ inches. What is its area?

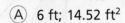

6. A rectangle has a width of 12 feet and an area of 196.8 square feet. What is its length?

_____

7. A rectangular flag consists of two right triangles. The area of each triangle is 6.6 square feet. What are the length and area of the flag?

Ⓐ 6 ft; 14.52 ft²   Ⓒ 3 ft; 14.52 ft²

Ⓑ 6 ft; 13.2 ft²   Ⓓ 3 ft; 13.2 ft²

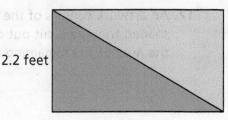

2.2 feet

8. A tile maker makes triangular tiles for a mosaic. Two triangular tiles form a square. What is the area of one of the triangular tiles?

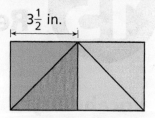

$3\frac{1}{2}$ in.

_____

9. The top of a school worktable is in the shape of a trapezoid. What is the area of the tabletop?

Ⓐ 7 ft²

Ⓑ 12 ft²

Ⓒ 14 ft²

Ⓓ 24 ft²

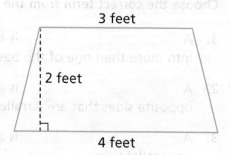

3 feet

2 feet

4 feet

10. What is the area of the figure shown?

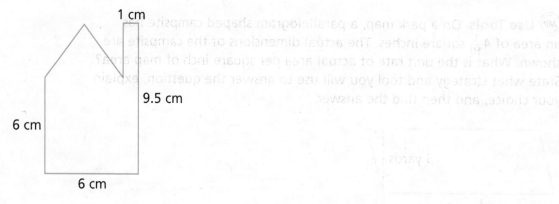

1 cm

9.5 cm

6 cm

6 cm

_____

11. A small plot of land is shaped like the figure shown. What is the area of the plot of land?

Ⓐ 43 yd²

Ⓑ 153 yd²

Ⓒ 306 yd²

Ⓓ 1,188 yd²

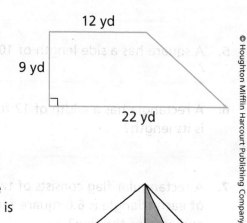

12 yd

9 yd

22 yd

12. An artwork consists of the triangles shown, where the shaded triangle is cut out of the larger triangle. What is the area of the remaining unshaded portion?

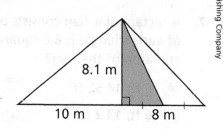

8.1 m

10 m   8 m

Surface Area and Volume

Pass the Popcorn

A company that makes microwave popcorn is redesigning its boxes. The diagram shows the company's current box size, with each face marked off in squares with a side length of 1 inch.

Use the diagram to answer the questions.

A. What is the volume of the company's current popcorn box? _____ cubic inches

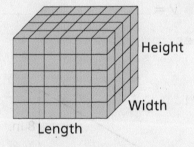

B. The company wants to keep the volume of its popcorn boxes the same, but decrease the width from 4 inches to 3 inches. What are a possible length and a possible height for the new box design?

Length: _____ inches   Height: _____ inches

 Turn and Talk

- Explain how you determined the volume of the company's current popcorn box.

- Explain how you determined a possible length and height for the new box design.

© Houghton Mifflin Harcourt Publishing Company • Image Credit: ©Africa Rising/Shutterstock

Are You Ready?

Complete these problems to review prior concepts and skills you will need for this module.

Explore Volume

Find the volume of each object by counting cubic units.

1.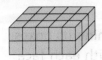

V = _____

2.

V = _____

3.

V = _____

4.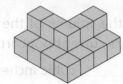

V = _____

Area of Quadrilaterals and Triangles

Find the area of each figure.

5.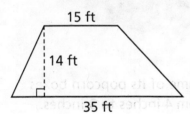

15 ft

14 ft

35 ft

A = _____

6.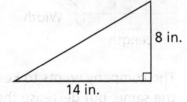

8 in.

14 in.

A = _____

7.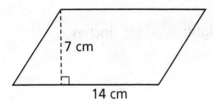

7 cm

14 cm

A = _____

8.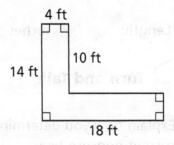

4 ft

10 ft

14 ft

18 ft

A = _____

9. The height of a parallelogram is 36 meters and the base is 6 meters. Find the area of the parallelogram.

_____

Name _____

Explore Nets and Surface Area

(I Can) use nets to find the surface area of prisms and pyramids.

Spark Your Learning

Caleb built a rectangular box to store his Dutch oven when camping.
He wants to paint the outside of the box, and has enough paint to
cover an area of 14 square feet. Does Caleb have enough paint?
Explain.

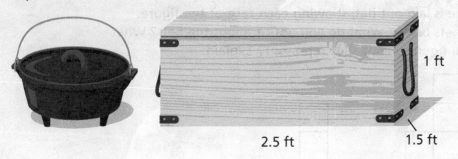

1 ft

2.5 ft   1.5 ft

Turn and Talk If Caleb decides not to paint the bottom of the storage box,
will he have enough paint to paint the storage box? Explain.

Build Understanding

1   A **solid figure** is a three-dimensional figure because it
has three dimensions: length, width, and height.

A.   A cube is a closed three-dimensional
figure. Look at the cube at the right.
How many faces does a cube have?

_____

B.   A *net* is the pattern made when the surface of a closed three-
dimensional figure is laid out flat, showing each face of the figure.
Look at the two nets below. What do you notice about the nets? What
three-dimensional figures might they represent? Explain.

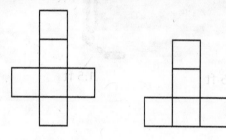

_____

_____

_____

C.   Trace both nets in Part B on a separate sheet of paper. Cut out each
net. Then fold the nets. Which net will fold into a closed three-
dimensional figure? What is the three-dimensional figure?

_____

D.   Write an equation to represent the area of one face of the cube.

_____

E.   If the edge of the cube measures 4 centimeters, what is the area of one
face of the cube?

_____

F.   What is the total area of all 6 faces of the cube?

_____

   Turn and Talk What do all six faces of the cube have in common? Is there
another way to calculate the total area of the faces?

2 ▶ Look at the square pyramid below. How many faces does the pyramid have? Explain how you know.

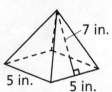

_____

_____

_____

A. A net of the pyramid above is shown. Fill in the dimensions.

B. What formula can you use to find the area of one triangular face?

_____

_____

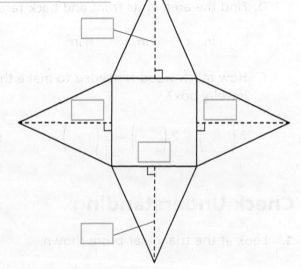

C. What is the area of one triangular face?

_____

D. What is the area of the square base?

_____

E. How can you find the surface area of the square pyramid?

_____

_____

F. What is the surface area of the square pyramid?

_____

 Turn and Talk Is there another way find the surface area? Explain.

3   Chandra is making a jewelry box and needs to know how much wood to buy.

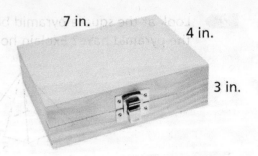

7 in.

4 in.

3 in.

A. Use the dimensions shown to label the side lengths of each face of the net.

B. Find the area of its right and left faces.

☐ in. × ☐ in. = ☐ in²

C. Find the area of its top and bottom faces.

☐ in. × ☐ in. = ☐ in²

D. Find the area of its front and back faces.

☐ in. × ☐ in. = ☐ in²

E. How much wood is needed to make the jewelry box?

2 (☐) + 2 (☐) + 2 (☐) = ☐ square inches

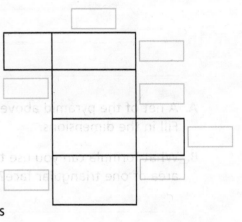

Check Understanding

1. Look at the triangular prism shown.

   A. This prism has _____ triangular faces and _____ rectangular faces.

   B. Draw a net to represent the prism.

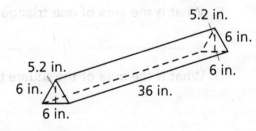

5.2 in.

6 in.

6 in.

5.2 in.

6 in.

36 in.

6 in.

   C. Find the surface area of the triangular prism.

   $2\left[\dfrac{1}{2}(\,\boxed{}\,)(\,\boxed{}\,)\right] + 3\left[\,\boxed{}\cdot\boxed{}\,\right] = \boxed{}$ in²

On Your Own

2. Keisha is helping her sister build triangular pyramids as containers to package her bracelets.

A. Draw and label a net that Keisha can use to fold and make the container.

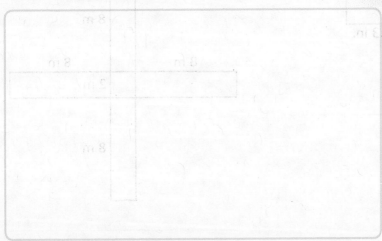

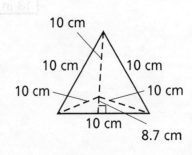

B. How much cardboard do they need for each container?

_____

(MP) **Reason** For Problems 3–5, tell whether the net can be folded into a cube. If not, explain.

3.

_____

4.

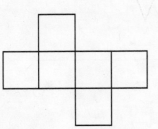

_____

5.

_____

For Problems 6–9, identify what solid figure the net folds into. Then find the surface area of the figure.

6.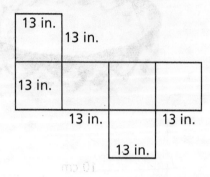

13 in.
13 in.
13 in.
13 in.   13 in.
13 in.

7.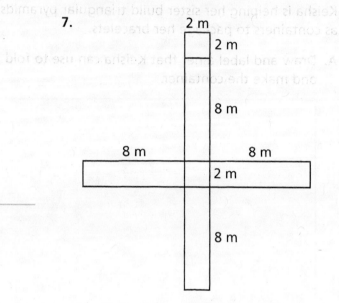

2 m
2 m
8 m
8 m   8 m
2 m
8 m

8.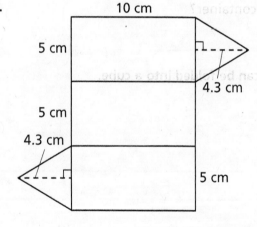

10 cm
5 cm
4.3 cm
5 cm
4.3 cm
5 cm

9.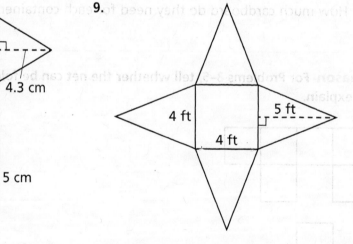

4 ft   5 ft
4 ft

I'm in a Learning Mindset!

How did I apply prior knowledge to finding the surface area of a square pyramid in Task 2?

Explore Nets and Surface Area

1. **MP Reason** George is building flower boxes to sell as gifts. Draw and label a net to represent the flower box. Then find the amount of material George needs for each box. Explain why you drew the net the way you did.

0.5 ft

1 ft

2 ft

2. **Math on the Spot** Find the surface area of the prism.

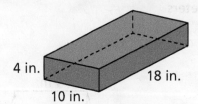

4 in.   18 in.   10 in.

For Problems 3–4, identify what solid figure the net folds into. Then find the surface area of the figure.

3.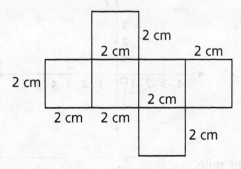

2 cm   2 cm   2 cm   2 cm   2 cm   2 cm   2 cm   2 cm

4.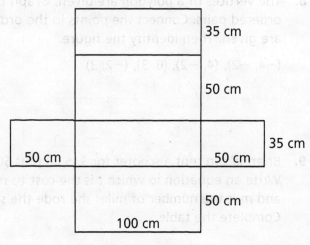

35 cm   50 cm   35 cm   50 cm   50 cm   50 cm   50 cm   100 cm

Test Prep

5. Match the net to its three-dimensional figure.

6. What is the surface area of a crate with a height of 2 meters, a length of 4 meters, and a width of 3 meters?

Ⓐ 18 square meters   Ⓒ 40 square meters

Ⓑ 26 square meters   Ⓓ 52 square meters

Spiral Review

7. Jem is carpeting a room. A drawing of the floor is shown. How much carpet will she use?

_____

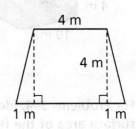

8. The vertices of a polygon are given. Graph the ordered pairs. Connect the points in the order they are given. Then identify the figure.

$(-4, -2)$, $(4, -2)$, $(6, 3)$, $(-2, 3)$

_____

9. Brianna can rent a scooter for $15.00 plus $0.50 per mile. Write an equation in which t is the cost to rent a scooter and m is the number of miles she rode the scooter. Complete the table.

_____

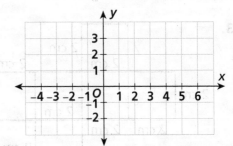

m	t
5	
10	
15	
20	

Name _____

Find Volume of Rectangular Prisms

(I Can) use the formulas $V = \ell wh$ or $V = Bh$
to find the volumes of rectangular prisms with
fractional edge lengths.

Spark Your Learning

The truck shown is delivering sand for a
sand sculpture competition. How many trips
must the truck make to deliver 15 cubic yards
of sand? Explain your reasoning.

5 ft

12 ft

3 ft

x	y

$\frac{1}{2}$ $\frac{1}{2}$

Turn and Talk Is there another formula that you could have used to find the
volume of the bed of the truck? Explain.

© Houghton Mifflin Harcourt Publishing Company • Image Credits: (t) ©Phil McDonald/Shutterstock; (inset) ©Miran Buric/Alamy

Build Understanding

1 ▶ A cube with edge length 1 unit and volume 1 cubic unit is filled with smaller cubes as shown. Find the **volume** of one small cube.

1 unit

A. How many small cubes are there? Explain how you know.

_____

B. How does the combined volume of the small cubes compare to the volume of the large cube?

_____

C. Complete the model.

Number of small cubes	•	Volume of one small cube	=	Volume of large cube
☐	•	?	=	☐

What is the volume of one small cube? ☐ cubic unit(s)

D. Complete the model.

Number of small cubes per edge	•	Edge length of one small cube	=	Edge length of large cube
☐	•	?	=	☐

What is the edge length of one small cube? ☐ unit(s)

E. The formula for volume of a rectangular prism is $V = \ell wh$, where ℓ and w are the length and width of the base and h is the height. Find the volume of one small cube using this formula.

$V =$ _____ = _____ cubic unit(s)

F. A cube with edge length $\frac{2}{3}$ unit is shown. The cube is filled with the same smaller cubes as used in Parts A–E.

Find the volume of the cube shown.

$V =$ _____ = _____ cubic unit(s)

$\frac{2}{3}$ unit

 Turn and Talk What is true about the edge lengths of a cube? How can you use this information to write a formula that uses exponents to find the volume of a cube?

© Houghton Mifflin Harcourt Publishing Company

Step It Out

You can find the volume of a rectangular prism using the formula $V = \ell wh$ or $V = Bh$ (where B represents the area of the prism's base, $B = \ell w$).

2 ▶ Josh would like to know how much flour his container can hold.

A. The length is _____ inches. The width is _____ inches.

   The height is _____ inches.

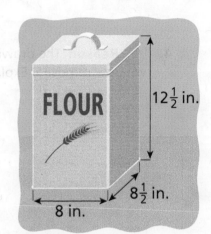

B. Substitute for the given variables and find the volume of the flour container.

$V = \ell wh$

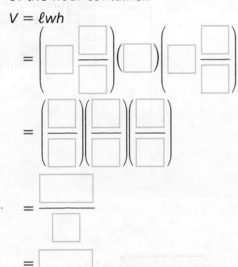

C. Josh's container can hold ⬜ cubic inches of flour.

 Turn and Talk Use the formula $V = Bh$ to find the volume of the flour container. Did you get the same volume? Will the two volume formulas always give the same result? Explain.

Check Understanding

1. What is the volume of the rectangular prism? Show your work.

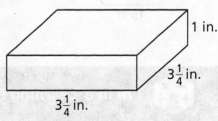

2. What is the volume of a rectangular prism that has a base area of $\frac{1}{8}$ square inch, and a height of $\frac{3}{4}$ inch?

On Your Own

How much cement does Trent need?

3. Trent is putting in a sidewalk that is $\frac{1}{18}$ yard thick, 9 yards long, and 1 yard wide. How many cubic yards of cement does he need?

_____

4. (MP) **Reason** The drawing shows a cinder block wall with a window removed. Explain how to find its volume.

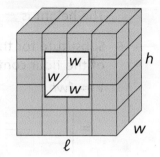

For Problems 5–8, find the volume of each figure.

5.

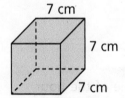
7 cm
7 cm
7 cm

6.

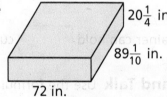
$20\frac{1}{4}$ in.
$89\frac{1}{10}$ in.
72 in.

7.

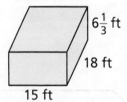
$6\frac{1}{3}$ ft
18 ft
15 ft

8.

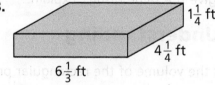
$1\frac{1}{4}$ ft
$4\frac{1}{4}$ ft
$6\frac{1}{3}$ ft

© Houghton Mifflin Harcourt Publishing Company • Image Credit: ©Randy Duchaine/Alamy

---

➖✖️➕➗ I'm in a Learning Mindset!

How did I use my prior knowledge of multiplying mixed numbers to find the volume of a rectangular prism?

_____

_____

Find Volume of Rectangular Prisms

1. **Open Ended** Keesha is building a raised flower bed around a tree. Explain how to find the volume of soil she needs in order to fill the flower bed. Then find the volume.

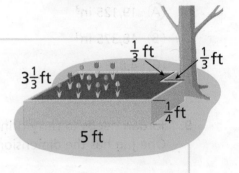

2. **Math on the Spot** An aquarium is shaped like a rectangular prism. The prism is $24\frac{1}{4}$ inches long, $12\frac{1}{2}$ inches wide, and 20 inches high. What is the volume of the aquarium?

_____

3. (MP) **Reason** Ray has 9 identical shoe boxes like the one shown. What is the total volume of all 9 shoe boxes?

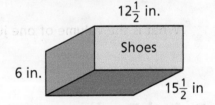

_____

For Problems 4–7, find the volume of each figure.

4.

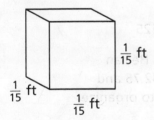

5.

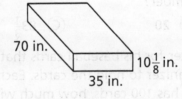

6.

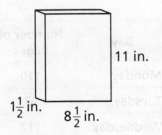

7.

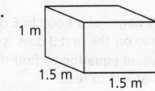

_____   _____

Test Prep

8. Anton is filling a fish tank with water. What volume of water does he need?

Ⓐ 19,125 in³

Ⓑ 18,375 in³

Ⓒ 4,815 in³

Ⓓ 90$\frac{1}{2}$ in³

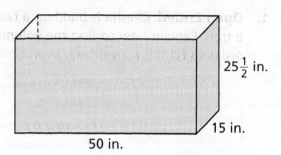

25$\frac{1}{2}$ in.

15 in.

50 in.

9. Jordan needs to carry drinking water to help people in a flooded area. One jug has the dimensions shown.

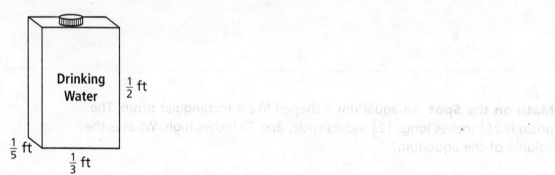

Drinking Water

$\frac{1}{2}$ ft

$\frac{1}{5}$ ft

$\frac{1}{3}$ ft

What is the volume of one jug for carrying the drinking water?

Spiral Review

10. 50 is 60% of what number?

Ⓐ 30 Ⓑ 20 Ⓒ 83$\frac{1}{3}$ Ⓓ 125

11. Tyrell buys an organizer for his baseball cards that costs $12.99. He can add pages to the organizer to hold the cards. Each page costs $2.75 and holds 9 cards. If Tyrell has 100 cards, how much will it cost him to organize them? Write and evaluate a numeric expression.

12. Greg has a goal to read 529 pages of a book in 6 days. The number of pages he read on the first 3 days is given in the table. Write and solve an equation to find the number of pages, *p*, Greg has left to read.

Day	Number of Pages
Monday	110
Tuesday	92
Wednesday	117

Name _____

Solve Volume Problems

(**I Can**) use equations to solve volume problems in which the volume or an edge length of a rectangular prism is unknown.

Step It Out

1 Lyon is making a toolbox as shown at the right.

A. What are the dimensions of the box?

Length: _____

Width: _____

Height: _____

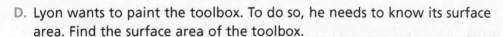

2.3 in.

3.4 in.   6.8 in.

B. Substitute the dimensions into the volume formula.

$V = \ell \times w \times h =$ ☐ $\times$ ☐ $\times$ ☐

C. What is the volume of the box?

☐ cubic inches, or ☐ in³

D. Lyon wants to paint the toolbox. To do so, he needs to know its surface area. Find the surface area of the toolbox.

$SA = 2\left(\Box \times \Box\right) + 2\left(\Box \times \Box\right) + 2\left(\Box \times \Box\right)$

$= 2\left(\Box\right) + 2\left(\Box\right) + 2\left(\Box\right)$

$= \Box + \Box + \Box$

$= \Box$ square inches

E. A tube of paint covers 40 square inches. How many tubes of paint should Lyon buy? Explain.

_____

_____

 Turn and Talk Why do you think volume is measured in cubic units?

2 A company makes cereal boxes with a volume of $432\frac{1}{4}$ cubic inches. The dimensions of one of the cereal boxes is shown. What is the width of the box?

A. How can you find the volume of the cereal box?

_____

B. Complete the equation to find the volume of the cereal box.

$9\frac{1}{2}$in.

14 in.

w in.

$V = \ell \times w \times h$

$432\frac{1}{4} = \dfrac{\boxed{}}{\boxed{}} \times w \times \boxed{}$

$\dfrac{1{,}729}{4} = \dfrac{\boxed{}}{\boxed{}} \times w \times \dfrac{\boxed{}}{1}$

$\dfrac{1{,}729}{4} = \dfrac{\boxed{}}{2} w$

$w = \dfrac{\boxed{}}{\boxed{}} \times \dfrac{\boxed{}}{\boxed{}}$

C. What is the width of the cereal box?

_____

 Turn and Talk In Task 2, if the width was given and the length was not, would the steps you used to find the length be different than the steps you used to find the width? Explain.

Check Understanding

1. A right rectangular prism is 10.25 yards long, 5.5 yards wide, and 2 yards tall. What is the volume of the prism?

_____

2. A large rectangular shipping container has a volume of $12\frac{3}{8}$ cubic feet. The shipping container is $2\frac{1}{5}$ feet long and $2\frac{1}{2}$ feet wide. What is the height of the shipping container?

_____

On Your Own

3 in.

3. What is the volume of the cube puzzle shown?

_____

4. A fish tank is filled halfway with water.

   A. What is the volume of the tank?

_____

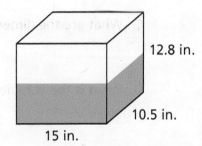

12.8 in.

10.5 in.

   B. What is the volume of the water in the tank?

_____

15 in.

5. A concert poster is shipped in the box shown.

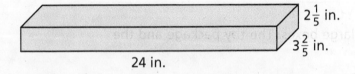

$2\frac{1}{5}$ in.

$3\frac{2}{5}$ in.

24 in.

   A. What is the volume of the poster box?

_____

   B. Show how you found your answer.

6. Carmen builds the dresser shown. The rectangular portion of the dresser has a volume of 27 cubic feet.

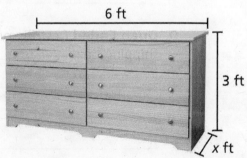

6 ft

3 ft

x ft

   A. How can you find the missing dimension?

_____

_____

   B. What is the missing dimension of the dresser?

_____

7. **(MP)** **Reason** A set of dishes comes in a cube-shaped box that has a surface area of 600 square inches.

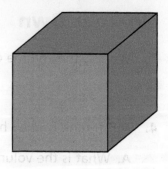

A. How do you find the surface area of a cube?

_____

_____

B. What is the area of each face of the cube?

_____

_____

C. What are the dimensions of the cube?

_____

D. What is the volume of the cube?

_____

8. A toy company ships packages in large boxes. The toy package and the shipping box are shown.

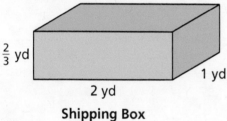

Shipping Box   **Toy Package**

A. What is the volume of the shipping box?

_____

_____

B. What is the volume of the toy package?

_____

_____

C. How many toy packages could fit in the shipping box?

_____

_____

D. **Open Ended** Describe one way you can arrange the packages in the shipping box.

_____

_____

_____

_____

Solve Volume Problems

1. (MP) **Reason** A cube-shaped box can be wrapped completely in gift wrap that measures 384 square inches. What is the volume of the box?

_____

2. **STEM** An architect builds a house like the one shown. What is the total volume of the house?

_____

3. An aquarium has a large fish tank with the dimensions shown. The tank has a volume of 585 cubic meters.

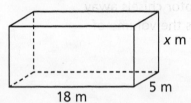

x m

5 m

18 m

What is the depth of the tank? _____

4. Joshua is organizing a garage using stackable containers like the one shown. He has a total of 12 containers. What is the combined total volume of the containers?

_____

5. **Math on the Spot** Aubrey has a suitcase with a volume of 2,200 cubic inches. The length of the suitcase is 25 inches and the width is 11 inches. What is the height of Aubrey's suitcase?

_____

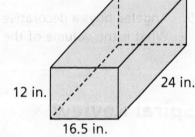

24 in.

12 in.

16.5 in.

6. A rectangular prism has a length of $2\frac{3}{5}$ inches and a width of $1\frac{2}{5}$ inches. If the prism has a volume of $10\frac{23}{25}$ cubic inches, what is the height of the prism? Explain how you found your answer.

19.6 ft

20 ft   15.42 ft

Test Prep

7. Students in an art class are given boxes to use for storage for their materials for the year. Shaun's box has a volume of 72 cubic inches. What is the unknown dimension?

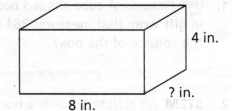

4 in.

? in.

8 in.

Ⓐ $2\frac{1}{4}$ in.

Ⓑ 9 in.

Ⓒ 18 in.

Ⓓ 60 in.

8. A sculptor buys a block of marble shaped like a rectangular prism to use for a sculpture. The original block of marble had a length of 3.5 meters, a width of 4 meters, and a height of 2.8 meters. If the sculptor chisels away a volume of marble that equals 12.2 cubic meters, what is the volume of the resulting sculpture?

Ⓐ 51.4 m³

Ⓑ 39.2 m³

Ⓒ 27.0 m³

Ⓓ 3.21 m³

9. Angelee buys a decorative photo box as shown. What is the volume of the photo box?

_____

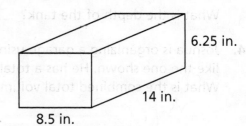

6.25 in.

14 in.

8.5 in.

Spiral Review

10. What is the area of the triangle?

_____

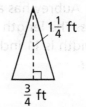

$1\frac{1}{4}$ ft

$\frac{3}{4}$ ft

11. Simplify the expression.

$3^2 - 2^2 + 1$

_____

12. Amanda earns $12 an hour babysitting. She spends $8 of her earnings on dinner later that evening. Write an expression to represent her total profit after babysitting for x hours and then eating dinner.

_____

Review

Vocabulary

Choose the correct term from the vocabulary box.

1. The total area of the faces of a three-dimensional object is the _____ .

2. A _____ is a two-dimensional pattern that can be folded into a solid figure.

3. A _____ is a solid with a polygon base and triangular faces that meet at a common vertex.

Concepts and Skills

4. The net shown can be folded to form a cube. What is the surface area of the cube formed by the net?

   _____

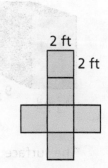

2 ft

2 ft

5. A cube has a surface area of 54 square centimeters. What is the volume of the cube?

   _____

6. **(MP) Use Tools** A painting set is shipped in the box shown. The surface area is printed with advertisements. What is the total area covered by advertisements? State what strategy and tool you will use to answer the question, explain your choice, and then find the answer.

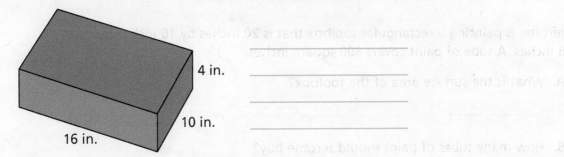

4 in.

10 in.

16 in.

7. A rectangular prism is 8 centimeters long, 11 centimeters wide, and 5.8 centimeters tall. What is the volume of the prism?

   (A) 88 cubic centimeters

   (B) 110.2 cubic centimeters

   (C) 396.4 cubic centimeters

   (D) 510.4 cubic centimeters

8. A box company makes cardboard boxes using flat templates like the one shown. Both squares are congruent, and the remaining four rectangular faces are congruent. What is the surface area of the cardboard box?

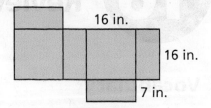

16 in.

16 in.

7 in.

_____

9. What is the volume of the rectangular prism formed by the net?

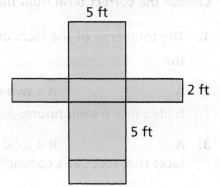

5 ft

2 ft

5 ft

Ⓐ 10 ft³

Ⓑ 50 ft³

Ⓒ 60 ft³

Ⓓ 90 ft³

10. What are the surface area and volume of the prism?

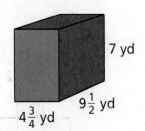

7 yd

$9\frac{1}{2}$ yd

$4\frac{3}{4}$ yd

The surface area is _____.

The volume is _____.

11. A casserole dish is in the shape of a rectangular prism. The dish is 6 inches wide, 12 inches long, and 5 inches deep. What is the volume of the dish?

_____

12. Jerome is painting a rectangular toolbox that is 20 inches by 10 inches by 8 inches. A tube of paint covers 300 square inches.

A. What is the surface area of the toolbox?

_____

B. How many tubes of paint should Jerome buy?

_____

13. A planter in the shape of a rectangular prism is 24 inches by 4 inches by 5 inches. How much dirt is needed to fill the planter?

_____

© Houghton Mifflin Harcourt Publishing Company

Unit 5

Data Collection and Analysis

Sales Director

A sales director manages a company's salespeople. The director helps develop strategies to increase sales of the company's products. For example, a sales director may help determine the best price to charge for a product by considering the company's cost to manufacture the product, the amount of profit the company hopes to earn, and the prices charged by other companies for similar products.

STEM Task:

The dot plot shows the total amounts of sales made so far this year by the four salespeople at a small wind turbine company. The company's sales goal for the year is $8 million. How much more is needed to reach the goal? Explain.

Sales (millions of dollars)

0.2 0.4 0.6 0.8 1 1.2 1.4 1.6 1.8

Learning Mindset

Resilience Monitors Knowledge and Skills

How do you know that you are learning? Whenever you approach a new topic or skill, it is important to pay attention to your understanding. Checking in with yourself before, during, and after learning keeps you focused and helps you identify and address difficulties before they become serious problems. Here are some questions you can ask yourself to monitor your learning.

- What am I trying to learn? What is the goal or objective?

- Why am I learning this? What will I know or be able to do after I learn this?

- How is the new topic connected to something I already know? What is the new information?

- What do I know that I can use next time?

- What have I learned from this effort?

- Can I explain or demonstrate to someone else what I have learned?

Reflect

Q How did you first make sense of the STEM Task? Did your understanding change as you worked on the task? If so, explain.

Q What did you learn from the STEM Task that you can use in your future learning?

Data Collection and Displays

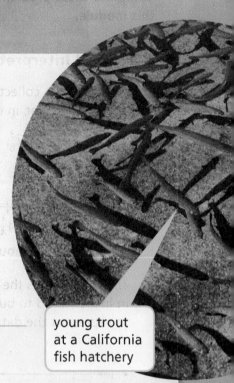

GOING FISHING

Fry, or baby fish, are measured at the hatchery. The weights of 12 fry are shown, in pounds:

$1\frac{1}{4}$, 1, $1\frac{3}{4}$, 2, $1\frac{1}{4}$, $1\frac{1}{2}$, $1\frac{1}{4}$, $1\frac{1}{2}$, $1\frac{1}{4}$, $\frac{3}{4}$, $2\frac{1}{4}$, 1

Make a line plot to show the data.

A. Organize the data from least to greatest.

_____

B. Use the data to make a line plot.

young trout at a California fish hatchery

 Turn and Talk

- Explain how you made the line plot.

- Compare reading the data from a list to reading the data on the line plot. Describe a strength and weakness for each type of display.

Are You Ready?

Complete these problems to review prior concepts and skills you will need for this module.

Make and Interpret Line Plots

1. William has a collection of paint jars. He measures the amount of paint in each jar, in cups. Use the data to complete the line plot.

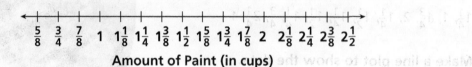

$1\frac{1}{4}$, $1\frac{3}{4}$, $2\frac{1}{2}$, $\frac{5}{8}$, $1\frac{1}{2}$, $2\frac{3}{8}$, $2\frac{1}{2}$, $1\frac{3}{4}$, $2\frac{1}{2}$, $\frac{5}{8}$, $1\frac{1}{2}$, $\frac{5}{8}$

Amount of Paint (in cups)

2. The table shows the widths of different stepping stones, in inches, used to build a path. Complete the line plot to represent the data from the table.

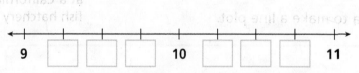

Widths of Stepping Stones (in inches)

Stepping Stone Widths (in inches)	
$10\frac{1}{4}$	$9\frac{3}{4}$
$10\frac{1}{2}$	11
$9\frac{1}{2}$	$10\frac{3}{4}$
10	$9\frac{1}{2}$
$10\frac{1}{4}$	$10\frac{1}{2}$

Plot Points on a Number Line

3. Plot and label each integer.

−10 −9 −8 −7 −6 −5 −4 −3 −2 −1 0 1 2 3 4 5 6 7 8 9 10

A. −8   B. 3   C. −5   D. 0

Division Involving Decimals

For Problems 4–6, divide.

4. $4)\overline{\$8.24}$ _____   5. $7)\overline{\$15.61}$ _____   6. $14)\overline{\$79.80}$ _____

For Problems 7–9, write the mixed number as a decimal.

7. $80\frac{2}{5}$ _____   8. $20\frac{4}{16}$ _____   9. $110\frac{9}{12}$ _____

Explore Statistical Data Collection

(**I Can**) identify a statistical question, and I can describe the attributes of a data set.

Spark Your Learning

Rani measured the heights of the seedlings she is growing. The heights were $\frac{3}{4}$ inch, $\frac{7}{8}$ inch, $\frac{1}{2}$ inch, $\frac{3}{4}$ inch, $\frac{5}{8}$ inch, $\frac{3}{4}$ inch, $\frac{7}{8}$ inch, $\frac{5}{8}$ inch, $\frac{1}{2}$ inch, $\frac{3}{4}$ inch, $\frac{1}{2}$ inch, and $\frac{1}{2}$ inch. How can Rani organize the information to present it to her science class?

Turn and Talk What are some other ways you could describe or organize the information shown in the list, such as by least height?

Build Understanding

When you measure the heights of your classmates, you are collecting data.

"What are the heights of my classmates?" is a statistical question, because height usually varies within a group of people. The data set will have multiple values, such as 54 inches, 48 inches, 51 inches, and so on. Statistical questions require multiple measurements in order to describe data sets, which can be both numeric and non-numeric quantities.

"What is Zoya's height?" is not a statistical question, because it asks for only one piece of information. The data set will have only a single value, such as 54 inches.

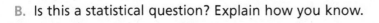

1 ▶ Read the question shown.

"How many hours do sixth-grade students spend on homework each week?"

A. Could this question yield a variety of different answers? Explain.

_____

_____

_____

B. Is this a statistical question? Explain how you know.

_____

_____

2 ▶ Read the question shown.

"How many siblings does Deion have?"

A. Could this question yield a variety of different answers? Explain.

_____

B. Is this a statistical question? Explain how you know.

_____

_____

_____

 Turn and Talk Is the question "How much does Alvin's cat weigh?" a statistical question? Explain. If it is not a statistical question, how can you change it to make it a statistical question?

One way to describe a set of data is by stating the number of observations, or measurements, that were made. Another method of describing data is to list the attributes, or characteristics, that were measured, such as color or length.

3 The table shows the results for some female runners in one semifinal heat of the 100-meter hurdles at the 2016 Summer Olympics.

Women's 100-meter hurdles, Summer Olympics, 2016

Runner	Time (in seconds)
Castlin	12.63
Simmonds	12.95
Billaud	13.03
Ofili	12.71
Pedersen	12.88

A. What attribute is being measured by the data in the table?

_____

_____

B. What is the unit of measurement for the data? _____

C. To what fraction of a unit are the times measured?

_____

D. How do you think the data values were measured?

_____

_____

E. How many runners are represented in the table? _____

F. How many observations, or measurements, were made? _____

Check Understanding

1. Is the following question a statistical question? Explain.

"Did it rain more in Miami or Orlando last month?"

_____

For Problems 2–4, use this table. It shows the masses of students' pets.

Dog	Beagle	Basset hound	Plott hound	Rat terrier	Pug
Mass (kilograms)	11.34	24.04	21.77	4.08	7.26

2. How many observations were made? _____

3. What attribute is being measured? _____

4. What is the unit of measurement for the data? _____

565

On Your Own

5. **(MP) Construct Arguments** Carrie asks the following questions:

"How many players on the soccer team scored goals during the season?"

"How many players per team in the soccer league scored more than 3 goals during the soccer season?"

Which is a statistical question and which is not? Explain your reasoning.

_____

_____

6. Max wants to design an experiment that will result in variable data. Which of these situations could result in a variety of data? Explain.

- measuring the temperature every day for a week
- measuring the average temperature of one week
- measuring the number of high tides for a day

_____

_____

7. The table shows information about buildings in Rome, Italy. Complete each statement about the data.

Building	Colosseum	Il Vittoriano	Pantheon
Height (meters)	157	230	43.28
Approx. age (hundreds of years)	19.38	1.07	18.92

The Colosseum
Rome, Italy

There are ☐ attributes.

The data were measured using _____.

There are ☐ observations.

 I'm in a Learning Mindset!

How do I explain the difference between statistical questions and non-statistical questions?

_____

566

© Houghton Mifflin Harcourt Publishing Company • Image Credit: ©Marco Rubino/Shutterstock

Name _____

Explore Statistical Data Collection

ONLINE

Video Tutorials and
Interactive Examples

1. Which of the following is not a statistical question? Explain.

   • What is the distance from home to places you regularly go?

   • What are the ages of your neighbor's pets?

   • How many days are there in March?

   • What is the time it takes each runner to finish a race at a track meet?

   _____

   _____

2. Light bulbs are labeled with the number of watts of electricity they use as shown in the table. What are the attributes, units of measurement, and number of observations?

Light bulb	A	B	C	D	E	F
Elect. used (watts)	6	18	40	100	60	20

Attributes: _____

Units of Measurement: _____

Number of Observations: _____

3. **Open Ended** Write two statistical questions that you could use to gather data about your family.

   _____

   _____

4. (MP) **Reason** Kate asks her friend what her favorite class at school is. How could she change her questioning so that she can collect statistical data?

   _____

   _____

5. Hector collected the data shown in the table for a basketball league. What are the attributes, units of measurement, and number of observations?

Team	A	B	C	D	E	F
Players	12	15	14	17	11	16
Average score (per game)	74	50	63	38	51	60
Average age of players	13.5	12.8	12.2	13.1	12.7	11.9

Attributes: _____

Units of Measurement: _____

Number of Observations: _____

Test Prep

6. Which of the following are statistical questions? Select all that apply.

   (A) How many total tomato plants are in a large garden pot?

   (B) How many cucumber plants are in each backyard garden in a neighborhood?

   (C) What was the low temperature in my town in December in 2000?

   (D) What percent of sixth grade students at a school don't like apple juice?

   (E) How many flights were delayed at the airport each day last year?

7. The data shown in the table were collected during an evaporation experiment. Which statement best describes the data collected?

Day	1	2	3	4	5	6	7
Water Depth (inches)	18	17.5	16.25	14	10.6	8.7	5.3

   (A) There are 7 observations and 1 attribute. The attribute was likely measured using a measuring cup.

   (B) There are 7 observations and 1 attribute. The attribute was likely measured using a ruler.

   (C) There is 1 observation and 7 attributes. The attributes were likely measured using a measuring cup.

   (D) There is 1 observation and 7 attributes. The attributes were likely measured using a ruler.

Spiral Review

8. A right triangle has an area of 54 square inches and a base of 12 inches. What is the height of the triangle?

9. What is the volume of a cube with an edge length of 7 centimeters?

10. Write an equation that can be described by the statement: y is equal to $\frac{1}{3}$ of x.

© Houghton Mifflin Harcourt Publishing Company

Name _____

Display Data in Dot Plots

(I Can) make a dot plot to display data, and use a dot plot to answer questions about data.

Step It Out

Statistical questions are answered by collecting and analyzing data. One way to understand a set of data is to make a visual display. A dot plot is a type of **line plot** that uses dots to show the number of times each value occurs.

Connect to Vocabulary

A **dot plot** is a visual display in which each piece of data is represented by a dot above a number line.

1 ▶ A pulse rate is the number of times a heart beats in a minute. The pulse rate for a group of 12-year-olds is taken before a physical education class. The results are shown in the table. Which pulse rate is the most common among the group?

Pulse Rates						
65	58	67	72	85	59	66
79	70	75	65	63	55	75
82	56	69	75	57	60	75

A. Complete the number line with an appropriate scale.

Pulse rates vary from ☐ to ☐ , so I should

use a scale from ☐ to ☐ .

☐ ☐ **59** ☐ ☐ ☐ **67** ☐ ☐ ☐ ☐ ☐ **79** ☐ ☐ ☐

B. For each piece of data, plot a dot above the number that corresponds to that data value.

C. Which pulse rate is the most common among the group of 12-year-olds? Explain how you know.

_____

_____

 Turn and Talk Are dot plots useful for a large volume of data? Explain.

© Houghton Mifflin Harcourt Publishing Company • Image Credit: ©Aleksandr Khakimullin/Alamy

2 A company's employees are rated for their customer service on a scale of 1–10, with 1 being very unhappy and 10 being very happy with the service. The customer service ratings for one day are shown in the dot plot. Use the dot plot to describe the data.

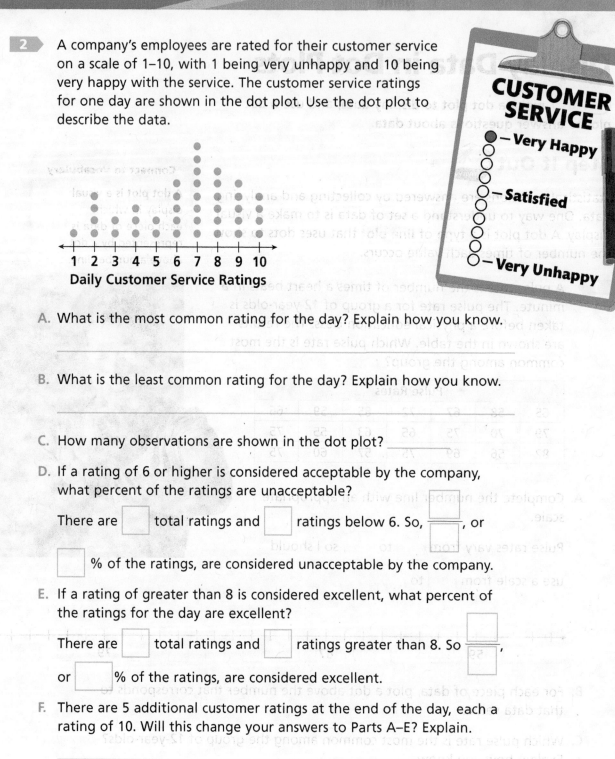

Daily Customer Service Ratings

A. What is the most common rating for the day? Explain how you know.

_____

B. What is the least common rating for the day? Explain how you know.

_____

C. How many observations are shown in the dot plot? _____

D. If a rating of 6 or higher is considered acceptable by the company, what percent of the ratings are unacceptable?

There are ☐ total ratings and ☐ ratings below 6. So, $\frac{☐}{☐}$, or

☐ % of the ratings, are considered unacceptable by the company.

E. If a rating of greater than 8 is considered excellent, what percent of the ratings for the day are excellent?

There are ☐ total ratings and ☐ ratings greater than 8. So $\frac{☐}{☐}$,

or ☐ % of the ratings, are considered excellent.

F. There are 5 additional customer ratings at the end of the day, each a rating of 10. Will this change your answers to Parts A–E? Explain.

_____

_____

_____

_____

 Turn and Talk How is a dot plot different from a number line? Explain.

Name _____

3 The recommended amount of water that each person should drink per day is shown. Students are asked to track how much water they actually drink in a day. The number of glasses of water they drank on a specific day is shown in the following list.

5, 7, 9, 7, 6, 1, 4, 2, 3, 0, 8, 5, 2, 5, 6, 7, 4, 8, 5, 6, 4, 3, 8, 6, 5

Drink 8 glasses of water per day.

A. Complete the dot plot to show the amount of water students drank per day.

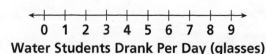

0 1 2 3 4 5 6 7 8 9
Water Students Drank Per Day (glasses)

B. What is the most common number of glasses of water students drank?

_____

C. How many students drank at least the recommended amount of water per day?

_____

D. How many observations are shown in the dot plot? _____

E. What percent of students did not drink at least the recommended amount of water per day?

_____

Check Understanding

Use the dot plot for Problems 1 and 2.

1. The shoe sizes of the players on a soccer team are shown in the list.

10.5, 11.5, 10, 9, 10.5, 10, 8, 9, 7.5, 8, 10.5, 11, 10,
10.5, 9.5, 8.5, 7, 8.5, 9, 9.5, 10, 10.5, 11

Complete the dot plot to show the shoe sizes of the players.

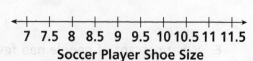

7 7.5 8 8.5 9 9.5 10 10.5 11 11.5
Soccer Player Shoe Size

2. A student is asked to make a dot plot with the list shown.

8, 11, 16, 27, 8, 10, 19, 21, 7, 12, 15, 16, 22, 13

How many observations will be shown in the dot plot? _____

On Your Own

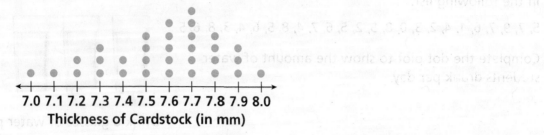

(MP) Attend to Precision For Problems 3–5, use this dot plot. It shows the thicknesses of sheets of cardstock, a type of paper.

Thickness of Cardstock (in mm)

3. What is the least thickness measured? _____

4. What is the greatest thickness measured? _____

5. What is the most common thickness measured? _____

6. A group of people is asked to count the number of coins in their pockets or wallets. The number of coins each person has is shown in the list.

   7, 10, 2, 0, 6, 8, 5, 3, 4, 0, 9, 1, 8, 7, 10, 0, 5, 7

   A. Complete the dot plot for the number of coins each person had.

   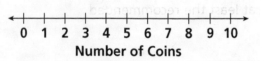

   Number of Coins

   B. What is the most common number of coins in a person's pockets?

   _____

   C. How many observations are shown in the dot plot?

   _____

   D. What percent of people had more than 5 coins in their pockets?

   _____

   E. What percent of people had fewer than 7 coins in their pockets?

   _____

Name _____

For Problems 7–10, use this information. A basketball team tracks the number of three-point shots it makes per game during a season, as shown in the dot plot.

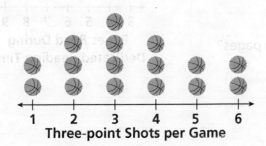

Three-point Shots per Game

7. In how many games did the team score at least 3 three-point shots?

_____

8. In how many games did the team score exactly 9 points from three-point shots?

_____

9. What is the most three-point shots made in a game? _____

10. In what percent of the games did the team score

at least 3 three-point shots? _____

11. The masses of a set of gemstones a jeweler has for jewelry are listed.

Gemstone masses (in grams): 0.2, 0.5, 0.1, 0.4, 0.7, 0.5, 0.3, 0.2, 0.1, 0.4, 0.2, 0.5, 0.2, 0.3, 0.1, 0.2, 0.6, 0.2, 0.6, 0.1

A. Make a dot plot to show the masses of the gemstones.

B. How many observations are shown in the dot plot? _____

C. What is the most common gemstone mass? _____

D. Which gemstone mass is the least common? _____

© Houghton Mifflin Harcourt Publishing Company • Image Credit: ©ALEXANDER V EVSTAFYEV/Shutterstock

Module 17 • Lesson 2

573

12. (MP) **Reason** The dot plot shows the numbers of pages students in a class read during their dedicated reading time.

A. How many students are in the class? _____

B. What percent of students read more than 6 pages? Explain your reasoning.

_____

_____

C. What fraction of the students read fewer than 5 pages? _____

D. How many total pages did all of the students read? Show your work.

Pages Read During Dedicated Reading Time

3 4 5 6 7 8 9

13. The table shows the heights of trees at a tree farm, to the nearest foot. Make a dot plot for the tree heights.

Tree type	Height (in feet)
Fraser fir	6, 7, 10, 11, 14, 8, 10, 13, 12, 7
Douglas fir	15, 14, 12, 16, 13, 11, 12, 15, 16, 18
Blue spruce	10, 12, 14, 9, 10, 8, 11, 12, 8, 10

Fraser Fir   Douglas Fir   Blue Spruce

Display Data in Dot Plots

1. The ages of campers who have attended a summer
camp for at least five years are listed.

13, 12, 15, 14, 16, 13, 15, 14, 15, 16, 15, 14, 12, 14, 16, 13, 15, 12, 14, 15

A. Complete the dot plot for the campers' ages.

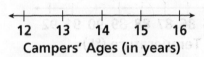

12   13   14   15   16
Campers' Ages (in years)

B. What is the most common age of the campers? _____

C. How many observations are shown in the dot plot? _____

D. (MP) **Attend to Precision** What percent of campers are
over the age of 14? _____

2. **STEM** A zoo has a population of endangered leaf-tailed
geckos. Each year, the zoo records the number of eggs
each female gecko lays and hatches. The data in the dot
plot show the number of eggs hatched in a year.

leaf-tailed gecko

A. What is the total number of eggs hatched in one year?
Explain how you found your answer.

_____

_____

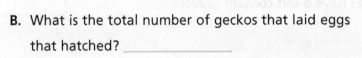

1 2 3 4 5 6 7 8
Eggs Hatched (in a year)

B. What is the total number of geckos that laid eggs

that hatched? _____

C. What is the greatest number of eggs laid and hatched

by one gecko? _____

D. What is the most common number of eggs hatched? _____

E. (MP) **Reason** One of the zoologists splits the data and considers the top
half of the data, or the 8 greatest observations. What percent of the
total eggs is under consideration? Explain your reasoning.

_____

_____

Test Prep

3. The chart shows the average daily temperatures for a week in a town. Which dot plot best represents the information in the table?

Average Daily Temperature							
Day	Sunday	Monday	Tuesday	Wednesday	Thursday	Friday	Saturday
Temperature (°F)	86	84	88	92	88	86	86

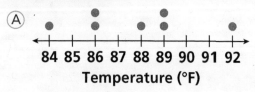

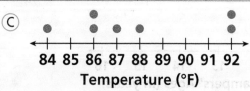

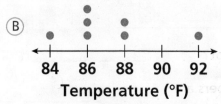

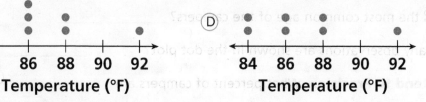

4. The dot plot shows the concentrations of salt in samples of sea water from around the world.

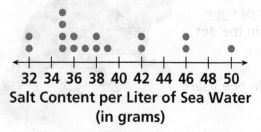

Salt Content per Liter of Sea Water (in grams)

A. How many samples were taken? _____

B. What fraction of the samples have a salt content greater

than 38 grams? _____

Spiral Review

5. A rectangular prism has a volume of 990 cubic inches. If it has a height of

11 inches and a width of 10 inches, what is its length? _____

6. Write an equation for the statement: A kilogram is equal to approximately 2.2 pounds. A cinder block weighs x pounds. A brick has a mass of 0.6 kilogram. What is the total mass in kilograms y of the cinder block and the brick?

_____

7. Evaluate the expression $3x^2 + 4x^3$ when $x = 4$. _____

Name _____

Make Histograms and Frequency Tables

(I Can) **make a histogram and frequency table, and I can answer questions about data displayed in these ways.**

Step It Out

When there is a large number of data values, it is helpful to group data into **intervals**. A histogram is a way to show the frequency of numeric data within those intervals.

1 ▶ A tae kwon do school teaches many ages of students. The ages of the students are shown in the histogram.

A. The height of each bar represents the

_____

in each age group.

B. You can find the total number of students that were included in the data set by

_____

the numbers of students in the age groups.

C. There are _____ students in the range from 25 to 28 years old.

D. There are _____ students from 9 to 16 years old.

E. The age range of _____ years old has the greatest number of students.

F. The difference between the number of students in the 13–16 year age range and the number of students in the 17–20 year age range is

_____ students.

 Turn and Talk Can you make a dot plot from a histogram? Explain.

A frequency table is used to organize data.

2 A salesperson hands out samples during work. The number of samples handed out each hour during the work week are tracked. Make a frequency table to represent the data.

Samples per Hour
7, 12, 15, 23, 8, 11, 10,
19, 21, 10, 16, 22, 13, 16,
27, 8, 12, 18, 24, 20

A. Write the data in order from least to greatest.

_____

_____

_____

B. The numbers vary from _____ to _____, so use a scale from 1 to 30.

Salesperson handing out food samples

C. Divide the data into six equal-sized intervals.

The first interval is 1 — ☐.

The second interval is ☐ — ☐.

The third interval is ☐ — ☐.

The fourth interval is ☐ — ☐.

The fifth interval is ☐ — ☐.

The sixth interval is ☐ — ☐.

D. Complete the frequency table.

Interval	1—5	6—10				
Frequency		0				

 Turn and Talk What is another way you could display the data from the frequency table?

3 A movie theater records the number of pretzels it sells per day for 2 weeks. The pretzel sales data are shown in the list. Make a histogram to represent the data.

11, 8, 21, 15, 28, 43, 37, 9, 12, 13, 17, 31, 50, 34

A. Order the data from least to greatest.

_____

B. The numbers vary from _____ to _____, so use a scale from 1 to 50.

C. Divide the data into five equal-sized intervals.

The first interval is 1—10.   The second interval is ☐ — ☐.

The third interval is ☐ — ☐.   The fourth interval is ☐ — ☐.

The fifth interval is ☐ — ☐.

D. Complete the frequency table.

Pretzels sold	Frequency
1—10	

E. Fill in the values in the histogram.

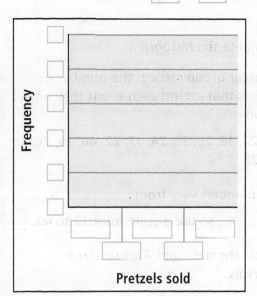

Pretzels sold

Check Understanding

1. A restaurant records the number of people who come in for breakfast for 15 days.

38, 59, 61, 33, 48, 54, 67, 29, 35, 49, 53, 21, 40, 66, 55

A. Use the data to complete the frequency table.

B. Describe how the histogram in Task 3 would look if the intervals were 11–30, 31–50, and 51–70.

_____

_____

Interval	Frequency
11—20	0
21—30	
	4
41—50	
51—60	

On Your Own

2. Jimena tutored students over the summer. She recorded the number of hours she tutored each week. Here are her data:

15, 24, 18, 26, 18, 21, 23, 12, 24, 25

A. Complete the frequency table.

Tutoring (hours)	Frequency
10–14	
	3
20–24	

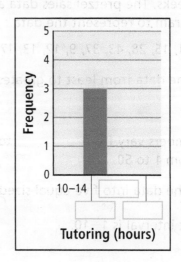

B. Complete the histogram.

3. A volunteer group records the number of volunteers that attend each event they host, as shown.

19, 30, 27, 18, 25, 38, 24, 17, 22, 40, 39, 26, 18, 37, 28

Volunteering is a great way to help out in your community.

A. The numbers vary from _____ to _____, so use a scale from 17 to 40.

B. Divide the data into 4 equal-sized intervals.

First interval: 17–22

Second interval: ☐–☐

Third interval: ☐–☐

Fourth interval: ☐–☐

Volunteers	Frequency

C. Complete the frequency table.

D. (MP) **Use Structure** If you drew a histogram for this data, which interval would have the shortest bar? _____

Name _____

4. Each team in a Hawaiian canoe racing regatta gains points for its finish times. The points each team earned are shown:

2, 6, 7, 5, 3, 4, 1, 8, 2, 9, 8, 6, 3, 5, 2, 4, 6

A. Use the data to complete the frequency table.

Interval	Frequency
1–3	
4–6	

B. How many bars will be used to represent the intervals in a histogram of the team points?

_____

C. What is the height of the tallest bar in the histogram?

_____

Regatta team points

D. Complete the histogram.

E. (MP) **Reason** Three other teams that competed were accidentally not included in the list. They earned 3, 2, and 8 points. How does this new information change the histogram? Is the second interval still the tallest bar? Explain.

_____

_____

_____

_____

5. In the high jump, athletes run and jump over a bar without knocking it down. The histogram shows the heights of the highest jumps of the top athletes in a state competition.

A. Which height range did the most athletes clear?

_____

B. How many athletes participated in the state competition?

_____

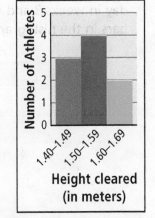

Height cleared (in meters)

Module 17 • Lesson 3

581

6. A florist delivers flowers each day. The table shows the numbers of flower deliveries for a two-week period.

Flower Deliveries		
Day	Deliveries (week 1)	Deliveries (week 2)
Monday	38	31
Tuesday	53	47
Wednesday	44	53
Thursday	35	39
Friday	51	48
Saturday	46	52
Sunday	32	35

A. Use the data from the table of delivery information to complete the frequency table.

Deliveries	Frequency
31–35	
36–40	
41–45	
46–50	
51–55	

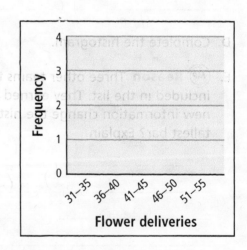

B. Complete the histogram.

C. (MP) **Reason** If the florist makes the same number of deliveries each day in weeks 3 and 4 as in weeks 1 and 2, how does this change the bars in the histogram? Explain.

_____

_____

_____

Make Histograms and Frequency Tables

1. A bakery records the number of loaves of bread it sells per hour for one day as shown.

   15, 17, 20, 22, 23, 25, 11, 12, 26, 13, 18, 21, 24, 28, 23, 18, 29, 24, 16

   A. Write the data in order from least to greatest.

   _____

   B. Complete the frequency table.

Number of loaves sold (per hour)	Frequency
11–15	

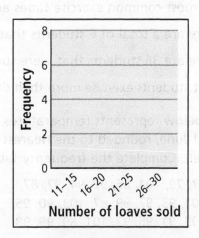

   C. Complete the histogam.

2. **Math on the Spot** The table shows survey results about the number of hours a week students spend studying. Make a histogram of the data.

	Number of Hours Spent Studying											
Hours	1	2	3	4	5	6	7	8	9	10	11	12
Number of students	1	1	4	2	6	8	10	10	12	7	2	3

   A. Complete the frequency table of the data.

   B. Draw a bar for each interval from the frequency table.

Hours	Number of students
1–2	2
3–4	
5–6	
7–8	
9–10	
11–12	

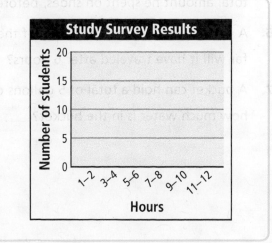

Test Prep

3. The histogram shows the amounts of time students spend exercising per day, rounded to the nearest hour. Which statements about the histogram are correct? Select all that apply.

   Ⓐ The least common amount of time spent exercising was 76–90 minutes.

   Ⓑ The most common exercise times are 1–15 minutes.

   Ⓒ There are a total of 6 students that exercise.

   Ⓓ There are 36 students that were surveyed.

   Ⓔ Most students exercise more than 60 minutes per day.

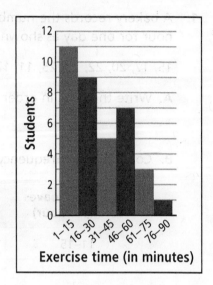

4. The list below represents temperatures for the month of June, rounded to the nearest degree Fahrenheit. Complete the frequency table.

   93, 85, 97, 79, 104, 88, 92, 94, 97, 87,
   78, 95, 101, 93, 97, 99, 87, 103, 90, 95,
   102, 97, 99, 91, 95, 92, 101, 89, 99, 98

Temperature (°F)	Days
71–80	

Spiral Review

5. Gustus bought three pairs of shoes. Each pair costs $19.98. What is the total amount he spent on shoes, before tax? _____

6. A car travels 220 miles in 4 hours. If the car travels at the same speed, how far will it have traveled after 6 hours? _____

7. A bucket can hold a total of 5 gallons of water. If the bucket is 45% full, how much water is in the bucket? _____

Name _____

Find Measures of Center

(**I Can**) find the mean, median, and mode of a set of data.

Step It Out

A **measure of center** is used to describe the middle of a data set.

1 ▶ Look at the stacks of counters shown. The heights of the
stacks from left to right are 8, 3, 7, 5, and 7.

A. Arrange the stacks in a row from shortest to tallest.
What is the height of the middle stack?

_____

B. What is the measure of center represented by the middle stack?

_____

C. What is the most common height for the stacks? Explain why.

_____

_____

D. What measure of center is given by the most common stack height?

_____

E. Rearrange the counters so that all of the stacks have the same number of
counters. Show your work. Now how many counters are in each stack?

_____

F. What measure of center is represented when all the stacks have the
same number of counters?

_____

 Turn and Talk If the first stack had 13 counters, instead of 8, which measures
of center would change?

Connect to Vocabulary

Mean is the sum of the items in a set of data divided by the number of items in the set; also called *average*.
Median is the middle number or mean (average) of the two middle numbers in an ordered set of data.
Mode is the number or numbers that occur most frequently in a set of data; when all numbers occur with the same frequency, we say there is no mode.

© Houghton Mifflin Harcourt Publishing Company

2 The data show the average price of gas (in dollars and cents) at some gas stations around the world. Find the mean, median, and mode of the data.

3.50	7.99	3.25	4.00	3.50	7.50	3.65	3.50	4.00

A. Complete the dot plot to represent the data.

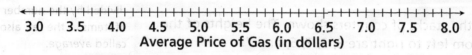

Average Price of Gas (in dollars)

B. How many observations of gas prices were made?

_____

C. Complete the equations to find the mean.

$3.50 + 7.99 + 3.25 + 4.00 + 3.50 + 7.50 + 3.65 + 3.50 + 4.00 = $ ☐

$$\frac{}{9} \approx \$\,☐$$

D. Write the data in order from least to greatest and circle the median.

_____

E. What is the mode of the data?

_____

 Turn and Talk Suppose the average gas prices had been given in a histogram instead of a table. Could you have found the mean, median, or mode?

Check Understanding

1. Zayn surveyed a group of people about how many times they ate at a restaurant last month. The results are: 4, 0, 21, 14, 12, 30, 8, 7, 8, 7, 7, 10, 14, 12. Find the mean, median, and mode of the data.

Mean: _____   Median: _____   Mode: _____

2. Find the mean, median, and mode of the data: 2.4, 1.9, 3.3, 3.5, 3.2, 2.7, 1.1, 20.9, 2.4.

Mean: _____   Median: _____   Mode: _____

On Your Own

3. Eric recorded the temperature forecast (in °F) for 10 days and wrote the information in a table.

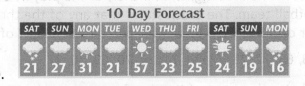

10 Day Forecast

SAT	SUN	MON	TUE	WED	THU	FRI	SAT	SUN	MON
21	27	31	21	57	23	25	24	19	16

21	27	31	21	57	23	25	24	19	16

A. Complete the dot plot to represent the data.

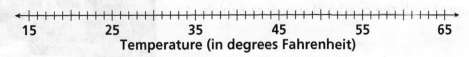

15   25   35   45   55   65

Temperature (in degrees Fahrenheit)

B. What is the mean of the data? _____

C. What is the median of the data? _____

D. What is the mode of the data? _____

4. (MP) **Attend to Precision** The 40-yard dash times, in seconds, for 7 runners are shown.

4.8, 5.3, 5.2, 6.4, 5.4, 5.3, 5.4

A. What is the mean of the data? _____

B. What is the median of the data? _____

C. What is the mode of the data? _____

D. Which of the measures of center has more than one possible value?

_____

5. (MP) **Reason** Look at the data: 0, 1, 2, 1, 2, 0, 1, 2, 0, 2, 1, 2, 1, 2. Which measure of center could best be used to describe the data? Explain.

_____

_____

6. **Open Ended** Describe a set of data that has no mode, one mode, and more than one mode.

_____

_____

7. A book has 20 pages, numbered from 1 to 20. Identify the mean, median, and mode for the page numbers.

_____

_____

8. The list shows the heights, in inches, of the players on a high school basketball team. The coach states that any of the three measures of center could be used to identify the typical height of the players.

69, 73, 68, 72, 75, 72, 78, 74, 74, 70, 69, 70, 72

A. What is the mean of the data? _____

B. What is the median of the data? _____

C. What is the mode of the data? _____

D. Do you agree with the coach's statement? Explain.

_____

_____

9. A thrift store has 11 bicycles for sale. The list shows the prices of the bicycles in dollars, in order from least to greatest.

12, 15, 15, 19, 20, 25, 26, 32, 32, 32, 34

A. Is the mode or median the more useful measure of center? Explain.

_____

_____

_____

B. The store receives a new bicycle that is in excellent condition, and has a price of $120. With the new bicycle included, does the mean, median, or mode of the prices change the most? Explain.

_____

_____

10. The set of numbers shown below includes an unknown value, n. The mean of the set is 8.

0, 4, 6, 12, 20, n

A. What is the value of n? _____

B. What is the median of the data? _____

C. What is the mode of the data? _____

Name _____

Find Measures of Center

1. Summer wants to know which cat food her cats prefer. She fed the cats and recorded the number of grams of food the cats ate each day. The results are: 60 grams, 63 grams, 61 grams, 58 grams, 65 grams, 60 grams, and 60 grams.

Which food do the cats prefer?

   A. How many days did Summer log the amount of food her cats ate? _____

   B. On average, how many grams of food did her cats eat each day? _____

   C. Which amount represents the mode of the data? _____

   D. What is the median of the data?

   _____

   E. Which measures of center are the same? _____

2. (MP) **Reason** Jackson recorded the following data: 2, 5, x, 2, 4, 3. If the mean of the data is 3, what is the value of x? Explain how you found your answer.

   _____

   _____

   _____

3. **Math on the Spot** Find the mean, median, and mode of the data set: 10, 6, 2, 3, 1, and 2.

   _____

For Problems 4–7, find the mean, median, and mode of the data set.

4. 17, 25, 23, 200, 14

   Mean _____

   Median _____

   Mode _____

5. 0.5, 1.4, 3.0, 7.0, 0.5, 1.8, 0.5

   Mean _____

   Median _____

   Mode _____

6. 1, 8, 5, 4, 1, 8, 5, 4

   Mean _____

   Median _____

   Mode _____

7. 0, 78, 99, 58, 65, 0, 47, 38, 227

   Mean _____

   Median _____

   Mode _____

Test Prep

8. The ages of dogs (in years) at a dog shelter are shown.

   7, 4, 6, 8, 8, 7, 3, 5, 4, 2

   What is the mode of the data? Select all that apply.

   Ⓐ 2 years

   Ⓑ 3 years

   Ⓒ 4 years

   Ⓓ 7 years

   Ⓔ 8 years

9. In their most recent tournament, the winning team's 6 members had the scores shown.

   70, 72, 74, 76, 80, 132

   Which statement is correct?

   Ⓐ The median is 74.

   Ⓑ The mean is 75.

   Ⓒ The median is 76.

   Ⓓ The mean is 84.

10. What is the median of the data?

    3, 5, 6, 7, 9, 6, 8, 7, 8, 12

    Ⓐ 6

    Ⓑ 7

    Ⓒ 7.1

    Ⓓ 8

Spiral Review

11. A parallelogram has a base of 13 centimeters and a height of 9.2 centimeters. What is the area of the parallelogram?

12. In which quadrant is the point $(-5, 1.7)$ located?

© Houghton Mifflin Harcourt Publishing Company

Name _____

Choose a Measure of Center

(I Can) choose an appropriate measure of center to describe a data set.

Step It Out

1 ▷ The table shows the numbers of songs downloaded in one week by some students.

12	13	10	9
13	44	15	12

A. What do you notice about the data in the table?

The data value of _____ is much _____ than the other data values in the table.

B. Complete the dot plot to represent the data.

Connect to Vocabulary

An **outlier** is a value much greater or much less than the other values in a data set. A set of data can have more than one outlier.

0   5   10   15   20   25   30   35   40   45   50
Number of Songs Downloaded

C. Which value in the data set is an outlier? Explain how you know?

_____

D. Find the mean, median, and mode with and without the outlier. Then complete the sentences.

The mean with the outlier is _____, and the mean without the

outlier is _____. The outlier makes the mean │ greater/less │.

The median with the outlier is _____, and the median without the

outlier is _____. The outlier makes the median │ greater/less │.

The mode with the outlier is _____, and the mode without the

outlier is _____. The outlier │ did/did not │ affect the mode.

Turn and Talk When the outlier is included, which measure of center is least representative of the data set? Why?

Step It Out

2 ▷ A group of friends decide to see who can balance themselves the longest on one foot with their eyes closed. The results, in seconds, are listed.

21, 21, 23, 11, 48, 21, 16, 15, 13

A. Complete the dot plot of the data.

21 s   21 s   23 s

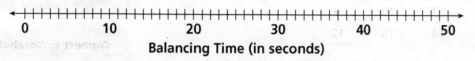

Balancing Time (in seconds)

B. Use the dot plot to complete the sentences.

The data value of _____ is an outlier.

The mean with the outlier is _____, and the mean without the outlier is about _____. The outlier made the mean | greater/less |.

The median with the outlier is _____, and the median without the outlier is _____. The outlier made the median | greater/less |.

The mode with the outlier is _____, and the mode without the outlier is _____. The outlier | did/did not | affect the mode.

C. The best measure of center for this data set is the median or the _____, because the outlier affects the _____ the most.

Check Understanding

1. Xavier drew 10 cards at random from a deck of numbered cards. The deck is composed of 3 sets of cards numbered 1 through 10 and three cards numbered 50. He recorded the numbers he drew: 8, 7, 9, 1, 10, 10, 50, 2, 5, 3. Find the mean, median, and mode of the data. What would happen to the mean, median, and mode if Xavier drew a 4 card instead of the 50 card?

_____

_____

2. Find the mean, median, and mode of the data: 0, 100, 25, 25, 25. Which outlier, 0 or 100, affects the data more? Why?

_____

_____

On Your Own

3. The table shows the masses (in kilograms) of eight gorillas.

155	157	160	158
44	160	156	154

A. What are the mean, median, and mode of the data?

_____

B. Which mass is the outlier of the data? _____

C. How does the outlier affect the mean, median, and mode?

_____

_____

_____

Adult male gorillas can have a mass of up to 220 kilograms.

D. Which measure of center best represents the data? Why?

_____

_____

4. (MP) **Attend to Precision** The circumference of a pumpkin is the distance around it. The following are circumferences (in inches) of some pumpkins growing in a pumpkin patch: 16, 12, 14, 17, 15, 9, 8, 5.

A. Make a dot plot of the data.

B. What is the mean of the data? _____

C. What is the median of the data? _____

D. What is the mode of the data? _____

E. Which measure or measures of center best represent this data? Explain.

_____

_____

_____

5. Simone's grandmother likes to give sweaters as gifts. She has eight grandchildren. The prices of the first seven sweaters she buys are shown.

A. How much does the 8th sweater cost if the mean price of all the sweaters is $40? _____

B. Complete the dot plot to represent the prices of the sweaters.

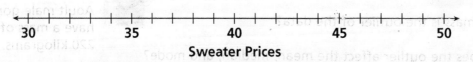

Sweater Prices

C. What are the median and mode of all the sweater prices?

_____

D. Which measure of center best represents the data? Explain.

_____

_____

6. The numbers of questions out of 20 that the students in a class got correct on a quiz are shown in the table.

Number of Questions Answered Correctly						
16	15	16	14	12	18	18
19	20	18	17	18	20	15
16	15	0	12	10	10	

A. Complete the dot plot of the data.

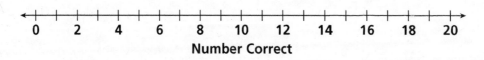

Number Correct

B. How does the outlier affect the data? Explain.

_____

_____

C. Which measure of center best represents the data? Why?

_____

_____

7. Open Ended Describe a data set that has the same mean, median, and mode.

_____

LESSON 17.5
**More Practice/
Homework**

ONLINE

Video Tutorials and
Interactive Examples

Choose a Measure of Center

1. **STEM** Rachel launched several model rockets and calculated the height, in feet, of each launch. The heights were: 75, 70, 80, 72, 84, 37, 65, 67, and 80.

   A. Complete the dot plot to represent the data.

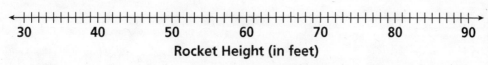

   Rocket Height (in feet)

   B. Find the mean, median, and mode of the heights.

   Mean: _____   Median: _____   Mode: _____

   C. How are the data affected by the outlier?

   _____

   _____

   D. Which measure of center best represents the data? Why?

   _____

   _____

   _____

Rachel's best rocket launch reached 84 feet in height!

2. **(MP) Reason** Hayden recorded the following measurements, in centimeters. He noted he was missing one measurement. If the mean is 1 centimeter, what is the value of the missing measurement? Explain how you found your answer.

   0.1, 0.2, 0.1, 0.2, 0.3, 0.1, 0.2.

   _____

   _____

3. **Math on the Spot** The dot plot shows the numbers of hours 15 people spent on the telephone in one week. Which measure of center best represents these data? Justify your answer.

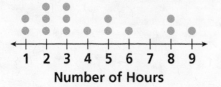

   Number of Hours

   _____

Test Prep

4. Identify any outliers in the data. Select all that apply.

   3, 8, 4, 7, 62, 10, 9, 59, 12

   (A) 3

   (B) 8

   (C) 10

   (D) 59

   (E) 62

5. The monthly rents for 8 apartments are shown.

   $650, $600, $800, $700, $600, $600, $750, $2,000

   Which measure of center best represents the data?

   _____

6. What is the mode of the data?

   0, 5, 8, 12, 14, 19, 11, 3

   (A) 0

   (B) 3

   (C) 5

   (D) No mode

7. A basketball team has scored the following numbers of points in games this season.

   65, 60, 58, 52, 50, 51

   Find the mean, median, and mode of the data.

   _____

Spiral Review

8. Find the surface area of a rectangular prism with a length of 6.1 centimeters, a width of 5.2 centimeters, and a height of 4 centimeters.

   _____

9. Write an equation to represent the data in the table.

x	−2	2	4
y	−4	4	8

   _____

Review

Vocabulary

Choose the correct term from the Vocabulary box.

1. A _____ is a graph that has bars that represent frequencies of numeric data within equal intervals.

2. A question that has many different or variable answers is called a _____.

3. The _____ is the sum of the values in a data set divided by the number of values in the set.

4. The middle number or mean of the two middle numbers in an ordered data set is called the _____.

> **Vocabulary**
>
> histogram
> mean
> median
> mode
> statistical question

Concepts and Skills

For Problems 5–6, use the dot plot shown.

5. Find the mode, median, and mean of the data.

   _____

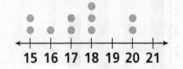

6. (MP) **Use Tools** What two data points could you remove from the plot to increase the mean but leave the median unchanged? State what strategy and tool you will use to answer the question, explain your choice, and then find the answer.

   _____

   _____

7. Which of these is a statistical question? Explain how you know.

   • What time did you go to bed last night?
   • What time do the students in your class go to bed?

   _____

   _____

8. The dot plot shows the amount each customer spent during a 1-hour period at a coffee shop. How many customers made a purchase at the coffee shop during that 1-hour period?

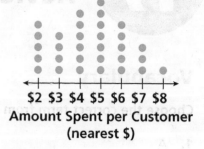

Amount Spent per Customer (nearest $)

_____

9. The frequency table gives the ages of students rounded to the nearest month. Which histogram correctly represents the data from the frequency table?

Age (in months)	Students
132–138	14
139–145	13
146–152	8
153–159	6

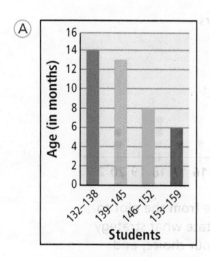

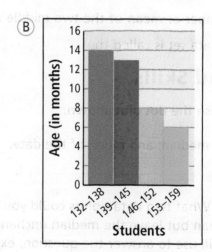

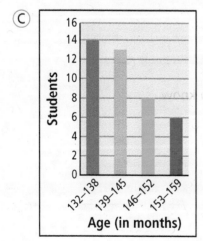

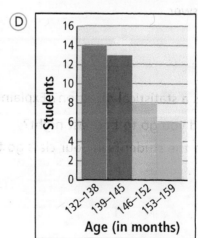

18

Variability and Data Distribution

Player Stats

Norah looked up her favorite college basketball player online. The player has played in 5 games so far this season. The information Norah found is shown.

PLAYER BIO	POINTS PER GAME
Player Name: S. Palmer	**Mean:** 22 points
Position: Guard	**Median:** 24 points
Height: 5 ft 8 in.	**Range (most points minus fewest points):** 20 points
Class: Junior	

Use the player's data to make a data set with a possible number of points the player could have scored in each game. Your data set should match the information Norah found about the player.

Game 1: _____ points   Game 2: _____ points

Game 3: _____ points   Game 4: _____ points

Game 5: _____ points

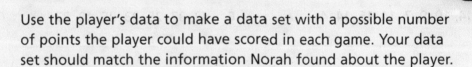 **Turn and Talk**

- Explain how you chose the values for your data set.

- Could the player have scored 0 points in one of the games? Explain your reasoning.

Are You Ready?

Complete these problems to review prior concepts and skills you will need for this module.

Compare and Order Whole Numbers

Order the numbers from least to greatest.

1. 21, 17, 7, 11, 20, 19, 10

2. 87, 78, 90, 85, 79, 82, 95

3. 101, 110, 107, 97, 111, 105, 102

4. 521, 518, 508, 512, 510, 501, 515

Mean

Find the mean for each set of data.

5. 14, 10, 9, 7, 14, 16, 14, 4   **6.** 42, 37, 25, 33, 25, 18, 37

7. 30, 75, 60, 10, 50, 85, 25, 45   **8.** 12, 20, 22, 15, 17, 18, 11, 23

9. The data show the heights, in inches, of the players on a basketball team. Find the mean of the heights.

74, 76, 67, 70, 76, 68, 73, 66, 70, 66, 64

Opposites and Absolute Value

Find the absolute value of the expression.

10. $|-6|$ **11.** $|26|$ **12.** $|-115|$

13. $|0|$ **14.** $|-100|$ **15.** $|134|$

Name

Explore Patterns of Data

(I Can) use a dot plot or histogram to describe the overall patterns in a data set, including clusters, gaps, peaks, and symmetry.

Spark Your Learning

Sharice is collecting data on the lengths of crocodiles for a science project. She thinks it would help to make a poster for her class so the students can understand her data at a glance. How should she display her data?

American crocodiles: 5.0 m, 4.5 m, 3.0 m, 4.5 m
Australian freshwater crocodiles: 2.5 m, 2.0 m, 2.0 m, 1.5 m
Orinoco crocodiles: 4.5 m, 4.5 m, 2.5 m, 2.5 m

Turn and Talk What are the advantages of visually organizing data?

Build Understanding

Seeing data sets represented as dot plots and histograms can help you find and understand overall patterns in the data.

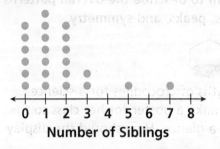

Number of Siblings

Students' Siblings

1 ▷ Mr. Ortega surveyed one of his classes to determine the number of siblings each of his students has. The results are summarized in the dot plot. What conclusions can you draw from the distribution of the data?

A. How many students did Mr. Ortega survey?

_____

B. A *cluster* is a group of data points that lie within a small interval. Does the dot plot have a cluster? If so, where?

_____

C. A *gap* is an interval that contains no data. Does the dot plot have any gaps or deviations from the overall pattern? If so, where?

_____

_____

D. A *peak* is a column of data points that is higher than the columns on either side. Does the dot plot have a peak? If so, where?

_____

E. Calculate the median of the data. How does it relate to the overall pattern?

_____

_____

F. Draw two conclusions from the survey results. Explain whether you used a cluster, a gap, a peak, or a mode to reach each conclusion.

_____

_____

_____

 Turn and Talk Suppose Mr. Ortega surveys all of his classes and summarizes the number of siblings in dot plots for each class. Would you expect the plots to look similar to the dot plot in Task 1 with respect to clusters and gaps? Explain.

2 The histogram shows the fuel efficiency, in miles per gallon, for cars sold at Max's Dealership.

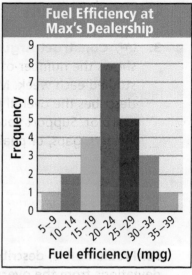

Fuel Efficiency at Max's Dealership

A. Is there a peak in the distribution? If so, where?

_____

B. Describe the overall pattern in how the data change.

_____

_____

_____

_____

C. If you draw a vertical line through the middle of the interval 20–24, the two sides of the histogram are close to mirror images. So the histogram is nearly symmetric. Is the pattern in Part B an indicator of symmetry? Does the data deviate from the overall pattern?

_____

_____

_____

Check Understanding

Describe the data set by identifying clusters, peaks, gaps, and symmetry. Draw one conclusion and explain how you reached it.

1.

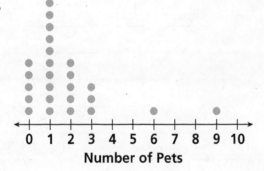

Number of Pets

2.

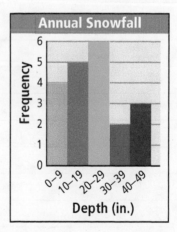

Annual Snowfall

Depth (in.)

_____

_____   _____

_____   _____

_____   _____

_____   _____

On Your Own

3. (MP) **Construct Arguments** The dot plot shows the number of hours that 40 students studied each week. Make a statement that describes the overall pattern of the data in the plot. Support your statement by describing clusters, gaps, or peaks.

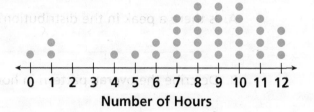

Number of Hours

_____

_____

_____

For Problems 4–5, describe any clusters, symmetry, peaks, and gaps or deviations from the overall pattern for the given distributions. Use the patterns you see to draw one conclusion about the data.

4.

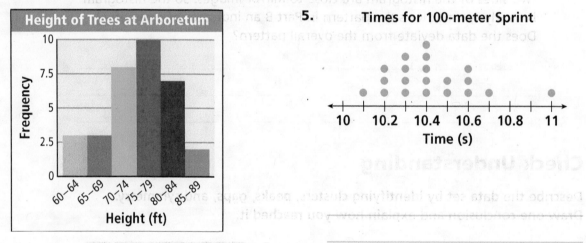

Height of Trees at Arboretum

5. **Times for 100-meter Sprint**

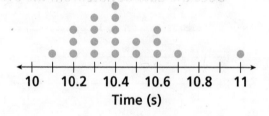

Time (s)

_____

_____

_____

_____

_____

_____

➖✖️➗ **I'm in a Learning Mindset!**

What can I apply from previous work to better understand patterns of data?

_____

Name _____

Explore Patterns of Data

ONLINE
Video Tutorials and
Interactive Examples

1. (MP) **Use Structure** The histogram shows the fuel efficiency (in miles per gallon) for some automobiles. Describe the overall pattern of the distribution. What conclusion can you draw?

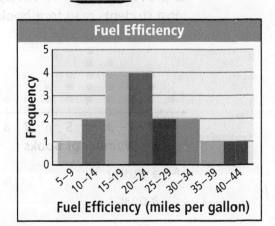

_____

_____

_____

_____

_____

2. Describe any clusters, gaps, deviations from the overall pattern, and peaks. State the mode. Draw a conclusion based on these patterns in the data.

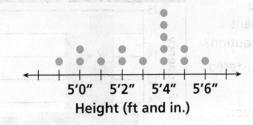

_____

_____

3. **Math on the Spot** The data set and dot plot display the grades of Professor Burger's students. Describe the shape of the data distribution.

Data Set	78	76	80	70	79	82	79	79	88
	74	78	82	79	75	80	83	84	76

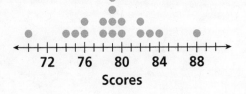

_____

_____

_____

© Houghton Mifflin Harcourt Publishing Company

Test Prep

4. The dot plot shows the distribution of books read last summer by students at the Parks School. Which pattern in the data helps you conclude that most students read four books?

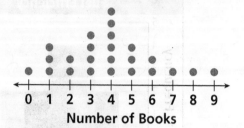

Number of Books

(A) a cluster

(B) a peak

(C) a gap

(D) no symmetry

5. In the survey from Problem 4, how many people were asked how many books they read last summer?

_____

6. The histogram shows the distribution of petal lengths for flowers in a botanical garden. What statement best summarizes the data distribution?

(A) Most petal lengths are clustered at 1–1.9 centimeters.

(B) There is a symmetry between the short and long petal lengths.

(C) The majority of petal lengths are greater than 3.9 centimeters.

(D) There is a gap between 2 and 3.4 centimeters.

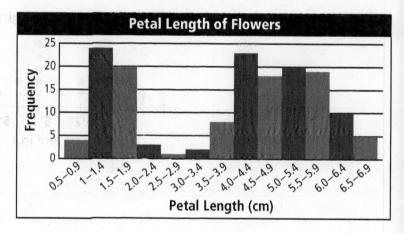

Spiral Review

7. Evaluate the expression for $x = 4$ and $y = 6$.

$4x - y + 15$

_____

8. Write an equation that models the data in the table.

x	1	2	3	4	5
y	7	14	21	28	35

9. Simplify the expression: $4a + 8 - 2a - 4 + 7b$.

_____

606

Name _____

Display Data in Box Plots

(I Can) make a box plot for a set of numerical data.

Spark Your Learning

Slavik is looking to buy new clothes for his best friend's weekend-long celebration. He wants to get the most for his money. He has gone to 7 stores and made a list of the prices for jeans, dress shirts, and sports jackets. He has $160 to spend. He needs to buy 1 of each item. What combination of items best fits his budget?

Store	Jeans	Dress shirt	Sports jacket
Addy's Fashions	$48	$38	$78
Garth's Warehouse	$39	$33	$69
Chester's Menswear	$29	$29	$54
L&P	$57	$45	$95
Dress to Impress	$68	$49	$89
Hallie's Superstore	$25	$20	$40
Kevin's Kicks and More	$33	$44	$85

Turn and Talk Why might it be better for Slavik to buy clothes that cost more, instead of buying all of his clothes at Hallie's Superstore?

Build Understanding

A **box plot** is a graph that shows how data are distributed by using the median, quartiles, least value and greatest value.

Connect to Vocabulary

The **lower quartile** is the median of the lower half of the data.

The **upper quartile** is the median of the upper half of the data.

1 ▷ Consider the prices for sports jackets that Slavik found: $78, $69, $54, $95, $89, $40, $85. Find the median, the lower quartile, and the upper quartile of the prices.

A. Explain how to find the median, then find the median.

_____

_____

_____

B. The lower quartile is the median of the lower half of the data or data to the left of the median. What is the lower half of the data? What is the lower quartile?

_____

_____

C. The upper quartile is the median of the upper half of the data or data to the right of the median. What is the upper half of the data? What is the upper quartile?

_____

_____

D. You can do Parts A to C by using the following display. Fill in the boxes with the prices in order from least to greatest.

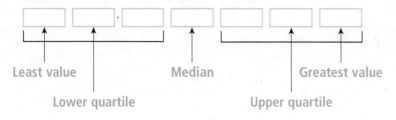

Least value   Median   Greatest value

Lower quartile   Upper quartile

E. So, the median is [ ], the lower quartile is [ ], and the upper quartile is [ ].

 Turn and Talk How would this process change if the data set had 8 values?

© Houghton Mifflin Harcourt Publishing Company

Step It Out

A box plot shows how the values in a data set are distributed, or spread out. It shows the data set divided into quarters, based on the quartiles and median.

2 The heights in feet of 10 roller coasters are 76, 35, 60, 42.5, 81, 79, 60, 78, 42, and 100. Make a box plot of these data.

A. Find the median, the lower and upper quartiles, the least value, and the greatest value. Start by ordering the data.

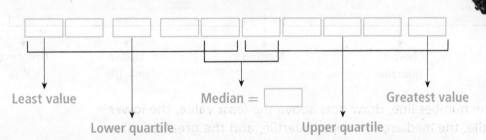

Least value

Lower quartile

Median =

Upper quartile

Greatest value

B. Draw the box plot above the number line. Start by putting dots above the least value, the lower quartile, the median, the upper quartile, and the greatest value. Then draw the box connecting the quartiles.

Draw a box connecting the quartiles.

Roller Coaster Heights

Draw a vertical line through the median.

35 40 45 50 55 60 65 70 75 80 85 90 95 100
Height (ft)

Draw segments connecting the least and greatest values to the box.

C. If the heights 122 feet and 127 feet were added to the data, how would the box plot change? Draw a new box plot to show the changes.

_____

Roller Coaster Heights

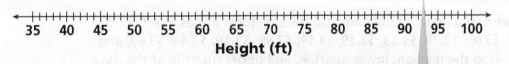

35 40 45 50 55 60 65 70 75 80 85 90 95 100 105 110 115 120 125 130
Height (ft)

3 The daily high temperatures for Cleveland, Ohio, for 15 days in December are: 66, 57, 56, 41, 34, 32, 35, 31, 34, 28, 23, 34, 30, 37, and 39 degrees Fahrenheit. Make a box plot to display the data.

Cleveland, Ohio

A. Find the median, the lower and upper quartiles, the least value, and the greatest value. Start by ordering the data.

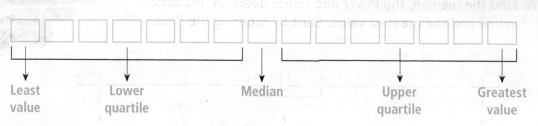

Least value   Lower quartile   Median   Upper quartile   Greatest value

B. On the number line, draw dots above the least value, the lower quartile, the median, the upper quartile, and the greatest value. Then draw a box and lines to complete the box plot.

December Temperatures in Cleveland, OH

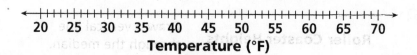

Temperature (°F)

Check Understanding

1. The price of a quart of soy milk at different stores are as listed: $2.99, $3.29, $3.09, $3.79, $3.59, $3.39, $3.59, $3.89, $3.19, $3.49, $3.69, and $3.29. Find the median, lower quartile, and upper quartile of the data.

2. The daily low temperature in degrees Farenheit for a week in Denver, Colorado, were: 37, 14, 23, 21, 27, 39, and 34. Make a box plot of the data.

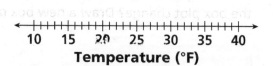

Temperature (°F)

3. The number of customers who entered a store each hour was recorded one Saturday: 5, 9, 15, 23, 27, 20, 16, 12, 14, and 18. Make a box plot of the data.

Number of Customers

On Your Own

4. **Geography** The heights (to the nearest foot) of coastal redwood trees over 340 feet tall are given below.

   359, 361, 363, 358, 368, 361, 366, 360,
   358, 359, 358, 366, 363, 364, 358, 363

   Giant sequoias in Kings Canyon National Park, CA

   A. Order the numbers from least to greatest.

   _____

   _____

   B. Find the median, lower quartile and upper quartile of the data set.

   Median: _____   Lower quartile: _____   Upper quartile: _____

5. The number of points a basketball player scored in each game this season so far are 16, 26, 23, 32, 19, 36, 18, 25, 30, 23, 47, 30, 16, 25, and 19.

   A. Find the median, lower quartile, and upper quartile of the data set.

   _____

   B. Make a box plot for the data set.

   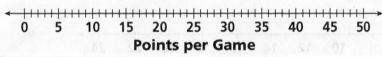

   Points per Game

6. (MP) **Use Structure** Describe the box plot using the lowest value, the quartiles, median, and the greatest value. What does the width of the box say about the data?

   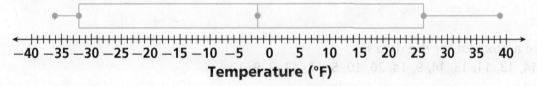

   Temperature (°F)

   _____

   _____

   _____

   _____

For Problems 7–8, find the median, lower quartile, and upper quartile of the data.

7. 27, 21, 24, 21, 26, 16, 24, 31, 0, 23   8. 4.9, 6.4, 3.6, 6.4, 4.6, 6.4, 4.2, 7.4

9. Andre likes to read a book in bed before he goes to sleep each night. For two weeks, he noted how many pages he read each night. He read 8, 12, 13, 6, 4, 19, 25, 7, 3, 18, 11, 15, 6, and 4 pages. Find the median, lower quartile and upper quartile of the data set. Then make a box plot for the data set.

_____

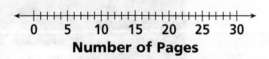

Number of Pages

10. (MP) **Attend to Precision** How can you find the median, lower quartile, and upper quartiles of a data set with 16 values? Explain.

_____

_____

_____

11. Open Ended Describe a situation that could be represented by the box plot shown.

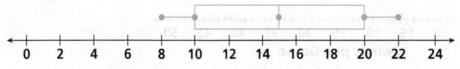

_____

_____

_____

12. Make a box plot for the data set.
11, 14, 13, 11, 13, 14, 9, 14, 20, 10, 5, 12, 17, 7, 9, 12

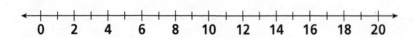

⬡ **I'm in a Learning Mindset!**

What steps did I use to find the upper and lower quartiles in Problem 5?

_____

_____

Display Data in Box Plots

1. Henry has taken a survey of the hourly wages of employees at a bakery. His results are shown. Find the median, lower quartile, and upper quartile of the data.

Hourly Wages ($)				
10.50	9.75	11.25	10.75	10.95
11.75	10.25	9.75	12.25	11.50

2. **STEM** A biologist is studying turkey vultures in Everglades National Park. Turkey vultures are one of the two vulture species native to the United States. The numbers of vultures the biologist spotted each day are 6, 9, 13, 8, 5, 12, 7, 18, 10, 14, 10 and 15. Make a box plot for the data set.

A turkey vulture has a wingspan of up to 6 feet.

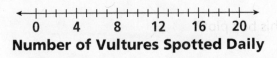
Number of Vultures Spotted Daily

3. **Math on the Spot** The number of matches won by a ping-pong team during each of the last 11 seasons are 7, 6, 8, 4, 0, 4, 8, 2, 3, 0, and 6. Use the data to make a box plot.

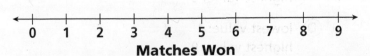
Matches Won

For Problems 4–5, find the median, lower quartile, and upper quartile of the data.

4. 5, 18, 7, 10, 14,
9, 2, 11, 13, 25, 16

5. 35, 28, 17, 60, 41, 36,
44, 55, 39, 50, 48, 19

6. Make a box plot for the data set.
25, 35, 5, 15, 85, 75, 65, 55, 45, 35, 25, 65, 75, 85

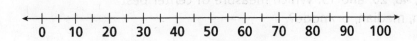

Test Prep

7. A softball team scored the following number of runs in the games they have played so far this year: 8, 5, 6, 9, 3, 1, 0, 4, 12, 14, 3, and 5. What are the lower and upper quartiles of these data?

   Ⓐ lower quartile = 1;
      upper quartile = 8.5

   Ⓒ lower quartile = 3;
      upper quartile = 8.5

   Ⓑ lower quartile = 1;
      upper quartile = 12

   Ⓓ lower quartile = 3;
      upper quartile = 12

8. Emile records the time he spends making dinner each night for 8 nights. What is the lower quartile of his data?

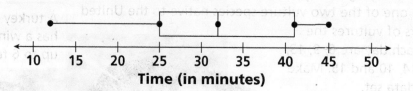

Time (in minutes)

9. What are the lowest and highest values on this box plot?

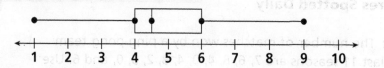

   Ⓐ lowest value: 1
      highest value: 6

   Ⓒ lowest value: 4
      highest value: 6

   Ⓑ lowest value: 4
      highest value: 9

   Ⓓ lowest value: 1
      highest value: 9

Spiral Review

10. Which of the following questions is a statistical question? Explain.

    • What time does school start at Lincoln Elementary?

    • What color is the principal's desk at King Middle School?

    • How did your classmates get to school today?

11. The number of hours Louisa worked each week over the summer were 19, 23, 18, 25, 16, 17, 21, 48, 20, and 13. Which measure of center best describes the data: mean, median, or mode?

Find Mean Absolute Deviation

(I Can) compute the MAD of a data set and use the MAD to describe data.

Step It Out

1 ▶ Helen and Jeff record the time, in minutes, they spent practicing piano this week.

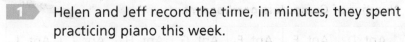 Piano Practice Chart (in minutes)					
Helen	35	25	30	20	40
Jeff	45	55	5	15	30

A. Compare the mean practice times for Helen and Jeff. Do the means help you to distinguish between the two sets of data? Explain.

_____

Connect to Vocabulary

Mean absolute deviation (MAD) is the mean of the distances between the data values and the mean of a data set.

B. You can use another statistical measure to compare two data sets, the mean absolute deviation, or MAD. To find MAD, first use absolute value to find the distance of each data value from the mean. Use the means you found in Part A.

Helen's times	35	25	30	20	40
Subtract	$\mid 35 - \_\_\_ \mid$	$\mid 25 - \_\_\_ \mid$	$\mid 30 - \_\_\_ \mid$	$\mid 20 - \_\_\_ \mid$	$\mid 40 - \_\_\_ \mid$
Distance from mean					
Jeff's times	45	55	5	15	30
Subtract	$\mid 45 - \_\_\_ \mid$	$\mid 55 - \_\_\_ \mid$	$\mid 5 - \_\_\_ \mid$	$\mid 15 - \_\_\_ \mid$	$\mid 30 - \_\_\_ \mid$
Distance from mean					

C. Find the mean absolute deviation for each data set by finding the mean of the distances in Part B.

D. Which data set has a greater mean absolute deviation? What does this tell you about the data?

_____

 Turn and Talk In Part B, why did you use absolute value to find the distance of each data value from the mean?

The mean absolute deviation (MAD) tells you the average distance of data values from the mean. It is a measure of how spread out, or varied, the data are. The data values whose distances to the mean are less than or equal to the MAD are *within the mean absolute deviation*.

2 ▶ Aaron surveyed the people in his apartment building to find out how many computers they owned. The mean of his data is 3 computers. The mean absolute deviation is 1.4. Find the values that fall within the MAD and the values that fall outside the MAD.

Number of Computers per Apartment									
Apt. A	Apt. B	Apt. C	Apt. D	Apt. E	Apt. F	Apt. G	Apt. H	Apt. I	Apt. J
1	5	3	2	7	3	2	1	2	4

A. Find the distance from the mean, 3, to each data value.

Value	1	5	3	2	7	3	2	1	2	4
Distance from mean										

B. If a data value's distance from the mean is less than or equal to the MAD of 1.4, then the value is *within the mean absolute deviation*. Which values from Aaron's survey fall within the mean absolute deviation?

_____

C. If a data value's distance from the mean is greater than the MAD of 1.4, then the value is *outside the mean absolute deviation*. Which values from Aaron's survey fall outside the mean absolute deviation?

_____

D. Another way to find the values that fall within the MAD is to add and subtract the MAD from the mean. This gives you the greatest and least values within the MAD. All values between the numbers will be within the MAD. For Aaron's data, find this range around the mean.

mean + MAD = 3 + ☐ = ☐   mean − MAD = 3 − ☐ = ☐

Values from _____ to _____ are within the MAD.

Check Understanding

For Problems 1–2, find the mean and the mean absolute deviation of each data set. Circle the values that fall within the mean absolute deviation.

1. 5 8 10 12 15 25 11 7 30 17   **2.** 9.5 10.5 11.25 10.75 9.25

Mean = _____ MAD = _____   Mean = _____ MAD = _____

Name _____

On Your Own

3. The table shows the number of hours two friends spent swimming laps each week. Which data set is more spread out?

	Week 1	Week 2	Week 3	Week 4	Week 5
Serena	6	11	10	8	5
Lisa	2	9	12	6	11

A. Find the mean for each data set.

_____

_____

B. Find the distance from the mean for each data value.

Serena's hours	6	11	10	8	5
Subtract	$\|6 - \_\_\_\_\|$	$\|11 - \_\_\_\_\|$	$\|10 - \_\_\_\_\|$	$\|8 - \_\_\_\_\|$	$\|5 - \_\_\_\_\|$
Distance from mean					

Lisa's hours	2	9	12	6	11
Subtract	$\|2 - \_\_\_\_\|$	$\|9 - \_\_\_\_\|$	$\|12 - \_\_\_\_\|$	$\|6 - \_\_\_\_\|$	$\|11 - \_\_\_\_\|$
Distance from mean					

C. (MP) **Attend to Precision** Calculate the MAD for both sets of data.

_____

_____

D. The data set for _____ is more spread out, because the mean

absolute deviation is _____ .

4. Ramon is a pumpkin farmer. He recorded the number of pumpkins he sold each week for 5 weeks. The mean is 782 pumpkins and the mean absolute deviation is 52. Give two possible values that are within the mean absolute deviation and two possible values that are outside the mean absolute deviation.

_____

_____

5. A group of people is being trained to standardize the scoring of diving competitions. The same dive was judged by 10 different trainees at the beginning and at the end of their training. The results are shown.

Scores at Beginning of Training									
7.5	8	10	6	9.5	6.5	8	8.5	9	9.5

Scores at End of Training									
8	8.5	9	7.5	8.5	8	8	8.5	8.5	8.5

A. Calculate the mean absolute deviation for the scores at the beginning of training.

B. Calculate the mean absolute deviation for the scores at the end of training.

C. Did the trainees make progress in standardizing their scores? Explain.

6. (MP) **Reason** Two students had the following scores on five history tests. Which set of scores shows more variation? Use the MADs to justify your answer.

Student A: 82, 90, 87, 91, 97

Student B: 84, 91, 89, 95, 91

Name _____

LESSON 18.3
More Practice/ Homework

ONLINE

Video Tutorials and
Interactive Examples

Find Mean Absolute Deviation

1. **STEM** A laboratory is studying brown anole lizards, which are native to Cuba and the Bahamas but are an invasive species in the southern United States from Florida to Texas. The length of 10 male lizards caught by researchers in Texas is shown in the table.

Length of Brown Anole Lizards (cm)				
17.9	20.3	20.1	20.2	18
19.4	18	20.2	20	17.9

Calculate the mean of the lengths of the lizards. Then calculate the mean absolute deviation.

A brown anole lizard

2. **Math on the Spot** Professor Burger ran the 50-yard dash four times and recorded his times in seconds as 6.8, 5.9, 6.2, and 6.7. What is the mean absolute deviation of Professor Burger's times?

_____

3. Several 2-pound bags of yellow onions at the supermarket are measured to see how much they actually weigh. Their weights are 2.1, 1.9, 2.3, 2.0, 2.4, 1.8, 2.1, and 2.2 pounds. What are the mean and the mean absolute deviation of the weights?

2.1 pounds

_____

_____

4. The mean of a data set is 9.4 and the mean absolute deviation is 1.2. List three data values that are within the MAD and three data values that are outside the MAD.

_____

_____

5. The mean of a data set is 4.5, and the mean absolute deviation is 0.8. Find the range around the mean that describes the values that fall within the mean absolute deviation.

_____

Test Prep

6. The prices of muesli cereal at different stores are shown in the table.

Cost ($)					
5.09	3.79	4.80	4.39	3.88	4.99

A. What is the mean price?

_____

B. What is the mean absolute deviation of the prices?

_____

7. The mean of a set of data is 4.03, and the mean absolute deviation is 2.69. Which data values are within the mean absolute deviation? Select all that apply.

Ⓐ 1.3   Ⓔ 5.8

Ⓑ 2.3   Ⓕ 6.7

Ⓒ 3.5   Ⓖ 7.5

Ⓓ 4.6   Ⓗ 8.6

8. Which of the following is closest to the mean absolute deviation of this data set: 2.1, 3.5, 4.6, 5.8, 3.9, 4.2, 2.8?

Ⓐ 0.89   Ⓒ 3.84

Ⓑ 1.6   Ⓓ 3.9

Spiral Review

9. What is the volume of a rectangular prism that is $3\frac{1}{2}$ inches wide, $5\frac{1}{2}$ inches long, and 9 inches high?

_____

10. Tyler collects data about how many animal companions (dogs, cats, birds, and so on) live at each house in his neighborhood. The numbers of animal companions are 1, 0, 2, 3, 2, 4, 12, 1, 2, and 3. Find the mean, median, and mode. What measure of center best describes the typical number of animal companions per household in his neighborhood? Explain.

_____

_____

_____

_____

_____

Name _____

Explore Measures of Variability

A Wi-Fi router

(I Can) interpret the range, IQR, and MAD of a data set.

Step It Out

A **measure of variability** is a single number used to describe how the values in a data set are spread out or vary. You have already learned about one measure of variability, the mean absolute deviation (MAD). Two other measures of variability are the range and the interquartile range.

1 The distributions of prices for Wi-Fi routers at two stores are shown in the box plots. Find and compare the ranges and interquartile ranges of the prices at each store.

Connect to Vocabulary

The **range** is the difference between the greatest and least values in a data set.

The **interquartile range (IQR)** is the difference between the upper and lower quartiles in a data set.

Wi-Fi Routers at Store A

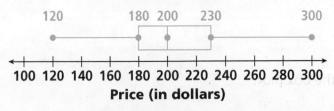

Price (in dollars)

Wi-Fi Routers at Store B

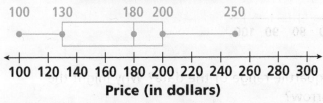

Price (in dollars)

A. To find the range, subtract the least value from the greatest value.

Range for Store A

$300 - 120 =$ ☐

Range for Store B

$250 -$ ☐ $=$ ☐

B. To find the IQR, subtract the lower quartile from the upper quartile.

IQR for Store A

$230 - 180 =$ ☐

IQR for Store B

$200 -$ ☐ $=$ ☐

C. Compare the ranges and the interquartile ranges for the two stores.

Store A has a greater _____, but

Store B has a greater _____.

Turn and Talk Can you tell the exact price of any of the routers at the two stores? If so, explain how.

© Houghton Mifflin Harcourt Publishing Company • Image Credit: ©Nelia Sapronova/Shutterstock

2 The number of visitors each day last week at a train exhibit hosted by a local museum were 29, 3, 45, 33, 30, 38, and 25 visitors.

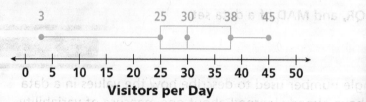

Visitors per Day

A. The range of the data is _____ visitors.

B. The interquartile range (IQR) of the data is _____ visitors.

C. Looking at the shape of the data distribution, which measure of variability, range or IQR, better describes how the values vary? Explain.

_____

_____

Check Understanding

1. Consider the data set shown in the box plot.

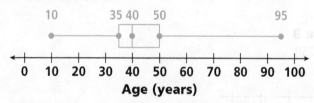

Age (years)

A. What are the range and interquartile range of the data? Why might the range be wide but the IQR narrow?

_____

_____

B. Compare the range and the IQR of the data in this plot with the range and the IQR from Part A.

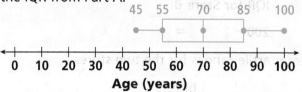

Age (years)

_____

2. A new swimming club has just started. The ages, in years, of its members are 39, 27, 51, 42, 33, 73, 49, and 46. What are the range and IQR of these data? Does one of these measures better describe how the values vary? Explain.

_____

_____

On Your Own

For Problems 3–6, use the box plot below. It summarizes the number of goals per game for one team in a field hockey tournament.

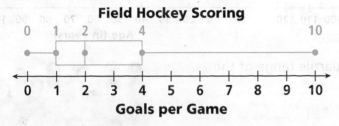

Field Hockey Scoring

Goals per Game

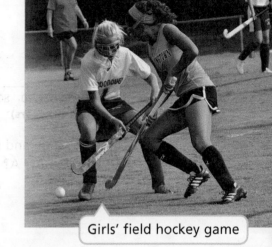

Girls' field hockey game

3. The range of the data is _____ goals.

The interquartile range of the data is _____ goals.

4. Looking at the shape of the distribution, which measure of variability, the range or the IQR, better describes how the values vary? Explain.

_____

_____

_____

5. Name one measure of variability for the data and give its value. What does this measure of variability tell you about the goals per game?

_____

_____

6. (MP) **Reason** Why might the range be wide but the IQR narrow?

_____

_____

_____

For Problems 7–8, find the range and interquartile range (IQR) for each box plot.

7.

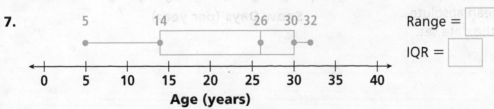

Age (years)

Range = ☐

IQR = ☐

8.

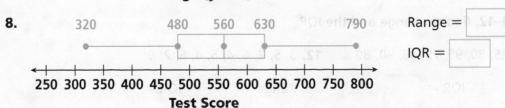

Test Score

Range = ☐

IQR = ☐

9. The box plots summarize data about the ages of the people who live in two counties.

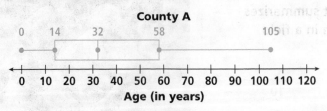

County A

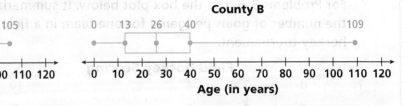

County B

A. What are the range and interquartile range of the population in County A?

_____

_____

B. What are the range and interquartile range of the population in County B?

_____

Ages vary from 0 to 105 in County A.

C. How do the range and interquartile range of the populations in the two counties compare?

_____

_____

D. (MP) **Reason** Which data set is likely to have the greater mean absolute deviation? Explain.

_____

_____

10. **Open Ended** Write a data set with 10 data values that could have the box plot shown. Then find the range, interquartile range, and mean absolute deviation of the data set.

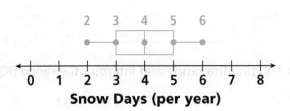

Snow Days (per year)

_____

_____

For Problems 11–12, find the range and the IQR.

11. 45, 85, 70, 25, 80, 95, 75, 85, 90, 80

Range = ☐   IQR = ☐

12. 3, 5, 2, 6, 4, 5, 4, 6, 2, 6

Range = ☐   IQR = ☐

Explore Measures of Variability

1. Darren counts the number of devices that are plugged into the
   wall in each room of his house and records them in a list:
   1, 2, 0, 6, 5, 3, 4, 3. What are the range and IQR of the data set?

   _____

2. During a gray September, the amounts of rainfall in
   millimeters per day over six days are 9.6, 3.7, 0.8, 6.2, 14.2,
   and 12.4. Find the range and interquartile range of the
   amounts of rainfall. Does one measure give you a better
   idea of how the values vary than the other? Explain.

   _____

   _____

   _____

14.2 millimeters rainfall today

3. The ages of people who competed in a road race last weekend are shown
   in the box plots. Interpret the differences in the range and the IQR for
   both groups to come to a conclusion about the runners.

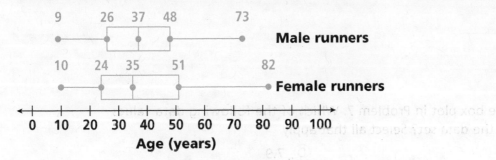

   _____

   _____

   _____

   _____

4. **Math on the Spot** Find the interquartile range for the data set. _____

   Data Set: 11, 5, 16, 20, 31, 27, 9, 15, 26

5. **Open Ended** Name a measure of variability and explain how it is
   calculated.

   _____

   _____

Test Prep

6. The box plot shows the number of grams of protein in several brands of protein bars. What are the range and interquartile range of the data?

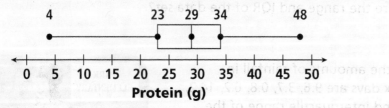

Protein (g)

Range = _____ grams

IQR = _____ grams

7. What are the range and interquartile range for the data set?

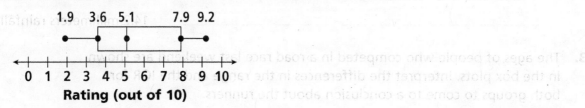

Rating (out of 10)

Range = _____

IQR = _____

8. Refer to the box plot in Problem 7. Which of the following data values *must* be in the data set? Select all that apply.

Ⓐ 1.9   Ⓓ 7.9

Ⓑ 3.6   Ⓔ 9.2

Ⓒ 5.1

Spiral Review

9. Juana and her friends have collected shells from the beach. The numbers of shells collected by each person are 4, 9, 7, 5, 12, 8, 6, and 5. What is the mean number of shells collected?

_____

10. A college student made videos showing his dorm life each week for two months. The numbers of weekly videos he recorded were 3, 9, 5, 2, 14, 6, 7, 5, and 8. What is the median number of weekly videos he recorded?

_____

Name _____

Describe Distributions

(I Can) choose an appropriate display for a data set and
compute the measures of center and variability.

Step It Out

1 ▶ The table shows the distance some students at Valley
Middle School live from a shopping mall.

Distance (miles)	0.01–2	2.01–4	4.01–6	6.01–8	8.01–10	10.01–12	12.01–14
Frequency (number of people)	2	4	6	9	8	5	1

A. What statistical question might these data have been collected to answer?

_____

_____

B. The histogram shows the data from the table. Describe the distribution
of the data by identifying clusters, peaks, gaps, and symmetry.

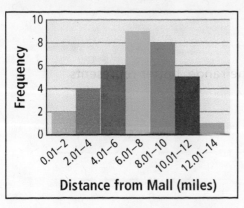

Distance from Mall (miles)

_____

_____

C. Draw one conclusion about the survey results based on a fact from
Part B. Explain.

_____

_____

 Turn and Talk What are the advantages and disadvantages of using a
histogram to analyze data?

The table below shows the daily high temperature in degrees Fahrenheit during Maria's 8-day family vacation.

Day	1	2	3	4	5	6	7	8
Temperature (°F)	40	66	72	75	80	72	66	77

A. Complete the box plot.

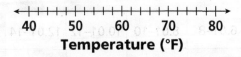

Temperature (°F)

B. Find each measure.

Mean: _____ Median: _____

Lower quartile: _____ Upper quartile: _____

Interquartile range: _____ Range: _____

C. Which measure of center, median or mean, better represents these data? Explain your reasoning.

_____

_____

D. Which measure of variability, the IQR or the range, better represents how the values vary? Explain.

_____

_____

Check Understanding

Draw one conclusion from the data. State whether you used a measure of center or fact about the shape or spread of the data to draw your conclusion.

1. **Mrs. Sanchez's Period 1 Math Quiz Results**

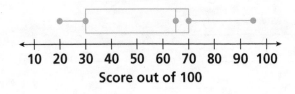

Score out of 100

2. **Hours Exercising per Week**

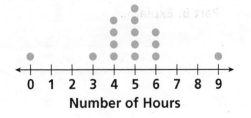

Number of Hours

_____

_____

On Your Own

3. The table shows the number of hours spent engaged in physical activity each week for 50 sixth-grade students.

Time (hours)	0–1.9	2–3.9	4–5.9	6–7.9	8–9.9	10–11.9
Frequency	3	6	8	10	13	10

A. What statistical question might these data have been collected to answer?

B. Why is a histogram a good way to show the data?

C. Complete the histogram to display the data.

D. Describe the distribution of data based on your histogram.

Time Spent in Physical Activity

Frequency

14
12
10
8
6
4
2
0

0–1.9 2–3.9 4–5.9 6–7.9 8–9.9 10–11.9

Time (hours)

E. **Open Ended** Write a statement that summarizes the data. Did you use a measure of variability, a measure of center, or the shape of the distribution as the basis for your statement? Explain.

4. The table summarizes the grade point averages (GPAs) for twelve students in the school band.

Student GPA's
4.0, 2.0, 2.33, 3.33, 3.67, 3.0, 2.67, 3.67, 3.0, 4.0, 2.67, 3.0

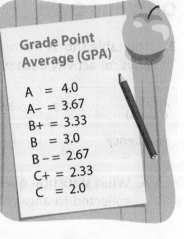

Grade Point Average (GPA)

A = 4.0
A− = 3.67
B+ = 3.33
B = 3.0
B− = 2.67
C+ = 2.33
C = 2.0

A. What statistical question might these data have been collected to answer?

_____

_____

B. Why might a box plot be a good way to display data about grade point averages?

_____

_____

_____

C. (MP) **Attend to Precision** Draw a box plot to display the data.

D. Describe the distribution of data based on your box plot.

_____

_____

_____

E. Write two or three sentences summarizing the data.

_____

_____

_____

_____

_____

_____

Name

LESSON 18.5
More Practice/ Homework

ONLINE
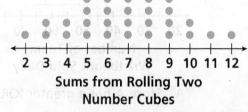
Video Tutorials and
Interactive Examples

Describe Distributions

1. The dot plot shows the sums of two number cubes for 36 rolls. Describe the distribution of the data. Which measure or measures of center best describe the data? Explain.

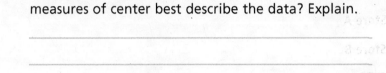

Sums from Rolling Two
Number Cubes

_____

_____

_____

_____

2. The histogram shows the age distribution for members in a small community band. Write a summary of the data. Be sure to consider the occurrence of peaks or gaps.

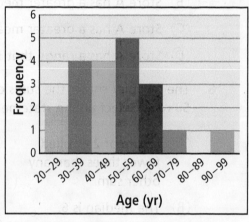

Age (yr)

_____

_____

3. **(MP) Construct Arguments** The box plot shows the annual snow depth for a ski resort over several winter seasons. Write a summary of the data. Draw one conclusion from a measure of variability or a measure of center. Explain how you reached your conclusion.

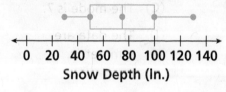

Snow Depth (In.)

_____

_____

_____

_____

_____

_____

4. Find the mean, median, and mode of the data shown in the dot plot. Which measure of center best describes the distribution? Explain.

Number of Books Read

_____

_____

_____

_____

Test Prep

5. The box plots show the distributions of wristbands sold at two stores for a local team. Which statement best describes the distributions for the stores?

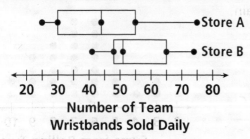

Number of Team Wristbands Sold Daily

Ⓐ Store A has a greater IQR than store B.

Ⓑ Store A has a greater median than store B.

Ⓒ Store A has a greater mean than store B.

Ⓓ Store A has a range that is less than that of store B.

6. The dot plot shows the sums of two number cubes for 50 rolls. Select all the statements that are true.

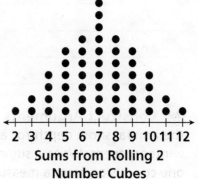

Sums from Rolling 2 Number Cubes

Ⓐ A sum of 2 is rolled fewer times than any other sum.

Ⓑ The median is 6.

Ⓒ The mode is 7.

Ⓓ The data are symmetric.

Ⓔ The shape of the distribution suggests that most sums are 8 or more.

Ⓕ 50% of the rolls are less than 8.

Ⓖ Most of the rolls are greater than 7.

Spiral Review

7. What is the opposite of −6?

8. Write an equation that models the data in the table below.

x	1	2	3	4	5
y	5.5	11	16.5	22	27.5

9. A parallelogram has a base length of 17 centimeters. The area is 85 square centimeters. What is the height of the parallelogram?

Review

Vocabulary

Choose the correct term from the Vocabulary box.

© Houghton Mifflin Harcourt Publishing Company

Vocabulary

box plot
interquartile range (IQR)
lower quartile
mean absolute deviation (MAD)
measure of variability
range
upper quartile

1. The mean distance of the data values from the mean of a

   data set is called the _____.

2. A _____ is a graph that shows
   the distribution of data using the median, quartiles, least
   value, and greatest value.

3. The median of the lower half of a data set is called the

   _____.

4. A single value used to describe how the values in a data set are spread out

   is a _____.

5. The _____ is the median of the upper half of a
   data set.

6. The difference between the greatest and least values in a data set is

   the _____.

7. The _____ is the difference between the upper
   and lower quartiles in a data set.

Concepts and Skills

8. (MP) **Use Tools** Give a set of 10 data values that has a mode of
   2, a gap between 2 and 5, and a cluster from 5 to 7. State what strategy
   and tool you will use to answer the question, explain your choice, and
   then find the answer.

   _____

   _____

9. Look at the histogram. Which statement best describes the data
   shown in the graph?

   (A) The data have a peak at 13 to 16.

   (B) The data have an outlier at 0 and 10.

   (C) The data have a cluster from 13 to 20.

   (D) The data are approximately symmetric.

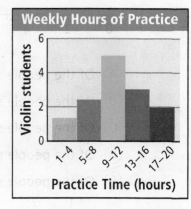

Weekly Hours of Practice

Practice Time (hours)

For Problems 10–15, use the following information.

Eight stores at the mall sell the same style of pants. The prices of the pants are $32, $35, $40, $38, $42, $37, $36, $80.

10. What is the median of the prices? _____

11. What is the lower quartile of the prices? _____

12. What is the upper quartile of the prices? _____

13. What is the range of the prices? _____

14. What is the interquartile range of the prices? _____

15. Does the range or the interquartile range better represent how the prices vary? Explain.

_____

_____

For Problems 16–19, use the dot plot. Round to the nearest tenth.

16. What is the mean of the data? _____

17. What is the mean absolute deviation of the data? _____

18. What is the median of the data? _____

19. Circle the points for the data values that fall within the mean absolute deviation.

20. Which statements describe the distribution of the data in the box plot? Select all that apply.

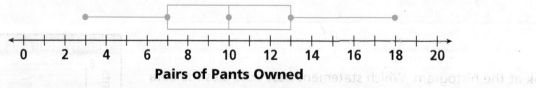

Pairs of Pants Owned

Ⓐ Of the people surveyed, $\frac{1}{2}$ own 7 to 13 pairs of pants.

Ⓑ Of the people surveyed, $\frac{1}{4}$ own 3 to 10 pairs of pants.

Ⓒ Of the people surveyed, $\frac{1}{2}$ own 13 to 18 pairs of pants.

Ⓓ Of the people surveyed, $\frac{1}{4}$ own 3 to 7 pairs of pants.

Ⓔ Of the people surveyed, $\frac{3}{4}$ own 10 to 18 pairs of pants.

UNIT 1

MODULE 1, LESSON 1
On Your Own

11. 1 13. −8

15. and 17.

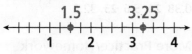

1.5   3.25

19.

−7 −4 2   2 4 7

2 °F is the opposite of −2 °F, −4 °F is the opposite of 4 °F, 7 °F is the opposite of −7 °F.

21.

−5 −2   4.5   10

23. 4.5 25. $2\frac{3}{4}$

More Practice/Homework

1A. 3 feet and −10 feet B. The opposite of 3 feet is −3 feet, which represents 3 feet below the surface of the water. The opposite of −10 feet is 10 feet, which represents 10 feet above the surface of the water.

3.

−1.7   −0.5   0.5   1.7
−0.3 0.3

5. 2 7. $\frac{1}{2}$ 9. C

11. A: −5; B: 0; C: −1; D: 4

13. A, B, D, E 15. < 17. >

MODULE 1, LESSON 2
On Your Own

3A.

−1.2   0.8 1.5   2.5
−1.25

B. >; <; > C. 2.5 > −1.25

5A.

Points of Interest	
Name	Location
City Park	−0.52
Courthouse	−1.5
Bookstore	1.25
Museum	0.75

B. The city park is to the left of the library; |−0.52| > |0|.

C. The bookstore is to the right of the courthouse; |1.25| < |−1.5|.
D. The museum is to the left of the bookstore; |0.75| < |1.25|.

9. > 11. <

More Practice/Homework

1A.   −1.3   −0.5   0.9   1.2

B. greater; right; less; left

3. $-\frac{6}{20}$ $-\frac{1}{20}$ $\frac{1}{20}$ $\frac{6}{20}$; <; >

5. $-\frac{2}{5}$ > −0.5; −0.5 < $-\frac{2}{5}$

7. A, B, D 9. 4,500 11. $6\frac{1}{2}$ feet

MODULE 1, LESSON 3
On Your Own

3A. Andy B. 6 miles 5. −234 °F
7. 1 9. 0

More Practice/Homework

1. The change from Monday to Tuesday 3. The Wednesday night game 5. −2 7. −4.05 9. 3.45
11. $\left|-\frac{1}{8}\right|$ 13. D 15. C 17. 228
19. 6.22

MODULE 1, LESSON 4
On Your Own

3A. 6 items B. 8; 9
C. 6; 6(8) + 6(9); 6(17) 5. $\frac{1}{3}$ > $\frac{1}{30}$ or $\frac{10}{30}$ > $\frac{1}{30}$ 7. potato salad 9. $\frac{15}{40}$, $\frac{4}{40}$; $\frac{15}{40}$ > $\frac{4}{40}$ or $\frac{4}{40}$ < $\frac{15}{40}$ 13. the key and the bowl 15. 60 17. 45 19. 8 21. 18 23. < 25. $\frac{24}{18}$ < $\frac{25}{15}$ or $\frac{25}{15}$ > $\frac{24}{18}$ 27. $-\frac{15}{21}$ < $-\frac{18}{42}$ or $-\frac{18}{42}$ > $-\frac{15}{21}$ 29. $\frac{11}{28}$ < $\frac{5}{12}$ or $\frac{5}{12}$ > $\frac{11}{28}$

More Practice/Homework

1. Martha; $\frac{5}{8}$ > $\frac{6}{15}$ or $\frac{6}{15}$ < $\frac{5}{8}$
3. after 30 minutes and after 60 minutes 5. 4 7. 6 9. $\frac{3}{21}$ < $\frac{14}{21}$; $\frac{1}{7}$ < $\frac{2}{3}$
11. $\frac{16}{24}$ > $\frac{12}{24}$; $\frac{4}{6}$ > $\frac{4}{8}$
13. $-\frac{14}{21}$ < $-\frac{3}{9}$ or $-\frac{3}{9}$ > $-\frac{14}{21}$ 15. B
17. 91 minutes 19. −10 21. 18

MODULE 1, LESSON 5
On Your Own

3. $\frac{1}{3}$, 0.5, $\frac{4}{6}$, $\frac{4}{5}$ 5. $-\frac{4}{5}$, −0.5, $\frac{3}{10}$, 0.7
7. −2.1, $-\frac{9}{10}$, 0.7, $1\frac{2}{5}$
9. $-4\frac{4}{10}$, $-1\frac{2}{5}$, 0, 1.2
11. −6, −4, 3.5, $6\frac{1}{3}$

More Practice/Homework

1. −2.7°, −2.65°, −0.1°, 0.09°, 1.48° 3. 0.01, 0.07, 0.38, $\frac{5}{10}$, $\frac{12}{10}$
5. $-4\frac{1}{2}$, −4.22, 0.8, $\frac{4}{3}$, 8.4
7. −3.25, 2.6, 5.75
9. −0.5, −0.41, $\frac{2}{4}$, $\frac{3}{5}$, $1\frac{1}{3}$ 11. <

MODULE 2, LESSON 1
On Your Own

7. 4 containers 9. 4 days
11. $2\frac{20}{25}$, or $2\frac{4}{5}$ Ångströms
13. $\frac{40}{10}$, or 4 cups that each hold $\frac{1}{5}$ liter 15. 10 earrings; 5,333 earrings 17. $\frac{5}{1}$, or 5 19. $\frac{9}{4}$
21. $\frac{12}{3}$, or 4 23. $\frac{55}{45}$, or $1\frac{2}{9}$
25. $\frac{35}{70}$, or $\frac{1}{2}$ 27. $\frac{45}{30}$, or $1\frac{1}{2}$

More Practice/Homework

1. 16 books 3. $\frac{3}{8} \div \frac{3}{4} = \frac{3}{8} \times \frac{4}{3} = \frac{12}{24} = \frac{1 \times 12}{2 \times 12} = \frac{1}{2}$; $\frac{3}{8} \div \frac{3}{4} = \frac{3}{8} \div \frac{6}{8} = \frac{3}{6} = \frac{1}{2}$ 5. $\frac{8}{7}$ 7. $\frac{1}{12}$ 9. $\frac{24}{8}$, or 3
11. $\frac{120}{8}$, or 15 13. $\frac{300}{18}$, or $\frac{50}{3}$
15. $\frac{14}{8}$, or $1\frac{3}{4}$ half cups
17. 2 small toys 19. −8 °F; −8 °F
21. −2.5, $-2\frac{1}{3}$, $-\frac{9}{4}$, 0, $2\frac{1}{2}$

MODULE 2, LESSON 2
On Your Own

3. $1\frac{1}{4}$ hours 5. $6\frac{1}{5}$ feet
7. 7 pieces 9. $\frac{26}{15}$, or $1\frac{11}{15}$
11. $\frac{6}{19}$ 13. 26 tarts 15. 34 tiles
17. $\frac{37}{8} \times \frac{2}{5}$ 19. $\frac{27}{5} \times \frac{8}{15}$

More Practice/Homework

1. 4 pieces 3. $\frac{3}{10}$ pound
5. 18 days 7. $\frac{11}{12}$ 9. $\frac{20}{21}$
11. $\frac{7}{10}$ 13. A 15. C 17. $\frac{16}{15}$, or $1\frac{1}{15}$

MODULE 2, LESSON 3
On Your Own
9. 7 cans 11. $42\frac{1}{4}$ square inches
13. $5\frac{3}{5}$ feet 15. $6\frac{3}{4}$ pounds
17. 52 plants 19. $3\frac{1}{10}$ 21. 6
23. $3\frac{1}{11}$

More Practice/Homework
1. twenty-six $1\frac{1}{2}$-pound bags
3. $5\frac{2}{3}$ feet 5. $12\frac{1}{2}$ 7. $10\frac{1}{4}$ 9. $2\frac{2}{3}$
11. B, D 13. B 15. $\frac{1}{2}$ 17. $\frac{3}{10}$

MODULE 2, LESSON 4
On Your Own
7. $1\frac{7}{12}$ pounds, subtraction
9A. $1\frac{1}{4}$ pints each B. $\frac{15}{16}$ pint each
11. 12 13. $7\frac{3}{10}$
15. Patty rides $6\frac{7}{12}$ miles.
17. 8 sixteenth notes 19. $6\frac{3}{4}$ 21. $\frac{2}{5}$
23. $5\frac{1}{12}$ hours 25. $4\frac{7}{8}$ cups
27. $5\frac{1}{9}$ 29. $3\frac{1}{3}$

More Practice/Homework
1. $5\frac{2}{5}$ hours 3. $\frac{19}{60}$
5. $1\frac{1}{2}$ pounds 7. $2\frac{13}{30}$ 9. $\frac{36}{37}$
11. $6\frac{1}{3}$ 13. C, E 15. A
17. 1.43

MODULE 3, LESSON 1
On Your Own
3. 1.21 miles 5. Add or
subtract from right to left.
7B. 320 squares C. 3.2 or 3.20
9. 4.231 11. 0.429 13. Write a
zero in the thousandths decimal
place of the number with two
decimal places to line up the
decimal places. 15. no
17. 3.58 19. 0.908

More Practice/Homework
1. 9.05 hours 3. 1.49 5. 8.94
seconds 7. 0.014 9. 3.64
11. 0.423 13. 6.942 15. 4.71
seconds 17. $\frac{3}{10}$ 19. $-12 < -2$ or
$-2 > -12$

MODULE 3, LESSON 2
On Your Own
3. 52.7 minutes 5A. 0.595 square
mile B. 0.6 C. 0.357 square mile
7. 0.32   0.4

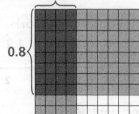

9. 40.29 11. If my product is a
lot greater or a lot less than my
estimate, I know I need to go
back and check the total number
of decimal places in the factors.
13. Multiply as you would with
whole numbers but count the
number of decimal places in the
factors. Make sure the product
has the same number of decimal
places. 15. 95.12 17. 68.643

More Practice/Homework
1. 65.7 inches 3. no 5. $2.29
7. 0.1686 9. 9.398 11. 10.87294
13. 0.414 inch 15. C 17. 4 days

MODULE 3, LESSON 3
On Your Own
3A. 36 boxes B. 1 box with
80 shirts 5. 23 liters 7. no
9. 50; 44 11. 64; 58; 2
13. 5; 4; 13 15. 16 school buses
17. 14 offices 19. 15 21. 19
23. 11 R200

More Practice/Homework
1. 19 reams 3. About 7.6
American football fields tall
5. 58 teams 7. 25 R 135 9. 17
11. 10 acres 13. $27 15. C
17. *M* and *P*

MODULE 3, LESSON 4
On Your Own
3. 9 members 5. 9 boxes 7. 5.8
9. 8.4 11. 32.6 13. 8.9 m
15. 57.8 miles per hour 17. $3.50
per pound 19. 0.38; 0.38; 0.38;
0.38 21. 5.6 23. 32.6

More Practice/Homework
1. 5 bookcases 3. 23.6 oz bottle
5. 7 miles per hour 7. 0.3 9. 12.6
11. 71 quarters 13. 3 bags
15. A, C, F 17. 238 boxes
19. 31.25 feet

MODULE 3, LESSON 5
On Your Own
5. $34.79 7. Gael did not line
up the decimal points in the
numbers. He actually harvested
84.75 pounds of potatoes.
9. 9 days 11. 0.525 centimeter
13. 0.5270 second 15. 47.4 ounces
17. 14.34 miles 19. 17.81
21. 7.15 23. 6.16

More Practice/Homework
1. $0.49 per ounce 3. 2 grams
5. 246.5 seconds 7. 7.6 cm
9. 9 homes 11. 26.1 hours 13. $\frac{8}{5}$
15. −86 meters

MODULE 4, LESSON 1
On Your Own
3.

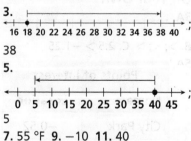

38
5.

5
7. 55 °F 9. −10 11. 40

More Practice/Homework
1. $750 3. decrease; 10 degrees;
endothermic 5. no 7. $47
9. positive 11. 7.658 13. $11.45

MODULE 4, LESSON 2

On Your Own

3. 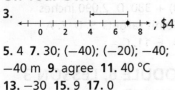 ; $4

5. 4 **7.** 30; (−40); (−20); −40;
−40 m **9.** agree **11.** 40 °C
13. −30 **15.** 9 **17.** 0

More Practice/Homework

1. −4
3.
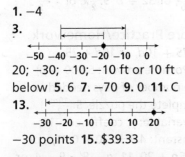
20; −30; −10; −10 ft or 10 ft
below **5.** 6 **7.** −70 **9.** 0 **11.** C
13.
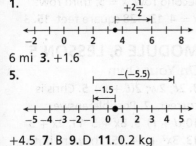
−30 points **15.** $39.33

MODULE 4, LESSON 3

On Your Own

5. −5 + 13 + (−5) = 3 **7.** 40 °F
9.

    +4

−3 −2 −1 0 1 2 3 ;
Evan added $2\frac{1}{2}$ + 4 instead of
$\left(-2\frac{1}{2}\right)$ + 4. The correct answer
is $1\frac{1}{2}$. **11B.** $19.25 **13.** Possible
answer: $-1\frac{1}{4}$; $\frac{1}{2}$ **15.** Possible
answer: −5; 5 **17.** increase of 7 °F

More Practice/Homework

1.

        +2½

−2 0 2 4 6 8
6 mi **3.** +1.6
5.
        −(−5.5)

      −1.5

−5 −4 −3 −2 −1 0 1 2 3 4 5
+4.5 **7.** B **9.** D **11.** 0.2 kg

MODULE 5, LESSON 1

On Your Own

3. −10 + (−15); She owes
$25. **5.** 11.50 + 0.25; $11.75
7. 3 **9.** $-\frac{13}{14}$ **11.** $3\frac{1}{2}$ **13.** −11 + 5;
6 floors **15.** $22\frac{1}{8} + \left(-16\frac{1}{5}\right) = 5\frac{37}{40}$;

$5\frac{37}{40}$, or 5.925 miles **17.** −46
19. $-12\frac{1}{8}$ **21.** 9.26

More Practice/Homework

1A. $75\frac{1}{2} + \left(-92\frac{1}{4}\right)$ **B.** $-16\frac{3}{4}$ ft, or
$16\frac{3}{4}$ ft below **3.** 28 + (−9);
$19 profit **5.** 15 **7.** 13.84 **9.** $-7\frac{17}{35}$
11. 0 **13.** 46.72 + (−24.61);
$22.11 **15.** C **17.** $-2\frac{1}{3}$ **19.** $9.49

MODULE 5, LESSON 2

On Your Own

5. −15 − 2; "−17 °F"
7A. −56.2 − 27.7; −83.9 points
9. 15.50 − 5.37; $10.13
11. 26 units **13.** 0.67 unit
15. 65.02 − (−9.78); $74.80
17. 41.7 + (−41.7); 0
19. $-13\frac{1}{4} + 10\frac{3}{4}$; $-2\frac{1}{2}$
21. 21.85 + (−6.03); 15.82
23. 0 + 5; 5

More Practice/Homework

1. 23 − (−12); 35 °F
3. $3\frac{1}{3} - 1\frac{2}{3}$; $1\frac{2}{3}$ mi **5.** $\frac{5}{12}$ **7.** −259
9. C **11.** 14,505 − (−282);
14,787 ft **13.** 32 **15.** 8.9 miles

MODULE 5, LESSON 3

On Your Own

7. The balance in his checking
account decreases by $500.
9. negative **11.** negative
13. negative **15.** −160 **17.** 90
19. 2 **21.** $\frac{1}{7}$ **23.** −6
25A.

−16 −14 −12 −10 −8 −6 −4 −2 0 2 4
−2 **B.** Negative

More Practice/Homework

1. Overall, missed landings on
aerial cartwheels lowered the
scores by 10 points. **3.** positive
5. negative **7.** Possible answer:
Let −10 ÷ (−5) = n. Then −10 =
−5 × n. For −5 × n to be
negative, n must be positive.
9. 43 **11.** $-4\frac{2}{3}$

13. A, C **15.** $43.52
17.

−8 −6 −4 −2 0 2 4 ; 1

MODULE 5, LESSON 4

On Your Own

5A. 0.45 h **B.** 23.4 mi
7A.

Fraction	Decimal
$\frac{1}{8}$	0.125
$\frac{2}{8}$	0.250
$\frac{3}{8}$	0.375

Possible answer: Each decimal
is 0.125 more than the previous
decimal. **B.** yes **9.** −8.5; Each
charge decreased the value of
the gift card by $8.50. **11.** 0.625
13. 0.777..., or $0.\overline{7}$
15. 10.3636..., or $10.\overline{36}$
17. Possible answer: $\frac{3}{-5}$, $-\left(\frac{3}{5}\right)$
19. Possible answer: $-7\frac{3}{5}$ =
$-\frac{38}{5} = \frac{-38}{5}$, −38 and 5 are
integers. **21.** −7.5

More Practice/Homework

1A. 0.5625 pound **B.** $13.50
3. 4.875 **5.** −0.6 **7.** −5.4
9A.

Fraction	Decimal
$\frac{1}{9}$	0.111...
$\frac{2}{9}$	0.222...
$\frac{3}{9}$	0.333...

Possible answer: Each decimal is
0.111... more than the previous
decimal. **B.** yes **11.** The values,
in order, are −8, 8, 6, and −6.
13. −11 + (−13) = −24; the
price decreased by $24 over the
two years.

MODULE 5, LESSON 5

On Your Own

3A. −3.76 °F; when elevation
increases by 0.2 mile,
temperature drops about 3.76 °F.

B. 3.76 °F; when elevation decreases by 0.2 mile, temperature increases about 3.76 °F. **C.** The temperature changes are opposites. **5.** $-12\frac{1}{2}$ feet per minute **7.** 5 containers; Possible answer: The quotient is $5\frac{1}{4}$ containers. So he can fill 5 whole containers and he'll have $\frac{1}{4} \times \frac{2}{3} = \frac{1}{6}$ cup of blueberries left over.

9. $\frac{\frac{-2}{4}}{\frac{-3}{4}}$, or $\frac{\frac{-1}{2}}{\frac{-3}{4}}$; $\frac{\frac{-1}{2}}{\frac{-3}{4}} = \frac{-1}{2} \div \frac{-3}{4} = \frac{-1}{2} \times \frac{4}{-3} = \frac{2}{3}$, and 2 and 3 are integers. **11.** $\frac{35}{36}$ **13.** -0.7 **15.** -0.8

More Practice/Homework

1. -20 ft **3A.** $4(3)(-12.50) = -150$; $-\$150$ **B.** 1 and 7, 2 and 6, 3 and 5, 4 and 4, 5 and 3, 6 and 2, 7 and 1 **C.** 9 **5.** $\frac{3}{2}$, or $1\frac{1}{2}$ **7.** -20 **9.** B

11.

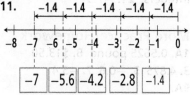

$(-1.4) + (-1.4) + (-1.4) + (-1.4) + (-1.4) = -7$

MODULE 5, LESSON 6
On Your Own

5A. LA: 543 ft; CA: 14,787 ft; IN: 937 ft; FL: 345 ft **B.** not reasonable; elevations are both negative; difference must be < -282 **7.** 0.4 **9.** 5.075 **11.** -6.2 **13A.** $9 - 3$; 6 **B.** $4 \cdot 6 + 6$; 30 **15A.** $20 - \left[2\frac{1}{2}(5.50) + 2(0.45)\right]$ **B.** $\$5.35$ **17.** $2\frac{1}{5}$ lb **19.** 0 **21.** $\frac{1}{2} \times \left(33 \times \frac{1}{11}\right)$; $1\frac{1}{2}$

More Practice/Homework

1. $11\frac{3}{4}$ ft, or 11.75 ft **3.** Commutative Property of

Addition; Associative Property of Addition; $\frac{1}{8}$ **5.** 10 loaves; about $\$0.88$ per loaf **7.** $(7 + 2.6)9 \div (4 - 2.8)$ **9.** C **11.** C **13.** -21.1°F

MODULE 5, LESSON 7
On Your Own

3A. 1.47 h **5.** 4 batches **7A.** Possible answer: $\$900$ **B.** no, too large **9A.** 5,760 m **B.** 5.76 km **C.** Possible answer: about 1 h 40 min **11A.** 157 in. **B.** 48 min

More Practice/Homework

1. Possible answer: $\$3,300$; underestimate **3A.** 23.9 min **5.** C **7.** C **9.** Nicolas; 7 ft **11.** 39 doses

UNIT 2

MODULE 6, LESSON 1
On Your Own

5A. 9^5 **B.** $\left(\frac{1}{8}\right)^3$ **7.** $\frac{1}{3} \times \frac{1}{3} \times \frac{1}{3} \times \frac{1}{3} \times \frac{1}{3} \times \frac{1}{3} \times \frac{1}{3}$ **9A.** 3; 5 **B.** $3 \times 3 \times 3 \times 3 \times 3 \times 3 \times 3 = 3^7$

More Practice/Homework

1. 12; 12; 8 **3A.** $3 \times 3 \times 3 \times 3 \times 3 \times 3 \times 3 \times 3$ **B.** $(3 \times 3 \times 3 \times 3) \times (3 \times 3 \times 3)$ **C.** The two expressions are equivalent. **5.** $2 \cdot 2 \cdot 2 \cdot 2 \cdot 2 \cdot 2 \cdot 2 \cdot 2 = 256$ **7.** 8^5 **9.** B, C, D **11.** 4^5; $4 \cdot 4 \cdot 4 \cdot 4 \cdot 4 = 1,024$ **13.** $\$59.94$ **15.** 216 cm³

MODULE 6, LESSON 2
On Your Own

5A. Possible answer: $2(2 + 1)$ **B.** Possible answer: $2(2 + 1 + 1)$ **C.** Possible answer: $3[2(2 + 1) + 2[2(2 + 1 + 1)]] = 34$ miles **7.** 9 **9.** 2 **11.** factors; 11 and 6; product **13.** $\frac{30}{5 + 7}$ **15.** $(12 \times 8) + 5$ **17A.** 2; 2^2; 11×2^3; 11×2^4 **B.** 176 dandelions **19.** 14 **21.** 15

More Practice/Homework

1A. Possible answer: $450 + 120$

B. Possible answer: $3(450 + 120)$ **C.** Possible answer: $3(450 + 120) + 380$ **D.** 2,090 inches **3.** 50 hit targets **5.** D **7.** A **9.** A, E **11.** C

MODULE 6, LESSON 3
On Your Own

5A. 21; y **B.** 25; 25; y **C.** Larry **7.** $\frac{32}{b}$, or $32 \div b$ **9.** $\frac{1}{2}x$, or $x \cdot \frac{1}{2}$

More Practice/Homework

1. $75 + 10d$, or $10d + 75$ **3.** Possible answer: $5,000 \div p$; the number of days needed to complete the puzzle **5.** $\frac{10m}{7}$ **7.** variable: y; coefficient: 11; constant: 4.5 **9.** $20 + 0.25p$, or $0.25p + 20$ **11.** $g - 8 - 9 - 4$, or $g - 21$ hours **13.** 13.97

MODULE 6, LESSON 4
On Your Own

7. 18 cubic inches **9.** 150; 125 **11.** 3 **13.** 13.25 **15.** Bill is correct. **17.** about 14.3 pounds **19.** 200 square centimeters **21.** $8\frac{3}{4}$ **23.** 16 **25.** 40 **27.** 138 **29.** 2 times **31.** $\frac{1}{8}$ **33.** 1,000 **35.** $\frac{1}{216}$

More Practice/Homework

1. 40 hours **3.** 18 **5.** 10.5 **7.** 37 **9.** 1 **11.** first row: $x = 3$; second row: $x = 5$; third row: $x = 4$ **13.** 128 square feet **15.** 3

MODULE 6, LESSON 5
On Your Own

3. 2ℓ; $2w$; $2(\ell + w)$ **5.** Chris is correct. **7.** Possible answer: $10(d + f)$ **9.** $8x + 5$ **11.** $2x + 3$ **13.** $3x^2 + 14$ **15.** They are both equivalent to $24x + 18y$. **17.** $2(5n + 9)$ **19.** Commutative; Associative **21.** not equivalent **23.** $4(6 + x)$ and $24 + 4x$ **25.** 3; 0; are not **27.** $4x + xy$ **29.** $8(3 + k)$ **31.** $7g^3 + g^3h$ **33.** equivalent

More Practice/Homework
1. $2n - 1$ **3.** no
5. $2(\ell w + \ell h + wh)$ **7.** equivalent
9. Commutative Property of
Addition **11.** First row: $2(3x + 2y)$;
Second row: $2(5x + 4y)$; Third row:
$3(2x + 3y)$ **13.** Possible answer:
$12(2x + 3y)$ **15.** -12

MODULE 6, LESSON 6
On Your Own
5. $7(2f + 3)$ **7.** $3(x - 10)$
9. $-1.3x - 15.2$ **11.** $4(7x) + (4)(3)$;
$28x + 12$ **13.** Possible answer: $2L$
$+ (L - 1)$ and $3L - 1$
15A. Possible answer: $3x + 5(2x)$
and $13x$ **B.** Possible answer: The
expression $3x + 5(2x)$ shows how
many regular-sized quilts (3) and
larger quilts (5) the customer
ordered. The expression $13x$
shows that the total material
used could also make 13 regular-
sized quilts. **17.** yes **19.** no
21. $2\left(5 - \frac{1}{4}x\right) + 2\left(5 - \frac{1}{4}x\right) +$
$\left(5 - \frac{1}{4}x\right) + \left(5 - \frac{1}{4}x\right)$; $30 - \frac{3}{2}x$
23. $-12s - 1\frac{2}{5}$ **25.** $24x - 56$
27. $18p + 9 = 9(2p + 1)$
29. Possible answer: $2(7x) + 2(3x)$;
it shows that the length is $7x$ and
the width is $3x$.

More Practice/Homework
1. $9\frac{3}{4}t - 1$ **3.** $6y - 5$ **5.** $77c + 21$
7. $-2.2s - 5$ **9.** D **11.** B, C
13. Positive

MODULE 7, LESSON 1
On Your Own
5. $3b = 27$; 9 blue marbles
7. $p + 20 = 85$; 65 pushups
9. Possible answer: An expression
represents one value and an
equation shows that two values
are equal. **11.** 5 **13.** 4 **15.** 3

More Practice/Homework
1. $23 = h - 12$; 35 members **7.** is

9. is not **11.** is not **13.** $15p = 300$,
or $\frac{300}{p} = 15$ **15.** $67 - h = 5$, or
$5 + h = 67$ **17.** Possible answer:
$9L = 72$; 8 inches **19.** $22.31
21. 21 **23.** 3

MODULE 7, LESSON 2
On Your Own
5. $b + 49 = 152.5$;
103.5 centimeters **7.** $14.85 +$
$c = 20$; $c = 5.15$; $5.15 **9.** 2
11. add; 75 **13.** subtract; 5.13
15. subtract; $\frac{3}{9}$, or $\frac{1}{3}$ **17.** $56 + c =$
200; $c = 144$ **19.** $1.27 + 3.74 \overset{?}{=}$
5.01; $5.01 \neq 5.1$; $g = 1.36$; $1.36 +$
$3.74 = 5.1$ **21.** 3.35

More Practice/Homework
1A. $s = 17$ **B.** $y = 41$ **C.** $x = 66$
5. is **7.** 55 **9.** 24 **11.** Add; 24; to
13. 23 miles **15.** $50t + 75$
17. 81 **19.** 1,000

MODULE 7, LESSON 3
On Your Own
3A. $2.4x = 33$ **B.** $13.75
5B. 14 ounces **7.** 2.5;

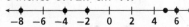

9. 15;

11. $\frac{x}{7} = 17.8$; 124.6 cm
13. $x = 19$ **15.** $x = 1\frac{1}{2}$

More Practice/Homework
1. $4p = 2.24$; $p = 0.56$; $0.56;

3A. $x = 14$ **B.** $w = 144$ **5.** $1.50r =$
18; $r = 12$; 12 times **7.** 19 **9.** 80
11. 20 inches **13.** D **15.** $2.49y$

MODULE 7, LESSON 4
On Your Own
3. 56 pretzel sticks **5A.** $x + 300 +$
$280 = 990$ **B.** 410 ft **7A.** $4\frac{2}{3}$ inches
B. $13\frac{5}{6}$ inches **11.** $3.29 + x =$
15.56; $x = 12.27$; $12.27
13A. $36 = 9w$ **B.** 4 inches

More Practice/Homework
1. $x + 44 = 90$; $x = 46$
3. $x + 40 = 64$; 24 blue floor
tiles **5.** $\frac{x}{5} = 4$; 20 baseball
cards **7.** $120 = 15w$;
8 inches **9.** 72.7 cm **11.**

MODULE 7, LESSON 5
On Your Own
5. $s > 761$ **7A.** $t > -9$ **B.** no
9. $y > -4$ **11A.** $h \leq 400$
B. yes **13.** $x \geq 100$
15.

More Practice/Homework
1B. $d \geq 500$
C.

3A.

B.

5. $x > 12$ **7.** $x > 48$

9. $5.16 **11.** -13.6 **13.** -6

MODULE 7, LESSON 6
On Your Own
7. B, C **9.** B, D
11. $x + (-4.5) = -12$; $x = -7.5$
13. $b = 85$ **15.** $m = -\frac{4}{7}$ **17.** $b = 7$
19. $h = 42$ **21.** $j = -29$
23. $z = -7.2$ **25.** $k = -\frac{3}{4}$
27. $m = 2.05$

More Practice/Homework
1. $y = -12.5$ **3.** $x = -21$
5. $z = -61$ **7.** $b = 3.52$
9. $p = -\frac{11}{28}$ **11.** $r = \frac{21}{16}$
13. A **15.** A **17.** 12.6
19. $431 + p = 487$; 56 pages

MODULE 8, LESSON 1
On Your Own
3A. C; s

© Houghton Mifflin Harcourt Publishing Company

B.

Shirts, s	Cost, C
3	$9.75
5	$16.25
8	$26.00
10	$32.50

C.

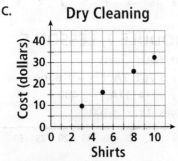

Dry Cleaning

D. separate points

5A.

Tina	Gary
2.5	7
5.5	10
7	11.5
10	14.5

B. 2.5; 7; 5.5; 10; 7; 11.5; 10; 14.5

C.

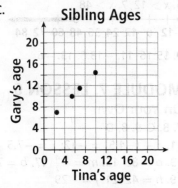

Sibling Ages

D. straight line **7.** $d = 57t$

More Practice/Homework

1. $C = 3p$ **3.** $m = 11n$
5. $y = x + 8$
7.

s	p
5	30
12	72
3.5	21
9	54

9. $m = 540h$ **11.** $y < 3$

[number line from 0 to 20 with open circle at 3]

MODULE 8, LESSON 2

On Your Own

3A. $e = 12.25h$ **B.** $238.88
5. $y = \frac{5}{2}x$ **7.** $y = x + 4.5$
9. $c = 9.75t$ **13.** $w = s - 1,392$;
9,866 steps **15.** $d = 250 - f$

More Practice/Homework

1. $y = \frac{1}{9}f$ **3.** $y = 3x$
5. $F = H - 35$ **7.** $c = 2.49p$
9. $a = 135c$ **11A.** $s = m + 28.75$
B. $49.75 **13.** $t = 30 - s$; t
15. Roberto; $1.77 **17.** 5-pound
bag: about $2.60 per pound;
12-pound bag: about $2.67 per
pound

MODULE 8, LESSON 3

On Your Own

3. $d = 24g$ **5.** $C = 45.25n$
7A. $C = 25n + 35$ **B.** 60; 85; 110;
135 **C.** after 5 months **9.** $y = x - 2$

More Practice/Homework

1A. $T = 4n$ **B.** $500 **3.** $y = 7.5x$
5. $y = x + 11.2$ **7B.** $y = 7x$ **9.** A
11. 3.5

UNIT 3

MODULE 9, LESSON 1

On Your Own

3. 3:2, 3 to 2, or $\frac{3}{2}$ **5.** 36:12, 36 to
12, $\frac{36}{12}$ **7.** no

More Practice/Homework

1. For every 7 botia loaches,
there are 20 African cichlids.
3. 4, for every; 4, for each; 4, per
5. 2:50, 2 to 50, or $\frac{2}{50}$; yes **7.** C
9. 30:1, 30 to 1, or $\frac{30}{1}$
11. $221 **13.** 2

MODULE 9, LESSON 2

On Your Own

5A.

Bracelets	2	3	4
Beads	32	48	64

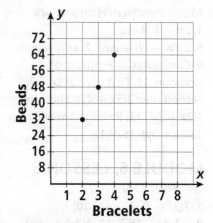

Bracelets

B. 16 beads to 1 bracelet
C. 160 beads
7. 45 minutes per practice;
135 min, or 2 h 15 min

9A.

Time (s)	3	6	9
Spins	60	120	180

20 spins per second

B.

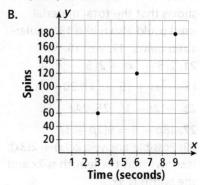

Time (seconds)

11. 9 grams per serving **13.** $80
per month

More Practice/Homework

1A. $30; \frac{90}{3} = \frac{30}{1}$, or $\frac{120}{4} = \frac{30}{1}$ **B.** no
3.

Time (h)	Cost ($)
2	50
4	100
6	150
8	200

5. 28 oz per can **7.** 30:1, or $\frac{30}{1}$,
or 30 parts iron per part
carbon **9.** D, E **11.** $168.10

MODULE 9, LESSON 3
On Your Own
3A.

Ratio for Each Runner	
Sprints	Laps
5	4
10	8
15	12
20	16

Ratio for Megan	
Sprints	Laps
11	8
22	16
33	24
44	32

B. Possible answer: The second row in table 1 and the first row in table 2 **C.** No **5.** Tim's paint mixture will be darker. **7.** no

More Practice/Homework
1A. $\frac{6}{14}, \frac{9}{21}, \frac{12}{28}$ **B.** $\frac{4}{10}, \frac{6}{15}, \frac{8}{20}$ **C.** Brookberry Farms **3.** no
5. A, C, D **7.** yes **9.** $-10 < |-10|$ or $|-10| > -10$

MODULE 9, LESSON 4
On Your Own
5A. $1.83 per foot **B.** about $54.90 **7A.** 60 meters per minute **B.** about 59.1 meters per minute **C.** Melanie **9.** 6 mi/h **13.** $90.00 **17A.** $9.60 per hour **B.** $384.00 **19.** $2\frac{1}{2}$ mi/h **21.** 10 c flour/1 c butter

More Practice/Homework
1. $7\frac{1}{2}$ hours **3.** Jen: $2\frac{2}{5}$ mi/h; Kamlee: 2 mi/h; Jen **5.** Franco's trough **7A.** 86 heartbeats per min **B.** 258 heartbeats **9.** $3\frac{1}{2}$ ft²/h **11.** 48-Pack **13.** $3\frac{1}{3}$ spools **15.** $22.23 **17.** the reef

MODULE 9, LESSON 5
On Your Own
5. 75 centimeters **7A.**

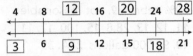

B. 44 **C.** $\frac{12}{21}$ **D.** $\frac{30}{70}$ **9A.** $\frac{5}{12}$, or 5 to 12, or 5:12 **B.** 72 turkey burgers **11A.** yes **B.** 35 free throws **13A.** 1.5 centimeters **B.** 36 centimeters

More Practice/Homework
1. $\frac{2}{3}$, or 2 to 3, or 2:3 **3.** $\frac{2}{2}$, or 2 to 2, or 2:2 **5.** yes **7.** 12 miles **9.** D **11.** 49 questions **13.** 0.466 yard **15.** −4, 3

MODULE 10, LESSON 1
On Your Own
3. 120; 40; 80 **5.** Music: 210, 35; News: 60, 10; Commercials: 60, 10; DJ talk: 30, 5

More Practice/Homework
1A. 1,800 calories
B. carbohydrates: 180°; protein: 72°; fat: 108° **5A.** $\frac{200}{500}$, or $\frac{2}{5}$
B. 144° **7.** $2\frac{1}{4}$ ounces

MODULE 10, LESSON 2
On Your Own
5. 5.6 kilometers **7.** yes
9. $\frac{63,360 \text{ inches}}{1 \text{ mile}}$ **11.** 36 **13.** 3,500
15. 6 **17.** Fiona **19.** 1.76 meters
21. 10 pints **23.** > **25.** >

More Practice/Homework
1. 12 quarts **3.** 40 quarts **5.** no
7. 5,000 m > 4,900 m; >
9. 15,840 ft = 15,840 ft; =
11. 450 mL < 4,200 mL; <
13. 420 centimeters, 4.3 meters, 4,600 millimeters, 0.04 kilometer
15. The gallon of milk
17. Mairead jogs farther, by 60 feet. **19.** 10 to 25, or 2 to 5
21. 14 units

MODULE 10, LESSON 3
On Your Own
3. Kathy does not have enough juice. **5.** 54.7 yards **7.** 5.5 pounds **9.** 3.1 **11.** 80.5 **13.** 236.8 **15.** 500 kilometers is longer. **17.** 68.3 miles per hour **19.** 5 feet 3 inches **21.** < **23.** > **25.** >

More Practice/Homework
1. yes **3.** no **5.** 8.6 meters **7.** 254 centimeters > 250 centimeters; > **9.** 3 miles < 3.1 miles; < **11.** 5 liters > 4.7 liters; > **13.** 10 feet, 4 meters, 200 inches, 600 centimeters **15.** $4.89 per kilogram **17A.** 36 **B.** 4 **C.** 9 red, 3 blue **19.** 36.5 kilometers

MODULE 11, LESSON 1
On Your Own
3. 6 (min); 20 (gal); yes **5.** yes

More Practice/Homework
1. yes **3.** no **5.** yes **7.** A **9.** $94.20

MODULE 11, LESSON 2
On Your Own
5. yes; $k = 21$ **7.** yes; $y = 7x$
9. no **11.** $k = 42$; $y = 42x$
13. 100; 300; 2

More Practice/Homework
1. yes; $k = 9$ **3.** The table represents a proportional relationship; $k = 24$; $y = 24x$
5. $k = 8$; $y = 8x$ **7.** Table 2 **9.** It takes 24 hours to build each chair. **11.** A **13.** yes

MODULE 11, LESSON 3
On Your Own
3A. It takes Yazmin 16 minutes to jog 1 mile. **B.** yes; 16; $y = 16x$
5. Proportional

More Practice/Homework
1A. yes **B.** $k = 15$ yd² per gal; $y = 15x$ **5.** B **7.** $3.50 per sandwich

MODULE 11, LESSON 4
On Your Own
3A. 30 ft³/min **B.** 1,800 ft³/h
C. $y = 1,800x$; 10,800 ft³ of water
D. 15,300 ft³ of water
5A. 384,000 ft/h **B.** 72.7 mi/h
C. $y = 72.7x$; 218.1 mi

More Practice/Homework
1. 5.7 mi/h **3.** 5.5 mi/h
5. 84.48 km **7.** $15 **9.** B **11.** >
13. −15, −5, −2, 1, 3, 8 **15.** 8

MODULE 12, LESSON 1
On Your Own
9. more **13.** 95% **15.** 620%
17. 34% **19A.** 6.5 miles **B.** 25%
21. 14.29%

More Practice/Homework
1. 55% **3.** 36% **5.** 20% **7.** 33%
9A. $\frac{3}{4}$ **B.** 75% **11.** B **13.** −3
15. seven-twelfths, or $\frac{7}{12}$

MODULE 12, LESSON 2
On Your Own
7. 36 square feet **9.** $30
11. 11,388.8 **13.** 21 **15.** 603
17. $9 per hour **19.** $24 **21.** 125
23. 10 **25.** 231

More Practice/Homework
1. 400 points **3.** 6.3 ounces
5. 54 **7.** 9 **9.** 27 **11.** popcorn: 56; pretzels: 42; milkshakes: 14
13. 56 marbles **15.** 20%
17. −12, −1, 0, 3 **19.** 0.019

MODULE 12, LESSON 3
On Your Own
5. 62.5% **7.** 20% giraffes; 80% zebras **9.** not reasonable
11. 12 **13.** 28.8 **15.** 100 **17.** 11
19. 90,000 gallons **21A.** 35
B. 196 students **C.** 0.35 **D.** 196

More Practice/Homework
1. 15 oysters **3.** $3.60 **5.** 24, 20%; 48, 40%; 72, 60%; 96, 80%
7. 40% **9.** 1,000 **11.** 20
13. B **15.** 48 people
17A. 20 **B.** 24 **C.** 9 **19.** 216 cm³

MODULE 13, LESSON 1
On Your Own
5. 69 students **7.** 2.5%
9A. 54 feet **B.** no
11. 56%; decrease **13.** 75%; increase **15.** 146.25 yd to 153.75 yd **17.** 14.7 to 15.3
19A. |1,592 m − 1,600 m| = 8 m
B. 0.5% **C.** 1.25%

More Practice/Homework
1. 30% **3.** 217 bacteria
5. 147 orders to 153 orders
7. increase of 87.5% **9.** A, D
11. D **13A.** 24 or $\frac{1}{24}$ **B.** $h = 24d$ or $d = \frac{1}{24}h$

MODULE 13, LESSON 2
On Your Own
3. $42 **5.** $133,860 **7A.** $y = 2.5x$
B. $30; $42 **C.** 75% **D.** $y = 0.75x$
9. $87.84 **11.** 150% **13.** $30,000
15A. Possible answer: $p − 0.08p$ and $0.92p$ **B.** 0.92

More Practice/Homework
1. 25% **3.** $120 **5.** $3.38
7. $352.00 **9.** $y = 3.4x$ **11.** B
13. C **15.** 237.5 g to 262.5 g

MODULE 13, LESSON 3
On Your Own
5. $290 **7.** $33.59 **9.** $900
11. $24.44 **13.** $250 **15.** $32.50

17. $676.18 **19.** $5.54
21. $y = 1.2x$ **23.** $y = 1.2x$; $207.18

More Practice/Homework
1. $89.10 **3.** $16.32 **5.** 7%
7. $166.07 **9.** $126.36
11. $256.10 **13.** $600
15. D **17.** 384 students

MODULE 13, LESSON 4
On Your Own
5. commission: $1,500; fees: $54
7. $141.60 **9.** $9,600 **11.** $1,637.50
13A. Irma also gets $11 for each delivery of pet supplies.
B. $4,044.80 **C.** Possible answer: In addition to a different base salary and a different commission rate for groceries, she will earn a commission rate for pet supplies instead of a fixed delivery fee. **D.** $3,597.26

More Practice/Homework
1. $6,500 **3.** $64,700 **5.** $1,925
7. $80,425 **9.** A, C, E **11.** $1,215
13. 7.5% **15.** $28.20

MODULE 13, LESSON 5
On Your Own
3A. $57.60 **B.** $576.00
5A. $7,047 **B.** $21,547
7. $26,000 **9A.** $30 **B.** $2,150
C. 17 years

More Practice/Homework
1. $3,955.00 **3.** $15,225 **5.** B
7. 9 years **9.** −1

UNIT 4

MODULE 14, LESSON 1
On Your Own
5. $P(−1, 3)$, $R(2, 3)$, $T(6, 3)$, $U(−4, −5)$, $Q(−1, −5)$, $S(6, −5)$
7. 4 units; yes **9.** no
11A. 40 units **B.** 320 miles

13. $4\frac{3}{5}$ units; I subtract because the points are in the same quadrant.

More Practice/Homework
1B. 9,000 miles **D.** Quadrant III
3A. 7 units **B.** 5 units **5.** *A*: (1.5, −1.75); *B*: (−1.75, 0.75); *C*: $(1\frac{1}{2}, 2\frac{1}{4})$; *D*: (0.75, −1); *E*: (2, 1); *F*: (−2.25, 2); *G*: $(-1\frac{3}{4}, -2)$ **7.** 2.9

MODULE 14, LESSON 2
On Your Own
3. It is a polygon; heptagon.
5. (3, 2) or (1, 5) **7B.** (−1, −1)
C. 5 units; 5 units **D.** Each side measures 5 units. **9.** polygon and octagon

More Practice/Homework
1. Not a polygon **3B.** (6, 3) or (0, 3) **5.** point (−2, 1) or point (1, −1) **7.** A, B, D, E **9.** 32 times

MODULE 14, LESSON 3
On Your Own
3A. 10; 6; 60 **B.** 30 heads of lettuce **C.** 5; 2; 10 **D.** 80 carrots
5. About 417 rectangles
9. 48 square units

More Practice/Homework
1A. 9 square units **B.** 36 square units **C.** 4 **3.** 18 units **5.** 4 units
7. 29 units **9.** C **11.** Quadrant III
13. Possible answer: $67 - c = 11$

MODULE 15, LESSON 1
On Your Own
5. 5 inches **7.** 10.5 square feet
9. $8\frac{1}{8}$ in² **11.** 42 cm² **13.** Bob is correct. **15.** 12 inches **17.** 8 ft
19. 4.5 in.

More Practice/Homework
1. 1,575 square meters
3. 15 in² per cm² **5.** 28.5 in²
7. 18 in² **9.** 24 square meters

11. 5 feet **13.** $9.1 - 6.4 = 2.7$, $2.7 \neq 2.61$. The correct solution is 9.01.

MODULE 15, LESSON 2
On Your Own
3. $19\frac{1}{8}$ square inches **5.** 16 feet
7. 17 in² **9.** 14.3 cm² **11.** 8 ft
13. 9 in.

More Practice/Homework
1. about 15.6 square feet
3. 8 centimeters **5.** 9 ft²
7. 8.75 in² **9.** D **11.** 21 feet **13.** $\frac{1}{8}$

MODULE 15, LESSON 3
On Your Own
3. 128 ft² **7.** 26 ft² **11.** 370 square feet **13.** 26 m² **17.** 75 cm²
19. 64 cm²

More Practice/Homework
1. 2,112 square feet **3.** 6 cases of flooring **5.** B, C, E **7.** $A = 8 \times 2 + (8 \times 2) \div 2$, or $A = 8 \times 3$ **9.** 0.8

MODULE 16, LESSON 1
On Your Own
3. no **5.** no **7.** rectangular prism; 72 m² **9.** square pyramid; 56 ft²

More Practice/Homework
1.

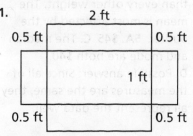

5 square feet **3.** cube; 24 cm²
7. 20 square meters
9. $t = 0.5m + 15$

MODULE 16, LESSON 2
On Your Own
3. $\frac{1}{2}$ yd³ **5.** 343 cm³ **7.** 1,710 ft³

More Practice/Homework
1. $4\frac{5}{36}$ ft³ **3.** $10,462\frac{1}{2}$ in³
5. $24,806\frac{1}{4}$ in³ **7.** 2.25 m³ **9.** $\frac{1}{30}$ ft³
11. $45.99

MODULE 16, LESSON 3
On Your Own
3. 27 in³ **5A.** $179\frac{13}{25}$ cubic inches
7A. Find the area of one face of the cube, then multiply by the number of faces, 6. **B.** 100 in²
C. 10 inches × 10 inches × 10 inches **D.** 1,000 in³

More Practice/Homework
1. 512 in³ **3.** 6.5 meters
5. 8 inches **7.** A **9.** 743.75 in³
11. 6

UNIT 5

MODULE 17, LESSON 1
On Your Own
5. The second question is a statistical question; the first question is not. **7.** 2; meters and hundreds of years; 6

More Practice/Homework
1. How many days are there in March? **5.** number of players, average score per game, and average age; players, points, and years; 18 **7.** B **9.** 343 cm³

MODULE 17, LESSON 2
On Your Own
3. 7.0 millimeters
5. 7.7 millimeters
7. 11 games
9. 6 **11B.** 20 observations **C.** 0.2 gram **D.** 0.7 gram

Selected Answers

More Practice/Homework

1A.

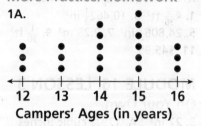

Campers' Ages (in years)

B. 15 years old
C. 20 observations **D.** 45%
3. B **5.** 9 inches **7.** 304

MODULE 17, LESSON 3
On Your Own

3A. 17; 40 **B.** Second interval:
23–28; Third interval: 29–34;
Fourth interval: 35–40 **C.** First
row: 17–22; 5; Second row:
23–28; 5; Third row: 29–34; 1;
Fourth row: 35–40; 4 **D.** interval
29–34 **5A.** 1.50–1.59 meters
B. 9 athletes

More Practice/Homework

1A. 11, 12, 13, 15, 16, 17, 18, 18,
20, 21, 22, 23, 23, 24, 24, 25, 26,
28, 29

B.

Number of loaves sold (per hour)	Frequency
11–15	4
16–20	5
21–25	7
26–30	3

C.

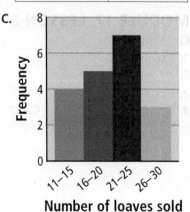

Number of loaves sold

3. A, B, D **5.** $59.94
7. 2.25 gallons

MODULE 17, LESSON 4
On Your Own

3B. 26.4 °F **C.** 23.5 °F **D.** 21 °F
5. The mean, because all of the
values are 0, 1, or 2, and there is
not much variation in the data.
7. The mean and median are
10.5. There is no mode. **9A.** The
median of $25 is more useful.
B. The mean changes the most.

More Practice/Homework

1A. 7 days **B.** 61 grams
C. 60 grams **D.** 60 grams
E. Median and mode **3.** mean:
4; median: 2.5; mode: 2 **5.** 2.1;
1.4; 0.5 **7.** 68; 58; 0 **9.** D
11. 119.6 cm²

MODULE 17, LESSON 5
On Your Own

3A. Mean: 143 kg, Median:
156.5 kg, Mode: 160 kg **B.** 44 kg
C. Without the outlier, the mean
increases to about 157 kg, the
median increases to 157 kg,
and the mode stays the same
at 160 kg. **D.** Possible answer:
the median. The mode is higher
than every other weight. The
mean is most affected by the
outlier. **5A.** $45 **C.** The median
and mode are both $40.
D. Possible answer: Since all of
the measures are the same, they
all represent the data well.

More Practice/Homework

1B. 70 feet; 72 feet; 80 feet
C. Without the outlier, the mean
height increases to about 74
feet, and the median height
to 73.5 feet. The mode stays
the same. **D.** Possible answer:
The median; Even though it
changes without the outlier,

it doesn't change as much as
the mean. The mode stays the
same, but it is higher than most
of the data values. **3.** Possible
answer: The median, because
it is closest to the largest group
of numbers of hours spent on
the telephone. **5.** The median
best represents the data. **7.** The
mean is 56, the median is 55,
and there is no mode. **9.** $y = 2x$

MODULE 18, LESSON 1
On Your Own

3. Possible answer: The majority
of students study for at least
8 hours each week.
5. Cluster from 10.2 to 10.4
seconds; gap or deviation from
the overall pattern between
10.7 and 11 seconds; peak at
10.4 seconds

More Practice/Homework

1. Possible answer: The
frequencies increase to a peak
at between 15 to 24 mpg and
then decrease. The data are not
symmetric. There are more cars
with fuel efficiency above 24
mph than below 15 mpg. Most
of the cars have fuel efficiencies
between 15 and 24 mpg.
3. Possible answer: The data
distribution is symmetric
around 79. **5.** 24 people **7.** 25
9. $2a + 7b + 4$

MODULE 18, LESSON 2
On Your Own

5A. median = 25; lower quartile
= 19; upper quartile = 30

B.

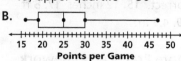

Points per Game

7. median = 23.5; lower quartile
= 21; upper quartile = 26

9. median = 9.5; lower quartile = 6; upper quartile = 15

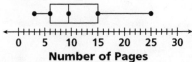

Number of Pages

More Practice/Homework
1. median: $10.85; lower quartile: $10.25; upper quartile: $11.50
3.

5. median = 40; lower quartile = 31.5; upper quartile = 49 **7.** C
9. D. **11.** median

MODULE 18, LESSON 3
On Your Own
3A. The mean for Serena's times is 8 hours. The mean for Lisa's times is 8 hours. **B.** Subtract (Serena): 8; 8; 8; 8; 8; Distance (Serena): 2; 3; 2; 0; 3; Subtract (Lisa): 8; 8; 8; 8; 8; Distance (Lisa): 6; 1; 4; 2; 3 **C.** Serena's MAD is 2 hours. Lisa's MAD is 3.2 hours. **D.** Lisa; greater
5A. 1.05 **B.** 0.34 **C.** yes

More Practice/Homework
1. Mean: 19.2 cm; MAD: 1 cm
3. mean = 2.1 pounds; MAD = 0.15 pound **5.** 3.7 to 5.3 **7.** B, C, D, E, F **9.** 173.25 cubic inches

MODULE 18, LESSON 4
On Your Own
3. 10; 3 **5.** Possible answer: IQR = 3 goals; The range of the middle half of the values is 3 goals. **7.** 27; 16 **9A.** range: 105 years; IQR: 44 years **B.** range: 109 years; IQR: 27 years

C. The range is slightly greater in County B, but the interquartile range is much greater in County A. **D.** County A **11.** Range = 70; IQR = 15

More Practice/Homework
1. Range = 6; IQR = 3
3. The range of ages and the interquartile range in ages are greater for female runners than male runners in this road race, so there is more variability in the ages of the female runners. **7.** 7.3; 4.3 **9.** 7 shells

MODULE 18, LESSON 5
On Your Own
3A. Possible answer: How many hours do sixth-grade students participate in physical activity each week? **B.** Possible answer: The data are presented as frequencies of values in equal intervals.
C.

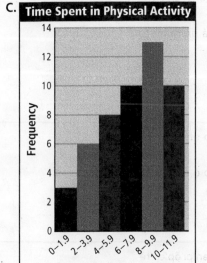

Time Spent in Physical Activity

D. Possible answer: The frequencies increase as the number of hours increases, reaching a peak at 8–9.9 hours. Then the frequency decreases. The data are not symmetrical and there are no outliers.
E. Possible answer: Most students are involved in physical activity for between 6 and 12 hours each week.

More Practice/Homework
1. The distribution is approximately symmetric. The mean, median, and mode all describe the data well, as they are all close to one another (between 6 and 7). **3.** Possible answer: The snow depths over the course of several winters range from 30 inches to 130 inches. 50% of the time, the snow depth was from 50 to 100 inches. **5.** A **7.** 6 **9.** 5 cm

Interactive Glossary

As you learn about each new term, add notes, drawings, or sentences in the space next to the definition. Doing so will help you remember what each term means.

Pronunciation Key

ă	add, map	g	go, log	n	nice, tin	p	pit, stop	û(r) burn, term
ā	ace, rate	h	hope, hate	ng	ring, song	r	run, poor	yōō fuse, few
â(r)	care, air	hw	which	ŏ	odd, hot	s	see, pass	v vain, eve
ä	palm, father	ĭ	it, give	ō	open, so	sh	sure, rush	w win, away
b	bat, rub	ī	ice, write	ô	taught, jaw	t	talk, sit	y yet, yearn
ch	check, catch	îr	tier	ôr	order	th	thin, both	z zest, muse
d	dog, rod	j	joy, ledge	oi	oil, boy	th	this, bathe	zh vision, pleasure
ĕ	end, pet	k	cool, take	ou	pout, now	ŭ	up, done	
ē	equal, tree	l	look, rule	ŏŏ	took, full	ōō	pull, book	
f	fit, half	m	move, seem	ōō	pool, food	ôr	cure	

ə the schwa, an unstressed vowel representing the sound spelled *a* in *above*, *e* in *sicken*, *i* in *possible*, *o* in *melon*, *u* in *circus*

Other symbols:
- - separates words into syllables
- ′ indicates stress on a syllable

A

absolute value [ăb′sə-lōōt′ văl′ōō] The distance of a number from zero on a number line; shown by | |

valor absoluto Distancia a la que está un número de 0 en una recta numérica. El símbolo del valor absoluto es | |

addend [ăd′ĕnd′] A number added to one or more other numbers to form a sum

sumando Número que se suma a uno o más números para formar una suma

Addition Property of Equality [ə-dĭsh′ən prŏp′ər-tē ŭv ĭ-kwŏl′ĭ-tē] The property that states that if you add the same number to both sides of an equation, the new equation will have the same solution

Propiedad de igualdad de la suma Propiedad que establece que puedes sumar el mismo número a ambos lados de una ecuación y la nueva ecuación tendrá la misma solución

My Vocabulary Summary

Addition Property of Opposites [ə-dǐsh'ən prǒp'ər-tē ŭv ǒp'ə-zǐt] The property that states that the sum of a number and its opposite equals zero

Propiedad de la suma de los opuestos Propiedad que establece que la suma de un número y su opuesto es cero

additive inverse [ăd'ǐ-tǐv ǐn-vûrs'] The opposite of a number; the sum of the number and its additive inverse is 0

inverso aditivo El opuesto de un número; la suma del número y su inverso aditivo es 0

algebraic expression [ăl'jə-brā'ǐk ǐk-sprěsh'ən] An expression that contains at least one variable

expresión algebraica Expresión que contiene al menos una variable

angle [ăng'gəl] A figure formed by two rays with a common endpoint called the vertex

ángulo Figura formada por dos rayos con un extremo común llamado vértice

area [âr'ē-ə] The number of square units needed to cover a given surface

área El número de unidades cuadradas que se necesitan para cubrir una superficie dada

Interactive Glossary

Associative Property of Addition [ə-sō′shə-tĭv prŏp′ər-tē ŭv ə-dĭsh′ən] The property that states that for all real numbers *a*, *b*, and *c*, the sum is always the same, regardless of their grouping

Propiedad asociativa de la suma Propiedad que establece que para todos los números reales *a*, *b* y *c*, la suma siempre es la misma sin importar cómo se agrupen

Associative Property of Multiplication [ə-sō′shə-tĭv prŏp′ər-tē ŭv mŭl′tə-plĭ-kā′shən] The property that states that for all real numbers *a*, *b*, and *c*, their product is always the same, regardless of their grouping

Propiedad asociativa de la multiplicación Propiedad que para todos los números reales *a*, *b* y *c*, el producto siempre es el mismo sin importar cómo se agrupen

average [ăv′ər-ĭj] The sum of the items in a set of data divided by the number of items in the set; also called *mean*

promedio La suma de los elementos de un conjunto de datos dividida entre el número de elementos del conjunto. También se le llama *media*

axes [ăk′sēz′] The two perpendicular lines of a coordinate plane that intersect at the origin (singular: axis)

ejes Las dos rectas numéricas perpendiculares del plano cartesiano que se intersecan en el origen

B

bar graph [bär grăf] A graph that uses vertical or horizontal bars to display data

gráfica de barras Gráfica en la que se usan barras verticales u horizontales para presentar datos

base (in numeration) [bās] When a number is raised to a power, the number that is used as a factor is the base

base (en numeración) Cuando un número es elevado a una potencia, el número que se usa como factor es la base

base (of a three-dimensional figure) [bās] A face of a three-dimensional figure by which the figure is measured or classified

base (de una figura tridimensional) La cara de una figura tridimensional, a partir de la cual se mide o se clasifica la figura

base (of a trapezoid) [bās] Either of two parallel sides of a trapezoid

base (de un trapecio) Cualquiera de los dos lados paralelos de un trapecio

base (of a triangle) [bās] Any side of a triangle

base (de un triángulo) Cualquier lado de un triángulo

Interactive Glossary

bisect [bī'sĕkt'] To divide into two congruent parts

trazar una bisectriz Dividir en dos partes congruentes

box plot [bŏks plŏt] A graph that shows how data are distributed by using the median, quartiles, least value, and greatest value; also called a box-and-whisker plot

gráfica de caja Gráfica para demostrar la distribución de datos utilizando la mediana, los cuartiles y los valores menos y más grande; también llamado gráfica de mediana y rango

C

capacity [kə-păs'ĭ-tē] The amount a container can hold when filled

capacidad Cantidad que cabe en un recipiente cuando se llena

Celsius [sĕl'sē-əs] A metric scale for measuring temperature in which 0 °C is the freezing point of water and 100 °C is the boiling point of water; also called *centigrade*

Celsius Escala métrica para medir la temperatura, en la que 0 °C es el punto de congelación del agua y 100 °C es el punto de ebullición. También se llama *centígrado*

center (of a circle) [sĕn'tər] The point inside a circle that is the same distance from all the points on the circle

centro (de un círculo) Punto interior de un círculo que se encuentra a la misma distancia de todos los puntos de la circunferencia

circle [sûr'kəl] The set of all points in a plane that are the same distance from a given point called the center

círculo Conjunto de todos los puntos en un plano que se encuentran a la misma distancia de un punto dado llamado centro

© Houghton Mifflin Harcourt Publishing Company

circle graph [sûr′kəl grăf] A graph that uses sectors of a circle to compare parts to the whole and parts to other parts

gráfica circular Gráfica que usa secciones de un círculo para comparar partes con el todo y con otras partes

coefficient [kō′ə-fĭsh′nt] The number that is multiplied by the variable in an algebraic expression

coeficiente Número que se multiplica por la variable en una expresión algebraica

commission [kə-mĭsh′ən] A fee paid to a person for making a sale

comisión Pago que recibe una persona por realizar una venta

commission rate [kə-mĭsh′ən rāt] The fee paid to a person who makes a sale expressed as a percent of the selling price

tasa de comisión Pago que recibe una persona por hacer una venta, expresado como un porcentaje del precio de venta

common denominator [kŏm′ən dĭ-nŏm′ə-nā′tər] A denominator that is the same in two or more fractions

denominador común Denominador que es común a dos o más fracciones

common factor [kŏm'ən fǎk'tər] A number that is a factor of two or more numbers

factor común Número que es factor de dos o más números

common multiple [kŏm'ən mŭl'tə-pəl] A number that is a multiple of each of two or more numbers

múltiplo común Un número que es múltiplo de dos o más números

Commutative Property of Addition [kŏm'yə-tā'tĭv prŏp'ər-tē ŭv ə-dĭsh'ən] The property that states that two or more numbers can be added in any order without changing the sum

Propiedad conmutativa de la suma Propiedad que establece que sumar dos o más números en cualquier orden no altera la suma

Commutative Property of Multiplication [kŏm'yə-tā'tĭv prŏp'ər-tē ŭv mŭl'tə-plĭ-kā'shən] The property that states that two or more numbers can be multiplied in any order without changing the product

Propiedad conmutativa de la multiplicación Propiedad que establece que multiplicar dos o más números en cualquier orden no altera el producto

complementary angles [kŏm'plə-měn'tə-rē ăng'gəls] Two angles whose measures add to 90°

ángulos complementarios Dos ángulos cuyas medidas suman 90°

My Vocabulary Summary

composite figure [kəm-pŏz′ĭt fĭg′yər] A figure made up of simple geometric shapes

figura compuesta Figura formada por otras figuras geométricas simples

congruent [kŏng′grōō-ənt] Having the same size and shape; the symbol for congruent is ≅

congruentes Que tiene el mismo tamaño y la misma forma, expresado por ≅

constant [kŏn′stənt] A number whose value does not change

constante Valor que no cambia

constant of proportionality [kŏn′stənt ŭv prə-pôr-shə-nălĭ-tē] A constant ratio of two variables related proportionally

constante de proporcionalidad Razón constante de dos variables que están relacionadas en forma proporcional

constraint [kən-strānt′] A restriction on the value(s) of a quantity or variable

restricción Una restricción del valor de una cantidad o variable

© Houghton Mifflin Harcourt Publishing Company

Interactive Glossary

My Vocabulary Summary

conversion factor [kən-vûr′zhən făk′tər] A rate in which two quantities are equal but use different units

factor de conversión Tasa a la cual dos cantidades son iguales, pero que usan diferentes unidades

coordinate grid [kō-ôr′dn-ĭt grĭd] A grid formed by the intersection of horizontal and vertical lines that is used to locate points

cuadrícula de coordenadas Cuadrícula formada por la intersección de líneas horizontales y líneas verticales que se usan por localizar puntos

coordinate plane [kō-ôr′dn-ĭt plān] A plane formed by the intersection of a horizontal number line, called the *x*-axis, and a vertical number line, called the *y*-axis

plano cartesiano Plano formado por la intersección de una recta numérica horizontal llamada eje *x* y otra vertical llamada eje *y*

coordinates [kō-ôr′dn-ĭts] The numbers of an ordered pair that locate a point on a coordinate graph

coordenadas Los números de un par ordenado que ubican un punto en una gráfica de coordenadas

customary system [kŭs′tə-mĕr′ē sĭs′təm] The measurement system often used in the United States

sistema usual de medidas El sistema de medidas que se usa comúnmente en Estados Unidos

D

data [dā′tə] A set of information collected about people or things, often to draw conclusions about them

datos Conjunto de información recopilada sobre personas u objetos, generalmente con el objetivo de obtener conclusiones acerca de los mismos

degree [dǐ-grē′] The unit of measure for angles or temperature

grado Unidad de medida para ángulos y temperaturas

denominator [dǐ-nŏm′ə-nā′tər] The bottom number of a fraction that tells how many equal parts are in the whole

denominador Número de abajo en una fracción que indica en cuántas partes iguales se divide el entero

dependent variable [dǐ-pĕn′dənt vâr′ē-ə-bəl] The output of a function; a variable whose value depends on the value of the input, or independent variable

variable dependiente Salida de una función; variable cuyo valor depende del valor de la entrada, o variable independiente

diagonal [di-ag′ə-nəl] A line segment that connects two nonadjacent vertices of a polygon

diagonal Segmento de recta que une dos vértices no adyacentes de un polígono

diameter [di-am′i-tər] A line segment that passes through the center of a circle and has endpoints on the circle, or the length of that segment

diámetro Segmento de recta que pasa por el centro de un círculo y tiene sus extremos en la circunferencia, o bien la longitud de ese segmento

---

dimension [dĭ-měn′shən] The length, width, or height of a figure

dimensión Longitud, ancho o altura de una figura

Distributive Property [dĭ-strĭb′yə-tĭv prŏp′ər-tē] For all real numbers, a, b, and c, $a(b + c) = ab + ac$ and $a(b - c) = ab - ac$

Propiedad distributiva Dado números reales a, b, y c, $a(b + c) = ab + ac$ y $a(b - c) = ab - ac$

---

dividend [dĭv′ĭ-děnd′] The number to be divided in a division problem

dividendo Número que se divide en un problema de división

Division Property of Equality [dĭ-vĭzh′ən prŏp′ər-tē ŭv ĭ-kwŏl′ĭ-tē] The property that states that if you divide both sides of an equation by the same nonzero number, the new equation will have the same solution

Propiedad de igualdad de la división Propiedad que establece que puedes dividir ambos lados de una ecuación entre el mismo número distinto de cero, y la nueva ecuación tendrá la misma solución

divisor [dĭ-vī′zər] The number you are dividing by in a division problem

divisor El número entre el que se divide en un problema de división

dot plot [dŏt plŏt] A visual display in which each piece of data is represented by a dot above a number line

diagrama de puntos Despliegue visual en que cada dato se representa con un punto sobre una recta numérica

E

equation [ĭ-kwā′zhən] A mathematical sentence that shows that two expressions are equivalent

ecuación Enunciado matemático que indica que dos expresiones son equivalentes

equilateral triangle [ē′kwə-lăt′ər-əl trī′ăng′gəl] A triangle with three congruent sides

triángulo equilátero Triángulo con tres lados congruentes

equivalent [ĭ-kwĭv′ə-lənt] Having the same value

equivalentes Que tienen el mismo valor

equivalent expression [ĭ-kwĭv′ə-lənt ĭk-sprĕsh′ən] Equivalent expressions have the same value for all values of the variables

expresión equivalente Las expresiones equivalentes tienen el mismo valor para todos los valores de las variables

Interactive Glossary

equivalent fractions [ĭ-kwĭv′ə-lənt frăk′shəns]
Fractions that name the same amount or part

fracciones equivalentes Fracciones que representan
la misma cantidad o parte

equivalent ratios [ĭ-kwĭv′ə-lənt rā′shōs] Ratios
that name the same comparison

razones equivalentes Razones que representan
la misma comparación

evaluate [ĭ-văl′yōō-āt′] To find the value of a
numerical or algebraic expression

evaluar Hallar el valor de una expresión
numérica o algebraica

exponent [ĭk-spō′nənt] The number that indicates
how many times the base is used as a factor

exponente Número que indica cuántas veces se
usa la base como factor

exponential form [ĕk′spə-nĕn′shəl fôrm] A
number is in exponential form when it is written
with a base and an exponent

forma exponencial Cuando se escribe un número
con una base y un exponente, está en forma
exponencial

expression [ĭk-sprĕsh'ən] A mathematical phrase that contains operations, numbers, and/or variables

expresión Enunciado matemático que contiene operaciones, números y/o variables

F

Fahrenheit [făr'ən-hīt'] A temperature scale in which 32 °F is the freezing point of water and 212 °F is the boiling point of water

Fahrenheit Escala de temperatura en la que 32 °F es el punto de congelación del agua y 212 °F es el punto de ebullición

factor [făk'tər] A number that is multiplied by another number to get a product

factor Número que se multiplica por otro para hallar un producto

fee [fē] A fixed amount or a percent of an amount

tarifa Cantidad fija o porcentaje de una cantidad

formula [fôr'myə-lə] A rule showing relationships among quantities

fórmula Regla que muestra relaciones entre cantidades

frequency [frē′kwən-sē] The number of times the value appears in the data set

frecuencia Cantidad de veces que aparece el valor en un conjunto de datos

frequency table [frē′kwən-sē tā′bəl] A table that lists items together according to the number of times, or frequency, that the items occur

tabla de frecuencia Una tabla en la que se organizan los datos de acuerdo con el número de veces que aparece cada valor (o la frecuencia)

G

greatest common factor (GCF) [grā′tĭst kŏm′ən făk′tər] The largest common factor of two or more given numbers

máximo común divisor (MCD) El mayor de los factores comunes compartidos por dos o más números dados

gratuity [grə-tī′-tē] A tip, or monetary percent that is given or paid in addition to the price of a service

gratificación Una propina o porcentaje monetario, que se da o paga además del precio de un servicio

H

height [hīt] In a triangle, the perpendicular distance from the base to the opposite vertex. In a trapezoid, the perpendicular distance between the bases

altura En un triángulo, la distancia perpendicular desde la base de la figura al vértice opuesto. En un trapecio, la distancia perpendicular entre las bases

hexagon [hĕk′sə-gŏn′] A six-sided polygon

hexágono Polígono de seis lados

histogram [hĭs′tə-grăm′] A bar graph whose bars represent the frequencies of numeric data within equal intervals

histograma Gráfica de barras que muestra las frequencias de los datos en intervalos iguales

I

Identity Property of Addition [ĭ-dĕn′tĭ-tē prŏp′ər-tē ŭv ə-dĭsh′ən] The property that states that the sum of zero and any number is that number

Propiedad de identidad de la suma Propiedad que establece que la suma de cero y cualquier número es ese número

Identity Property of Multiplication [ĭ-dĕn′tĭ-tē prŏp′ər-tē ŭv mŭl′tə-plĭ-kā′shən] The property that states that the product of 1 and any number is that number

Propiedad de identidad de la multiplicación Propiedad que establece que el producto de 1 y cualquier número es ese número

independent variable [ĭn′dĭ-pĕn′dənt vâr′ē-ə-bəl] The input of a function; a variable whose value determines the value of the output, or dependent variable

variable independiente Entrada de una función; variable cuyo valor determina el valor de la salida, o variable dependiente

Interactive Glossary

inequality [ĭn´ ĭ-kwŏl´ĭ-tē] A mathematical sentence that shows the relationship between quantities that are not equal

desigualdad Enunciado matemático que muestra una relación entre cantidades que no son iguales

integer [ĭn´tĭ-jər] An element of the set of whole numbers and their opposites

entero Un miembro del conjunto de los números cabales y sus opuestos

interquartile range (IQR) [ĭn´tûr-kwôr´tĭl´ rānj] The difference between the upper and lower quartiles in a data set, representing the middle half of the data

rango intercuartil (RIC) Diferencia entre el cuartil superior y el cuartil inferior de un conjunto de datos, que representa la mitad central de los datos

interval [ĭn´tər-vəl] The space between marked values on a number line or the scale of a graph

intervalo El espacio entre los valores marcados en una recta numérica o en la escala de una gráfica

inverse operations [ĭn-vûrs´ ŏp´ə-rā´shəns] Operations that undo each other: addition and subtraction, or multiplication and division

operaciones inversas Operaciones que se cancelan mutuamente: suma y resta, o multiplicación y división

My Vocabulary Summary

isosceles triangle [ī-sŏs'ə-lēz' trī'ăng'gəl] A triangle with at least two congruent sides

triángulo isósceles Triángulo que tiene al menos dos lados congruentes

L

least common denominator (LCD) [lēst kŏm'ən dĭ-nŏm'ə-nā'tər] The least common multiple of two or more denominators

mínimo común denominador (m.c.d.) El mínimo común múltiplo de dos o más denominadores

least common multiple (LCM) [lēst kŏm'ən mŭl'tə-pəl] The smallest number, other than zero, that is a multiple of two or more given numbers

mínimo común múltiplo (m.c.m.) El menor de los múltiplos (distinto de cero) de dos o más números

like fractions [līk frăk'shəns] Fractions that have the same denominator

fracciones semejantes Fracciones que tienen el mismo denominador

like terms [līk tûrms] Terms with the same variables raised to the same exponents

términos semejantes Términos con las mismas variables elevadas a los mismos exponentes

Interactive Glossary

My Vocabulary Summary

My Vocabulary Summary

line plot [līn plŏt] A number line with marks or dots that show frequency

diagrama de puntos Recta numérica con marcas o puntos que indican la frecuencia

lower quartile [lou'ər kwôr'tĭl'] The median of the lower half of a set of data

cuartil inferior La mediana de la mitad inferior de un conjunto de datos

M

magnitude [măg'nĭ-tōod'] The distance of a number from zero on a number line, also referred to as the absolute value

magnitud La distancia a la que está un número de 0 en una recta numérica, también se conoce como el valor absoluto

markdown [märk'doun'] The amount of decrease in a price

margen de descuento Cantidad en la que disminuye un precio

markup [märk'ŭp'] The amount of increase in a price

margen de aumento Cantidad en la que aumenta un precio

mean [mēn] The sum of the items in a set of data divided by the number of items in the set; also called *average*

media La suma de todos los elementos de un conjunto de datos dividida entre el número de elementos del conjunto

mean absolute deviation (MAD) [mēn ăb'sə-lōot' dē'vē-ā'shən] Mean of the distances between the data values and the mean of the data set

desviación absoluta media (DAM) Distancias medias entre los valores de datos y la media del conjunto de datos

My Vocabulary Summary

measure of center [mězh'ər ŭv sĕn'trəl tĕn'dən-sē] A measure used to describe the middle of a data set; the mean, median, and mode are measures of center

medida central Medida que se usa para describir el centro de un conjunto de datos; la media, la mediana y la moda son medidas centrales

measure of variability [mězh'ər ŭv vâr'ē-ə-bĭl'ĭ-tē] A single value used to describe how the values in a data set are spread out

medida de variabilidad Valor que se usa para describir cómo se dispersan los valores en un conjunto de datos

median [mē'dē-ən] The middle number, or the mean (average) of the two middle numbers, in an ordered set of data

mediana El número intermedio, o la media (el promedio), de los dos números intermedios en un conjunto ordenado de datos

metric system [mĕt'rik sis'təm] A decimal system of weights and measures that is used universally in science and commonly throughout the world

sistema métrico Sistema decimal de pesos y medidas empleado universalmente en las ciencias y por lo general en todo el mundo

minuend [mĭn'yoo-ĕnd'] The first number in a subtraction sentence

minuendo El primer número en una oración de resta

My Vocabulary Summary

My Vocabulary Summary

mixed number [mĭkst nŭm′bər] A number made up of a whole number that is not zero and a fraction

número mixto Número compuesto por un número cabal distinto de cero y una fracción

mode [mōd] The number or numbers that occur most frequently in a set of data; when all numbers occur with the same frequency, we say there is no mode

moda Número o números más frecuentes en un conjunto de datos; si todos los números aparecen con la misma frecuencia, no hay moda

Multiplication Property of Equality [mŭl′tə-plĭ-kā′shən prŏp′ər-tē ŭv ĭ-kwŏl′ĭ-tē] The property that states that if you multiply both sides of an equation by the same number, the new equation will have the same solution

Propiedad de igualdad de la multiplicación Propiedad que establece que puedes multiplicar ambos lados de una ecuación por el mismo número y la nueva ecuación tendrá la misma solución

Multiplication Property of Zero [mŭl′tə-plĭ-kā′shən prŏp′ər-tē ŭv zîr′ō] The property that states that for all real numbers a, $a \times 0 = 0$ and $0 \times a = 0$

Propiedad de multiplicación del cero Propiedad que establece que para todos los números reales a, $a \times 0 = 0$ y $0 \times a = 0$

multiplicative inverse [mŭl′tə-plĭ-kā′tĭv ĭn-vûrs′] One of two numbers whose product is 1

inverso multiplicativo Uno de dos números cuyo producto es igual a 1

N

negative number [nĕgʹə-tĭv nŭmʹbər] A number less than zero

número negativo Número menor que cero

net [nĕt] An arrangement of two-dimensional figures that can be folded to form a solid figure

plantilla Arreglo de figuras bidimensionales que se doblan para formar un cuerpo geométrico

numerator [nōōʹmə-rā´tər] The top number of a fraction that tells how many parts of a whole are being considered

numerador El número de arriba de una fracción; indica cuántas partes de un entero se consideran

numerical expression [nōō-mĕrʹĭ-kəl ĭk-sprĕsh´ən] An expression that contains only numbers and operations

expresión numérica Expresión que incluye sólo números y operaciones

O

opposites [ŏpʹə-zĭt] Two numbers are opposites if, on a number line, they are the same distance from 0 but on different sides

opuestos Dos números que están a la misma distancia de cero en una recta numérica

My Vocabulary Summary

order of operations [ôr′dər ŭv ŏp′ə-rā′shəns] A rule for evaluating expressions: first perform the operations in parentheses, then compute powers and roots, then perform all multiplication and division from left to right, and then perform all addition and subtraction from left to right

orden de las operaciones Regla para evaluar expresiones: primero se resuelven las operaciones entre paréntesis, luego se hallan las potencias y raíces, después todas las multiplicaciones y divisiones de izquierda a derecha y, por último, todas las sumas y restas de izquierda a derecha

ordered pair [ôr′dərd pâr] A pair of numbers that can be used to locate a point on a coordinate plane

par ordenado Par de números que sirven para ubicar un punto en un plano cartesiano

origin [ôr′ə-jĭn] The point where the *x*-axis and *y*-axis intersect on the coordinate plane; (0, 0)

origen Punto de intersección entre el eje *x* y el eje *y* en un plano cartesiano: (0, 0)

outlier [out′lī′ər] A value much greater or much less than the others in a data set

valor atípico Un valor mucho mayor o menor que los demás valores de un conjunto de datos

P

parallelogram [păr′ə-lĕl′ə-grăm′] A quadrilateral with two pairs of parallel sides

paralelogramo Cuadrilátero con dos pares de lados paralelos

My Vocabulary Summary

My Vocabulary Summary

pentagon [pĕn′tə-gŏn′] A five-sided polygon

pentágono Polígono de cinco lados

percent [pər-sĕnt′] A ratio comparing a number to 100

porcentaje Razón que compara un número con el número 100

percent change [pər-sĕnt′ chānj] The amount stated as a percent that a number increases or decreases

porcentaje de cambio Cantidad en que un número aumenta o disminuye, expresada como un porcentaje

percent decrease [pər-sĕnt′ dĭ-krēs′] A percent change describing a decrease in a quantity

porcentaje de disminución Porcentaje de cambio en que una cantidad disminuye

percent error [pər-sĕnt′ ĕr′ər] A special case of percent change in which the amount over or under an expected amount is expressed as a percent of the expected amount

porcentaje de error Caso especial de porcentaje de cambio en que la cantidad esperada por encima o por debajo se expresa como un porcentaje de la cantidad esperada

My Vocabulary Summary

My Vocabulary Summary

percent increase [pər-sĕnt′ ĭn-krēs′] A percent change describing an increase in a quantity

porcentaje de incremento Porcentaje de cambio en que una cantidad aumenta

perimeter [pə-rĭm′ĭ-tər] The distance around a polygon

perímetro Distancia alrededor de un polígono

plane [plān] A flat surface that has no thickness and extends forever

plano Superficie plana que no tiene ningún grueso y que se extiende por siempre

point [point] An exact location that has no size

punto Ubicación exacta que no tiene ningún tamaño

polygon [pŏl′ē-gŏn′] A closed plane figure formed by three or more line segments that intersect only at their endpoints

polígono Figura plana cerrada, formada por tres o más segmentos de recta que se intersecan sólo en sus extremos

positive number [pŏz′ĭ-tĭv nŭm′bər] A number greater than zero

número positivo Número mayor que cero

principal [prĭn′sə-pəl] The initial amount of money borrowed or saved

capital Cantidad inicial de dinero depositada o recibida en préstamo

prism [prĭz′əm] A polyhedron that has two congruent polygon-shaped bases and other faces that are all parallelograms

prisma Poliedro con dos bases congruentes con forma de polígono y caras con forma de paralelogramo

proportion [prə-pôr′shən] An equation that states that two ratios are equivalent

proporción Ecuación que establece que dos razones son equivalentes

proportional relationship [prə-pôr′shə-nəl rĭ-lā′shən-shĭp′] A relationship between two quantities in which the ratio of one quantity to the other quantity is constant

relación proporcional Relación entre dos cantidades en que la razón de una cantidad a la otra es constante

pyramid [pĭr′ə-mĭd] A three-dimensional figure with a polygon base and triangular sides that all meet at a common vertex

pirámide Figura tridimensional cuya base es un polígono; tiene caras triangulares que se juntan en un vértice común

Q

quadrant [kwŏd′rənt] The x- and y-axes divide the coordinate plane into four regions. Each region is called a quadrant

cuadrante El eje x y el eje y dividen el plano cartesiano en cuatro regiones. Cada región recibe el nombre de cuadrante

quadrilateral [kwŏd′rə-lăt′ər-əl] A polygon with four sides and four angles

cuadrilátero Polígono que tiene cuatro lados y cuatro ángulos

quartile [kwôr′tĭl] Three values, one of which is the median, that divide a data set into fourths

cuartil Cada uno de tres valores, uno de los cuales es la mediana, que dividen en cuartos un conjunto de datos

quotient [kwō′shənt] The result when one number is divided by another

cociente Resultado de dividir un número entre otro

R

radius [rā′dē-əs] A line segment with one endpoint at the center of a circle and the other endpoint on the circle, or the length of that segment

radio Segmento de recta con un extremo en el centro de un círculo y el otro en la circunferencia, o bien la longitud de ese segmento

range [rānj] In statistics, the difference between the greatest and least values in a data set

rango (en estadística) Diferencia entre los valores máximo y mínimo de un conjunto de datos

rate [rāt] A ratio that compares two quantities measured in different units

tasa Una razón que compara dos cantidades medidas en diferentes unidades

ratio [rā′shō] A comparison of two quantities by division

razón Comparación de dos cantidades mediante una división

rational number [răsh′ə-nəl nŭm′bər] A number that can be written in the form $\frac{a}{b}$, where a and b are integers and $b \neq 0$

número racional Número que se puede expresar como $\frac{a}{b}$, donde a y b son números enteros y $b \neq 0$

reciprocal [rĭ-sĭp′rə-kəl] One of two numbers whose product is 1

recíproco Uno de dos números cuyo producto es igual a 1

Interactive Glossary

rectangle [rĕk′tăng′gəl] A parallelogram with four right angles

rectángulo Paralelogramo con cuatro ángulos rectos

reflection [rĭ-flĕk′shən] A transformation of a figure that flips the figure across a line

reflexión Transformación que ocurre cuando se invierte una figura sobre una línea

regular polygon [rĕg′yə-lər pŏl′ē-gŏn′] A polygon with all sides of the same length and all angles of the same measure

polígono regular Un polígono con todos los lados de la misma longitud y todos los ángulos de la misma medida

retail price [rē′tāl′ prīs] The amount an item is sold for after a company adds a markup

precio de venta al por menor Cantidad en la que se vende un artículo después que una compañía le agrega un aumento de precio

rhombus [rŏm′bəs] A parallelogram with all sides congruent

rombo Paralelogramo en el que todos los lados son congruentes

right angle [rīt ăng′gəl] An angle that measures 90°

ángulo recto Ángulo que mide exactamente 90°

right triangle [rīt trīˈănggˈgəl] A triangle containing a right angle

triángulo rectángulo Triángulo que tiene un ángulo recto

S

sales tax [sāl tăks] A percent of the cost of an item that is charged by governments to raise money

impuesto sobre la venta Porcentaje del costo de un artículo que los gobiernos cobran para recaudar fondos

scale [skāl] The ratio between two sets of measurements

escala La razón entre dos conjuntos de medidas

scale drawing [skāl drôˈĭng] A drawing that uses a scale to make an object smaller than or larger than the real object

dibujo a escala Dibujo en el que se usa una escala para que un objeto se vea mayor o menor que el objeto real al que representa

set [sĕt] A group of items

conjunto Un grupo de elementos

Interactive Glossary

My Vocabulary Summary

My Vocabulary Summary

simple interest [sǐm′pəl ǐn′trǐst] A fixed percent of the principal, found using the formula $I = Prt$, where P represents the principal, r the rate of interest, and t the time

interés simple Un porcentaje fijo del capital. Se calcula con la fórmula $I = Cit$, donde C representa el capital, i, la tasa de interés y t, el tiempo

simplest form (of a fraction) [sǐm′pəl-ǐst fôrm] When the numerator and denominator of a fraction have no common factors other than 1

mínima expresión (de una fracción) Una fracción está en su mínima expresión cuando el numerador y el denominador no tienen más factor común que 1

simplify [sǐm′plə-fī] To write a fraction or expression in simplest form

simplificar Escribir una fracción o expresión numérica en su mínima expresión

solid figure [sŏl′ǐd fǐg′yər] A three-dimensional figure

cuerpo geométrico Figura tridimensional

solution of an equation [sə-lōō′shən ǔv ən ǐ-kwā′zhən] A value or set of values that make an equation true

solución de una ecuación Valor o valores que hacen verdadera una ecuación

solution of an inequality [sə-loo′shən ŭv ən ĭn′ĭ-kwŏl′ĭ-tē] A value or set of values that make an inequality true

solución de una desigualdad Valor o valores que hacen verdadera una desigualdad

sphere [sfîr] A three-dimensional figure with all points the same distance from the center

esfera Figura tridimensional en la que todos los puntos están a la misma distancia del centro

statistical question [stə-tĭs′tĭ-kəl kwĕs′chən] A question that has many different, or variable, answers

pregunta estadística Pregunta con muchas respuestas o variables diferentes

Subtraction Property of Equality [səb-trăk′shən prŏp′ər-tē ŭv ĭ-kwŏl′ĭ-tē] The property that states that if you subtract the same number from both sides of an equation, the new equation will have the same solution

Propiedad de igualdad de la resta Propiedad que establece que puedes restar el mismo número de ambos lados de una ecuación y la nueva ecuación tendrá la misma solución

subtrahend [sŭb′trə-hĕnd′] The number that is subtracted from another number in a subtraction sentence

sustraendo el número que se resta de otro número en una oración de resta

supplementary angles [sŭp′lə-mĕn′tə-rē ăng′gəls] Two angles whose measures have a sum of 180°

ángulos suplementarios Dos ángulos cuyas medidas suman 180°

© Houghton Mifflin Harcourt Publishing Company

Interactive Glossary

My Vocabulary Summary

My Vocabulary Summary

surface area [sûr′fəs âr′e-ə] The sum of the areas of the faces, or surfaces, of a three-dimensional figure

área total Suma de las áreas de las caras, o superficies, de una figura tridimensional

T

term (in an expression) [tûrm] The parts of an expression that are added or subtracted

término (en una expresión) Las partes de una expresión que se suman o se restan

tip [tĭp] Another word for gratuity, a monetary percent that is given or paid in addition to the price of a service

propina Otra palabra para gratificación, que es un porcentaje de dinero que se da o se paga adicionalmente al precio de un servicio

transformation [trăns′fər-mā′shən] A change in the size or position of a figure

transformación Cambio en el tamaño o la posición de una figura

trapezoid [trăp′ĭ-zoid′] A quadrilateral with at least one pair of parallel sides

trapecio Cuadrilátero con al menos un par de lados paralelos

My Vocabulary Summary

triangle [trī′ăng′gəl] A three-sided polygon

triángulo Polígono de tres lados

U

unit rate [yōō′nĭt rāt] A rate in which the second quantity in the comparison is one unit

tasa unitaria Una tasa en la que la segunda cantidad de la comparación es una unidad

---

unlike fractions [ŭn-līk′ frăk′shəns] Fractions with different denominators

fracciones distintas Fracciones con distinto denominador

---

upper quartile [ŭp′ər kwôr′tīl′] The median of the upper half of a set of data

cuartil superior La mediana de la mitad superior de un conjunto de datos

---

V

variable [vâr′ē-ə-bəl] A letter or symbol used to represent a quantity that can change

variable Símbolo que representa una cantidad que puede cambiar

---

My Vocabulary Summary

variation (variability) [vâr′ē-ā′shən] The spread of values in a set of data

variación (variabilidad) Amplitud de los valores de un conjunto de datos

vertex (vertices) [vûr′těks′] On an angle or polygon, the point where two sides intersect

vértice (vértices) En un ángulo o polígono, el punto de intersección de dos lados

vertical angles [vûr′tĭ-kəl ăng′gəls] A pair of opposite congruent angles formed by intersecting lines

ángulos opuestos por el vértice Par de ángulos opuestos congruentes formados por líneas secantes

volume [vŏl′yo͞om] The number of cubic units needed to fill a given space

volumen Número de unidades cúbicas que se necesitan para llenar un espacio

X

***x*-axis** [ěks ăk′sĭs] The horizontal axis on a coordinate plane

eje *x* El eje horizontal del plano cartesiano

My Vocabulary Summary

x-coordinate [ĕks kō-ôr′dn-ĭt] The first number in an ordered pair; it represents the distance to move right or left from the origin, (0, 0)

coordenada *x* El primer número en un par ordenado; indica la distancia que debes avanzar hacia la izquierda o hacia la derecha desde el origen, (0, 0)

Y

y-axis [wī ăk′sĭs] The vertical axis on a coordinate plane

eje *y* El eje vertical del plano cartesiano

y-coordinate [wī kō-ôr′dn-ĭt] The second number in an ordered pair; it represents the distance to move up or down from the origin, (0, 0)

coordenada *y* El segundo número en un par ordenado; indica la distancia que debes avanzar hacia arriba o hacia abajo desde el origen, (0, 0)

Index

careers
astronomer, 319
event organizer, 1
marketing manager, 481
sales director, 559
visual artist, 197

center
measures of. *See* measures of center

Check Understanding, appears in every lesson. *See, for example,* 8, 16, 23, 29, 36, 48, 56, 62, 69, 80, 86, 92, 98, 104

circle graph, 363–368, 385–386

clusters, 602, 603, 604, 605

coefficients
in algebraic expressions, 216, 245

combinatorics, 1

commissions
proportional reasoning in determining, 467–472, 479

common denominator, 15, 29, 30, 31, 34, 36, 37, 39, 42
rewriting fractions with a, 29, 31, 36, 39
in writing equivalent ratios, 370, 380

Commutative Property
of Addition, 144, 180, 185, 230, 235, 236, 237, 238, 242
of Multiplication, 158, 230

compare
decimals, 4, 78
percent ratios, 423–430
rational numbers
on a number line, 13–20
using LCM and GCF, 27–34
ratios and rates, 337–342
whole numbers, 4

compass rose, 529

complex fractions
computing unit rates involving, 347–348

composite figures, 525, 533
finding area of, 525–532

constant of proportionality, 396, 397, 398, 399, 400, 401, 402, 406, 407, 419
markup rate as, 457, 459

constant rates, 391, 392, 394, 396, 414

constants
in algebraic expressions, 216, 245

constraints, 278. *See also* inequalities

conversion factor, 385, 386
converting between measurement systems with, 371, 372, 373, 378, 379

coordinate plane, 485–508
finding distance on the, 485–492
finding perimeter and area on the, 501–506

graphing polygons on the, 493–500
graphing rational numbers on the, 485–492
ordered pairs on the, 4, 294, 298, 300, 310, 484, 486
origin on the, 404, 486, 507
quadrants in the, 486
reflections on the, 486
x-axis on the, 485, 486, 507
x-coordinate on the, 486
y-axis on the, 486, 507
y-coordinate on the, 486

coordinates, 486, 507

cubes, 444, 538, 542, 546. *See also* represent
edge length of, 538, 546
faces of, 63
surface area of, 63, 224, 554
volume of, 224, 444, 546, 554

cubic units, 206, 444, 536, 551

customary measurements
capacity in, 370, 378
length in, 370, 378
weight in, 370, 378

D

data, 564. *See also* measures of center
attributes of, 565
in box plots, 607–614
collection and displays of, 561–598
in dot plots, 559, 569–576, 591–595, 605, 606, 633, 634
in histograms and frequency tables, 577–584
in line plots, 561–562, 563, 569
mean absolute deviation and, 615–620
observations of, 565
patterns of, 601–606
statistical, 563–568
variability and distribution of, 599–634

data set, 622. *See also under* represent
distribution of, 627–632
interquartile range of, 626
mean absolute deviation of, 626
range of, 626

decagon
perimeter of, 240

decimals. *See also* multi-digit decimals
comparing, 4, 78
multi-digit, 77–110
addition of, 44, 78, 79–84, 140
division of, 97–102, 140, 322
multiplication of, 78, 85–90, 140
operations with, 103–108
subtraction of, 79–84, 140

multiply by whole numbers, 448
ordering, 36
place value of, 78, 79, 85
as rational numbers, 36
writing as fractions, 422
writing fractions as, 165–172, 422
writing rational numbers as, 165–172

denominators
common. *See* common denominator
division of fractions with like and unlike, 45–52
least common multiple in adding and subtracting fractions with unlike, 67–74

density, 349

dependent variables, 296, 297, 299, 303, 304, 317

diagonals, 520, 521

diagrams. *See also* represent
tape, 324, 325, 352, 355
tree, 201, 202

difference, 25, 35, 37, 40, 44, 80, 81, 82, 83, 108, 109, 112, 113, 120, 128, 133, 136, 138, 139, 140, 143. *See also* subtraction

discounts, 455–460

distance
finding, on the coordinate plane, 485–492

distributions
describing, 627–632

Distributive Property, 230
in evaluating numerical expressions, 210
in simplifying algebraic expressions, 230–236, 238, 239, 240

dividend, 55, 98, 101, 109, 159, 163. *See also* division

division
with decimals, 97–102, 140, 322
dividend in, 55, 98, 101, 109, 159, 163
divisor in, 62, 69, 97, 98, 101, 109, 159, 163
of fractions, 43–76, 140
with like and unlike denominators, 45–52
unit, 44
of integers, 165–172
long, 97
of mixed numbers, 53–60
of multi-digit decimals, 97–102
in order of operations, 209
quotient in, 26, 44, 47, 48, 51, 55, 56, 59, 60, 76, 84, 91–97, 99, 100, 101, 108, 109, 110, 140, 157,159–164, 166, 167, 176, 177, 178, 210, 211, 217, 219, 254, 270, 290, 322, 336, 342, 364, 438
of rational numbers, 157–164, 173–178

© Houghton Mifflin Harcourt Publishing Company

pentagons in, 235, 240, 242, 244, 494, 497, 499, 528
  graphing on the coordinate plane 493–500
  perimeter and area of, 501–506
  vertices of, 493, 494, 495, 497, 498, 499, 502, 503, 506, 507, 508, 520, 544
prisms in
  rectangular, surface area of, 228, 542, 543
  rectangular, volume of, 224, 273, 545–550
pyramids in, 539, 557
  square, 539, 542
  triangular, 541
rectangles in,
  area of, 57, 63, 65, 102, 104, 225, 234, 274, 276, 510, 515, 527
  classifying figures as, 484
  length of, 63, 100, 104, 225, 232, 234, 242, 243, 274, 276, 280, 356, 502, 503, 510, 512, 522
  perimeter of, 222, 232, 242, 362
  width of, 63, 100, 104, 225, 232, 234, 242, 243, 274, 276, 280, 356, 502, 503, 510, 512, 522
rhombuses in, 483, 498
  vertices of, 498
square pyramids in, 539, 542
  base in, 539
  faces in, 539
  surface area of, 539, 542
squares in
  area of, 516
  classifying figures as, 484
  perimeter of, 102, 272
surface area in, 63, 224, 228, 235, 437
  exploring, 537–544
  using nets in finding, 537–544
  volume and, 535–558
trapezoids in, 512, 533
  base of, 512, 513, 514, 515, 516, 517, 518
  developing and using formulas for, 511–518
  height of, 512, 513, 514, 515, 516, 517, 518
triangles in,
  acute, 510
  area of right, 502, 520, 521
  base of, 224, 501, 502, 522, 523, 524
  developing and using formula for area of, 519–524
  equilateral, 264
  height of, 224, 501, 502, 522, 523, 524
  hypotenuse in right, 495
  isosceles, 497, 523
  obtuse, 510
  perimeter of, 231, 273, 276

right, 510
volume in,
  of cubes, 224, 444, 546, 554
  problem solving and, 551–556
  of rectangular prisms, 224, 273, 545–550
  surface area and, 535–558
Glossary, G2–G37
grams, 378
graphs. *See also under* represent
  bar. (*See* histograms)
  for inequalities, 277–284
  origin in, 404, 486, 507
  of polygons on the coordinate plane, 493–500
  of rational numbers on the coordinate plane, 485–492
  representing equations in, 295–302
  representing ratios and rates with, 329–336
  writing equations from, 309–316
gratuities
  equations in determining, 461–466, 479–480
greater than (>), 4, 12, 15, 20, 26, 32, 78, 138, 164, 195, 277, 278, 281, 283, 284, 342, 374, 375, 382, 383, 418, 492
greater than or equal to (≥), 277
greatest common factor (GCF), 28, 29, 30, 31, 41, 42, 242, 328, 358
  comparing rational numbers using, 27–34
grids. *See under* represent

hectares, 84, 108
hexagons, 229, 302, 531
histograms, 577–584, 603, 604, 605, 606, 629. *See also* frequency tables; represent: histograms
  as symmetric, 603
hypotenuse, 495

Identity Property of Multiplication, 181
independent variables, 296, 297, 299, 303, 304, 317
inequalities, 16, 17, 277, 291. *See also under* represent
  completing with > or <, 4, 12, 15, 16, 17, 18, 19, 20, 32, 78, 277, 374, 375, 382, 383, 418
  constraints and, 278
  graphing, 277–284
  solutions of an, 278, 291

variables in, 277–284
  writing, 15, 20, 22, 23, 26, 29, 30, 31, 32, 33, 35, 84, 90, 186, 277–284, 302, 537
integers, 7. *See also* rational numbers
  comparing and ordering on a number line, 13–20
  division of, 165–172
  graphing on a number line, 6, 8, 10, 11, 23
  identifying and interpreting, 5–12
  inequalities, 16
  opposites, 6, 10
  as rational numbers, 7
interest
  proportional reasoning in calculating simple, 473–478
interquartile range (IQR), 621, 622, 623, 624, 625, 626, 628, 633
inverse
  multiplicative, 47, 75
inverse operations, 159
Inverse Property of Multiplication, 181
IQR. *See* interquartile range (IQR)

LCM. *See* least common multiple (LCM)
Learning Mindset
  perseverance, 2, 10, 18, 24, 50, 58, 118, 126, 146, 154, 162, 170, 176, 320, 326, 334, 366, 374, 382, 392, 400, 408, 428, 436
  resilience, 198, 204, 212, 218, 252, 260, 268, 300, 560, 566, 588, 604, 612, 618
  strategic help-seeking, 482, 490, 498, 516, 522, 542, 548
least common multiple (LCM), 27, 29, 31, 32, 33, 41, 42, 58, 67, 68
  addition and subtraction of fractions with unlike denominators, 67–74
  comparing rational numbers using, 27–34
length
  customary measurements of, 370, 378
  metric measurements of, 370, 378
less than (<), 4, 12, 15, 20, 26, 32, 78, 138, 164, 195, 277, 278, 281, 283, 284, 342, 374, 375, 382, 383, 418, 492
less than or equal to (≤), 277
linear expressions
  adding, subtracting, and factoring, with rational coefficients, 237–244
line plots
  making and interpreting, 561–562, 563, 569
lines of latitude, 24

points. *See also* ordered pairs (points)
identifying, on a coordinate plane, 4, 294, 300, 484
plotting, on a number line, 114–115, 116, 117, 118, 119, 122, 123, 124, 125, 126, 127, 128, 129, 130, 131, 132, 133, 134, 135, 136, 137, 138, 142, 143, 150, 151, 164, 248, 562

polygons, 494
on the coordinate plane, 483–508
graphing, 493–500
vertex of, 494

positive numbers, 6, 18, 24, 41, 113, 120, 122, 123, 135, 150, 151, 152, 285, 486
absolute value of, 22
addition or subtraction of, on a number line, 113–120, 137–138
on number lines, 6
writing, 6

positive sign (+), 6

prerequisite skills. *See also* Are You Ready?
adding and subtracting fractions, 112
adding fractions and decimals, 44, 78, 140
analyzing patterns and relationships, 294, 322
classifying quadrilaterals, 484
classifying triangles, 510
comparing and ordering whole numbers, 4, 600
comparing decimals, 4, 78
dividing with decimals, 322, 562
dividing fractions and mixed numbers, 140, 388
dividing with unit fractions and whole numbers, 44
dividing with whole numbers, 78
estimating and finding area, 510
evaluating simple numerical expressions, 200
exploring volume, 536
expressions with variables, 248
factors, 44
finding area of quadrilaterals and triangles, 536
finding percent or whole, 448
identifying points on a coordinate grid, 4, 294, 484
making and interpreting line plots, 562
mean, 600
multiplication of decimals by whole numbers, 448
multiplying decimals, 140
multiplying fractions, 44
multiplying or dividing in finding equivalent fractions, 322, 362
multiplying with decimals, 78
one-step equations, 388
opposites and absolute value, 112, 600

ordered pairs on the coordinate plane, 388
place value of decimals, 78
plotting points on a number line, 248, 562
ratio language, 362, 388
rational numbers on number lines, 112
relating fractions and decimals, 422
representing equivalent ratios, 362
using ratio and rate reasoning, 448
writing and interpreting numerical expressions, 140, 200
writing decimals as fractions, 422

prices
retail, 455

principal
simple interest and, 473, 479

prisms
rectangular
surface area of, 228, 542, 543
volume of, 224, 273, 545–550

problem solving, 247–292
adding, subtracting, and factoring, with rational coefficients, 237–244
addition and subtraction equations in, 255–262
algebra tiles in, 257, 264
bar models in, 249
determining correct operations in word problems, 103
diagrams in, 250, 252, 253, 256, 257, 259, 260, 261, 271, 272, 273, 274, 275, 276
graphing polygons on the coordinate plane, 493–500
multiplication and division equations in, 263–270
of multi-step problems
with rational numbers, 187–194
number lines in, 255, 266, 267, 269, 270, 276, 277, 278, 279, 280, 281, 282, 283, 284, 292
one-step equations in, 271–276
percent, 439–444
ratios and rates in, 448
tables in, 283
volume in, 551–556
writing and graphing inequalities in, 277–284
writing equations to represent situations, 249–254

products, 26, 44, 52, 85, 86, 87, 88, 89, 90, 103, 109, 140, 158, 159, 160, 161, 163, 172, 177, 200, 208, 210, 211, 217, 218, 219, 246, 302, 448. *See also* multiplication
of rational numbers, 157–164

properties of operations
Addition Property of Equality, 284

Associative Property of Addition, 179, 180, 185, 230, 237, 238
Associative Property of Multiplication, 181, 230, 235
Commutative Property of Addition, 144, 180, 185, 230, 235, 236, 237, 238, 242
Commutative Property of Multiplication, 158, 230
Distributive Property, 210, 230–236, 238, 239, 240
Division Property of Equality, 265, 271
Multiplication Property of Equality, 265
Subtraction Property of Equality, 258, 271, 272

proportional reasoning
in calculating markups and markdowns, 455–460
in determining commissions and fees, 467–472
percent in, 449–454
simple interest, 473–478
solving ratio and rate problems using, 351–358

proportional relationships, 387–420
computing unit rates involving complex fractions in, 347–348
equations for, 397, 398, 405, 411, 412, 413
percent (%) in, 447–480
recognizing on graphs, 403–410
recognizing in tables, 395–402
solving rate problems with, 411–418

proportionality
constant of, 396, 397, 398, 399, 400, 401, 402, 406, 407, 419

pyramids, 539, 557
square, 539, 542
base in, 539
faces in, 539
surface area of, 539
triangular, 541

Q

quadrants, 486, 507
quadrilaterals, 512
area of, 503, 536
classifying figures as, 484
perimeter of, 503
quantity
strategies to find percent of a, 431–438
quartile. *See* lower quartile; upper quartile

Index

Tables of Measures, Symbols, and Formulas

LENGTH

1 meter (m) = 1,000 millimeters (mm)

1 meter = 100 centimeters (cm)

1 meter ≈ 39.37 inches

1 kilometer (km) = 1,000 meters

1 kilometer ≈ 0.62 mile

1 inch = 2.54 centimeters

1 foot (ft) = 12 inches (in.)

1 yard (yd) = 3 feet

1 mile (mi) = 1,760 yards

1 mile = 5,280 feet

1 mile ≈ 1.609 kilometers

CAPACITY

1 liter (L) = 1,000 milliliters (mL)

1 liter = 1,000 cubic centimeters

1 liter ≈ 0.264 gallon

1 kiloliter (kL) = 1,000 liters

1 cup (c) = 8 fluid ounces (fl oz)

1 pint (pt) = 2 cups

1 quart (qt) = 2 pints

1 gallon (gal) = 4 quarts

1 gallon ≈ 3.785 liters

MASS/WEIGHT

1 gram (g) = 1,000 milligrams (mg)

1 kilogram (kg) = 1,000 grams

1 kilogram ≈ 2.2 pounds

1 pound (lb) = 16 ounces (oz)

1 pound ≈ 0.454 kilogram

1 ton = 2,000 pounds

TIME

1 minute (min) = 60 seconds (s)

1 hour (h) = 60 minutes

1 day = 24 hours

1 week = 7 days

1 year (yr) = about 52 weeks

1 year = 12 months (mo)

1 year = 365 days

1 decade = 10 years

© Houghton Mifflin Harcourt Publishing Company

Tables of Measures, Symbols, and Formulas

SYMBOLS

$=$	is equal to	10^2	ten squared
$\neq$	is not equal to	10^3	ten cubed
$\approx$	is approximately equal to	2^4	the fourth power of 2
$>$	is greater than	$\lvert-4\rvert$	the absolute value of -4
$<$	is less than	$\%$	percent
$\geq$	is greater than or equal to	$(2, 3)$	ordered pair (x, y)
$\leq$	is less than or equal to	$\degree$	degree

FORMULAS

Perimeter and Circumference

Polygon	$P = $ sum of the lengths of sides
Rectangle	$P = 2\ell + 2w$
Square	$P = 4s$
Circle	$C = \pi d$ or $C = 2\pi r$

Area

Rectangle	$A = \ell w$ or $A = bh$
Parallelogram	$A = bh$
Triangle	$A = \frac{1}{2}bh$
Trapezoid	$A = \frac{1}{2}h(b_1 + b_2)$
Square	$A = s^2$
Circle	$A = \pi r^2$

Volume

Right Prism	$V = \ell wh$ or $V = Bh$
Cube	$V = s^3$
Pyramid	$V = \frac{1}{3}Bh$

Surface Area

Right Prism	$S = Ph + 2B$
Cube	$S = 6s^2$
Square Pyramid	$S = \frac{1}{2}P\ell + B$